COMPUTATIONAL INTELLIGENCE IN SOFTWARE ENGINEEING

ADVANCES IN FUZZY SYSTEMS — APPLICATIONS AND THEORY

Honorary Editor: Lotfi A. Zadeh (*Univ. of California, Berkeley*)
Series Editors: Kaoru Hirota (*Tokyo Inst. of Tech.*),
George J. Klir (*Binghamton Univ.–SUNY*),
Elie Sanchez (*Neurinfo*),
Pei-Zhuang Wang (*West Texas A&M Univ.*),
Ronald R. Yager (*Iona College*)

Advances in Fuzzy Systems — Applications and Theory   Vol. 16

COMPUTATIONAL INTELLIGENCE IN SOFTWARE ENGINEERING

W Pedrycz
University of Alberta

J F Peters
University of Manitoba

World Scientific
Singapore • New Jersey • London • Hong Kong

Published by

World Scientific Publishing Co. Pte. Ltd.

P O Box 128, Farrer Road, Singapore 912805

USA office: Suite 1B, 1060 Main Street, River Edge, NJ 07661

UK office: 57 Shelton Street, Covent Garden, London WC2H 9HE

British Library Cataloguing-in-Publication Data
A catalogue record for this book is available from the British Library.

COMPUTATIONAL INTELLIGENCE IN SOFTWARE ENGINEERING
Advances in Fuzzy Systems — Applications and Theory, Vol. 16

ISBN 981-02-3503-8

This book is printed on acid-free paper.

Printed in Singapore by Uto-Print

CONTENTS

PREFACE

With the rapidly growing demand for new software systems having increasing complexity and size, it is not amazing that the software crisis recognized several decades ago is still with us. As a discipline, software engineering is striving to meet the continuously growing challenges in the area by establishing sound and complete methodologies as well as crystallizing in more specific and fully reliable products (Pedrycz and Peters, 1998). While some extremely useful paradigms have been announced and promoted including software reusability and portability, formal verification methods, to name a few, their transfer into everyday projects is still very slow and limited. Similarly, a number of software measures whose use could (potentially) lead to more reliable products have never been fully exploited in practice.

The recently emerging area of Computational Intelligence (CI) provides a software designer and software professional with a unique conceptual and algorithmic opportunity by taking advantage of the currently developed and already highly mature technologies of fuzzy sets, rough sets, neural networks and evolutionary computation including genetic algorithms. In general, the main objective of CI is to establish a highly coherent design and analysis environment (Bezdek, 1992; Pedrycz, 1997; Peters and Pedrycz, 1998; Pedrycz, Peters and Ramanna, 1998; Peters and Ramanna, 1998a) through a series of synergistic links that give rise to neurofuzzy systems, evolutionary neural networks, fuzzy genetic schemes, granular rough decision systems, and many others in the context of software engineering (see Fig. 1). It is essential to elaborate in brief on these main conceptual and functional pillars of CI.

CI technologies have been used separately and in various combinations to solve problems stemming from increasingly complex of forms of software systems description and analysis. This chapter gives a brief introduction to four CI technologies with natural ties to software engineering: fuzzy, rough, neural and evolutionary computing. The intent in introducing CI technologies in software engineering is to address the needs arising during various phases of software development and analysis which involves imprecise measurement and uncertain information.

Examples of the applications of CI technologies in software engineering are summarized

x

in Fig. 1. Fuzzy sets have been used in object-oriented design (Pedrycz and Sosnowski, 1998) and software quality management (Ebert, 1993). Neural networks have been used in connection with software testing (Mayrhauser and others, 1995; Mayrhauser and others, 1998) and software reuse (Merkl, 1993; Merkl, 1998). Rough sets have used in assessing software quality (Peters and Ramanna, 1998a; Peters and Ramanna, 1998b) and estimating software cost (Peters and Ramanna, 1996). Evolutionary computing techniques have been used in the study of the evolution of competing programs (Koza, 1993). The micro-cubes along the surface of the CI sphere in Fig. 1 are suggestive of points of convergence of these methodologies that have been used in software engineering. Examples of the combined used of CI technologies can be found in assessing software quality (Peters and Ramanna, 1998b) and in describing and analyzing intelligent systems (Gudwin and Gomide, 1998). Other applications of CI technolgies in software engineering can be found in (Pedrycz and Peters, 1997; Pedrycz, Peters, and Ramanna, 1998).

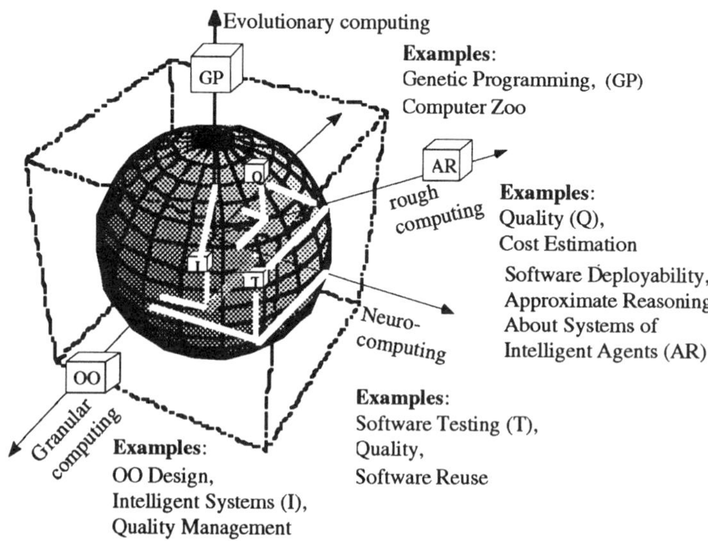

Fig. 1 CI in SE Sphere

CI technologies dovetail with the reality of software system design. For example, an inherent factor of software complexity calls for various approaches capable of handling uncertainty, linguistic evidence, and experimental data. A variety of illustrative examples of the application of CI in software engineering are contained in this volume.

Neural networks (Minsky and Pappert, 1969; Rumelhart and McClelland, 1986) offer a powerful and distributed computing architecture equipped with significant learning abilities. They help represent highly nonlinear and multivariable relationships that can be learned from experimental data. Neural networks have become instrumental in carrying out a vast number of different prediction tasks.

Granular computing forms a key methodology for representing and processing linguistic or, in general, non-numeric information. It supports a diversity of mechanisms of knowledge representation focusing on a relevant selection of information granules and delivering suitable mechanisms aimed at their processing. Fuzzy sets (Zadeh, 1973) exploit imprecision in an attempt to make system's or process' complexity manageable. Rough sets (Pawlak, 1991) help exploit the notions of discernability, indiscernability, and approximate reasoning.

The concept of evolutionary computation (Fogel et al., 1966; Holland, 1975; Koza, 19xx) embraces genetic algorithms, evolutionary computation and evolutionary strategies. All of them are biologically - inspired methodologies exploiting an idea of population-oriented development that is aimed at global system optimization.

The book is intended to become a comprehensive and fully updated source on CI portrayed as a new and useful paradigm in software engineering. It is aimed at practitioners in the area addressing the needs of those fully familiar with software engineering and CI No prerequisites are necessary. The book addresses the needs of undergraduate students in a number of courses in Computer Science and Computer Engineering curricula in the area of software analysis and design. There are a number of graduate offerings that could highly benefit from the book; these pertain to more advanced aspects of Software Engineering. The book could be helpful in courses devoted to new innovative aspects of computing and software design. The readers interested in the development of advanced software layers for the Internet can find the material stimulating.

The contributions in this volume come with a number of carefully arranged exercises that help the reader reflect over the material and gain a better insight into the essence of the discussed approaches. This volume is divided into three sections. This taxonomy is driven by the main technologies of CI. Part I is devoted to meurocomputing and SE.

Part II deals with evolutionary methods in the setting of software synthesis and analysis. In Part III, we concentrate on the synergy between software engineering and granular computing represented here mainly by fuzzy sets and rough sets. The assumed organization of the material carries an unavoidable level of ambiguity. Simply, some contributions span across a number of areas embracing granular models, learning abilities implied by neural mechanisms and evolutionary behavior associated with genetic algorithms. Nevertheless, by and large, we have achieved a reasonably high level of coherency of classification resulting therein.

We are confident that in the coming years the ideas of CI will find a solid place in the realm of Software Engineering as an essential and powerful platform of synthesis and analysis. We are highly grateful to the authors for their generous contributions that are indisputably located at the frontiers of this rapidly progressing area. Our thanks go the Natural Sciences and Engineering Council of Canada (NSERC) which through operating, strategic as well as industry-university grants generously supported this project. The professional and on-time help of all folks from the World Scientific was also instrumental in assuring a smooth progress of the project. We hope that the readers will find this volume thought-provoking, inspiring, and intellectually refreshing.

References

J. C. Bezdek, On the relationship between neural networks, pattern recognition and intelligence, J. Approximate Reasoning, 6, 1992, 85-107.

C. Ebert, An approach to fuzzy data analysis for software quality control, Proc. 1st European Congress onb Fuzzy and Intelligent Technologies, EUFIT'93, Aachen, September 7-10, 1993, pp. 1156-1161.

R.R.Gudwin and F.A.C. Gomide, Object network: A formal model to develop intelligent systems. In W. Pedrczy and J.F. Peters (Eds.), Computational Intelligence in Software Engineering. Singapore, World Scientific, 1998.

J.R. Koza, Genetic Programming: On the Programming of Computers by Means of Natural Selection. Cambridge, MA, The MIT Press, 1993.

D. Merkl, Structuring software for reuse--The case of self-organizing maps. In Proc. of the Int. Joint Conf. on Neural Networks (IJCNN'93), Nagoya, Japan, 1993.

D. Merkl, Self-organizing maps and software reuse. In W. Pedrycz and J.F. Peters (Eds.), Computational Intelligence in Software Engineering. Singapore, World Scientific, 1998.

A. von Mayrhauser, Ch. Anderson, R.Mraz, Using a neural network to predict test case effectiveness, Proc. IEEE Aerospace Applications Conf., Snowmass, CO, Feb. 1995.

A. von Mayrhauser, C.W. Anderson, T. Chen, R.Mraz, C.A. Gideon, On the promise of neural networks to support software testing. In W. Pedrczy and J.F. Peters (Eds.), Computational Intelligence in Software Engineering. Singapore, World Scientific, 1998.

W. Pedrycz, J.F. Peters, "Computational intelligence in software engineering", IEEE Canadian Conf. on Electrical & Computer Engineering (CCECE'97), May, 1997, pp. 253-257.

W. Pedrycz, J.F. Peters, S. Ramanna, Design of a Software Quality Decision System: A Computational Intelligence Approach, IEEE Canadian Conf. on Electrical & Computer Engineering (CCECE'98), May, 1998a [to appear].

W. Pedrycz, J.F. Peters, Software Engineering: An Engineering Approach, J. Wiley, N. York, 1998 (to appear)

W. Pedrycz, Computational Intelligence: An Introduction. CRC Press, Boca Raton, Fl, 1997

J.F. Peters, W. Pedrycz, Computational Intelligence. In Webster (Ed.), Encyclopedia of Electronic and Electrical Engineering. New York, John Wiley [to appear].

J.F. Peters and S. Ramanna, A rough sets approach to assessing software quality: Concepts and rough Petri net models. In: Rough-Fuzzy Hybridization: New Trends in Decision-Making, edited by L. Polkowski and A. Skowron. Physica Verlag, a division of Springer Verlag [to appear].

J.F. Peters and S. Ramanna, Software Deployability Decision System Framework: A Rough Sets Approach, Proc. IPMU'98, Paris, France, July 1998.

J.F. Peters and S. Ramanna, Application of Choquet Integral in Software Cost Estimation. IEEE Int. Conf. on Fuzzy Systems, New Orleans, 1996, 862-866.

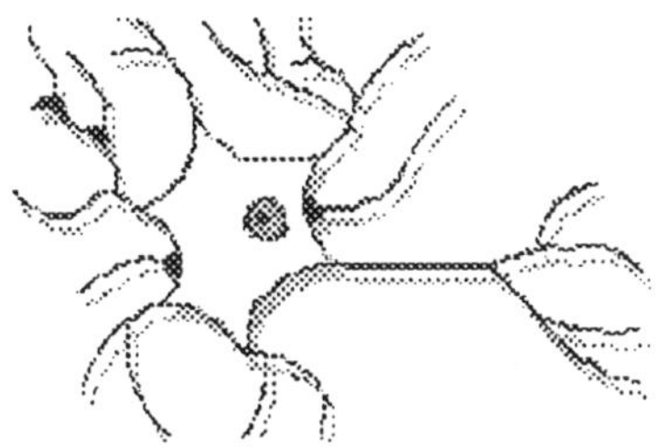

NEUROCOMPUTING
IN SOFTWARE ENGINEERING

This section is concerned with the development of software constructs and description or prediction their quality by exploiting various techniques of neurocomputing. The most outstanding features of neural networks such as learning, approximation and prediction abilities have been found highly appealing in many crucial tasks of software engineering including testing, organization of visualization of software modules, and inductive computing.

This section is comprised of four papers. First, von Mayerhauser et al. report on the use of neural networks in the problem of software testing with an intent of improving the level of test coverage. The use of self-organizing map in the essential problem of software reusability is studied by Merkl. The issue of prediction of software quality formulated in the setting of neural networks is studied by Khoshgoftaar and Allen. The paper by Partridge deals with inductive computing regarded as a new and attractive approach to the SE development. It reveals a number of interesting neural network-based implementation links.

ON THE PROMISE OF NEURAL NETWORKS TO SUPPORT SOFTWARE TESTING

Anneliese von Mayrhauser, Charles W. Anderson

Computer Science Department, Colorado State University, Fort Collins, CO 80523

Tom Chen

Electrical Engineering Department, Colorado State University, Fort Collins, CO 80523

Richard Mraz

HQ USAF/DFCS, 2354 Fairchild Hall, Suite 6K41, U. S. Air Force Academy, CO 80840

C. A. Gideon

Computer Science Department, Colorado State University, Fort Collins, CO 80523

This chapter explores the possibilities of using neural networks to support various software testing activities. They range from automated test generation to evaluation of automatically generated test cases for their effectiveness in meeting test criteria or finding faults. Our motivation is that it would be useful to have a mechanism that is able to learn, based on past history, to predict test cases are either likely to increase desired coverage items, or which test cases are likely to yield more coverage or failures versus those that are not going to increase coverage or fault exposure. *rewrite previous sentence* Such approaches show particular promise for large scale software as they do not require extensive structural analysis. In this chapter, we describe experiments involving the testing of a large software system and of a large VHDL design and summarize our assessment of the capabilities of neural networks for testing and their current limitations.

1 Introduction

Software testing still consumes major resources in a software product's lifecycle. A myriad of testing methods exist ranging from white box testing methods for unit testing to black box methods for system testing[34,4]. Methods are usually associated with testing criteria, that identify what to test and how we know that we are done. Examples include branch testing, dataflow testing, etc. Coverage metrics measure compliance with testing criteria and identify which parts of the code have not been adequately tested. An example of a coverage analyzer is the Free Software Foundation's *gct* tool. Often, testing methods are associated with their own test case or test suite generation tools (e. g. ASSET[30] and dataflow testing[29], *Sleuth*[36] and domain based testing[38]). Test generation tools may aim for forcing compliance or only approximate it (then coverage measurement tools evaluate how well test data meets the testing criterion). While test data generation from some formal representation (syntactic or semantic) of the object under test can be very simple and cheap, forcing test criteria compliance is quite often expensive or only partially feasible. Examples are test generation tools based on symbolic execution that ensure various types of white box testing coverage[33]. This should come as no surprise: the general test data generation problem is undecidable[16]. In practice, many test data generation systems make simplifying assumptions, either in terms of the power of the language for which they generate test data[10,15,45], or the information they consider in driving test data generation. Effects of such simplification include: (1) the generated test data may not completely satisfy a test criterion, (2) the test data set may be larger than necessary, (3) the test data generation system may only be able to generate test data for a subset of the programming language. Simplification is obviously not a problem when test data are effective (reveal faults). This makes it very important to evaluate a test generation method experimentally and/or analytically. Analytical evaluation considers whether the testing criteria meet adequacy properties[27,42]. They describe properties any testing criteria should have to be considered adequate. They do not, however, guarantee high failure yields. Thus experimental evaluation of testing techniques is also important. Examples of such evaluations include[43,44,14].

When the number of tests to be run can become very large, test case reduction[10,39] becomes desirable. Prudent test case reduction prunes a test set by eliminating those test cases that are not likely to increase compliance with a testing criteria (e. g. increase branch coverage) or, that are not likely to yield any failures. Figure 1 summarizes our discussion.

We present our investigations into the use of Neural Networks for software testing from two perspectives:

1. System testing (black box testing).
Test generation mechanisms[2,3,5,6,11,13,15,22,26,35,36,37,38] are able to generate thousands of test cases in a very short amount of time. It may not be immediately obvious whether the test generation tool generates effective test cases. We used a neural net to learn failure behavior of test cases. This can be used to filter out test cases in any newly generated set that would not likely expose any faults, thus effectively pruning the number of tests to be run without sacrificing effectiveness. A trained neural net might also be used to emphasize severe error exposure in test cases, or to minimize the number of test cases that need to be run.

We used a neural network as a classifier to learn about the system under test and to predict the fault exposure capability of newly generated test cases.

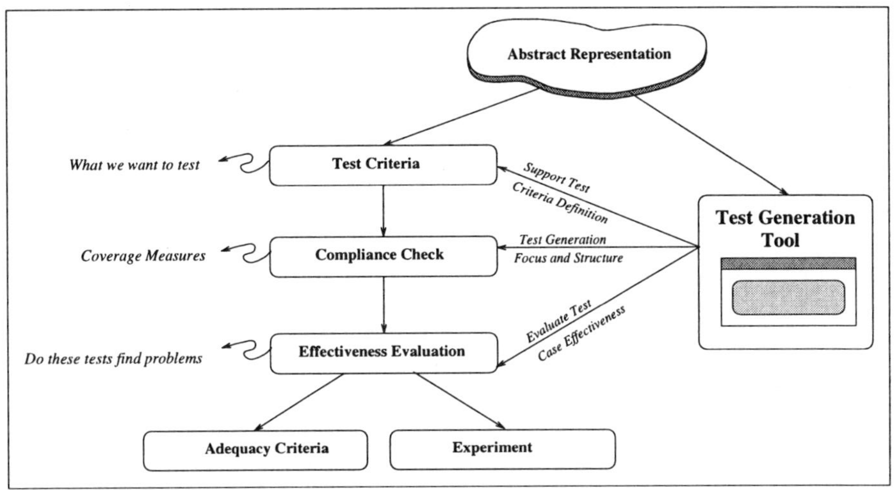

Figure 1: Relating Test Generation with Test Criteria, Coverage, and Effectiveness

We describe attributes of test cases to the neural network as inputs and relate them to resulting faults (neural network outputs). Inputs are test case length and various coverage metrics relevant to the testing strategy used. Outputs are levels of severity of faults detected. They range from severe (level 1) to "correct operation" (level 4). Then, we trained the network to recognize relationships between test case descriptors and faults. Once trained, the network acts as a fault predictor for new test cases. Related work includes the use of neural networks to predict quality in a manufacturing process[1].

2. White box testing.

The objective of whitebox testing criteria is to fulfill various types of coverage criteria such as branch coverage, dataflow coverage, decision coverage, etc. In order to support whitebox testing, a neural net would have to support either test generation that will increase coverage or be able to reduce newly generated test data by eliminating coverage duplicates. In either case, the neural net must be able to learn existing coverage and recognize tests that would not increase coverage. Ideally, we'd also like it to help in generating test data that will increase coverage.

We decided to investigate these questions using a special purpose language, VHDL. VHDL is a hardware description language that has most of the statement types of other programming languages (including concurrency) and much simpler data structures. Since our plan was to investigate the possibility of predicting branch coverage, choosing this language avoided the complexities of some other languages while still providing necessary statement types to fruitfully investigate white box test coverage (specifically branch coverage) and test generation.

We report results from a study designed to answer the following questions:

1. Given a method of producing plausible tests, can a neural network predict which tests are most likely to produce the desired coverage? If this is indeed the case, we can use the neural net to

   - filter out (possibly automatically generated test cases) that are not likely to increase coverage and thus will not add to the fault revealing capabilities of an existing test suite, reducing the test effectiveness of the test set, and

   - reduce the already existing set by throwing out "coverage duplicates" and thus keep test cases to a minimum while still achieving coverage goals.

2. Can the trained neural network be used to generate new test cases that result in new coverage not produced by existing test cases?

While our experiment considered VHDL as the language of choice, it is reasonable to expect that the results will carry over to other programming languages as well.

Section 2 provides background on neural network classifiers and their use to predict failures. Section 3 evaluates how well neural networks work when used as test effectiveness predictors for system testing. As example testing technique we use Domain Based Testing [36] and its associated test data generation tool *Sleuth* [38]. The results are useful in two ways. First, they point out which tests are likely to trigger what types of incidents. Second, for those test suites that the neural net has identified as not revealing any problems, the neural net analysis can also provide information about what test variables to change so as to produce effective results. This is the first step towards prescribing successful test generation, where success is defined as finding faults. Section 4 describes our efforts related to white box testing. We first provide some background on VHDL and its use in hardware design, the testing criteria used, and the example VHDL code we used for the analysis. Then we describe the experimental design and the training results for the network. Section 5 discusses what we learned and the advice we can give when using neural net classifiers to guide test case generation to either increase fault exposure, or to increase test coverage.

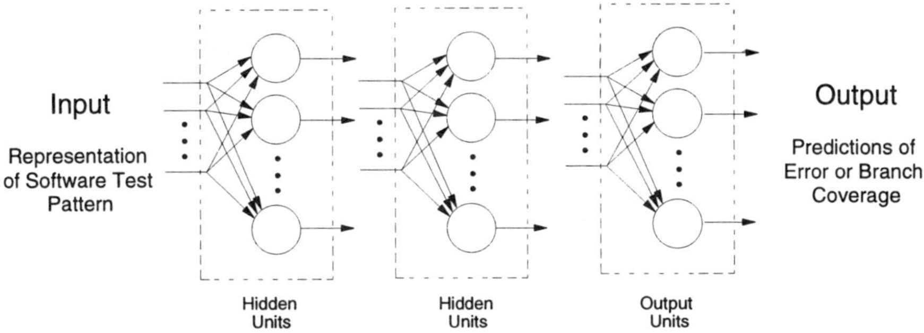

Figure 2: The Neural Network Architecture Used in All Experiments Reported Here. The Networks Contained Either One or Two Hidden Layers

2 Background on Neural Networks

2.1 Training

The neural network architecture used for our experiments is shown in Figure 2. The circles represent the computational units of the network. The interconnections represent scalar values passed as input to each unit. Each unit has a unique vector of weights corresponding to its input vector. The computation performed by the units is a weighted sum of their inputs and a nonlinear *squashing* function that restricts the range of the output to be between 0 and 1. We used the typical *sigmoid* squashing function. Let the inputs to a unit be x_i, the weights be w_i, and the output of the unit be y. The weighted sum and sigmoid function are combined to produce the unit's output:

$$y = \frac{1}{1 + e^{-\sum_i x_i w_i}}.$$

The network consists of two or three layers of units. The units in the initial layers are called *hidden units*, because the outputs of these units are used internal to the network to transform the input into another representation for the *output unit*. The output of the output unit is taken as the classification of the current input pattern.

To train the network, a set of training patterns and corresponding correct outputs is repetitively presented to the network. After each pass through the training data, called an *epoch*, the weights are adjusted to reduce the error between the correct output and the actual output of the network. To determine how to adjust each weight, we applied the error backpropagation algorithm [31]. This algorithm calculates the gradient of an error function with respect to each weight, then adjusts the weights in the negative gradient direction to reduce the error. The error function is the squared error summed over all training patterns:

$$E = \sum_p (z^{(p)} - y^{(p)})^2$$

where p is an index into the set of training patterns, $z^{(p)}$ is the correct output for pattern p, and $y^{(p)}$ is the output of the network for pattern p.

The gradient of E with respect to the weights results in the following expressions. Let $h_i^{(p)}$ signify the output of hidden unit i when the network receives input pattern p. To change the weights of the output unit, we sum the following $\Delta w_i^{(p)}$'s

$$\Delta w_i^{(p)} = c(z^{(p)} - y^{(p)})h_i^{(p)}$$

over all training patterns and, at the end of the epoch, add the result to the weights in the output unit. The constant c is a scale factor that is chosen empirically to produce weight changes that are not too large nor too small. If too large, the network would converge quickly to a suboptimal local minimum; if too small, the time required for the network to converge would be impractically long. Similarly, we sum the $\Delta w_{ij}^{(p)}$'s for hidden unit j, given by

$$\Delta w_{ij}^{(p)} = c_h(z^{(p)} - y^{(p)})h_j^{(p)}(1 - h_j^{(p)})x_i^{(p)}$$

where $x_i^{(p)}$ is a component of the input pattern given to the network. The hidden units have their own scale factor, c_h.

2.2 The Overfitting Problem

Although this algorithm is designed to minimize the squared error over a training set, the true goal of this procedure is to find a set of weights for which the squared error is minimized over a novel set of data, i.e., data to which the network was not trained. Only if the algorithm is able to find a model (the network and weights) that generalizes well to this *test set* can we say that the model captures the regularities present in the data. This problem has been called the overfitting problem—the network too closely matches the training data and does not interpolate and extrapolate well to novel data. The is usually tested by dividing the data into a *training* and a *testing* set. The network is trained to convergence on the training set, after which the error on the testing set is calculated and used as an estimate of how well the network will perform on novel data.

To limit the amount of overfitting, one may repetitively train networks, starting with very simple ones and continuing with more complex ones containing more hidden units. At some point, the test error will no longer increase with increases in network complexity. Alternatively, one may train a single network and decrease the complexity of a trained network through pruning, or by limiting the growth in complexity during training, or by terminating the training when the network begins to overfit. Each is described below.

A trained network that overfits may be pruned by removing weights and units that have minimal effect on the network's error. This may be performed by sequentially setting each weight to zero and testing the error of the resulting network. Methods that require less computation rely on measures of utility for each weight[18,23,28]. For example, the Hessian of the error with respect to the weights for a given input pattern is the sensitivity of the error with respect to each weight[18].

The complexity of the function learned by a neural network is related to the number of hidden units and the number of weights of magnitude significantly different from zero. One way to limit the growth of complexity during training is to add an error term that biases the gradient search for weight values to regions in the weight space of low-magnitude weights. Weigend, Rumelhart, and Huberman[41] developed a term that penalizes large magnitude weights and applied this to several time series prediction problems.

A final method for controlling overfitting is more dependent on the data than the previous two. The data is divided into three parts, two for training and testing, and the third for determining when the network is overfitting. The third part is called the *validation* set. After each pass through the training data, the error on the validation set is calculated. Initially, the error on the training and validation set decreases. As the network begins to overfit, the error on the validation set begins to increase. Training continues for some fixed number of epochs. The weight values at the epoch for which the validation error is minimal are taken as the best values. The network with these weights is applied to the test set to obtain our estimate of performance on novel data. Weigend[40] used this technique on a time-series prediction problem and found it to be useful even for very small networks.

For the experiments in VHDL testing, we used early stopping with a validation set because the size of our data sets were large. For the system testing experiments, we used the first method, of starting with simple networks, because our data was limited. For the latter case, we followed a Leave-One-Out-Method (LOOM). LOOM removes one vector from the data set. The single vector is called the *test vector* and the remaining patterns are called the *training set*. We train the network using the training set and evaluate its classification on the test vector. The training procedure is repeated for each choose-one-test-vector, train, evaluation cycle. When training on the system testing data, we used LOOM to experimentally calculate the best network topology (number of hidden units) by starting with simple networks and repeating for networks with more hidden units. LOOM is useful for training any neural network, but the amount of computation is prohibitive for large data sets.

A trained network can be used to predict the output (in our case severity of failure in the system testing study, or branch coverage in the white box testing example) of a given input stimulus by performing the standard output calculations in a forward (from input to output) direction. However, the network can also be used in a backwards direction to predict an input which will produce a given output (fault severity or coverage). This is done by "inverting" the network—calculating the gradient of the squared error of the network's output with respect to its input. A gradient search can then be performed in the network's input space to find inputs which, when passed through the network in the forward direction, produce output that most matches the desired output.

3 System Testing

3.1 Input Representation

Once a software test generator creates a test case, we would like to evaluate its fault exposure potential. If the test case does not expose faults, then we don't need to run it. We used a neural network classifier to make this decision. This required to determine how to represent test cases and resulting fault severity output to the neural net for training purposes.

Thus, the first decision prior to the training process is to determine how to represent training inputs to the neural net. The choice of input representation is important. If the input is too detailed, the search space for the Neural Net is too large, resulting in a linear model and weak predictability. If the data is too summarized, the net training may benefit from the smaller input space, but struggle with conflicting information as test cases that run without failure and those that cause failures may be mapped to the same (summarized) neural net input (i. e. the same inputs can cause different outputs).

We decided to map test cases into test metrics derived from the application domain model the test generator uses. This reduces the search space compared to presenting the neural net with the actual test case representation.

Figure 3 shows how to train the neural network. Test case metrics are extracted from the test case. Metrics measure test case length, command frequencies, and parameter use frequencies. An "oracle" classifies any errors

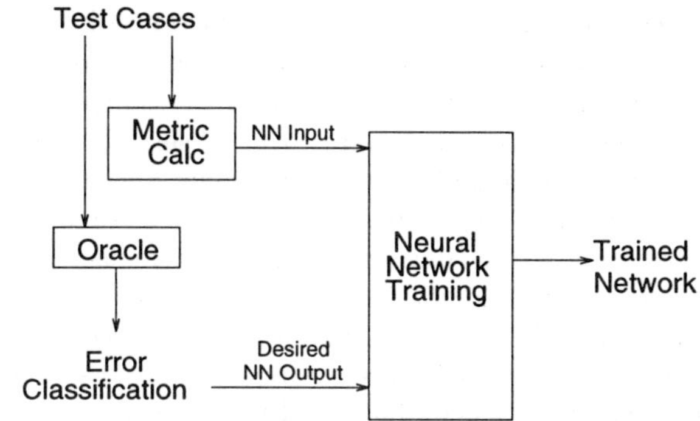

Figure 3: Neural Net Test Effectiveness Predictor : Training Phase

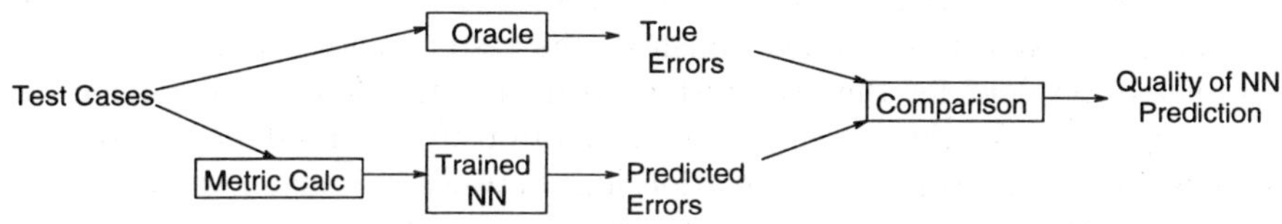

Figure 4: Neural Net Test Effectiveness Predictor : Evaluation Phase

exposed by the test case. The oracle is an objective arbiter to whether a given test case exposes a fault. In practice, testers act as arbiters, but in our controlled laboratory experiment we defined a synthetic test oracle.

The network uses test case metrics (input pattern) and the error classification (output pattern) for training. Once trained, the network predicts the fault exposure of new test cases. Figure 4 shows how we evaluate the effectiveness of the neural classifier. Given a test case, the test oracle identifies the actual faults exposed by the test case and the neural network predicts the fault exposure. Comparing the two, we measure how well the neural net acts as a test case effectiveness predictor.

3.2 Test Data Generation

Using the *Sleuth* test generator[36,38], we defined six test objectives from which 180 data vectors were generated, 30 for each test objective. Each test objective is associated with a set of test criteria. For the experiment, we trained and tested the neural network on a set of commands commonly used to control an automated tape library. This includes commands for mounting and

12

dismounting tapes, and for moving tapes between tape silos.

The first test objective is to test the application for normal or valid operation (mounting and dismounting tapes, moving tapes around, etc.). All rules representing sensible application use are to be observed. Systematic feature testing must go beyond testing of "normal" behavior and test invalid or pathological use of the software. Test objectives 2-6 reflect this by systematically disregarding various types of rules of sensible system use. The second test objective is to disregard the `Mount-Dismount` scripting rules. The robot tape library requires `Mount` and `Dismount` commands to be sequenced properly. It does not make sense to issue a `Dismount` request unless a tape was `Mounted` earlier in the command sequence. The third test objective is to test for faults in the `Enter-Drain` sequences. The `Enter` command allows a test engineer to insert new tapes into the robot tape library through a door called a Cartridge Access Port (CAP). The door is a shared resource and it is assigned to one tester at a time. When finished, the tester issues a `Drain` command to release the door for the next tester. Test objective four is to disregard all scripting rules. In this case, the test generator creates random lists of commands, but within commands, relationships between parameter values are still enforced during the parameter value selection for test commands. The next test objective explicitly disregards such intracommand rules. Intracommand rules specify how to choose parameter values within a single command. Sometimes the value of one parameter constrains the choices of other parameters in the same command. For instance, when moving tapes within the same "silo", it is usually not allowed to move tapes to the very slots they just came from (meaning that in a move command the slot identifier parameter where the tape is now and where it should be moved, must be different). The last test objective is to disregard any and all rules. This effectively generates random sequences of commands and parameter values. Thus, the six test objectives represent a variety of sensible and erroneous system uses.

3.3 Test Oracle

The test oracle acts as an impartial, objective arbiter to determine whether a given test case (i.e., sequence of commands) exposes a fault and if so, the type of fault. The oracle for this study was automated. When used in the field, the test oracle is replaced by testers who judge the results of running a test case.

Table 1 specifies characteristics of ten hypothetical faults in an automated tape library, representing six different aspects of the application domain. These ten hypothetical faults cause failures at three different severity levels. Severity 1 is the most severe and Severity 3 the least. Severity 4 represents no-fault. For each fault, Table 1 gives the symptom and the specification how to recognize it (fault indicator column), as well as the severity of the problem. For a detailed description of the faults see von Mayrhauser et al. 1995 [39].

Table 1: Test Oracle Specification

Fault Type	Symptom	Fault Indicators	Sev
Sequencing Fault	1. Incorrect mount order	Test Case Length $\geq$ 30 MOUNT Freq = DISMOUNT Freq	S3
	2. Incorrect command sequencing	Test Case Length $\geq$ 20 MOUNT Freq < DISMOUNT Freq	S2
	3. CAP not released	Test Case Length $\geq$ 10 ENTER Freq > DRAIN Freq	S2
Command Fault	4. Inconsistent database	Test Case Length > 30 CDS Freq $\geq$ 5 `disable` Parameter > 3	S1
Command & Parameter Fault	5. Unusually high delay to put 000 online	`MODIFY 000 ONLINE` MODIFY Frequency $\leq$ 3	S3
	6. System stays offline	`MODIFY 000 ONLINE` MODIFY Frequency > 3	S2
Object Fault (Pass Through Port)	7. Lost tape	Test Case Length > 30 Number of PTP Moves > 8	S1
Intracommand Rule Fault	8. No warning issued for violating rule.	Test Case Length $\leq$ 15 LSM1 = LSM2 AND Panel1 = Panel2	S3
	9. Tape moved to wrong destination panel	Test Case Length > 15 LSM1 = LSM2 AND Panel1 = Panel2	S2
Command Interaction	10. Inconsistent database	Ratio: MOUNT Freq to MOVE Freq > 0.8 Test Case Length $\geq$ 30	S1

3.4 Neural Network Training

We trained four neural nets using error backpropagation with unipolar sigmoid units, one for each fault severity level. Each network had 21 input nodes and one output node. The number of hidden units was calculated experimentally to achieve the best Root Mean Square (RMS) error during training.

The test data set for neural net training included 180 observations, thirty test cases for each of the six test objectives. Table 2 shows the 21 metrics used as input to the neural net and lists the four output severity levels. These inputs relate to coverage metrics for Domain Based Testing, i.e., we wanted to explore with the fault revealing capabilities of the testing technique itself, to which extent coverage measures of a test case work in training a neural network to recognize effective test cases. The first input calculates the length of the test case, the next ten inputs represent the frequency of each command in the test case, and the last ten inputs count the number of unique values for each parameter. The output vector identifies fault severity levels 1-4.

Table 2: Input Vector Descriptions

Index	Description
1.	Test Case Length
2.	CDS Frequency
3.	DISMOUNT Frequency
4.	DISPLAY Frequency
5.	DRAIN Frequency
6.	EJECT Frequency
7.	ENTER Frequency
8.	MODIFY Frequency
9.	MOUNT Frequency
10.	MOVE Frequency
11.	SRVLEV Frequency
12.	acs Frequency
13.	cap Frequency
14.	cc Frequency
15.	drive Frequency
16.	dsn Frequency
17.	host Frequency
18.	lsm Frequency
19.	pp Frequency
20.	rr Frequency
21.	volser Frequency

3.5 Training Results

We trained all four networks (one for each severity level) using LOOM to experimentally calculate the best network topology (number of hidden units).

Table 3 lists the best topology for each network. Best results for Fault Severity 1 through 3 were obtained with networks having single hidden units. For Severity 4, best results were for five hidden units.

When it is discovered that test accuracy is not improved with more than one hidden unit, two possibilities exist. One possibility is that there is an almost linear relationship between the features used to represent the test cases and the presence or absence of the error. The second, more likely, possibility is that there is an insufficient amount of data to support learning a more complex relationship. For example, this would be the case if the desired function is a four-period sine curve, but only four samples of this function are available. Another example would be a simpler, but noisy function, such as a one-period

Table 3: Network Topologies

Severity	Input Units	Hidden Units	Output Units
S1	21	1	1
S2	21	1	1
S3	21	1	1
S4	21	5	1

sine curve with added noise. Again, four samples are insufficient for approximating the curve. Given the high classification accuracies reported in Table 5, it appears that approximately linear relationships do exist between test case features and Severity 1, 2, and 3 errors, but not for Severity 4 errors.

The results from training all four networks are listed in Table 4. The second column shows how well each network predicted individual fault severities. The Severity 4 (no error) predicted the best with 94.4%, and the second-best predictor was the Severity 1 (most severe fault) net, with 91.7%. Incorrectly classified tests were either: *False Positive*, *False Negative*, and *Other Incorrect*. A False Positive response is recorded for severity 1-3 errors when the network predicts a fault that doesn't truly exist. For S4 (no error), a false positive means that the neural network predicted no error, when the test case would have uncovered one. For severity classes 1-3, a False Negative response predicts Severity 4 (no fault exposed) when the test case indicates a fault. Other Incorrect refers to tests that were classified by the neural net as exposing a fault, but of the wrong type. We use this information to analyze three test data generation objectives.

Table 4: Neural Network Prediction Results

Sev.	Correct Class	False +	False −	Other Incorrect
S1	165 (91.7%)	0	0	15
S2	161 (89.4%)	7	0	12
S3	149 (82.8%)	18	12	1
S4	170 (94.4%)	3	0	7

Objective 1: Reduce Number of Test Cases. One goal for test data generation is to reduce the number of test cases run on the system under test. Each test case consumes machine time and resources. Testers must evaluate each test case to determine whether a fault was exposed. To reduce testing

time and cost, we need to run tests that are likely to identify a fault. This is particularly important with automated test data generation systems that easily and quickly generate thousands of test cases.

A tester could use the neural net classifier to reduce the number of test cases. The neural net classifies each test case. Severity 4 predictions need not be run. Two things that help us achieve this objective are automated test data generation and low cost of test case evaluation. Automated test data generators like *Sleuth* generate test cases quickly. They can generate tests much more quickly than it takes to run them. Likewise, a neural network predictor evaluates a test case in a single forward-pass through the net. The key to meeting this objective is a predictor that is good at the binary decision: `Does this test case expose a fault or not?` We aren't concerned about misclassification of the individual fault severity but we must keep False Positive predictions for severity levels 1-3 to a minimum. It is also advantageous to keep False Positive low for Severity 4.

Our study shows that the neural net has a low False Positive and Negative prediction rates. This suggests that the neural net can be used to reduce the number of test cases. With these results we could reduce the number of test cases to be run by 30%.

Objective 2: Emphasize Severe Error Exposure. Another goal for test data generation is to create tests that expose the most severe system faults. The cost to fix such problems once the product is in the field is high. To make matters worse, severe faults are often the most difficult to isolate, identify, and expose.

A tester could meet this test data generation objective using a neural net to evaluate tests before they are run. If the net predicts high severity (e.g., Severity 1 or 2 for our tests), then the test should be run. We also have the advantage of automated test data generation and a fast test evaluation. The key to achieving this objective is an accurate fault prediction at the higher levels of severity. We are concerned about misclassification of tests at lower severity levels. If the net tends to classify test cases with a lower fault severity than truly exists, then tests will not run that should. If misclassified with higher fault severity than truly exists, then we will run tests that need not run. We also require the neural net to have a low False Negative prediction. If tests that are likely to expose faults are classified as Severity 4, we will not run them, but we should.

Data from the empirical study suggests that the neural network can be used to identify tests for severe error exposure. The network predicts Severity 1 and Severity 2 faults well, and its False Negative rate is low. Only 12 out of 180 vectors were False Negative. We did not find any tests in which the network predicted a higher severity fault than really existed.

Objective 3: Minimize Number of Test Cases. Beyond objectives 1 and 2 we may be able to reduce tests further by concentrating on test cases that expose errors at multiple severity levels. One way to rank a test case as more effective than another is to count the number of fault severity levels the test exposes. If one test exposes multiple severity levels (say, Severity 2 and 3), it should be ranked higher than a test that exposes a single level (i.e., Severity 2). It exposes multiple severity levels, meets several test criteria, and thus further reduces the total test set. To achieve this objective, we need accurate test case effectiveness prediction. We emphasize the accuracy of the neural net prediction because we want to keep those tests that identify multiple severity levels. If the net misclassified a multi-severity test as a single severity test, then it may not be ranked high enough to be included in the test set.

The data set for the experimental study contains 60 multi-severity tests. The neural net fails to predict all faults in 26 of the 60 multi-severity tests. When failing to predict every fault, these 26 tests could be ranked incorrectly and some of them could be eliminated from the minimal test set. The variability in these classifications can be explained by our choice of input representation. The neural network only gets summarized information via the metrics in Table 2. It sees a "filtered" picture of each test case. This may not be precise enough to predict multi-severity level tests accurately. What these results indicate, however, is that the neural network produces remarkably good "coarse" level predictions (i.e., Test Data Objectives 1 and 2) despite the limited metric information. In particular, the network effectively screens no-yield test cases (Test Objective 1) and identifies high severity tests (Test Objective 2). This result also indicates that we need to add other test case metrics to improve neural net predictions.

4 White Box Testing

4.1 VHDL Branch Coverage

VHDL is a language to describe the behavioral design of hardware. Currently designers verify behavioral models through extensive functional simulations. However, for large behavioral models with several thousand lines of code, a large number of tests may show significant overlap in what portion of the model they cover, thus reducing the likelihood of uncovering new faults in the model. Therefore, white box testing of VHDL models using certain coverage metrics can provide useful guidance to minimize overall test effort while achieving maximum coverage. Model coverage in VHDL is similar to test coverage in software. Analogous to software metrics like branch coverage, we define coverage measures for VHDL. Insofar as VHDL is a language to express the behavior of a 'machine', it can be considered software. We use the term *testing* in the software sense to refer to validation of VHDL behavioral models (VHDL software). Human effort is often required to produce test cases and inspect results. Substantial computing resources are also required; simulations of final VLSI (Very Large Scale Integration) designs may require days of computing time.

We studied how well a neural network can be trained to predict coverage from a given test input, as a prelude to building a system for automatically generating tests for VHDL behavioral models.

For the experiments reported here, we chose a software test coverage metric called "branch coverage" [17]. A design is said to be fully covered only when the tests force execution of every branch in the model. Consider the following fragment from a VHDL model. Comments begin with "–".

```
1 – All flags are FALSE at beginning of simulation.
2 IF (x = '0') THEN
3     – flag1 := TRUE; (inserted by compiler)
4     a <= p;
5 ELSE
6     – flag2 := TRUE; (inserted by compiler)
7     a <= q;
8 END IF;
```

Lines 4 and 7 are branches in the flowchart of this model. Branch coverage requires that each branch must be executed at least once. In order to determine which branches are covered, the VHDL compiler inserts flag-setting statements into the model as shown in italics on lines 3 and 6 of the code fragment. After simulating the model with a set of test stimuli, the flags indicate which branches have been executed. If all branch flags are TRUE, the test has achieved 100% branch coverage.

We chose a VHDL model of a VLSI chip for visual object recognition [32]. This model has about 3,700 lines of VHDL code. The code is of the same character and complexity as is found in microprocessors and thus represents a realistic problem.

In addition to the selection of the input data, the experiment had to consider how many clock ticks each input set was going to be applied. For hardware design where devices and chips may exercise some of their functionality only after a certain number of 'steps' (clock ticks) this is an important consideration. An example of such a situation would be the design of a counter.

4.2 Experiment with 3 Clock-ticks

To investigate automated generation of stimuli for behavioral designs, we randomly generated 400 independent tests, ran them through the simulator, and recorded the results for later training and analysis by a neural network. Each test run consisted of the following steps:

1. The simulator was reset, and the branch coverage flags set to FALSE.

2. The clock input (of the simulated VLSI device) was set high and the simulation time advanced a few nanoseconds in order to allow the device to respond and stabilize.

3. The 36 inputs (not including the clock input) were set to a random state (each bit randomly set to 0 or 1 with 50% probability), and the state of each of these input bits was recorded in a file. The simulation time was advanced again.

4. The clock input was set low, and time was advanced.

5. Steps 3 and 4 are repeated two more times.

This model generated 505 coverage flags; 450 of them were constant over all test runs, with 148 of the branches always covered and 302 of them never covered. This is not surprising, as some branches will always be covered by any clock activity, and some branches will never be covered with just 1 1/2 clock cycles (3 clock ticks). The mean coverage over all 400 patterns is 169.8 with a standard deviation of 4.6. The range is from 155 to 182. Constant branch flags (those that were always covered or never covered) were eliminated from the collected data, leaving 55 bits of coverage data for use in training and analysis of the neural net. Thus, each test produced 36 x 3, or 108, bits representing the stimulus to the device, and 55 bits representing the coverage results from that stimulus.

Three clock ticks(1.5 cycles) is a small amount of activation for testing a complex VLSI circuit. New tests with widely varying sizes of sets of random inputs (10 - 400) show very little difference in the number of branches covered leading to the suspicion that few enough branches may be potentially exercised in three clock ticks that testing coverage has reached a plateau.

4.3 Higher Number of Clock Ticks

Tests using greater numbers of clock ticks, up to 15, and generating up to 1000 test cases indicates slightly higher levels of coverage. For 7 clock ticks(3.5

20

cycles), coverage reaches 219 branches. Similar results were obtained for 5 and 15 clock ticks. Apparently, there is a plateau of coverage for each number of clock ticks that can be reached.

From these 1000 random inputs, only 300 were used to train the neural network. The 300 inputs covered 217 of the 219 branches. Thus, there are 2 branches that we knew could be covered with 7 clock ticks that are not covered by the training examples presented to the neural network. As before, we reduce the neural net training problem by eliminating the branches that are always covered (161) and the branches which are never covered (286). This leaves 58 branches for training the neural network. Two of these are not covered by the 300 test cases used to train the network.

This way we can test whether the neural network is able to find test cases that would cover two 'new' branches of which it knows nothing.

4.4 Neural Net Training

For our experiments we used standard, feedforward neural networks consisting of one or two hidden layers and one output layer, all containing units with sigmoidal activation functions. Inputs are the states of the binary stimuli used to test the circuit and outputs are predictions of whether or not particular branches intex the circuit will be covered. The network is trained using the error back-propagation algorithm[31] and data splitting explained earlier.

Runs with three clock-ticks

A number of different neural network architectures were tested. Performance of each was measured by the percent of branch coverage flags correctly predicted as being covered or not. A network output greater than 0.5 is taken as a prediction that the corresponding branch would be covered.

Figure 5 shows the percent correct versus the network architectures. Architectures are indicated by a pair of numbers giving the number of hidden units in each layer. A zero for the second number represents a network with a single hidden layer. Plotted values are averages over 20 training runs, each with different initial weight values and different selections of training, validation and test data.

The figure shows that even a network with a single hidden unit can, on average, correctly predict 82% of the branch coverage flags. A network with a single hidden unit is practically a linear function. The addition of up to 60 hidden units, however, improves performance to almost 88% correct. Larger networks might result in even higher accuracy, but this has not been tested.

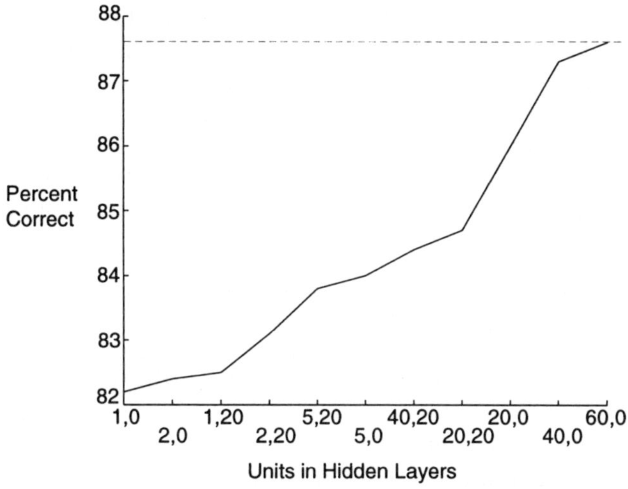

Figure 5: Fraction of Coverage Flags Correctly Predicted, Averaged Over 20 Runs.

A count of correct and incorrect predictions made by a 40,0 network are shown in Table 5. The test data consists of 80 cases of 55 branch flags each, for a total of 4,400 flags to be predicted. The table shows that out of these 4,400, 1,558 of the covered branches and 2,394 of the uncovered branches were correctly predicted, making a total of 3,952, or 89.8%, correct predictions. The table also shows that the network produced 248 false positives (predicted coverage for uncovered branches) and 200 false negatives (no predicted coverage for covered branches).

Table 5: Results for a 40,0 Network

		Actual Data	
		Covered	Not Covered
Network	Covered	1,558	200
Prediction	Not Covered	248	2,394

Thus, the neural network is able to predict coverage with fairly high accuracy. A related question is whether one can use the inverted neural network to generate new test stimuli.

A random input stimulus was supplied to the neural network. This input stimulus was incrementally modified by performing a gradient-based minimization search, where the gradient is of the squared difference between the network's output and the desired coverage. The desired coverage was set to either all branches covered or all branches uncovered. This process was repeated 5 times with a desired coverage of all branches, and 4 times with a desired coverage of no branches. The resulting input stimuli were then passed through the VHDL simulator and the resulting coverage recorded. The generated input stimuli consist of real-valued components. To pass the generated input stimuli through the simulator, these values are converted to binary values by setting them to 1 if greater than 0.5 and to 0 if not.

Table 6 summarizes the results. Input stimulus 1 is predicted by the network to cover 181 branches. When applied to the VHDL simulator, 185 branches were covered. Recall that the largest number of branches covered by any single test in our initial 400 stimuli is 182, so this procedure has discovered a new test stimulus that covers more branches than any previous single stimulus. This table also shows that those test stimuli generated to maximize coverage do indeed cover more branches than those stimuli generated to minimize coverage.

Table 6: Predicted and Actual Number of Branches Covered

	Input	Branches Covered	
	Stimuli	Predicted	Actual
	1	181	185
	2	181	182
Maximized	3	179	178
Coverage	4	178	181
	5	183	176
	6	156	155
Minimized	7	156	155
Coverage	8	157	156
	9	156	161

This result relates to individual test stimuli, but how well does the coverage produced by the set of 5 generated test stimuli compare to that of the initial 400 stimuli? The initial set of 400 stimuli covers 203 branches. The set of generated stimuli, numbered 1–5 in Table 6 covers 196 (96.6%) of these while 7 remain uncovered. Inspection of exactly which branches are covered by each test stimulus reveals that the 5 generated test stimuli do not cover any additional branches that were not covered by the initial set of 400 stimuli.

Runs with higher numbers of clock ticks

Analogous to the first experiment, the network is trained and inverted. This inversion of the neural network means that the neural network's input space of test data is searched for vectors that most closely produce the desired branch coverage. The calculated test cases from the inverted network are vectors of real values between 0 and 1. Inspection revealed that most of the values had migrated to a 0 or a 1 during training. The simulator accepts vectors of probabilities for inputs. Setting the inputs in a vector to 0's and 1's allow for the testing of a specific input vector. In the earlier experiment, the rest of the inputs in the vector were set to 0 or 1 based on a threshold value (.5) before being tested on the simulator. In addition to these individual tests this study presented the real valued vectors to the simulator and produced sets of 50 simulations. Using these probability vectors as inputs for generating test cases for the simulator should cause inputs about which the neural network is least confident to be varied the most.

The data was run on networks with various learning rates and topologies ranging from 2 to 80 hidden nodes and 1 or 2 hidden layers. All of the networks showed the error on the training data decaying to less than .02 while the minimum validation error was reached quickly at approximately .27-.28. This indicates that the networks learned the training data well but were less than excellent in generalizing to new data. This may indicate that the training data did not contain enough information.

Of the 300 randomly generated test inputs the maximum coverage by any one test was 207 branches and the minimum coverage for any one test was 180. The mean coverage for the 300 inputs was 193.4 branches. The tests generated by the neural network by setting the output to maximized coverage produced results similar to the experiment with three clock ticks.

Table 7 shows the results of coverage produced by 5 test cases generated by training and then inversion of the neural network based on the 300 random tests described above, using a target of maximized coverage(all 1's).

Table 7: Results for Tests to Maximize Coverage

Tests	Predicted Coverage	Actual Coverage	50 Test Case Totals
1	199	203	206
2	198	204	209
3	199	193	207
4	198	204	206
5	198	205	205

The predicted coverage is the number of branches that the network predicts will be covered by the calculated test case. The output of the inverted network is actually a vector of probability values for the inputs in the input vector. The column of actual coverage values is the number of branches covered by setting each input in the input vector to 0 or 1 based on a threshold value (.5) before being tested on the simulator. The last column is the cumulative coverage generated by leaving each of the vectors of probabilities as values between 0 and 1, and setting the simulator to produce 50 tests based on each vector. The minimum number of branches covered by any of the calculated tests was 191. The maximum number of branches covered by any single calculated test was 206. The mean number of covered branches for all generated tests was 200.88. A relatively poor convergence value for test 3 is reflected in the lower actual coverage. The results show that the network learned to identify and created inputs that would produce coverages that were on the average better than random testing. However, the 5 calculated tests combined only covered 206 out of the 219 known branches that could be covered. Examination of the random tests revealed that all 219 branches could be covered by as few as 4 of the tests. No new branches were covered that were not covered by the random tests.

Table 8: Results for Tests Generated to Minimize Coverage

Tests	Predicted Coverage	Actual Coverage	50 Test Case Totals
1	187	190	191
2	186	190	197

Table 8 shows two tests with the target set to minimized coverage (all 0's). The inverted network did not converge well with the desired coverage set all 0's. It is possible that the network contained insufficient information about that part of the input space. The predicted coverage of outputs hovered closely to .5 indicating that the network was not sure of its prediction. No new branches were covered. This indicates that increases in coverage are not likely going to come from this process. Test vectors with low likelihood given existing data will not produce rare or entirely new test stimuli in terms of resulting coverage.

5   Assessment and Conclusions

Without a doubt, our studies show that neural nets can be used to enhance current testing approaches, because they trained very well in all cases. This would make it possible for the neural net to act as a filter with various objectives. First, such a filter could weed out test cases that are not likely to find faults. Second, the net could be used to identify test cases that are likely to find particular types of faults. In either case, generation of new test cases that are presented to the trained neural net for classification, can be generated by any of a number of generation mechanisms from random to manual.

The success of using a neural net to enhance testing efforts hinges on the following factors.

The Choice of Input Representation. The system testing study indicates that the chosen test case metrics worked very well in the classification of tests that would not reveal any errors, as well as in the classification of severity 1 errors. For the other error classes, the input representation may need more information. This conclusion is suggested by the combination of the relatively low accuracies of the networks and the finding that accuracy does not increase with more than one hidden unit. These two results often indicate noisy data containing little information about the relationship between inputs and desired outputs of the neural network or any function approximator. The input representation should be expanded to include additional metrics of the test cases that are suspected to relate more strongly to the predictions of errors.

In the white box testing study, the bit representation of the input was too detailed. While it did not affect training and forward use of the network (as when using it as a filter), the inverted network indicated that the net had too little knowledge to be of use in generating new test cases. The input space was too large. This indicates that the net needs a more compact input representation. Using the bit representation is also problematic when test cases are of a varying number of clock ticks, resulting in variable-length input vectors to the neural networks. We also suggest to include clock cycles as one of the inputs to train on, as it affects whether or not internal states can be reached by the code. In general, training a neural net on input information that includes retained state would lead to higher accuracy.

Type of Neural Network. We have found that it is possible to train a neural network to predict fault exposure or branch coverage of newly generated tests. The trained network can also be used to generate a much smaller validation suite by using the inverted neural network. In the whitebox testing study, we reduced 400 test stimuli to 5 stimuli to cover 96.6% of the same branches. Training with additional stimuli or larger networks might increase this percentage.

Our method of inverting the network did not, however, produce test stimuli that obtain any new branch coverage. This is not too surprising, because the new test stimuli produced by inverting the network is based only on data about branches that have already been covered. To produce new coverage we must generate test stimuli that differ from existing test stimuli.

We plan to combine what the neural net has learned with heuristics to identify inputs that are considered 'different' from the ones that cause the current coverage (e. g. Cartesian or Hamming distance of new inputs compared to old ones [20]). A second approach is to include information about the relationships among branches, gleaned from the VHDL model, to focus our search for tests that will cover particular, key branches.

A third approach is to use active learning algorithms. Active learning algorithms have produced some encouraging results in improving learning and should be readily adaptable to the problem of generating new test cases that will increase coverage.

The primary question of active learning is how to choose which input to try next. There are many heuristics for choosing the next input including where we don't have data or have a high degree of uncertainty, where we expect it to change our model or where we previously found data that resulted in learning [9]. Various active learning algorithms [25,19,7,8,24] using methods including optimal experiment design, version space training, statistically based locally weighted regression and Bayesian query construction have shown promise in minimizing generalization errors. Some methods have been shown to work well on small sample situations but may have computational cost problems on larger situations [9,7].

The Bayesian approach requires that the prediction for a test case be based on all possible values for the network parameters, weighted by the probability of each set of parameters values in light of the training data. While conventional backpropagation is an optimization problem, Bayesian training and prediction is an integration problem [24]. Specifically, we plan to consider the methods used by Paas and Kindermann [25] in Bayesian query construction using Markov Chain Monte Carlo methods.

Branch coverage is just one of several posssible testing criteria. A good active learning, predictive model should also be applicable to the other structural testing metrics.

Size of Training Data. The amount of training data needed and the choice of data representation are strongly related. The dimensionality of the data space is determined by the number of components in the data representation. A fixed amount of data is, in general, spread much more sparsely in a higher-dimensional space, making it more difficult to find the interrelationships among the data components and the desired outputs. If the amount of data is limited, then more effort must be directed toward finding a small representation. It is difficult to devise a rule of thumb for the amount of data needed, because it depends strongly on the complexity of the function that must be learned, which is usually not known a priori.

Nature of Training Data. In the system testing study, we used test data that were generated based on an operational profile and based on specific test objectives. This worked very well for training purposes. The quality of the data used to train the net affects what the net can learn. Data that concentrates on a small portion of the search space results in a neural net that is well trained on that small portion of the search space, making generalization difficult.

In the white box testing study, the input stimuli were generated randomly. The results might have been different, had we chosen test stimuli that were not random. This needs further exploration. Since neural nets require a certain amount of data to train, it may be a good use of the net to wait until a plateau of coverage has been reached with a number of test stimuli that is large enough to train the net. This means that we are using the trained net when other approaches to increase coverage further have failed. If this works, the neural net would be successful in the hardest part of the test task, when other techniques not longer work.

Combined Heuristics. Neural nets do not assume any knowledge about the software under test other than the relationships on which they were trained. There may be other information available that, in combination with the net may improve yield. We believe that ultimately, a combination of test generation methods using functional, random, and extrapolation heuristics will be most helpful in increasing software testing yield.

Acknowledgements

This work was partially supported by the National Science Foundation through grant MIP-9628770 and by the Colorado Advanced Software Institute (CASI), and StorageTek. CASI is sponsored in part by the Colorado Advanced Technology Institute (CATI), an agency of the state of Colorado. CATI promotes advanced technology teaching and research at universities in Colorado for the purpose of economic development.

References

1. Charles W. Anderson, Judy A. Franklin, and Richard S. Sutton. "Learning a Nonlinear Model of a Manufacturing Process Using Multilayer Connectionist Networks," *Proc. of the 5th IEEE International Symposium on Intelligent Control*, Philadelphia, PA, September 1990, pp. 404–409.

2. J. Bauer and A. Finger. "Test Plan Generation Using Formal Grammars", *Procs. Fourth International Conference on Software Engineering*, 1979, pp. 425-432.

3. Franco Bazzichi and Ippolito Spadafora. "An Automatic Generator for Compiler Testing," *IEEE Transactions on Software Engineering*, 1982:8(4), pp.343-353.

4. B. Beizer; *Software Testing Techniques*, Van Nostrand Reinhold, New York, NY, 1990.

5. A. Celentano and S. Crespi Reghizz i and P. Della Vigna and C. Ghezzi and G. Gramata and F. Savoretti. "Compiler Testing using a Sentence Generator," *Software-Practice and Experience*, 1980:10, pp.987-918.

6. Tsum S. Chow. "Testing Software Design Modeled by Finite State Machines," *Proceedings of the First COMPSAC*, 1977, pp. 58-64.

7. David Cohn, Les Atlas, Richard Ladner. (1994) Improving Generalization with Active Learning. Machine Learning, 15(2):201-221.

8. David A. Cohn. (1994) Neural Network Exploration Using Optimal Experiment Design. In J. Cowan et al., eds., Advances in Neural Information Processing Systems 6. Morgan Kaufmann.

9. David A. Cohn, Zoubin Ghahramani, Michael I. Jordan.(1995) Active Learning with Statistical Models. In G. Tessauro, D. Touretzky, and T. Leen, eds., Advances in Neural Information Processing Systems 7. MIT Press, Cambridge, MA.

10. DeMillo, R., A.; Offutt, A., J.; "Constraint-Based Automatic Test Data Generation", *IEEE Transactions on Software Engineering SE-17*, 9(Sept. 1991), pp. 900–910.

11. A.G. Duncan and J.S. Hutchison, "Using Attributed Grammars to Test Designs and Implementations," *Proceedings of the Fifth International Conference on Software Engineering*, 1981, pp. 170-177.

12. Laurene Fausett. *Fundamentals of Neural Networks*. Prentice Hall: Englewood Cliffs, New Jersey, 1994.

13. S. Fujiwara, G. von Bochman, F. Khendek, M. Amalou, and A. Ghedamsi. "Test Selection Based on Finite State Models", *IEEE Transactions on Software Engineering SE-17*, no. 10(June 1991), pp. 591-603.

14. P. Frankl, S. Weiss; "An experimental comparison of the effectiveness of

branch testing and data flow testing", *Transactions on Software Engineering vol. 19*, no. 8(August 1993), pp. 774–787.

15. Higashino, T., v. Bochman, G.; "Automatic Analysis and Test Case Derivation for a Restricted Class of LOTOS Expressions with Data Parameters", *IEEE Transactions on Software Engineering SE-20*, 1(January 1994), pp. 29–42.

16. W. Howden; *Functional Testing and Analysis*, McGraw-Hill, New York, NY, 1987.

17. J. Huang. An approach to program testing. *ACM Computing Surveys*, 7:113–128, September 1975.

18. Y. LeCun, J. S. Denker, and S. A. Solla. Optimal brain damage. In D. S. Touretzky, editor, *Advances in Neural Information Processing Systems*, volume 2, page 598. Morgan Kaufmann, San Mateo, CA, 1990.

19. D. MacKay. (1992) Information-Based Objective Functions for Active Data Selection. Neural Computation 4, p.590- 604.

20. Y. Malaiya. Antirandom Testing: Getting the Most out of Black-Box Testing. In *Proceedings Symposium on Software Reliability Engineering*, Oct. 1995, Toulouse, France.

21. J.L. McClelland, D.E. Rumelhart, and the PDP Research Group. *Parallel Distributed Processing: Exploration in the Microstructure of Cognition*, vol 1. MIT Press, 1986.

22. P. Maurer. "Generating Test Data with Enhanced Context-Free Grammars", *IEEE Software*, July 1990, pp. 50-55.

23. M. C. Mozer and P. Smolensky. Skeletonization: A technique for trimming the fat from a network via relevance assessment. In D. S. Touretzky, editor, *Advances in Neural Information Systems*, volume 1, pages 107–115. Morgan Kaufmann, San Mateo, CA, 1989.

24. R. M. Neal.(1992) Bayesian Training of Backpropagation Networks by the Hybrid Monte Carlo Method. Tech Report CRG-TR-92-1, Dept. of Computer Science, Univ. of Toronto.

25. Gerhard Paass, Jorg Kindermann. (1995) Bayesian Query construction for Neural Network Models. In G. Tesauro, D. Touretzky, and T. Leen, eds., Advances in Neural Information Processing Systems 7. MIT Press, Cambridge, MA.

26. P. Purdom. "A Sentence Generator for Testing Parsers", *BIT*, 12(3), 1972, pp. 366-375.

27. A. Parrish, S. Zweben; "Analysis and Refinement of Software Test Data Adequacy Properties", IEEE Transactions on Software Engineering vol. 17, no. 6(June 1991), pp. 565–581.

28. S. Ramachandran and L. Pratt. Information measure based skeletoni-

sation. In *Advances in Neural Information Systems*, volume 4. Morgan Kaufmann, San Mateo, CA, 1992.

29. Rapps, S.; Weyuker, E., J.; "Data Flow Analysis Techniques for Test Data Selection" *Procs. Sixth Int. Conf. Software Engineering*, IEEE Computer Society, Tokyo, Japan, Sept. 1982, pp. 272–277.

30. Rapps, S.; Weyuker, E., J.; "Selecting Software Test Data using Data Flow Information", *IEEE Transactions on Software Engineering SE-11*, 4(April 1985), pp. 367–375.

31. D. E. Rumelhart, G. E. Hinton, and R. W. Williams. Learning internal representations by error propagation. In D. E. Rumelhart, J. L. McClelland, and The PDP Research Group, editors, *Parallel Distributed Processing: Explorations in the Microstructure of Cognition*, volume 1. Bradford, Cambridge, MA, 1986.

32. Maureen Schaffer and Tom Chen. A VLSI architecture for 2D object classification based on tree matching. In *Proceedings of the International Conference on Computer Architectures for Machine Perception*, September 1995.

33. Gmeiner, L.; Voges, U.; von Mayrhauser, A.; "SADAT–An Automated Testing Tool", *IEEE Transactions on Software Engineering SE-6*, 3(May 1980), pp. 286–290.

34. A. von Mayrhauser; *Software Engineering: Methods and Management*, Academic Press, Boston, MA, 1990.

35. A. von Mayrhauser, S. Crawford-Hines; "Automated Testing Support for a Robot Tape Library", *Procs. IEEE Computer Society International Symp. on Software Reliability Engineering*, Denver, Nov. 1993, pp. 6–14.

36. Anneliese von Mayrhauser, Jeff Walls, and Richard Mraz, "Testing Applications Using Domain Based Testing and *Sleuth*," *Proceedings of the Fifth International Software Reliability Engineering Symposium,* Monterey, November 1994, pp. 206–215.

37. Anneliese von Mayrhauser, Richard Mraz, Jeff Walls, and Pete Ocken. "Domain Based Testing: Increasing Test Case Reuse," *Proc. of the International Conference on Computer Design*, Boston, October 1994, pp. 484–491.

38. Anneliese von Mayrhauser, Jeff Walls, and Richard Mraz. "*Sleuth*: A Domain Based Testing Tool", *Proc. of the International Test Conference*, October, 1994.

39. von Mayrhauser, A.; Anderson, Ch.; Mraz, R.; "Using A Neural Network to Predict Test Case Effectiveness", *Procs. IEEE Aerospace Applications Conference*, Snowmass, CO, Feb. 1995

40. Andreas S. Weigend. On overfitting and the effective number of hidden

units. In M. C. Mozer, P. Smolensky, D. S. Touretzky, J. L. Elman, and A. S. Weigend, editors, *Proceedings of the 1993 Connectionist Models Summer School*, pages 335–342, 1994.

41. Weigend, Rumelhart, and Huberman. Generalization by weight-elimination with application to forecasting. In Richard P. Lippmann, John E. Moody, and David S. Touretzky, editors, *Advances in Neural Information Processing Systems*, volume 3, pages 875–882. Morgan Kaufmann, 1991.

42. E. Weyuker; "Axiomatizing Software Test Data Adequacy", *IEEE Transactions on Software Engineering vol. 12*, no. 12(Dec. 1986), pp. 1128–1138.

43. E. Weyuker; "The Cost of Data Flow Testing: An Empirical Study", *IEEE Transactions on Software Engineering vol. 16*, no. 2(Feb. 1990), pp. 121–128.

44. E. Weyuker; "More Experience with Data Flow Testing", *IEEE Transactions on Software Engineering vol. 19*, no. 9(Sep. 1993), pp. 912–919.

45. Weyuker, E., Goradia, T., Singh, A.; "Automatically Generating Test Data from a Boolean Specification", *IEEE Transactions on Software Engineering SE-20*, 5(May 1994), pp. 353–363.

46. Jacek M. Zurada. *Introduction to Artificial Neural Systems*. West Publishing: St. Paul, 1992.

Exercises

1. The test case representation shown in Table 2 does not produce a unique input vector for every test case. Identify some tests that will be represented by exactly the same input vector. Do they represent similar types of operation of the system being tested? Are the likely to exhibit the same failure severity?

2. Discuss the possible ramifications of reducing the representation in Table 2 to only the first 11 features—those that indicate command frequency.

3. Neural networks are capable of learning nonlinear relationships between their input and output. Discuss why using the correlation between individual inputs and desired outputs would not be sufficient for determining which inputs can be thrown out.

4. Explain why pruning can increase the generalization ability, which is the performance on new data, of a neural network.

5. Using an early-stopping procedure, if you find that one hidden unit is enough for your data, what should you be concerned with? Describe two ways of dealing with this concern.

6. If, in addition to a trained neural network, you also have a control flow graph, how could you use the control flow graph with the neural network to do a better job of generating test cases that uncover new branches than with the neural network alone? What if you also have a data flow graph?

7. SEMESTER PROJECT: Choose a small command language, such as a subset of the Unix command language. Construct an oracle for this language. Define an input representation for test cases like the one in this chapter. Define at least one alternative representation. Determine how consistent the data is given your representations, i.e., how many test cases are represented by identical input vectors for each representation. Which of your representations is likely to result in the best prediction of errors?

Considering how much data you collect, would you use LOOM or early-stopping for your project? Why?

Train a neural network using your best representations. Evaluate the results in the manner illustrated in this chapter.

NEURAL NETWORKS
FOR SOFTWARE QUALITY PREDICTION

T.M. KHOSHGOFTAAR, E.B. ALLEN
Empirical Software Engineering Laboratory
Department of Computer Science and Engineering
Florida Atlantic University
777 W. Glades Road
Boca Raton, FL 333431, USA
E-mail: taghi@cse.fau.edu

Society's reliance on large complex computer systems mandates high reliability. Reliable software is a necessary component. Controlling faults in software requires that one can predict problems early enough to take preventive action. Software metrics are a basis for such predictions. This study systematically presents a methodology for developing models that predict software quality factors with special emphasis on artificial neural network models. The individual details of this methodology may be familiar, but the whole modeling process must be integrated to produce successful predictions of software quality. We use two case studies to illustrate each step. One case study predicted the number of faults to be discovered in each module, and the other predicted whether each module would be considered *fault-prone*. The first case study was based on a sample of modules from a military command, control and communications system. We developed a quantitative neural network model, and for comparison, we developed a multiple linear regression model on the same data. The neural network approach produced a better quantitative model. The second case study was based on very large telecommunications system. We modeled modules reused with changes from the previous release, representing over seven million lines of code. We compared a classification neural network model with a nonparametric discriminant model, and found the classification neural network model was more accurate.

1 Introduction

High reliability is essential for many computer systems. Much of a system's reliability rests on the reliability of its software. Failures, faults, and errors are three important software quality metrics. In this context, a *failure* is a departure of program execution from its specified behavior due to a *fault*. An *error* is a human action that results in a *fault*, or defect, in the software product.

Controlling faults in software presupposes that one can predict problems early enough in the life cycle to take preventive action before the software goes into operation. Software metrics are a foundation for such predictions.[1,2] Many organization rush to collect volumes of software metric data without a plan for utilizing it in the course of development. Collecting software metrics is not enough. One must translate measurements into predictions. The objective of this paper is to present a methodology for doing so.

Software quality models are the tools needed for predicting a quality factor, such as faults, based on the experience of an earlier project and metrics of the current product and development process. We develop models based on data from a completed past project where the quality factor is available for each module. A *module* is lowest level of software for which we have data.

A *model* is an equation (or algorithm) where the dependent variable is a function of one or more independent variables. If one supplies values for the independent variables, then one can calculate the value of the dependent variable. A software quality model has independent variables that may be measured earlier in the life cycle than the dependent variable. Thus, the calculated dependent variable value is a *prediction* of what one expects its measured value to be.

Our goal is to develop models that will predict quality factors related to faults for each module. Total faults are directly measurable only after software has become operational. In contrast, software product metrics and process metrics can be measured during development. A suitable software quality model can make predictions when it is not too late to take compensatory actions. A software quality model that predicts a measure of reliability for each module enables developers and managers to focus resources on the most trouble-prone modules early in the software life cycle. Consequently, operational reliability can be significantly improved by quality predictions.

This paper gives details of a modeling methodology that we have successfully used numerous times to develop models that predict some aspect of software quality.[3,4,5,6,7] The individual steps may be familiar from texts or the literature, but we present the complete methodology in one place to help practitioners develop robust quality models. As examples of this methodology, we review results from two of our recent studies.[8,9]

A variety of statistical techniques are used in software quality modeling.[10] Models are often based on a statistical relationship between a measure of quality and measures of software attributes, namely, software metrics. However, relationships between software product and process metrics and quality factors are often complex and nonlinear, limiting the accuracy of conventional approaches. Artificial neural networks are adept at modeling nonlinear functional relationships that are difficult to model with other techniques, and thus, are attractive for software quality modeling.

The large set of software product metrics used in published case studies includes many interrelated members. Statistical models are often based on assumptions that seldom hold for large subsets of this set. For example, multiple linear regression analysis assumes among other things, that the independent variables have no linear relationships, and that the errors are uncorrelated and exhibit constant variance.[11] Large collections of product metrics can violate these assumptions. The absence of the data assumptions typical of statistical techniques, suggests that neural network techniques are more apt than statistical techniques for developing models based upon software product metric data. Our case studies each compared a neural network model to a competing statistical model. Our research group has applied neural networks to software quality models since 1992.[12]

In our first case study, we applied a neural network to predict a quantity, the number of faults discovered for each software module. A military software system provided data for quantitative modeling. When predicting a quantity, we have found neural networks are often better than multiple linear regression models. We applied both neural network and multiple linear regression methods to develop quantitative models based upon these data. Each model predicts the number of faults that testing and operation will uncover in each module, based upon software product metric values for each module. We found that the neural network approach produced a better quantitative model in terms of both quality of fit and predictive quality.[8]

We have also applied neural networks to software quality classification models.[5,13,14,15] The goal of such models is identification of fault-prone modules, rather than prediction of the number of faults. In the technical literature, various classification techniques have been used to identify fault-prone software, including discriminant analysis,[16,17] classification trees,[18] fuzzy classification,[19] and pattern recognition.[20]

In our second case study, we compared a classification neural network to nonparametric discriminant analysis. We modeled a set of modules representing over seven million lines of code. The set consisted of those modules reused with changes from the previous release. The dependent variable was membership in the classes of *fault-prone* or *not fault-prone modules*. The independent variables were principal components of nine measures of software design attributes. Compared to a nonparametric discriminant model, the classification neural network model had better predictive accuracy.

2 Neural Networks

Advances in learning algorithms for neural networks and parallel computation have led to renewed research in statistical pattern classification.[21,22] Researchers have applied neural networks to both time varying patterns and static patterns in software engineering.[23] In this paper, we focus on feedforward multilayer perceptron neural networks, trained by the backpropagation algorithm. Neural network research has also investigated many other paradigms, architectures, and training algorithms.[24,25]

A neural network is a set of interconnected neurons each having a number of inputs, an output, and a transformation function. The multilayer perceptron model arranges these neurons in layers: one layer for input variables, one for output variables, and between these layers at least one hidden layer. Each neuron performs a transformation on the sum of its inputs to produce an output. Each neuron in the input layer receives one input variable. Each neuron in the first hidden layer receives the output of each neuron in the input layer. Each neuron in succeeding hidden layers receives the output of each neuron in the preceding hidden layer. Each neuron in the output layer receives the output of each neuron in the final hidden layer. The output layer neurons provide the output variable values.

Each of the neuron-to-neuron connections carries a variable weight quantifying the connection strength. Let W_{ij} be the connection weight between neurons i and j. As previously noted, each input-layer neuron receives its input directly from a single input variable, and thus there are no neuron-to-neuron connections at the inputs to these neurons. Let in_j be the value of the input variable for input-layer neuron j. Then the summed input at a neuron j is given by

$$Net_j = \begin{cases} in_j & \text{if } j \text{ is an input-layer neuron} \\ \sum_{i=1}^{n} W_{ij}Out_i - \theta_j & \text{otherwise} \end{cases} \tag{1}$$

where θ_j is the threshold of neuron j having n neural inputs. The output of neuron j is given by the logistic function

$$Out_j = \begin{cases} Net_j & \text{if } j \text{ is an input-layer neuron} \\ 1/(1 + e^{-Net_j/T}) & \text{otherwise} \end{cases} \tag{2}$$

where T adjusts the gain of the function.

The network learns by finding a vector of interconnection weights that minimizes its error on the training data set, a data set having known inputs and known outputs. After minimizing the error on the training data, the network can predict the outputs for data having known inputs and unknown outputs. These actions, learning and predicting, occur in the two phases of neural network activity shown in Figure 1.

Figure 2 gives a low-level view of a typical hidden- or output-layer neuron, j, getting n inputs from the neurons of the previous layer. Note the additional input from the neuron labeled $n + 1$. This extra neuron acts as an input neuron in the sense that it passes its input, a constant -1, to its output with no transformation. The connection weight to the extra neuron represents the threshold value of neuron j, that is, $\theta_j = W_{(n+1)j}$, and

$$Net_j = \sum_{i=1}^{n} W_{ij}Out_i - \theta_j = \sum_{i=1}^{n+1} W_{ij}Out_i$$

Using this implementation, the training phase establishes the neuron thresholds in the same manner as the interconnection weights.

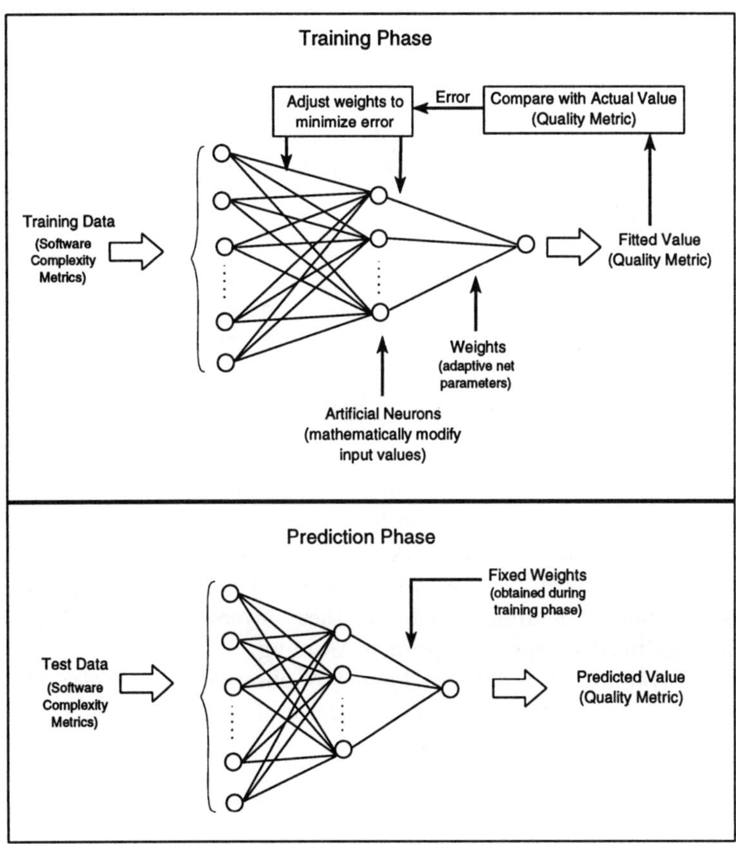

Figure 1: Two Phases of Neural Network Operation

38

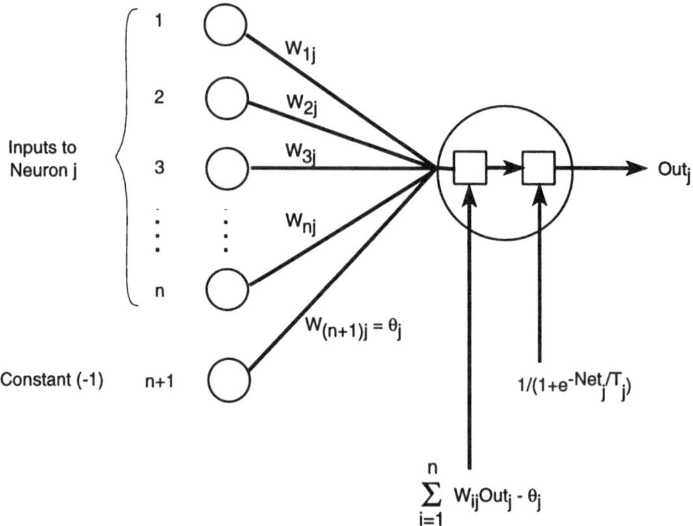

Figure 2: Artificial Neuron

A neural network's topology, that is the number of hidden layers, and the numbers of neurons in each of these layers, affects its behavior. For example, more hidden layers allow the network to develop higher order internal features. Network topology selection is a complex task. The number of hidden layers, and the numbers of neurons in each of these layers can vary independently. The topology must be specified prior to training.

During training on a data set having N observations, a network with M output layer neurons attempts to find a vector of connection weights, $\mathbf{W}$, that minimizes

$$E(\mathbf{W}) = \sum_{p=1}^{N} \sum_{i=1}^{M} (d_{pi} - Out_{pi})^2 \, ,$$

where d_{pi} and Out_{pi} are, respectively, the desired and actual output values of ith output layer neuron on the pth observation. In this study, the neural networks achieve this using a backpropagation learning algorithm.[26] At the beginning of the training phase, $\mathbf{W}$ is a random vector. The network iterates through the training data adjusting $\mathbf{W}$. Let $W_{ij}(n)$ be the interconnection strength between neuron i in layer $(l-1)$ and neuron j in layer l after the nth iteration through the training data set. The following relationship adjusts the weights:

$$W_{ij}(n+1) \quad = \quad W_{ij}(n) + \eta Out_i \delta_j + \alpha(W_{ij}(n) - W_{ij}(n-1))$$

where η and α set the learning and momentum rates, respectively, and δ_j gives the error contribution for neuron j. For the output layer,

$$\delta_j \;=\; (d_j - Out_j)Out_j(1 - Out_j)$$

Unlike the output layer neurons, the desired output for the hidden layer neurons is not known. However, since the error contribution of the hidden layer neurons propagates to the output layer, backward propagation of error allows estimation of the hidden layer neuron error contributions,

$$\delta_j \;=\; \left(\sum_k \delta_k W_{jk}\right)Out_j(1 - Out_j)$$

where k is the running index for the neurons in layer $(l+1)$.

The algorithm iterates through all of the inputs until a desired error tolerance is achieved or until the user defined maximum number of iterations is reached. If the desired error tolerance is achieved, the network is said to have converged and it is ready for the prediction phase. If the network does not converge, one could repeat the training phase after varying a learning parameter, η or α, or after selecting a new training data set. Larger values of η increase the learning rate, but also amplify oscillations. Larger values of α attenuate oscillations, but also decrease the learning rate. By dynamically adjusting the learning parameters,[27,28] and modifying the error function,[29] researchers have improved neural network convergence. Recently, our research team has used genetic algorithms to select automatically a preferred neural network architecture and parameter set.[30,31]

3 Case Studies

In the sections that follow, two case studies serve as examples of our methodology. The goal of Example 1 was to predict the number of faults discovered in each module.[8] However, sometimes it is not necessary to predict the exact number of faults. The goal of Example 2 was simply to predict whether each module was *not fault-prone* or *fault-prone*, in other words, to predict class membership of each module.[9]

3.1 Example 1: Military System

The Command and Control Communications System (CCCS) is a large military telecommunications system implemented in Ada. We randomly selected 282 software modules for our experiment. Generally, a module was an Ada package. The providers of the CCCS data set collected *faults*, the number of faults tracked during the system integration and test phase, and during the first year of deployment. They also collected software product metric data from the program text. Table 1 describes the software product metrics used in this case study.

Table 1: CCCS Metrics

η_1	Number of unique operators [32]
η_2	Number of unique operands [32]
N_1	Total number of operators [32]
N_2	Total number of operands [32]
$VG1$	McCabe's cyclomatic number, i.e., one more than the number of decision nodes in the control flow graph [33]
$VG2$	Extended cyclomatic complexity $VG2 = VG1 +$ number of logical operators
LOC	Number of lines of code
$ELOC$	Number of executable lines of code

Table 2: Telecommunications System Profile — Changed Modules

Application	Telecommunications
Language	PROTEL
Changed Modules	7 thousand
Lines of Code	7 million
Executable Statements	6 million
Control Flow Graph Edges	2 million
Source Files	18 thousand

3.2   Example 2: Telecommunication System

We studied a very large commercial telecommunications software system consisting of almost 13 million lines of code. The system was programmed in PROTEL, a high level language similar to Pascal. A *module* was defined as a set of source code files that work together to perform a function. A source code file may have multiple procedures.

In some software development environments, models based on metrics of product attributes alone do not give useful accuracy. Information regarding the reuse history of each module can be helpful in quality models.[34,35] Since modules reused from a prior release are likely to have a fault distribution different from equivalent new or unchanged modules, this case study modeled only the classification of modules reused with changes as a function of design metrics. We limited the scope of the case study to this subset of modules, summarized in Table 2, representing about seven million lines of code. Other modules were not considered in this study, such as new modules or modules reused without changes, because separate models would be more accurate.

A *fault* was defined as a reported problem that caused a change in the code. Data on faults in each module were collected covering unit test, system test,

Table 3: Telecommunications System Metrics

Call Graph Metrics	
UCT	Unique procedure calls to others
TCT	Total procedure calls to others
NDI	Distinct files included
Control Flow Graph Metrics	
VG	McCabe cyclomatic complexity [33]
NL	Loops
$IFTH$	If-then structures
$NELTOT$	Total nesting level
$PSCTOT$	Total number of vertices within the span of loop or if-then structures
$RLSTOT$	Total edges plus vertices within loop structures

See references[34,39] for detailed definitions of the metrics.

beta test, and operations. We considered only total faults for each module. We defined the *not fault-prone* group, G_1, as those modules with *faults* < 3, and the *fault-prone* group, G_2, as those with *faults* ≥ 3. About 14% of the modules were in G_2. Other studies identify the proportion of high risk modules anywhere from about 5% to about 20%.[36,37] Another criterion for *fault-prone* group membership might be appropriate in another situation.

Data were collected on almost seven thousand changed modules using the DATRIX software analyzer.[38,39] We selected the design metrics listed in Table 3. Software design metrics allow detection of fault-prone modules well before the testing phase. A number of studies have evaluated software design metrics as inputs to software quality models.[40,41] A *call graph* depicts dependencies among procedures. Call graph metrics can be collected as early as the high level design phase.[42] A *control flow graph* depicts the flow of control of an algorithm with a graph made of edges and vertices. Those based on a control flow graph can be collected as soon as the detailed design of algorithms is complete. These metrics can be reconfirmed thereafter, as the software is coded, and maintained. Note that one could select other software metrics to characterize the software. The selected metrics illustrate the methodology and its potential as a tool for management, but our methodology is not dependent on any particular set of metrics.

4 Methodology

Suppose we have measurements on a sample of n software modules, using a set of m software metrics, $X_j, j = 1, \ldots, m$. Let $\mathbf{X}$ be the $n \times m$ matrix of measurements. The following is a summary of our methodology which is applicable to a wide variety of mathematical modeling techniques.

1. Transform the raw data, if necessary.

   Modeling of some data sets may benefit from the following steps.

   (a) Standardize measurements to a mean of zero and a variance of one for each metric. Many raw software metrics have incompatible units of measure. This step converts them all to a unit of one standard deviation.

   (b) Perform principal components analysis on the standardized product metrics to produce domain metrics.

2. Prepare data sets.

   This step assumes that data from only one project is available, having a sufficiently large number of modules for meaningful statistical results.

   Merge product metrics or domain metrics with quality factor values into one data set. Randomly split the data into *fit* and *validation* data sets.

   The first example's *training* data set was the entire *fit* data set. Example 2 split the *fit* data set into a *training* data set and a *test* data set, as explained below.

3. Develop models.

   (a) Develop a neural network model based on the *training*, and, if applicable, *test* data sets.

   (b) Develop a statistical model based on the *fit* data set.

4. Predict the dependent variable of each module in the *validation* data set using the statistical model and the neural network model.

5. Evaluate predictive quality by comparing predictions to actual values.

Several statistics indicate a quantitative model's quality of fit and predictive quality by considering its performance on, respectively, the fit and the validation data.[43] Narula and Wellington found that the average relative error, ARE, is appropriate for quantifying the predictive quality of a model.[44] Shen, et al., established the utility of this statistic in comparing software metric-based models for identifying error-prone software.[45] Levitin indicated that ARE provides more information than the model's average absolute error.[46] We apply ARE in this study, and thus limit our discussion to this statistic.

Some notation is helpful in discussing a model's ARE. For n observations, the dependent variable values, y_i, $1 \leq i \leq n$, will have corresponding predicted and residual values, $\hat{y}_i$ and $e_i = y_i - \hat{y}_i$, respectively. A model's ARE for n observations is the average absolute ratio of the residual value to the dependent variable value,

$$ARE = \frac{1}{n} \sum_{i=1}^{n} |e_i/(y_i + 1)|$$

In our application, the dependent variable is the number of software faults. Thus $y_i \geq 0$, $i \geq 1$. To avoid undefined results where $y_i = 0$, we add one to y_i in the denominator.[43]

A classification model is evaluated by the portions of modules that are assigned to the wrong class. *Type I* misclassifications classify *not fault-prone* modules, those in G_1, into the *fault-prone* group, G_2. *Type II* misclassifications classify *fault-prone* modules, those in G_2, into the *not fault-prone* group, G_1. The overall misclassification rate is all misclassifications divided by the number of modules.

The models developed in Step 3 can be used to forecast the quality of modules from a subsequent release or a similar system developed in the same environment. At the beginning of coding, one could make software measurements and then forecast which modules will probably need extra attention during the remainder of development. Step 4 simulates such utilization with the *validation* data set. The following sections discuss each of these steps in more detail.

4.1 Transformation of Raw Data

Example 1 did not transform the raw data. A modeling study with raw data is instructive, and moreover, the amount of data was small enough that training times of the neural network were reasonable without transformation. The Transformation step was performed in Example 2, because the data set was much larger.

Standardization. A mathematical model should have a form such that the dependent variable's unit of measure is a function of the units of measure of the independent variables and the units of measure of the parameters. Since software metrics have a variety of units of measure, any modeling methodology must reconcile the units of measure. In order to simplify the units of measure of parameters and to maximize modeling flexibility without loss of information, we standardize software metric data. The unit of measure becomes one standard deviation.

Let the population mean of the jth metric be estimated by the average, $\bar{x}_j$, of a set of measurements, $x_{1j}, \ldots, x_{nj}$, and let the population standard deviation of the jth metric be estimated by the sample standard deviation, s_j. A *standardized* metric is defined as

$$Z_j = \frac{X_j - \bar{x}_j}{s_j} \tag{3}$$

for all $j = 1, \ldots, m$. Thus, all Z_j have a mean of zero and a variance of one. Let $\mathbf{Z}$ be the $n \times m$ matrix of standardized measurements where z_{ij} is an element, each row corresponds to a module, and each column is a standardized metric.

Principal components analysis. Software product metrics are often highly correlated with one another, because they measure related attributes of the software. Unfortunately, if the independent variables of a linear model are highly correlated, estimates of the model parameters may not be stable. In other words, insignificant variations in the data may result in drastically different parameter estimates. Principal components analysis is a technique for transforming multivariate data into variables that are not correlated, and thus, they result in a more robust model.[47] We have also investigated whether or not principal components analysis of input metric data is beneficial to neural network models that predict the number of design changes, the number of faults in code, and code churn.[48,49,6] When the original data are software metrics, we call the new principal component variables *domain metrics*.

Principal components analysis is also a data reduction technique. Even though the number of domain metrics could be the same as the number of product metrics, a stopping rule chooses a few domain metrics that represent most of the variability in the data. In other words, given m product metrics, a stopping rule chooses $p \ll m$ domain metrics, and ignores the remaining domain metrics because they have insignificant variation across the data set.[47]

Recall that we have m product measurements on each of n modules. Principal components analysis performs the following calculations, given an $n \times m$ matrix of standardized metric data, $\mathbf{Z}$.[47]

1. Calculate the covariance matrix, $\boldsymbol{\Sigma}$, of $\mathbf{Z}$.

2. Calculate eigenvalues, λ_j, and eigenvectors, $\mathbf{e}_j$, of $\boldsymbol{\Sigma}$, $j = 1, \ldots, m$.

3. Reduce the dimensionality of the data. In Example 2, we chose to explain at least 95% of the total variance of the original standardized metrics. Choose the minimum p such that $\sum_{j=1}^{p} \lambda_j / m \geq 0.95$.

4. Calculate a standardized transformation matrix, $\mathbf{T}$, where each column is defined as

$$\mathbf{t}_j = \frac{\mathbf{e}_j}{\sqrt{\lambda_j}} \text{ for } j = 1, \ldots, p \tag{4}$$

5. Calculate domain metrics for each module, where

$$D_j = \mathbf{Z}\mathbf{t}_j \tag{5}$$
$$\mathbf{D} = \mathbf{Z}\mathbf{T} \tag{6}$$

The end result is an $n \times p$ matrix of domain metric data, $\mathbf{D}$, where each domain metric, D_j, has a mean of zero and a variance of one. Since they are orthogonal, the domain metrics are suitable as independent variables in linear models.

We have shown elsewhere that principal components analysis can also improve the performance of discriminant software quality models.[50] Moreover, we found that if correlated raw software metrics were used directly, our classification neural network models did not train satisfactorily, but transforming raw data with principal components analysis facilitated training.[30,51] Since they are orthogonal, the domain metrics are attractive as independent variables in discriminant and neural network models.

For the telecommunications system in Example 2, given the nine software design metrics, principal components analysis retained four domains under the stopping rule that we retain components which account for 95% or more of the total variance. Table 4 shows the relationship between the original metrics and the domain metrics. Each table entry is the correlation between the metrics. The largest correlation in each row is **bold**.

4.2 *Prepare Data Sets*

Modeling software typically requires data to be organized in tabular form where each row includes the candidate independent variable values and the dependent variable value for one observation. For each CCCS module in Example 1, the raw software product metrics were independent variables and the number of faults is the dependent variable. For each telecommunications system module in Example 2, domain metrics (transformed software product metrics) were independent variables and the module's class was the dependent variable. These were merged into one data set for each case study where each row consists of data on a module.

Whenever possible, we prefer to use data from two similar projects to develop and validate a software quality model.[6] When there is data on only one large project, we simulate two projects by impartially splitting the modules into two subsets: a subset for developing the model, and a subset for evaluating its predictive quality. If the number of modules is small for the selected

Table 4: Domain Pattern

Metric	D_1	D_2	D_3	D_4
PSCTOT	**0.884**	0.313	0.275	-0.009
NELTOT	**0.853**	0.362	0.335	0.012
IFTH	**0.665**	0.601	0.374	0.013
TCT	0.360	**0.853**	0.307	0.005
UCT	0.359	**0.838**	0.367	0.001
VG	0.617	**0.632**	0.416	-0.005
NL	0.290	0.407	**0.841**	-0.046
RLSTOT	0.418	0.316	**0.827**	-0.019
NDI	0.003	0.004	-0.030	**0.999**
Eigenvalues	2.85	2.69	2.12	1.00
% Variance	31.67%	29.89%	23.56%	11.11%
Cumulative	31.67%	61.56%	85.12%	96.23%

Changed Modules

modeling technique, then alternative methods for model evaluation must be investigated.[11,47,52] Validation data do not contribute to model development, and thus, application of the model to the validation data gives an indication of the model's predictive quality.

Considering sample sizes, we chose to put two thirds of the modules in the *fit* data set, and the remaining third in the *validation* data set. The *fit* data set was used to estimate statistical model parameters, and to configure and train a neural network model. The *validation* data set was used to evaluate the predictive accuracy of both models.

In Example 1, we impartially partitioned the data into two subsets: 188 modules in the *fit* data set, and 94 modules in the *validation* data set.

In Example 2, the data set was impartially divided into a *fit* data set with 4,648 modules and a *validation* data set with 2,324 modules. We found that the distribution of faults was extremely skewed toward few faults. About 51% of the modules had no faults. Only 14% of the modules in the *fit* data set were *fault-prone*. Such a lopsided distribution presents difficulties for the backpropagation training algorithm, which attempts to extract essential features from the input. When using the entire *fit* data set for training, candidate models did not converge to an acceptable identification rate in a manageable number of epochs. When there are features in the training set that are rare, they may not influence the formation of the weight set sufficiently in training to be recognized when they occur in validation. We constructed the *training* set to increase their influence without introducing false data.

We randomly selected one third of the modules from the *fit* data set to become the *test* data set of 1,549 modules, which was used to evaluate alternative neural network architectures. The *training* data set consisted of a subset of the remaining 3,099 modules in the *fit* data set. This subset was carefully designed considering the characteristics of the data set. Our *training* data set was derived by combining all of the available *fault-prone* modules with an equal number of randomly selected *not fault-prone* modules. We limited the number of *not fault-prone* modules with zero faults to a small sample of five, to avoid giving undue weight to those patterns. The other *not fault-prone* modules in the *training* data set had more than zero faults. The selections were uniformly random without replacement. The *training* data set included all 425 *fault-prone* modules, five randomly selected modules with zero faults, and 420 randomly selected *not fault-prone* modules with at least one fault, for a total of 850 modules.

4.3 Develop Models

Train quantitative neural network model.   The neural network in Example 1 was constructed with logistic-function units that yield an output between 0.0 and 1.0 so the input data were scaled to this range by dividing each product metric value by the metric's highest observed value. We determined the network topology for the model experimentally. After training networks having 1, 2, and 3 hidden layers, we found that, with a fixed number of hidden layer neurons equal across all hidden layers, a single hidden layer gave the best results. For Example 1, we trained single hidden layer networks having 5, 10, 11, ..., 19, 20, 25, and 30 hidden layer neurons. The network with 16 hidden layer neurons gave the best results.

The networks trained using backward error propagation. Training began with connection weights initialized to random values between -1.0 and 1.0. The learning and momentum rates were $\eta = 1.5$ and $\alpha = 0.7$, respectively. When the *fit* data set was resubstituted into the model, the quality of fit was $ARE = 33.33\%$ with a standard deviation of 23%.

Fit multiple linear regression model.   *Stepwise regression.* Even though we may have a long list of candidate independent variables, it is possible that some do not significantly influence the dependent variable. If an insignificant variable is included in the model, it may add noise to the results and may cloud interpretation of the model. For example, if a coefficient, a_j for the jth variable in a linear model is not significantly different from zero, then it is best to omit that term from the model. The process of determining which variables are significant is called *model selection.*

Of several model selection techniques available for multiple linear regression, we used the *stepwise regression* method[52] with the *fit* data set. Having specified a list of candidate independent variables, variables are entered into the model in an incremental manner, based on an F test from analysis of variance which is recomputed for each change in the current model. Begin with no variables in the model. Add the variable not already in the model with the best significance level, as long as its significance is better than the threshold. Then remove the variable already in the model with the worst significance level, as long as its significance is worse than the threshold. Repeat these steps until no variable can be added to the model.

The best model identified during model selection included $VG1$, $VG2$, η_1 and η_2.

Estimating parameters. Many models have a general mathematical form with parameters that must be chosen so that the *fit* data set matches the model as closely as possible. This step consists of estimating the values of such parameters.

When using a mathematical model, the parameters are known, the independent variable values are known, and one then calculates dependent variable values. In contrast, when estimating model parameters, the independent variable values are known, the dependent variable values are known, and one must solve for the best estimate of the unknown parameter values by minimizing some overall measure of error.

Example 1 applied multiple linear regression to predict the number of faults to be discovered in each module. Since this is a very common statistical technique, a brief description of our application will suffice here.

A multivariate linear model is an equation where the dependent variable, y, is a linear function of the independent variables, $x_1, \ldots, x_p$. Suppose there are n observations in the *fit* data set, and the subscript i indicates data for the ith observation. In general, a multivariate linear model has the following form.

$$\hat{y}_i = a_0 + a_1 x_{i1} + \ldots + a_p x_{ip} \tag{7}$$

$$y_i = a_0 + a_1 x_{i1} + \ldots + a_p x_{ip} + e_i \tag{8}$$

where $x_{i1}, \ldots, x_{ip}$ are the independent variables' values, $a_0, \ldots, a_p$ are parameters to be estimated, $\hat{y}_i$ is the predicted value of the dependent variable, y_i is the dependent variable's actual value, and $e_i = y_i - \hat{y}_i$ is the error for the ith observation. In Example 1, the number of faults is the dependent variable, and the raw product metrics are independent variables. We estimate the parameters, $a_0, \ldots, a_p$, using the *least squares* method. This method chooses a set of parameter values that minimizes $\sum_{i=1}^{n} e_i^2$.[47] The model was

$$\hat{y}_i = 1.0537 - 0.425\, N_1 + 0.0306\, N_2$$
$$- 0.2632\, VG1 + 0.2314\, VG2 \tag{9}$$

Table 5 gives the model details.

Table 5: Regression Model Parameters

Parameter	Estimate	Std Dev	Probability
Intercept	1.0537	0.3560	0.0035
N_1	-0.0425	0.0260	0.0405
N_2	0.0306	0.0029	0.0001
$VG1$	-0.2632	0.0302	0.0001
$VG2$	0.2314	0.0304	0.0001

Table 6: Regression Model Analysis of Variance

Source	Degrees of Freedom	Sum of Squares	Mean Square	F Statistic
Regression	4	2981.819	745.455	129.019
Error	183	1057.346	5.778	
Total	187	4039.165		

Table 6 gives the regression model analysis of variance for the fitted model. The model was significant ($p < .01$) overall. When we resubstituted the *fit* data set into the model, the quality of fit was $ARE = 62.49\%$ with a standard deviation of 82%.

Train classification neural network model. An artificial neural network is composed of computational processing elements with weighted connections. In this section, we refer to each computational processing element as a *unit*. Each unit has a number of inputs, an activation function and an output. The multilayer perceptron model arranges these units in layers: one layer for system input variables, another for system output variables, and between these layers one or more hidden layers. We use a feed-forward multilayer perceptron network and the backpropagation training algorithm.[24] Table 7 summarizes our architecture which was experimentally determined; details are explained below.

The input layer has one unit for each input variable, $D_j, j = 1, \ldots, 4$. We use one hidden layer, noting that what can be achieved in function approximation with more than one hidden layer can also be achieved with one.[53] There are two units in the output layer, one for each class. The output unit with the greatest value indicates the class selected by the network. All connections go forward from the input layer toward the output layer.

The activation function is the logistic function, with a *temperature* parameter, T, that controls how sharply the function changes from 0 to 1.

Each input value, d_{ij}, in the *training* data set, the *test* data set, and the

Table 7: Classification Neural Network Summary

Architecture	
Class	Perceptron
Connections	Feedforward
Layers	3
Input units	4
Hidden units	19
Output units	2
Unit Details	
Activation function	Logistic
Temperature	$T = 125$
Training	
Mode	Supervised
Algorithm	Backpropagation
Weight updates	Continuous
Learning Rate	$\eta = 0.5$
Momentum Rate	$\alpha = 0.38$

validation data set was scaled to the closed unit interval $[0, 1]$.

The network learns by finding a vector of connection weights that minimizes the sum of squared errors on the *training* data set. One pass through all of the training observations is called an *epoch*. After training, the network should be able to predict the output values for a data set having known input values and unknown output values.

We trained the network with a continuous backpropagation learning algorithm, where the weights are adjusted after each observation is fed forward through the network. Our experience with this data set indicated that the continuous procedure was more suitable for this system than updating weights only at the end of each epoch as was done in Example 1. The learning and momentum parameters were η and α, respectively.[24]

Various neural network architectures were tested. The number of units in the hidden layer, the temperature (T), learning rate (η), and momentum rate (α) were adjusted to find a preferred combination. For each architecture, the training algorithm iterated through all of the *training* data set modules until the maximum number of epochs was reached. At the end of each epoch, the *test* data set was presented to the network. Misclassification rates and the network details were recorded, providing a basis for comparing architectures and specific models. We found that there is a trade-off between the desired degree of accuracy for *fault-prone* classification balanced against the degree of *not fault-prone* accuracy. We chose approximately equal misclassification

Table 8: Classification Neural Network Test

Number of Observations/Percent

Group	Model		
Actual	G_1	G_2	Total
G_1	959	377	1336
	71.8%	28.2%	100.0%
G_2	62	151	213
	29.1%	70.9%	100.0%
Total	1021	528	1549
Percent	65.9%	34.1%	100.0%

Overall misclassification rate: 28.3%

Changed Modules

rates. A different balance might be desirable in another situation.

Table 8 shows the results of classifying the *test* data set. This indicates quality of fit. The Type I misclassification rate was 28% and the Type II misclassification rate was about 29%. The overall misclassification rate was 28.3%.

Fit nonparametric discriminant model. *Stepwise discriminant analysis.* Recall that the purpose of Example 2 was to classify modules as belonging to either the *not fault-prone* group or the *fault-prone* group. We used *stepwise discriminant analysis* model selection at the 5% significance level to choose the domain metrics, D_j, that should be included as independent variables in the discriminant model.[47]

Variables are entered into the model in an iterative manner, based on an F test from analysis of variance which is recomputed for each change in the current model. Begin with no variables in the model. Add the variable not already in the model with the best significance level, as long as its significance is better than the threshold (5%). Then remove the variable already in the model with the worst significance level, as long as its significance is worse than the threshold (5%). Repeat these steps until no variable can be added to the model. The final result is a subset of $D_j, j = 1, \ldots, p$, that are significantly related to the module class.

The stepwise model selection process found the first three domain metrics significant at the 5% significance level, but not D_4, and therefore, the inputs to the discriminant model were D_1, D_2, and D_3.

Estimating parameters. Example 2 applied nonparametric discriminant analysis, a standard statistical technique, to predict the membership of each module in the *not fault-prone* group (G_1) or the *fault-prone* group (G_2). The goal was to define a *discriminant function* that assigns a module to one of two classes, given values for the independent variables. We defined the selected domain metrics, D_j, as independent variables, and the group membership as the dependent variable. We estimated a *discriminant function* based on the *fit* data set. Parametric discriminant analysis has been applied to software metric data in other studies.[16] The following gives details on how we estimate a nonparametric discriminant function.[47]

Consider the following notation. Let $\mathbf{d}_i$ be the vector of the ith module's independent variables. Let G_1 and G_2 be mutually exclusive groups, and let n_k be the number of modules in group $G_k, k = 1, 2$. Let $\mathbf{S}_k$ be the covariance matrix for all samples in G_k, and let $|\mathbf{S}_k|$ be its determinant. Let $f_k(\mathbf{d}_i)$ be the multivariate probability density giving the probability that an module, $\mathbf{d}_i$, is in G_k, and let $\hat{f}_k(\mathbf{d}_i|\lambda)$ be an approximation of $f_k(\mathbf{d}_i)$, where λ is a parameter. From a Baysian probability viewpoint, let π_k be the prior probability of membership in G_k. We choose the prior probability, π_k, to be the proportion of *fit* modules in G_k.

Since the density functions, f_k, are not likely to conform to the normal distribution, we use nonparametric discriminant analysis. Let λ be a smoothing parameter in this context. We select the multivariate normal kernel on vector $\mathbf{u}$ with modes at $\mathbf{v}$. This is the most commonly used kernel, and has been studied the most mathematically.[54]

$$
\begin{aligned}
K_k(\mathbf{u}|\mathbf{v}, \lambda) \quad &= \quad (2\pi\lambda^2)^{-n_k/2}|\mathbf{S}_k|^{-1/2} \\
&\quad \exp(\quad (-1/2\lambda^2)(\mathbf{u} - \mathbf{v})'\mathbf{S}_k^{-1}(\mathbf{u} - \mathbf{v}))
\end{aligned} \tag{10}
$$

Let $\mathbf{d}_{kl}, l = 1, \ldots, n_k$ be a vector of independent variable values for the lth observation in group G_k. The estimated density function is given by the multivariate kernel density estimation technique.

$$
\hat{f}_k(\mathbf{d}_i|\lambda) = \frac{1}{n_k} \sum_{l=1}^{n_k} K_k(\mathbf{d}_i|\mathbf{d}_{kl}, \lambda) \tag{11}
$$

The estimated discriminant function is given by

$$
\text{Assign } \mathbf{d}_i \text{ to} \begin{cases} G_1 & \text{if } \frac{\hat{f}_1(\mathbf{d}_i|\lambda)}{\hat{f}_2(\mathbf{d}_i|\lambda)} > \frac{\pi_2}{\pi_1} \\ G_2 & \text{otherwise} \end{cases} \tag{12}
$$

This classification rule minimizes the total number of misclassifications.[47]

Model fit is judged by resubstituting the *fit* data into the discriminant function, and calculating the Type I, Type II, and overall misclassification rates.

Table 9: Discriminant Analysis Fit
Number of Observations/Percent

Group Actual	Model G_1	G_2	Total
G_1	4010 100.0%	0 0.0%	4010 100.0%
G_2	34 5.3%	604 94.7%	638 100.0%
Total	4044	604	4648
Percent	87.0%	13.0%	100.0%
Prior	86.3%	13.7%	

Overall misclassification rate: 0.7%
Changed Modules

The discriminant procedure used the *fit* data set to estimate the multi-variate density functions, $\hat{f}_1, \hat{f}_2$, and thus, the discriminant function per Equation (12). We empirically determined the kernel density estimation smoothing parameter to be $\lambda = 0.005$. The discriminant function was then used to classify each module in the *fit* data set. Table 9 summarizes the results. No member of the *not fault-prone* group was misclassified, and about 5% of the *fault-prone* group were misclassified, for an overall misclassification rate of less than 1%. This represents excellent quality of fit.

4.4 Making Predictions

After a model has been developed and given a set of independent variable values, a model can calculate a value of the dependent variable. Since the independent variables are known earlier than the actual value of the dependent variable, the calculated value is a *prediction*. For evaluating a model, we use the *validation* data set, where the actual values of the dependent variable are known, but have not been used in the modeling process.

4.5 Evaluating Predictive Quality

Having predicted the value of the dependent variable for each module in the *validation* data set, one should evaluate how well the model has performed. Various statistical techniques give an overall comparison of the predicted values and the actual values. If the number of modules is small then splitting the data into *fit* and *validation* data sets may not yield statistically meaningful results.

In such situations, alternative approaches should be investigated such as PRESS statistics and cross-validation.[52,47]

Example 1 predicted the number of faults to be discovered in each module. Since we know the actual number of faults, y_i, for the ith module, we validate that the predictions, $\hat{y}_i$, are sufficiently accurate for the needs of the current project.

Example 2 predicted the membership of each module in the *not fault-prone* group and the *fault-prone* group. A measure of predictive quality should summarize the proportions of correct or incorrect predictions. We apply the same measures to prediction as we did to quality of fit, namely, Type I, Type II, and overall misclassification rates. The penalty for Type I misclassifications is wasting extra effort reviewing and testing modules that are actually not fault-prone. The penalty for Type II misclassifications is the risk of more faults in the released software, due to the lack of extra attention. Since the cost of faults in released software is often very high, we prefer that the Type II misclassification rate be lower than the Type I rate.

Quantitative neural network model. The predictive quality of the quantitative neural network model was $ARE = 39.80\%$ with a standard deviation of 28%. Training using several different random weight initializations produced nearly identical results.

Multiple linear regression model. The predictive quality of the multiple linear regression model was $ARE = 58.77\%$ with a standard deviation of 62%.

Classification neural network model. Table 10 shows the results of classifying the *validation* data set with the classification neural network model. The Type I misclassification rate was 26% and the Type II misclassification rate was about 27%. The overall misclassification rate was 26.2%. Thus, the weight set developed from the *training* data set with crossvalidation from the *test* data set, as shown in Table 8, generalized successfully when applied to the *validation* data set, as shown in Table 10.

Assuming that the development of the next release is similar to the release studied here, suppose the project is about to begin the coding phase, and suppose that 1,000 modules are being changed. Based on proportions in the *fit* data set, we expect about 862 to be *not fault-prone* and about 138 to be *fault-prone* modules. We could measure those modules and apply the neural network developed here. Per Table 10, we would expect the model to identify about 325 modules as *fault-prone* ($32.5\% \times 1,000$). We could then give this set of modules more intense design reviews and additional testing. We would expect to waste design review time on 224 modules that are actually *not fault-prone* ($26\% \times 862$). We would expect the model to identify correctly about 101

Table 10: Neural Network Validation
Number of Observations/Percent

| Group | Model | | Total |
Actual	G_1	G_2	Total
G_1	1482	522	2004
	74.0%	26.0%	100.0%
G_2	86	234	320
	26.9%	73.1%	100.0%
Total	1568	756	2324
Percent	67.5%	32.5%	100.0%

Overall misclassification rate: 26.2%
Changed Modules

modules that are actually *fault-prone* (73.1% × 138), but fail to identify only 37 *fault-prone* modules (26.9% × 138). The extra reviews and testing would probably discover many faults earlier than otherwise would have occurred.

Nonparametric discriminant model. The discriminant function developed using *fit* data was used to classify each observation in the *validation* data set. Table 11 summarizes the results. About 28% of the *not fault-prone* modules were misclassified, and about 39% of the *fault-prone* modules were misclassified, for an overall misclassification rate of less than 30%.

The classification rule in Eq. 12 minimizes the total number of misclassifications,[47] and thus, assumes that Type I and Type II misclassifications have equal costs. In software engineering, the cost of letting a fault go undetected until late in the life cycle is often much more than the cost of an extra design review, or extra tests.[55] Suppose the cost of a Type II misclassification is ten times the cost of a Type I misclassification. In other words, the direct cost of extra reviews or tests per module is one unit. Suppose the same 1,000 modules are being changed as was analyzed above, and we apply the discriminant model. The direct cost of reliability enhancement for modules identified by the model as *fault-prone* would be about 324 units. This effort would detect faults in 83 = (1000)(194/2324) modules for a cost-avoidance of 830 units, and would waste effort on 241 = 324 − 83 units. There would remain 54 = (1000)(126/2324) *fault-prone* modules that would be discovered late in development according to the standard development process. The profit of using the model would be 506 = 830 − 324, and the return on investment (ROI) would be 2.56 : 1 = 830 : 324. Since the error rates of the neural network model are even better, a similar analysis would show that it would be an even better investment.

Table 11: Discriminant Analysis Validation
Number of Observations/Percent

Group	Model		
Actual	G_1	G_2	Total
G_1	1444	560	2004
	72.1%	27.9%	100.0%
G_2	126	194	320
	39.4%	60.6%	100.0%
Total	1570	754	2324
Percent	67.6%	32.4%	100.0%

Overall misclassification rate: 29.5%
Changed Modules

5   Conclusions

Modern software systems are so large and complex that high reliability is difficult to achieve. To reduce the cost of a software development effort, and to increase the reliability of the resulting product, some software engineers apply systematic software development techniques. Quantitative modeling is one of these techniques. By applying past experience to build quantitative models early in the development cycle, software engineers can identify quality problems that will materialize late in this cycle. With this information they can take actions to reduce and prepare for the quality risks of the product.

Many organizations begin to collect software metrics with the hope of improving the reliability of their products. Metrics are often collected without knowing how to utilize them. This paper is aimed to bridge the gap between collecting data and making predictions. Predictions of software faults for each module is an important tool for focusing development resources and maximizing their effectiveness.

This paper systematically presents a modeling methodology, with emphasis on developing neural network models that predict software quality factors. The individual details of this methodology may be familiar, but the whole modeling process must be integrated to produce successful predictions of software quality.

The examples demonstrate the kind of useful results that software quality models can produce. Timely predictions of fault related quality factors can be used to give extra attention to problem modules, and to make realistic plans for testing and support. The case studies presented here used neural network methods which produced quantitative models having better predictive quality than models produced with traditional statistical methods.

Table 12: Summary of Quantitative Models

Quality	Model	ARE	Std Dev
Fit	Regression	0.6249	0.82
	Neural net	0.3333	0.23
Predictive	Regression	0.5877	0.62
	Neural net	0.3980	0.28

Table 13: Summary of Classification Models
Misclassification Rates (%)

Model	Fit/Test			Validation		
	Type I	Type II	Overall	Type I	Type II	Overall
Discriminant	0.0	5.3	0.7	27.9	39.4	29.5
Neural Network	28.2	29.1	28.3	26.0	26.9	26.2

For Example 1, we evaluated the quantitative neural network model's ARE values on both the training and the validation data, as shown in Table 12. This table reveals that, for both data sets, the neural network approach produced the model having better quality of fit and predictive quality. The difference in these statistics is significant ($p < 0.01$).

For Example 2, Table 13 summarizes the misclassification rates of the discriminant model and classification neural network. The neural network had a much smaller Type II misclassification rate, namely, the proportion of *fault-prone* modules mistakenly classified as *not fault-prone*. For many software development environments, Type II misclassifications are more serious, because they risk releasing software with undetected faults, which in turn may cause operational failures. Therefore, the neural network model had an important advantage over the discriminant model.

These models can be used to forecast the quality of modules from a subsequent release or a similar system developed in the same environment.[6] At the beginning of coding, one could make software measurements and then predict which modules will probably need extra attention during the remainder of development. This can help management focus resources on those modules that cause the bulk of problems.

Acknowledgments

We thank John P. Hudepohl, Stephen J. Aud, Jean Mayrand, Bruno Lague, and their team, for collecting the telecommunications system data. We thank Hemant B. More and Robert Hochman for conducting the experiments. We thank the research team at Florida Atlantic University for helpful discussions and for performing related research, in particular, Abhijit S. Pandya, Peter J. Guasti, David L. Lanning, Robert M. Szabo, and Ronald Weir. This work was supported in part by a grant from Nortel. The findings and opinions in this paper belong solely to the authors, and are not necessarily those of the sponsor. Moreover, our results do not in any way reflect the quality of the sponsor's software products. DATRIX is a trademark of Bell Canada.

References

1. Norman E. Fenton and Shari Lawrence Pfleeger. *Software Metrics: A Rigorous and Practical Approach*. PWS Publishing, London, 2d edition, 1997.
2. John C. Munson and Taghi M. Khoshgoftaar. Software metrics for reliability assessment. In Michael Lyu, editor, *Handbook of Software Reliability Engineering*, chapter 12, pages 493–529. McGraw-Hill, New York, 1996.
3. Taghi M. Khoshgoftaar and Edward B. Allen. Predicting faults from an information theory based software metric. In Hoang Pham, editor, *Proceedings of the Second ISSAT International Conference on Reliability and Quality in Design*, pages 210–214, Orlando, FL, March 1995. International Society of Science and Applied Technologies.
4. Taghi M. Khoshgoftaar, Edward B. Allen, Kalai S. Kalaichelvan, and Nishith Goel. Predictive modeling of software quality for very large telecommunications systems. In *Proceedings of the International Communications Conference*, volume 1, pages 214–219, Dallas, TX, June 1996. IEEE Communications Society.
5. Taghi M. Khoshgoftaar, David L. Lanning, and Abhijit S. Pandya. A comparative study of pattern recognition techniques for quality evaluation of telecommunications software. *IEEE Journal on Selected Areas in Communications*, 12(2):279–291, February 1994.
6. Taghi M. Khoshgoftaar, Robert M. Szabo, and Peter J. Guasti. Exploring the behavior of neural network software quality models. *Software Engineering Journal*, 10(3):89–96, May 1995.
7. Taghi M. Khoshgoftaar, Robert M. Szabo, and Timothy G. Woodcock. An empirical study of program quality during testing and maintenance. *Software Quality Journal*, 3(3):137–151, September 1994.
8. Taghi M. Khoshgoftaar, Abhijit S. Pandya, and David L. Lanning. Application of neural networks for predicting faults. *Annals of Software Engineering*, 1:141–154, 1995.
9. Taghi M. Khoshgoftaar, Edward B. Allen, John P. Hudepohl, and Stephen J. Aud. Applications of neural networks to software quality

modeling of a very large telecommunications system. *Transactions on Neural Networks*, 8(4):902–909, July 1997.

10. Norman F. Schneidewind. Methodology for validating software metrics. *IEEE Transactions on Software Engineering*, 18(5):410–422, May 1992.

11. William R. Dillon and Matthew Goldstein. *Multivariate Analysis: Methods and Applications*. John Wiley & Sons, New York, 1984.

12. Taghi M. Khoshgoftaar, Abhijit S. Pandya, and Hemant B. More. A neural network approach for predicting software development faults. In *Proceedings of the Third International Symposium on Software Reliability Engineering*, pages 83–89, Research Triangle Park, NC USA, October 1992. IEEE Computer Society.

13. Taghi M. Khoshgoftaar, Edward B. Allen, John P. Hudepohl, and Stephen J. Aud. Software metric-based neural network classification models of a very large telecommunications system. In Steven K. Rogers and Dennis W. Ruck, editors, *Applications and Science of Artificial Neural Networks II*, volume 2760 of *Proceedings of SPIE*, pages 634–645, Orlando, FL, April 1996. SPIE—International Society for Optical Engineering.

14. Taghi M. Khoshgoftaar and David L. Lanning. A neural network approach for early detection of program modules having high risk in the maintenance phase. *Journal of Systems and Software*, 29(1):85–91, April 1995.

15. Taghi M. Khoshgoftaar, David L. Lanning, and Abhijit S. Pandya. A neural network modeling methodology for detection of high-risk programs. In *Proceedings of the Fourth International Symposium on Software Reliability Engineering*, pages 302–309, Denver, CO, November 1993. IEEE Computer Society.

16. John C. Munson and Taghi M. Khoshgoftaar. The detection of fault-prone programs. *IEEE Transactions on Software Engineering*, 18(5):423–433, May 1992.

17. V. Rodriguez and W. T. Tsai. Evaluation of software metrics using discriminant analysis. *Journal of Information and Software Technology*, 29(3):245–251, May 1987.

18. Richard W. Selby and Adam A. Porter. Learning from examples: Generation and evaluation of decision trees for software resource analysis. *IEEE Transactions on Software Engineering*, 14(12):1743–1756, December 1988.

19. Christof Ebert. Classification techniques for metric-based software development. *Software Quality Journal*, 5(4):255–272, December 1996.

20. Lionel C. Briand, Victor R. Basili, and William M. Thomas. A pattern recognition approach for software engineering data analysis. *IEEE Transactions on Software Engineering*, 18(11):931–942, November 1992.

21. T. Tolleneare. SuperSAB: Fast adaptive back-propagation with good scaling properties. *Neural Networks*, 3:561–573, 1990.

22. T. P. Vogl, J. K. Mangis, A. K. Rigler, W. T. Zink, and D. L. Alkon. Accelerating the convergence of the back-propagation method. *Biological Cybernetics*, 59:257–263, 1988.

23. Nachimuthu Karunanithi and Yashwant K. Malaiya. Neural networks for software reliability engineering. In Michael Lyu, editor, *Handbook of Software Reliability Engineering*, chapter 17, pages 699–728. McGraw-Hill, New York, 1996.

24. Philip D. Wasserman. *Neural Computing: Theory and Practice.* Van Nostrand Reinhold, New York, 1989.

25. Anil K. Jain and Jianchang Mao. Artificial neural networks: A tutorial. *Computer*, 29(3):31–44, March 1996.

26. D. E. Rumelhart, G. E. Hinton, and R. J. Williams. *Parallel Distributed Processing: Explorations in the Microstructure of Cognition*, volume 1, chapter Learning Internal Representations by Error Propagation, pages 318–362. MIT Press, Cambridge, MA, USA, 1986.

27. R. Jacobs. Increased rates of convergence through learning rate adaptation. *Neural Networks*, 1:295–307, 1988.

28. R. Pedone and D. Parisi. Learning the learning parameters. In *Proceedings of the Internation Joint Conference on Neural Networks*, pages 2033–2037, Singapore, 1991.

29. A. van Ooyen and B. Niemhuis. Improving the convergence of the back-propogation algorithm. *Neural Networks*, 5:465–471, 1992.

30. Robert Hochman, Taghi M. Khoshgoftaar, Edward B. Allen, and John P. Hudepohl. Using the genetic algorithm to build optimal neural networks for fault-prone module detection. In *Proceedings of the Seventh International Symposium on Software Reliability Engineering*, pages 152–162, White Plains, NY, October 1996. IEEE Computer Society.

31. Robert Hochman, Taghi M. Khoshgoftaar, Edward B. Allen, and John P. Hudepohl. Evolutionary neural networks: A robust approach to software reliability problems. In *Proceedings of the Eighth International Symposium on Software Reliability Engineering*, pages 13–26, Albuquerque, NM USA, November 1997. IEEE Computer Society.

32. Maurice H. Halstead. *Elements of Software Science.* Elsevier, New York, 1977.

33. Thomas J. McCabe. A complexity measure. *IEEE Transactions on Software Engineering*, SE-2(4):308–320, December 1976.

34. Taghi M. Khoshgoftaar, Edward B. Allen, Kalai S. Kalaichelvan, and Nishith Goel. Early quality prediction: A case study in telecommunications. *IEEE Software*, 13(1):65–71, January 1996.

35. Taghi M. Khoshgoftaar, Edward B. Allen, Kalai S. Kalaichelvan, and Nishith Goel. The impact of software evolution and reuse on software quality. *Empirical Software Engineering: An International Journal*, 1(1):31–44, 1996.

36. G. LeGall, M. F. Adam, H. Derriennic, B. Moreau, and N. Valette. Studies on measuring software. *IEEE Journal of Selected Areas in Communications*, 8(2):234–245, February 1990.

37. Adam A. Porter and Richard W. Selby. Empirically guided software development using metric-based classification trees. *IEEE Software*, 7(2):46–54, March 1990.

38. Jean Mayrand and François Coallier. System acquisition based on software product assessment. In *Proceedings of the Eighteenth International Conference on Software Engineering*, pages 210–219, Berlin, March 1996.

39. Pierre N. Robillard, Daniel Coupal, and François Coallier. Profiling software through the use of metrics. *Software—Practice and Experience*, 21(5):507–518, May 1991.

40. Barbara A. Kitchenham, Lesley M. Pickard, and S. J. Linkman. An evaluation of some design metrics. *Software Engineering Journal*, 5(1):50–58, January 1990.

41. Wayne M. Zage and Dolores M. Zage. Evaluating design metrics on large-scale software. *IEEE Software*, 10(4):75–80, July 1993.

42. Barbara A. Kitchenham. An evaluation of software structure metrics. In *Proceedings of the International Computer Software and Applications Conference (COMPSAC)*, pages 369–376, Chicago, IL, 1988.

43. Taghi M. Khoshgoftaar, John C. Munson, Bibhuti B. Bhattacharya, and Gary D. Richardson. Predictive modeling techniques of software quality from software measures. *IEEE Transactions on Software Engineering*, 18(11):979–987, November 1992.

44. S. C. Narula and J. F. Wellington. Prediction, linear regression and the minimum sum of relative errors. *Technometrics*, 19:185–190, May 1977.

45. Vincent Y. Shen, Tze-Jie Yu, Stephen M. Thebaut, and Lorri R. Paulsen. Identifying error-prone software — An empirical study. *IEEE Transactions on Software Engineering*, SE-11(4):317–323, April 1985.

46. A. Levitin. The L_1 criteria in data analysis and the problem of software size estimation. In *Proceedings of Twenty-First Symposium on the Interface of Computing Science and Statistics*, pages 382–383, 1989.

47. G. A. F. Seber. *Multivariate Observations*. John Wiley and Sons, New York, 1984.

48. Taghi M. Khoshgoftaar and Robert M. Szabo. Improving neural network predictions of software quality using principal components analysis. In *Proceedings of the International Conference on Neural Networks*, pages 3295–3300, Orlando, FL, June 1994. IEEE Computer Society.

49. Taghi M. Khoshgoftaar and Robert M. Szabo. Predicting software quality during testing using neural network models: A comparative study. *International Journal of Reliability, Quality, and Safety Engineering*, 1(3):303–319, September 1994.

50. Taghi M. Khoshgoftaar and Edward B. Allen. Multivariate assessment of complex software systems: A comparative study. In *Proceedings of the First International Conference on Engineering of Complex Computer Systems*, pages 389–396, Fort Lauderdale, FL, November 1995. IEEE Computer Society.

51. M. M. Nelson and W. T. Illingworth. *A Practical Guide to Neural Nets*. Addison-Wesley, Reading, MA, 1990.

52. Raymond H. Myers. *Classical and Modern Regression with Applications*. Duxbury Series. PWS-KENT Publishing, Boston, 1990.

53. Andrei N. Kolmogorov. On the representation of continuous functions of many variables by superposition of continuous functions of one variable and addition. *American Mathematical Society Translations*, 28:55–59, 1963. Originally published in *Doklady Akademii Nauk SSSR* 114:953–956, 1957 [in Russian].

54. Bernard W. Silverman. *Density Estimation for Statistics and Data Analysis*. Chapman and Hall, London, 1986.

55. Taghi M. Khoshgoftaar and Edward B. Allen. The impact of costs of misclassification on software quality modeling. In *Proceedings of the Fourth International Software Metrics Symposium*, pages 54–62, Albuquerque, NM USA, November 1997. IEEE Computer Society.

Problems

1. Principal components analysis has been performed on a data set, resulting in the following domain pattern.

Domain Pattern

Metric	Domain 1	Domain 2
N_2	0.90650	0.40314
N_1	0.90241	0.42068
LOC	0.88923	0.39994
$ELOC$	0.87983	0.44468
η_2	0.76635	0.58308
η_1	0.40602	0.90972
Eigenvalues	3.953055	1.864772

List all the software metrics that strongly correlate with the second domain metric.

2. The principal components analysis in Problem 1 resulted in the following standardized transformation matrix, **T**.

Metric	Domain 1	Domain 2
N_2	0.37179	-0.24400
N_1	0.34825	-0.20546
LOC	0.35964	-0.23069
$ELOC$	0.30054	-0.13353
η_2	0.04072	0.26228
η_1	-0.65691	1.30095

A software module from a project similar to that in Problem 1 has these standardized measurements, z_i:

$$\begin{aligned}
N_2 &= -0.38485 \\
N_1 &= -0.40943 \\
LOC &= -0.41983 \\
ELOC &= -0.45814 \\
\eta_2 &= -0.42401 \\
\eta_1 &= -0.13556
\end{aligned}$$

What are the domain metric values, d_{ij}, for this module?

3. Why is correlation among software metrics an important issue in statistical software quality modeling?

4. For a classification model that identifies *fault-prone* and *not fault-prone modules*, what is a Type I error and what is a Type II error?

5. Why is the *data splitting* technique sometimes used in software quality modeling?

6. Collect software product metrics data from a project in your organization, and the associated problem history.

7. Use the data set collected in Problem 6 to conduct a two-class neural network classification experiment similar to Example 2 in this chapter.

8. Use the data set collected in Problem 6 to conduct a three-class classification neural network experiment with the classes *fault-prone, medium-faults,* and *not fault-prone.*

   (a) What is the accuracy of the neural network model?

   (b) How does the complexity of the network compare to the network developed in Problem 7?

SELF-ORGANIZING MAPS AND SOFTWARE REUSE

DIETER MERKL

Institut für Softwaretechnik
Technische Universität Wien
Resselgasse 3/188, A-1040 Wien, Austria
dieter@ifs.tuwien.ac.at

Abstract

Software reuse is the process of building new systems from existing components instead of developing these systems from scratch. For a long time now software reuse is repeatedly acknowledged for playing an essential role in overcoming the so-called software crisis, i.e. the late delivery of then still faulty software products. Current development practice as for example object-oriented analysis, design, and programming should in principle assist the proliferation of the reuse idea. However, before existing components may be considered for reuse they have to be found in a software library. As ever in any area relying on the retrieval of particular objects from a large data store, the process of retrieval may turn out to be rather cumbersome, especially when a large number of objects is contained in the data store and the success of the whole operation is dependent on the retrieval of a small number of relevant objects. With this work we address the assistance of such a retrieval process by means of using a connectionist representation of the contents of the software library. More precisely, we rely on the self-organizing map for software library organization. What makes this model especially attractive for an information retrieval task such as software library organization is the topology preserving learning process leading to a highly intuitive similarity visualization.

1 Introduction

The field of software reuse is concerned with the technological and organizational issues arising from the usage of already existing software components to build new applications. Software reuse is widely acknowledged for equipping the software industry with the tools and techniques to enhance both productivity—due to the substantial amount of work that may be saved when a component is reused instead of redeveloped—and quality—due to the fact that the component is used and tested in many different contexts. In other words, software reuse is widely promoted as a panacea for the software crisis, i.e. low productivity of the software industry combined with the inability to satisfy the needs of the customers. For an eloquent treatment of the software crisis and suggestions to address it we refer to [1].

As the technological basis to make software reuse operational, the developers have to be equipped with so-called software libraries that store the various reusable items. In order to be useful, such a library should provide a large number of reusable components within a wide spectrum of application domains. These components may be either reused as they are or may be adapted to the specific needs of the application at hand. We should note that software reuse is not necessarily restricted to the reuse of code. In a much broader sense we regard all products of the software development process as candidates for reuse; examples are process models, requirements analysis, designs, code, documentation, test plans and test data. In this work, however, we restrict ourselves to code as the reusable entities.

Searching for a stored item in a possibly large software library may turn out as a tricky task. The vicious ingredients are an often ill-defined target description of the needed software component on the one hand. On the other hand, the thus following bad initial retrieval results may lead to the "insight" from the users of the library, i.e. the software developers, that developing the needed component from scratch is faster and easier. Consequently, the issue of software library organization is of central concern for the success of the whole idea of software reuse. The basic question is, how should a software library be structured in order to facilitate the retrieval process most? In general, software libraries should be organized in such a way that locating the most appropriate component is easy for the users. Particularly, the library should provide assistance to the user in locating components that meet some specified functionality. A large variety of approaches to software library organization have been suggested in the literature, yet an agreed-upon standard is still not in sight.

In this work we will present an approach to software library organization based on connectionist models. The central aim is to make the semantic relationship of the stored software components as intuitively accessible to the user as possible. By semantic relationship we refer to the functional closeness of the various components which is, obviously, of interest to the actual software developer. As a simple example consider the case where one is looking for a component capable of sorting a number of data items. In general, we would expect a component implementing a *QuickSort* routine to be functionally similar to a component implementing a *MergeSort* routine and a component implementing a *BubbleSort* routine—which of them is best suited for the application at hand may only be determined with deeper knowledge about the system that is to be developed, like the number and the location of the data items to be sorted. We would expect further that these components are functionally dissimilar to a component implementing, say, a string comparison routine such as the *Boyer-Moore algorithm.*

In order to assess the functional similarity of the various software components, we rely on an automatically derived software representation obtained from the textual description of the various components as present in the software manual. We have chosen a keyword-based software representation where the various keywords are extracted by means of full-text indexing of the software manual. Based on such a software representation, we use the self-organizing map, i.e. an unsupervised neural network model, to determine the mutual similarity of the software components and to organize the library accordingly. As a highly convenient benefit, the software components are arranged within a two-dimensional grid of neurons where similarity corresponds to geographical closeness. Hence, the functional similarity of two software components is expressed in terms of spatial closeness of the neurons representing these components—a concept that is intuitively accessible for the user.

The remainder of this work is organized as follows. In Section 2 we give a brief overview of software reuse. A particular aspect of software reuse is described in Section 3 in greater detail, namely approaches to software library organization. Section 4 contains a description of self-organizing maps, the neural network model we rely on for software library organization. The experimental environment for our study in software library organization is described in Section 5. Our approach to software library organization is outlined in Section 6. In particular we give experimental results from organizing a software library with self-organizing maps. We describe an alternative visualization technique that enables a more intuitive similarity representation. Additionally, we show results from using the growing grid model, i.e. a neural network model based on the self-organizing map with adaptive architecture that develops according to the specific requirements of the input data. Finally, we provide some conclusions in Section 7.

2 Software Reuse

Software productivity has been steadily increasing over the past three decades. This increase, however, is still not enough to close the gap between the demands placed on the software industry and what the current state of practice is able to deliver[2,3]. The reuse of software products is one of the few realistic alternatives to bring about the gains of productivity and quality that the software industry needs to meet today's challenging requirements. Software reuse involves building software that is reusable in design and building systems with reusable software components. Software reuse includes reusing both the products of previous software projects and the processes developed to produce them. Thus, a wide spectrum of approaches to software reuse have been suggested [4] ranging from *building block* approaches, i.e. reusing and assembling specific products, to *generative* approaches, i.e. reusing processes of previous software development.

The notion of reusability is an old idea that proved to be highly effective in a wide range of applications. As solutions to current problems are found, these solutions are tried in solving similar new problems. Typically, the old solutions are modified, combined, and adapted to solve the new problem. As some solutions are used time and again to solve the same type of problem, these solutions tend to get accepted, generalized, and standardized. Especially the engineering disciplines are full of examples for successful implementation and execution of the reuse idea in an industrial fashion. The development of large and complex systems relies heavily on the reuse of standardized components because it is impossible otherwise. We refer to civil engineering, mechanical engineering, electrical engineering, aircraft construction, etc. for areas that may be characterized by having a highly mature reuse culture. Software engineering is deliberately omitted from this list. The general idea of reusing software components in order to build new systems and the knowledge of its anticipated benefits is well established in literature since three decades, the practical wide-range implementation of this idea, however, is still in its infancy.

Contrary to this knowledge, the typical situation in a large number of development projects is marked by little exchange of information between departments relative to on-going work and production. Hence, when—rarely enough—shared requirements are discovered it is often too late to take advantage of them. Poor coordination between project teams developing similar products causes them to choose their architectures independently, which makes later reuse difficult if not impossible.

The failure to build a few reusable products instead of many specialized products also results in a growing proportion of effort dedicated to maintenance instead of development of new products. Even worse, the proportion of perfective maintenance, i.e. the adaptation of a software system to new or changed requirements, is by far the largest part of the overall maintenance tasks [5]. In other words, much effort is invested in adaptation and evolution of software systems while sticking to the technological framework of the existing one—with all its limitations and possible design flaws. This is aggravated by monolithic systems in which it is increasingly difficult to isolate and replace specific functionalities. Continuously maintaining software by ad hoc patching is also inferior to replacing larger units. Nevertheless, company internal budgeting policies frequently discourage the production, marketing, and support of reusable components. The usual picture is that managers believe reuse is an important issue, but think it will happen by itself, and thus do little to encourage it, like rewarding the reuse of components, the insertion of components originating from the project into the software library, or discouraging the redevelopment of components. The role of management is frequently reactive, trying to meet deadlines and minimizing cost and time over-runs, rather than visionary, forecasting opportunities and threats.

Moreover, insufficient time is dedicated to the earlier phases of the development process such as analysis and design. During these phases the possibility for identifying the reusability of existing components and defining new reusable components is at its greatest. This chance all too often flows by unnoticed. Software development is not considered as an investment over the whole life span of the product line, but rather as a one-shot development ending when the first release is out of the door and further duty is with the maintenance group.

The widespread misconception is that since it is easy to fix the software, we can start to implement now, and adjust the system later. This is in strong contrast to the traditional manufacturing industries, where a mistake in design is very costly to correct in later development phases. In general, the quality of a system is rarely increased by bug fixes, and often the final product does not correspond to the initial specification.

However, some sort of reuse is performed in most organizations. This reuse originates from individuals who reuse their own components developed during earlier projects or pick up solutions from other developers. Additionally, especially with the widespread usage of object-oriented programming languages, at least the utilization of standard libraries becomes habitual.

From all this it should be obvious that software reuse has a wide spectrum of targets—the question of software library organization which will be further detailed in this work is just one aspect. Reuse is not an end in itself, but it definitely is a means of achieving the general objectives of the company. Companies today are faced with new and more challenging market pressures. In response, companies have to reduce the time-to-market with new or enhanced products, increase the diversity of products available to the customers, and enhance the standardization and interoperability of the products. Reuse is a promising way to achieve such objectives.

In this work we cannot, however, cover the scope of software reuse in sufficient detail, we may just refer the interested reader to the extensive literature on this topic. In particular we left out important issues such as new organizational structures to assist software reuse [6,7,8], new software process models incorporating software reuse explicitly [9,10,11], the analysis of reuse costs and reusability metrics [12,13,14,15,16,17,18,19,20], the generative approach to software reuse, i.e. application generators, [21,22,23], or the wide area of object-oriented system development with all its positive implications for software reuse [24,25,26]. Good starting points for a more thorough treatment of software reuse are [27,28,29,30,31,32].

3 Organization of Software Libraries

Software libraries are repositories where software components are stored and searched. Hence, they represent a highly valuable resource for the software engineer. Several usage patterns for software libraries can be observed. An engineer can study library components to become familiar with a programming language or more generally with a particular programming style, look for common patterns of usage of a particular component, get acquainted with the requirements of a particular application domain, or—last but not least—reuse library components instead of rewriting them from scratch.

A variety of different approaches to software library organization assisting the software engineer in locating appropriate components have been suggested during the last years. These approaches may roughly be classified into three large groups with are outlined below.

The first group of approaches relies on knowledge-based systems for software library organization. Here the similarity between software components is explicitly encoded by means of a knowledge-representation formalism as, for instance, semantic networks. These approaches share in common that the knowledge-base has to be designed manually. Moreover, the knowledge-base has to be developed anew for each new application domain. Even worse, the knowledge-base has to be adapted manually each time a new component is inserted into the library—a situation that is to be expected to occur quite often especially when software reuse has its well established position within the development process. This laborious task has its benefits in increased retrieval efficiency, yet at the expense of losing generality. We do not want to go into more detail concerning knowledge-based approaches, we just refer to [33,34,35] for prominent proponents of this direction of research.

Secondly, a number of approaches are based on a formal specification describing the functional properties of software components. The abstract nature of formal specifications allows to focus on that aspects of a component which are presumably the most important ones for later retrieval. Following such an approach, better retrieval results in terms of finding appropriate components can be anticipated. The price for these retrieval results, however, is expensive in that the formal specification has to be developed manually. Recent achievings in this direction of research are presented in [36,37,38].

Finally, ideas from information retrieval and library science have been utilized relying on the textual description of the software components as found in the software reference manual. These approaches count for their high degree of automatization and general applicability. In the remainder of this Section we will give a more detailed account on information retrieval approaches to software library organization.

As usual in information retrieval approaches the various documents, i.e. manual pages describing the software components, have to be mapped onto a representation language. This process is termed *indexing* in the information retrieval literature. The representation language might consist of predefined terms or keywords, i.e. indexing with a controlled vocabulary, or might consist of terms that are extracted from the document at hand, i.e. full-text indexing. In the remainder of this work we will use the words *term* and *keyword* interchangeably to refer to entities that are selected to represent a document.

Controlled vocabularies are beneficial in the sense that the set of possible keywords is well-defined and the user of the library has less degrees of freedom in describing her or his information needs. In particular, each component and each search request is described by using a set of relevant keywords taken from a predefined catalogue. The obvious drawback of a controlled vocabulary is that the assignment of a particular keyword is done manually and is thus rather expensive because highly skilled personnel is required. Furthermore, the process of keyword selection is highly subjective by nature since different people tend to assign different keywords to describe the same object—a phenomenon known as the *vocabulary problem* in information science research [39].

The utilization of controlled vocabularies has found some attraction in the form of *faceted classification* [40,41,42] in the software reuse community. Such a classification schema consists of a set of categories, i.e. the so-called facets, each of which has several predefined keywords that may possibly be filled in. Thus, the classification schema remains flexible with respect to extensibility because components derived from new applications may easily be classified by using the same categories, just the keywords might need an adjustment, especially when components from a new application domain are added to the software library. The selection of appropriate categories, however, is done in a manual process and represents thus a rather expensive task. In [43] a hypertext interface to a library with objects described by means of facted classification is presented. While such an interface certainly is useful for the software engineer, the general problem of manually derived component descriptions is not addressed.

Full-text indexing on the other hand is done automatically and is hence less subjective. Commonly, the document representation is restricted to those words that appear with sufficient frequency within the document and within the whole document collection. In other words, terms that are expected to provide the best discrimination between documents are used in the representation language [44]. As the major shortcoming we have to note that a particular keyword is used to represent the document only if it is found in that document. Consequently, the retrieval process is susceptible to omissions of relevant documents. A number of papers have been published on the utilization of uncontrolled vocabularies to represent software components. As one example we refer to [45] describing an environment where the full-text of the software documentation is accessed in order to extract the keywords for software representation. In [46] the usage of *lexical affinities* [47], i.e. pairs of frequently co-occurring keywords, is suggested in order to improve the retrieval result. These approaches using full-text indexing are typically combined with statistical cluster analysis to find groups of similar software components. Such a group is then presented together as a retrieval result. In [48,49] the usage of self-organizing maps instead of conventional cluster analysis is suggested because of improved retrieval results. The utilization of fuzzy clustering techniques for software library organization is described in [50].

In Figure 1 we provide a simple pictorial representation of the software retrieval process. On the left hand side, we show the description of the needed software component starting with an information requirements statement that is formalized into a query expression. Essentially, the formalization comprises the transformation of the requirements statement into search terms for the component library. On the right hand side, we show the various reusable software components. The starting point is the component as such that has to be formalized in order to be comparable to the information requests. The comparison between the query and the component representation is termed *matching process* in the figure. Depending on the chosen retrieval model a set of components will be selected as the retrieval result and shown to the user of the library. An overview of different retrieval models may be found in [51,52,53,54]. In our work we use the *vector-space* model where queries and components are represented by means of vectors of keyword occurrences [55]. Depending on the similarity between query vector and component vectors several software components are retrieved as the query result. In particular we rely on the Euclidean vector norm for similarity analysis. Other comparison methods, like the Cosine of the angle between the vectors, should work comparatively well.

A prototypical component-based reuse process is shown in Figure 2. This process starts with an informal description of the needed subsystem that is further transformed into a set of search terms. This search terms are used to query the component library. Assume, that the retrieval result of this initial query returns no reusable components—not a particularly satisfying yet not an uncommon initial result. The reason for such a rather dissatisfying result might be due to an inappropriate selection of search terms or due to the non-existence of appropriate

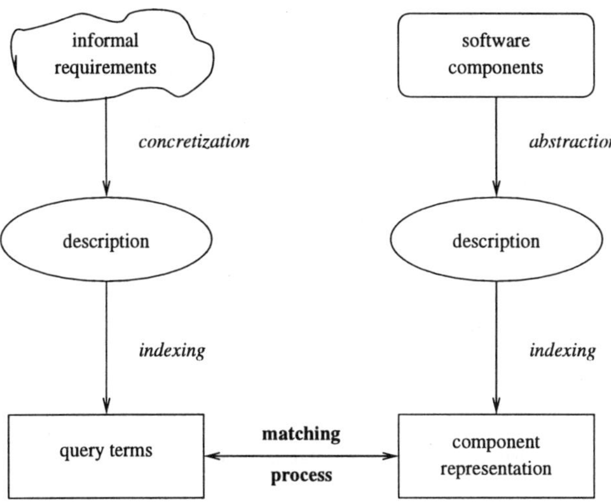

Figure 1: Process model of software retrieval

components in the library. In either case, the retrieval process may be continued with a more detailed subsystem design and thus with a more specific description of the needed components. In our picture we assume that the original subsystem is further decomposed into a number of smaller subsystems for which reusable components are requested from the library. This second retrieval result contains a number of possibly relevant components which are referred to as *candidate components* in the figure. One of those may be reused as such, i.e. the component can be used without modification. Two other components may be reused as well. In the first case, the component has to be adapted in order to be useful. In the second case, it is sufficient to adapt the specification of the component in order to be reusable. In other words, in this case a modification of the subsystem's design enables the reuse of an existing component. In our example one component of the subsystem has to be developed from scratch. This new component and the two adapted components are now candidates for inclusion in the component library for reuse in further projects. Such an inclusion, however, has to be accompanied with careful design and analysis of the components. With such a reuse process model development *with* reuse and development *for* reuse are tied together in a nice and natural fashion.

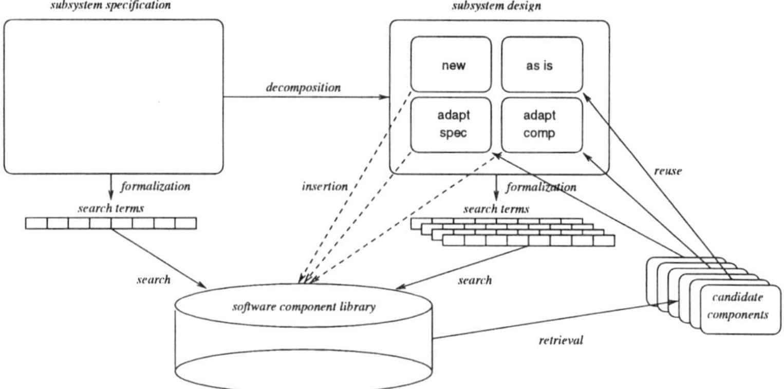

Figure 2: Component-based software reuse

4 Self-Organizing Maps

The *self-organizing map* as proposed in [56,57] and described thoroughly in [58] is one of the most distinguished unsupervised artificial neural network models. This model consists of a layer of input units each of which is fully connected to a grid of output units. These output units are arranged in some topology where the most common choice is represented by a two-dimensional grid.

Input units receive the input patterns x, $x \in \Re^n$, and propagate them as they are onto the output units. Each of the output units i is assigned a weight vector m_i. These weight vectors have the same dimension as the input data, $m_i \in \Re^n$. In the initial setup of the model prior to training, the weight vectors are filled with random values.

During each learning step, the unit c with the highest activity level with respect to a randomly selected input pattern x is adapted in a way that it will exhibit an even higher activity level at future presentations of that specific input pattern. Commonly, the activity level of a unit is computed as the Euclidean distance between the input pattern and that unit's weight vector. Hence, the selection of the winner c may be written as given in Expression (1).

$$c : ||x - m_c|| = \min_i\{||x - m_i||\} \tag{1}$$

Adaptation takes place at each learning iteration and is performed as a gradual reduction of the difference between the respective components of the input vector and the weight vector. The amount of adaptation is guided by a learning-rate α that is gradually decreasing in the course of time. This decreasing nature of adaptation strength ensures large adaptation steps in the beginning of the learning process where the weight vectors have to be tuned from their random initialization towards the actual requirements of the input space. Furthermore, the ever smaller adaptation steps towards the end of the learning process enable a fine-tuned input space representation.

As an extension to standard competitive learning, units in a time-varying and gradually decreasing neighborhood around the winner are adapted, too. Pragmatically speaking, during the learning steps of the self-organizing map a set of units around the winner is tuned towards the currently presented input pattern enabling a spatial arrangement of the input patterns such that alike inputs are mapped onto regions close to each other in the grid of output units. Thus, the training process of the self-organizing map results in a topological ordering of the input patterns. According to [59] we may thus refer to the self-organizing map as a neural network model performing a spatially smooth version of k-means clustering.

The neighborhood of units around the winner may be described implicitly by means of a neighborhood-kernel h_{ci} taking into account the distance—in terms of the output space—between unit i under consideration and unit c, the winner of the current learning iteration. This neighborhood-kernel assigns scalars in the range of $[0, 1]$ that are used to determine the amount of adaptation ensuring that nearby units are adapted more strongly than units further away from the winner. A Gaussian may be used to define the neighborhood-kernel as given in Expression (2) where $||r_c - r_i||$ denotes the distance between units c and i within the output space with r_i representing the two-dimensional vector pointing to the location of unit i within the grid.

$$h_{ci}(t) = e^{-\frac{||r_c - r_i||}{2 \cdot \delta(t)^2}} \tag{2}$$

It is common practice that in the beginning of the learning process the neighborhood-kernel is selected large enough to cover a wide area of the output space. The spatial width of the neighborhood-kernel is reduced gradually during the learning process such that towards the end of the learning process just the winner itself is adapted. Such a reduction is done by means of the time-varying parameter δ in Expression (2). This strategy enables the formation of large clusters in the beginning and fine-grained input discrimination towards the end of the learning process.

In combining these principles of self-organizing map training, we may write the learning rule as given in Expression (3). Please note that we make use of a discrete time notation with t denoting the current learning iteration. The other parts of this expression are α representing the time-varying learning-rate, h_{ci} representing the time-varying neighborhood-kernel, x representing the currently presented input pattern, and finally m_i denoting the weight vector assigned to unit i.

$$m_i(t+1) = m_i(t) + \alpha(t) \cdot h_{ci}(t) \cdot [x(t) - m_i(t)] \qquad (3)$$

A simple graphical representation of a self-organizing map's architecture and its learning process is provided in Figure 3. In this figure the output space consists of a square of 36 units, depicted as circles. One input vector $x(t)$ is randomly chosen and mapped onto the grid of output units. In the second step of the learning process, the winner c is selected. Consider the winner being the unit depicted as the black node in the figure. The weight vector of the winner, $m_c(t)$, is now moved towards the current input vector. This movement is symbolized in the input space in Figure 3. As a consequence of the adaptation, unit c will produce an even higher activation with respect to input pattern x at the next learning iteration, $t+1$, because the unit's weight vector, $m_c(t+1)$, is now nearer to the input pattern x in terms of the input space. Apart from the winner, adaptation is performed with neighboring units, too. Units that are subject to adaptation are depicted as shaded nodes in the figure. The shading of the various nodes corresponds to the amount of adaptation and thus, to the spatial width of the neighborhood-kernel. Generally, units in close vicinity of the winner are adapted more strongly and consequently, they are depicted with a darker shade in the figure.

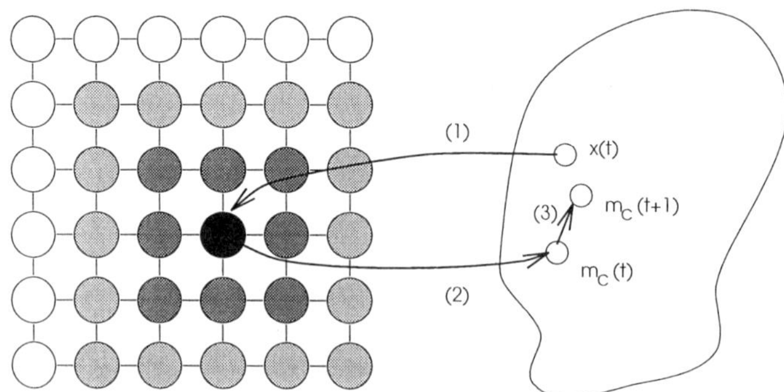

Figure 3: Architecture and training process of a self-organizing map

5   The Experimental Software Library

5.1   The NIH class library

Throughout the remainder of this work we will use the various components of the NIH Class Library[60], the NIHCL in short, as a sample software component library. The NIHCL is a collection of classes developed in the C++ programming language. The class library covers classes for storing and retrieving arbitrarily complex data structures on disk like OIOifd and OIOostream, generally useful data types such as String, Time, and Date, and finally a number of container classes as, for example, Set, Dictionary, and OrderedCltn. A more complete description of the class library may be found in[61].

In an information retrieval approach to software library organization the task of similarity recognition between the various software components is replaced by similarity recognition between natural language documents describing these components, i.e. their respective manual pages. However, since natural language processing is still far from understanding arbitrarily complex document structures, the various documents have, in a first step, to be mapped onto some representation language in order to be comparable. Still one of the most widely used representation languages is single-term full-text indexing[53]. Roughly speaking, the documents are represented by the set of words they are built of. As a result, the various text documents are represented by vectors of equal dimension. Each vector component corresponds to a keyword from the representation language, and each vector entry in a particular component relates to the importance of that very keyword in describing the component at hand. In its most basic form, i.e. binary single-term indexing, an entry of one indicates that this specific keyword was extracted from the description of the component at hand. Contrary to that an entry of zero means that the corresponding keyword is not contained in that component's description[54]. A simple example of binary single-term indexing is provided in Table 1.

	$Keyword_1$	$Keyword_2$	$\cdots$	$Keyword_n$
$Component_1$	1	1		0
$Component_2$	0	1		0
$Component_3$	0	0		1
$\cdots$				
$Component_m$	1	0		1

Table 1: Binary indexing of software components

Assuming a suitable representation, the similarity between two documents corresponds to the distance between their vector representations, i.e. the rows in Table 1. The benefit of such a vector-based representation is the ease of implementing a best-match retrieval strategy, where the retrieved software components may be ranked according to decreasing similarity between the vector representing the actual query, i.e. the description of the needed software component, and the vectors representing the various text documents describing the components stored in the archive.

In order to obtain the final document representation, we accessed the full-text of the various manual pages describing NIHCL classes. As an illustrative example we refer to Figure 4 containing a portion of the textual description of class Set as provided in [60].

Set – UNORDERED COLLECTION OF NON-DUPLICATE OBJECTS

Base Class: `Collection`
Derived Classes: `Dictionary`, `IdentSet`
Related Classes: `Iterator`
A Set is an unordered collection of objects. The objects cannot be accessed by a key as can the objects in a `Dictionary`, for example. Unlike a Bag, in which equal objects may occur more than once, a Set ignores attempts to add any object that duplicates one already in the Set. A Set considers two objects to be duplicates if they are `isEqual()` to one another.
Class Set is implemented using a hash table with open addressing. `Set::add()` calls the virtual member function `hash()` and uses the number returned to compute an index to the hash table at which to begin searching, and `isEqual()` is called to check for equality.

Figure 4: NIHCL manual entry of class set

The natural language text of the various manual pages describing the classes is accessed and full-text indexed in order to generate a binary vector-space representation of the documents. Just to provide the exact figure, the indexing process identified 489 distinct content terms and thus, each component is represented by a 489-dimensional feature vector. During the indexing process we excluded terms contained in a small stopword list—mostly articles, pronouns, and conjunctions—and terms that occurred in less than two documents. These vectors are subsequently used as the input data to the self-organizing map.

5.2   Cluster analysis: The baseline for comparison

In order to provide the baseline for the discussion of the results achieved with unsupervised neural networks, we will first show the classification results from statistical cluster analysis [62]. Table 2 contains the result from k-means clustering where the software components are assigned to 4 clusters. The limitation of statistical cluster analysis is quite obvious from that result. There are two clusters with a large number of components. As a consequence, the functional closeness of these components is questionable to say the least. Especially *Class 3* contains a broad variety of rather unrelated components. On the other hand, two clusters consist of a very small number of components. It is obvious that these clusters are too specialized to be useful.

	Software Components
Class 1	Arraychar, ArrayOb, Assoc, AssocInt, Bag, Collection, Dictionary, Heap, IdentDict, IdentSet, Iterator, KeySortCltn, Link, LinkedList, LookupKey, OrderedCltn, SeqCltn, Set, SortedCltn, Stack
Class 2	Vector
Class 3	Bitset, Class, Date, Exception, FDSet, Float, Integer, LinkOb, Nil, Object, OIOifd, OIOin, OIOistream, OIOnihin, OIOnihout, OIOofd, OIOostream, OIOout, Point, Random, ReadFromTbl, StoreOnTbl, Time
Class 4	Range, Regex, String

Table 2: k-means clustering of the NIHCL—4 clusters

A result from k-means clustering where the software components are assigned to 10 clusters is shown in Table 3. Here the separation comes closer to the functionality of the components but the result is still not completely satisfying. *Class 1*, *Class 6*, and *Class 8* contain mostly components implementing data structures. Some of the assignments are, however, not justifyable within their particular cluster like AssocInt, LookupKey, and ArrayOb. *Class 9* contains mostly data types—the exclusion of String and Vector from that cluster, however, is far from natural. A completely satisfying cluster is formed with *Class 2* consisting exclusively of file I/O components.

	Software Components
Class 1	Arraychar, Assoc, Bag, Bitset, Dictionary, Heap, IdentDict, IdentSet, KeySortCltn, OrderedCltn, SeqCltn, Set, SortedCltn, Stack
Class 2	OIOifd, OIOin, OIOistream, OIOnihin, OIOnihout, OIOifd, OIOostream, OIOout, ReadFromTbl, StoreOnTbl
Class 3	Iterator
Class 4	Vector
Class 5	Object
Class 6	AssocInt, Link, LinkedList, LinkOb, LookupKey
Class 7	Class, Exception, Nil, Regex
Class 8	ArrayOb, Collection
Class 9	Date, FDSet, Float, Integer, Point, Random, Range, Time
Class 10	String

Table 3: k-means clustering of the NIHCL—10 clusters

6 Unsupervised Learning in Software Library Organization

6.1 Results with the standard self-organizing map model

A typical result from the application of self-organizing maps to data describing reusable software components is provided in Figure 5. In this case we have used a 10×10 self-organizing map to represent the software library. Generally, the graphical representation may be interpreted as follows. Each output unit of the self-organizing map is represented by means of either a dot or a class name. The class name appears where the respective unit is winner of the input pattern representing that specific software component. Contrary to that, a dot marks units that have not won the competition for an input pattern. These units, however, have their important role in determining the spatial range of the various data clusters.

In the upper right part of the map we recognize the arrangement of all classes performing file I/O, these classes are designated by the 'OIO'-part of their respective class name. The region itself is organized in such a way that a class performing an input operation is mapped neighboring its output counterpart, e.g. OIOifd and OIOofd.

Just below the file I/O region we find a large area of the map consisting of the various classes representing data structures. Within this large region we recognize a smaller area in the lower middle of the map com-

81

Integer	.	Point	.	String	.	OIOofd	.	OIOout	OIOin
Float	.	.	Range	.	.	OIOifd	.	OIOostream	OIOistream
Random	.	Date	.	Vector	.	.	OIOnihout	OIOnihin	.
.	Time	.	Class	.	.	ReadFromTbl	StoreOnTbl	.	.
Nil	.	FDSet	.	.	Exception	.	.	ArrayOb	.
.	Collection	.	.	Object	.	.	Arraychar	.	Bitset
Iterator	.	Link	LinkOb	.	.	Regex	.	.	.
SeqCltn	.	LinkedList	.	.	SortedCltn	.	Bag	.	Heap
.	.	.	.	LookupKey	.	Dictionary	.	IdentSet	.
OrderedCltn	Stack	.	AssocInt	Assoc	KeySortCltn	.	IdentDict	.	Set

Figure 5: 10×10 *Self-Organizing Map* representation of the NIHCL

prising classes that allow an access to their elements via a key-attribute, i.e. Dictionary, IdentDict, and KeySortCltn. Within this particular area we find the classes that actually implement this type of access, i.e. Assoc, AssocInt, and LookupKey. Please note that this important relationship was never obvious with the results of statistical cluster analysis as presented above.

Finally, we want to shift the attention towards the upper left-hand side of the map where the classes representing data types are located. Again, their arrangement reflects their mutual similarity. As some examples we refer to the assignment of Date and Time, String and Vector, and Float and Integer to geographically close units, respectively. Their class names are fully self-contained, we thus refrain from a detailed discussion of the functionality of these classes. Furthermore, please note the placement of class Random, a random number generator producing (pseudo-) random numbers of Float data type. This class is mapped onto a unit neighboring the basic numerical data types Float and Integer.

A lot more interesting areas may be located in this representation. We cannot, however, cover them in detail here, we rather refer to [63] especially for a comparison of these results with those obtained from statistical cluster analysis.

However, in case one is not familiar with the NIHCL as such it is still problematic to identify regions of functionally similar C++ classes. From the pure two-dimensional representation as provided in Figure 5 a casual user might for instance conclude that the classes Point and String or String and OIOofd are of comparable similarity since they are located at units of equal distance in the upper middle of the final map. The similarity of the former two classes is evident in that both classes represent data types. The latter pair, however, is formed from two completely unrelated classes, the one being a data type, the other a file I/O class. Such a representation might be misleading for the unexperienced user of the software library, to say the least. With a novel visualization technique, outlined in the next subsection, we are addressing exactly this type of misleading representation.

6.2 Adaptive coordinates for improved similarity representation in self-organizing maps

We extended the basic learning rule in order to capture the movements of the various weight vectors within a two-dimensional 'virtual' output space for subsequent visualization of the clustering result. We will refer to this extension as the *adaptive coordinate* visualization technique[64,65].

The initial setup of the 'virtual' output space is such that each of the output units of the self-organizing map is shown in its position within the two-dimensional grid defined by the neural network architecture. In other words, the initial coordinates $\langle ax_i, ay_i \rangle$ of the unit i are identical to the unit's position within the grid of the map. In the beginning of each learning step the distances between the weight vectors and a randomly selected input pattern are stored in a table, $Dist(t)$, where the distance of a particular unit i is denoted as $Dist_i(t)$. After the adaptation of weight vectors the new distance table is calculated, $Dist(t+1)$. As the next step, the relative change in distance according to the actual learning iteration is computed for every unit i, i.e. Δ_{Dist_i}. This computation is given in Expression (4).

$$\Delta_{Dist_i}(t+1) = \frac{Dist_i(t) - Dist_i(t+1)}{Dist_i(t)} \qquad (4)$$

The movement of the various weight vectors within the input space due to the adaptation process is performed analogously within the 'virtual' output space. Pragmatically speaking, the adaptive coordinates $\langle ax_i, ay_i \rangle$ are used in order to mimic the movement of this unit's weight vector during the training process. Since the presented input signal was mapped onto the winning unit c, no adaptation of the position of the winning unit is performed, with c now being the representative of the selected input signal in terms of the 'virtual' output space. This unit's position is further used as an attractor for other units in the neighborhood of the winner. The adaptive coordinates of all units but the winner are now moved by the fraction given in $\Delta_{Dist_i}(t+1)$ towards the position of the winning unit c given by $\langle ax_c, ay_c \rangle$. Note that the larger the width of the neighborhood-kernel the more units' coordinates are adapted—this is similar to the adaptation process of weight vectors in the basic learning rule.

In Expression (5) we provide the exact formulation of adaptation performed with the ax-coordinate of unit i. The calculation of the new

ay-coordinate of unit i, ay_i, is performed analogously.

$$ax_i(t+1) = ax_i(t) + \Delta_{Dist_i}(t+1) \cdot (ax_c(t) - ax_i(t)) \tag{5}$$

In Figure 6 we present a highly idealized schematic representation of the effect of the adaptive coordinate visualization technique. The upper part of this figure is already known from Figure 3. The shaded nodes represent units that are subject to weight vector adaptation and are thus also subject to coordinate adaptation. The adaptive coordinates of these units are moved closer to the winner as shown in the lower part of Figure 6. Units that are not adapted due to the limited range of the neighborhood-kernel do not change their location within the 'virtual' output space.

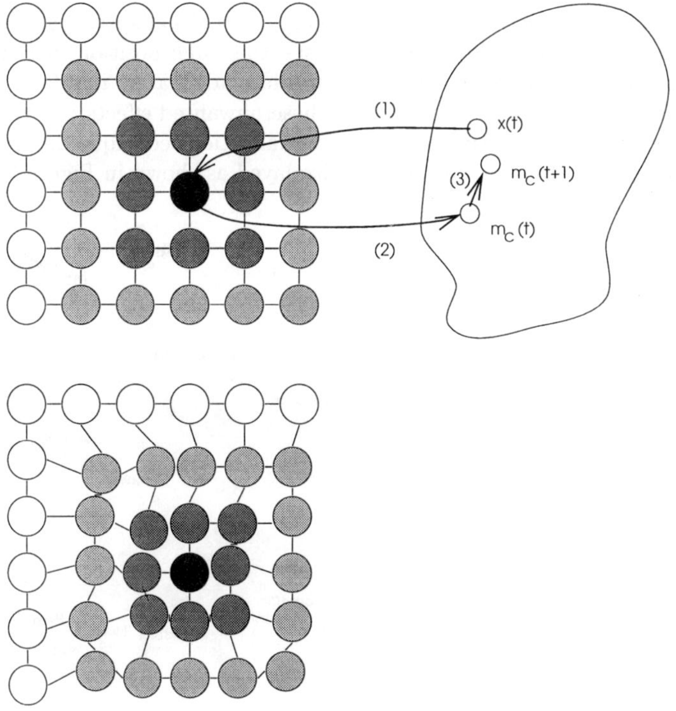

Figure 6: Adaptive coordinate visualization technique

Thus, the clustering of units around the winning unit resembles the clustering of the units' weight vectors around the presented input signal after the current training cycle. After convergence of the training process the clusters learned by the self-organizing map can be visualized by using the coordinates $\langle ax_i, ay_i \rangle$ to plot the position of unit i in the 'virtual' output space.

We have to note that we usually do not start with coordinate adaptation right from the beginning of the learning process. We rather wait until the first stage of rough clustering is finished when the neighborhood-kernel has a width of, say, half the initial one. The reason for the later beginning of coordinate adaptation is simply the fact that during the initial phases of the learning process the weight vector adaptation results in a rough ordering of the input patterns and the necessary evolution of the random initial weight vector positions towards the actual requirements of the input data set. Starting that early would mean that the rather large movements of weight vectors are repeated with the adaptive coordinates. Moreover, due to the large adaptation movements affecting a wide area of the network, chances are high that the adaptive coordinates of each unit converge towards—almost—the same position in the 'virtual' output space. Starting with coordinate adaptation in a later stage of the learning process ensures that these unwanted effects are avoided.

By using the adaptive coordinate visualization technique the training result of the self-organizing map is displayed as shown in Figure 7.

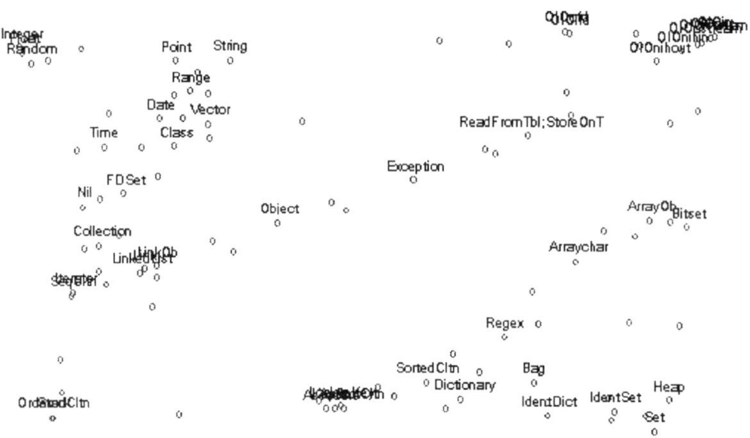

Figure 7: *Adaptive coordinate* representation of a 10×10 *self-organizing map*

The most obvious observation from the result as depicted in Figure 7 is that the regions we described for Figure 5 are readily recognizable thanks to the fact that they are better separated graphically. Consider for example the pairs Point and String or String and OIOofd. These pairs have been identified as a sample area of misleading visualization in the conventional output space representation. With the adaptive coordinate visualization technique they are now separated substantially in the output space. There is certainly no longer the risk that these classes might be considered as being comparably similar.

Moreover, some parts of the final map contain such highly similar classes that the learning process allocates a fairly condensed region in the map for them. As an example consider the file I/O classes in the right upper part of Figure 7. For convenient comparison we show an enlarged visualization of this area in Figure 8. A similar observation holds true for the left upper part of the map containing the various classes implementing data types, and here especially for the area containing the classes Integer, Float, and Random. This region is enlarged in Figure 9. The fact that these software components belong to a fairly homogeneous group is even stressed by using the adaptive coordinate technique for output space visualization.

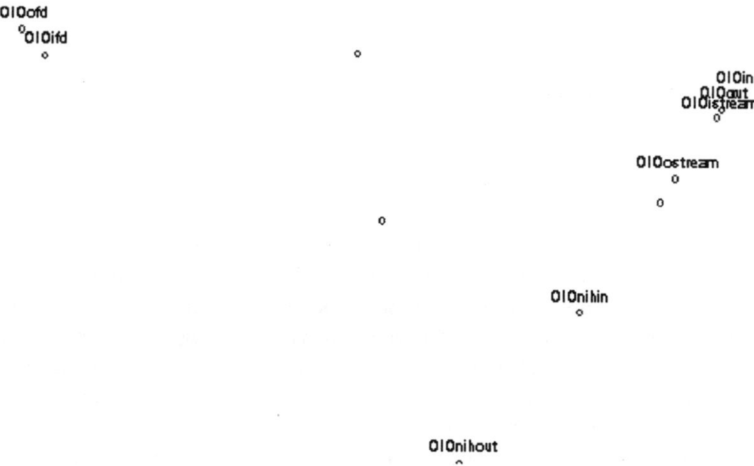

Figure 8: Right upper region of Figure 7

6.3 Results with the growing grid model

When using the self-organizing map as the underlying model for software library organization we have to define the dimension of the output space in terms of the number of units in advance. This might be somewhat difficult when the contents of the library is not known exactly. A model that overcomes this limitation by relying on an adaptive architecture

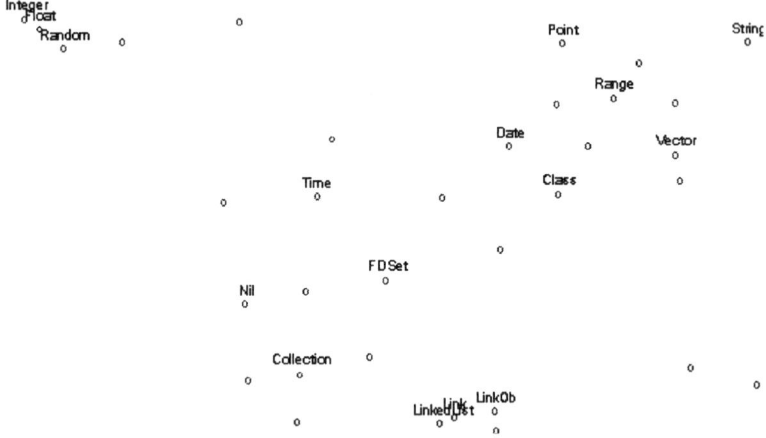

Figure 9: Left upper region of Figure 7

that grows according to the specific needs of the input space is the only recently suggested *growing grid* [66]. The training process starts with a square of just four units and the network grows in the course of the training process in order to improve the representation of the input space. The growth process retains the rectangular structure of the output space.

During each learning iteration the winner as well as its neighboring units are adapted in order to resemble the current input pattern more closely. This adaptation strategy is thus similar to self-organizing maps. The first remarkable difference in the training processes is that the growing grid model is trained with a fixed value of the learning-rate and constant neighborhood-kernel as opposed to the time-varying behavior of their counterparts in self-organizing maps. The second difference is marked by in the so-called *signal counter*, where for each unit the number of times this very unit served as the winner is recorded. This figure represents an indication for the location in the output space where the input space is not represented adequately. The underlying assumption is that if a unit serves often as the winner it represents a number of—presumably—different input patterns. Ever after a fixed number of training iterations the unit with the highest signal counter is selected and either a new row or a new column is inserted depending of the direction of that unit's most dissimilar neighbor. The dissimilarity of two units, obviously, is calculated as the distance between their respective weight vectors.

The growth process is symbolized in Figure 10. On the left hand side of the figure we find the architecture of the network before insertion. On the right hand side, the architecture after insertion of a column of units in between the unit with the highest signal counter, depicted as a black node, and its most dissimilar neighbor, depicted as a hatched node, is shown.

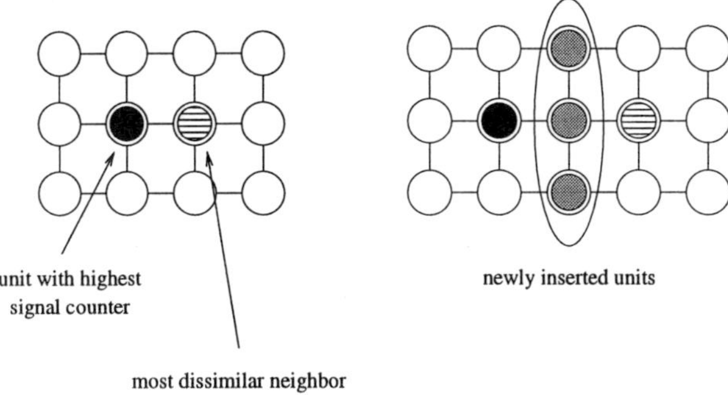

Figure 10: Growth process during *growing grid* training

Subsequently, the weight vectors of the new units are initialized and the signal counter values are redistributed between already existing and newly inserted units. The growth process terminates when a sufficiently exact input pattern representation is reached in terms of the mean quantization error, i.e the mean of the remaining deviation of input vector and best matching weight vector after training. After the termination of the growth process the training continues with weight vector finetuning according to the standard self-organizing map training rule.

As a consequence, the growing grid model is able to exhibit the characteristic benefit of self-organizing maps, namely the visualization of input data similarity in terms of geographical closeness within the grid of output units. As a specific benefit of the growing grid model we have to stress the fact that the model determines an appropriate number of units within the framework of an unsupervised training process.

In Figure 11 a typical result of the growing grid model trained with the NIHCL data is depicted. This figure shows the input pattern representation after termination of the growth process with a 6 × 14 grid and before finetuning. It is quite obvious that the overall input space representation resembles that from self-organizing maps as shown above. The major difference is that some units represent a rather large number of input patterns, e.g. the file I/O classes in the lower right corner.

The benefit of the finetuning process is the better separation of input patterns within the grid of units as can be seen in Figure 12.

Point	Random	Float Integer Range	Date FDSet Time	.	Regex String
.	Exception	.	.	.	Vector
Nil	.	.	.	.	.
.	.	.	Link	.	Object
.	.	Class	.	.	.
ReadFromTbl StoreOnTbl	.	.	Iterator	Collection	.
.	Stack	.	.	.	.
.	IdentSet	LinkedList	.	.	Arraychar Arrayob
LinkOb	.	Bag OrderedCltn SeqCltn	.	.	.
.	SortedCltn	.	Heap	.	Bitset
AssocInt Dictionary IdentDict	KeySortCltn	.	.	.	.
Assoc LookupKey Set	.	.	.	.	.
.	.	.	.	.	OIOifd OIOin OIOistream OIOofd OIOostream OIOout
.	.	OIOnihin OIOnihout	.	.	.

Figure 11: 6 × 14 *Growing grid* representation of the NIHCL before finetuning

FDSet Nil	Exception	Random	.	.	Float Integer Point Range
.	.	Date Time	.	.	.
Link	Class	.	.	Vector	.
.	.	.	Object	.	String
Collection Iterator	.	.	.	.	Regex
.	.	ArrayOb	Arraychar Set	.	Bitset
Bag IdentSet	.	.	.	.	.
.	Heap	.	.	.	OIOifd OIOofd
SortedCltn	OrderedCltn Stack	.	.	ReadFromTbl StoreOnTbl	.
.	SeqCltn	.	.	.	.
IdentDict	.	LinkedList	.	.	.
KeySortCltn	.	.	.	.	OIOin OIOout
.	.	LinkOb	.	.	OIOistream OIOostream
Assoc AssocInt Dictionary	LookupKey	.	.	.	OIOnihin OIOnihout

Figure 12: 6 × 14 *Growing grid* representation of the NIHCL after finetuning

The observation of the training process of the growing grid model is highly valuable for exploratory data analysis of the software library. In particular it is noteworthy that the overall discrimination into classes implementing data types, container classes, and classes handling file I/O is easily observable in that these classes are mapped onto the same—or a small number of—units respectively during the early stages of the training process when the network is small. In this sense it is rather straight forward to determine functional correspondences even in unknown libraries.

7   Conclusions

In this work we described the utilization of unsupervised neural networks, in particular self-organizing maps, for software library organization. The reason for using this particular type of neural network may be found in its ability to reveal the similarity of software components in a highly intuitive fashion in terms of spatial distance within a two-dimensional plane. We have shown, that the self-organizing map is capable of arranging a number of reusable software components according to their mutual functional closeness where similar components are shown in geographically near regions of the two-dimensional output space of the self-organizing map. The results of a novel visualization technique for self-organizing maps provides a highly accessible representation of similarity where clusters containing similar components are tied together more closely within the two-dimensional plane. Such a library representation has its benefits when developers look for a particular component during the development process of a software system. Additionally, the self-organizing map can be used easily for interactive exploration of the software library—a feature that is of vital importance in software reuse. For exploratory analysis of the contents of the software library we suggested the utilization of the growing grid model which represents, pragmatically speaking, a self-organizing map with adaptive architecture that develops according to the requirements of the input data space.

Acknowledgments

Thanks are due to Andreas Rauber for long and fruitful discussions on cluster visualization for self-organizing maps and the implementation of the adaptive coordinate visualization technique. Additional thanks go to Wolfgang Liedl for providing a prototype implementation of the Growing Grid model.

References

1. F. P. Brooks. No silver bullet—Essence and accidents of software engineering. *IEEE Computer*, 20(4), 1987.
2. B. Boehm. Improving software productivity. *IEEE Software*, 4(6), 1987.
3. B. J. Cox. Planning the software revolution. *IEEE Software*, 7(6), 1990.
4. E. Horowitz and J. B. Munson. An expansive view of reusable software. *IEEE Transactions on Software Engineering*, 10(5), 1984.
5. H. van Vliet. *Software Engineering: Principles and Practice*. John Wiley & Sons, Chichester, UK, 1993.
6. V. R. Basili, G. Caldiera, F. McGarry, R. Pajerski, G. Page, and S. Waligora. The software engineering laboratory—An operational software experience. In *Proceedings of the Int'l Conference on Software Engineering (ICSE'92)*, Melbourne, Australia, 1992.
7. M. A. Cusumano. The software factory: A historical interpretation. *IEEE Software*, 6(2), 1989.
8. Y. Matsumoto. Experiences from software reuse in industial process control applications. In *Proceedings of the Int'l Workshop on Software Reusability*, Lucca, Italy, 1993.
9. B. Henderson-Sellers and J. M. Edwards. The object-oriented systems life cycle. *Communications of the ACM*, 33(9), 1990.
10. R. Prieto-Diaz. Integrating domain analysis and reuse in the software development process. In *Proceedings of the Annual Workshop on Methods and Tools for Reuse*, Syracuse, NY, 1990.
11. M. A. Simos. The domain-oriented life cycle: Toward an extended process model for reusability. In W. Tracz, editor, *Software Reuse: Emerging Technology*. IEEE Computer Society Press, Piscataway, NJ, 1990.
12. B. H. Barnes and T. B. Bollinger. Making reuse cost-effective. *IEEE Software*, 8(1), 1991.
13. S. Chidamber and C. Kemerer. A metrics suite for object oriented design. *IEEE Transactions on Software Engineering*, 20(6), 1994.
14. N. Fenton. *Software Metrics: A Rigorous Approach*. Chapman & Hall, London, UK, 1991.
15. W. B. Frakes and C. Terry. Reuse level metrics. In *Proceedings of the Int'l Conference on Software Reuse (ICSR'94)*, Rio de Janeiro, Brazil, 1994.
16. W. B. Frakes and C. Terry. Software reuse and reusability metrics models. Technical Report TR-95-07, Virginia Polytechnic Institute and State University, Falls Church, VA, 1995.
17. M. Hitz. Measuring reuse attributes in object-oriented systems. In *Proceedings of the Int'l Conference on Object-Oriented Information*

Systems, Dublin, Ireland, 1995.

18. M. Hitz and B. Montazeri. Chidamber & Kemerer's metrics suite: A measurement theory perspective. *IEEE Transactions on Software Engineering*, 22(4), 1996.

19. J. Margono and T. E. Rhoads. Software reuse economics: Cost benefit analysis on a large-scale ADA project. In *Proceedings of the Int'l Conference on Software Engineering (ICSE'92)*, Melbourne, Australia, 1992.

20. J. S. Poulin, J. M. Caruso, and D. R. Hancock. The business case for software reuse. *IBM Systems Journal*, 32(4), 1993.

21. C. T. Cleaveland. Building application generators. *IEEE Software*, 5(4), 1988.

22. L. S. Levy. A metaprogramming method and its economic justification. *IEEE Transactions on Software Engineering*, 12(2), 1986.

23. S. K. Misra and P. J. Jalics. Third-generation versus fourth-generation development. *IEEE Software*, 5(4), 1988.

24. I. Jacobson. *Object Oriented Software Engineering: A Use Case Driven Approach*. Addison-Wesley, Reading, MA, 1992.

25. J. Rumbaugh, M. Blaha, W. Premerlani, F. Eddy, and W. Lorensen. *Object Oriented Modeling and Design*. Prentice-Hall, Englewood Cliffs, NJ, 1991.

26. R. Wirfs-Brock and R. E. Johnson. Surveying current research on object-oriented design. *Communications of the ACM*, 33(9), 1990.

27. T. J. Biggerstaff and A. J. Perlis, editors. *Software Reusability*. Addison-Wesley, Reading, MA, 1989.

28. W. B. Frakes and S. Isoda. Success factors of systematic reuse. *IEEE Software*, 11(5), 1994.

29. E.-A. Karlsson, editor. *Software Reuse: A Holistic Approach*. John Wiley & Sons, Chichester, UK, 1995.

30. C. W. Krueger. Software reuse. *ACM Computing Surveys*, 24(2), 1992.

31. H. Mili, F. Mili, and A. Mili. Reusing software: Issues and research directions. *IEEE Transactions on Software Engineering*, 21(6), 1995.

32. W. Schäfer, R. Prieto-Diaz, and M. Matsumoto, editors. *Software Reusability*. Ellis Horwood, New York, 1994.

33. P. Devanbu, R. J. Brachman, P. J. Selfridge, and B. W. Ballard. LaSSIE—A knowledge-based software information system. *Communications of the ACM*, 34(5), 1991.

34. E. Ostertag, J. Hendler, R. Prieto-Diaz, and C. Braun. Computing similarity in a reuse library. *ACM Transactions on Software Engineering and Methodology*, 1(3), 1992.

35. G. Spanoudakis and P. Constantopoulos. Similarity for analogical software reuse—A conceptual modeling approach. In *Proceedings*

of the Int'l Conference on Advanced Information Systems Engineering (CAiSE'93), 1993.

36. B. H. C. Cheng and J.-J. Jeng. Reusing analogous components. *IEEE Transactions on Knowledge and Data Engineering*, 9(2), 1997.

37. R. Mili, A. Mili, and R. T. Mittermeir. Storing and retrieving software components: A refinement based approach. *IEEE Transactions on Software Engineering*, 23(7), 1997.

38. A. M. Zaremski and J. M. Wing. Signature matching: A tool for using software libraries. *ACM Transactions on Software Engineering and Methodology*, 4(2), 1995.

39. G. W. Furnas, T. K. Landauer, L. M. Gomez, and S. T. Dumais. The vocabulary problem in human-system communications. *Communications of the ACM*, 30(11), 1987.

40. R. Prieto-Diaz and P. Freeman. Classifying software for reusability. *IEEE Software*, 4(1), 1987.

41. R. Prieto-Diaz. Implementing faceted classification for software reuse. *Communications of the ACM*, 34(5), 1991.

42. E.-A. Karlsson, S. Sørumgård, and E. Tryggeseth. Classification of object-oriented components for reuse. In *Proceedings of the Int'l Conference on Technology of Object-Oriented Systems (TOOLS'92)*, 1992.

43. T. Isakowitz and R. J. Kauffman. Supporting search for reusable software objects. *IEEE Transactions on Software Engineering*, 22(6), 1996.

44. G. Salton and C. Buckley. Term weighting approaches in automatic text retrieval. *Information Processing & Management*, 24(5), 1988.

45. Y. F. Chang and C. M. Eastman. An information retrieval system for reusable software. *Information Processing & Management*, 29(5), 1993.

46. Y. S. Maarek, D. M. Berry, and G. E. Kaiser. An information retrieval approach for automatically constructing software libraries. *IEEE Transactions on Software Engineering*, 17(8), 1991.

47. Y. S. Maarek and F. A. Smadja. Full-text indexing based on lexical relations: An application—Software libraries. In *Proceedings of the Int'l ACM SIGIR Conference on Research and Development in Information Retrieval (SIGIR'89)*, Cambridge, MA, 1989.

48. D. Merkl. Structuring software for reuse—The case of self-organizing maps. In *Proceedings of the Int'l Joint Conference on Neural Networks (IJCNN'93)*, Nagoya, Japan, 1993.

49. D. Merkl, A M. Tjoa, and G. Kappel. Learning the semantic similarity of reusable software components. In *Proceedings of the Int'l Conference on Software Reuse (ICSR'94)*, Rio de Janeiro, Brazil, 1994.

50. W. Pedrycz and J. Waletzky. Fuzzy clustering in software reusability. *Software–Practice and Experience*, 27(3), 1997.

51. W. B. Frakes and R. Baeza-Yates, editors. *Information Retrieval: Data Structures and Algorithms*. Prentice Hall, Englewood Cliffs, NJ, 1992.

52. G. Salton and M. J. McGill. *Introduction to Modern Information Retrieval*. McGraw-Hill, New York, 1983.

53. G. Salton. *Automatic Text Processing: The Transformation, Analysis, and Retrieval of Information by Computer*. Addison-Wesley, Reading, MA, 1989.

54. H. R. Turtle and W. B. Croft. A comparison of text retrieval models. *Computer Journal*, 35(3), 1992.

55. D. L. Lee, H. Chuang, and K. Seamons. Document ranking and the vector-space model. *IEEE Software*, 14(2), 1997.

56. T. Kohonen. Self-organized formation of topologically correct feature maps. *Biological Cybernetics*, 43, 1982.

57. T. Kohonen. The self-organizing map. *Proceedings of the IEEE*, 78(9), 1990.

58. T. Kohonen. *Self-organizing maps*. Springer-Verlag, Berlin, 1995.

59. B. D. Ripley. *Pattern Recognition and Neural Networks*. Cambridge University Press, Cambridge, UK, 1996.

60. K. E. Gorlen. *NIH class library reference manual*. National Institutes of Health, Bethesda, MD, 1990.

61. K. E. Gorlen, S. Orlow, and P. Plexico. *Abstraction and Object-Oriented Programming in C++*. John Wiley & Sons, New York, 1990.

62. A. K. Jain and R. D. Dubes. *Algorithms for Clustering Data*. Prentice Hall, Englewood Cliffs, NJ, 1988.

63. D. Merkl. A connectionist view on document classification. In *Proceedings of the Australasian Database Conference (ADC'95)*, Adelaide, Australia, 1995.

64. D. Merkl and A. Rauber. On the similarity of eagles, hawks, and cows—Visualization of similarity in self-organizing maps. In *Proceedings of the Int'l Workshop on Fuzzy-Neuro-Systems*, Soest, Germany, 1997.

65. D. Merkl and A. Rauber. Alternative ways for cluster visualization in self-organizing maps. In *Proceedings of the Workshop on Self-Organizing Maps*, Espoo, Finland, 1997.

66. B. Fritzke. Growing Grid: A self-organizing network with constant neighborhood range and adaptation strength. *Neural Processing Letters*, 2(5), 1995.

Exercises

1. Which artifacts of the software development process are usually considered to be reusable?

2. Why is the software retrieval process usually considered to be an iterative one where the early retrieval results normally are not the most satisfying ones?

3. Discuss the differences between the vector-space model of information retrieval and the Boolean retrieval model.

4. What are the benefits of using the self-organizing map as compared to more conventional clustering methods?

5. What are the limitations of the standard self-organizing map visual representation of a software library?

6. Discuss the feasibility of using the adaptive coordinate visualization technique together with the growing grid artificial neural network model.

7. Discuss the benefits that growing neural networks like the growing grid model have to offer for software library organization.

THE CASE FOR AN INDUCTIVE COMPUTING SCIENCE[a]

D. PARTRIDGE

*Department of Computer Science, University of Exeter
Exeter EX4 4PT, UK
E-mail: derek@dcs.exeter.ac.uk*

In the past few decades a science of computing has begun to emerge from the conglomeration of ad hoc techniques, and partially understood principles that governed the production of software once it became a widespread activity. Great strides forward in hardware technology have outstripped the relatively slow development of a necessary, complementary, software technology. However, early realization of this need for a science to underpin software development has led to much effort towards producing it. A central plank of the resultant formal infrastructure is logical deduction. It is almost axiomatic within computing science proper that the basis for software science should be logic, and, moreover, it should be deductive logic. This chapter first justifies the claim that a deductive use of logic is seen as having an exclusive claim to be the basis for computing science. Even where the formal requirements are more relaxed, programming is invariably viewed as a deductive type of process – i.e. reasoning from the general to the particular. Second, it presents a number of computing activities, peripheral to the mainstream effort, that use a process of induction rather than deduction. Thirdly, it argues that there is now an undeniable claim for the developing science of computing to admit an inductive paradigm into the fold and to give it a place alongside the deduction-based one. Lastly, admission of this radical alternative is expected to have a profound effect on the future development of both computing science theory and practice. Some of these expected repercussions are outlined.

---

[a]This chapter is based on an earlier article, *The Case for Inductive Programming*, which appeared in *IEEE Computer*, January, 1997

1 Introduction

Ever since the late '60s, when profound problems with the embryonic discipline of software production were generally acknowledged by the similarly youthful community of computing scientists and software technologists, much effort has been focused on the development of a formal science to underpin software production. Considerable progress has been made on all fronts: from the management of commercial software production, through the development of a software-engineering infrastructure (e.g. design methodologies, life-cycle models, better programming languages), to a formal science of computing that includes formal bases for programming languages, for data structures, and for the notion of a correct program. It is this last development that we will focus on. There is much more to computer science than program correctness, but many of the other developments are either supportive of, or would benefit from the achievement of, a situation where programs were routinely guaranteed to be correct. It should be clarified at the outset that "correct" in this context means "conforms to the specification" which may not be everything that the practicing software developer would like, but it would be a great step forward nevertheless.

A major claim in this chapter is that this step forward, although by no means sorted out in detail, is seen by the computing science community to be an advance that must be based on deductive logic rather than inductive logic (simple examples contrasting deductive and inductive logic are provided in Figure 1). Several reasons for this situation exist. Firstly, deductive logic is the only way to provide a guarantee of correctness. Secondly, the nature of programming, constructing an elaborate symbol structure in some formally-defined language, bears many similarities to the notion of mathematical proof. Knuth [1], a founding father of the science of computation, put it thus in the Preface to the first of his seminal volumes:

The construction of a computer program from a set of instructions is very similar to the construction of a mathematical proof from a set of axioms.

Deduction, rather than induction, is the implicit framework underlying software production, even outside of the esoteric world of academic computing science. Deduction in this loose usage means reasoning from the general to the specific, and, in this particular case, I refer to the practice of generating specific implementations of general specifications – i.e. the classic notion crudely summarized as 'programming.'

deductive logic	inductive logic
premise: *all swans are white*	fact: *P is white and P is a swan*
fact: *X is a swan*	fact: *Q is white and Q is a swan*
	fact: *R is white and R is a swan*
conclusion: *X is white*	conclusion: all swans are white
if the axiom and fact are true then the conclusion is true	if all the facts are true then the conclusion may still be false

Figure 1: Simple examples contrasting deductive and inductive logic

There are, however, a number of induction-based techniques for the production of what are not always thought of as programs as such but rather implementations that compute useful quantities. Inductively generated implementations might be, for example, decision trees or neural networks. They are typically not programs in the classical sense of a list of instructions, and, whereas a decision tree might be readily transformable into a list of condition-action rules, most neural networks admit no such simple transformation – they may be implementations of functions, but they don't appear to be much like the classical notion of a program[2]. These induction techniques are to be found within the fringe activities pursued by persons who tend to view computers as no more than a means to an end; computation per se is typically not their main concern. Those who employ inductive techniques may be exploring a philosophy of cognition, they may be developing a theory of adaptive behavior, or they may simply be finding a way around a particularly awkward problem.

The use of inductive programming techniques occurs for diverse reasons and is thus to be found under a variety of labels, such as 'rule induction', 'cased-based learning', 'genetic algorithms', and 'connectionism'. Under the banner of 'machine learning', a subfield of AI, a good many of these inductive techniques can be found (as well as much else, see Kodratoff and Michalski[3] for a representative sample).

Inductive programming is not currently considered to be part of the core of computing science by anyone, not by the induction-using specialists themselves, and certainly not by those whose prime goal is the further development of a science of computing. This article argues that this exclusivity in computing science, although easily explainable, is insupportable and undesirable for the future development of computing, both as a theoretical science and as a purely practical endeavour. The time has come for a new major branch to be added to the tree of computing science, a fresh branch very close to the root.

2 Deduction as the Framework of Computing

In deductive programming, the program is a specific implementation of a general specification. In inductive programming, the program constitutes a generalization of a set of specific behaviors.

In the formal area of computing science, the belief is that the symbol structures that are programs should be derived from the problem specification by a process that will guarantee correctness. According to this view, programming clearly ought to be a deductive process, for this is the only process that can guarantee correctness of the symbol structure derived. A somewhat weaker view holds that programs may be derived from specifications in a less rigorous manner (thus giving more licence to flair and intuition, and perhaps sheer luck). This leaves the task of proving that the resultant program is correct. The proven program (or, perhaps more accurately, algorithm) is then a specific witness to the general truth of the specification couched as a theorem. This type of proof leans heavily on the notion of proof in mathematics; it is thus based on logical deduction (as illustrated in Figure 2).

general problem specification: *sort(L,S), where*
L and S are both <u>lists</u>, and
S is a <u>permutation</u> of L, and
S is <u>ordered</u>
(note: all underlined terms must be precisely defined)

$\rightarrow$ deductive logic $\rightarrow$

a specific formal mechanism:*quicksort algorithm*
guaranteed correct

Figure 2: Deductive programming — the formal extreme

The software practitioners, who must do the best they can with the tools available here and now, find little use for formal deductive logic. Formal deductive proofs often become extremely complex and difficult. Nevertheless, the practice of software technology, which is often at pains to distance itself from proofs of correctness and associated formal abstractions, is following and continuing to develop its own strategies that echo the deductive philosophy. These strategies are inconsistent with an inductive approach. In other words, conventional programming can be reduced to a process of deriving a particular specific result from a combination of general 'givens', primarily a specification and a programming language. A specific <u>how</u> is derived from a more general <u>what</u> (as illustrated in Figure 3).

a general specification: *sort lists into ascending order*
(**what** is desired)

→ program development →

a specific solution: *a quicksort program*
(**how** it is to be achieved)

tested for correctness

Figure 3: Deductive programming — the usual method

Conventional software construction involves building up a program from an abstract design. Guesswork and inspiration (not to mention perspiration) may often be important components of the program-development methodology, but the subsequent justification is expected to be a rational one, i.e. one that attempts to explain the outcome as a reasonable derivation from the givens, in this case the specification or the design, together with the programming language. This is not a process of logical deduction, but it is a process of reasoned argument from accepted general premises to a derived specific result, which contrasts sharply with an inductive process of deriving a more general structure from the commonalities within a collection of specific instances.

Figures 4 and 5 compare and contrast the deductive and inductive approaches to programming. The question that Figure 4 suggests is, if the program is actually derived from a set of behaviors, then what is the purpose of the resultant program? For, presumably, the specific results that it can compute are already available. The missing information is, of course, that the derived program should be a <u>generalization</u> of the set of behaviors used to

$$\boxed{Specification \rightarrow \mathbf{PROGRAM} \leftarrow Set\ of\ Behaviors}$$

$$\underline{\mathbf{DEDUCTIVE}} \qquad\qquad \underline{\mathbf{INDUCTIVE}}$$

Figure 4: The complementary nature of deductive and inductive programming

derive it; it should be capable of computing a larger set than the one used to obtain it in the first place. Figure 5 makes this explicit: the inductive approach begins with a set of example behaviors and generates an implementation that is capable of computing a larger set of behaviors. And different inductive techniques embody different generalization characteristics.

$$\underline{\text{the deductive approach}}$$

$$Specification \rightarrow \mathbf{PROGRAM} \rightarrow Set\ of\ Behaviors$$

$$\underline{\text{the inductive approach}}$$

$$Subset\ of\ Behaviors \rightarrow \mathbf{PROGRAM} \rightarrow Set\ of\ Behaviors$$

Figure 5: Deductive and inductive programming

3   Examples of Inductive Methods

As examples of inductive programming techniques we can consider two, rather different, ones: automatic induction of decision trees to implement human expertise, and the training of neural nets to implement various functions.

In expert systems technology the goal is to instantiate the problem-solving abilities of a human expert (say, a medical diagnostician) within a computer program. Attempts to achieve this goal typically aim to elicit the decision rules that the human expert supposedly uses, and to codify them as a set of IF-THEN rules within the expert-system software – this is then the so-called 'knowledge base.' Skipping over the many fine points of expert systems technology, the picture is completed by adding a logical-inference based mechanism to operate on this knowledge base and generate expert diagnoses.

One of the problems that this scheme quickly encountered was that human experts were not very expert at articulating the rules that (supposedly) embody their expertise; in fact, they prove to be very bad at it. This means that this process of knowledge acquisition turns into a long, drawn out one of codifying what the expert says, running the system to see where it fails, asking the expert to modify the knowledge base, and running it again. This iterative process of knowledge refinement can go on for a long time, with no guarantee of convergence, or even of substantial improvement. This problem has been termed 'the knowledge-acquisition bottleneck.'

It was pointed out by Michie[4] that, although human experts are bad at articulating their general rules, they are very good at deciding on specific cases – this is, after all, what their expertise is essentially. So why not collect a set of specific decisions (e.g. a certain set of symptoms implies a specific diagnosis) and use an automatic induction algorithm to generate the general rules embodied in this set of examples? As automatic induction algorithms had already been developed within AI, why not exploit them together with the human expert's strengths to inductively program expert systems?

This method of inductive programming has been used with some success. For example, in the development of an expert system for the early diagnosis of disease in soybean crops (Michalski and Chilausky [5]) the inductively programmed system proved to be more reliable than the human experts who supplied the example diagnoses! Another example is described in Figure 6.

In a totally different area, but still loosely under the umbrella of AI, a variety of inductive approaches to programming can be found in the guise of training neural networks to exhibit certain behaviors. Some connectionists (to use a popular handy label for those who implement neural networks) work with this paradigm because they believe that it will avoid problems that traditional deductive programming has run into when attempting to model cognitive phenomena; others are interested in the persuasive similarity between these network implementations and the architecture of the human brain; and still others implement with networks simply because traditional deductive programming has failed them. Together with the variety of reasons for taking up this inductive method there is a wide variety of alternative ways to pursue it.

The general idea is to set up a network that is rich enough (i.e. enough nodes and inter-node connections) to embody the desired function, and then to train it (using an error-feedback algorithm to modify the inter-node connections) to accurately compute the training set of input-output pairs. At this point, a properly trained network will have learnt a general function for which the training set is a representative sample of specific behaviors. In sum, the trained network has been inductively programmed to implement a general function. There are still many outstanding problems with this inductive method. For example, what is a 'representative' training set, and precisely what function has a trained network learned? These, and many other questions, remain to be answered (as similar open questions remain within the method of inductively generating expertise), but this is not the point. The point is that there are existence proofs of the viability of several types of inductive approaches to programming.

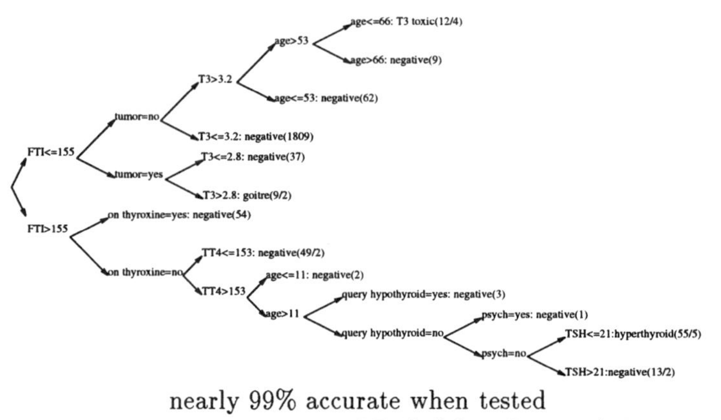

Figure 6: An example of rule-based inductive programming

Suffice it to say that network training is another inductive-style of programming, and that it has also been shown to work in a wide variety of application areas. In addition, it too has been shown to work better on some problems than traditional deductive programming, e.g. human face recognition as implemented in the WISARD system (Aleksander[7]). The general scheme using neural computing is illustrated in Figure 7, and a detailed example is given in Figure 8. Widrow, Rumelhart and Lehr[8] describe a large number of neural computing applications in industry, business and science.

<u>INDUCTIVE PROGRAMMING</u>
in neural computing

input:
a set of input-output pairs
— a training set

→neural net learning algorithm→

result:
a trained network that generalizes
the training set data

Figure 7: The general scheme for inductive software development using neural networks

4   The Neglect of Inductive Methods

Evidence for the neglect of inductive programming by computing scientists is easy to find. Choose any book that purports to cover the fundamentals of computing science and you will find lots on deductive methods, either formal deduction or, more loosely, use of a

NETtalk — a system that pronounces English

input:
50,000 examples of English words and
and their correct pronunciations;
a *Multilayer Perceptron* network (MLP)
comprising an input layer of 7 sets of units
(each set capable of inputting one character)
one 'hidden' layer of 80 units
an output unit (capable of outputting
a subset of the 29 articulatory features
required to specify the required range of
phonemic pronunciations),
link weights randomly initialised

→backpropagation algorithm→

result:
a network with link weights adjusted
such that it correctly computes the training set,
and generalizes to good pronunciation of English
— successful on 95% of subsequent tests

3 features output (f2, f11, f23) as pronunciation of "G" in "ROUGHLY"

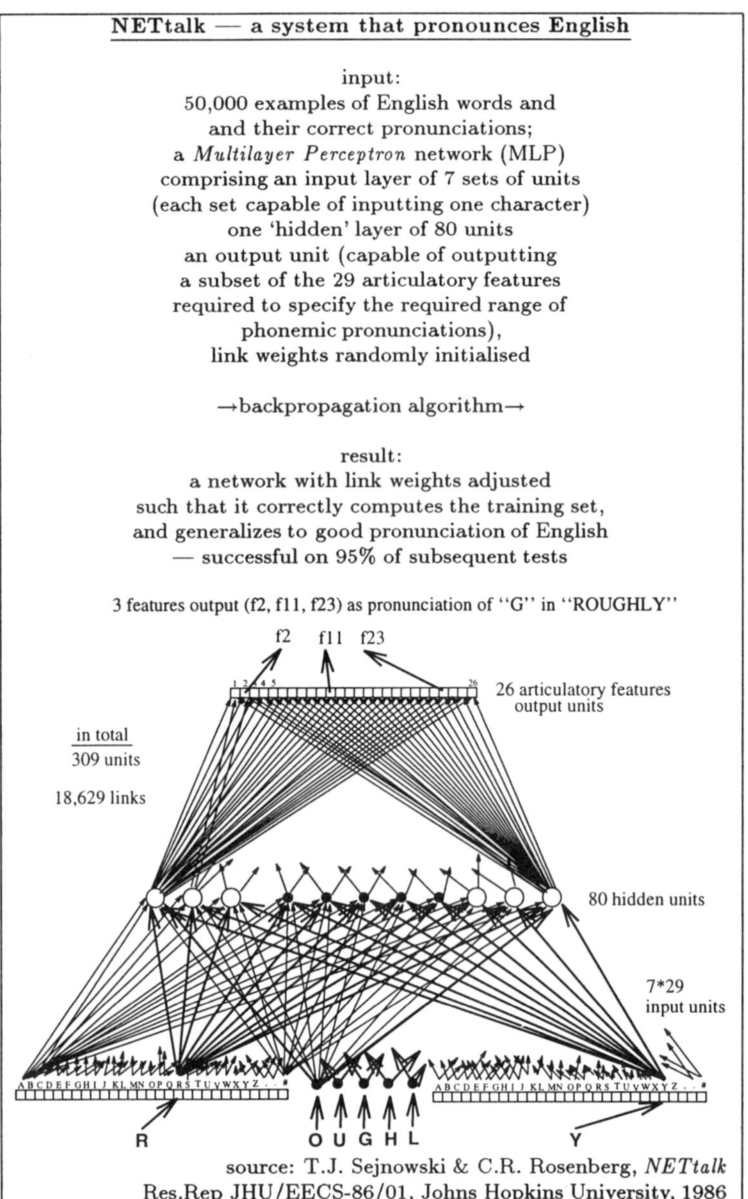

source: T.J. Sejnowski & C.R. Rosenberg, *NETtalk*
Res.Rep JHU/EECS-86/01, Johns Hopkins University, 1986

Figure 8: An example of inductive programming using neural networks

deductive framework, but you will not find anything on inductive methods. I think it is safe to say that there is an absence of consideration of inductive programming in virtually all basic computing science books which points up quite clearly the claimed bias of the computing science community.

Mention, and even detailed description, of inductive methods is quite easy to find in the literature. But in terms of basic books, mention must be sought in AI and AI-related books. Occurrences of inductive methods are to be found in the leading computing science journals. Michie[9], for example, makes a full and eloquent case for the practice of a logic-based science of automatic induction of rules; and Gallant[10] explains and provides a formal treatment of a 'localist' approach to connectionism – in a 'localist' network each node represents an obvious element of the problem, which can be contrasted with 'non-localist' or 'distributed' networks where this is not the case.

But these references tend to be expositions of interesting techniques and algorithms for solving certain classes of problem. They are not presented as manifestations of an alternative way to compute, in general. They are viewed as one-off considerations with no real impact on the fabric of computing science proper, and certainly no claim to be demonstrations of a notion that should be fundamental to the development of the science of computing. Michie[9] limits his discussion to "the computer induction of decision rules" (abstract), but he does point out that this technique is being extended to "inductive program generation," and that researchers "have established points of contact with the formal methods school" (p. 563).

Inductive techniques are somewhat *ad hoc*. However, formal methods to underpin inductive techniques are emerging, but they have yet to be viewed, accepted, and then developed, as a fundamental alternative to complement deductive computing science. Researchers working on "inductive logic programming" (see survey in Lavrač and De Raedt [11]), and a number of AI-oriented researchers in automatic programming have begun to explore formal inductive-logic methods for program synthesis (e.g. Kodratoff [12]). Kodratoff, Franova and Partridge [13] include use of inductive logic as part of their "certification cycle" for automatically checking the correctness of partially synthesized programs. So there has been some progress in the direction being advocated here. But it is all a far cry from the development of inductive methods as a legitimate subfield of computing science on a par with deductive schemes.

The computer scientist might explain this situation of neglect in the following way: inductive methods have arisen as subfields of AI along with many other dubious practices. They are, at best, interesting diversions for the serious computing scientist, and at worst total irrelevancies, unwanted distractions from the real goal of the development of a science to support robust and reliable computing, a science that is deduction based. This sort of reason, together with a number of better ones, accounts for the situation of neglect of inductive methods by the computing science community.

5 Reasons for the Neglect

The primary reason for ignoring induction as a basis for a science of programming is that induction is a technique which, by its very nature, can never be guaranteed to deliver a correct result. It is thus fundamentally inferior to deduction for the projected use.

There are essentially two ways to undermine this charge: one can challenge both the possibility and potential utility of the certainty that deduction can supposedly deliver. It is only the extreme formalist approach that really aspires to provide absolute guarantees, and it remains an open question whether it can really be made to work effectively. A semi-formal approach to deduction, which is all that most realists aim for, can only deliver something less than certainty. And anything less than certainty is uncertainty. It then becomes a more open question whether deductive uncertainty is better or worse than inductive uncertainty. So the deductivists may be aiming for a more lofty goal, but if it is either unreachable or unusable in practice (both of which are debatable at this point in time), inductive programming will have been dismissed from a standpoint of misplaced faith.

Even if the goals of the formal computing scientists are realized beyond their wildest dreams, it is still likely that there will be a useful role for an induction-based science of software engineering. For, as will be discussed later, complete, prior specification is a foundation stone of the formal deductive approach, yet some problems will always be more satisfactorily 'specified' in terms of a set of behaviors than as a conventional, abstract specification. AI problems, such as natural-language processing, are extreme examples of such *data-defined problems*[14], but so are many conventional software engineering problems. Real-world problems tend to be manifest as a set of specific data relationships, e.g. 'when we observe these readings on the sensors we want to close the control valve down, but when we observe these other readings we want to open it up.' Classical software engineering technology takes such a set of specific input-output mappings as the starting point for the process of developing an abstract specification of the problem, and the resultant specification may be a good or bad abstraction of the original, data-defined problem. Inductive methods open the possibility of implementing such data-defined problems directly from the definitional data mappings without a need to first embark on the abstraction process and any distortions that it may introduce.

The products of inductive methods, that is, the resultant implementations (which may be, for example, decision trees or trained networks) have tended to be conceptually opaque – the developers cannot inspect the implementation and rationalise its behavior. The use of such 'black-box' software can only aggravate the problems that beset the software engineer already. This is certainly a drawback, but it is by no means a necessary characteristic of inductive methods. This lack of comprehensibility is an area of major concern in AI. Michalski himself (a developer of the soybean disease diagnosis system[5] has framed a "comprehensibility principle" which requires that the domain experts can understand the inductively generated decision trees. Two special issues of *Applied AI* in 1994, which focused on applications of machine learning, contained numerous examples in which comprehensibility was the key issue.

Michie[6], for example, has modified the inductive process to one of "structured induction" so that it yields comprehensible decision trees. Gallant[10] provides an algorithm to generate IF-THEN type rules from his localist neural networks. One promising approach to comprehensibility is to exploit problem-specific information within the initial conditions for network training, and thereby prestructure the final trained version.

Neural computing is fundamentally a process of statistical approximation. As a result, accurate statistical models can be developed for input-output relationships. It is, for example, possible to compute "error bars" on network outputs and so have a meaningful 'confidence' associated with every computation (see Bishop[15]).

In addition, under the aegis of an inductive-programming paradigm where alteration of a program (either to remove a bug or to extend its scope) is done by more training with further examples, it is not at all clear that a mental grasp of operational detail will be anything like as critical as it is in conventional programming. A novel paradigm wreaks drastic changes to what is needed and to what is possible (see Partridge[2] for the upheavals introduced by non-localist neural computing).

Dijkstra, who is very reluctant to countenance inductive methods, has commented on neural networks as computing "with an uncertain probability an otherwise ill-defined function" (personal communication). He is entirely correct about the current state of affairs. What this seems to mean to him is that it is not worth bothering to divert effort away from further development of the formal deductive approach. What it ought to mean to the computing science community is that inductive methods represent a challenging alternative; an alternative with *prima facie* evidence of practical viability, although sorely in need of investigation to determine its real scope and limitations as a radically new software technology.

6   The Relative Merits of Inductive Programming

As well as the known weaknesses associated with inductive methods for software production, there are some clear strengths. First and foremost, inductive methods can be used in cases where deductive ones cannot, and these cases are not at all rare. The advantages of an inductive method become clear as soon as the application problem is one where more is known of what the desired software should do in terms of specific behaviors than is known about the abstract specification of the problem in general. For such data-defined problems the available information (i.e. a set of specific behaviors) is already the right sort of information for programming a solution using an inductive method. It is not at all useful for deductive programming. For the deductive programmer the next step is to try to capture these desired behaviors in an abstract specification. This process can vary in difficulty from hard to virtually impossible. At the hard end of the spectrum, techniques such as prototyping have been devised to assist in the framing of a good specification for the problem.

It is, in fact, not at all uncommon for problems to be first formulated as a set of behaviors. Users often characterize their problems in terms of a list of things that the computer should do for them. The systems analyst then works with the user to elicit the full requirements from which an abstract specification is generated to feed into the deductive programming process. It may be that by using inductive programming the software engineer can tap into the problem at an earlier stage thereby avoiding the necessity for someone to go through the difficult task of generating an abstract specification from the data (Michie's approach to programming human expertise is a case in point).

In AI all this is more commonplace simply because the generation of an accurate abstract specification is often the more difficult option, which is why inductive methods have arisen in this domain. In fact, such performance-mode specifications are sometimes considered to be characteristic of AI and a feature of many software problems (e.g. Partridge[17]). To take the face recognition problem, referenced earlier as the the WISARD system: we are all good human face recognizers, but how we do it is an almost total mystery. We know very little about which features (in a pattern recognition sense) we use, and equally little about how we use them to effect recognition. To deductively program a system to recognize a certain set of people's faces, requires that first many of these awkward questions must be answered in fine detail. To inductively program the same system, it is not at all clear that such answers are needed at all.

Another positive effect of inductive programming is that it favourably alters the economics of software production: it uses more computer time (for the automatic inductive generalization) and less software-engineer time (it avoids much of the deductive algorithm-design stage). Given that automatic induction tends to be orders of magnitude faster that manual algorithm design, this shift in the economics of software production could be substantial. Michie[9] provides a tabulation of this efficiency gain for one large, inductively generated, commercial software system (see Table 1).

Related to the last point, absence of manual algorithm design should mean absence of human design misconceptions. It is clear that some creative input to the final program will inevitably be lost when the implementation is largely an automatic process of induction, but it is also clear that some of this loss will be beneficial. The radical shift in the economics of implementation development

Table 1: The relative economics of inductive software engineering, adapted from D. Michie, *The Computing Journal*, 34(6), 1991, 559-565

system name	application area	size (no. of rules)	development (man-yrs)	maintenance (man-yrs/yr)	inductive tool
MYCIN	medical diagnosis	400	100	N/A	N/A
XCON	computer sys. configuration	8,000	180	30	N/A
GASOIL	hydrocarbon separation	2,800	1	0.1	ExpertEase & Extran 7
BMT	configuring fire protection equip. in buildings	$> 30,000$	9	2.0	1st Class & RuleMaster

opens up the possibility of multiversion software systems. Multiversion systems are ones in which the overall system functionality is duplicated in a set of alternative versions. The implied change is that reliable software will be engineered through an advantageous distribution of the inevitable errors rather than through attempts to eliminate error completely.

Given the expectation that no single version will be totally correct, the goal is to generate a *diverse* set of versions such that common errors do not run through the version set. Maximum diversity is achieved when each error is restricted to just one version, and minimum diversity occurs when all errors are duplicated in all versions. Given a diverse version set, it is then possible to construct a system that is more reliable than any of the individual versions — by using a majority-vote strategy, for example[16].

Quite apart from the prohibitive cost of programming the same problem repeatedly, empirical studies have shown that a disappointingly low level of diversity results. Automatic induction of versions undermines the cost constraint, but how do you introduce and control the required diversity?

In neural computing the nature of the implemented version (i.e. the trained network) is determined by the initial conditions — the training set, the configuration of the network and the values of a variety of parameters. So by exploring the diversity effects of the elements of the initial conditions, the diversity generating potential of the various options can be determined. The result is that version sets of networks can be systematically engineered to be diverse [16].

We are currently exploiting these special characteristics of inductive neural computing to guide the development of a methodology for engineering inductively generated multiversion neural-net software systems. A multiversion system is composed of a set of alternative implementations — the multi-versions — and the system outcome for any input is typically determined by applying a *decision strategy* to the set of individual version results (e.g. majority vote).

Figure 9 illustrates this methodology. Having decided that a given problem is potentially implementable as a neural-net system (module 1, in Fig. 9), the available data is organized into training, acceptance, and validation sets, and suitable neural-net types are identified (module 2). Prototyping experiments are then used to determine the most effective net architectures and the individual reliability and diversity levels to be expected (module 3). Given this basic information, a multiversion system is designed to support the required system reliability — version set(s) diversity characteristics and decision strategy such as majority vote (module 4). One productive strategy for engineering diversity is 'overproduce and select' — i.e. generate more diverse trained nets than the final system requires (module 5), and then select maximally diverse subsets for the final multiversion software system (module 6) using, say, a heuristic procedure. The finished system is then validated and a *de facto* specification is constructed (module 7).

In Figure 10 a character recognition example is illustrated. This is a difficult task, which is based upon a publicly available data set (see Exercise 1). The randomly distorted characters appear to defy 100% recognition, but the results of several different inductive techniques have been published. It would appear to be a particularly difficult problem to solve with deductive programming and no such programmed solution has yet been published. The prototyping experiments (module 3) indicate that Multilayer Perceptron (MLP) nets can be trained to deliver up to 88% correctness while Radial Basis Function (RBF) nets deliver only about 50% correctness. However, the experiments also indicate that there is a high diversity between these two types of neural-net implementation.

Consequently, the system design (module 4) is to use both types of neural network together with a 'maximum in agreement' strategy to obtain an optimal system. Variation in the architecture of the individual networks, the training sets used, and the random initialization of the network weights results in a pool of trained networks, both MLP and RBF nets (module 5).

A heuristic is then used (in conjunction with the 'acceptance set', module 2) to select from this pool nine individual nets that are highly diverse (module 6). The nine individual versions selected, five MLPs and four RBF nets, exhibit individual performances from 88.62% down to 33.77% (an RBF net) as illustrated in Figure 10.

But because of the high diversity among these nine versions, 0.73 on a scale of zero to one, the 'maximum in agreement' outcome is significantly better than any individual version can deliver, as shown in Figure 10.

7   Concluding Remarks

It is undeniable that some problems can be implemented inductively, and even that some problems are more easily and more satisfactorily implemented inductively. Inductive programming can be made to work. Its many undoubted problems are not a reason for exclusion from the science of computing; they should be a spur to research and development of inductive programming techniques. Gone is the age when certain phenomena, especially ones that we create within formally defined frameworks, can be pushed aside as deep mysteries which are best left alone. Such is the hall-

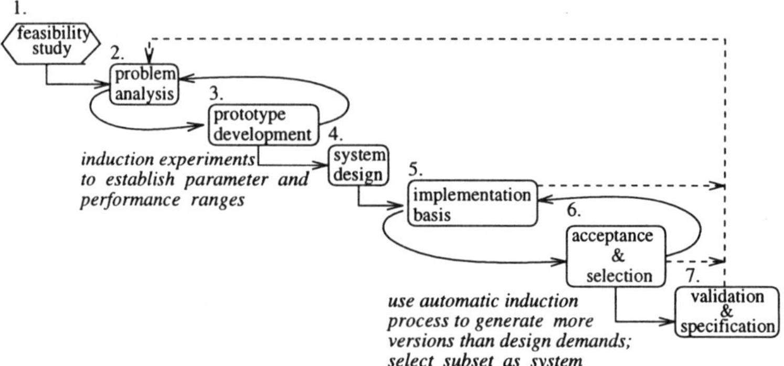

Figure 9: a methodology for inductive software engineering with neural networks, adapted from D.Partridge and W.B.Yates, *Proc. Artificial Neural Networks Conference*, Cambridge, p. 353, 1995

mark of superstition and blind ignorance, it is anathema to the scientific mind. The fact that inductive programming leads to the implementation of ill-defined functions in a difficult-to-comprehend representation should be viewed as a challenge by computing scientists, not a reason to ignore the demonstrated latent power that resides in this alternative way to compute.

The current, quite lamentable, state of affairs with respect to our sparse knowledge of inductive methods for software development is not a good reason for ignoring them. As there is ample evidence that they can be used to produce useful software, and, moreover, software in situations where deductive approaches are less effective. The rational response is to work towards a science of inductive programming. Some computing scientists should be working to transform the current hit-and-miss craft of inductive programming into a sound technology. Such a technology would need to be based on a better understanding of inductive techniques such that: the scope and limitations of the inductive products can be systematically determined (if not predicted in advance of the induction); and inadequate induction products can be systematically

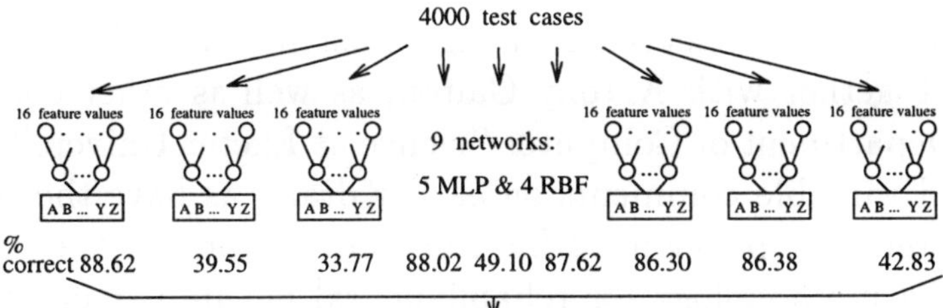

A randomly ordered set of 20,000 images of
uppercase characters, each randomly distorted
e.g.

ABC

Each image transformed into a 16-valued feature vector

input:
First 16,000 feature vectors

→use methodology of Figure 9→

9 trained networks, diversity 0.73 in range (0,1)

4000 test cases

16 feature values 16 feature values 16 feature values 16 feature values 16 feature values 16 feature values

9 networks:
5 MLP & 4 RBF

A B … Y Z   A B … Y Z   A B … Y Z   A B … Y Z   A B … Y Z   A B … Y Z

% correct 88.62   39.55   33.77   88.02 49.10 87.62   86.30   86.38   42.83

majority in agreement is 93.47% correct

(originally published result is 82.7% correct)
Frey & Slate 1991 *J. Machine Learning*

source: D. Partridge & W. B. Yates, Engineering multiversion
neural-net systems, *Neural Computation*, in press

Figure 10: Character recognition: **OCR9** — an example multiversion system

improved. Implicit in these requirements for a 'proper science' is a detailed and accurate knowledge of the generalization characteristics of each induction technique — i.e. the manner in which it extrapolates from, and interpolates between, the specific examples it processes. While much is known about this subject for certain types of inductive techniques, there is much still to be learnt before a sound basis for a predictive technology, spanning a variety of techniques, is available.

All computing scientists should acknowledge that there is another way to develop software. Deductive approaches may be the most generally useful option, but they are not the only option, and indeed sometimes they are inferior to inductive methods. Computing scientists, as individuals, may continue to focus exclusively on a deductive methodology, but computing science and software engineering, as general disciplines, should be obliged to include inductive methods. Currently this is not the case.

Acknowledgments

This chapter was developed from a suggestion made by Ajit Narayanan, and he together with Antony Galton, as well as other colleagues in the Department of Computer Science at Exeter University, have provided valuable comments on earlier drafts as have the referees of the precursor paper in *IEEE Computer*. Work on the development of a methodology for reliable neural net implementations is supported by the EPSRC (grant number GR/K78607).

References

1. D. E. Knuth, *The Art of Computer Programming*, vol. I, Addison-Wesley: Reading, Mass., (1968).
2. D. Partridge, "On the difficulty of really considering a radical novelty", *Minds and Machines*, Vol. 5, pp. 391-410, (1995).

3. Y. Kodratoff and R. S. Michalski, editors *Machine Learning III*, Morgan Kaufmann, San Mateo, CA, (1990).

4. D. Michie, "The state of the art in machine learning", in D. Michie (Ed.) *Introductory Readings in Expert Systems*, Gordon and Breach, London, pp. 208-229, (1982).

5. R. S. Michalski and R. L. Chilausky, "Knowledge acquisition by encoding expert rules versus computer induction from examples: a case study involving soybean pathology", In D. Partridge (Ed.) *Artificial Intelligence and Software Engineering*, Ablex, Norwood, NJ, pp. 491-520, (1991).

6. D. Michie, "The superarticulacy phenomenon", in D. Partridge and Y. Wilks (Eds.) *The Foundations of AI: A Sourcebook*, Cambridge University Press, Cambridge, UK, pp. 411-439, (1990).

7. I. Aleksander, W. V. Thomas and P. A. Bowden, "WISARD – a radical step forward in image recognition", *Sensor Review*, July, pp. 120-124, (1984).

8. B. Widrow, D. E. Rumelhart and M. A. Lehr, Neural Networks: applications in Industry, Business and Science, *Communications of the ACM*, vol. 37, no. 3, 93-105, (1994).

9. D. Michie, "Methodologies from machine learning in data analysis and software", *The Computing Journal*, Vol. 34, No. 6, pp. 559-565, (1991).

10. S. I. Gallant, "Connectionist Expert Systems", *Communications of the ACM*, Vol. 31, No. 2, pp. 152-169, (1988).

11. N. Lavrač and L. De Raedt, "Inductive logic programming: a survey of European research", *AI Communications*, Vol. 8, No. 1, pp. 3-19, (1995).

12. Y. Kodratoff, "A class of functions synthesized from a finite number of examples and a Lisp program scheme", *Int. J. of Computer & Information Science*, Vol. 8, pp. 489-521, (1979).

13. Y. Kodratoff, M. Franova and D. Partridge, "Why and How Program Synthesis?", In *Analogical and Inductive Inference,* K.P. Janke (Ed.), Springer-Verlag, pp. 45-59, (1989).
14. D. Partridge and W. B. Yates, Data-defined problems and multiversion neural-net systems, *Journal of Intelligent Systems*, vol. 7, nos. 1-2, 19-32 (1997).
15. C. M. Bishop, *Neural Networks for Pattern Recognition,* Clarendon Press: Oxford, UK (1995).
16. D. Partridge and W. J. Krzanowski, Software Diversity: practical statistics for its measurement and exploitation, *Information and Software Technology,* vol. 39, 707-717 (1997).
17. D. Partridge, *Engineering Artificial Intelligence Software,* Intellect Books, Oxford, UK, (1992).

Exercises

Exercise 1

The database of 20,000 character image vectors, illustrated earlier in Figure 10, is publicly available at *aha@ics.uci.edu* as part of the machine learning database maintained at UC Irvine. The original study was conducted by Frey and Slate (*Machine Learning,* vol. **6**, 161-182, 1991) who applied Holland-style adaptive classifiers to the problem. That study also contains examples of the character images which show clearly how difficult (perhaps impossible) some will be to recognize correctly. The best systems so far published, which are neural networks, achieve 96-97% accuracy, on the final 4,000 feature vectors as the test set.

The problem is to access this database, together with a copy of Frey and Slate's original study (which gives full details of the features extracted), and to construct a recognition system.

From a study of this problem it will quickly become apparent that a conventionally programmed approach will be extremely difficult — although it would be instructive to try. Inductive techniques would seem to be the only viable option.

Exercise 2

Another way to experiment with inductive technologies is to first construct a data generator — i.e. a conventionally programmed implementation. Having done this, the purpose of subsequent experiments with inductive technologies is to explore the various technologies and the options within each technology. Given below is a simple, well-defined problem that is, nevertheless, difficult to implement 'correctly' using the statistical approximation techniques that neural networks embody.

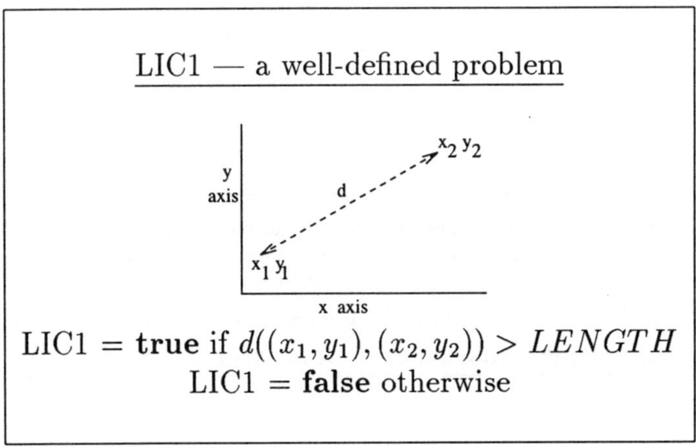

$$\text{LIC1} = \mathbf{true} \text{ if } d((x_1, y_1), (x_2, y_2)) > LENGTH$$
$$\text{LIC1} = \mathbf{false} \text{ otherwise}$$

The task is to write a data generator for LIC1, i.e. a program that generates sets of input values and the corresponding output. These data sets can then be used to train neural networks and to test for the accuracy of the trained nets. An example of the quality of inductive implementations is given below.

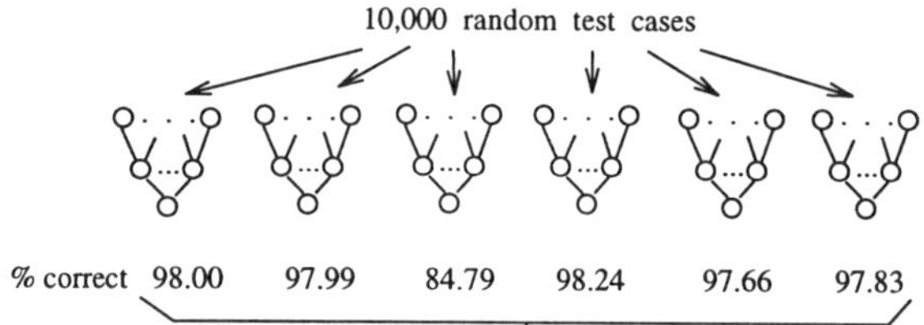

input:
5 real-values in range (0,1) to 6 decimal places
$x_1, y_1, x_2, y_2, LENGTH$

$\rightarrow$use methodology of Figure 9$\rightarrow$

6 trained networks, diversity 0.85 in range (0,1)

source: D. Partridge & W. B. Yates, Engineering multiversion neural-net systems, *Neural Computation*, **8**, 869-893, 1997

EVOLUTIONARY COMPUTING
IN SOFTWARE ENGINEERING

Evolutionary computing delivers an exciting opportunity to automate software development, especially at the phase of automatic programming. Evolutionary techniques have demonstrated their crucial role in the problems of global optimization which are omnipresent and highly visible in software design.

There are three papers in this sections. In the first, Skipper elaborates on the computer ZOO-an interesting artificial life simulator dealing with a family of breeding species-programs. In the second, genetic programming is used by Koza and al. in order to design electric circuits - an important endeavor developed along the line of automatic programming. Khoshgoftaar et al. discuss an application of genetic programming to the problem of software quality prediction.

AUTOMATIC CREATION OF COMPUTER PROGRAMS FOR DESIGNING ELECTRICAL CIRCUITS USING GENETIC PROGRAMMING

J. R. Koza

Computer Science Dept., Stanford University, Stanford, CA 94305
E-mail: koza@cs.stanford.edu
http://www-cs-faculty.stanford.edu/~koza/

F. H Bennett III

Visiting Scholar, Computer Science Dept., Stanford University, Stanford, CA 94305
E-mail: forrest@evolute.com

D. Andre

Computer Science Division University of California, Berkeley, CA
E-mail: dandre@cs.berkeley.edu

M. A. Keane

Martin Keane Inc., 5733 West Grover, Chicago, Illinois 60630
E-mail: makeane@ix.netcom.com

One of the central goals of computer science is to get computers to solve problems starting from only a high-level statement of the problem. The goal of automating the design process bears many similarities to the goal of automatically creating computer programs. The design process entails creation of a complex structure to satisfy user-defined requirements. The design process is usually viewed as requiring human intelligence. Indeed, design is a major activity of practicing engineers. For these reasons, the design process offers a practical yardstick for evaluating automated programming (program synthesis) techniques. In particular, the design (synthesis) of analog electrical circuits entails the creation of both the topology and sizing (numerical values) of all of a circuit's components. There has previously been no general automated technique for automatically designing an analog electrical circuit from a high-level statement of the circuit's desired behavior. This paper shows how genetic programming can be used to automate the design of both the topology and sizing of a suite of five prototypical analog circuits, including a lowpass filter, a tri-state frequency discriminator circuit, a 60 dB amplifier, a computational circuit for the square root, and a time-optimal robot controller circuit. All five of these genetically evolved circuits constitute instances of an evolutionary computation technique solving a problem that is usually thought to require human intelligence.

1. Introduction

Genetic programming addresses one of the central goals of computer science – program synthesis (automatic programming). Paraphrasing Arthur Samuel (1959), this goal concerns

How can computers be made to do what needs to be done, without being told exactly how to do it?

When we use the terms "program synthesis" or "automatic programming" and talk about the goal of getting computers to solve problems starting from only a high-level statement of the problem, we mean a system that

- produces an entity that runs on a computer (i.e., is either a computer program or something that can be easily converted into a program),
- solves a wide variety of problems in a wide range of fields,
- requires the human user to supply a minimum of information in advance,
- is problem independent in the sense that the user does not have to alter the basic operation of the system for each new problem,
- scales well to ever-larger problems,
- has a mechanism for implementing the full range of useful programming constructs (or suitable substitutes for them) such as arithmetic operations, conditional operations, logical operations, internal memory, parameterizable subroutines, data structures, iteration, recursion, hierarchical compositions of subprograms, multiple inputs, and multiple outputs,
- is open-ended in the sense that it does not require the user to prespecify the size, shape, and form of the solution,
- does not require the user to decompose the problem into subproblems in advance or to identify and reward the achievement of prespecified subgoals,
- does not rely on discretionary human intervention and unmistakably distinguishes between what the user must provide in advance and what the system delivers,
- produces results that are reproducible and has no hidden steps, and
- is capable of producing results that are competitive with those produced by human programmers, mathematicians, and specialist designers.

Speaking about artificial intelligence, Samuel (1983) provided an alternative statement of the last point above,

"[T]he aim [is] ... to get machines to exhibit behavior which if done by humans would be assumed to involve the use of intelligence."

Over the past four decades, the field of artificial intelligence has been dominated by the belief that this goal can be achieved by representing knowledge with some suitable representation, depositing the knowledge into a computer in the form of a knowledge base, and then manipulating the knowledge using logic.

However, the existence of a strongly asserted belief for more than four decades does not preclude the possiblity that there may be alternative ways of achieving the goal of program synthesis that do not rely on knowledge or logic.

Natural selection and evolution offers an alternative way to get computers to solve problems from a high-level statement of the problem in the form of genetic programming. Genetic programming is an extension of the genetic algorithm (Holland 1975) in which the population consists of computer programs. Genetic programming is described in the books *Genetic Programming: On the Programming of Computers by Means of Natural Selection* (Koza 1992) and *Genetic Programming II: Automatic Discovery of Reusable Programs* (Koza 1994a).

Genetic programming is different from other approaches to artificial intelligence, machine learning, adaptive systems, automated logic, expert systems, and neural networks in the following four fundamental ways:

- representation – namely the space of computer programs,
- the role of knowledge – namely none,
- the role of logic – namely none, and
- the mechanism for searching the space of possible solutions (programs) – namely evolutionary and natural selection.

Specifically, the representation used by genetic programming is that of computer programs. Knowledge and logic play no role during the search. The search mechanism is based on evolution and natural selection.

As to representation, genetic programming operates in the space of possible computer programs and does not employ surrogate structures such as if-then rules, Horn clauses, decision trees, propositional logic, frames, formal grammars, conceptual clusters, concept sets, numerical weight vectors (for neural nets), vectors of numerical coefficients for polynomials (or other fixed expressions), classifier system rules, binary decision diagrams, production rules, expert system rules, or linear chromosome strings (as used in the genetic algorithm). Tellingly, computers are not commonly programmed using any of these surrogate structures. Human programmers do not commonly regard any them as being useful or suitable for ordinary programming. Our view is that if we are really interested in getting computers to solve problems without explicitly programming them, the structures that we should be using are *computer programs*. That is, we should be conducting the search for a solution to the problem of program synthesis in the space of computer programs. Computer programs offer the flexibility to perform computations on variables of many different types, perform iterations and recursions, store intermediate results in data structures of various types (indexed memory, matrices, stacks, lists, rings, queues, named memory, relational memory), perform alternative calculations conditionally based on the outcome of other calculations, perform groups of operations in a hierarchical way, and to employ parameterizable, reusable, hierarchically callable subprograms (i.e., subroutines). Subroutines and iteration are particularly important because they involve reusing code and we believe that reusing code is the precondition for scalability in automatic programming.

Of course, once we say that what we really want and need is a computer program, we are immediately faced with the problem of how to locate the desired program in the space of possible programs. That is, we need a way to fruitfully search program space. As will be seen, genetic programming provides a problem-independent way to automatically create a computer program to solve a problem.

Knowledge has no explicit role in genetic programming. There is no knowledge representation; there is no explicit knowledge base in genetic programming; and there is no manipulation of knowledge in genetic programming – by logic or any other means. The practitioners of genetic programming are not against knowledge; they simply say that no one seems to know how to effectively represent it or to productively manipulate it. In any event, an explicit knowledge base is not needed when using genetic programming.

The vast majority of the research in artificial intelligence is based on approaches that are logically sound, correct, consistent, justifiable, deterministic, orderly, parsimonious, unequivocal, and decisive. Since computer science is founded on logic, it is almost second nature for computer scientists to unquestioningly assume that every problem-solving technique should have these characteristics. However, logic has no role in evolution in nature and it has no role in genetic programming. Genetic programming does not proce4ed in logical steps and operates by actively harboring (indeed encouraging) clearly inconsistent and contradictory approaches to solving the problem.

When the goal is automatic programming, we believe that the illogical principles of evolution and natural selection should be used instead of the principles of conventional knowledge-based and logic-driven artificial intelligence. We do not say that "knowledge is the enemy" or "logic considered harmful," but simply that neither knowledge nor logic are allies in the goal of achieving automatic programming.

Concerning its methodology for automatically creating computer programs, genetic programming uses a time-tested method – it evolves them. Starting with a primordial ooze of thousands of randomly created computer programs, a population of computer programs is progressively evolved over many generations by applying the operations of Darwinian fitness proportionate reproduction, crossover (sexual recombination), and occasional mutation.

The goal of automating the design process bears many similarities to the goal of automatically creating computer programs.

The design process entails creation of a complex structure to satisfy user-defined requirements. The design requirements specify "what needs to be done." A satisfactory design tells us "how to do it."

The design process is usually viewed as requiring human intelligence. Indeed, design is a major activity of practicing engineers. For these reasons, engineering design offers a practical yardstick for evaluating automated programming techniques.

In electrical engineering, for example, the design process typically involves the creation of an electrical circuit that satisfies a set of user-specified design goals. The design process for analog circuits begins with a high-level description of the circuit's desired behavior and entails creation of both the topology and the sizing of a satisfactory circuit. The topology comprises the gross number of components in the circuit, the type of each component (e.g., a resistor), and a list of all connections between the components. The sizing involves specifying the values (typically numerical) of each of the circuit's component.

Considerable progress has been made in automating the design of certain categories of purely digital circuits; however, the design of analog circuits and mixed analog-digital circuits has not proved as amenable to automation (Rutenbar 1993). Describing "the analog dilemma," Aaserud and Nielsen (1995) noted

"Analog designers are few and far between. In contrast to digital design, most of the analog circuits are still handcrafted by the experts or so-called 'zahs' of analog design. The design process is characterized by a combination of experience and intuition and requires a thorough knowledge of the process characteristics and the detailed specifications of the actual product.

"Analog circuit design is known to be a knowledge-intensive, multiphase, iterative task, which usually stretches over a significant period of time and is performed by designers with a large portfolio of skills. It is therefore considered by many to be a form of art rather than a science."

There has been extensive previous work on the problem of circuit design using simulated annealing, artificial intelligence, and other techniques as described in detail in Koza, Bennett, Andre, Keane, and Dunlap 1997, including work using genetic algorithms (Kruiskamp and Leenaerts 1995; Grimbleby 1995; Thompson 1996). However, there has previously been no general automated technique for synthesizing an analog electrical circuit from a high-level statement of the desired behavior of the circuit.

This paper presents an approach to the automatic design of both the topology and sizing of analog electrical circuits. Section 2 presents design problems involving five prototypical analog circuits. Section 3 describes the method. Section 4 details required preparatory steps. Section 5 shows the results for the five problems. Section 6 cites other circuits that have been designed by genetic programming.

2. Five Problems of Analog Circuit Design

This paper applies genetic programming to a suite of five problems of analog circuit design. The circuits comprise a variety of types of components, including transistors, diodes, resistors, inductors, and capacitors. The circuits have varying numbers of inputs and outputs.

(1) Design a lowpass filter having a one-input, one-output composed of capacitors and inductors and that passes all frequencies below 1,000 Hz and suppresses all frequencies above 2,000 Hz.

(2) Design a tri-state frequency discriminator (source identification) circuit having one input and one output that is composed of resistors, capacitors, and inductors and that produces an output of 1/2 volt and 1 volt for incoming signals whose frequencies are within 10% of 256 Hz and within 10% of 2,560 Hz, respectively, but produces an output of 0 volts otherwise.

(3) Design a computational circuit having one input and one output that is composed of transistors, diodes, resistors, and capacitors and that produces an output voltage equal to the square root of its input voltage.

(4) Design a time-optimal robot controller circuit having two inputs and one output that is composed of the above components and that navigates a constant-speed autonomous mobile robot with nonzero turning radius to an arbitrary destination in minimal time.

(5) Design an amplifier composed of the above components and that delivers amplification of 60 dB (i.e., 1,000 to 1) with low distortion and low bias.

3.   Design by Genetic Programming

The circuits are developed using genetic programming in which the population consists of computer programs. Multipart programs consisting of a main program and one or more reusable, parametrized, hierarchically-called subprograms can be evolved using automatically defined functions (Koza 1994a, 1994b). Architecture-altering operations (Koza 1995) automatically determine the number of such subprograms, the number of arguments that each possesses, and the nature of the hierarchical references, if any, among such automatically defined functions. For current research in genetic programming, see Kinnear 1994, Angeline and Kinnear 1996, Koza, Goldberg, Fogel, and Riolo 1996, Koza et al. 1997, and Banzhaf, Nordin, Keller, and Francone 1997.

A computer program is not a design. Genetic programming can be applied to circuits if a mapping is established between the program trees (rooted, point-labeled trees – that is, acyclic graphs – with ordered branches) used in genetic programming and the line-labeled cyclic graphs germane to electrical circuits. The principles of developmental biology, the creative work of Kitano (1990) on using genetic algorithms to evolve neural networks, and the innovative work of Gruau (1992) on using genetic programming to evolve neural networks provide motivation for mapping trees into circuits by means of a growth process that begins with an embryo. For circuits, the embryo typically includes the inputs and outputs of the particular circuit being designed and a test harness of fixed components (such as source and load resistors). The embryo also contains modifiable wires. Until these wires are modified, the circuit does not produce interesting output. An electrical circuit is developed by progressively applying the functions in a circuit-constructing program tree to the modifiable wires of the embryo (and, during the developmental process, to new components and modifiable wires). See also Brave 1996.

The functions in the circuit-constructing program trees are divided into four categories: (1) connection-modifying functions that alter the circuit topology, (2) component-creating functions that insert components into the circuit, (3) arithmetic-performing functions that appear in subtrees as argument(s) to the component-creating functions and specify the numerical value of the component, and (4) automatically defined functions that appear in the function-defining branches and potentially enable certain substructures of the circuit to be reused (with parameterization).

Each branch of the program tree is created in accordance with a constrained syntactic structure. Branches are composed of construction-continuing subtrees that continue the developmental process and arithmetic-performing subtrees that determine the numerical value of components. connection-modifying functions have one or more Construction-continuing subtrees, but no arithmetic-performing subtree. component-creating functions have one or more construction-continuing subtrees and typically have one arithmetic-performing subtree. This constrained syntactic structure is preserved using structure-preserving crossover with point typing (see Koza 1994a).

3.1.   The Embryonic Circuit

An electrical circuit is created by executing a circuit-constructing program tree that contains various component-creating and topology-modifying functions. Each tree in the population creates one circuit. The specific embryo used depends on the number of inputs and outputs.

Figure 1 shows a one-input, one-output embryonic circuit in which **USOURCE** is the input signal and **UOUT** is the output signal (the probe point). The circuit is driven by an incoming alternating circuit source **USOURCE**. There is a fixed load resistor **RLOAD** and a fixed source resistor **RSOURCE** in the embryo. In addition to the fixed components, there is a modifiable wire **Z0** between nodes 2 and 3. All development originates from this modifiable wire.

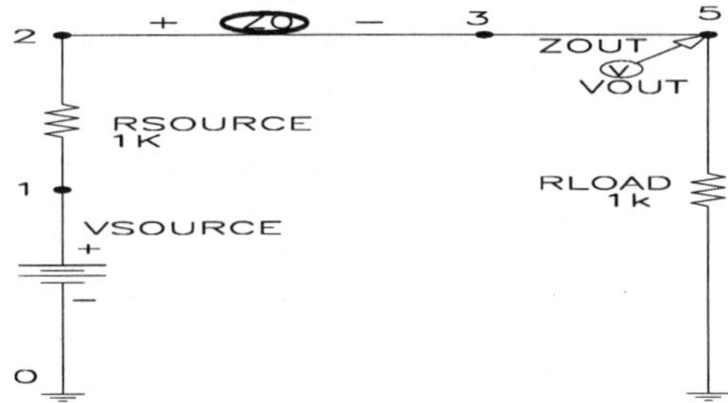

Figure 1 One-input, one-output embryo.

3.2. Component-Creating Functions

Each program tree contains component-creating functions and connection-modifying functions. The component-creating functions insert a component into the developing circuit and assign component value(s) to the component.

Each component-creating functions has a writing head that points to an associated highlighted component in the developing circuit and modifies that component in a specified manner. The construction-continuing subtree of each component-creating functions points to a successor function or terminal in the circuit-constructing program tree.

The arithmetic-performing subtree of a component-creating functions consists of a composition of arithmetic functions (addition and subtraction) and random constants (in the range -1.000 to +1.000). The arithmetic-performing subtree specifies the numerical value of a component by returning a floating-point value that is interpreted on a logarithmic scale as the value for the component in a range of 10 orders of magnitude (using a unit of measure that is appropriate for the particular type of component.

The two-argument resistor-creating R function causes the highlighted component to be changed into a resistor. The value of the resistor in kilo Ohms specified by its arithmetic-performing subtree.

Figure 2 shows a modifiable wire **Z0** connecting nodes 1 and 2 of a partial circuit containing four capacitors (**C2**, **C3**, **C4**, and **C5**). The circle indicates that **Z0** has a writing head (i.e., is the highlighted component and that **Z0** is subject to subsequent modification). Figure 3 shows the result of applying the R function to the modifiable wire **Z0** of figure 2. The circle indicates that the newly created **R1** has a writing head so that **R1** remains subject to subsequent modification.

Similarly, the two-argument capacitor-creating C function causes the highlighted component to be changed into a capacitor whose value in micro Farads is specified by its arithmetic-performing subtrees.

The one-argument Q_D_PNP diode-creating function causes a diode to be inserted in lieu of the highlighted component. This function has only one argument because there is no numerical value associated with a diode and thus no arithmetic-performing subtree. In practice, the diode is implemented here using a pnp transistor whose collector and base are connected to each other. The Q_D_NPN function inserts a diode using an npn transistor in a similar manner.

There are also six one-argument transistor-creating functions (Q_POS_COLL_NPN, Q_GND_EMIT_NPN, Q_NEG_EMIT_NPN, Q_GND_EMIT_PNP, Q_POS_EMIT_PNP, Q_NEG_COLL_PNP) that insert a bipolar junction transistor in lieu of the highlighted component and that directly connect the collector or emitter of the newly created transistor to a fixed point of the circuit (the positive power supply, ground, or the negative power supply). For example, the Q_POS_COLL_NPN function inserts a bipolar junction transistor whose collector is connected to the positive power supply.

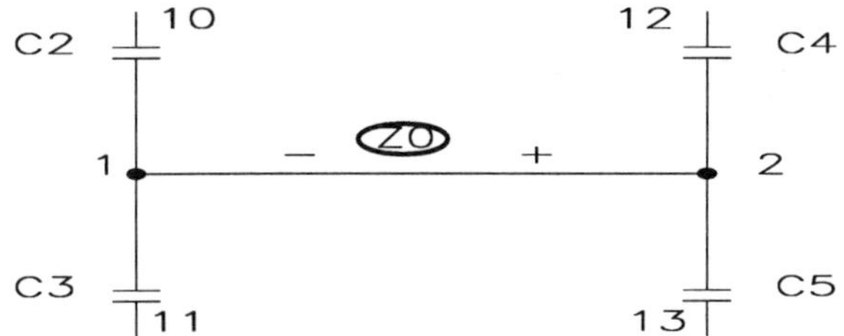

Figure 2 Modifiable wire Z0.

Each of the functions in the family of six different three-argument transistor-creating Q_3_NPN functions causes an npn bipolar junction transistor to be inserted in place of the highlighted component and one of the nodes to which the highlighted component is connected. The Q_3_NPN function creates five new nodes and three new modifiable wires. There is no writing head on the new transistor, but there is one on the new modifiable wires. There are 12 members (called Q_3_NPN0, ..., Q_3_NPN11) in this family of functions because there are two choices of nodes (1 and 2) to be bifurcated and then there are six ways of attaching the transistor's base, collector, and emitter after the bifurcation. Similarly the family of 12 Q_3_PNP functions causes a pnp bipolar junction transistor to be inserted.

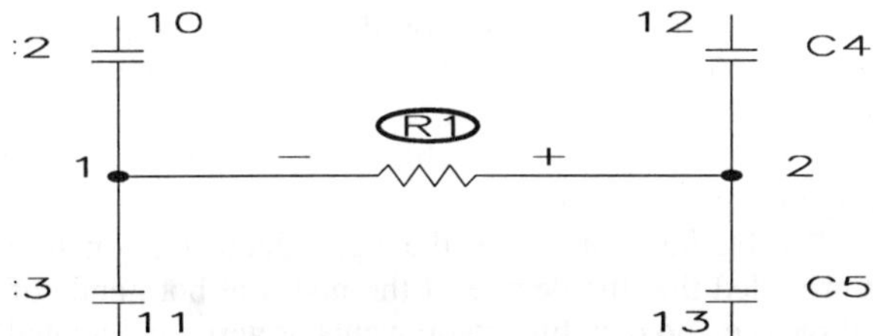

Figure 3 Result of applying the R function.

3.3. Connection-Modifying Functions

Each connection-modifying function in a program tree points to an associated highlighted component and modifies the topology of the developing circuit.

The three-argument SERIES division function creates a series composition of the highlighted component (with a writing head), a copy of it (with a writing head), one new modifiable wire (with a writing head), and two new nodes.

The four-argument PSS parallel division function creates a parallel composition consisting of the original highlighted component (with a writing head), a copy of it (with a writing head), two new modifiable wires (each with a writing head), and two new nodes. Figure 4 shows the result of applying PSS to resistor R1 from figure 3.

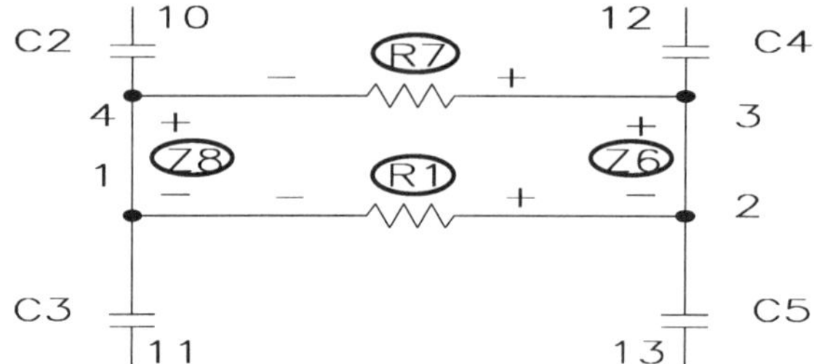

Figure 4 Result of the PSS function.

The one-argument polarity-reversing FLIP function reverses the polarity of the highlighted component.

There are six three-argument functions (T_GND_0, T_GND_1, T_POS_0, T_POS_1, T_NEG_0, T_NEG_1) that insert two new nodes and two new modifiable wires, and then make a connection to ground, positive power supply, or negative power supply, respectively.

There are two three-argument functions (PAIR_CONNECT_0 and PAIR_CONNECT_1) that enable distant parts of a circuit to be connected together. The first PAIR_CONNECT to occur in the development of a circuit creates two new wires, two new nodes, and one temporary port. The next PAIR_CONNECT creates two new wires and one new node, connects the temporary port to the end of one of these new wires, and then removes the temporary port.

The one-argument NOOP function has no effect on the highlighted component; however, it delays activity on the developmental path on which it appears in relation to other developmental paths in the overall program tree.

The zero-argument END function causes the highlighted component to lose its writing head, thereby ending that particular developmental path.

The zero-argument SAFE_CUT function causes the highlighted component to be removed from the circuit provided that the degree of the nodes at both ends of the highlighted component is three (i.e., no dangling components or wires are created).

4. Preparatory Steps

Before applying genetic programming to a problem of circuit design, seven major preparatory steps are required: (1) identify the suitable embryonic circuit, (2) determine the architecture of the overall circuit-constructing program trees, (3) identify the terminals of the program trees, (4) identify the primitive functions contained in these program trees, (5) create the fitness measure, (6) choose parameters, and (7) determine the termination criterion and method of result designation.

4.1.　　Embryonic Circuit

The embryonic circuit used on a particular problem depends on the circuit's number of inputs and outputs.

For example, in the robot controller circuit, the circuit has two inputs, **VSOURCE1** and **VSOURCE2**, not just one. Moreover, each input needs its own separate source resistor (**RSOURCE1** and **RSOURCE2**). Consequently, the embryo has three modifiable wires **Z0**, **Z1**, and **Z2** in order to provide full connectivity between the two inputs and the one output. All development then originates from these three modifiable wires.

There is often considerable flexibility in choosing the embryonic circuit. For example, an embryo with two modifiable wires (**Z0** and **Z1**) was used for the lowpass filter. In some problems, such as the amplifier, the embryo contains additional fixed components because of additional problem-specific functionality of the harness (as described in Koza, Bennett, Andre, and Keane 1997).

4.2.　　Program Architecture

Since there is one result-producing branch in the program tree for each modifiable wire in the embryo, the architecture of each circuit-constructing program tree depends on the embryonic circuit. One result-producing branch was used for the frequency discriminator and the computational circuit; two were used for lowpass filter problem; and three were used for the robot controller and amplifier. The architecture of each circuit-constructing program tree also depends on the use, if any, of automatically defined functions. Automatically defined functions and architecture-altering operations were used in the frequency discriminator, robot controller, and amplifier. For these problems, each program in the initial population of programs had a uniform architecture with no automatically defined functions. In later generations, the number of automatically defined functions, if any, emerged as a consequence of the architecture-altering operations.

4.3.　　Function and Terminal Sets

The function set for each design problem depended on the type of electrical components that were used to construct the circuit. Capacitors, diodes, and transistors were used for the computational circuit, the robot controller, and the amplifier. Resistors were used for the frequency discriminator. When transistors were used, functions to provide connectivity to the positive and negative power supplies were also included,.

For the computational circuit, the robot controller, and the amplifier, the function set, $\mathcal{F}_{\text{ccs-initial}}$, for each construction-continuing subtree was

$\mathcal{F}_{\text{ccs-initial}}$ = {R, C, SERIES, PSS, PSL, FLIP, NOOP, T_GND_0, T_GND_1,
　　　T_POS_0, T_POS_1, T_NEG_0, T_NEG_1, PAIR_CONNECT_0,
　　　PAIR_CONNECT_1, Q_D_NPN,　Q_D_PNP, Q_3_NPN0, ...,

```
Q_3_NPN11, Q_3_PNP0, ..., Q_3_PNP11, Q_POS_COLL_NPN,
Q_GND_EMIT_NPN, Q_NEG_EMIT_NPN, Q_GND_EMIT_PNP,
Q_POS_EMIT_PNP, Q_NEG_COLL_PNP}.
```

For the npn transistors, the Q2N3904 model was used. For pnp transistors, the Q2N3906 model was used.

The initial terminal set, $T_{ccs\text{-}initial}$, for each construction-continuing subtree was

$$T_{ccs\text{-}initial} = \{\texttt{END}, \texttt{SAFE\_CUT}\}.$$

The initial terminal set, $T_{aps\text{-}initial}$, for each arithmetic-performing subtree consisted of

$$T_{aps\text{-}initial} = \{\mathfrak{R}\},$$

where $\mathfrak{R}$ represents floating-point random constants from -1.0 to $+1.0$.

The function set, F_{aps}, for each arithmetic-performing subtree was,

$$F_{aps} = \{+, -\}.$$

The terminal and function sets were identical for all result-producing branches for a particular problem.

For the lowpass filter and frequency discriminator, there was no need for functions to provide connectivity to the positive and negative power supplies.

For the frequency discriminator, the robot controller, and the amplifier, the architecture-altering operations were used and the set of potential new functions, $F_{potential}$, was

$$F_{potential} = \{\texttt{ADF0}, \texttt{ADF1}, ...\}.$$

The set of potential new terminals, $T_{potential}$, for the automatically defined functions was

$$T_{potential} = \{\texttt{ARG0}\}.$$

The architecture-altering operations changed the function set, F_{ccs} for each construction-continuing subtree of all three result-producing branches and the function-defining branches, so that

$$F_{ccs} = F_{ccs\text{-}initial} \cup F_{potential}.$$

The architecture-altering operations generally changed the terminal set for automatically defined functions, $T_{aps\text{-}adf}$, for each arithmetic-performing subtree, so that

$$T_{aps\text{-}adf} = T_{aps\text{-}initial} \cup T_{potential}.$$

4.4.   Fitness Measure

The fitness measure varies for each problem. The high-level statement of desired circuit behavior is translated into a well-defined measurable quantity that can be used by genetic programming to guide the evolutionary process. The evaluation of each individual circuit-constructing program tree in the population begins with its execution. This execution progressively applies the functions in each program tree to an embryonic circuit, thereby creating a fully developed circuit. A netlist is created that identifies each component of the developed circuit, the nodes to which each component is connected, and the value of each component. The netlist becomes the input to the 217,000-line SPICE (Simulation Program with Integrated Circuit Emphasis) simulation program (Quarles, Newton, Pederson, and Sangiovanni-Vincentelli 1994). SPICE then determines the behavior of the circuit. It was necessary to make considerable modifications in SPICE so that it could run as a submodule within the genetic programming system.

4.4.1   Lowpass Filter

A simple *filter* is a one-input, one-output electronic circuit that receives a signal as its input and passes the frequency components of the incoming signal that lie in a specified range (called the *passband*) while suppressing the frequency components that lie in all other frequency ranges (the *stopband*).

The desired lowpass LC filter should have a passband below 1,000 Hz and a stopband above 2,000 Hz. The circuit is driven by an incoming AC voltage source with a 2 volt amplitude. If the source (internal) resistance **RSOURCE** and the load resistance **RLOAD** in the embryonic circuit are each 1 kilo Ohm, the incoming 2 volt signal is divided in half.

The *attenuation* of the filter is defined in terms of the maximum signal in its stopband relative to the reference voltage (half of 2 volt here). A *decibel* is a unitless measure of relative voltage that is defined as 20 times the common (base 10) logarithm of the ratio between the voltage at a particular probe point and a reference voltage.

In this problem, a voltage in the passband of exactly 1 volt and a voltage in the stopband of exactly 0 volts is regarded as ideal. The (preferably small) variation within the passband is called the *passband ripple*. Similarly, the incoming signal is never fully reduced to zero in the stopband of an actual filer. The (preferably small) variation within the stopband is called the *stopband ripple*. A voltage in the passband of between 970 millivolts and 1 volt (i.e., a passband ripple of 30 millivolts or less) and a voltage in the stopband of between 0 volts and 1 millivolts (i.e., a stopband ripple of 1 millivolts or less) is regarded as acceptable. Any voltage lower than 970 millivolts in the passband and any voltage above 1 millivolts in the stopband is regarded as unacceptable.

A fifth-order *elliptic (Cauer) filter* with a modular angle Θ of 30 degrees (i.e., the arcsin of the ratio of the boundaries of the passband and stopband) and a reflection coefficient ρ of 20% is required to satisfy these design goals.

Since the high-level statement of behavior for the desired circuit is expressed in terms of frequencies, the voltage **UOUT** is measured in the frequency domain. SPICE performs an AC small signal analysis and report the circuit's behavior over five decades (between 1 Hz and 100,000 Hz) with each decade being divided into 20 parts (using a logarithmic scale),so that there are a total of 101 fitness cases.

Fitness is measured in terms of the sum over these cases of the absolute weighted deviation between the actual value of the voltage that is produced by the circuit at the probe point **UOUT** and the target value for voltage. The smaller the value of fitness, the better. A fitness of zero represents an (unattainable) ideal filter.

Specifically, the standardized fitness is

$$F(t) = \sum_{i=0}^{100} \left(W(d(f_i), f_i) d(f_i) \right)$$

where f_i is the frequency of fitness case i; $d(x)$ is the absolute value of the difference between the target and observed values at frequency x; and $W(y,x)$ is the weighting for difference y at frequency x.

The fitness measure is designed to not penalize ideal values, to slightly penalize every acceptable deviation, and to heavily penalize every unacceptable deviation. Specifically, the procedure for each of the 61 points in the 3-decade interval between 1 Hz and 1,000 Hz is as follows: If the voltage equals the ideal value of 1.0 volt in this interval, the deviation is 0.0. If the voltage is between 970 millivolts and 1 volt, the absolute value of the deviation from 1 volt is weighted by a factor of 1.0. If the voltage is less than 970 millivolts, the absolute value of the deviation from 1 volt is weighted by a factor of 10.0. The acceptable and unacceptable deviations for each of the 35 points from 2,000 Hz to 100,000 Hz are similarly weighed (by 1.0 or 10.0).

For each of the five "don't care" points between 1,000 and 2,000 Hz, the deviation is deemed to be zero.

The number of "hits" for this problem (and all other problems herein) is defined as the number of fitness cases for which the voltage is acceptable or ideal or that lie in the "don't care" band (for a filter).

Many of the random initial circuits and many that are created by the crossover and mutation operations in subsequent generations cannot be simulated by SPICE. These circuits receive a high penalty value of fitness (10^8) and become the worst-of-generation programs for each generation.

For details, see Koza, Bennett, Andre, and Keane 1996b.

4.4.2   Tri-state Frequency Discriminator

Fitness is the sum, over 101 fitness cases, of the absolute weighted deviation between the actual value of the voltage that is produced by the circuit and the target value.

The three points that are closest to the band located within 10% of 256 Hz are 229.1 Hz, 251.2 Hz, and 275.4 Hz. The procedure for each of these three points is as follows: If the voltage equals the ideal value of 1/2 volts in this interval, the deviation is 0.0. If the voltage is more than 240 millivolts from 1/2 volts, the absolute value of the deviation from 1/2 volts is weighted by a factor of 20. If the voltage is more than 240 millivolts of 1/2 volts, the absolute value of the deviation from 1/2 volts is weighted by a factor of 200. This arrangement reflects the fact that the ideal output voltage for this range of frequencies is 1/2 volts, the fact that a 240 millivolts discrepancy is acceptable, and the fact that a larger discrepancy is not acceptable.

Similar weighting was used for the three points (2,291 Hz, 2,512 Hz, and 2,754 Hz) that are closest to the band located within 10% of 2,560 ,Hz.

The procedure for each of the remaining 95 points is as follows: If the voltage equals the ideal value of 0 volts, the deviation is 0.0. If the voltage is within 240 millivolts of 0 volts, the absolute value of the deviation from 0 volts is weighted by a factor of 1.0. If the voltage is more than 240 millivolts from 0 volts, the absolute value of the deviation from 0 volts is weighted by a factor of 10. For details, see Koza, Bennett, Lohn, Dunlap, Andre, and Keane 1997b.

4.4.3   Computational Circuit

SPICE is called to perform a DC sweep analysis at 21 equidistant voltages between –250 millivolts and +250 millivolts. Fitness is the sum, over these 21 fitness cases, of the absolute weighted deviation between the actual value of the voltage that is produced by the circuit and the target value for voltage. For details, see Koza, Bennett, Lohn, Dunlap, Andre, and Keane 1997a.

4.4.4   Robot Controller Circuit

The fitness of a robot controller was evaluated using 72 randomly chosen fitness cases each representing a different target point. Fitness is the sum, over the 72 fitness cases, of the travel times. If the robot came within a capture radius of 0.28 meters of its target point before the end of the 80 time steps allowed for a particular fitness case, the contribution to fitness for that fitness case was the actual time. However, if the robot failed to come within the capture radius during the 80 time steps, the contribution to fitness was 0.160 hours (i.e., double the worst possible time).

SPICE performs a nested DC sweep, which provides a way to simulate the DC behavior of a circuit with two inputs. It resembles a nested pair of FOR loops in a computer program in that both of the loops have a starting value for the voltage, an increment, and an ending value for the voltage. For each voltage value in the outer loop, the inner loop simulates the behavior of the circuit by stepping through its range of voltages. Specifically, the starting value for voltage is –4 volt, the step size is 0.2 volt, and the ending value is +4 volt. These values correspond to the dimensions of the robot's world of 64 square meters extending 4 meters in each of the four directions from the origin of a coordinate system (i.e., 1 volt equals 1 meter). For details, see Koza, Bennett, Keane, and Andre 1997.

4.4.5　60 dB Amplifier

SPICE was requested to perform a DC sweep analysis to determine the circuit's response for several different DC input voltages. An ideal inverting amplifier circuit would receive the DC input, invert it, and multiply it by the amplification factor. A circuit is flawed to the extent that it does not achieve the desired amplification, the output signal is not perfectly centered on 0 volts(i.e., it is biased), or the DC response is not linear. Fitness is calculated by summing an amplification penalty, a bias penalty, and two non-linearity penalties – each derived from these five DC outputs. For details, see Bennett, Koza, Andre, and Keane 1996.

4.5.　Control Parameters

The population size, M, was 640,000 for all problems. Other parameters were substantially the same for each of the five problems and can be found in the references cited above.

4.6.　Implementation on Parallel Computer

Each problem was run on a medium-grained parallel Parsytec computer system (Andre and Koza 1996) consisting of 64 80-MHz PowerPC 601 processors arranged in an 8 by 8 toroidal mesh with a host PC Pentium type computer. The distributed genetic algorithm was used with a population size of $Q = 10,000$ at each of the $D = 64$ demes (semi-isolated subpopulations). On each generation, four boatloads of emigrants, each consisting of $B = 2\%$ (the migration rate) of the node's subpopulation (selected on the basis of fitness) were dispatched to each of the four adjacent processing nodes.

5.　Results

In all five problems, fitness was observed to improve over successive generations. A large majority of the randomly created initial circuits of generation 0 were not able to be simulated by SPICE; however, most were simulatable after only a few generations. Satisfactory results were generated in every case on the first or second trial. When two runs were required, the first produced an almost satisfactory result. This rate of success suggests that the capabilities of the approach and current computing system have not been fully exploited.

5.1.　Lowpass Filter

Many of the runs produced lowpass filters having a topology similar to that employed by human engineers. For example, in generation 32 of one run, a circuit (figure 5) was evolved with a near-zero fitness of 0.00781. The circuit was 100% compliant with the design requirements in that it scored 101 hits (out of 101). After the evolutionary run, this circuit (and all evolved circuits herein) were simulated anew using the commercially available MicroSim circuit simulator to verify performance. This circuit had the recognizable ladder topology (46) of a Butterworth or Chebychev filter (i.e., a composition of series inductors horizontally with capacitors as vertical shunts).

Figure 6 shows the behavior in the frequency domain of this evolved lowpass filter. As can be seen, the evolved circuit delivers about 1 volt for all frequencies up to 1,000 Hz and about 0 volts for all frequencies above 2,000 Hz.

In another run, a 100% compliant recognizable "bridged T" arrangement was evolved. In yet another run using automatically defined functions, a 100% compliant circuit emerged with the recognizable elliptic topology that was invented and patented by Cauer. When invented. the Cauer filter was a significant advance (both theoretically and commercially) over the Butterworth and Chebychev filters.

Thus, genetic programming rediscovered the ladder topology of the Butterworth and Chebychev filters, the "bridged T" topology, and the elliptic topology.

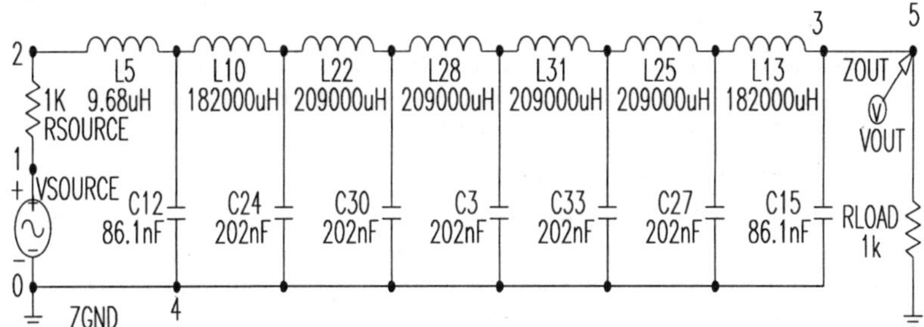

Figure 5 Evolved 7-rung ladder lowpass filter.

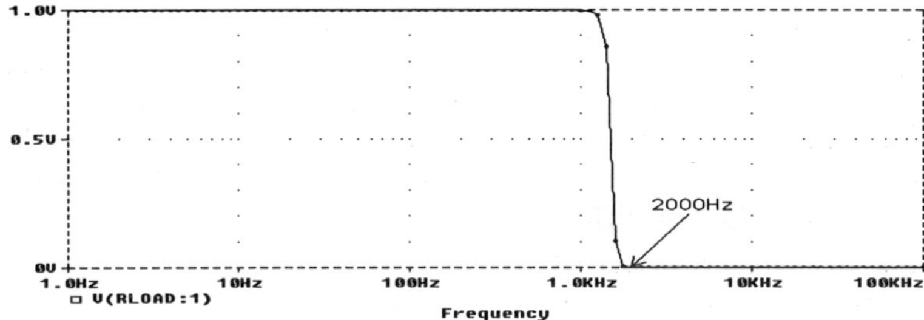

Figure 6 Frequency domain behavior of genetically evolved 7-rung ladder lowpass filter.

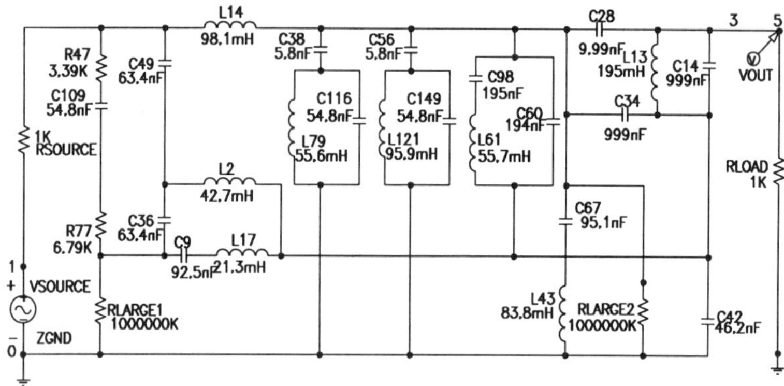

Figure 7 Evolved frequency discriminator.

5.2. Tri-state Frequency Discriminator

The evolved three-way tri-state frequency discriminator circuit from generation 106 scores 101 hits (out of 101). Figure 7 shows this circuit (after expansion of its automatically defined functions). The circuit produces the desired outputs of 1 volt and 1/2 volts (each within the allowable tolerance) for the two specified bands of frequencies and the desired near-zero signal for all other frequencies.

5.3. Computational Circuit

The genetically evolved computational circuit for the square root from generation 60 (figure 8), achieves a fitness of 1.68, and has 36 transistors, two diodes, no capacitors, and 12 resistors (in addition to the source and load resistors in the embryo). The output voltages produced by this best-of-run circuit are almost exactly the required values.

5.4. Robot Controller Circuit

The best-of-run time-optimal robot controller circuit (figure 9) appeared in generation 31, scores 72 hits, and achieves a near-optimal fitness of 1.541 hours. In comparison, the optimal value of fitness for this problem is known to be 1.518 hours. This best-of-run circuit has 10 transistors and 4 resistors. The program has one automatically defined function that is called twice (incorporated into the figure).

5.5. 60 dB Amplifier

The best circuit from generation 109 (figure 10) achieves a fitness of 0.178. Based on a DC sweep, the amplification is 60 dB here (i.e., 1,000-to-1 ratio) and the bias is 0.2 volt. Based on a transient analysis at 1,000 Hz, the amplification is 59.7 dB; the bias is 0.18 volts; and the distortion is very low (0.17%).

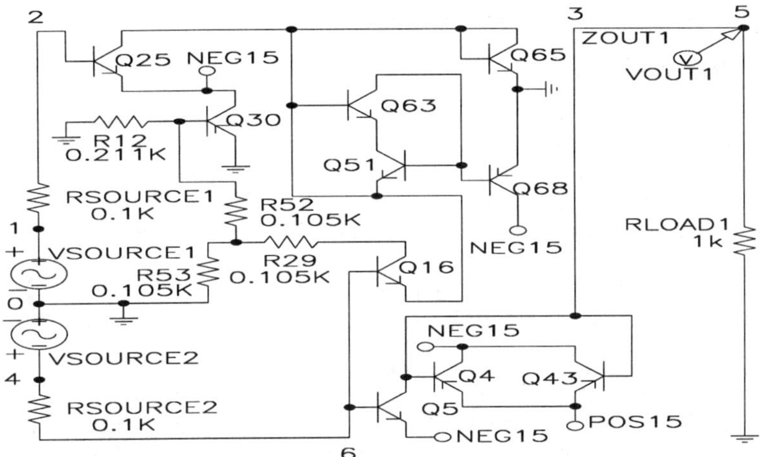

Figure 9 Evolved robot controller.

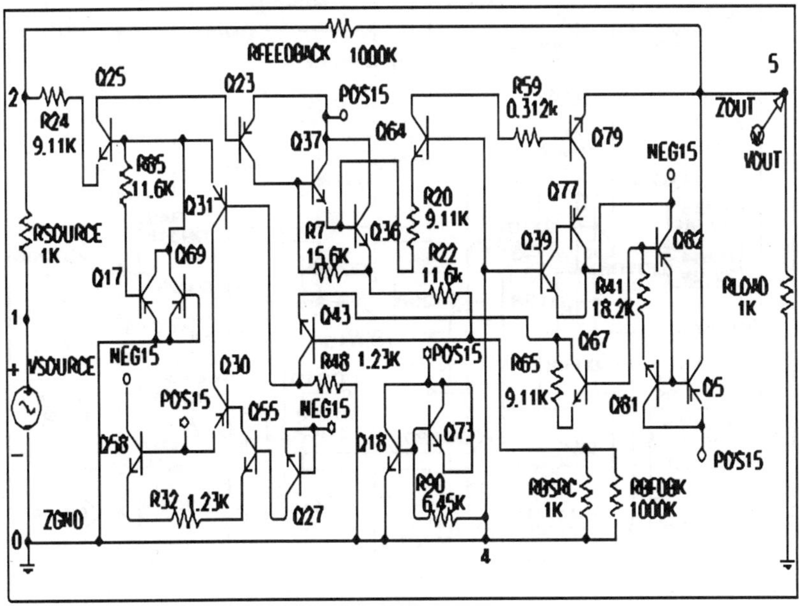

Figure 10 Genetically evolved amplifier.

Based on an AC sweep, the amplification at 1,000 Hz is 59.7 dB; the flatband gain is 60 dB; and the 3 dB bandwidth is 79, 333 Hz. Thus, a high-gain amplifier with low distortion and acceptable bias has been evolved.

6. Other Circuits

Numerous other circuits have been similarly designed, including asymmetric bandpass filters (Koza, Bennett, Andre, and Keane 1996c), crossover filters (Koza, Bennett, Andre, and Keane 1996a), comb filters (Koza, Andre, Bennett, and Keane 1996), amplifiers (Koza, Bennett, Andre, and Keane 1997), a temperature sensor, and a voltage reference circuit (Koza, Bennett, Andre, Keane, and Dunlap 1997).

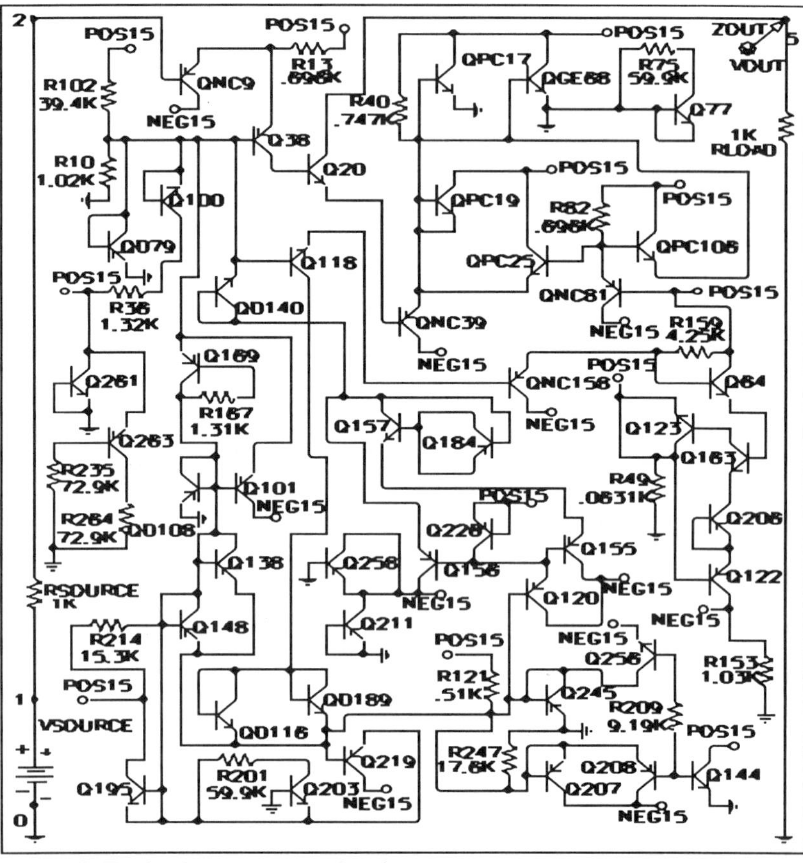

Figure 8 Evolved square root circuit.

7. Conclusion

Genetic programming evolved the topology and sizing of five different prototypical analog electrical circuits.

References

Aaserud, O. and Nielsen, I. Ring. 1995. Trends in current analog design: A panel debate. *Analog Integrated Circuits and Signal Processing.* 7(1) 5-9.

Andre, David and Koza, John R. 1996. Parallel genetic programming: A scalable implementation using the transputer architecture. In Angeline, P. J. and Kinnear, K. E. Jr. (editors). 1996. *Advances in Genetic Programming 2.* Cambridge: MIT Press.

Angeline, Peter J. and Kinnear, Kenneth E. Jr. (editors). 1996. *Advances in Genetic Programming 2.* Cambridge, MA: The MIT Press.

Banzhaf, Wolfgang, Nordin, Peter, Keller, Robert E., and Francone, Frank D. 1998. *Genetic Programming – An Introduction.* San Francisco, CA: Morgan Kaufmann and Heidelberg: dpunkt.

Bennett III, Forrest H, Koza, John R., Andre, David, and Keane, Martin A. 1996. Evolution of a 60 Decibel op amp using genetic programming. In Higuchi, Tetsuya, Iwata, Masaya, and Lui, Weixin (editors). *Proceedings of International Conference on Evolvable Systems: From Biology to Hardware (ICES-96).* Lecture Notes in Computer Science, Volume 1259. Berlin: Springer-Verlag. Pages 455-469.

Brave, Scott. 1996. Evolving deterministic finite automata using cellular encoding. In Koza, John R., Goldberg, David E., Fogel, David B., and Riolo, Rick L. (editors). 1996. *Genetic Programming 1996: Proceedings of the First Annual Conference, July 28-31, 1996, Stanford University.* Cambridge, MA: MIT Press. Pages 39–44.

Grimbleby, J. B. 1995. Automatic analogue network synthesis using genetic algorithms. *Proceedings of the First International Conference on Genetic Algorithms in Engineering Systems: Innovations and Applications.* London: Institution of Electrical Engineers. Pages 53–58.

Gruau, Frederic. 1992. *Cellular Encoding of Genetic Neural Networks.* Technical report 92-21. Laboratoire de l'Informatique du Parallélisme. Ecole Normale Supérieure de Lyon. May 1992.

Holland, John H. 1975. *Adaptation in Natural and Artificial Systems.* Ann Arbor, MI: University of Michigan Press.

Kinnear, Kenneth E. Jr. (editor). 1994. *Advances in Genetic Programming.* Cambridge, MA: The MIT Press.

Kitano, Hiroaki. 1990. Designing neural networks using genetic algorithms with graph generation system. *Complex Systems.* 4(1990) 461–476.

Koza, John R. 1992. *Genetic Programming: On the Programming of Computers by Means of Natural Selection.* Cambridge, MA: MIT Press.

Koza, John R. 1994a. *Genetic Programming II: Automatic Discovery of Reusable Programs.* Cambridge, MA: MIT Press.

Koza, John R. 1994b. *Genetic Programming II Videotape: The Next Generation.* Cambridge, MA: MIT Press.

Koza, John R. 1995. Evolving the architecture of a multi-part program in genetic programming using architecture-altering operations. In McDonnell, John R., Reynolds, Robert G., and Fogel, David B. (editors). 1995. *Evolutionary Programming IV: Proceedings of the Fourth Annual Conference on Evolutionary Programming.* Cambridge, MA: The MIT Press. Pages 695–717.

Koza, John R., Andre, David, Bennett III, Forrest H, and Keane, Martin A. 1996. Use of automatically defined functions and architecture-altering operations in automated circuit synthesis using genetic programming. In Koza, John R., Goldberg, David E., Fogel, David B., and Riolo, Rick L. (editors). 1996. *Genetic Programming 1996: Proceedings of the First Annual Conference.* Cambridge, MA: The MIT Press.

Koza, John R., Bennett III, Forrest H, Andre, David, and Keane, Martin A. 1996a. Four problems for which a computer program evolved by genetic programming is competitive with human performance. *Proceedings of the 1996 IEEE International Conference on Evolutionary Computation.* IEEE Press. Pages 1–10.

Koza, John R., Bennett III, Forrest H, Andre, David, and Keane, Martin A. 1996b. Automated design of both the topology and sizing of analog electrical circuits using genetic programming. In Gero, John S. and Sudweeks, Fay (editors). *Artificial Intelligence in Design '96.* Dordrecht: Kluwer. Pages 151-170.

Koza, John R., Bennett III, Forrest H, Andre, David, and Keane, Martin A. 1996c. Automated WYWIWYG design of both the topology and component values of analog electrical circuits using genetic programming. In Koza, John R., Goldberg, David E., Fogel, David B., and Riolo, Rick L. (editors). 1996. *Genetic Programming 1996: Proceedings of the First Annual Conference.* Cambridge, MA: The MIT Press.

Koza, John R., Bennett III, Forrest H, Andre, David, and Keane, Martin A. 1997. Evolution using genetic programming of a low-distortion 96 Decibel operational amplifier. *Proceedings of the 1997 ACM Symposium on Applied Computing, San Jose, California, February 28 – March 2, 1997.* New York: Association for Computing Machinery. Pages 207 - 216.

Koza, John R., Bennett III, Forrest H, Andre, David, Keane, Martin A, and Dunlap, Frank. 1997. Automated synthesis of analog electrical circuits by means of genetic programming. *IEEE Transactions on Evolutionary Computation.* 1(2). Pages 109 – 128.

Koza, John R., Bennett III, Forrest H, Keane, Martin A., and Andre, David. 1997. Automatic programming of a time-optimal robot controller and an analog electrical circuit to implement the robot controller by means of genetic programming. *Proceedings of 1997 IEEE International Symposium on Computational Intelligence in Robotics and Automation.* Los Alamitos, CA; Computer Society Press. Pages 340 – 346.

Koza, John R., Bennett III, Forrest H, Lohn, Jason, Dunlap, Frank, Andre, David, and Keane, Martin A. 1997. Automated synthesis of computational circuits using genetic programming. *Proceedings of the 1997 IEEE Conference on Evolutionary Computation.* Piscataway, NJ: IEEE Press. 447–452.

Koza, John R., Bennett III, Forrest H, Lohn, Jason, Dunlap, Frank, Andre, David, and Keane, Martin A. 1997b. Use of architecture-altering operations to dynamically adapt a three-way analog source identification circuit to accommodate a new source. In Koza, John R., Deb, Kalyanmoy, Dorigo, Marco, Fogel, David B., Garzon, Max, Iba, Hitoshi, and Riolo, Rick L. (editors). 1997. *Genetic Programming 1997: Proceedings of the Second Annual Conference* San Francisco, CA: Morgan Kaufmann. 213 – 221.

Koza, John R., Deb, Kalyanmoy, Dorigo, Marco, Fogel, David B., Garzon, Max, Iba, Hitoshi, and Riolo, Rick L. (editors). 1997. *Genetic Programming 1997: Proceedings of the Second Annual Conference* San Francisco, CA: Morgan Kaufmann.

Koza, John R., Goldberg, David E., Fogel, David B., and Riolo, Rick L. (editors). 1996. *Genetic Programming 1996: Proceedings of the First Annual Conference.* Cambridge, MA: The MIT Press.

Koza, John R., and Rice, James P. 1992. *Genetic Programming: The Movie.* Cambridge, MA: MIT Press.

Kruiskamp Marinum Wilhelmus and Leenaerts, Domine. 1995. DARWIN: CMOS opamp synthesis by means of a genetic algorithm. *Proceedings of the 32nd Design Automation Conference.* New York, NY: Association for Computing Machinery. Pages 433–438.

Quarles, Thomas, Newton, A. R., Pederson, D. O., and Sangiovanni-Vincentelli, A. 1994. *SPICE 3 Version 3F5 User's Manual.* Department of Electrical Engineering and Computer Science, University of California, Berkeley, CA. March 1994.

Rutenbar, R. A. 1993. Analog design automation: Where are we? Where are we going? *Proceedings of the l5th IEEE CICC.* New York: IEEE. 13.1.1-13.1.8.

Samuel, Arthur L. 1959. Some studies in machine learning using the game of checkers. *IBM Journal of Research and Development.* 3(3): 210–229.

Samuel, Arthur L. 1983. AI: Where it has been and where it is going. *Proceedings of the Eighth International Joint Conference on Artificial Intelligence.* Los Altos, CA: Morgan Kaufmann. Pages 1152 – 1157.

Thompson, Adrian. 1996. Silicon evolution. In Koza, John R., Goldberg, David E., Fogel, David B., and Riolo, Rick L. (editors). 1996. *Genetic Programming 1996: Proceedings of the First Annual Conference.* Cambridge, MA: MIT Press.

THE COMPUTER ZOO – EVOLUTION IN A BOX

J. SKIPPER

Thorsmosen 2, DK-3500 Vaerlose, DENMARK
E-mail: Jakob.Skipper@copenhagen.ncr.com

The Computer Zoo is an artificial life simulator and its purpose is to recreate life in a computer. It does so be breeding new species of little programs using evolution and natural selection. The programs are written in a specially designed programming language *Czoo*, which is more resistant to mutations than a traditional programming language. The mutant programs show spontaneous symbiosis, parasites, self-assembly of flocks of programs, punctuated equilibria, and traces of predatory behavior.

1   Modeling Life

As the title of this paper suggests, it describes a project with a very ambitious goal: the creation of evolution in a completely artificial system. The medium chosen for re-creating evolution is a computer. It may not be the only possible medium for this – or even the best – but it is handy.

Note that it is a model of evolution, not of the nature. Other authors have instead modeled the interaction of species in the nature explicitly, for example by defining foxes, rabbits, grass etc. and then letting the foxes eat the rabbits under the control of a handful of rules.

The Computer Zoo does not represent the nature directly in the model. Instead it is in itself a complete *electronic ecosystem* including digital creatures to live in it. These creatures have nothing to do with rabbits or foxes and they 'live' under completely different conditions. Yet the digital creatures show some of the same behaviors as real animals.

One common consensus from the First Conference on Artificial Life in Santa Fe[1] was that artificial life should be created by the use of local interactions among individuals rather than by global control. For example, lions eat zebras that they find in the neighborhood without regard to how many zebras there are in the world. From this arises a global balance between lions and zebras that can be described by a predator-prey equation.

It would be global control if the predator-prey equation was the basic rule used to decide if a lion was allowed to eat a given zebra. Obviously, this is not a natural model for lions, since they tend to cut the math classes.

In real life, a crucial part of the environment for an animal is the other animals and plants in the habitat. Evolution ensures that the animals adapt not only to the slowly changing climatic and geological conditions, but also to the other animals, who are themselves being changed by evolution. As the lion develops new, ingenious hunting techniques, the zebra must learn how to run faster. The pace of the evolution is set by the fastest evolving species, so a species must evolve quickly, simply to keep its niche and to survive. This is known as the Red Queen hypothesis (L. van Valen[2]).

This interaction with other species is a driving force in the evolution. If the creatures did not interact, they would evolve until optimum in the given environment and then stay there. But when the creatures interact, the environment is constantly changing and so must the inhabitants do. This creates the open-ended evolution. Therefore The Computer Zoo is designed to allow the digital creatures to interact with each other.

This approach follows the tradition established by earlier models of evolution, such as the Coreworld by Rasmussen et al.[3] and the Tierra simulator by Thomas Ray.[4]

In the Computer Zoo, a digital creature is just a program, but it is not a traditional program. Traditional programming languages are far too sensitive to random mutations. Instead The Computer Zoo uses a new language *Czoo* designed specifically for this purpose.

At the beginning of time, the Zoo contains just one single ancestor program living in this electronic world. But this program reproduces again and again, and soon there are more than enough to fill the available space. The reproduction process is not always successful. Random mutations occur now and then, and along the way the mutations give rise to new and better 'species' of programs that outperform and eradicate the original ancestor program.

In the following I will describe first the Czoo language and the environment, then the anticipated and actual results from running The Computer Zoo.

2 Defining the Zoo

But first we must define a system in which evolution may take place. Such a definition must include a description of both the digital creatures (genetic code), their relations to the environment they live in, and the characteristics of that environment. In computer terms we would call it the programming language, the operating system API, and the operating system architecture.

The environment must be rich enough to allow a wide variety of possible species to exist, reproduce, and evolve, but on the other hand it should not be overly unrestricted, as this would lead to a total chaos. Chris Langton[5] has shown how a one-dimensional cellular array should be balanced at a point between order and chaos to evolve long transients in time. The Computer Zoo is based on the assumption the same is true for other complex systems.

2.1 Language Principles

The first thing to define in the Zoo is the language that the programs (digital creatures) are written in. A traditional programming language like C or Pascal is very sensitive to random mutations in the code. Change a random bit, and chances are the program falls completely apart. This is because the number of functional programs is microscopic compared to the number of possible programs. This fact is usually referred to as the 'brittleness problem', and the Czoo language is designed to reduce it. The basic principle is to use an assembly-like language with 32 instructions but with no constant operands.

Other principles are:

- The world is two-dimensional rather than the usual one-dimensional memory space of computers. This allows interesting moving patterns and gives many more opportunities for interaction.

- Memory comes in chunks of 16 words and can be moved freely around in the two-dimensional world. They are referred to by templates instead of traditional addresses.

- Programs consist of a set of memory blocks. Flow of execution is controlled by special jump templates (32-bit words) saying where to continue execution.

- Programs interact by sending events (or messages) to itself and to other programs nearby.

- Programs can also interact by running pieces of each others code.

The following sections describe these characteristics of Czoo. A more detailed description is given by Skipper[6].

The Instruction Set

The instruction set used in Czoo resembles a traditional assembly language. The code is a string of instructions with no compound constructs like `begin ... end`, `for ... do` etc. But there is one important difference: Czoo has no constant operands. If a constant like 42 is needed in a program, it has to be constructed from zero by shifting, incrementing, and adding.

A language with no constant operands was first introduced by Thomas Ray[4] in his Tierra language. The objective is to reduce the *real* size of the instruction set. With a large instruction set it is highly unlikely that a random mutation in the code creates a useful instruction. As Ray points out, the size of an instruction set is not just the number of op-codes. Two instructions like `add 1` and `add 2` have different semantics even if they have the same op-code. They are therefore really different instructions.

The Coreworld[3] use the language Redcode taken from the game Core War[7]. It has only 10 op-codes, but most instructions have one or two operands and four addressing modes. Thomas Ray calculates the real number of instructions in Redcode to be about 10^{11}. In contrast, the Czoo language has 32 instructions and none of them have operands.

In addition to traditional instructions like **add**, **push**, etc., Czoo has a set of special purpose instructions like **alloc** (allocates a memory cell), **split** (creates a new program from all the data cells and starts running it), and **kill** (immediately kills the program executing it).

The full instruction set is listed in appendix A.

Two-dimensional World

As mentioned earlier, The Computer Zoo is based on local interactions rather than global control. But then we need a meaning to the words local and global, which means we must have some kind of topology or geography in the model.

Both the Coreworld[3] and the Tierra simulator[4] use as topology a conventional one-dimensional memory. To improve local interactions, The Computer Zoo uses a two-dimensional grid instead. Every program has at a given time a position on the grid, as well as a direction it is facing. There are eight possible directions: north, north east, east etc. Two or more programs may share the same grid position. To enable the programs to move around on the grid, the instruction set contains the three instructions **forward**, **turnleft**, and **turnright**.

When we have a geography, we also need a measure of distance. Otherwise we could not say what is local and what is not. In the Zoo, the distance between two programs is the maximum of the vertical and the horizontal distance on the grid. Therefore a program has the distance 1 to all its eight neighbor grid points.

Memory Cells

Since we have discarded the linear memory model as our topology and replaced it with a two-dimensional grid, we need some other way to organize the memory. The Computer Zoo chops memory into small, independent pieces of 16 words each. These chunks are named *memory cells* and they contain the code and the data of the programs in the Zoo. The words are 32 bits wide, but when they contain code we only use the lower 5 bits.

A memory cell has a position on the grid and moves around together with the program that owns it. Therefore it is impossible to refer to it using a traditional addresses. Instead The Computer Zoo uses associative addressing.

For every cell, the Zoo calculates a 32-bit word called the *cell template*. This is the name of the cell and is used by the code to address this specific memory cell. It is computed from the 16 instructions in the cell by xor'ing and

<table>
<tr><td>Cell template</td></tr>
<tr><td>Primary jump template</td></tr>
<tr><td>Conditional jump template</td></tr>
<tr><td>Instruction 1</td></tr>
<tr><td>⋮</td></tr>
<tr><td>Instruction 16</td></tr>
</table>

Figure 1: *A single memory cell. The cell template works as a label to identify the cell and it is computed from the lower 5 bits of each of the 16 instruction words.*

rotating the five instruction bits in a way so that a mutation of a single bit in an instruction results in a change of a single bit in the template. Whenever an instruction is changed, for instance by a mutation, the cell template also changes. Note that this template is not unique—the algorithm maps 80 bits into 32, giving $2^{48} \approx 3 \cdot 10^{14}$ different possible memory cells having the same template.

This cell name is then used to make jumps from the code in one cell to the code in another. Every memory cell has two jump templates: the *primary jump template* and the *conditional jump template*. They are used to find the next memory cell with code to execute. Whenever a program has executed the 16 instructions in a memory cell, it uses the primary jump template to find the next cell to execute. The winner is the cell with the name (cell template) having the closest match to the jump template. 'Closest' means the number of different bits (Hamming distance) between two templates. If no cell template matches the jump template within a certain limit called the *template tolerance*, the jump fails and the program dies.

By establishing a sequence of matching cell and jump templates we can create an endless loop. But sometimes we want to make conditional jumps, and for this purpose the memory cells also contain a conditional jump template. The instruction set contains two conditional instructions: `if` and `ifnot`. They skip the rest of the instructions in the cell when the `flag` register is true or false, respectively. The next cell to execute is then selected by using the conditional jump template instead of the primary.

The two instructions `if` and `ifnot` are the only instructions for program sequencing. The use of templates makes explicit loop, repeat, and jump instructions superfluous.

As a cell and a jump template may match even if they are not equal, this scheme introduces some fault tolerance. The jump can be resolved correctly even if one of the templates is partly changed by mutations.

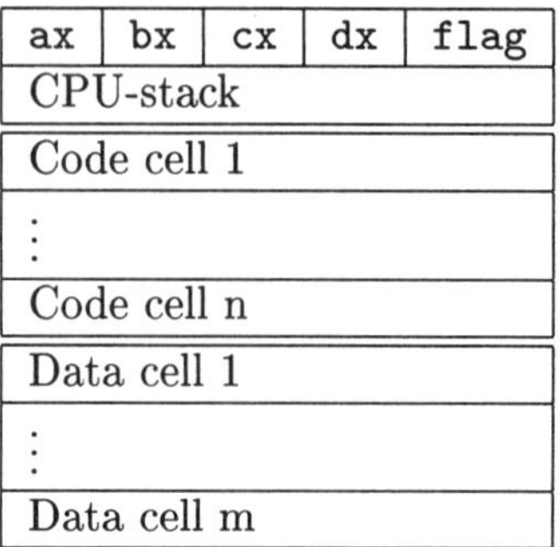

Figure 2: *A program consists of four general purpose registers, a flag register, a CPU-stack, one or more code cells, and zero or more data cells.*

Programs

A program consists of one or more memory cells containing code, and zero or more cells containing data. A data cell is identical to a code cell. The only difference is the way it is used by the program. The data cells typically hold an offspring program under construction, but they may hold any type of data. Just like the code cells, the data cells are addressed using a template.

In addition to memory cells, each program has its own instances of the four general purpose CPU registers `ax`, `bx`, `cx` and `dx`, and the boolean `flag` register. The latter is set and cleared to indicate success and failure of certain instructions. Finally a program has a CPU-stack, which is just a statically allocated data cell. At any given time, one register is the current stack register and one is the prefix register. Both point to a memory cell (code or data) by holding a cell template.

Events

Until now the focus has been on a single program, paying no attention to its interactions with other programs. But as pointed out in the beginning of this paper, interaction between the digital creatures is essential to evolution. This interaction is implemented using events and remote execution, to be explained below.

The combination of cell and jump templates controls the program flow through the memory cells. This simple principle can be reformulated using *events*, and the new scheme can easily be extended to include interactions among programs.

An event is a message sent from one program to another (possibly the same). It is a 32 bit number, and the receiving program reacts by using it as a jump template. The result is that it executes the code in the memory cell with the cell template that best matches the event.

In other words, a program reacts to an event by executing some code, depending on the value of the event. It is very similar to object oriented programming. If a program is an object, you invoke a methode ($\approx$ code cell) by sending it a message ($\approx$ event).

Execution starts when a program receives an event, and the best matching code cell is executed. When the execution of the instructions in the cell has finished, the program sends a new event taken from either the primary or the conditional jump template. The program then receives its own event, sparks off the execution of a new cell, and the process is repeated.

With this new view on the same thing we can now introduce talking programs. When the event is created, it is broadcasted to all the programs within some distance called the *event radius*. As a consequence, not only the originating program but also a number of other programs nearby receive the event and possibly execute some code selected by the event.

When this event broadcasting is enabled, a program may receive more events than it can handle. The events are then queued for the program for later processing. There is no limit of the number of queued events. This could cause a continuous, unlimited growth in the queue size, but the experiments have shown that this does not happen in practice.

If a program has received an event that does not match any cell template, the event is simply discarded and the next in the queue is used instead. If the queue runs empty, the program does not know what to do next, so then it dies.

The concept of events can easily be expanded. The Computer Zoo could for example raise events to signal external conditions such as the presence of an unallocated memory cell. The programs could then develop code to react sensibly. This aspect has not been investigated.

Remote Execution

As described above, one program may use broadcasting of events to affect the program flow of another program. But a program may also execute code belonging to another program. This is called *remote execution*. It is in some sense the opposite scheme of event broadcasting; a program does not broadcast its jump templates, it 'imports' the cell templates of other programs.

When a program receives an event (from itself or from another program), it searches all its own code cells for the best match. But if we use remote execution, it also searches the code cells of all other programs within event radius. If the best match is a cell owned by some other program, this foreign code is executed. The scheme is illustrated in figure 3. Remote execution turns out to be a very important facility, as we shall see in section 3.

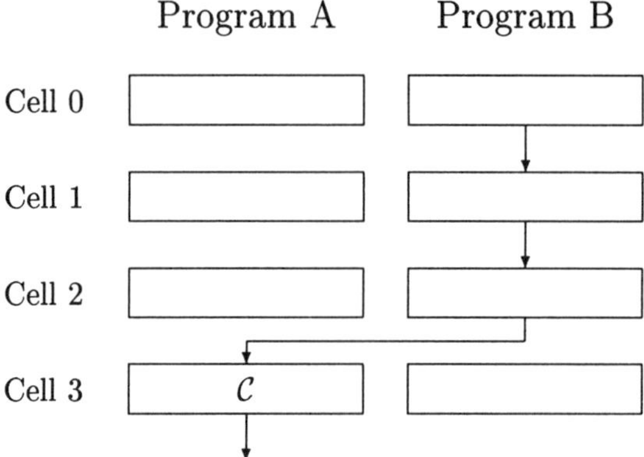

Figure 3: *Remote execution. Program B executes remotely the code of cell C in program A. It then continues execution using the jump template stored in cell C and it is therefore likely to continue executing A's code. But since A may also execute B's code remotely, the execution of the two programs can become deeply interweaved.*

Remote Collection

Remote execution is a way for a program to read and use the code cells of other programs. It has a parallel when the memory cells are treated as data, called *remote collection*. When reading a memory cell as data (being either a code or a data cell), the program searches all cells of all programs within the event radius (instead of just its own cells) for the best match, and then reads the desired data from it.

2.2 The Environment

The programs described in the previous sections run in a large multiprocessing simulator. It could also be called the environment, the electronic ecosystem, the operating system, or the world of the programs. This simulator has some adjustable properties that affect the behavior of the programs.

Memory Management

First of all there is memory allocation. Memory is a limited resource to any computer program including Czoo programs. There is a fixed amount of memory cells available to the programs. All unallocated memory cells go into a big, central pool from which the programs allocate new cells, and into which the cells belonging to dead programs go.

Mortality

When programs replicate they use memory and in very little time all the available memory cells are allocated. To allow further replication, some programs must die and thus release their allocated memory.

A program may die because of an execution error, because it executed a special suicide instruction `kill`, or it can be terminated by the simulator. When a program asks for more memory and no more memory cells remain in the pool, the Zoo automatically terminates the oldest program so that all of its memory cells are returned to the pool.

Mutations

The ancestor program would be the only program species in the simulator if it had not been for mutations. The Computer Zoo implements two different kinds of mutations: point mutation and erroneous duplication. The main difference is the time when the mutations occur.

Point mutation is the simplest form. With uneven intervals the simulator flips a random bit in a random memory cell, changing either an instruction, some data, or a jump template. As a result, even a program that was correct when started may after a while degenerate due to mutations.

Erroneous duplication takes place during the process of copying a single memory cell. The instruction set contains a `duplicate` instruction that copies an entire memory cell onto another previously allocated memory cell. This duplication is not always correct. With a small probability, the simulator flips a random bit in the cell, or it either deletes or inserts a random instruction at a random place. Erroneous duplication only affects new programs. Once a program has started running it never changes (except if point mutation is also used).

2.3 What The Zoo Can Do

So far I have described how the world is seen by a program running in the Zoo. The chosen architecture has some interesting consequences that will be summarized in the following section. These are the anticipated capabilities of the Zoo. The actually demonstrated capabilities are described later in section 3.

Redundancy and Resilience

In Czoo, memory cells are addressed with a template where a certain number of bits are allowed to be wrong. This means that a Czoo program may potentially continue to work even if some of the code is changed by mutations. They are fault resilient.

The same scheme also allows for redundancy in a program by duplicating vital program parts. If a program owns multiple copies of a code cell and one of these is mutated, the cell template is also changed. But then the unchanged copy of the cell is (probably) a better match for the jump templates in the program, and this unchanged cell is selected for execution before the mutated one.

Sexual Reproduction

A program reproduces (makes copies of itself) by copying its memory cells, and these cells are addressed by templates. But when we use remote collection (meaning it may instead reach the memory cells of other programs), the resulting offspring program will be a combination of memory cells from one, two, or even many different programs.

This is actually sexual reproduction, but it is implicit. The programs are not 'aware' that they reproduce sexually, and there is no performance penalty for a program to reproduce sexually.

When using remote collection, the program makes an offspring assembled of pieces taken from various other programs. In biology, this is called cross-over. In a traditional programming language cross-over would almost certainly lead to a disabled offspring. But in Czoo it is different. First of all, the cell templates ensure that the code taken from another program resembles the original code of the parent. Secondly, when we copy the code one cell at a time, cross-over does not happen in the middle of that cell, only between cells.

Sensing and Communication

When a program receives and processes an event we can say that it senses the event. This view is especially useful when the program receives events that it did not issue itself (when using event broadcasting). We can say that the program sees another approaching program when it reacts to the events issued by this other program. It may also recognize other program species by their events and take appropriate action. Likewise, a program can issue events that may trick other programs into believing something else has happened. This opens up an enormous range of possible interactions between the programs.

Note that the use of events equips the programs with a sensing apparatus and not with an explicit appearance (such as for instance explicitly adding the concept of color), because the appearance is completely determined by the character of the observer's senses. We humans recognize a zebra on the stripes, but that is only because our main sense is our sight. Had our main sense been the sense of smell, we would describe the appearance of a zebra very differently.

A Czoo program has many different appearances: a pattern of events emerging from it, a written representation in the Czoo language, a bit pattern in the memory etc. But since Czoo programs sense events they recognize each other from the issued events.

Because programs may exchange events, they can also be said to communicate. In principle it should be possible to evolve programs that communicate by sending various events to each other.

Predatory Behavior

The possibility of predatory behavior is one consequence of the design of the Zoo. A program is called a predator if it kills other programs in the hunt for more memory. There is actually (at least) two ways to be a predator, corresponding to the two kinds of interaction: remote execution and event broadcasting. These two kinds could be called 'setting up a trap' and 'shooting poisoned arrows'. I have concentrated on the former since that is by far the easiest to detect.

Consider the picture in figure 4. The predator owns a code cell that it never executes itself, and this cell contains a `kill` instruction, which causes the executing program to instantly die. Another program within event radius (the prey) executes this code remotely and dies during the execution. The predator then allocates the memory of the prey, using the memory allocation instruction `alloc`.

Instead of an explicit `kill` instruction, the fatal code could cause an execution error or it could simply mess things up in a way so that the prey will make an execution error later (poisoning).

This kind of predatory behavior is very passive. The predator just sets up the trap and then waits for the prey to do the work. But the opposite scheme is also possible when using event broadcasting instead of remote execution. The predator then sends an event that is lethal to the prey by sparking off execution of some code in the prey that causes it to die.

These two methods can be combined. The predator issues an event that causes the prey to execute a fatal code cell owned by the predator. This requires the predator to be immune to the fatal code, since it itself receives the event and therefore executes the code.

Predatory behavior is only an evolutionary advantage to a program if memory is scarce and the memory allocation scheme ensures that the predator is the program most likely to allocate the memory released from the prey. More about memory allocation in section 3.5.

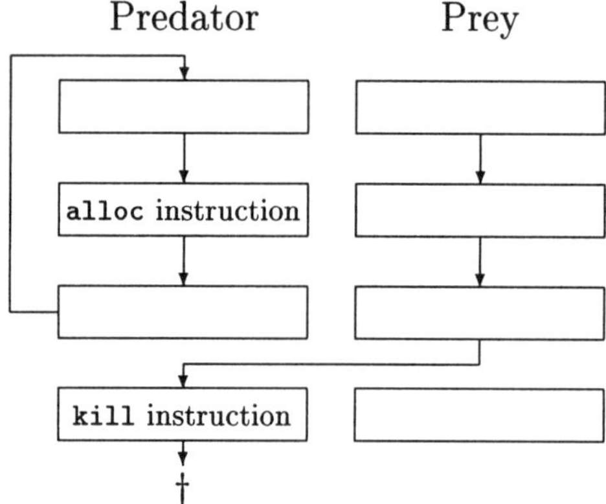

Figure 4: *Program flow when a prey due to remote execution falls into the trap set up by the predator.*

2.4 Relations to Biology

The Computer Zoo as described above is a piece of artificial life, but it is not designed to resemble the biological life in any way However, some of the concepts have been inspired by the nature and the human DNA.

The human DNA can be viewed as a long string of nucleotides, just like a traditional assembly language program is a long string of instructions. But the DNA string is divided into functional substrings, and each substring codes for some specific character of the individual. During the reproduction process cross-over is more likely to occur between two such functional substrings than in the middle of a string.

A natural model of this in a program is to divide the code into smaller parts that go relatively intact through the reproduction process. This was the idea behind the memory cells. The concept is simplified in the Zoo by giving all cells a fixed length.

The use of templates in the cells was inspired by Thomas Ray, but he was inspired by biochemistry. When two protein molecules in a biological cell interact, they do not specify the coordinates or address of each other. Instead they are brought together by diffusion, and they react when their surfaces match.

3 Running the Zoo

Now that I have described how the Zoo is designed, I will then describe the results observed from actual trial runs with the system. A run starts with an ancestor program. I have used the same simple ancestor program in all the

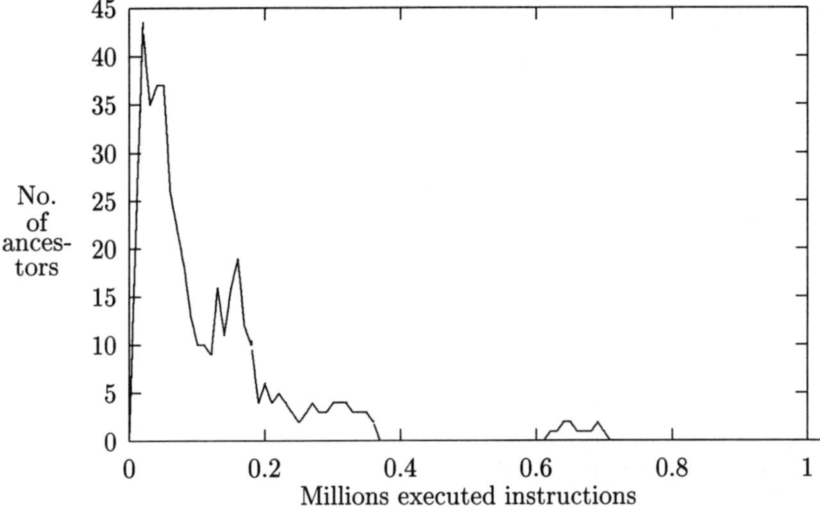

Figure 5: *Number of copies of the ancestor program. Notice how the ancestor is eradicated by mutants, but reappears for a short while before it disappears forever.*

runs. It is loaded into the Zoo and starts running and reproducing itself again and again. The ancestor dominates for a short while, but then other mutated programs take over (see figure 5).

3.1 Symbiosis and Parasites

One very common result of the runs is the development of parasite programs similar to what happens in Thomas Ray's Tierra simulator. It happens when using remote execution and no broadcasting of events.

For a short while the ancestor totally dominates the entire Zoo. But the system quickly destabilizes and a lot of small programs appear. Typically it happens after a few hundred thousand instructions.

These small programs contain just a single code cell so they do not themselves have all the code necessary to replicate. Instead they use remote execution to execute the code of other programs in the neighborhood. Since there is only one cell to copy, the replication is much faster.

These small parasitic programs cannot replicate alone, they are dependent on each other and the hosts. This dependence on other programs is the trade-off for an improved reproduction speed.

```
"igakgissas" (lt. gray   ), cnt=41, len=1/0, preys=0/0, bal=-5
0 :igakgissas CELL isidgaskok(-) isibfahkek(-)
      SPLIT . . . . . . TURNRIGHT TURNRIGHT . . . . . . TURNRIGHT


"igakgiskas" (lt. green  ), cnt=43, len=1/0, preys=0/0, bal=-5
0 :igakgiskas CELL isidgaskok(-) isibfahkek(-)
      SPLIT FORWARD . . . . . TURNRIGHT . . . . . . . TURNRIGHT


" littamref" (lt. gray   ), cnt=37, len=1/0, preys=0/0, bal=-5
0 : littamref CELL oketnovlen(-) isarbisfob(-)
        SELF KILL TURNRIGHT PREFIX-CX MOVSP ZERO? ADD SHL
        MOVSP STACK-AX TURNRIGHT PREFIX-CX DEC IFNOT SPLIT SPLIT
```

Figure 6: *The code of three parasites. The 'igakgissas' and 'igakgiskas' parasites are variations of a cell from the ancestor program, but turn-instructions have entered and changed the moving pattern of the program.*
The 'littamref' program illustrates how a parasite may lose all of its functional code and run completely on code belonging to other programs.
The cell name ('littamref', 'igakgissas', etc.) is the 32-bit cell template translated to a character representation.

3.2 Moving and Flock Formation

The one-cell parasite programs depend on begin close to their hosts. This causes them to cluster in one big flock on the screen (see the screen dumps in figure 7).

The ancestor program is constructed to move forward all the time. A program that does so will sooner or later fall out of the flock. If it is a parasite, it dies because there are no fellow programs with the code it needs. It simply dies of loneliness.

As a countermeasure the parasites start moving in circles and spirals, thereby reducing the chance of 'getting lost'. The circle-moving programs soon dominate and cause the flock to decrease in size. This has already developed in two of the programs shown in figure 6.

3.3 Punctuated Equilibria

The Zoo also shows punctuated equilibria. Punctuated equilibria is an expression originally used by Gould and Eldredge [8] to describe the paleobiological evolution. Their hypothesis was that evolution did not happen gradually. Instead there were longer periods of relative stability, punctuated with irregular intervals by short periods of turbulent changes.

Looking at the example in figure 8, it is evident that at any given time, the Zoo is either dominated by programs of length 4 (having four memory cells

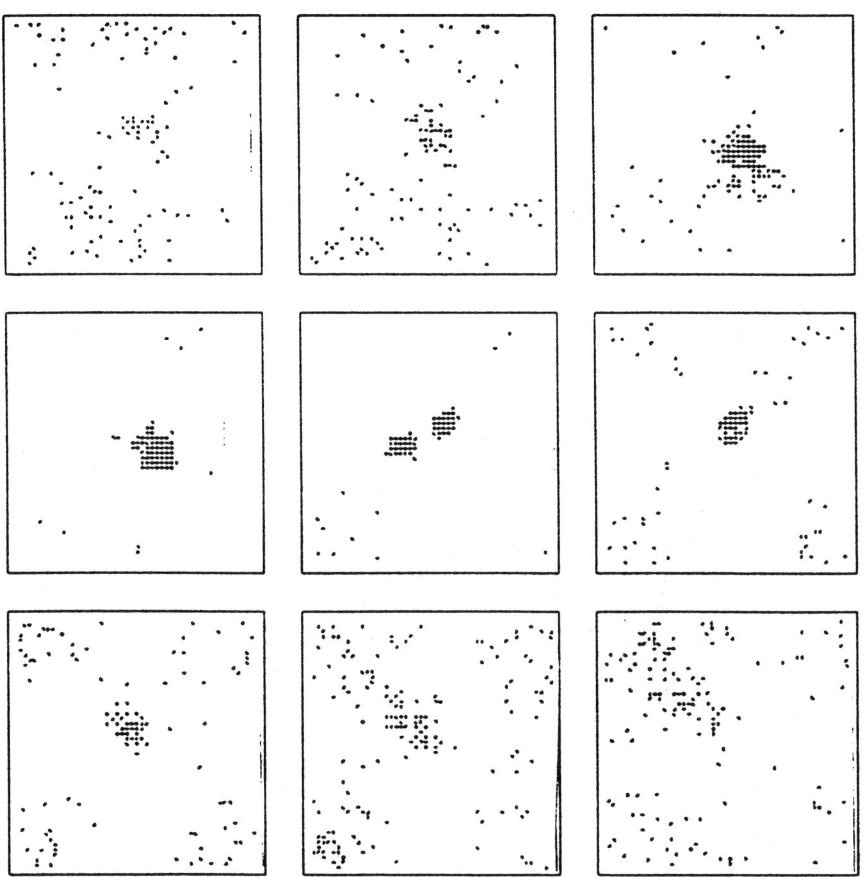

Figure 7: *Reproduction of nine actual screen shots showing the self-assembly and subsequent disintegration of a flock. Notice how the flock is temporarily divided in two.*

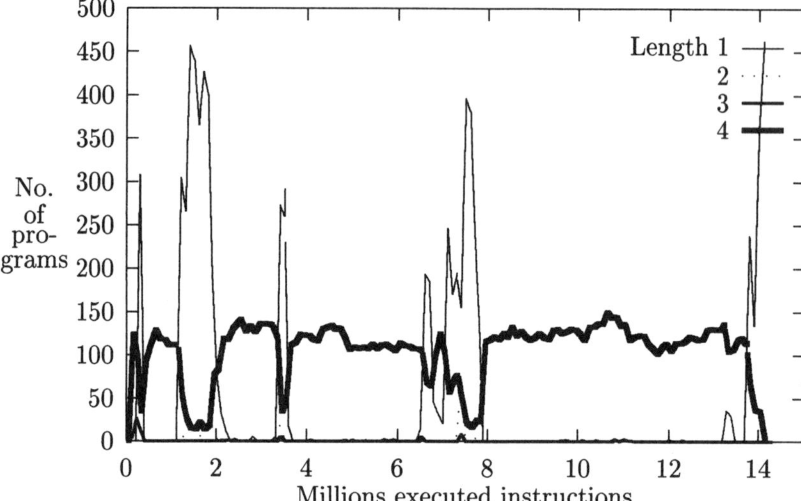

Figure 8: *Punctuated equilibria. The graph shows the number of programs of the lengths 1 to 4 during the run. Notice the sudden and irregular changes between 1-dominance and 4-dominance.*

of code), or dominated by programs of length 1, or in the transition between the two. It is interesting that the transition phases are short with dramatic changes.

As an example, consider the transition that happens around 1 million instructions. 4-length programs rule the world for a while, but suddenly they are almost eradicated by 1-length programs, who then rule the world for another million instructions until they equally suddenly disappear again leaving room for the 4-lengths to return.

This behavior can be explained by the appearance of a new and more competitive group of programs (the 1-lengths). They reproduce much faster, which gives them a competitive advantage. They outgrow the slower 4-lengths and therefore quickly take over the world. But as they are less robust, they tend to die out after a while.

The 1-length programs are most likely parasitic programs described above in section 3.1. They use the code of each other and of the four-cell hosts and are therefore dependent on having a critical mass of useful programs around to survive. If the density of programs drops too low, the community breaks down completely and all the parasites die very quickly. It could happen for example because of random fluctuations in the number of programs, or if they move too far apart from each other on the grid. This gives room for more robust programs carrying all their code around. They grow in numbers and rule the world until the parasites get together again.

Such a sudden takeover may happen many times during a run with irregular intervals.

In the example above, the takeover takes less than 200,000 instructions. The 1-lengths have a reproduction time of about 60 instructions. With a max population size of 450, the takeover happens in the time it takes for the entire population to reproduce about seven times.

In comparison, the 4-lengths have a reproduction time of about 140 instructions and a max population of 125, so this population may reproduce itself about four times in the same period. In other words: they disappear in only four generations.

3.4 Predatory Behavior

The Zoo has shown spurious appearances of predators, but the evolved predators are too unstable to survive for longer periods of time.

In an attempt to measure predatory activity, the Zoo updates a *prey count* for each program. It is reset when the program is born, and incremented every time another program dies executing the code of the first program.

Figure 9 shows the maximum and average prey counts of a run. Notice how the prey counts suddenly increase violently but quickly drop again. This

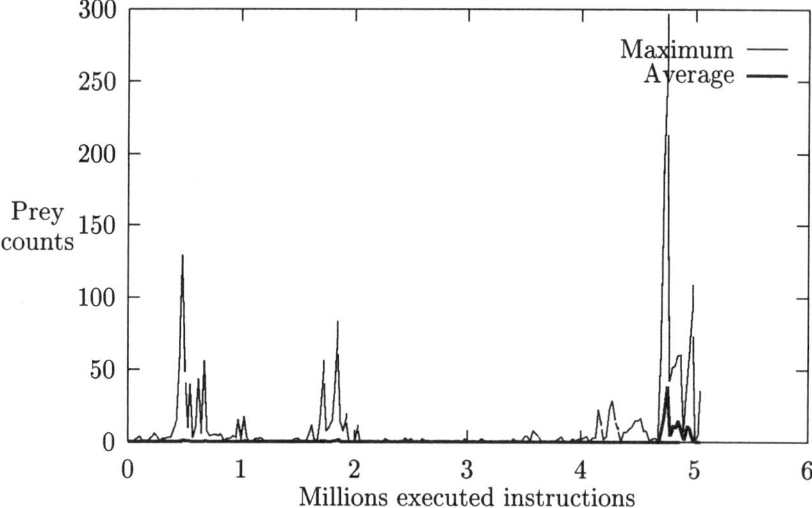

Figure 9: *Prey counts. Graph showing the maximum and average prey counts of the programs in the Zoo.*

suggests that one or more predators occurred, but also that they did not reign the Zoo for very long time. Their sudden death could be because they end up killing themselves, or simply because they run out of prey. Or it could be a program that coincidentally cause other programs to die, but with no evolutionary advantage to itself.

3.5 Increasing Locality

An important buzz-word in artificial life is *local*. As many relations and interactions as possible between players in the artificial world should be local rather than global. But in the Zoo both mortality and memory allocation is handled globally. Therefore I tried to change the environment to be more local.

In the new version, every unallocated memory cell was assigned a position on the grid just like the programs. In other words, when a program dies and releases a couple of memory cells, these cells would be deposited on the spot where the program died, rather than going into a central pool.

In addition the `alloc` instruction was changed so that there had to be an unallocated memory cell within event radius from the program. If not, the `alloc` instruction failed, setting the `flag` register accordingly. This means that a program has move around in search of memory.

The mortality was also changed. Ideally the simulator should never forcibly terminate any program at all. The programs ought to live until they die by themselves or are killed by a predator. I tried that, but it slowed down the evolution too much, so a different strategy was chosen as a compromise. The `alloc` instruction no longer caused the simulator to kill the oldest program. Instead the simulator would now and then insert a `kill` instruction in a random memory cell belonging to a random program.

This new setup ought to be better for predators. When the simulator automatically kills enough programs to supply memory, there is no evolutionary advantage in being a predator. And having all memory handled globally has the consequence that any program may allocate the memory a predator has released from a dead prey. Local memory and the `kill` insertion strategy should therefore evolve more predators.

But that was not the case. The best results concerning predators were done with the original configuration of the environment, despite its expected lack of encouragement for the programs to develop predatory behavior. The reason for this is not understood.

4   Conclusion

The Computer Zoo demonstrates that it is possible to create evolution among computer programs. It is not fair to claim true open-ended evolution since the programs always die out after a while.

But in a sense there is open-ended evolution anyway. The observed evolution has no end point, meaning that no 'optimal' creature that cannot be improved has turned out (so far). The fitness of a given program depends on the other programs in the Zoo at any given time. Therefore the evolution may in principle continue forever.

There are probably many reasons why this does not happen in practice. The death of the programs in the Zoo usually coincides with the appearance of predators or parasites. For some reason they cause the number of programs to drop, and if it reaches zero it will never rise again. It is quite possible that a larger grid with more memory cells and programs would enable the Zoo to live longer.

The concept of remote execution seems to be essential to the evolution. All the results mentioned in the previous section are achieved using remote execution. Thomas Ray's Tierra Simulator does also use what is actually a variation of remote execution. And he has also found symbiosis. His parasite programs are quite similar to our one-cell programs as both kinds use other program's code to reproduce without affecting the host.

The behaviors documented in this article are all phenomena that have biological parallels. But it is quite possible that there are many other odd behaviors in the Zoo with no biological counterpart that cannot be described in simple biological terms like 'parasite' and 'predator'. Unfortunately it is very hard to detect because we do not know what to look for. For further progress with the Zoo it is essential to develop better analysis tools that do more work than just extracting and dumping megabytes of data. What we need is a tool to analyze the interactions between the programs. Given such a tool, I am convinced we could find many more interesting program species.

4.1 Alive or Not

The Computer Zoo is a computerized model of evolution and it shows many interesting characteristics normally found only among living organisms. But how close should a model be before you can say that it is really itself alive?

To answer that, we need a good definition of what we mean with 'alive'. There are many suggestions for a definition, the but there is no consensus on which is the best. Below is a short summary of Carl Sagans[9] thorough treatment of the subject. He sets up five classes of definitions of life.

- *Physiological.* A physiological definition defines a living system as one being able to perform a number of functions like eating, metabolizing, excreting, breathing, moving, growing, reproducing and responding to external stimuli. But there are many counterexamples. For instance can a car be said to eat, metabolize, excrete, breathe, move and respond to external stimuli. And on the other hand there are some bacteria that do not breathe at all.

- *Metabolic.* Under a metabolic definition a living system has a definite boundary and it is continually exchanging material with its surroundings, but without altering its general properties, at least over some period of time. A counterexample of this is a spore. There are examples of seeds and spores that remain dormant for hundreds of years with no metabolic activity, yet may revive one day. Another example is a flame. It has a well defined, fixed boundary and it exchanges oxygen and products of combustion with the surroundings. Yet no one calls a flame alive. Flames also have a well-known capacity for growth.

- *Biochemical.* A biochemical definition sees living organisms as systems that contain reproducible hereditary information coded in nucleic acid molecules and that metabolize by controlling the rate of chemical reactions using proteinaceous catalysts known as enzymes. There are hints of counterexamples to this definition also. Furthermore, a definition strictly in chemical terms rules out beforehand the possibility of live forms based on other media than ours.

- *Genetic.* A genetic definition of life is quite simple: a system capable of evolution by natural selection. This definition places great emphasis on the replication, and it is independent of the particular choice of constituent molecules.

- *Thermodynamic.* A thermodynamic definition sees life as the order that arises spontaneously when energy flows through a system. Most life on earth is dependent on the flow of sunlight, which is utilized by plants to construct complex molecules from simpler ones. The second law of thermodynamics states that the universe as a whole moves toward a state of total disorder. Living systems might then be defined as localized regions where there is a continuous increase in order, at the expense of a larger decrease in the order of the universe outside.

In The Computer Zoo there is evolution and it is based on natural selection (it is not the Computer Zoo simulator itself that decides which programs survive). Therefore it is a true living system according to a genetic definition of life. In other words: *The digital creatures in The Computer Zoo are just as much alive as a zebra.* It is just silicon-based life rather than carbon-based.

Acknowledgements

I would like to thank professor Benny Lautrup from The Niels Bohr Institute for help and inspiration during the entire development process of The Computer Zoo, and also thanks to Thomas Ray for inspiring me to make the Computer Zoo and for critical comments on my early drafts of the system. And finally thanks to Claus Emmeche for many interesting comments on the Zoo from a more philosophical point of view.

References

1. Langton, Christopher G. 1987. *Artificial life: Proceedings of an Interdisciplinary Workshop on the Synthesis and Simulation of Living Systems.* Addison-Wesley, ISBN 0-201-09346-4 and 0-201-09356-1 (pbk.)
2. van Valen, L. 1973. *A new evolutionary law.* Evolutionary Theory 1, pp. 1–30.
3. Rasmussen, Steen, Carsten Knudsen, Rasmus Feldberg, Morten Hindsholm. 1990. *The Coreworld: Emergence and evolution of cooperative structures in a computational chemistry.* Physica D 42, North-Holland, pp. 111–134.
4. Ray, Thomas S. 1991. *An approach to the Synthesis of Artificial Life.* In Artificial Life II, edited by Christopher G. Langton, Charles E. Taylor, J. Doyne Farmer, Steen Rasmussen. Addison-Wesley.
5. Langton, Christopher G. 1990. *Computation at the edge of chaos: Phase transitions and emergent computation.* Physica D 42, North-Holland, pp. 12–37.

6.Skipper, J. 1991. *The Computer Zoo — Evolution in a Box.* Unpublished thesis from The Niels Bohr Institute, Blegdamsvej 17, DK-2100 Copenhagen O, Denmark.

7.Dewdney, A.K. 1984. *Computer recreations: In the game called Core War hostile programs engage in a battle of bits.* Scientific American 250, pp. 14–22.

8.Gould, S.J., N. Eldredge. 1977. *Punctuated equilibria: The tempo and mode of evolution reconsidered.* Paleobiology vol 3,2, pp. 115–151.

9.Sagan, Carl. *Life* Encyclopedia Britannica 15th ed., Macropaedia, Vol. 10.

A   The Czoo instruction set

add, dec, inc, neg, shl, zero, zero?
Arithmetic operations on the current stack top.

alloc
Allocate a new data cell.

copy
Move data from one stack to another.

duplicate
Copy an entire memory cell onto another previously allocated data cell.

forward, turnleft, turnright
Move and turn the program 45 degrees on the two-dimensional grid.

if, ifnot
Jump using conditional jump template if **flag** is set or cleared, respectively.

kill
Commit suicide instantly.

movps, movsp
Move data between the prefix and the stack registers.

nop
No operation.

null
Clear the stack register so that the new current stack is the CPU-stack.

pop, push
Move data between current stack top and prefix register.

prefix-ax, prefix-bx, prefix-cx, prefix-dx
Change the current prefix register to be **ax**, **bx**, **cx**, or **dx**, respectively.

self
Instruction for self inspection.

split
Create a new program from all the data cells owned by a program, and start running it.

stack-ax, stack-bx, stack-cx, stack-dx
Change the current stack register to be **ax**, **bx**, **cx**, or **dx**, respectively.

Exercises

1. The Computer Zoo fulfills the requirements to be called 'living' if we accept a genetic definition of life (section 4.1). What would we have to define to decide if it also fulfills the requirements of a physiological or a metabolic definition? Can the Computer Zoo also be said to be a living system according to those two definitions? Is it a meaningful thing to discuss?

2. The digital creatures in The Computer Zoo can move using the instructions `forward`, `turnleft`, and `turnright`. If we instead had the instructions `north`, `west`, `south`, and `east`, how would that affect the way the creatures move around? Keeping in mind that parasite programs must stay close together, how would this affect creation of parasites?

3. The cell template is calculated by a magic algorithm from the code in the memory cell. When the code changes, so does the template. When resolving a jump, it is allowed to have some bits difference between the jump and the cell template. What happens if this difference is zero? If it is 32?

4. The evolution in The Computer Zoo is open-ended rather than goal oriented, meaning that there is no final goal for the evolution such as an optimal program and no the best answer to a given question. A new run creates new results and new evolved programs, and could in principle run forever.

   Let's imagine that we wanted to use the same principles to evolve useful programs instead of manually writing them. How would you have to create the new Zoo to evolve these programs? Remember to consider the impact of the fact that interactions between programs is a driving factor in the evolution in the Computer Zoo.

AN APPLICATION OF GENETIC PROGRAMMING TO SOFTWARE QUALITY PREDICTION

AUTHORS:
T. M. Khoshgoftaar, M. P. Evett, E. B. Allen, and P.-D. Chien
Empirical Software Engineering Laboratory
Department of Computer Science and Engineering
Florida Atlantic University
777 W. Glades Road
Boca Raton, FL 333431, USA
E-mail: taghi@cse.fau.edu

ABSTRACT:

Because highly reliable software is becoming an essential ingredient in many systems, software developers apply various techniques to discover faults early in development, such as more rigorous reviews, more extensive testing, and strategic assignment of key personnel. Our goal is to target reliability enhancement activities to those modules that are most likely to have problems. This paper presents a methodology that incorporates genetic programming for predicting the order of software modules based on the expected number of faults. This is the first application of genetic programming to software engineering that we know of. We found that genetic programming can be used to generate software quality models whose inputs are software metrics collected earlier in development, and whose output is a prediction of the number of faults that will be discovered later in development or during operations. We established ordinal evaluation criteria for models, and conducted an industrial case study of software from a military communications system. Case study results were sufficiently good to be useful to a project for choosing modules for extra reliability enhancement treatment.

KEYWORDS: genetic programming, evolutionary computation, software quality, software reliability, fault-prone modules, software metrics, software engineering

AN APPLICATION OF GENETIC PROGRAMMING
TO SOFTWARE QUALITY PREDICTION

T.M. KHOSHGOFTAAR, M.P. EVETT, E.B. ALLEN, P.-D. CHIEN
Empirical Software Engineering Laboratory
Department of Computer Science and Engineering
Florida Atlantic University
Boca Raton, FL 33431 USA
E-mail: taghi@cse.fau.edu

Because highly reliable software is becoming an essential ingredient in many systems, software developers apply various techniques to discover faults early in development, such as more rigorous reviews, more extensive testing, and strategic assignment of key personnel. Our goal is to target reliability enhancement activities to those modules that are most likely to have problems. This paper presents a methodology that incorporates genetic programming for predicting the order of software modules based on the expected number of faults. This is the first application of genetic programming to software engineering that we know of. We found that genetic programming can be used to generate software quality models whose inputs are software metrics collected earlier in development, and whose output is a prediction of the number of faults that will be discovered later in development or during operations. We established ordinal evaluation criteria for models, and conducted an industrial case study of software from a military communications system. Case study results were sufficiently good to be useful to a project for choosing modules for extra reliability enhancement treatment.

1   Introduction

Highly reliable software is becoming an essential ingredient in many systems. Public safety and the fabric of modern life depend on software-intensive systems. We can ill afford for important systems to fail due to inadequate software reliability.

Correcting software faults late in the development life cycle is often very expensive. Consequently, software developers apply various techniques to discover faults early in development.[1] Reliability improvement techniques include more rigorous design and code reviews, automatic test case generation to support more extensive testing, and strategic assignment of key personnel.

Our goal is to target reliability enhancement activities to those modules that are most likely to have problems. Prior research has shown that software product and process metrics[2] collected early in the software development life cycle can be the basis for reliability predictions.[3,4,5,6,7,8,9,10,11] Predicting the exact number of faults in each module is often not necessary; previous research has focused on classification models to identify *fault-prone* and *not fault-prone* modules.[12,13,14,15,16] However, such models require that *fault-prone* be defined before modeling, usually via a threshold on the number of faults expected, and software development managers often do not know an appropriate threshold at the time of modeling. In such cases, a prediction of the rank-order of modules, from the least to the most fault-prone, is more useful.[17,18] With a predicted rank-order in hand, one can select as many from the top of the list for reliability enhancement as resources will allow.

This study presents a methodology for producing models that predict the number of faults expected in each module, but we use the prediction only to order the modules. Our evaluation of a model is based on ordinal criteria, rather than the amount of error in the predicted number of faults. In the context of reliability enhancement strategies, the accuracy of predictions of numbers of faults is only indirectly relevant to decisions to target fault-prone modules for reliability enhancement treatments, such as extra reviews, or more intense testing. In this context, it is sufficient to rank the most fault-prone modules. We present an industrial case study to illustrate our methodology.

Genetic programming, abbreviated GP for remainder of this paper, is a type of machine learning — a technique for autonomously determining a solution to a given problem. For example, artificial neural networks, a machine learning paradigm, learn patterns from a set of training data.[19] (Carbonell gives an overview of the machine learning literature.[20]) More particularly, GP is an adaptive search technique, examining a space of potential solutions for good solutions, where "good" can have many meanings, including optimal, near-optimal, etc. In this study, the problem to be solved is to find a model that accurately predicts the rank-order of modules according to the number of faults that will be discovered later in the life cycle. A potential solution is a function mapping modules to numbers which are the basis for ordering the modules. The space of all such functions is often infinite or extremely large. The task of an adaptive search technique is to navigate through that space, examining only a tiny fraction of it, yet still discovering a model in that space that provides acceptable performance.

GP is a member of the *evolutionary computation* family of adaptive search techniques, whose defining characteristic is an adaptation mechanism loosely based upon neo-Darwinian natural selection. GP is closely related to *genetic algorithms*.[21,22] Although genetic algorithms have been applied to software testing and software quality modeling for several years,[23,24,25] this study is the first application of GP to software engineering that we know of.

The following sections present background on GP, our software quality modeling methodology,[26] an ordinal approach to model evaluation, specification of the GP system used in the case study, case study results, and conclusions. Because this study only introduces the application of GP to software engineering, there are many opportunities for future research.

2 Genetic Programming

A GP system, like other evolutionary computation systems, consists of several basic components.[a]

1. A *population* is a set of potential solutions to the given problem.

2. An *individual* is an element of the population, a potential solution. Each evolutionary computation technique uses its own representation of individuals. In genetic algorithms, each individual is a genotype, such as a "chromosome" (usually a binary string), that uniquely describes a function or program, its phenotype. In GP, each individual is an actual program, and thus, the genotype and phenotype are equivalent. In this study, an individual is a program whose inputs are a software module's set of software product measurements and whose output is a prediction of the number of faults that will be discovered later.

3. A *fitness function* objectively measures the quality of an individual. This is usually a function mapping each individual to a numeric value. This function is not constrained to any particular mathematical form. The value of the fitness function for an individual is referred to as its *fitness*.

   An important type of fitness function is one that measures an individual's performance against desired performance represented by an *objective function* or *oracle*.[b] The fitness function used in this study is presented in Section 3.3.

2.1 Overview of the Algorithm

The similarity of GP to natural selection and evolution derives from how it manipulates its population. This process generally consists of the following steps.

1. *Creation of initial population* — Generate the initial population via a random process.

2. *Evaluation* — Apply the fitness function to every individual, obtaining the *fitness* of each.

3. *Termination test* — Determine whether the GP process should halt. The termination criterion includes the detection of any individual that completely solves the given problem. In addition, because there is usually no guarantee that such an individual will be found within an acceptable

---

[a]The terminology of GP is meant to reflect its natural systems roots.
[b]The term "oracle" is borrowed from computational theory.

amount of time, or that one even exists, the GP process also terminates after some predefined number of iterations, to prevent infinite looping or arbitrarily long execution.

4. *Selection* — Select a subset of the current population as the basis for a new population. In general, one chooses those individuals with good fitness relative to others in the population. The specific methods used in this study are presented in Section 2.2.

5. *Population redefinition* — Create a new population via a set of *genetic operations*. In this study, each member of the new population is created by one of the following operations. Each method is used to create a section of the population.

   - *Reproduction*: Selected individuals are copied directly into the new population without modification. (This is also called *Darwinian reproduction*.)

   - *Sexual recombination*: The selection step chooses a subset of the population for membership in a *mating pool, M*. Two or more individuals of the mating pool, called *parents*, are randomly selected, and then integrated in some way to form new individuals, called *offspring*, that usually differ from their parents. The most common type of sexual recombination in GP is *cross-over* based on two parents.

   - *Mutation*: Each selected individual is altered randomly, and then put in the new population

6. Loop back to Step 2.

Each loop through the GP process is called a *generation*. The entire set of iterations from population initialization to termination is called a *run*. At termination, the result of the GP process is the *best-of-run* individual.

Under the right circumstances, the mating pool will tend to consist of better and better individuals, over successive generations. These circumstances are not completely understood, but the fitness function is particularly important, as is the property that the merging of two high-value individuals is more likely to yield another high-value individual than is the merging of two random individuals. Consequently, the population as a whole tends to maximize its value over successive generations, i.e., the average fitness value increases. If all goes well, a GP system will yield an individual which solves or nearly solves the given problem.

In general (and this is a very broad generalization), GP systems tend to perform better as population size increases, and to a lesser extent, as run size (i.e., the number of generations), increases. Like neural networks and other machine learning paradigms, GP systems don't necessarily converge, i.e. find a solution; they may get stuck in a local maximum. Runs provide a rather crude mechanism for dealing with such situations. Generally, a GP experiment completes several runs, recording the best solutions found during each run. The population usually is reinitialized with each run.

2.2 Details

There is insufficient space to fully describe the GP process. More detail can be found elsewhere.[27,22,28,29] A brief explanation of some elements of the technique are in order however.

Individuals. The individuals of a GP system are programs. Consequently, it is necessary to be able to randomly generate programs during the population initialization phase and to create novel programs for new generations, via sexual recombination and mutation. All the generated programs must be "correct" in the sense that they compile and execute. Also, no program execution should yield infinite looping, otherwise the GP system might never complete fitness evaluation.

GP satisfies these restrictions by representing each program as an *s-expression*,[c] which is a tree structure for which the internal nodes are operators or functions of as many arguments as the nodes have children, and the leaves are constants, variables, or functions of zero arguments.

Evaluation. An s-expression is executed by evaluating the nodes of the tree in a left-to-right postorder traversal, providing the value of a node as an argument to its parent node in the tree, and returning the value of the root node as the value of the s-expression. Figure 1 shows two s-expressions. The evaluation of the left s-expression would proceed as follows.

1. The "2" node represents the constant value 2, and so the evaluation of that node is 2.

2. The "x" node is a variable, representing an independent variable of the problem space. In this context, that variable has a numeric value. For this example, let x evaluate to 6.

3. The "×" node represents the multiplication operation, and evaluates to the product of the values returned by its children (2 from step 1 and 6 from step 2), 12.

---

[c] "S-expression" is a term taken from the LISP programming language. Indeed, the original implementation of GP was in LISP.[22] Although most current GP research uses C or C++ implementations, those systems still encode individuals as s-expressions.

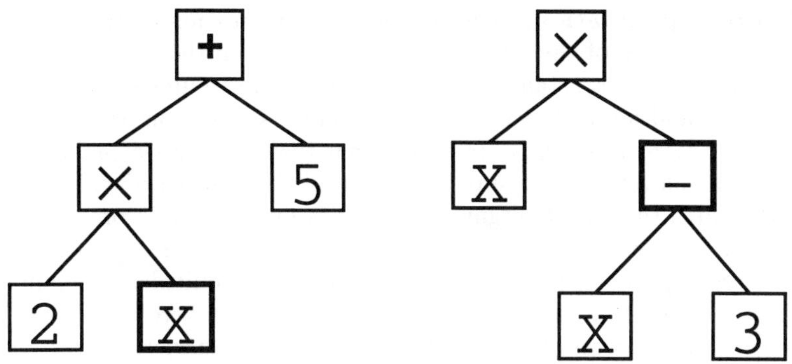

Each tree is an s-expression representing a program of one independent variable. The left represents $(2 \times x) + 5$ and the right represents $x \times (x - 3)$.

Figure 1: S-expression examples

4. The "5" node represents the constant value 5, and so the evaluation of that node is 5.

5. The "+" node represents arithmetic addition, so its evaluation yields the sum of the values of its two children nodes (12 from step 3 and 5 from step 4), 17.

The s-expressions of Figure 1 represent functions of a single independent variable, x. In many applications of GP, such as that reported here, calculation of the fitness function for an individual may involve evaluation of its s-expression over many *observations*, the set $\mathcal{O}$, each of which will provide its own values for the independent variables. For Figure 1, each observation typically would provide a different value for x.

Raw fitness, f_{raw}, is defined as a function of the results of the evaluation of the s-expression over the elements of $\mathcal{O}$. We define *standardized fitness*, f_{std}, as a transformation of raw fitness such that smaller values are better.[28] Adjusted fitness, f_{adj}, is a transformation of standardized fitness such that $f_{adj}(i)$ for individual i has a value in $[0, 1]$, where 1 corresponds to a perfect solution to the problem.

$$f_{adj}(i) = \frac{1}{1 + f_{std}(i)} \tag{1}$$

The adjusted fitness function is the basis for the Evaluation step in the GP algorithm. The fitness value is usually stored with the corresponding individual, and the population is sorted by these values to increase the efficiency of later steps.

Creation of a population. During the random creation of the first generation, the identities of the leaf nodes are chosen from the *terminal set*, $\mathcal{T}$, consisting of variables, constants, and functions with no arguments, while those of the internal nodes are chosen from the *function set*, $\mathcal{F}$, consisting of functions of one or more arguments. To ensure that the resulting s-expressions are executable, the data types of the return values of the children of each internal node must match those of its arguments. This is most easily accomplished by ensuring that all elements of the terminal and function sets evaluate to the same data type (such as real numbers) — i.e., by using equivalent domain and range spaces — and that is the case in the work reported here.[d]

The generative process can be implemented in various ways to create random trees of different sizes and shapes. The *full-tree* method generates only full trees, for which the length of every non-back-tracking path between a terminal node and the root is equal to the maximum depth. The *grow* method selects any member of $\mathcal{T}$ or $\mathcal{F}$ for the root, then recursively generates children from $\mathcal{T}$ or $\mathcal{F}$ for randomly selected function nodes that are leaves. This study uses a mixture of the full-tree method and the grow method. Other methods are discussed in the literature.[22]

Selection. The purpose of selection is to choose a set of individuals, $\mathcal{M}$, from the population for genetic operators to process. This study used the following selection methods.

The *fitness-proportionate* method randomly selects an individual with probability based on the proportion of the total adjusted fitness of the population accounted for by that individual's adjusted fitness. In particular, the probability of selection, $\Pr(i)$, for a particular individual i is given by

$$\Pr(i) = \frac{f_{adj}(i)}{\sum_j f_{adj}(j)} \, , i \in \mathcal{M} \tag{2}$$

where $\sum_j f_{adj}(j)$ is the total population fitness. Consequently, an individual with a larger portion of the overall fitness has a better chance of being selected.

The *tournament* selection method chooses a small set of candidate individuals, $\mathcal{C}$, according to a uniform random distribution, to participate in a "tournament". The individual with the highest fitness from among the tournament participants is selected.

$$i \in \mathcal{M} \text{ such that } f_{adj}(i) = \max_{k \in \mathcal{C}} f_{adj}(k) \tag{3}$$

This procedure is repeated for each selection. Our system uses the same tournament size, $n_t = 7$ as Koza.[28]

---

[d]Some GP systems use heterogeneous data types, based Montana's strongly typed GP.[30]

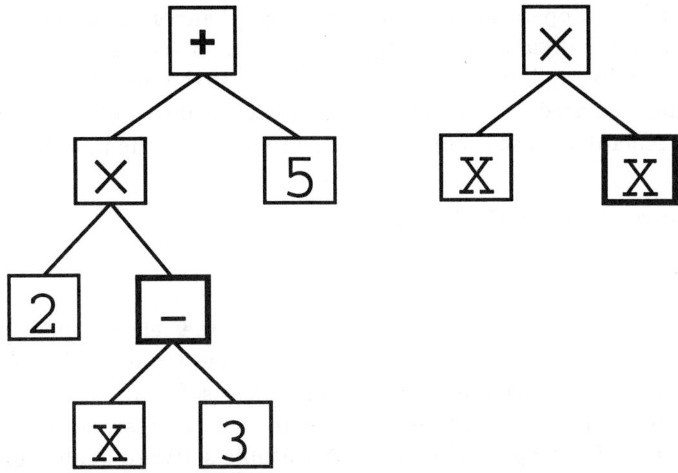

The s-expressions resulting from cross-over applied at the cross-over points indicated by the bold boxes in Figure 1. The left s-expression represents $(2 \times (x - 3)) + 5$ and the right represents $x \times x$.

Figure 2: Example result of cross-over

Population redefinition. For each member of the new population, a genetic operation is chosen according to a probability distribution: the probability of reproduction, p_r, the probability of cross-over, p_c, and the probability of mutation, p_m, where $p_r + p_c + p_m = 1$. Genetic operations are the mechanism for creating a new population based on selected individuals from the current population. Each type of genetic operation may have a different selection method.

The *reproduction* operator copies a selected individual's tree structure, without alteration, into the new population.

Cross-over is the main operator in genetic programming for improving the overall fitness of the population. Our GP system uses a simple binary *cross-over* operator to effect sexual recombination. Cross-over is applied to two individuals from the mating pool, $\mathcal{M}$. A node is randomly selected in each such individual as the *cross-over point* of each. As an example, let the s-expressions in Figure 1 be the two individuals, and let the bold node in each indicate the cross-over points. Cross-over is accomplished by swapping the subtrees headed by the cross-over points, resulting in two new s-expressions. Figure 2 shows the results of the cross-over. Provided that the data types of the cross-over point nodes are the same (which is, perforce, the case with a homogeneously typed system like ours), cross-over will yield compilable, executable programs.

The *mutation* operator introduces random changes to individuals in the population. An individual is selected by applying a selection method, and a mutation point is randomly chosen. The subtree at the mutation point is then removed and replaced with a randomly generated subtree at that point. The subtree is generated in the same manner as the trees in the initial population.

3 Software Quality Modeling

3.1 Methodology

Our goal is to develop a model that will predict the relative quality of each module, in particular, their order according to the number of faults. Most quality factors are directly measurable only after software has become operational. The number of faults is no different. In contrast, software metrics can be measured during development. A suitable software quality model can make predictions when it is not too late to take compensatory actions, such as reliability enhancement activities.

An *observation* is a software module represented by a tuple of software measurements, $\mathbf{x}_j$. The dependent variable of a model is the number of faults, $F(j)$, for observation j. The s-expressions resulting from a GP system are *models*. Let $\widehat{F}_i(\mathbf{x}_j)$ be the estimate of $F(j)$ by model i. We develop software quality models based on data from a completed past project where measurements and the number of faults are available for each module, using the following methodology.

1. Impartially split the available data into *training* and *validation* data sets.

2. Make multiple runs.

   (a) Train a GP system using the *training* data set to yield a best model for each run, as defined below.

   (b) Use each best-of-run model to predict the number of faults in the *validation* modules, and order them accordingly. Make multiple runs.

   (c) Evaluate each best-of-run model using ordinal criteria.

3. Summarize the model evaluations over the runs.

Comparison to a random ordering indicates whether the GP result is really different from a random ordering result. Moreover, a random ordering emulates the development strategy that takes random samples for extra reviews or other reliability enhancement treatments. Comparison to the actual ordering indicates how close the model is to a perfect model.

3.2 Ordinal Evaluation

An individual is a model that predicts the number of faults in a software module, given a set of software product measurements. Because we do not expect perfect accuracy in Step 2c of our modeling methodology, we evaluate a model's usefulness by its ability to approximately order modules from the most fault-prone to the least fault-prone.

According to Pareto's Law applied to software engineering, 20% of the modules will typically account for about 80% of the faults. These proportions were true for our case study, where more than 70% of the modules had zero or only one fault. The purpose of the model should be to identify the top 20% of the fault-prone modules. Moreover, resources may be limited for reliability enhancement treatments. Thus, in this study, a manager will probably be interested in reviewing less than 25% of the modules. In this context, let $\mathcal{C}$ be management's preferred set of cutoff percentiles of modules ranked by faults, and let n_c be the number of percentiles in $\mathcal{C}$. In these terms, Pareto's Law implies that the modules above the 80th percentile (i.e., the top 20% of the modules) have 80% of the faults. In the case study, we chose 90, 85, 80, and 75 percentiles. Another project might choose different percentiles, but this set illustrates our methodology.

Let G_{tot} be the total number of actual faults in the validation data set's software modules. The following is our ordinal evaluation procedure used in Step 2c for each model. Given an individual, i, and a validation data set indexed by j:

1. Determine the perfect ranking of modules, $\mathbf{R}$, by ordering modules according to $F(j)$. Let $R(j)$ be the percentile rank of observation j.

2. Construct a random ranking of the modules, $\mathbf{R'}$. Let $R'(j)$ be the percentile rank of observation j.

3. Determine the predicted ranking, $\widehat{\mathbf{R}}_i$, by ordering modules according to $\widehat{F}_i(\mathbf{x}_j)$. Let $\widehat{R}_i(j)$ be the percentile rank of observation j.

4. For each cutoff percentile value of interest, $c \in \mathcal{C}$:

   (a) Calculate the sum of actual faults, G_c, in modules above the cutoff for $\mathbf{R}$.

   $$G_c = \sum_{j:R(j) \geq c} F(j) \qquad (4)$$

   (b) Calculate the sum of actual faults, G'_c, in modules above the cutoff for $\mathbf{R'}$.

   $$G'_c = \sum_{j:R'(j) \geq c} F(j) \qquad (5)$$

(c) Calculate the sum of actual faults in modules above the cutoff, $\widehat{G}_c(i)$, for $\widehat{\mathbf{R}}_i$.

$$\widehat{G}_c(i) = \sum_{j:\widehat{R}_i(j)\geq c} F(j) \tag{6}$$

5. Calculate the percentage of faults accounted for by each ranking, namely, G_c/G_{tot}, G'_c/G_{tot}, and $\widehat{G}_c(i)/G_{tot}$.

6. Calculate how closely the faults accounted for by the random and model rankings match those of the perfect ranking as ratios, G'_c/G_c and $\widehat{G}_c(i)/G_c$. Let

$$\phi_c(i) = \frac{\widehat{G}_c(i)}{G_c} \tag{7}$$

The percentage of all faults gives us insight into the importance of this percentile level. The percentage of the actual faults, $\phi_c(i)$, for a percentile level c, indicates the accuracy of the ranking.

3.3 A Genetic Programming Model

This section specifies the GP system used by this study. Much of the terminology is explained in Section 2.

S-expressions. The set of primitive functions consists of

$$\mathcal{F} = \{+, -, \times, /, \sin, \cos, \exp', \log\} \tag{8}$$

where $\exp'(x) = \exp(\sqrt{x})$ to lessen the risk of arithmetic overflow. Divide ($/$), modified exponentiation ($\exp'$), and natural logarithm ($\log$), are protected from invalid inputs. The set of terminals, $\mathcal{T}$, consists of the available software product metric variables and an ephemeral random constant generator function.

The maximum depth of an s-expression tree is limited to 17 levels, adapted from Koza.[22] Without such a limit, the s-expression could grow indefinitely.

Initial population. We use the *half-and-half* method, where 50% of individuals are created using the *full-tree* method, and 50% are created using the *grow* method. The *population size* is constant at 2,000 individuals.

Fitness function. The fitness function is applied to each individual in each generation. In some GP system, the fitness of an individual can be influenced by that of its ancestors, but here it is not. Thus, we omit the generation of an individual from our notation.

Raw fitness of individual i is defined as a logarithmic/exponential function of the absolute errors in predictions of faults.

$$f_{raw}(i) = \log \left(\sum_{j \in \mathcal{O}} \exp |(\widehat{F}_i(\mathbf{x}_j) - F(j))| \right) \tag{9}$$

where j is an index over all observations, $\mathcal{O}$, in the training data set. This functional form is a starting point for further research. Because our goal is to minimize error, we let *standardized fitness* simply be equal to raw fitness

$$f_{std}(i) = f_{raw}(i) \tag{10}$$

Recall that adjusted fitness has a value in $[0, 1]$, where 1 is the best, and is defined per Eq. 1 as

$$f_{adj}(i) = \frac{1}{1 + f_{std}(i)} \tag{11}$$

This f_{adj} is the fitness function used in our GP system.

Run termination criterion. A run is terminated if an individual i with $f_{adj}(i) = 1$ is encountered, a "perfect" solution to the problem, or when the maximum number of generations is reached. The maximum number of generations is 50, which is typical of GP systems.[22]

Selection and population redefinition. The probability of cross-over is $p_c = 0.90$. The probability of reproduction is $p_r = 0.09$. The probability of mutation is $p_m = 0.01$. These values are typical of GP systems.[22]

Reproduction. The *fitness-proportionate* method is used to select candidates for reproduction.

Cross-over. The *tournament* selection method is used to choose each parent for cross-over. The tournament size is $n_t = 7$ individuals.[28] One cross-over node in each parent's s-expression is independently chosen using a uniform probability distribution. If cross-over creates an offspring that violates the maximum depth of tree parameter, the result is discarded and new cross-over points are chosen until a pair of valid offspring are produced.

Mutation. The *fitness-proportionate* method is used to select candidates for mutation. A mutation point is randomly chosen. When mutation produces a tree that violates the maximum depth of tree parameter, the result is discarded and the mutation process is repeated with the same parent until a valid offspring is produced.

Best-of-run identification. We use a modification of Ryan's Pygmy technique [31] to limit the effects of overfitting in our system.[e] This entails using a function different from our fitness function to select the individual returned as the result of the GP system. The GP system keeps a record during each run of the *best-so-far* individual, i_{bsf}, according to the fitness function. Recall that we evaluate models based on the percentage of actual faults, $\phi_c(i)$, in the validation data set. Let

$$g(i) = \frac{1}{n_c} \sum_{k \in \mathcal{C}} \phi_k(i) \tag{12}$$

where $\phi_k(i)$ is as defined in Eq. eq:phi but calculated using the training data set. This give equal emphasis to each cutoff percentile of interest. The GP system also keeps a record during each run of the individual with the best value of $g(i)$ so far, i_g. Whenever a new best-so-far, i_{bsf}, is identified, if $g(i_{bsf}) > g(i_g)$, we let $i_g = i_{bsf}$.

We define the *best-of-run* individual as the best-so-far individual with the best percentage of actual faults, averaged over the percentile levels of interest.

$$i_{bor} \text{ such that } \phi_{bor} = g(i_{bor}) = \max_i g(i) \tag{13}$$

4 Case Study

4.1 System Description

The Command and Control Communications System, CCCS, was a large military data communications system written in Ada. Generally, a module was an Ada package, consisting of one or more procedures. The developers had collected software product metrics from the source code of each module. Practical constraints limited the number and selection of metrics. Table 1 lists the software metrics used in this study. Another project might have a different set.[32] Our purpose is to present a methodology that can be adapted to a variety of projects.

We randomly selected 282 modules for our experiment. Applying data splitting, we impartially partitioned this data into two subsets, two thirds of the modules (188) for training the GP system, and the remaining third (94 modules) for validating the predictive accuracy of the best model from each run. The top 20% of the modules contained 82.2% of the faults.

4.2 Empirical Results

We ran the GP system specified above for multiple runs, using all the observations in the training data set as input. The set of *software quality models*

---

[e]Ryan[31] uses the technique to limit population convergence.

Table 1: Software Product Metrics

Symbol	Description
η_1	Number of unique operators [33]
N_1	Total number of operators [33]
η_2	Number of unique operands [33]
N_2	Total number of operands [33]
$V(G)$	McCabe's cyclomatic complexity [34]
$V_2(G)$	Extended cyclomatic complexity
	$V_2(G) = V(G) +$ number of logical operators
LOC	Lines of code
$ELOC$	Executable lines of code

consisted of the *best-of-run* individuals from each run.

For each model, we ranked the observations in the validation data set by the actual number of faults, $F(j)$, to create the list, **R**. We randomly ordered the observations in the validation data set to form the ranking, **R'**. We used each software quality model to predict the number of faults, $\hat{F}_i(\mathbf{x}_j)$, for each module, j, in the validation data set, and then we ordered the modules by predicted faults, forming a ranking, $\widehat{\mathbf{R}}_i$.

We evaluated the rankings at cutoff percentile values of 75%, 80%, 85%, and 90%. If a run did not achieve a minimally satisfactory best-of-run percentage of actual faults, $\phi_{bor} \geq \phi_0$, over the training data set, then it was not included in the analysis below. The threshold was $\phi_0 = 0.70$, which is somewhat less than the accuracy implied by Pareto's Law. We made 30 runs of the GP system, of which 5 were unsatisfactory over the training data set. The evaluation below is based on the 25 satisfactory models applied to the validation data set. Table 2 is a statistical summary over the 25 models of the percentage of actual faults at each percentile level, $\phi_c(i)$, calculated over the validation data set. Table 3 shows the more detailed evaluation results averaged over the 25 models.

The first section of Table 3 shows the averaged sum of faults for each range of percentiles of fault-prone modules. The second section of the table shows the corresponding number from the first section divided by the total number of faults in all modules, G_{tot}. In each of the percentile ranges studied, the model is much closer to the actual proportion of faults than the random selection ordering. Thus, we conclude that the model is much better than a random sampling strategy. The third section of the table shows $\phi_c(i)$ averaged over the best-of-run models, namely, the corresponding number from the first section divided by the actual number of faults, G_c, on its row. The average percent of actuals, $\widehat{G}_c/G_c$, was almost 85% of a perfect model for the 75, 80,

Table 2: Statistical Summary

$\phi_c(i)$ for best-of-run models

Rank $\geq$ %-ile c	Median	Mean	Std Dev
90	82.89%	79.42%	8.18%
85	85.08%	84.82%	9.65%
80	86.87%	84.75%	9.27%
75	87.32%	85.74%	5.72%

Summarized over 25 runs

Validation data set

Table 3: Average Model Results

Rank $\geq$ %-ile c	Ranking		
	Actual	Random	Model
	Faults, $\overline{G_*}$		
	G_c	G'_c	$\overline{\widehat{G}_c}$
90	152	23	120.6
85	181	37	153.52
80	198	47	167.81
75	213	60	182.63
	% of Faults, $\overline{G_*}/G_{tot}$		
90	63.07%	9.65%	50.07%
85	75.10%	15.43%	63.70%
80	82.16%	19.63%	69.63%
75	88.38%	25.01%	75.78%
	% of Actual, $\overline{G_*}/G_c$		
90	100%	15.30%	79.42%
85	100%	20.54%	84.82%
80	100%	23.89%	84.75%
75	100%	28.29%	85.74%

Averaged over 25 runs

Validation data set

$$G_{tot} = 241$$

and 85 percentile ranges, and almost 80% for the 90 percentile range. This indicated how closely the averaged sum of predictions for a range of percentiles approaches perfection.

5 Conclusions

This study is the first that we know of to apply genetic programming to software engineering. In particular, GP can be used to generate software quality models whose inputs are software metrics collected earlier in development, and whose output is a prediction of the number of faults that will be discovered later in development or during operations.

We established ordinal evaluation criteria, rather than the amount of error, for the models produced by the GP system. This is especially appropriate for targeting reliability enhancement activities to the most fault-prone modules.

We conducted an industrial case study of software from a military communications system. The GP system used a conventional terminal set, function set, and fitness function.[28] Case study results were sufficiently good to be useful to a project for choosing modules for extra reliability enhancement treatment.

Future work may include the following research topics.

- Predict the number of faults, for comparison to statistical models[35] and neural network models.[36,37]

- Experiment with other fitness functions that more closely reflect ordinal evaluation criteria for software engineering.

- Experiment with two consecutive releases to validate model results, instead of using data splitting.

Acknowledgments

This work was supported in part by a grant from Nortel. The findings and opinions in this study belong solely to the authors, and are not necessarily those of the sponsor. We thank Douglas Zongker, Bill Punch, and Bill Rand of Michigan State University for implementing the lil-gp system, which formed the kernel of our GP system.

References

1. John P. Hudepohl, Stephen J. Aud, Taghi M. Khoshgoftaar, Edward B. Allen, and Jean Mayrand. EMERALD: Software metrics and models on the desktop. *IEEE Software*, 13(5):56–60, September 1996.

2. Norman E. Fenton and Shari Lawrence Pfleeger. *Software Metrics: A Rigorous and Practical Approach*. PWS Publishing, London, 2d edition, 1997.

3. John C. Munson and Taghi M. Khoshgoftaar. Software metrics for reliability assessment. In Michael Lyu, editor, *Handbook of Software Reliability Engineering*, chapter 12, pages 493–529. McGraw-Hill, New York, 1996.

4. Taghi M. Khoshgoftaar and Edward B. Allen. Predicting faults from an information theory based software metric. In Hoang Pham, editor, *Proceedings of the Second ISSAT International Conference on Reliability and Quality in Design*, pages 210–214, Orlando, FL, March 1995. International Society of Science and Applied Technologies.

5. Taghi M. Khoshgoftaar and Edward B. Allen. An information theoretic approach to predicting software faults. *International Journal of Reliability, Quality and Safety Engineering*, 5, 1998. Forthcoming.

6. Taghi M. Khoshgoftaar, Edward B. Allen, Kalai S. Kalaichelvan, and Nishith Goel. The impact of software evolution and reuse on software quality. *Empirical Software Engineering: An International Journal*, 1(1):31–44, 1996.

7. Taghi M. Khoshgoftaar and John C. Munson. Predicting software development errors using software complexity metrics. *IEEE Journal on Selected Areas in Communications*, 8(2):253–261, February 1990.

8. Taghi M. Khoshgoftaar and Paul Oman. Software metrics: Charting the course. *Computer*, 27(9):13–15, September 1994. Guest editors of special issue on software metrics.

9. David L. Lanning and Taghi M. Khoshgoftaar. The impact of software enhancement on software reliability. *IEEE Transactions on Reliability*, 44(4):677–682, December 1995.

10. Robert M. Szabo and Taghi M. Khoshgoftaar. An assessment of software quality in a c++ environment. In *Proceedings of the Sixth International Symposium on Software Reliability Engineering*, pages 240–249, Toulouse, France, October 1995. IEEE Computer Society.

11. Taghi M. Khoshgoftaar, K. Ganesan, Edward B. Allen, Fletcher D. Ross, Rama Munikoti, Nishith Goel, and Amit Nandi. Predicting fault-prone modules with case-based reasoning. In *Proceedings of the Eighth International Symposium on Software Reliability Engineering*, pages 27–35, Albuquerque, NM USA, November 1997. IEEE Computer Society.

12. Taghi M. Khoshgoftaar and Edward B. Allen. The impact of costs of misclassification on software quality modeling. In *Proceedings of the Fourth International Software Metrics Symposium*, pages 54–62, Albuquerque, NM USA, November 1997. IEEE Computer Society.

13. Taghi M. Khoshgoftaar, Edward B. Allen, Nishith Goel, Amit Nandi, and John McMullan. Detection of software modules with high debug code churn in a very large legacy system. In *Proceedings of the Seventh International Symposium on Software Reliability Engineering*, pages 364–371, White Plains, NY, October 1996. IEEE Computer Society.

14. Taghi M. Khoshgoftaar, Edward B. Allen, Kalai S. Kalaichelvan, and Nishith Goel. Early quality prediction: A case study in telecommunications. *IEEE Software*, 13(1):65–71, January 1996.

15. Taghi M. Khoshgoftaar, David L. Lanning, and Abhijit S. Pandya. A comparative study of pattern recognition techniques for quality evaluation of telecommunications software. *IEEE Journal on Selected Areas in Communications*, 12(2):279–291, February 1994.

16. John C. Munson and Taghi M. Khoshgoftaar. The detection of fault-prone programs. *IEEE Transactions on Software Engineering*, 18(5):423–433, May 1992.

17. Taghi M. Khoshgoftaar, John C. Munson, and David L. Lanning. Alternative approaches for the use of metrics to order programs by complexity. *Journal of Systems and Software*, 24(3):211–221, March 1994.

18. Niclas Ohlsson and Hans Alberg. Predicting fault-prone software modules in telephone switches. *IEEE Transactions on Software Engineering*, 22(12):886–894, December 1996.

19. Taghi M. Khoshgoftaar, Edward B. Allen, John P. Hudepohl, and Stephen J. Aud. Applications of neural networks to software quality modeling of a very large telecommunications system. *Transactions on Neural Networks*, 8(4):902–909, July 1997.

20. J. Carbonell, editor. *Machine Learning, Paradigms and Methods*. MIT Press, Cambridge, MA, 1990.

21. J. Holland. *Adaptation in Natural and Artificial Systems*. University of Michigan Press, Ann Arbor, MI, 1975.

22. John R. Koza. *Genetic Programming: On the Programming of Computers by Means of Natural Selection*. MIT Press, Cambridge, MA, 1992.

23. Robert Hochman, Taghi M. Khoshgoftaar, Edward B. Allen, and John P. Hudepohl. Using the genetic algorithm to build optimal neural networks for fault-prone module detection. In *Proceedings of the Seventh International Symposium on Software Reliability Engineering*, pages 152–162, White Plains, NY, October 1996. IEEE Computer Society.

24. B. F. Jones, H.-H. Sthamer, and D. E. Eyres. Automatic structural testing using genetic algorithms. *Software Engineering Journal*, 12(5), May 1995.

25. Marc Roper. Computer aided software testing using genetic algorithms. In *Conference Proceedings of the Tenth International Software Quality Week*, San Francisco, CA USA, May 1997. Software Research Institute.

194

Paper 9T1.

26. Taghi M. Khoshgoftaar, Edward B. Allen, Kalai S. Kalaichelvan, and Nishith Goel. Predictive modeling of software quality for very large telecommunications systems. In *Proceedings of the International Communications Conference*, volume 1, pages 214–219, Dallas, TX, June 1996. IEEE Communications Society.

27. P. Angeline and K. E. Kinnear, editors. *Advances in Genetic Programming, Vol. II*. MIT Press, Cambridge, MA, 1996.

28. John R. Koza. *Genetic Programming II: Automatic Discovery of Reusable Programs*. MIT Press, Cambridge, MA, 1994.

29. John R. Koza, D. E. Goldberg, D. B. Fogel, and R. L. Riolo, editors. *Proceedings of the First Annual Conference on Genetic Programming*, Cambridge, MA, 1996. MIT Press.

30. D.J. Montana. Strongly typed genetic programming. *Evolutionary Computation*, 3(2):199–230, 1995.

31. C. Ryan. Pygmies and civil servants. *Advances in Genetic Programming*, 1994.

32. Taghi M. Khoshgoftaar, Edward B. Allen, Robert Halstead, Gary P. Trio, and Ronald Flass. Process measures for predicting software quality. In *Proceedings of the IEEE High-Assurance Systems Engineering Workshop*, Washington, DC, August 1997. IEEE Computer Society. Forthcoming.

33. Maurice H. Halstead. *Elements of Software Science*. Elsevier, New York, 1977.

34. Thomas J. McCabe. A complexity measure. *IEEE Transactions on Software Engineering*, SE-2(4):308–320, December 1976.

35. Taghi M. Khoshgoftaar, Bibhuti B. Bhattacharyya, and Gary D. Richardson. Predicting software errors during development using non-linear regression models: A comparative study. *IEEE Transactions on Reliability*, 41(3):390–395, September 1992.

36. Taghi M. Khoshgoftaar, Abhijit S. Pandya, and Hemant B. More. A neural network approach for predicting software development faults. In *Proceedings of the Third International Symposium on Software Reliability Engineering*, pages 83–89, Research Triangle Park, NC USA, October 1992. IEEE Computer Society.

37. Taghi M. Khoshgoftaar, Abhijit S. Pandya, and David L. Lanning. Application of neural networks for predicting faults. *Annals of Software Engineering*, 1:141–154, 1995.

Problems

1. Draw the tree corresponding to this expression:

$$(((((y + 3) - z) + (x - 1)) * ((x * (2)) + 4)) + \sin(4))$$

2. Suppose two identical individuals are selected for mating in the GP system, each s-expression being equal to the one specified in Problem 1.

   (a) What offspring will result if the cross-over points are the first '-' and the fourth '+' operators (reading left to right)?

   (b) How many possible distinct offspring can these two parents yield via cross-over?

3. Provide three different GP function and terminal sets for the software quality domain. Compare and contrast the pros and cons of each function set in terms of their appropriateness to the domain, and the expected efficacy of a GP system using them.

4. Because a GP system is stochastic, each run can yield a different solution (best-of-run individual). There are a number of possible methods to increase the probability that the GP system described in this chapter will create an accurate software quality predictor. Candidates include, but are not limited to 1) having a run yield a set of individuals, rather than just one, 2) combining the results of of several runs somehow, 3) adding a validation phase, etc.

   (a) Why is each of these methods likely to increase the expected accuracy of the result?

   (b) What method do you prefer, and why?

5. GP systems are very compute-intensive. How might parallel processing be used to accelerate processing of the system described in this chapter?

6. This chapter uses a fitness function based on predictors of the ordinal ranking on the basis of expected number of faults, rather than on a simple classifier, mapping each training observation to *fault-prone* or *not-fault-prone.*

   (a) How should a classifier fitness function measure the quality of the classifications?

   (b) How would a classifier fitness function drive the evolutionary process?

   (c) What are some advantages and disadvantages of the fitness function used in this chahpter compared to a classifier?

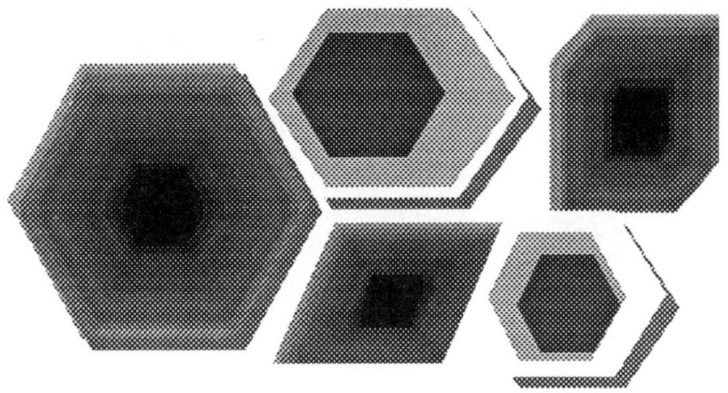

GRANULAR COMPUTING
IN SOFTWARE ENGINEERING

This section embraces a series of chapters that dwell on some aspects of granular computing. The diversity of the area is strongly reflected in the section. The first three papers revolve around the notion of objects; Gudwin and Gomide discuss object networks, Polkowski and Skowron are concerned with approximate reasoning exploiting the notions of rough sets, and Pedrycz and Sosnowski discuss a design with fuzzy objects regarded as a generalization of object-oriented design. In the sequel, the next three papers are focused on software management and quality: Ebert and Baisch look at a number of techniques (including fuzzy classifiers and neural networks) in the problem of cost-effective software project management. Gray and MacDonell discuss the use of various techniques of logic in the setting of quantifying software development effort. Peters and Ramanna elaborate on time-constrained software cost control system by exploiting techniques of rough sets and fuzzy logic. The design aspects of rule-based systems are studied by McCoy and Levary. Finally Cui and Kandel discuss a certain optimization problem arising in the area of databases.

OBJECT NETWORK : A FORMAL MODEL TO DEVELOP INTELLIGENT SYSTEMS

R.R. GUDWIN, F.A.C. GOMIDE
DCA-FEEC-UNICAMP, Caixa Postal 6101
13.083-970 – Campinas – SP – Brasil
e-mails: gudwin@dca.fee.unicamp.br
gomide@dca.fee.unicamp.br

ABSTRACT: The aim of this work is to introduce an approach based on a generalization of the object-oriented paradigm for system modeling and implementation. The key concept is object network, a set of connected places containing objects modeling the characteristics and properties of a given system. Object network has a naturally distributed structure, is derived from a general and formal approach for a theory of objects, and provides a framework particularly suitable for computational intelligence. An object network has both, formal and representational power needed to develop and to implement intelligent systems.

1   Introduction

Attempts to develop artificially intelligent systems have a long and rich history. The last quarter of century has revealed a number of fundamental insights, from approaches to machine reproduction behavior, control and communication in the animal and machine, to artificial intelligence and, more recently, computational intelligence. In particular, computational intelligence has come up as a field embracing neural networks, evolutionary computation, fuzzy systems, artificial life, probabilistic reasoning.

Intelligent systems may be viewed as a class of systems in which intelligence arises as a consequence of some kind of embedded knowledge, learning and adaptation. From the computational point of view, intelligent systems depend on architectures for information processing, that is, architectures to determine how they perceive an environment, to recognize and interpret the objects in it, and to specify subsequent actions based on objects recognition. Clearly, a central issue in computational intelligence is the very basic notion of object.

Generally speaking, an object is an identifiable entity that plays a role in an environment. In computational terms, an object is an identifiable entity that plays a visible role in providing a service to a user or program[1] under request. Therefore, it is intuitively reasonable to think about a computational object as a means to model physical and, more abstractly, non-physical objects of an environment. A computational object explicitly embodies an abstraction characterized by the behavior of certain requests. Services may access or modify information associated with objects. Services are described independently of the form of data and algorithms used to implement the services. Behavior, in particular, can have several implementations.

Although a considerable effort in object-oriented programming, there is still no commonly accepted formal definition of the object-oriented approach. For instance, Wand[2] suggests a formal model in which the object-oriented paradigm is shifted from implementation-driven to modeling-driven. Wolczko[3] suggests a formal, meta-language specification in which object-oriented programming languages should adhere to.

Despite the numerous approaches and languages for object-oriented programming available today, they still lack formal and representational power which is mandatory within intelligent systems framework. For instance, any intelligent system should be able to dynamically create and destroy objects; to associate objects into a higher abstraction levels to assemble time variant cognitive concepts; to cooperate, to compete and to change its own structure to achieve adaptation and learning capabilities.

In this work, we introduce the notion of object network aiming at not only to provide a more general and formal approach for a theory of objects, but also as a computational framework to develop intelligent systems. After this brief introduction, the paper proceeds presenting a mathematical theory of objects. Next, the idea of an object system is developed, followed by the central concept of object network. An object network has both, formal and representational power needed to develop and to implement intelligent systems, a feature that is not available in most current approaches.

2   Foundations for a Mathematical Theory of Objects

In this section we build the formal body of the theory that is addressed here. It starts by introducing some preliminary definitions used as a base for further developments. After, we discuss conceptual objects, followed by its formal definition. This discussion is first related to the object as an individual, and next by the study of its interaction with other objects, to compose object systems. At the end we define the object network, and its extensions developed to enhance the representation power of classes of knowledge.

2.1   Preliminary Definitions

Here, we introduce the concepts and definitions used as a formal background for further developments. The focus here is on the main issues and definitions only. For a more in depth coverage the reader is referred to the work of Gudwin[4,5,6,7] . The definitions assume a discrete set N associated with time instants, or algorithm steps when convenient. Extensions to the continuous case may be possible, but it will not be considered here. Usually N is the set of natural numbers, but in general it can be any countable set.

A remark concerning notation: no distinction between a function and its graph will be made. Therefore, both $f : A \rightarrow B$ and $f \subset A \times B$ will be used to express a function f.

Definition 1 – **Tuples** : Let q_1 , q_2 , ... , q_n be generic elements of the sets Q_1 , Q_2 , ... , Q_n respectively. A tuple is a structure joining q_1 , q_2 , ... , q_n into a single element denoted by $q = (q_1 , q_2 , ... , q_n)$.

A tuple with n elements is an n-tuple, or tuple for short. The elements of a tuple are called components. They can be identified by the indices associated with the order in which they appear. Note that a tuple component can be itself a tuple. In this case they are called complex tuples. For example $q = (q_1 , (q_{21} , q_{22} , q_{23}), q_3 , q_4 , q_5)$ is a complex tuple. To simplify notation we may assign $q_2 = (q_{21} , q_{22} , q_{23})$ turning the original tuple into $q = (q_1 , q_2 , q_3 , q_4 , q_5)$.

Definition 2 - **Tuple Arity:** Let $q = (q_1 , q_2 , ... , q_n)$ be a tuple. The **arity** of q, $Ar(q)$, is the number of tuple's components: $Ar(q) = n$.

Examples: $q = (a,b,c)$, $Ar(q) = 3$; $q = (a,(b,c),d)$, $Ar(q) = 3$; $q = ((a,b,c),(d,(e,f),g))$, $Ar(q) = 2$.

Definition 3 - **Reference Index:** Let q be tuple. To identify an individual component of q we associate a reference index to each of its element. For a simple tuple the reference index will be a number i, $1 \leq i \leq Ar(q)$. For a complex tuple the reference index will be a simple tuple i with each element i_k corresponding to a sub-index of level k. The value of the sub-indices ranges between one and the arity of the tuple at level k. The reference index can also be used to identify the domain of the components. For example, let $s \in S$ be simple, and $c \in C$ complex tuples. Thus the reference indices and the component domains are found as follows:

$s = (a,b,c)$, $S = S_A \times S_B \times S_C$
$i=1 \rightarrow s_i = a$, $S_i = S_A$
$i=2 \rightarrow s_i = b$, $S_i = S_B$
$i=3 \rightarrow s_i = c$, $S_i = S_C$
$c = (a,(b,d))$, $C = C_A \times (C_B \times C_C)$
$i=1 \rightarrow c_i = a$, $C_i = C_A$
$i=2 \rightarrow c_i = (b,d)$, $C_i = C_B \times C_C$
$i=(2,1) \rightarrow c_i = b$, $C_i = C_B$
$i=(2,2) \rightarrow c_i = d$, $C_i = C_C$
$c = (a,(b,(s,d,(e,f),g),h))$, $C = C_A \times(C_B \times (C_C \times C_D \times (C_E \times C_F) \times C_G) \times C_H)$
$i=(2,1) \rightarrow c_i = b$, $C_i = C_B$
$i=(2,2,3) \rightarrow c_i = (e,f)$, $C_i = C_E \times C_F$
$i=(2,2,3,2) \rightarrow c_i = f$, $C_i = C_F$
$i=(2,3) \rightarrow c_i = h$, $C_i = C_H$
$i=2 \rightarrow c_i = (b,(s,d,(e,f),g),h)$, $C_i = C_B \times (C_C \times C_D \times (C_E \times C_F) \times C_G) \times C_H$

Definition 4 - **Induction Formula** : Let $q = (q_1 , q_2 , ... , q_n)$ be a tuple and k be an expression defined by the following syntax

$k \leftarrow [\,i\,]$
$i \leftarrow i , i$
$i \leftarrow [\,i , i\,]$

where i is a reference index of q. The expression k is called an induction formula.

Examples:　　$k = [\,i_1 , [\,i_2 , i_3 , i_4\,] , i_5\,]$
　　　　　　　$k = [\,[i_1 , i_2\,], [i_3 , [i_4 , i_5\,]\,]\,]$
　　　　　　　$k = [i_1 , i_2 , i_3\,]$
　　　　　　　where i_j are reference indices of q.

Definition 5 - **Induction of a tuple:** Let $q = (q_1 , q_2 , ... , q_n)$ be a tuple in $Q = Q_1 \times ... \times Q_n$ and k be an induction formula. The induction of q according k is defined as the new tuple $q_{(k)}$ induced by the induction formula. The induced tuple $q_{(k)}$ is found from k by changing brackets and each reference index i_j into parenthesis and q_{i_j} of the original tuple q. The domain $Q_{(k)}$ of $q_{(k)}$ is found similarly.

Examples:　　$q = (a,b,c,d)$, $Q = Q_1 \times Q_2 \times Q_3 \times Q_4$, $k = [1,3,4,2\,]$,
　　　　　　　$q_{(k)} = (a,c,d,b)$, $Q_{(k)} = Q_1 \times Q_3 \times Q_4 \times Q_2$

$q = (a,b,c,d)$, $Q = Q_1 \times Q_2 \times Q_3 \times Q_4$, $k = [4,1]$,
$q_{(k)} = (d,a)$, $Q_{(k)} = Q_4 \times Q_1$

$q = (a,b,c,d)$, $k = [\,1, [2, 3]\,, 4\,]$,
$q_{(k)} = (a, (b,c), d)$, $Q_{(k)} = Q_1 \times (Q_2 \times Q_3)\times Q_4$

$q = (a,(b,c),d)$, $Q = Q_1 \times (Q_2 \times Q_3)\times Q_4$,$k = [1,(2,1),(2,2),3]$,
$q_{(k)} = (a,b,c,d)$, $Q_{(k)} = Q_1 \times Q_2 \times Q_3 \times Q_4$

$q = (a, (b,c), d)$, $Q = Q_1 \times (Q_2 \times Q_3)\times Q_4$, $k = [3,2]$,
$q_{(k)} = (d,(b,c))$, $Q_{(k)} = Q_4 \times (Q_2 \times Q_3)$

$q = (a, (b,c), d)$, $Q = Q_1 \times (Q_2 \times Q_3)\times Q_4$, $k = [3,2,(2,1)]$,
$q_{(k)} = (d,(b,c),b)$, $Q_{(k)} = Q_4 \times (Q_2 \times Q_3) \times Q_2$

Definition 6 - **Sub-tuple:** A tuple $q_{(k)}$ is called a sub-tuple of q if k has only one pair of brackets, and each reference index in k is unary and appears only once in k.

Definition 7 – **Relation:** If R_1 , ... , R_n are sets and $R = \{(r_{i1}, ... , r_{in})\}$, $i = 1, ... , M$, is a set of M tuples with arity $n > 1$ such that $\forall i \in \{1, ... ,M\}$, $\forall k \in \{1, ... , n\}$, $r_{ik} \in R_k$, then the set R, $R \subseteq R_1 \times ... \times R_n$ is a relation in $R_1 \times ... \times R_n$,

Definition 8 – **Projection:** Let $R = \{r_i\}$, $r_i = (r_{i1}, ... , r_{in})$ be an n-ary relation in $R_1 \times ... \times R_n$ and k be an induction formula with unary indices $k = [k_1, k_2, ... , k_m]$, $k_i \in \{1, ... , n\}$, $k_i \neq k_j$, if $i \neq j$, $i = 1, ... , m$, $j = 1, ... , m$, $m \leq n$. The projection of R on $R_{k_1} \times ... \times R_{k_m}$,denoted by $R \downarrow R_{k_1} \times ... \times R_{k_m}$ (alternatively, $R_{(k)}$) is the relation obtained by the union of all sub-tuples $r_{i(k)} = (r_{ik_1}, ..., r_{ik_m})$ of R originated from the induction of R's tuples according to k, $R_{(k)} = \cup\, r_{i(k)}$.

Examples: $A = \{1, 2\}$ $B = \{a,b,c\}$ $C = \{\alpha, \beta, \gamma\}$. $R = \{(1,a,\beta), (2,c,\alpha), (2,b,\beta), (2,c,\beta)\}$
   $R \downarrow A \times C = \{\,(1,\beta), (2,\alpha), (2, \beta)\,\}$
   $R \downarrow C \times B = \{\,(\beta,a), (\alpha,c), (\beta,b), (\beta,c)\}$

Definition 9 - **Free Projection:** Let $R = \{r_i\}$, $r_i = (r_{i1}, ... , r_{in})$ be an n-ary relation defined in $U = R_1 \times ... \times R_n$ and k be an induction formula. The free projection of R in $U_{(k)}$, $R \downarrow U_{(k)}$ (alternatively, $R_{(k)}$) is the relation obtained by the union of all sub-tuples $r_{i(k)}$ originated by the induction of the tuples from R according to k: $R_{(k)} = \cup\, r_{i(k)}$.

NOTE: Free projection is a generalization of projection. Recall that in a projection, the induction formula has unary indices only. This implies in tuples defined only over the main dimensions of the original tuple. In free projection, any element, in whatever level of a tuple, can be used to define the inducted tuple. Clearly, with the proper induction formula free projection becomes standard projection.

Definition 10 - **Cylindrical Extension:** Let $R = \{ (r_{i1}, r_{i2}, \dots, r_{in}) \}$ be an n-ary relation in $R_1 \times \dots \times R_n$. The cylindrical extension P of R in $P_1 \times \dots \times P_m$, denoted by $P = R \uparrow P_1 \times \dots \times P_m$, where $\forall k \in \{1, \dots, n\}$ $\exists P_j = R_k$, $1 \le j \le m$, is the greatest (in the sense of the greatest number of elements) relation $P \subseteq P_1 \times \dots \times P_m$ such that $P \downarrow R_1 \times \dots \times R_n = R$.

Example: $A = \{1, 2\}$ $B = \{a,b,c\}$ $C = \{\alpha, \beta, \gamma\}$. $R = \{ (1,a), (2,c) \}$
$\qquad R \uparrow A \times B \times C = \{ (1,a,\alpha), (2,c,\alpha), (1,a,\beta), (2,c,\beta), (1,a,\gamma), (2,c,\gamma) \}$
$\qquad R \uparrow C \times A \times B = \{ (\alpha,1,a), (\alpha,2,c), (\beta,1,a), (\beta,2,c,), (\gamma,1,a,), (\gamma,2,c,).$

NOTE: As in projection, the order of elements in tuples of the cylindrical extension it is not the same as in the original tuples.

Definition 11 – **Junction:** Let R and S be two relations in $R_1 \times \dots \times R_n$ and $S_1 \times \dots \times S_m$, respectively, and $P = P_1 \times \dots \times P_o$ an universe where $\forall i \in \{1, \dots, n\}$ $\exists P_k = R_i$, and $\forall j \in \{1, \dots, m\}$ $\exists P_h = S_j$, $o \le n + m$. The junction of R and S under P, denoted by $R * S \mid_P$, is $R * S \mid_P = R \uparrow P \cap S \uparrow P$.

NOTE: If there is a $R_i = S_j$ then there may be only one set P_k with elements in tuples of R*S. In this case, for the tuples to be included in junction, the value of such element in the tuple in R and S should be the same (see first example).
NOTE: If $\forall i,j$, $R_i \ne S_j$, then $R*S \mid_P \downarrow R_1 \times \dots \times R_n = R$ and $R * S \mid_P \downarrow S_1 \times \dots \times S_m = S$.
Example: $A = \{1, 2\}$ $B = \{a,b,c\}$ $C = \{\alpha, \beta, \gamma\}$. $R = \{ (1,a), (2,c) \}$ $S = \{(a,\alpha), (b,\beta)\}$
$\qquad R * S \mid_{A \times B \times C} = \{ (1,a,\alpha) \}$
$\qquad R * S \mid_{A \times B \times B \times C} = \{(1,a,a,\alpha), (1,a,b,\beta), (2,c,a,\alpha), (2,c,b,\beta) \}$

Definition 12 – **Variable:** Let N be a countable set with a generic element n (comprising some type of time measure), and $X \subseteq U$. A variable x of type X is a function $x : N \to X$. Note that a function is also a relation and hence it can be expressed as a set. Thus, $x \subset N \times X$.

Examples: $N = \{1, 2, 3\}$, $X = \{a, b, c \}$, $x(1) = a$, $x(2) = b$, $x(3) = c$ or
$\qquad x = \{ (1, a), (2, b), (3, c) \}$

Definition 13 - **Composed Variable:** Let x be a variable of type X. If the elements of X are n-tuples with n > 1, then x is called a composed variable (or structure).

The value of a composed variable, in a particular instant of time, will always be a tuple. The individual value of each sub-element of this tuple can be obtained by its reference index, the field of the variable. If $X = X_1 \times ... \times X_n$, then each field of x can be viewed as a free projection on $N \times X_i$, i.e., it is a standard variable of type X_i.

Example: N={1, 2, 3}, $X_1 = \{a,b\}$, $X_2 = \{c,d\}$ $X = X_1 \times X_2 = \{ (a,c),(a,d),(b,c),(b,d)\}$

$$x = \{ (1,(a,c)) , (2,(a,d)), (3, (a,d)) \}$$

$$x \downarrow N \times X_1 = \{ (1,a) , (2,a), (3, a) \}$$

$$x \downarrow N \times X_2 = \{ (1,c) , (2,d), (3, d) \}$$

2.2 *The Conceptual Object*

Before to mathematically define an object, we briefly describe the conceptual object. Our concept of object is closely related to its intuitive physical meaning. Ontologically, an object is an entity of the real world and is characterized by its properties. The properties are its attributes[2] . Based on a frame of reference, it is possible to find attributes distinguishing different objects. Thus attributes describe the objects. This view of objects does not consider that, in addition to its existence, the objects also "act" in real world. Therefore, a mathematical concept of object must model its active aspect.

The conceptualization of object cannot, in principle, be made in an independent way. Although we can imagine the existence of an object by itself, we should also consider its capability to interact with different objects. In other words, to introduce the main concepts about objects, we have to discuss object systems. An object system is a set of interacting entities.

The object components that allow interaction are shown in figure 1.

Each active object is assumed to have two types of interfaces: input and output interfaces, as in figure 1. The input interface is composed by a collection of gates (input gates). Within an object we find its internal states. These states are divided in 4 regions. The first is a copy of the input interface whereas the second comprises internal variables. The third region is a copy of the output interface, and the fourth region is a set of transformation (internal) functions. The output interface, similarly to the input one, is composed by a collection of output gates.

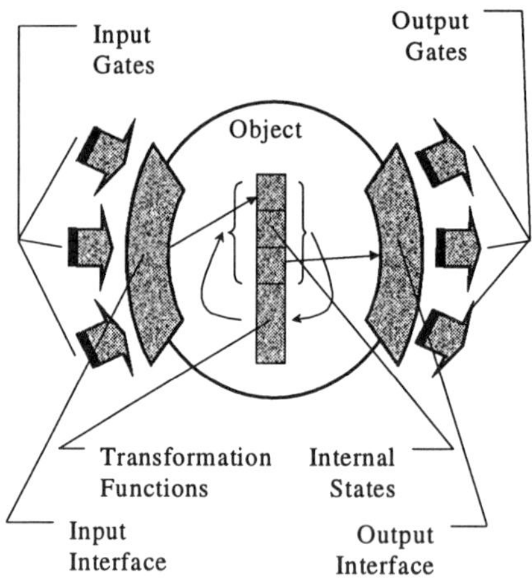

Figure 1 – The Conceptual Object

The interaction among objects is regulated by a mechanism called triggering, and is performed by active objects. In this mechanism, some objects are first bound to the active object, through the input gates, starting what is called the assimilation phase. In this phase, the active object copies the internal states of binding objects to its internal states. After assimilation, the bounded objects can be destroyed or released back to the system. If they are destroyed, we have a destructive assimilation (or consumption). Otherwise, a non-destructive assimilation. In the second phase of triggering, the active object uses one of the transformation functions to change its internal states. Both, input and output, are in the internal states. This is called the transformation phase. After the transformation phase, some of the active object internal states are copied into the output interface. Next, another set of objects is bound to the output gates, and their internal states are changed to those present in the output interface. This last phase is called either generation phase, or regeneration phase, depending on the objects that are bound to output gates. If the bounded objects are existing objects, then this process is called regeneration because it alters the internal states of bounded objects. However, this last phase can also create a new object, not part of the object system. In this case, the last phase creates this new object, fills its internal states with the information of the output interface, and releases it to the system. This process is called generation.

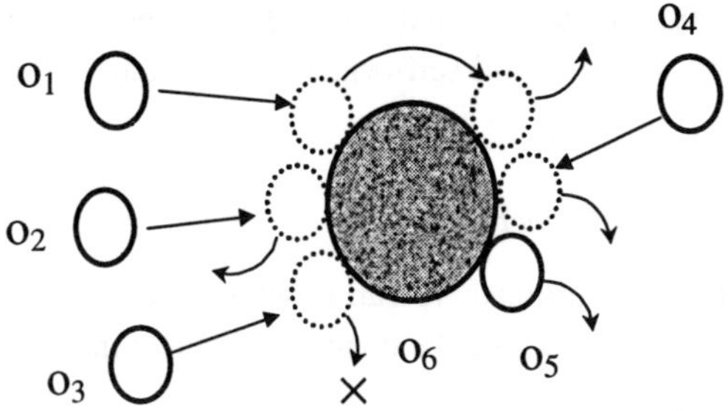

Figure 2 – Object Interactions

The triggering mechanism may allow different kinds of behavior, as illustrated in figure 2. In this example, object o_6 is the active object performing the triggering process. Objects o_1, o_2 and o_3 are the objects to be assimilated in the triggering. Objects o_1 and o_4 are regenerated, and o_5 is generated. Note that o_1 is, at the same time, assimilated and regenerated. Object o_2, after assimilation, is released back to the system but o_3 is destroyed.

To control the triggering process, there is a special function associated with each object called the selection function. This function decides which objects are to be bound to input gates, which objects are to be bound to output gates, and which internal function is to be used in the triggering process. The control strategy of an object system is dictated by the selection functions.

Note, however, that the selection functions do have some restrictions. These restrictions concern the transformation functions requirements, as well as some problems involving synchronization. Each transformation (internal) function requires a minimum set of objects to start the triggering procedure. Therefore, the selection function must consider the simultaneous availability of all objects needed to enable a transformation function. The synchronization problems that may appear are related to multiple active objects binding the same object. For assimilation bindings, there should be a guarantee that only one active object is performing a destructive assimilation. If some assimilated object is also being regenerated, it must be regenerated by only one active object. And cannot be destructively assimilated in this case. In this sense, there should be a global policy for the selection functions, assuring that those constraints are satisfied.

With an appropriate implementation of selection functions, objects can become autonomous entities, i.e., independent of an external synchronization mechanism. Synchronism, despite being useful sometimes, is not a requirement in object systems. The behavior of real objects, with asynchronous and parallel activities can be modeled. Note that both assimilated and (re)generated objects are not necessarily passive. This allows adaptive and self-organizing systems to be modeled by object systems.

2.3   The Mathematical Object

Using the preliminary definitions, we can now proceed to define the mathematical concepts involving objects, turning the conceptual object into a mathematical one.

Definition 14 – **Class:** A class C is a set whose elements c_i are tuples of the type:

$$(v_1, v_2, \dots, v_n, f_1, f_2, \dots, f_m), n \geq 0, m \geq 0$$

where $v_i \in V_i$, and f_j are functions

$$f_j : \bigtimes_{p \in P_j} V_p \to \bigtimes_{q \in Q_j} V_q.$$

Here $\bigtimes$ means the Cartesian product, $P_j \subseteq \{1, \dots, n\}$ and $Q_j \subseteq \{1, \dots, n\}$.

Definition 15 – **Object:** Let C be an non-empty class and c be a variable of type C. Thus c is an object of class C.

It is worth noting that an object, as a variable, supports objects composed by parts which are objects themselves. In addition, if n=1 and m=0 then the tuple reduces to a single element. Hence a standard variable (a primitive object) is an object. For an empty class n=m=0 and there is no object. Clearly structures are also object. As it will be seen later, a structure is a passive object.

Definition 16 - **Instance of an Object:** Let c be an object of class C. The instance c(n) is the value of c at n.

C is a set of tuples. Therefore the instance of an object is an element of C, i.e. a tuple.

Definition 17 - **Superclass and Subclass:** Let C be a class. The set D whose elements are sub-tuples of the elements of C belonging to the same universe, and each element in C is associated with one element of D and D is itself a class, is called a superclass of C. In this case C is a subclass of D.

Note that a class can be defined from primitive classes. Since class is a relation, another class can be generated by the cylindrical extension of a class, by the junction of two or more classes, or by both junction and cylindrical extensions. In all cases, the primitive classes are superclasses of the newly generated class. Moreover, for a given a class its cylindrical extension is a subclass of itself. The junction of two classes is a subclass of both of them. Any class is a subclass of empty class. Therefore a hierarchy of classes is induced by projections, junctions and cylindrical extensions (figure 3).

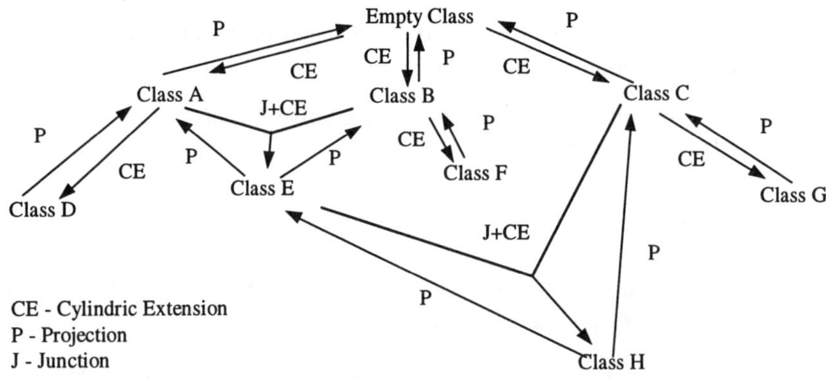

Figure 3 - Example of Class Hierarchy

Definition 18 - **Sub-object:** Let c be an object of class C and d an object of class D a superclass of C. If for any n the instance of d is a sub-tuple of the instance of c, then d is a sub-object of c.

In other words, d is the free projection of c in $N \times D$, i.e. $d = c \downarrow N \times D$.

Definition 19 - **Active and Passive Objects:** An object c of a class C is called an active object if $m > 0$. If $m = 0$, then c is a passive object.

Definition 20 - **Input Interface:** Let c be an active object of a class C and I a superclass of C, defined by:

$$I = \bigtimes_i V_i, \forall i \in \{1,...,n\} \text{ such that} \begin{cases} \exists f_j, \ 1 \le j \le m \text{ where } i \in P_j \\ \forall f_1, \ 1 \le l \le m \ \ i \notin Q_1 \end{cases}$$

The input interface i of the object c is the passive object generated by the free projection of c in $N \times I$, i.e. $i = c \downarrow N \times I$.

Definition 21 - **Function Specific Input Interfaces:** Let c be an active object of class C, i its input interface, and I^j a superclass of I and C such that :

$$I^j = \bigtimes_i V_i, \forall i \in \{1,...,n\} \text{ such that, for } f_j, i \in P_j \text{ and } \forall l \in \{1,...,m\}, i \notin Q_l$$

The specific input interface for function j of c, i^j, is the free projection of c in $N \times I^j$.

Note that $i^j = c \downarrow N \times I^j = i \downarrow N \times I^j$. If the elements of class C have m functions, then there exist m function specific input interfaces. Each i^j is a sub-object of i and c.

Definition 22 - **Output Interface:** Let c be an active object of class C and O a superclass of C characterized by:

$$O = \bigtimes_i V_i, \forall i \in \{1,...,n\} \text{ such that} \begin{cases} \exists f_j, 1 \leq j \leq m \text{ where } i \in Q_j \\ \forall f_l, 1 \leq l \leq m \quad i \notin P_l \end{cases}$$

The output interface o of object c is the passive object generated by the free projection of c in $N \times O$, i.e. $i = c \downarrow N \times O$.

Definition 23 -**Function Specific Output Interfaces:** Let c be an active object of a class C, o its output interface, and O^j is a superclass of O and C such that :

$$O^j = \bigtimes_i V_i, \forall i \in \{1,...,n\} \text{ such that for } f_j \, i \in Q_j \text{ and } \forall l \in \{1,...,m\}, i \notin P_l$$

The output interface specific for function j of c, o^j, is the free projection of c in $N \times O^j$.

Clearly, $o^j = c \downarrow N \times O^j = o \downarrow N \times O^j$ and if the elements of class C have m functions, then there exist m function specific input interfaces. Each o^j is a sub-object of o and c.

Definition 24 - **Existence of Objects:** An object c is said to exist at n if the function which maps instances of c in C is defined for $n \in N$.

2.4 *Interaction Among Objects*

After formally defining the concepts involving objects, we now proceed to define the concepts necessary to provide objects interaction.

Definition 25 - **Generation and Destruction of Objects:** An object is generated at n if it does not exist at n and does exist at n+1. An object is destroyed (destructively assimilated) at n if it does exist at n but does not exist at n+1.

Definition 26 - **Enabling Scope of Functions:** Consider an active object c from a class $C = \{ (v_1, v_2, \dots, v_n, f_1, f_2, \dots, f_m) \}$, a function f_j of C, and i^j an input interface specific for function f_j. Let β be the arity of instances of i^j, gi an input index function for f_j, $gi : \{1, \dots, \beta\} \to \{1, \dots, n\}$ mapping each component from instances of the input interface specific for f_j to a component in instances of c, and $B = \{0,1\}$. An enabling scope for f_j is a set of tuples $H = \{(h_t, b_t)\}$, $t = 1, \dots, \beta$, where h_t is an object of class $V_{gi(t)}$ and $b_t \in B$ is a boolean value indicating if object h_t should ($b_t = 1$) or should not ($b_t = 0$) be destroyed when c triggers.

Definition 27 - **Generative Scope of Functions:** Assume an active object c of class $C = \{ (v_1, v_2, \dots, v_n, f_1, f_2, \dots, f_m) \}$, a function f_j of C, an output interface o^j specific or function f_j, α the arity of instances of o^j, and an output index function for f_j, $go : \{1, \dots, \alpha\} \to \{1, \dots, n\}$ mapping each component from instances of output interface specific for f_j to a component in instances of c. A generative scope for f_j is a set of objects $S = \{s_u\}$, $u = 1, \dots, \alpha$, where s_u is an object of class $V_{go(u)}$.

Definition 28 - **Enabling of an Active Object:** An active object of class C is enabled at n if all objects belonging to an enabling scope of one of its functions f_j do exist at n. Function f_j is said to be enabled at n.

Definition 29 - **Triggering of an Active Object:** Consider the following:

    a)-an object c from a class C,

    b)- the instance of c at n, $c(n) = (v_1(n), \dots, v_n(n), f_1(n), \dots, f_m(n))$,

    c)-a function f_j of c at n, enabled by $H = \{(h_t, b_t)\}$,

    d)-a generative scope $S = \{s_u\}$ for f_j such that if $s \in S$, then or s does not exist at n, or $s \in H$,

    e)-p, the number of values such that $k \in P_j$, $k = 1, \dots, n$, (P_j from def. 14)

    f)-a domain index function $gd : (1, \dots, p\} \to \{1, \dots, n\}$ for f_j,

    g)-the projection of f(.) on V_k, $f(.)\downarrow V_k$,

    h)-β, α, gi e go as before.

    Triggering an active object at n means:

    1)- determination of c's instance at instant n+1, given the instance of c at n and the instances of h_t at n:

$$
v_i(n+1) = \begin{cases} v_i(n) & \text{if } i \notin P_j \text{ and } i \notin Q_j \\ h_{gi^{-1}(i)}(n) & \text{if } i \in P_j \text{ and } i \notin Q_j \\ f_j(w_1, \dots, w_b)\downarrow V_i & \text{if } i \in Q_j \end{cases}
$$

$$\text{where } w_r = \begin{cases} h_{gi^{-1}(gd(r))}(n), & \text{if } gd(r) \in P_j \\ v_{gd(r)}(n), & \text{if } gd(r) \notin P_j \end{cases}$$

2)- destruction ($b_t = 1$) of object h_t , (h_t , b_t) $\in$ H ,at n,

3)-generation, at n , of the objects of S those do not exist at n,

4)-determination of the instances of the objects of S, at n+1, according to the instances of c at n+1:

$$s_u(n+1) = v_{go(u)}(n+1)$$

2.5   *Object Systems*

Knowing what objects are and which mechanisms allow objects interaction we can define an object system.

Definition 30 - **Object System:** Assume the following:

a)-c_i are objects of class C_i , $i = 1, \dots , \delta$,

b)-$\mathcal{C} = \bigcup_i c_i$,

c)-$\Theta_i = \{ 0, \dots , m_i \}$ where m_i is the number of functions for object c_i,

d)-$B = \{0,1\}$,

e)-γ_i , $0 \le i \le \delta$, $\delta > 0$, are selection functions $\gamma_i : N \to 2^{C \times B} \times 2^C \times \Theta_i$ which, for each object c_i at n, select an enabling scope H_i , a generative scope S_i and a function index such that $\forall (c,b) \in H_i$, if $b = 1$, then $(\forall k \ne i)((c,1) \notin H_k)$, $\forall c \in S_i$, $(\forall k \ne i)(c \notin S_k)$ and $(\forall k)((c,1) \notin H_k)$. H_i is an enabling scope and S_i is a generative scope for function $\gamma_i(n) \downarrow \Theta_i$. If c_i is a passive object or, at n $\nexists H_i \ne \varnothing$ or $\nexists S_i \ne \varnothing$, then $\gamma_i(n) = (\varnothing, \varnothing, 0)$. The third index is null to indicate that no function is to be executed. The meaning of these conditions are grasped as follows. An object of an enabling scope programmed to be destroyed must be destroyed by only one active object. If an object is part of a generative scope of an active object, then it cannot be in any other generative scope. If the object in question is passive, or if active it does not have an enabling scope for any of its functions, then its selection function must do nothing.

An object system Ω is a set of pairs $\{\omega_i\}$, $\omega_i = (c_i , \gamma_i)$, such that :

1)-for n=0, there exists at least one ω_i with an object c_i defined,

2)-for n>0 all active objects c_i with $\gamma_i(n) \ne (\varnothing, \varnothing, 0)$, i.e. objects whose selection functions are in the form $\gamma_i(n) = (H_i, S_i, j)$ may trigger according to its enabling scope H_i and the generative scope S_i , using its j-th internal function,

3)-for n>0, all objects c_i which exist at n and do not have its instance at (n+1) determined by item 2, may have c_i (n+1) = c_i (n).

The definition of an object system may be viewed from two different perspectives. In the first, it provides a recursive way of building an object system. In the second view, comprising a given collection of objects, it works as a specification. To call a given set of objects an object system, the values of its instances (and their existence at different times) should be associated with each other according to the laws of triggering and regeneration of objects given by items 2 and 3 of definition 30. These laws determine, at each time instant, the values of the instances (or its inexistence) based on their previous values. The objects that interact at each instant are determined according to the selection functions, which define the enabling scopes, the generative scopes, and the functions to be triggered for each active object. Therefore, the selection function plays a fundamental role in the object system dynamics.

Objects are functions and there are, in principle, no restrictions on their form. For a set of objects the functions can be any. An object system has, as opposed to a set of objects, a clear recursive nature. The recursiveness is not simple because objects may be *partial* functions, i.e. they do not have to be defined for any value of its domain. This leads to the fundamental question about the computability[8,9] of object systems, certainly a desirable property. An object system being computable means that we can determine, for each $n \in N$, the values of the instances for the existing objects at n. Conditions for computability of object systems are given as follows. Assume Ω an object system with a finite number of elements ω_i , with all its selection functions γ_i computable, and all internal functions of all objects c_i of ω_i computable. Then Ω is computable.

These are sufficient conditions only. An object system does not need to necessarily have a finite number of objects to be computable. If for adjacent instants n and n+1 the number of existing objects is finite, then the system is computable.

An object system fulfilling the previous conditions can be viewed as the limit of a (possibly infinite) sequence of objects systems Ω_1 , Ω_2 , ... , each Ω_i with a finite number of objects defined on a finite and incremental domain N_i. That is: $N_0 = \{0\}$, and $N_i = N_{i-1} \cup \{i\}$.

Consequently, each object system Ω_i is computable and the whole sequence is computable as well. The infinite object is the i-th element of this sequence when $i \rightarrow \infty$. Hence, the object system is computable, although infinite.

214

2.6 *Object Network*

An object network is a special type of object system in which additional restrictions concerning interactions are included. To distinguish object network and object system let us assume places and arcs whose roles are similar to those used in Petri nets[10,11] context. Objects in places can only interact with objects in places connected through arcs. Thus, at each instant, the objects defined should be at one place. For each place there is a set of places connected with through input arcs. These places are called the input gates of the place. Analogously, each place has a set of places connected with it by means of output arcs, called output gates. For each field of output interface of objects in this place there should exist one corresponding output gate. With those conditions we can see that, for each place, there should be only objects of the same class. Remember that objects can be of two types: passive and active. Passive objects do not have functions in its tuples and are only used to store information. Active objects do have functions in its tuples, and perform the task of transitions in the object network. Each place can only have objects of the same class. In this sense, we can say that there are passive and active places if the objects that can be put in a place are passive or active, respectively. Apart of those special characteristics, an object network is similar to an object system.

Object networks can be put in a graphical form, with places being represented by circles and arcs by lines. Passive places are indicated by circles. Active places are indicated by double circles, and instances of objects by black tokens, as in figure 4.

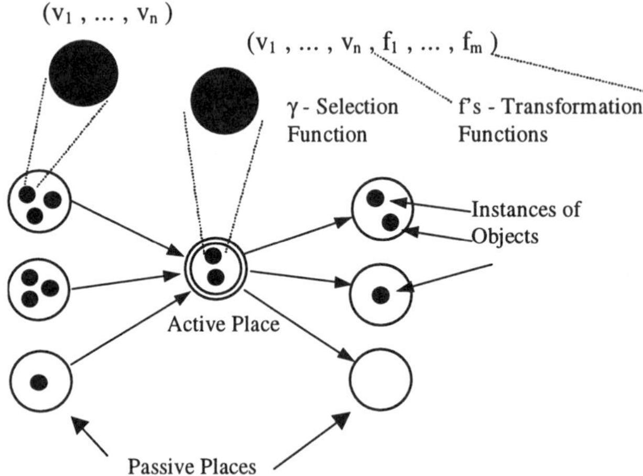

Figure 4 : Example of an Object Network

Observe that, differently than in Petri nets, the tokens are instances of objects that have individuality, i.e., they are not a marking on the place, but are related to objects with attributes and eventually transforming functions. Again, active objects, which perform the role of transitions, are also mobile and changeable. This gives an object net great power of representation, allowing modeling of systems that are not suitable to be modeled by Petri nets, e.g., adaptive systems.

As for an object system, the basic behavior in an object network is the triggering of active objects. Triggering an active object corresponds to the generation of new instances of objects in places directly connected to the place where the active object is through output arcs. To be triggered, an object must first have an enabling scope, that is, a set of object instances put in the input gates, enabling one of the object functions. To select an enabling scope, there is a selection function that selects, from the object instances available, those that are to be used for triggering. After triggering, object instances may be put in one ore more output gates of the place where the active object is. This is also determined by the selection function. The object instances used as an enabling scope may (or not) be destroyed for the next time instant.

Definition 31 - **Object Network:** Assume the following:

a)- a set of classes $\Sigma = \{C_i\}$

b)- a set of objects $C = \{c_i\}$, where c_i are objects from a class C_i, $C_i \in \Sigma$, $0 \leq i \leq \delta, \delta > 0$.

c)- $\Pi = \{\pi_i\}$ a set of places π_i

d)- A, a set of arcs $A = \{a_i\}$

e)-η a node function $\eta : A \to \Pi \times \Pi$

f)-ξ a localization function $\xi : N \times C \to \Pi$, which relates to each object $c \in C$, for each instant n, a place π.

g)-$F(\pi)$ a mapping $\Pi \to 2^\Pi$, defined by $F(\pi) = \cup \pi_k$ where $k \in K$, $K = \{k \mid \exists\, a_j \in A$ such that $\eta(a_j) = (\pi_k,\pi)\}$.

h)-$V(\pi)$ a mapping $\Pi \to 2^\Pi$, defined by $V(\pi) = \cup \pi_k$ where $k \in K$, $K = \{k \mid \exists\, a_j \in A$ such that $\eta(a_j) = (\pi,\pi_k)\}$.

i)- $X(\pi)$ a mapping of connections $\Pi \to 2^\Pi$, such that $X(\pi) = F(\pi) \cup V(\pi)$.

j)-$\Xi = \Xi(\pi)$ a mapping of classes $\Pi \to \Sigma$, such that $\forall \pi \in \Pi$ for each field v_i of input interface of objects from class $\Xi(\pi)$, being v_i an object from class C, $\exists \pi_k$, $\pi_k \in F(\pi)$, such that $\Xi(\pi_k) = C$, and for each field v_i of output interface of objects

216

from class $\Xi(\pi)$, being v_i an object from class C, $\exists \pi_k$, $\pi_k \in V(\pi)$, such that $\Xi(\pi_k) = C$.

k)- i^i the input interface of an object from class $\Xi(\pi_i)$.

l)-o^i the output interface of an object from class $\Xi(\pi_i)$.

m)-∂_i the number of fields in i^i and ρ_i the number of fields in o^i.

n)-the function fpi_i the attribute function for input gates of objects which are at a place π_i, defined $fpi_i : \{1, ... , \partial_i\} \rightarrow A$ and $fpi = \{fpi_i\}$.

o)-$fpo_i = \{1, ... , \rho_i\} \rightarrow A$ the attribute function for output gates of objects that are at a place π_i and $fpo = \{fpo_i\}$

p)-$\Theta_i = \{0, ... , m_i\}$, where m_i is the number of function for object c_i

q)-$\gamma = \{\gamma_i\}$, $0 \le i \le \delta$, $\delta > 0$, which elements are selection functions $\gamma_i : N \rightarrow 2^{C \times B} \times 2^C \times \Theta_i$ that for each object c_i, in an instant n, select an enabling scope H_i, a generative scope S_i and the index for the function to be executed by the object, having as a restriction that $\forall(c,b) \in H_i$, $\xi(n,c) = \pi$, $\pi \in F(\xi(n,c_i))$, if $b = 1$, $(\forall k \ne i)((c,1) \notin H_k)$, $\forall c \in S_i$, $\xi(n+1,c) = \pi$, $\pi \in V(\xi(n,c_i))$, $(\forall k \ne i)(c \notin S_k)$ and $(\forall k)((c,1) \notin H_k)$. More than that, H_i should be an enabling scope and S_i should be a generative scope for function f_k, $k = \gamma_i(n) \downarrow \Theta_i$. If c_i is a passive object or, for a given n, $\nexists H_i \ne \varnothing$ or $\nexists S_i \ne \varnothing$ then $\gamma_i(n) = (\varnothing, \varnothing, 0)$. The third index being 0 does mean that no function is going to be executed. Those conditions are analogous to the selection function for an object system, added by the following conditions: Any object belonging to the enabling scope of another object should be connected to the place where the active object is by an input arc. Any object belonging to the generative scope of an active object should be put in a place that is connected to the place where the active object is by means of an output arc.

An object network $\Re$ is a tuple $\Re = (\Sigma, \Pi, \Xi, A, \eta, fpi, fpo, C, \xi, \gamma)$, such that:

1)- an objects system $\Omega = \{(c_i, \gamma_i)\}$ is determined by choosing $c_i \in C$ and $\gamma_i \in \gamma$, $0 \le i \le \delta$,

2)-for each object $c_i \in C$ with a function f_j being triggered at n, being this object at n at a place $\pi = \xi(n,c_i)$, the objects s_i^k belonging to the generative scope S_i indicated by $\gamma_i(n)$ should have a localization function defined by:

$$\xi(n+1,s_i^k) = \pi^k$$

where π^k should be such that $\eta(fpo_\pi(k')) = (\pi,\pi^k)$ and k' is the index of the k-th field of the input interface specific to function f_i of c_i referred at the output interface of c_i.

Alike an object system, an object network can be seen as a specification comprising the trajectories over time for a given set of objects. In the same way, an important class of object networks are those that are computable. Again, we can determine a computable object network iteratively, generating a sequence of object networks $\Re_0$, $\Re_1$, ... , where each $\Re_i$ contains a finite number of objects, defined over incremental domains N_i. Each object network from the sequence is equivalent to the previous, being its objects added by a temporal instance, according to the laws of triggering, the selection function defined for the last instance and the localization function. The procedure is similar to the one used for objects systems with infinite number of objects, included the conditions for localization functions. With this methodology, one can determine, for each instant $n \in N$, the instance of any object that exists in n. The initial objects network from the sequence, $\Re_0$ has a special denomination, being called the kernel of an object network. In its kernel, objects and localization functions are defined only for instance n=0, and the selection function should be computable, being described by an algorithm γ'.

Definition 32 - **Kernel of an Object Network:** We define the kernel of an object network as an objects network $\Re_0 = (\Sigma, \Pi, \Xi, A, \eta, \text{fpi}, \text{fpo}, C^0, \xi^0, \gamma)$, where

- $\Sigma, \Pi, \Xi, A, \eta$, fpi and fpo are as in the Definition of objects network and
- $C^0 = \{c_i'\}$ is a set of objects defined only for n=0.
- ξ^0 is a localization function $\xi^0 : N \times C^0 \to \Pi$, defined only for n=0.
- γ is a selection function determined by means an algorithm γ'.

Starting with a kernel, new finite object networks are computed in sequence. Each algorithm step generates a new network that is, fundamentally, the previous one increased by the definition of new values for C, ξ and γ. The new C is the old one plus the objects to be generated at step n, according to γ. The new ξ is also the old one, defined now also for instant n, again according to γ. The algorithm γ' incrementally defines function γ. At each step the algorithm defines new instances for the current objects and new values for localization function and selection function such that for each instant n, we obtain new C, ξ and γ corresponding to a new finite objects network. Finite networks correspond to some element of such a sequence. Infinite networks (both networks with a finite number of objects, defined in infinite domains, or networks with an infinite number of objects), are considered as the limit element i of the sequence, when $i \to \infty$. An example of such algorithm is described in figure 5. Note that each new network in the sequence includes the previous one increased by the definition of a new time instant.

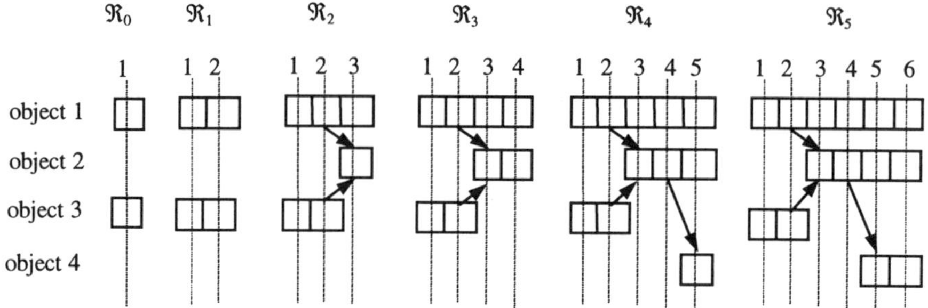

Figure 5 - Example of an Evolution Sequence

Examples of main algorithms described through pseudo-codes are the following:

procedure Main:

{Define $\mathcal{C}$, composed by objects c_i given in $\mathcal{C}^0$.

Define localization function ξ, composed by the tuples in ξ^0.

Define $\gamma = \varnothing$

For n from 0 to final

   {Apply γ' to determine $\gamma(n)$ and refresh γ.

   For all active objects c_i existing at n:

     {Calculate $\gamma_i(n) = (H_i, S_i, f)$.

     If $H_i = \varnothing$, go to next object

     If $H_i \neq \varnothing$:

       {execute function f, generating a new instance $c_i(n+1)$

       refresh c_i : $c_i = c_i(n) \cup c_i(n+1)$.

       For all $s_i^k \in S_i$

         {If $s_i^k \notin \mathcal{C}$ generate a new empty object and add to $\mathcal{C}$

         calculate the value for $s_i^k(n+1)$ from $c_i(n+1)$ and refresh s_i^k.

         determine $\xi(n+1, s_i^k) \in V(\xi(n, c_i))$ and refresh ξ.

         }

       }

     }

   For all objects c_i such that $(c_i, 1)$ does not appear at any other enabling scope and c_i is not at   neither generative scope

     $c_i(n+1) = c_i(n)$.

   }

}

Procedure γ'
{For each active object c_i
    {For each function f_j of active object c_i
        {Generate a new empty enabling scope for function f_j
        For each field k of input interface specific to f_j
            {check if in the place pointed by the arc fpo(k) does exist:
                no object, one object or more than one object
            If there is no object, delete the enabling scope(s) and go to next function
            If there is only one object, put it into the enabling scope(s).
            If there is more than one object, do as many copies of the enabling scope
              as the number of objects and put one object into each enabling scope.
            }
        For each enabling scope calculate a performance index
        }
    }
For each active object c_i
    {Do a list ordered by the performance index containing the function and the
    enabling scope.
    }
For each active object c_i
    {Choose the first element in the list as the function and enabling scope for the
        object
    Check if is there any conflict with other objects choices.
    If is there a conflict, use a decision criterion. The looser object chooses than the
        next in its list. If the own object c_i belongs to the enabling scope of another
        object, cancel its enabling scope and reorganize the list.
    }
For each active object c_i with an enabling scope different from empty
    {Create an empty generative scope for c_i
    For each field k of output interface specific to function f_j chosen
        {If is there an object in C not defined at n-1 and n for the desired class,
            put it into the generative scope, else create a new object for the desired
            class and include it.
        }
    }
  Returns, for each object, the enabling scope, the generative scope and the function
  chosen
}

2.7   *Extensions*

To enhance its representation power, additional definitions are developed to allow different classes of concepts. Those concepts are used mainly within computational semiotics theory[4,5,6,7]. They are presented next.

Definition 33 - **Temporal Restriction for Objects:** Let N be a set of time instants, S a class and o:N→S an object of type S. Let N' $\subseteq$ N . The temporal restriction of object o to N', denoted by o $\Downarrow$ N' corresponds to the object o':N→S such that if $(n,s) \in$ o and $n \in$ N', $(n,s) \in$ o'. Otherwise, $(n,s) \notin$ o'.

Example: N = { n_1 , n_2 , n_3 }, S = $\mathfrak{R}^3$, o = { (n_1 , (0,0,0)) , (n_2 , (0,1,0)) , (n_3 , (1,2,2)) }.

N' = { n_2 , n_3 } → o' = { (n_2 , (0,1,0)) , (n_3 , (1,2,2)) }.

Definition 34 -**Set Variable:** Let N be an enumerable set, with a generic element n and X $\subseteq$ U a subset of U. We define a **set variable** x of type X as a function $x : N \rightarrow 2^X$.

Examples: Let N = {1,2,3} and X = {1,2,3,4} . An example of a set variable x of type X is :

x = { (1, {1,2}) , (2, {2,3,4}) , (3, {1,3}) }

Assume now $X^2 = X \times X$. Thus, a set variable x' of type X^2 is, for example,

x' = { (1, { (1,2),(2,3),(2,4),(3,3) }) , (2, {(2,3),(4,1),(1,1)}) , (3, {(1,3),(2,1) }) }

Note, in the last example, that the value of x for each $n \in$ N corresponds to a relation. In this case, if we set R_1 = { (1,2),(2,3),(2,4),(3,3) }, R_2 = {(2,3),(4,1),(1,1)} and
R_3 = {(1,3),(2,1) }, we get, for short, x' = { (1,R_1) , (2,R_2), (3, R_3) }.

Definition 35 - **Generic Object:** Let C be a non-empty class. Let c be a set variable of type C. The variable c is called a **generic object** of class C.

Definition 36 - **Case of a Generic Object:** Let c be a generic object of class C. An object c' of type C is said to be a case of generic object c if $\forall n \in$ N, $c'(n) \in$ c(n).

Definition 37 - **Fuzzy Object:** Let N be an enumerable set with a generic element n, X a class, $\tilde{X}$ a fuzzy set defined onto X and $2^{\tilde{X}}$ the set of all fuzzy sets onto X. We define a **fuzzy object** x of type X as a function $x : N \rightarrow 2^{\tilde{X}}$.

If X is a passive class, $X = X_1 \times ... \times X_m$, $\widetilde{X}$ will be, in general, an m-ary fuzzy relation. In some cases, it is interesting to use not a generic fuzzy relation, but a fuzzy relation formed by the cartesian product of different fuzzy sets. In this case, $\widetilde{X}$ may be represented by a tuple of m fuzzy sets. If X is an active class, $\widetilde{X}$ would consider as fuzzy only the fields that are not functions. The m-ary fuzzy relation, in this case, will be represented by the (fuzzy) cartesian product of all elements that are not functions.

Note that a fuzzy object can represent any (standard) object $o = \{ (n,x) \mid \forall n \in N, x \in X\}$ if we take, for each $n \in N$, a fuzzy set that is a singleton in $x \in X$.

Since a passive object corresponds to a fuzzy relation, it is possible to define operations involving fuzzy objects. The same occurs with active objects, because the operations are related with non-function fields only.

Definition 38 - **Union of Fuzzy Objects:** Let x' and x'' be two fuzzy objects of type X, defined in N such that $\forall n \in N$, if x'(n) is defined, x''(n) is also defined. The union x of x' and x'' is a fuzzy object such that $\forall n \in N$, x(n) = x'(n) S x''(n), where S is a matrix operator which applies a triangular co-norm, element to element, in the m-ary relational matrices. Operator S applies only to non-function fields of the corresponding tuples.

Definition 39 - **Intersection of Fuzzy Objects:** Let x' and x'' be two fuzzy objects of type X, defined in N, such that $\forall n \in N$, if x'(n) is defined, x''(n) is also defined. The intersection x of x' and x'' is a fuzzy object such that $\forall n \in N$, x(n) = x'(n) T x''(n), where T is a matrix operator which applies a triangular norm, element to element, in the m-ary relational matrices. Again, operator T applies only to the non-function fields of the tuples.

For the sake of computational implementation, it is important to stress that both generic objects and fuzzy objects can be transformed into objects. Suppose that the values of their instances (which are sets or fuzzy sets) are represented by discriminating functions, functions that are approximated by multilayer neural networks. We can generate a standard object whose attributes are the parameters of such neural network. In this case, we represent a generic object (or a fuzzy object), by a standard object. To use a generic knowledge in this form, however, the arguments used to manipulate it must be modified to deal with generic/fuzzy objects in such a representation.

Definition 40 - **Meta-Object:** Let N be an enumerable set, with a generic element n; V be an enumerable set where each $v \in V$ is a variable of type N defined over the occurrence space T, $v : T \rightarrow N$; R be a set of restrictions for the values of variables V (possibly empty) and X be a class. A **meta-object** x of type X is a function $x : V \rightarrow X$.

Examples : Let T = { 1,2, ... } , N = {1,2,3,4,5,6}, V = { v_1 , v_2 , v_3 }, such that v_1 , v_2 , v_3 : T $\rightarrow$ N , R = $\varnothing$, and X = $X_1 \times X_2$, X_1 = {1,2,3,4}, X_2 = {a,b,c}. An example of a meta-object x' of type X_1 is x' = { (v_1 , 1) , (v_2 , 3) }. Other example of a meta-object x'' of type X is x'' = { (v_1 , (1,a)) , (v_2 , (3,a)) }.

Definition 41 - **Instance of a Meta-Object:** Let x be a meta-object of type X. An **instance** of x is an object x' where the variables of x are substituted for the values provided by specific instances of such variables in the occurrence space.

Examples: Consider the meta-objects x' and x'' as in the example above. An instance of x', doing v_1 = 1 and v_2 = 2 is x''' = { (1 , 1) , (2 , 3) }. Other example, for v_1 = 2 and v_2 = 5, x''' = { (2 , 1) , (5 , 3) }. An instance of x'', for v_1 = 1 and v_2 = 4 is x''' = {(1 , (1,a)), (4 , (3,a))}.

Definition 42 - **Occurrence of a Meta-Object in an Object:** Consider an object o from class X, and a meta-object o' from class X'. An occurrence o'' of meta-object o' in o is an object o'' such that o'' is at the same time a sub-object from an instance of o' and a temporal restriction of a sub-object of o.

Examples: Assume an object x of type X, x = { (1,(1,a)) , (2,(3,b)) , (3,(3,a)), (4,(1,c)) , (5,(2,b)), (6,(3,a)). As in the example above, for v_1 = 1 and v_2 = 2, we have an instance x''' = { (1,1), (2,3) } which is a temporal restriction of sub object x ↓ X_1 of x to N = {1,2}. This is an occurrence of x' in x. Other occurrences for this case do exist, for v = (v_1 , v_2) = (1,3), v = (1,6), v = (4,6). Not so obvious is the case for v = (4,2) and v = (4,3). Meta-object x'' does also occur in x, but there exist only two occurrences, for v = (1,3) and v = (1,6) respectively.

When the restriction R for a meta-object is not empty, domain variables may have restrictions to its values. One way of representing restrictions is by means of algebraic equations and/or inequations using domain variables. In this case the occurrence of meta-objects in objects does consider such restrictions for the determination of possible instances for the meta-object.

Example: In the example above, assume that $v_2 = v_1 + 1$. In this case, there exists only one occurrence of x' in x for $v = (1,2)$, because the restriction is violated for the other cases. Note that here, the meta-object x'' does not occur in x.

Other example could be $v_2 > v_1$. Viewing the inequality as a restriction in the example of Definition 6, we avoid non-intuitive cases $v = (4,2)$ and $v = (4,3)$ as occurrences.

Following the definition, an occurrence does not need to be, necessarily, a meta-object instance, but any sub-object of the former. With this, from the same meta-object there may be different occurrences in different objects, with each object from a different class, but sharing a field of the instance of the meta-object.

Definition 43 - **Occurrence of a Meta-Object in a Generic Object:** Let x be a generic object from class X, and x' a meta-object from class X'. An occurrence x'' of the meta-object x' in x is an object x'' such that x'' is an occurrence for any case of x.

Definition 44 - **Occurrence of a Meta-Object in a Fuzzy Object:** Let o be a fuzzy object from class X, and o' a meta-object from class X'. An occurrence o'' of the meta-object o' in o is a fuzzy object o'' such that o'' corresponds to the intersection of a sub-object from an instance of o', described as a fuzzy object by means of singletons, and a temporal restriction of a fuzzy sub-object of o.

Example: Consider the following fuzzy sets
$a_1 = \{ 1/0.2, 2/0.8, 3/0.6 \}$, $a_2 = \{ 1/0.1, 2/0.2, 3/0.9 \}$, $a_3 = \{ 1/0, 2/0.15, 3/0.3 \}$,
$b_1 = \{ 5/0.3, 6/0.4, 7/0.1 \}$, $b_2 = \{ 5/0.4, 6/0.4, 7/0.8 \}$, $b_3 = \{ 5/0.1, 6/0.9, 7/0.8 \}$,
$c_1 = \{ 15/0.2, 18/0.9 \}$, $c_2 = \{ 15/0.3, 18/0.8 \}$, $c_3 = \{ 15/0.7, 18/0.1 \}$, the fuzzy
object $x = \{ (1,(a_1,b_1,c_1)), (2,(a_2,b_2,c_2)), (3,(a_3,b_3,c_3)) \}$, and the meta-object
$x' = \{ (v_1, (2,5,15)), (v_2, (3,7,18)) \}$. For $v_1 = 1$ and $v_2 = 3$, there is an instance of
meta-object x' which is $x'' = \{ (1, (2,5,15)), (3, (3,7,18)) \}$. Thus, for $a'_1 = \{1/0,$
$2/1, 3/0 \}$, $b'_1 = \{5/1, 6/0, 7/0 \}$ and $c'_1 = \{15/1, 18/0 \}$, $a'_2 = \{1/0, 2/0, 3/1 \}$,
$b'_2 = \{5/0, 6/0, 7/1 \}$ and $c'_2 = \{15/0, 18/1 \}$ we have the representation of x'' by
the fuzzy object $x''' = \{ (1, (a'_1, b'_1, c'_1)), (3, (a'_2, b'_2, c'_2)) \}$. An occurrence of
x' in x, in this case, can be found to be $x'''' = (x \Downarrow \{1,3\})$ T x''', i.e.,
$x'''' = \{ (1, (a''_1, b''_1, c''_1)), (3, (a''_2, b''_2, c''_2)) \}$, where, taking the minimum
as triangular norm, we have: $a''_1 = a_1$ T $a'_1 = \{1/0, 2/0.8, 3/0 \}$, $b''_1 = b_1$ T b'_1
$=\{5/0.3, 6/0, 7/0 \}$, $c''_1 = c_1$ T $c'_1 = \{15/0.2, 18/0 \}$, $a''_2 = a_3$ T $a'_2 =$
$\{1/0, 2/0, 3/0.3 \}$, $b''_2 = b_3$ T $b'_2 = \{5/0, 6/0, 7/0.8 \}$, $c''_2 = c_3$ T $c'_2 =$
$\{15/0, 18/0.1 \}$.

224

Definition 45 - **Generic Meta-Object:** Let N be an enumerable set, with generic element n, V be an enumerable set, where each $v \in V$ is a variable of type N, R be a set of restrictions on the variables of V (possibly empty) and X be a class. A **generic meta-object** x of type X is a function $x : V \to 2^X$.

Definition 46 - **Case of a Generic Meta-Object:** Let x be a generic meta-object from class X. A meta-object x' of type X is a case of generic meta-object x if $\forall v \in V, x'(v) \in x(v)$.

Definition 47 - **Occurrence of a Generic Meta-Object in an Object:** Assume x as a generic meta-object of type X and x' an object of type X'. An occurrence x'' of x in x' is an object x'' such that x'' is an occurrence of any case of x in x'.

Definition 48 - **Occurrence of a Generic Meta-Object in a Generic Object:** Let x be a generic meta-object of type X and x' a generic object of type X'. An occurrence x'' of x in x' is a generic object x'' such that x'' is the union of all occurrences of any case of x in cases of x'.

Definition 49 - **Occurrence of a Generic Meta-Object in a Fuzzy Object:** Let x be a generic meta-object of type X and x' a fuzzy object of type X'. An occurrence x'' of x in x' is a fuzzy object x'' such that x'' is the intersection of a sub-object of x, viewed as fuzzy object, and a temporal restriction of a sub-object of x'.

Example: Consider the fuzzy sets a_1 = { 1/0.2, 2/0.8, 3/0.6 },
a_2 = { 1/0.1, 2/0.2, 3/0.9 }, a_3 = { 1/0.1, 2/0.15, 3/0.3 }, b_1 = { 5/0.3, 6/0.4, 7/0.1 },
b_2 = { 5/0.4, 6/0.4, 7/0.8 }, b_3 = { 5/0.1, 6/0.9, 7/0.8 }, c_1 = { 15/0.2, 18/0.9 },
c_2 = { 15/0.3, 18/0.8 }, c_3 = { 15/0.7, 18/0.1 }, the fuzzy object x = { $(1,(a_1,b_1,c_1))$,
$(2,(a_2,b_2,c_2))$, $(3,(a_3,b_3,c_3))$, and the generic meta-object x' = { $(v_1 ,([2,3],[5,6],15))$,
$(v_2 , ([1,2],[6,7],18))$ }. For $v_1 = 1$ and $v_2 = 3$, we have an instance of the generic meta-object x', x'' = { $(1 , ([2,3],[5,6],15))$, $(3 , ([1,2],[6,7],18))$ }. Thus, for
a'_1 = { 1/0, 2/1, 3/1 }, b'_1 = {5/1, 6/1, 7/0 } and c'_1 = {15/1, 18/0 },
a'_2 = { 1/1, 2/1, 3/0 }, b'_2 = {5/0, 6/1, 7/1 } and c'_2 = {15/0, 18/1 } we get a representation of x'' by the fuzzy object x''' = { $(1, (a'_1 , b'_1 , c'_1))$,
$(3, (a'_2 , b'_2 , c'_2))$ }. An occurrence of x' in x, in this case, can be found through
x'''' = $(x \Downarrow \{1,3\})$ T x''', i.e., x'''' = { $(1, (a''_1, b''_1 , c''_1))$,
$(3, (a''_2 , b''_2 , c''_2))$ }, where, taking again the minimum as a triangular norm, we have: $a''_1 = a_1$ T a'_1 = { 1/0, 2/0.8, 3/0.6 }, $b''_1 = b_1$ T b'_1 = {5/0.3, 6/0.4, 7/0 },
$c''_1 = c_1$ T c'_1 = { 15/0.2, 18/0 }, $a''_2 = a_3$ T a'_2 = { 1/0.1, 2/0.15, 3/0 },
$b''_2 = b_3$ T b'_2 = {5/0, 6/0.9, 7/0.8 }, $c''_2 = c_3$ T c'_2 = {15/0, 18/0.1 }.

Definition 50 - **Fuzzy Meta-Object:** Let N be an enumerable set, with a generic element n, V be an enumerable set, where each $v \in V$ is a variable of type N, R be a set of restrictions over the variables in V (possibly empty), X a class, $\tilde{X}$, a fuzzy set defined over X and $2^{\tilde{X}}$, the set of all fuzzy sets defined on X. A **fuzzy meta-object** x of type X is a function $x : V \rightarrow 2^{\tilde{X}}$.

Definition 51 - **Occurrence of a Fuzzy Meta-Object in an Object:** Let x be a fuzzy meta-object of type X and x' an object of type X'. An occurrence x'' of x in x' is a fuzzy object x'' such that x'' is the intersection of a sub-object of x and a temporal restriction of a sub-object of x' described as a fuzzy object.

Definition 52 - **Occurrence of a Fuzzy Meta-Object in a Generic Object:** Let x be a fuzzy meta-object of type X and x' a generic object of type X'. An occurrence x'' of x in x' is a fuzzy object x'' such that x'' is the intersection of a sub-object of x and a temporal restriction of a sub-object of x' described as a fuzzy object.

Definition 53 - **Occurrence of a Fuzzy Meta-Object in a Fuzzy Object:** Let x be a fuzzy meta-object of type X and x' a fuzzy object of type X'. An occurrence x'' of x in x' is a fuzzy object x'' such that x'' is the intersection of a sub-object of x and a temporal restriction of a sub-object of x'.

Note that the definitions of occurrence of fuzzy meta-objects are the same, wherever being in an object, generic object or fuzzy object. In all cases, the representation of object or generic object is first converted to a fuzzy object, and next the definition for an occurrence of a fuzzy meta-object in a fuzzy object is used.

In our examples of occurrences, we showed only meta-objects with two variables, i.e., $V = \{v_1, v_2\}$. But this is not a requirement. The use of meta-objects with two variables is particularly useful to represent events, i.e. sudden changes between two states. But other types of occurrences do exist, as e.g. an unitary occurrence that represents a single state. This kind of occurrence is useful, e.g., to obtain information about some attribute of the object during its existence. Meta-objects with more than 2 variables are used to represent tendencies or behaviors as, e.g., an increasing or decreasing behavior, or a periodic behavior. The formal model herein stated allows the representation of occurrences with all those subtle differences.

To use meta-objects (and its generic and fuzzy extensions) in the framework of object networks, we have to convert them to objects. But first, all objects that are to

226

be related to the meta-objects have to be modified to handle some kind of memory. This is showed in figure 6.

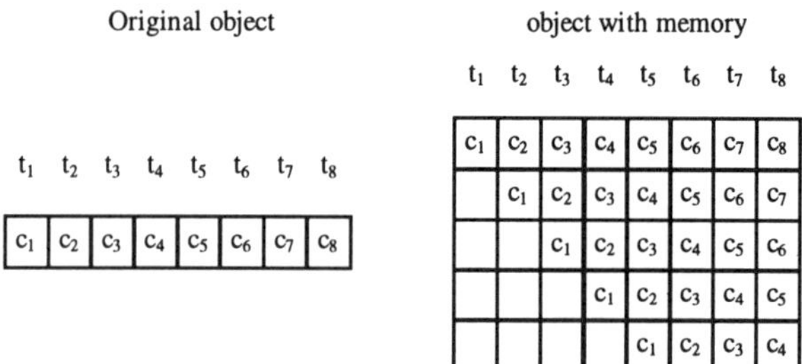

Figure 6 - Assembling Memory in an Object

Once the related objects are equipped with memory, we can modify the meta-object to become an object. This transformation is shown in figure 7.

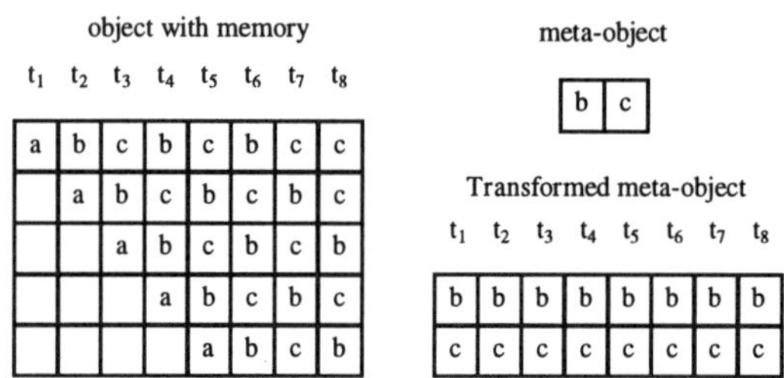

Figure 7 - Transformation of a meta-object into an object

Now, to check the occurrence of a meta-object in an object (and its variations), we use an active object that is fed both with the modified meta-object and the object with memory. Its active function is responsible for doing the respective computations.

In real systems, object memory can not be infinite. An alternative strategy for this problem is to use hierarchical memory using occurrence knowledge to generate a higher level memory. An example is shown in figure 8.

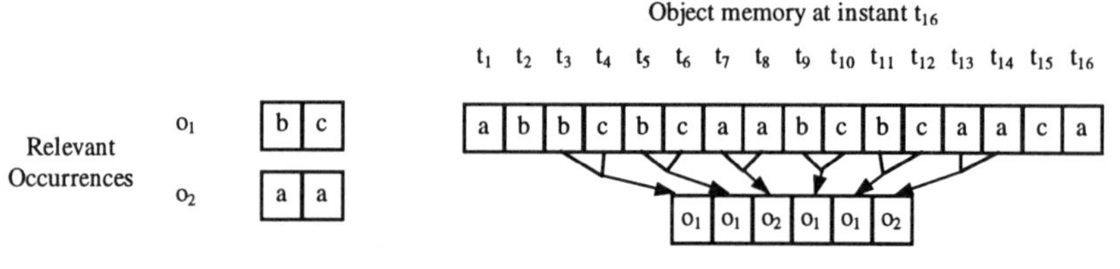

Figure 8 - Composition of a Higher Level Memory

As it can be seen in the example, a higher level memory has a smaller size. This may lead to information loss because higher-level memory stores only the occurrences considered to be relevant. The procedure to generate higher level memories can be successively applied, creating many levels, in a complex hierarchy.

3   Computational Intelligence and Object Nets

In this session we provide examples to show how we can implement and computational intelligence[12,13] techniques with object networks.

From computational semiotics[4,5,6,7], we know that there are three main functions used to build intelligent systems: deductive, inductive and abductive functions, also called arguments. Arguments are described by means active objects in an object network.

3.1   Fuzzy Systems

A general fuzzy production system is shown in figure 9.

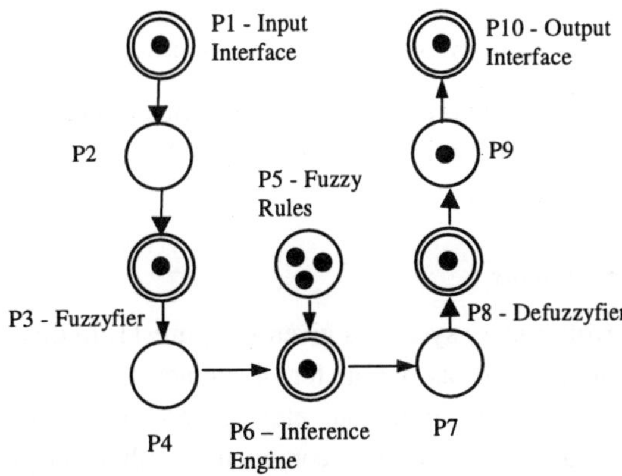

Figure 9 – Fuzzy System

The main argument in a fuzzy production system is the deductive argument in P6, called the inference engine. The other arguments in P1, P3, P8 and P10 are also deductive arguments, but their only task is to convert knowledge into a suitable format.

228

3.2 Neural Networks

Figure 10 shows the representation of a self-organizing neural network by an object network. Note that this neural network has two main arguments. The deductive argument works during the feedforward phase when it generates an output from an input. The learning function is an inductive argument that performs the self-organization of the neural network. It acts considering the input, and modifying the neural structure (i.e., the weights and offsets of the neural net) to perform learning.

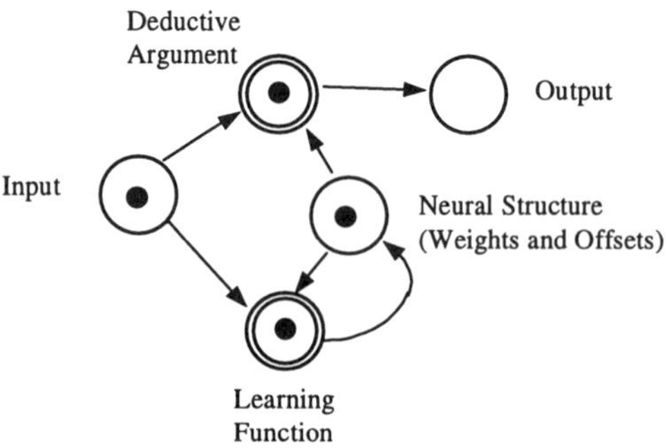

Figure 10 – Self-Organizing Neural Network

Other types of neural networks (like supervised neural networks) would have a similar representation including, in this case, a place for the desired output feeding the learning function argument.

3.3 Evolutionary Systems

An example of an evolutionary system is given in figure 11. In this example, there is an original population used as input for 4 inductive arguments (performing crossover, mutation, inductive mutation, etc), generating new sub-populations. Those 4 new sub-populations are used, in conjunction with the original population to fed an abductive argument that will choose the new population (and destroy the old one). The best individual of this new population is extracted by an abductive argument to generate a solution, and the new population is redirected again to the beginning through a feedback deductive argument that simply moves the new population from the new population place to the original population place.

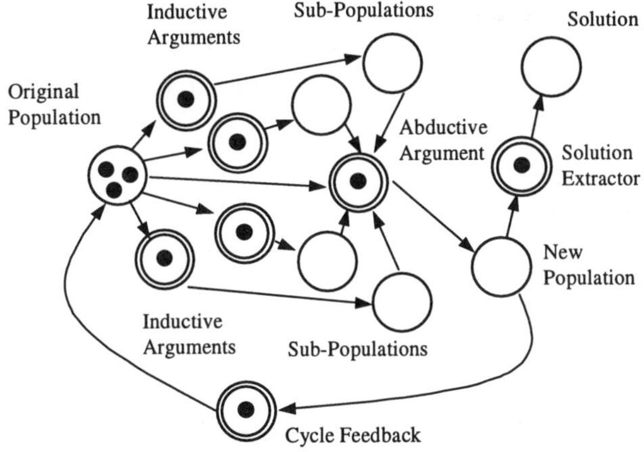

Figure 11 – Evolutionary System

3.4 *Hybrid Systems*

Soft computing techniques can be enlarged using not only its three main constituents (i.e., fuzzy systems, neural networks and evolutive systems), but (with object networks) hybrid systems can be constructed as well from the tools provided by the basic types of arguments associated with the three operations with knowledge: knowledge extraction, knowledge generation and knowledge selection.

4 Object Networks and Software Engineering

Object-oriented modeling approach has been extensively to specify, visualize, construct and document software, databases, business and many other systems. However, it is important to point out the difference between object-oriented programming and object-oriented modeling. Object-oriented programming basically involves adding inheritance and dynamic binding to programming. Object-oriented modeling comprises a software engineering methodology used to properly specificy complex software systems[14]. There are several object-oriented modeling methodologies proposed in the literature. Among them, we should mention the OMT[15] (Object Modeling Technique), one of the earliests to gain popularity and the UML[16] (Unified Modeling Language), derived from OMT and other technologies, which is being viewed as a new standard amongst software developers using object technology.

Most of the modeling techniques use a set of diagrams to capture the meaning of the system being modeled. For example, in figure 12, we summarize the diagrams used by UML. To each kind of diagram it is attached a corresponding semantics, used to specificy a part of the system.

Use case diagram		
Class diagram		
Behavior diagrams	Statechart diagram	
	Activity diagram	
	Interaction diagrams	Sequence diagram
		Collaboration diagram
Implementation diagrams	Component diagram	
	Deployment diagram	

Figure 12 – Diagrams used by UML

The choice of diagrams to be used in a system modeling has a profound influence on how a problem is approached and how a solution is developed. As a general tool, UML provides different types of diagrams to allow different types of systems to be specified.

Intelligent systems are a special kind of software systems, whose particularities make them very difficult to be modeled by generic methodologies like UML or OMT. These methodologies still lack diagrams to adequately manage some characteristics of inteligent systems. A strong limitation of these approaches concerns their use of a limited scope of the object-oriented paradigm, which is, the idea of a set of objects that exchange messages. Although being the usual meaning of what is an object system, it does not convey the whole expressiveness of the paradigm. The formalization of what is an object and an object system introduced in this paper attempts to surpass this limitation by considering messages also as objects. In this sense, our formalization subsumes the usual conceptualization, and embraces a more abstract view of what an object is. It allows a representation for adaptation, self-organization and parallelism, important issues when modeling intelligent behavior, which are not easyly tackled by generical modeling tools. When put together with higher order models of intelligence, like semiotics and computational intelligence, the object networks appear as a promising tool for modeling intelligent systems.

The design and implementation of an autonomous vehicle controller, example developed under this paradigm can be found in the work of Gudwin[4,6]. In this example, the task is to navigate a vehicle in an unknown environment, by interactively building an internal model for the environment, and using the model to make control decisions about the next actions to be performed.

5   Conclusion

The notion of object network has been introduced with the purpose to provide a modeling and implementation framework for computational intelligence. Beginning with a general and formal approach, put in the form of a foundation for a theory of objects, the idea of an object system was developed, followed by the key concept of object network. Object network has the formal and representational power needed to deal with intelligent systems. Several potential applications have been envisioned including control of autonomous vehicles using computational semiotics methodology[4,5,6].

Acknowledgements

The second author acknowledges CNPq, the Brazilian National Research Council for grant #300729/86-3.

References

1. A.Snyder, "The Essence of Objects:Concepts and Terms" - *IEEE Software*, pp. 31-42, Jan. (1993).
2. Y. Wand, "A Proposal for a Formal Model of Objects" - *in Object-Oriented Concepts, Databases and Applications*, W. Kim and F. Lochovsky, eds., (ACM Press, New York, pp. 537-559, 1989).
3. M.I.Wolczko, - *Semantics of Object-Oriented Languages* – (Ph.D. Thesis - Technical Report Series UMCS-88-6-1 - Department of Computer Science, University of Manchester, Manchester M13 9PL, England, 1988).
4. R.R.Gudwin, *Contribuições ao Estudo Matemático de Sistemas Inteligentes* – Ph.D. Thesis - DCA-FEEC-UNICAMP, Maio (1996) (in portuguese)
5. R.R.Gudwin and F.A.C.Gomide, *Computational Semiotics : An Approach for the Study of Intelligent Systems - Part I : Foundations* – (Technical Report RT-DCA 09 – DCA-FEEC-UNICAMP, 1997).
6. R.R.Gudwin and F.A.C.Gomide, *Computational Semiotics : An Approach for the Study of Intelligent Systems - Part II : Theory and Application* – (Technical Report RT-DCA 09 – DCA-FEEC-UNICAMP, 1997).
7. R.R.Gudwin and F.A.C.Gomide, *An Approach to Computational Semiotics* – (Proceedings of the ISAS'97 – Intelligent Systems and Semiotics : A

Learning Perspective – International Conference – Gaithersburg, MD, USA - 22-25 September, 1997).

8. M. Davis, *Computability & Unsolvability* (McGraw-Hill Book Company, New York, 1958).

9. R.L.Epstein and W.A.Carnielli, *Computability : Computable Functions, Logic and the Foundations of Mathematics* (Wadsworth & Brooks/ Cole Advanced Books & Software - Pacific Grove, California, USA,1989).

10. K.Jensen, - "Coloured Petri Nets : A High Level Language for System Design and Analysis" - *Lecture Notes in Computer Science 483 - Advances in Petri Nets*, pp. 342-416, (1990).

11. T.Murata, - "Petri Nets : Properties, Analysis and Applications" - *Proceedings of the IEEE*, vol. 77, n. 4, April (1989).

12. L.Zadeh, – "Soft Computing and Fuzzy Logic", *IEEE Software*, vol. 11, n. 6, pp. 48-56, (1994).

13. J.Zurada, R.J.Marks II, and C.J.Robinson, - *Computational Intelligence - Imitating Life* – (IEEE Press, USA, 1994).

14. S. Sigfried – *Understanding Object-Oriented Software Engineering* – (IEEE Press, USA, 1995).

15. J.Rumbaugh, M.Blaha, W.Premerlani and F. Eddy - *Object-Oriented Modeling and Design* – (Prentice Hall, USA, 1991).

16. M. Fowler, K. Scott - *Uml Distilled : Applying the Standard Object Modeling Language* - (Addison-Wesley Object Technology Series, USA, 1997).

Exercises

1. Assume we are interested in modeling an industrial oven and consider that, for our purposes, the following list of attributes fully describes an oven: Width (w), Height (h), Depth (d), Weight (p), Color (c), Temperature (t), Number of heaters (nh), Clean State (cl), Age (a) and Conservation State (cs).

Notice that some of the attributes are static, as Width, Height, Depth, Weight, Color and Number of heaters. Width, Height and Depth are given in cm, Weight in kg, Color by a triplet (R,G,B), and Number of heaters is an integer number. Temperature is a dynamic attribute, ranging from 0 to 200 °C. Age is also a dynamic attribute, ranging from 0 to 50 years. Clean State and Conservation State are normalized dynamic attributes, ranging from 0 to 1. A clean state of 0 means that the oven is totally dirty. A clean state of 1 means a totally clean oven. The same holds with the Conservation State: 0 means a spoiled (useless) oven, whereas 1 means a perfect working oven.

Now, suppose that the dynamic attributes are as given by the functions depicted in figure 13:

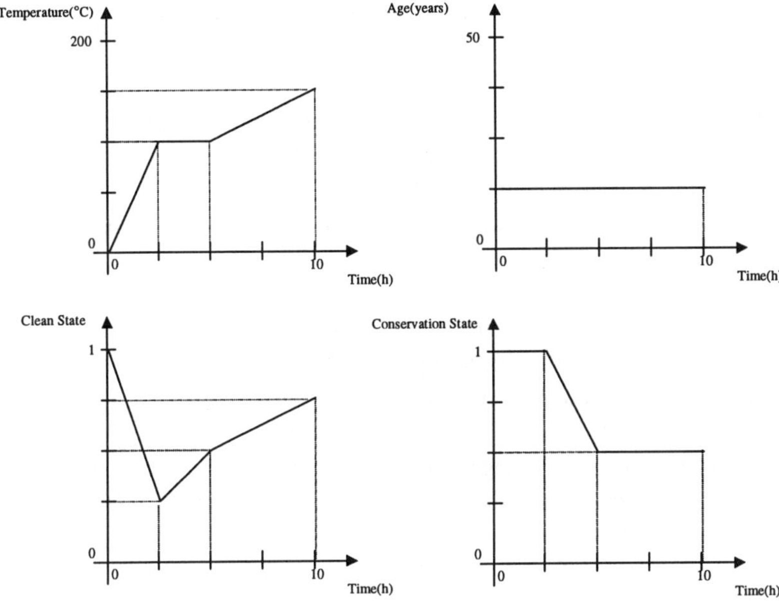

Figure 13 – Dynamic Attributes of Industrial Oven

Based on the formal definition of object, define the classes involved and the mathematical object "oven" that models the industrial oven in the period of time indicated in the figure 13.

2. Consider the object model for an industrial oven developed in exercise 1. We want to model the verb "to warm" and to use it associated with the oven. The purpose to answer the questions: Did the oven warm ? When ?

Based on the formal definition of meta-object, build a (fuzzy/generic) meta-object to model the verb "to warm". Next, find the occurrences of such meta-object in the object "oven".

234

3. Assume the meta-object developed in exercise 2 and the object developed in exercise 1. Transform the meta-object "to warm" into an object, and the object "oven" into an object with memory. Next, build an object network that is able to compute if (and when) something has warmed, and feed it with the object "oven" to obtain the answer.

4. Consider the graphs of object networks illustrated in figures 9, 10 and 11, illustrating examples of a fuzzy system, a neural network and an evolutionary system. Provide a formal definition of the kernel for each object network, and develop them through a sequence of object networks, until reaching object networks with 10 time steps.

5. Recall the example of an object network depicted in figure 10, which represents a neural network with unsupervised learning. Develop the graph for an object network for a neural network with supervised learning.

6. Let N be the set of integers and R the set of reals. Let it be a class C_1 representing instances of rhematic knowledge pieces given by $C_1 = \{(v_1,v_2)\}$, where $v_1 \in N$ corresponds to a flag indicating the rhematic knowledge type, as follows: 0 - sensorial piece of knowledge, 1 – designative piece of knowledge, 2 – prescriptive piece of knowledge and $v_2 \in R_n$ corresponds to the set of attributes characterizing the rhematic knowledge pieces (do not care, by now, about it). Let it be a class C_2, representing instances of objects of type sensor, given by $C_2 = \{(v_3,v_4,f_1)\}$, where $v_3 \in N$ corresponds to a timer indicating the time instant, $v_4 \in C_1$ corresponds to the output interface and f_1 is a function $f_1:N \to N \times C_1$, that for each time instant updates the internal timer and generates an object of type C_1 corresponding to a sensorial piece of knowledge (flag=0). Let it be a class C_3 representing instances of objects of type actuator, given by $C_3 = \{(v_5, v_6, f_2)\}$, where $v_5 \in N$ is a timer, $v_6 \in C_1$ is the input interface and f_2 is a function $f_2:N \times C_1 \to N$, that for each time instant updates the internal timer and destructively assimilate an object of type C_1, corresponding to a prescriptive piece of knowledge (flag=2). Let it be a class C_4, representing instances of objects of type reasoners, given by $C_4 = \{(v_7, v_8, f_3, f_4)\}$, where $v_7 \in C_1$ is the input interface, $v_8 \in C_1$ is the output interface, f_3 is a function $f_3 : C_1 \to C_1$, that destructively assimilates sensorial pieces of knowledge (flag=0), generating designative pieces of knowledge (flag=1), and f_4 is a function $f_4 : C_1 \to C_1$, that destructively assimilates designative pieces of

knowledge (flag = 1), generating prescriptive pieces of knowledge (flag=2). Let it be the kernel of an object network given by:

$\mathfrak{R}_0 = (\Sigma, \Pi, \Xi, A, \eta, \text{fpi}, \text{fpo}, \mathcal{C}^0, \xi^0, \gamma)$

$\Sigma = \{ C_1, C_2, C_3, C_4 \}$,

$\Pi = \{\pi_1, \pi_2, \pi_3, \pi_4\}$,

$\Xi = ((\pi_1, C_2), (\pi_2, C_3), (\pi_3, C_1), (\pi_4, C_4) \}$,

$A = \{ a_1, a_2, a_3, a_4\}$,

$\eta = \{ (a_1, (\pi_1, \pi_3)), (a_2, (\pi_3, \pi_4)), (a_3, (\pi_4, \pi_3)), (a_4, (\pi_3, \pi_2)) \}$,

$\text{fpo}_{\pi 1}(1) = a_1$, $\text{fpi}_{\pi 2}(1) = a_4$, $\text{fpi}_{\pi 4}(1) = a_2$, $\text{fpi}_{\pi 4}(2) = a_2$, $\text{fpo}_{\pi 4}(1) = a_3$, $\text{fpo}_{\pi 4}(2) = a_3$,

$\mathcal{C}^0 = \{ c_1, c_2, c_3 \}$, where c_1 is of type C_2, c_2 is of type C_3 and c_3 is of type C_4,

$Nu = (o, r)$ is a default value, $Nu \in C_1$,

$c_1 = \{ (0, (0, Nu, f_1)) \}$,

$c_2 = \{ (0, (0, Nu, f_2)) \}$,

$c_3 = \{ (0, (Nu, Nu, f_3, f_4)) \}$,

$\xi^0 = \{ (0, c_1, \pi_1), (0, c_2, \pi_2), (0, c_3, \pi_4) \}$.

Using this data, do the following:

a)   Draw the graph for the object network.

b)   Evolve the network $\mathfrak{R}_0$ for 6 steps (until $\mathfrak{R}_6$), using an arbitrary selection function γ (arbitrated step by step), assuming that the knowledge type requirements (if sensorial, designative or prescriptive) are sustained.

c)   Speculate on an asynchronous (distributed) algorithm that should be used for the determination of all instances of γ.

7. Think about the implications of using synchronous (centralized) and asynchronous (distributed) selection functions, assuming that an object network is allowed to have two active objects competing to destructively assimilate the same object. Speculate on how to generate an asynchronous selection function dealing with this problem.

Approximate Reasoning about Complex Objects in Distributed Systems: Rough Mereological Formalization *

Lech Polkowski[1] and Andrzej Skowron[2]

[1] Institute of Mathematics, Warsaw University of Technology
Pl. Politechniki 1, 00-665 Warsaw, Poland
e-mail: polk@mimuw.edu.pl
[2] Institute of Mathematics, Warsaw University
Banacha 2, 02-097 Warsaw, Poland
e-mail: skowron@mimuw.edu.pl

Abstract. We propose an approach to approximate reasoning by systems of intelligent agents based on the paradigm of rough mereology. In this approach, the knowledge of each agent is formalized as an information system (a data table) from which similarity measures on objects manipulated by this agent are inferred. These similarity measures are based on rough mereological inclusions which formally render degrees for one object to be a part of another. Each agent constructs in this way its own rough mereological logic in which it is possible to express approximate statements of the type: *an object x satisfies a predicate Ψ in degree r*. The agents communicate by means of mereological functors (connectives among distinct rough mereological logics) propagating similarity measures from simpler to more complex agents; establishing these connectives is the main goal of negotiations among agents. The presented model of approximate reasoning entails such models of approximate reasoning like fuzzy controllers, neural networks etc. Our approach may be termed analytic, in the sense that all basic constructs are inferred from data.

keywords: *rough sets, rough mereology, synthesis and analysis of complex objects, distributed systems, multi–agent systems, software quality*

1 Introduction

Approximate reasoning concerns synthesis of a solution to a given problem in the case when our knowledge about the context of the problem is insufficient

---

* This is an extended version of the lecture delivered at the Workshop: Logic, Algebra and Computer Science (LACS) held in the Banach International Mathematical Center in Warsaw on December 16, 1996.

to bring forth an exact solution e.g. when our knowledge is incomplete or uncertain, or the problem is formulated in an imprecise (e.g. natural) language.

Many formal models of approximate reasoning are described in the literature e.g. Dempster-Schafer theory of evidence [40], [41], [44], bayesian reasoning [26], [41], belief networks [26], [41], many-valued logics [13] and fuzzy logics [13], non-monotonic logics [41] and neural network logics [19].

We can extract from these formal models a general scheme for approximate reasoning.

It is manifest that this scheme encompasses classical models of reasoning adopted in mathematical logic [22]: the process of derivation of a formula from instances of axioms can be regarded as a synthesis process of a complex artifact from simple inventory parts and each application of a derivation rule (e.g. *Modus ponens*) can be regarded as an action of an agent applying its specialized operation to simpler objects in order to construct a more complex object.

At the end we discuss possible applications of the proposed formalism to quality software assessment [3], [6], [21], [27], [28].

1.1 A formal model of approximate reasoning

We present a formal model of approximate reasoning about processes of synthesis of complex objects. This approach have been developed and presented in [17], [29], [30], [32]–[38]. Our research has been stimulated by the demand for solutions of the following groups of problems concerned with the treatment of:

1. Poorly defined, poorly understood or incomplete design specifications.
2. Negotiations among interacting goals and constraints.
3. Decomposition of problems into subproblems (including the problem of formation of a hierarchical scheme for solving the problem).
4. Adaptation problems (including redesign and reuse problems).
5. Problems of knowledge representation and reasoning about knowledge.

These groups of problems are considered in [1] as the most important in the area of automated design and manufacturing.

Design as well as manufacturing processes involve the space of specifications and the space of structures. These spaces are present in our approach at each local process site and they meet each other at the inventory level where primitive (indecomposable) specifications are converted into primitive (inventory) constructs.

Our analysis can be applied to the following fields concerned with complex systems:

6. Computer-aided design [1], [39], [49] or computer-aided manufacturing [1], [5], [16], [49]. In this field, a complex system is synthesized , or designed, from elementary subsystems.

7. Adaptive control of complex systems [15], [20], [33]. In this field, a given specification (constraint) is maintained by adaptive adjustment of specifications for some subsystems.

8. Business re-engineering [2], [25] (including software reuse). In this area, a complex system is adaptively modified according to a current requirement.

9. Cooperative and distributive problem solving [9], [10], [11, [12], [16], [39], [49], [55], [56]. In this field a complex system of local agents is organized from a set of agents in order to synthesize a solution to a problem.

The accessible knowledge on the basis of which constructs in the synthesis process are selected and classified (evaluated) is as a rule incomplete, poorly defined, or inconsistent. In consequence, we are bound to evaluate the basic ingredients of the synthesis process approximately only, in terms of values of some uncertainty measures which express a degree in which a given construct satisfies a given specification and in terms of some functors which propagate uncertainty measures along the synthesis scheme.

The general scheme for approximate reasoning can be represented by the following tuple

$$Appr\_Reas = (Ag, Link, U, St, Dec\_Sch, O, Inv, Unc\_mes, Unc\_prop)$$

where

(i) The symbol Ag denotes the set of agent names.

(ii) The symbol $Link$ denotes a set of non-empty strings over the alphabet Ag; for $v(ag) = ag_1 ag_2 ... ag_k ag \in Link$, we say that $v(ag)$ defines an *elementary synthesis scheme* with the *root ag* and the *leaf agents*

$$ag_1, ag_2, ..., ag_k.$$

The intended meaning of $v(ag)$ is that the agents $ag_1, ag_2, .., ag_k$ are the children of the agent ag which can send to ag some simpler constructs for assembling a more complex artifact. The relation $\leq$ defined via $ag \leq ag'$ iff ag is a leaf agent in $v(ag')$ for some $v(ag')$ is usually assumed to be at least an ordering of Ag into a type of an acyclic graph; we assume for simplicity that $(Ag, \leq)$ is a tree with the root $root(Ag)$ and leaf agents in the set $Leaf(Ag)$.

(iii) The symbol U denotes the set $\{U(ag) : ag \in Ag\}$ of *universes* of agents.

(iv) The symbol St denotes the set $\{St(ag) : ag \in Ag\}$ where $St(ag) \subset U(ag)$ is the set of *standard objects* at the agent ag.

(v) The symbol O denotes the set $\{O(ag) : ag \in Ag\}$ of *operations* where $O(ag) = \{o_i(ag)\}$ is the set of *operations at ag*.

(vi) The symbol *Dec_Sch* denotes the set of *decomposition schemes*; a particular decomposition scheme *dec_sch$_j$* is a tuple

$$(\{st(ag)_j : ag \in Ag\},\ \{o_j(ag) : ag \in Ag\})$$

which satisfies the property that if $v(ag) = ag_1 ag_2 ... ag_k ag \in Link$ then

$$o_j(ag)(st(ag_1)_j, st(ag_2)_j, .., st(ag_k)_j) = st(ag)_j \text{ for each } j.$$

The intended meaning of *dec_sch$_j$* is that when any child ag_i of ag submits the standard construct $st(ag_i)_j$ then the agent ag assembles from

$$st(ag_1)_j, st(ag_2)_j, .., st(ag_k)_j$$

the standard construct $st(ag)_j$ by means of the operation $o_j(ag)$.

The rule *dec_sch$_j$* establishes therefore a decomposition scheme of any standard construct at the agent *root(Ag)* into a set of consecutively simpler standards at all other agents. The standard constructs of leaf agents are *primitive (inventory) standards*. We can regard the set of decomposition schemes as a skeleton about which the approximate reasoning is organized. Any rule *dec_sch$_j$* conveys a certain knowledge that standard constructs are synthesized from specified simpler standard constructs by means of specified operations. This ideal knowledge is a reference point for real synthesis processes in which we deal as a rule with constructs which are not standard: in adaptive tasks, for instance, we process new, unseen yet, constructs (objects, signals).

(vii) The symbol *Inv* denotes the *inventory set* of primitive constructs. We have $Inv = \cup\{U(ag) : ag \in Leaf(Ag)\}$.

(viii) The symbol *Unc_mes* denotes the set $\{Unc\_mes(ag) : ag \in Ag\}$ of *uncertainty measures of agents*, where $Unc\_mes(ag) = \{\mu_j(ag)\}$ and $\mu_j(ag) \subseteq U(ag) \times U(ag) \times V(ag)$ is a relation (possibly function) which determines a distance between constructs in $U(ag)$ valued in a set $V(ag)$; usually, $V(ag) = [0,1]$, the unit interval.

(ix) The symbol *Unc_prop* denotes the set of *uncertainty propagation rules* $\{Unc\_prop(v(ag)) : v(ag) \in Link\}$; for $v(ag) = ag_1 ag_2 ... ag_k ag \in Link$, the set $Unc\_prop(v(ag))$ consists of functions $f_j : V(ag_1) \times V(ag_2) \times ... \times V(ag_k) \longrightarrow V(ag)$ such that
if $\mu_j(ag_i)(x_i, st(ag_i)_j) = \varepsilon_i$ for $i = 1, 2, .., k$

$$\text{then } \mu_j(ag)(o_j(x_1, x_2, .., x_k), st(ag)_j) = \varepsilon \geq f_j(\varepsilon_1, \varepsilon_2, .., \varepsilon_k).$$

The functions f_j relate values of uncertainty measures at the children of ag and at ag.

This general scheme may be adapted to the particular cases.

As an example, we will interpret this scheme in the case of a fuzzy controller [13]. In its version due to Mamdani [20], in its simplest form, we have two agents: *input, output*, and standards of agents are expressed in terms of linguistic labels like *positively small, negative, zero* etc. Operations of the agent *output* express the control rules of the controller e.g. the symbol

$$o(positively, small, negative) = zero$$

is equivalent to the control rule of the form
if $st(input)_i$ *is positively small and* $st(input)_j$ *is negative*
$$\textbf{then } st(output)_k \textit{ is zero.}$$
Uncertainty measures of agents are introduced as fuzzy membership functions [13], [54] corresponding to fuzzy sets representing standards i.e. linguistic labels. An input construct (signal) $x(input)$ is fuzzified i.e. its distances from input standards are calculated and then the fuzzy logic rules are applied [13]. By means of these rules uncertainty propagating functions are defined which allow for calculating the distances of the output construct $x(output)$ from the output standards. On the basis of these distances the construct $x(output)$ is evaluated by the defuzzification procedure.

Knowledge is represented in our approach by means of rough set theory [22]. This theory assumes that constructs in a given universe are perceived by means of the available information, expressed in the form of values on these objects of certain attributes (features), and in consequence these constructs which bear the same information about them are perceived as identical and form collections of indiscernible constructs. The resulting granularity of knowledge is the effect of incompleteness of knowledge. We are not able therefore to discuss individual constructs but their collections consisting of pairwise indiscernible objects; in consequence, we discuss not the membership relation but the containment relation. The counterpart of the notion of a fuzzy membership function would be the more general notion of a partial containment.

The formal treatment of partial containment is provided by the notion of a rough inclusion [29], [32], [34]. Rough inclusions are construed as most general functional objects conveying the intuitive meaning of the relation of being a part in a degree. In particular, it turns out that the relation of being a part in the greatest possible degree is the relation of being a (possibly, improper) part in the sense of mereology of Stanislaw Leśniewski [18]. We can regard therefore a rough inclusion as a tool by means of which we extend the mereological relation of being an ingredient to a weaker relation (of being a part to a degree) over all pairs of objects in the universe. In this way, we create a family of similarity measures on pairs of objects.

In mereology of Leśniewski the notions of a (possibly improper) part, of a subset and of an element are equivalent (see [18]) and therefore we can

242

interpret rough inclusions as global fuzzy membership functions on the universe of discourse which satisfy certain general requirements (stemming from our intuition).

We take rough inclusions of agents as measures of uncertainty in their respective universes.

Remark 1.1. Any non-leaf agent ag is able to establish a local decomposition scheme of complex constructs in its universe into some simpler parts by means of its rough inclusion $\mu(ag)$ and the relation *part* (of being a (proper) part) in the induced model of mereology of Leśniewski.

Remark 1.2. The mereological relation of being a part is not transitive globally over the whole synthesis scheme as distinct agents use distinct mereological languages.

The process of synthesis by a scheme of agents of a complex object x which is an approximate solution to a requirement Φ consists in our approach of the two communication stages viz. the top - down communication/negotiation process and the bottom - up synthesis process. We outline the two stages here.

In the process of top - down communication, a requirement Φ received by the scheme from an external source is decomposed into approximate specifications of the form

$$(\Phi(ag), \varepsilon(ag))$$

for any agent ag of the scheme. The intended meaning of the approximate specification $(\Phi(ag), \varepsilon(ag))$ is that a construct $z \in U(ag)$ satisfies $(\Phi(ag), \varepsilon(ag))$ iff there exists a standard $st(ag)$ with the properties that $st(ag)$ satisfies the predicate $\Phi(ag)$ and

$$\mu(ag)(z, st(ag)) \geq \varepsilon(ag).$$

The uncertainty bounds of the form $\varepsilon(ag)$ are defined by the agents viz. the root agent $root(Ag)$ chooses $\varepsilon(root(Ag))$ and $\Phi(root(Ag))$ as such that according to it any construct x satisfying $(\Phi(root(Ag)), \varepsilon(root(Ag)))$ should satisfy the external requirement Φ in an acceptable degree. The choice of $(\Phi(root(Ag)), \varepsilon(root(Ag)))$ can be based on the previous learning process; the other agents choose their approximate specifications in negotiations within each elementary scheme $v(ag) \in Link$. The result of the negotiations is successful when there exists a decomposition scheme dec_sch_j such that for any $v(ag) \in Link$, where $v(ag) = ag_1 ag_2 ... ag_k ag$, from the conditions

$\mu(ag_i)(x_i, st(ag_i)_j) \geq \varepsilon(ag_i)$
and
$st(ag_i)_j$ satisfies $\Phi(ag_i)$ for $i = 1, 2, .., k$,
it follows that
$\mu(ag)(o_j(x_1 x_2, .., x_k), st(ag)_j) \geq \varepsilon(ag)$
and
$st(ag)_j$ satisfies $\Phi(ag)$.

The uncertainty bounds $\varepsilon(ag)$ are evaluated on the basis of uncertainty propagating functions whose approximations are extracted from information systems of agents.

The synthesis of a complex object x is initiated at the leaf agents: they select primitive constructs (objects) and calculate their distances from their respective standards; then, the selected constructs are sent to the parent nodes of leaf agents along with vectors of distance values. The parent nodes synthesize complex constructs from the sent primitives and calculate the new vectors of distances from their respective standards. Finally, the root agent $root(Ag)$ receives from its children the constructs from which it assembles the final construct and calculates the distances of this construct from the root standards. On the basis of the found values, the root agent classifies the final construct x with respect to the root standards as eventually satisfying $(\Phi(root(Ag)), \varepsilon(root(Ag))$.

Our approach is analytic: all logical components (uncertainty measures, uncertainty functions etc.) necessary for the synthesis process are extracted from the empirical knowledge of agents represented in their information systems; it is also intensional in the sense that rules for propagating uncertainty are local as they depend on a particular elementary synthesis scheme and on a particular local standard.

We conclude this section with a concise rendering of basic notions of rough set theory.

1.2 Rough set theory preliminaries

An *information system* is a pair $A = (U, A)$ where U is a finite set called the *universe of objects* and A is a finite set of *attributes*; any attribute $a \in A$ is a mapping on the universe U. We denote by the symbol V_a the range of the attribute a; the set V_a is called the *value set* of a. We let $V = \cup\{V_a : a \in A\}$.

In consequence of the above assumption some objects may become indiscernible. For an object $x \in U$, we define for a set $B \subseteq A$ the *information vector* $Inf_B(x) = \{(a, a(x)) : a \in B\}$. We say that objects $x, y \in U$ are *B-indiscernible* when $Inf_B(x) = Inf_B(y)$; the *B-indiscernibility relation* $IND(B)$ is defined as follows: $IND(B) = \{(x,y) \in U \times U : Inf_B(x) = Inf_B(y)\}$. The relation $IND(B)$ is an equivalence relation and we denote by the symbol $[x]_B$ the equivalence class of this relation which contains x. We will use the term *concept* for subsets of the universe U; for a concept $X \subseteq U$, we define the two approximations of X relative to a set $B \subseteq A$:

$$\underline{B}X = \{x \in U : [x]_B \subseteq X\} \text{ and } \overline{B}X = \{x \in U : [x]_B \cap X \neq \emptyset\}.$$

The set $BN_B(X) = \overline{B}X - \underline{B}X$ is called the $B-boundary\ region$ of X. In the case when $BN_B(X) = \emptyset$ the concept X is said to be *B-exact*, otherwise X

is *B-rough*. The concepts $\overline{B}X$, $\underline{B}X$ and $BN_B(X)$ have clear epistemic interpretation viz. the concept $\overline{B}X$ collects all objects which belong certainly in X, the concept $U - \overline{B}X$ collects all objects which certainly do not belong in X and the concept $BN_B(X)$ collects all objects which are vague with respect to X i.e. have representatives both in X and in the complement of X. It follows that $BN_B(X)$ is a non-sharp boundary of X in the sense of Frege (cf.[23]).

Given a concept X, the numerical characterization of a degree in which an object x belongs in the concept X relative to the knowledge represented by an attribute set $B \subseteq A$ is provided by the rough membership function $\mu_{X,B}$ [24]. For $B \subseteq A$, $X \subseteq U$ and $x \in U$, we let

$$\mu_{X,B}(x) = \frac{\|X \cap [x]_B\|}{\|[x]_B\|}$$

where $\|Z\|$ denotes the cardinality of a set Z. In the case when $B = A$ we use the symbol μ_X instead of the symbol $\mu_{X,A}$.

We can extend the rough membership function μ_X to the function μ_U on the power set $\exp(U)$ of U. To this end, we define $\mu_U : \exp(U) \times \exp(U) \longrightarrow [0,1]$ by letting

$$\mu_U(X,Y) = \frac{\|X \cap Y\|}{\|X\|} \text{ in case } X \neq \emptyset \text{ and } \mu_U(\emptyset, Y) = 1.$$

We denote by the symbol *Stand* the class of pairs of the form (U, μ_U) where U is a finite set and μ_U is the standard rough inclusion on the set U.

The reader will find in [31], [42], [43], [46], [47] a thorough discussion of rough set-theoretic tools for decision rules generation and for synthesis of adaptive decision systems.

2 Mereology of Stanisław Leśniewski

The importance for logic of the fundamental study of relations of being a part was already stressed by Aristotle (*Metaphysics*, Book IV). The first modern mathematical system based on the notion of the relation of *being a (proper) part* was proposed by Stanisław Leśniewski [18]. We recall here the basic notions of the mereological system of Leśniewski; in the next section the mereological system of Leśniewski will be extended to the system of approximate mereological calculus called *rough mereology*.

We consider a finite set U; we assume that U is non-empty. A binary relation *part* on the set U will be called the *relation of being a (proper) part* in the case when the following conditions are fulfilled

(P1) (*irreflexivity*) for any $x \in U$, it is *not* true that x *part* x;

(P2) (*transitivity*) for any triple $x, y, z \in U$, if x *part* y and y *part* z, then x *part* z.

It follows obviously from (P1) and (P2) that the following property holds

(P3) for any pair $x, y \in U$, if x *part* y then it is not true that y *part* x.

In the case when x *part* y we say that the object x is a (*proper*) *part* of the object y. The notion of being (possibly) an improper part is rendered by the notion of an ingredient [18]; for objects $x, y \in U$, we say that the object x is a *part-ingredient* of the object y when either x *part* y or $x = y$. We denote the relation of being a *part*-ingredient by the symbol *ingr*(*part*); hence we can write

(I1) for $x, y \in U$, x *ingr*(*part*) y iff x *part* y or $x = y$.

It follows immediately from the definition that the relation of being an ingredient has the following properties:

(I2) (*reflexivity*) for any $x \in U$, we have x *ingr*(*part*) x;
(I3) (*weak antisymmetry*) for any pair $x, y \in U$, if x *ingr*(*part*) y and y *ingr*(*part*) x then $x = y$;
(I4) (*transitivity*) for any triple $x, y, z \in U$, if x *ingr*(*part*) y and y *ingr*(*part*) z then x *ingr*(*part*) z i.e. the relation *ingr*(*part*) is a partial order on the universe U.

We will call any pair (U, *part*), where U is a finite set and *part* a binary relation on the set U, which satisfies the conditions (P1) and (P2), a *pre-model of mereology*.

We now recall the notions of a set of objects and of a class of objects [18]. For a given pre-model (U, *part*) of mereology and a property m which can be attributed to objects in U, we say that an object x is an object m (x *object* m, for short) when the object x has the property m. The property m is said to be non-void when there exists an object $x \in U$ such that x *object* m. Consider a non-void property m of objects in a set U where (U, *part*) is a pre-model of mereology.

An object $x \in U$ is said to be a *set of objects with the property* m when the following condition is fulfilled:

(SETm) for any $y \in U$, if y *object* m and y *ingr*(*part*) x then there exist $z, t \in U$ with the properties: z *ingr*(*part*) y, z *ingr*(*part*) t, t *ingr*(*part*) x and t *object* m.

We will use the symbol x *set* m to denote the fact that an object x is a set of objects with the property m.

Assume that x *set* m; if, in addition, the object x satisfies the condition

(CLm) for any $y \in U$, if *y object m* then *y ingr(part)* x then we say that the object x is *a class of objects with the property m* and we denote this fact by the symbol *x class m*.

We will say that a pair $(U, part)$ is a model of mereology when the pair $(U, part)$ is a pre-model of mereology and the condition

(EUC) for any non-void property m of objects in the set U, there exists a unique object x such that *x class m* holds.

The following proposition [18] recapitulates the fundamental metamathematical properties of mereology of Leśniewski; observe that in mereology there is no hierarchy of objects contrary to the Cantorian naive set theory. We denote for an object $x \in U$ by the symbol *ingr(x)* the property of being an ingredient of x (non-void in virtue of (I2)) and for a property m, we denote by the symbol $s(m)$ the property of being a set of objects with the property m.

Proposition 2.1. The following equivalencies hold:

(i) *x class(s(m))* if and only if *x class m*;

(ii) *x class(ingr(x))*;

(iii) *x set(s(m))* if and only if *x set m*.

We recall the notions of an *element* and of a *subset* in mereology of Leśniewski. For $x, y \in U$, we will say that

(EL) the object x is an element of the object y (x *el* y, for short) when there exists a non-void property m such that *x object m* and *y class m*
and

(SUB) the object x is a *subset* of the object y (x *sub* y, for short) when for any $z \in U$, if *z ingr(part)* x then *z ingr(part)* y.

The following proposition is a consequence of (I4) and Proposition 2.1(ii).

Proposition 2.2. The following are equivalent for any pair x, y of objects:

(i) *x ingr y*;

(ii) *x sub y*;

(iii) *x el y*.

3 Rough Mereology

An approximate mereological calculus called rough mereology has been proposed (cf. e.g. [28–39]) as a formal treatment of the hierarchy of relations of being a part in a degree. We begin with an exposition of rough mereological calculus in the form of a rough mereological logic L_{rm}.

We begin with the syntactical part.

3.1 Syntax of L_{rm}

We have the following basic ingredients of the syntactic part of the logic L_{rm}.

Variables: $x, x_1, x_2, ...,$ $y, y_1, y_2, ...,$ $z, z_1, z_2, ...$ of type *set_element* and r, $r_1, r_2, ...,$ $s, s_1, s_2, ...$ of type *lattice_element*;

Constants: ω of type *lattice_element*;

Predicate symbols, function symbols: $\leq$ of type (*lattice_element, lattice_element*) and μ of type (*set_element, set_element, lattice_element*);

Auxiliary symbols: propositional connectives: $\vee$, $\wedge$, $\Longrightarrow$, $\neg$, quantifier symbols: $\forall$, $\exists$ and commas, parentheses.

Formulae: atomic formulae are of the form $\mu(x, y, r)$, $s \leq r$ and formulae are built from atomic formulae as in the predicate calculus.

Axioms: the following are axioms of L_{rm}

(A1) $\forall x.\mu(x, x, \omega)$;

(A2) $\forall x.\forall y.\{\mu(x, y, \omega) \Longrightarrow \forall s.\forall r.\forall z.[\mu(z, x, s) \wedge \mu(z, y, r) \Longrightarrow (s \leq r)]\}$;

(A3) $\forall x.\forall y.\{\mu(x, y, \omega) \wedge \mu(y, x, \omega) \Longrightarrow$
$\qquad \forall s.\forall r.\forall z.[\mu(x, z, s) \wedge \mu(y, z, r) \Longrightarrow (s \leq r)]\}$;

(A4) $\exists x.\forall y.\mu(x, y, \omega)$;

(A5) $\forall x.\forall y.\{[\forall z.[[\exists u.\neg(\mu(z, u, \omega)) \wedge \mu(z, x, \omega)] \Longrightarrow$
$\qquad \exists t.(\exists w.(\neg \mu(t, w, \omega)) \wedge \mu(t, z, \omega) \wedge \mu(t, y, \omega)] \Longrightarrow \mu(x, y, \omega)\}$;

and the axiom schemata $(A6)_n$ for n = 2,3,.... where

$(A6)_n$

$\forall x_1.\forall x_2....\forall x_n.\exists y.(\alpha_n(x_1, x_2, ..., x_n, y) \wedge$
$\qquad \beta_n(x_1, x_2, ..., x_n, y) \wedge \gamma_n(x_1, x_2, ..., x_n, y))$

where

$\alpha_n(x_1, x_2, .., x_n, y) : \forall z.\{[\exists t.(\neg \mu(z, t, \omega)) \wedge \mu(z, y, \omega)] \Longrightarrow$
$\qquad \exists x_i.\exists w.[(\exists u.(\neg \mu(w, u, \omega))) \wedge \mu(w, z, \omega) \wedge \mu(w, x_i, \omega)]\}$;

$\beta_n(x_1, x_2, .., x_n, y) : \mu(x_1, y, \omega) \wedge \mu(x_2, y, \omega) \wedge ... \wedge \mu(x_n, y, \omega)$;

$\gamma_n(x_1, x_2, .., x_n, y) :$
$\qquad \forall z.\{[\alpha_n(x_1, x_2, .., x_n, z) \wedge \beta_n(x_1, x_2, .., x_n, z)] \Longrightarrow \mu(y, z, \omega)\}$.

3.2 Semantics of L_{rm}

We will call an *interpretation* of L_{rm} a triple $M = (U^M, L^M, F^M)$ where U^M is a finite set, L^M is a (complete) lattice with the lattice partial order $\leq^M$ and with the greatest element Ω^M and F^M is a mapping which assigns to constants and predicate symbols of L_{rm} their denotations in M in the following manner: $F^M(\omega) = \Omega^M$, $F^M(\leq) = \leq^M$ and $F^M(\mu) = \mu^M \subseteq U^M \times U^M \times L^M$, where the relation $\mu^M \subseteq U^M \times U^M \times L^M$ is a function i.e. $\mu^M : U^M \times U^M \longrightarrow L^M$.

An M-value assignment g is a mapping which assigns to any variable x of L_{rm} of type *set_element* the element $g(x) \in U^M$ and to any variable r of L_{rm} of type *lattice_element* the element $g(r) \in L^M$. For an M-value assignment g, a variable x of L_{rm} of type *set_element* and an element $u \in U^M$, we denote by the symbol $g[u/x]$ the M-value assignment defined by the conditions: $g[u/x](v) = g(v)$ in case $v \neq x$ and $g[u/x](x) = u$; the same convention will define $g[p/r]$ in case of a variable r of type *lattice_element* and $p \in L^M$.

For a formula α of L_{rm}, we denote by the symbol $[\alpha]^{M,g}$ the meaning of the formula α in the model M relative to an M-value assignment g by the following conditions

(M1) $[\mu(x,y,r)]^{M,g} = true$ iff $\mu^M(g(x),g(y)) = p$ for some $p \geq^M g(r)$;

(M2) $[s \leq r]^{M,g} = true$ iff $g(s) \leq^M g(r)$;

(M3) $[\alpha \vee \beta]^{M,g} = true$ iff $[\alpha]^{M,g} = true$ or $[\beta]^{M,g} = true$;

(M4) $[\neg\alpha]^{M,g} = true$ iff $[\alpha]^{M,g} = false$;

(M5) $[\exists x.\alpha]^{M,g} = true$ iff there exists $u \in U^M$ such that $[\alpha]^{M,g[u/x]} = true$;

(M6) $[\exists r.\alpha]^{M,g} = true$ iff there exists $p \in L^M$ such that $[\alpha]^{M,g[p/r]} = true$.

It follows that the intended meaning of a formula $\mu(x,y,r)$ is that *the object x is a part of the object y in degree at least r.*

A formula α is *true in an interpretation M* iff α is M,g-true (i.e. $[\alpha]^{M,g} = true$) for any M-value assignment g.

An interpretation M is a *model* of L_{rm} iff all axioms (A1)-(A6) are true in M.

We will give the basic deduction rules for L_{rm}; recall that a deduction rule in the form $\frac{\alpha,\beta,...}{\psi}$ is said to be *valid in a model M* iff for any M-value assignment g if the premises $\alpha,\beta,...$ are M,g - true then the conclusion ψ is M,g-true. The deduction rule is *valid* when it is valid in any model M of L_{rm}. We have the following valid deduction rules

$$(D1) \quad \frac{\mu(x,y,\omega),\mu(y,z,\omega)}{\mu(x,z,\omega)};$$

$$(D2) \quad \frac{\mu(y,z,\omega),\neg\mu(y,x,\omega)}{\neg\mu(z,x,\omega)};$$

$$(D3) \quad \frac{\mu(x,y,\omega),\neg\mu(z,y,\omega)}{\neg\mu(z,x,\omega)}.$$

We show the consistency of the axiom system (A1)-(A6) by revealing a class of models of L_{rm}. We denote by *Stand* the class consisting of pairs (U,μ_U) where U is a finite set and μ_U is the standard rough inclusion on the set $\exp(U)$. For a pair $M = (U,\mu_U)$, we let $L^M = [0,1]$, the unit interval, $\leq^M = $ *the natural linear ordering on* [0,1], $\mu^M = \mu_U$ and $U^M = \exp(U)$. Then we denote by

Stand_Mod the class of triples $M^* = (U^M, L^M, F^M)$ where $M = (U, \mu_U)$ and $F^M(\omega) = 1$, $F^M(\leq) = \leq^M$ and $F^M(\mu) = \mu_U$. We have the following statement whose proof is straightforward.

Proposition 3.1. Any $M^* = (U^M, L^M, F^M)$ in *Stand_Mod* is a model of L_{rm}.

4 Rough Inclusions

In this section we are concerned with the structure in models of L_{rm} induced by rough inclusions. We show that in any model of L_{rm} we have a canonical model of mereology of Leśniewski introduced by means of the rough inclusion of this model. One can apply the Tarski idea of fusion of sets [51] in order to define in a model of L_{rm} the structure of a (complete) Boolean algebra which contains isomorphically the quasi-boolean structure (without the least (zero) element) corresponding to the model of mereology of Leśniewski. We show that the rough inclusion satisfies with respect to boolean operations of join and meet the same formal conditions which the rough membership function satisfies with respect to the set-theoretic operations of union and intersection.

We study relations of rough inclusions with many-valued logic and fuzzy logic; in particular, we show that when the rough inclusion is regarded as a fuzzy membership function then any fuzzy containment induced by a residual implication [13] is again a rough inclusion and, moreover, the hierarchy of objects set by the induced model of mereology of Leśniewski is invariant under these fuzzy containment operators.

We are concerned also with the problem of consistency of deduction rules of the form

$$(D_f) \quad \frac{\mu(x, y, r), \mu(y, z, s)}{\mu(x, z, f(r, s))}$$

where f is a functional symbol of type (*lattice_element, lattice_element, lattice_element*).

We demonstrate the consistency of (A1)-(A6)+(D_f) by revealing a class of models in which the deduction rule (D_f) is valid under an appropriate interpretation of f.

Given a model M of L_{rm}, $M = (U^M, L^M, F^M)$, we will call the function $\mu^M : U^M \times U^M \longrightarrow L^M$ the M-rough inclusion. We define a relation $congr(\mu^M)$ on the set U^M by letting $u \ congr(\mu^M) \ w$ iff $\mu^M(u, w) = \Omega^M = \mu^M(w, u)$ for $u, w \in U^M$. The following proposition, whose proof follows immediately by (A2) and (A3), establishes the basic properties of the relation $congr(\mu^M)$ and demonstrates it to be a μ^M−congruence.

Proposition 4.1. The relation $congr(\mu^M)$ is an equivalence relation on the set U^M and we have

(i) if $u\ congr(\mu^M)\ w$ then $\mu^M(v,w) = \mu^M(v,u)$;
(ii) if $u\ congr(\mu^M)\ w$ then $\mu^M(u,v) = \mu^M(w,v)$

for any triple $u, v, w \in U^M$.

It follows from this proposition that the rough inclusion can be factored throughout the relation $congr(\mu^M)$ i.e. we define the quotient set

$$U_\mu^M = U^M / congr(\mu^M)$$

and the quotient function

$$\mu_\sim^M : U_\mu^M \times U_\mu^M \longrightarrow L^M$$

by letting $\mu_\mu^M(u_\mu, w_\mu) = \mu^M(u, w)$; clearly, the pair $(U_\mu^M, \mu_\sim^M)$ introduces a model $M_\sim$ of L_{rm}. In the sequel we will always work with a fixed reduced model $M_\sim$. We denote by the symbol n_μ the *null object* i.e. the object existing in virtue of (A4) and such that $\mu_\sim^M(n_\mu, w_\mu) = \Omega^M$ for any $w_\mu \in U_\mu^M$. We will write $u_\mu \neq_\mu n_\mu$ to denote the fact that the object u_μ is not the null object. Let us recall that the existence of a null object in a model of mereology of Leśniewski reduces the model to a singleton, as observed in Tarski [50]. In the sequel, for simplicity of notation, we will write μ in place of $\mu_\sim^M$, U in place of U_μ^M, u in place of u_μ etc. We will call the rough inclusion μ a *strict rough inclusion* when it satisfies the condition $\mu(x, n) = 0$ for any non-null object x; we observe that any standard rough inclusion is strict.

We now show how the rough inclusion μ introduces in U a model of mereology of Leśniewski. To this end, we define a binary relation $part(\mu)$ on the set U by letting

$u\ part(\mu)\ w$ iff $\mu(u, w) = \Omega^M$ and it is not true that $\mu(w, u) = \Omega^M$.

Then we have the following proposition whose straightforward proof is omitted:

Proposition 4.2. The relation $part(\mu)$ satisfies the conditions (P1) and (P2) i.e. it is a relation of being a (proper) part in the sense of Leśniewski.

We now define in the model $M_\sim$ for any collection Ψ of objects in U, the notions of a set of objects in Ψ and of a class of objects in Ψ. We will say then that $u \in U$ is a *set of objects in Ψ, u set Ψ* for short, when

(S1) for any $w \neq_\mu n$ such that $w\ ingr(part(\mu))\ u$ there exist $v \neq_\mu n$ and $t \in \Psi$ such that $v\ ingr(part(\mu)\ )\ w$, $v\ ingr(part(\mu))\ t$, $t\ ingr(part(\mu)\ )\ u$.

If in addition, we have

(S2) $t\ ingr(part(\mu)\ )\ u$ for any $t \in \Psi$;

(S3) for any t, if t satisfies (S1) and (S2) with Ψ then $u\ ingr(part(\mu)\ )\ t$

then we say that u is a *class of objects in* Ψ, u *class* Ψ, for short. It follows from (A6) that for any collection Ψ there exists a unique object u such that u *class* Ψ and there exists objects of the form *set* Ψ.

We sum up the last few observations.

Proposition 4.3. For any model $M = (U^M, L^M, F^M)$ of L_{rm}, the pair $(U_\mu^M - \{n_\mu\}, part(\mu_\sim^M))$ is a model of mereology of Leśniewski.

4.1 Rough inclusion vs. fuzzy containment

In this section we will reveal some of the basic connections between rough mereology and many-valued logic [13], announced above. We recall that a *t-norm* T is a mapping $\mathsf{T} : [0,1] \times [0,1] \longrightarrow [0,1]$ which satisfies the conditions $\mathsf{T}(r,1) = r$, $\mathsf{T}(r,s) = \mathsf{T}(s,r)$, if $r \leq s$ then $\mathsf{T}(r,t) \leq \mathsf{T}(s,t)$ and $\mathsf{T}(r, \mathsf{T}(s,t)) = \mathsf{T}(\mathsf{T}(r,s),t)$. A *residual implication* $\overrightarrow{\mathsf{T}}$ induced by a t-norm T is a mapping $\overrightarrow{\mathsf{T}} : [0,1] \times [0,1] \longrightarrow [0,1]$ which satisfies the condition

$$\mathsf{T}(r,s) \leq t \text{ iff } r \leq \overrightarrow{\mathsf{T}}(s,t).$$

Clearly, when a t-norm T is a continuous mapping then we have a unique residual implication

$$\overrightarrow{\mathsf{T}}(s,t) = \sup\{r : \mathsf{T}(r,s) \leq t\}.$$

We consider a model $M_\sim$ of L_{rm}. As the induced model of mereology has the property that the notions of a set and of a subset are equivalent, we can interpret the value $\mu(u,w)$ as the value of a fuzzy membership function $\mu_w(u)$ in the sense of fuzzy set theory [51]. The partial containment can be expressed in this theory [13] by means of a many-valued implication viz. for a given many-valued implication $I : [0,1] \times [0,1] \longrightarrow [0,1]$, the induced partial containment function $\sigma_I(u,w)$ is defined by the formula: $\sigma_I(u,w) = \inf\{I(\mu_u(z), \mu_w(z)) : z \in U\}$. We show that when the implication I is a residual implication $\overrightarrow{\mathsf{T}}$ induced by a continuous t-norm T then the resulting function σ_T is a rough inclusion and, moreover, the function σ_T preserves the relation $ingr(part(\mu))$

Our next proposition reads as follows.

Proposition 4.4. For a continuous t-norm T and a model $M_\sim$ of L_{rm} with the strict rough inclusion μ, the function

$$\text{(i)} \quad \sigma_\mathsf{T}(u,w) = \inf\{\overrightarrow{\mathsf{T}}(\mu_u(z), \mu_w(z)) : z \in U\}$$

is a rough inclusion; moreover, we have

$$\text{(ii)} \quad \sigma_\mathsf{T}(u,w) = 1 \text{ iff } \mu(u,w) = 1.$$

We denote by $M_\top$ the model which is produced from a model $M_\sim$ with a strict rough inclusion μ by replacing μ with $\sigma_\top$. By the symbol $Stand\_Mod(\top)$ we denote the class of models of the form $M_\top$ where M is a standard model of L_{rm}.

We now formulate the consistency of the deduction rule of the form (D_f); the symbol $\mathrm{Con}((A1)\text{-}(A6)+(D_f))$ denotes the consistency of (D_f) i.e. the existence of the model of L_{rm} in which (D_f) is valid under a plausible interpretation of the function symbol f. We extend the syntax of the L_{rm} by adding a functional constant symbol f of type

$$(lattice\_element,\ lattice\_element,\ lattice\_element).$$

we extend accordingly the domain of F^M. Then we have

Proposition 4.5. $\mathrm{Con}((A1)\text{-}(A6)+(D_f))$; more specifically, the deduction rule (D_f) is valid in any model M in $Stand\_Mod(\top)$ where $F^M(f) = \top$.

Now, we are ready to present a general scheme for synthesis of approximate solutions to a given requirement. We begin with introductory remarks which provide a motivation and explain our methodological assumptions.

5 Approximate Reasoning in Distributed Systems: Methodology

We will start from a general scheme for reasoning with uncertainty by a system of intelligent cooperating agents. We begin with an account of the structure of an agent.

5.1 The agent structure

We will discuss here the structure of a single agent ag in a scheme S of agents.

A *pre-rough inclusion* μ_o on a set U is any function

$$\mu_o : U \times U \to [0,1]$$

which satisfies the following conditions:

(i) $\mu_o(x,x) = 1$;

(ii) if $\mu_o(x,y) = 1$ then $\mu_o(z,y) \geq \mu_o(z,x)$ for any $z \in U$;

(iii) $\mu_o(x,y) = \mu_o(y,x)$.

We recall that a *t-conorm* $\bot$ [13] is a function $\bot : [0,1] \times [0,1] \to [0,1]$ such that $\bot$ is increasing coordinate-wise, commutative, associative and $\bot(r,0) = r$. We extend the operators $\top, \bot$ over the empty set of arguments and over singletons by adopting the following convention : $\top(\emptyset) = 1, \bot(\emptyset) = 1, \top(r) =$

$r = \perp(r)$. We observe that by the associativity and commutativity of $\top$ and $\perp$, the values $\top(x_1, ..., x_k)$ and $\perp(x_1, ..., x_k)$ are defined uniquely for any finite set of arguments. We have the following proposition, whose straightforward proof is omitted.

Proposition 5.1. For any *pre-rough inclusion* μ_o on the set U, the function

$$\mu(A, B) = \top\{\perp\{\mu_0(a, b) : b \in B\} : a \in A\}$$

defined for any pair A, B of finite subsets of U, is a rough inclusion on the universe $U^{<\omega}$ of finite subsets of U.

We will work from now rather with pre - rough inclusions. Any interpretation of L_{rm} in which requirements for μ_0 are satisfied is called a *pre - model* of L_{rm}.

We now define formally the ingredients of our scheme of agents.

We consider an agent ag in the scheme. We will call the *label of the agent* ag the tuple

$$lab(ag) = (\mathsf{A}(ag), M(ag), L(ag), Link(ag), O(ag), St(ag),$$
$$Unc\_rel(ag), H(ag), Unc\_rule(ag), Dec\_rule(ag))$$

where

1. $\mathsf{A}(ag) = (U(ag), A(ag))$ is an information system of the agent ag.
2. $M(ag) = (U(ag), [0, 1], F(ag))$ is a pre - model of L_{rm} with a quasi-rough inclusion $F(ag)(\mu) = \mu_o(ag)$ in the universe $U(ag)$.
3. $L(ag)$ is a set of unary predicates in a predicate calculus interpreted in the set$U(ag)$.
4. $St(ag) = \{st(ag)_1, ..., st(ag)_n\} \subset U(ag)$ is the set of standard objects at ag.
5. $Link(ag)$ is a collection of strings of the form $ag_1 ag_2 ... ag_k ag$; the intended meaning of a string $ag_1 ag_2 ... ag_k ag$ is that $ag_1, ag_2, .., ag_k$ are children of ag in the sense that ag can assemble complex objects (constructs) from simpler objects sent by $ag_1, ag_2, ..., ag_k$. In general we can assume that for some agents ag we may have more than one element in $Link(ag)$ which represents the possibility of re-negotiating the synthesis scheme.
6. $O(ag)$ is the set of operations at ag; any $o \in O(ag)$ is a mapping from the cartesian product $U(ag_1) \times U(ag_2) \times ... \times U(ag_k)$ into the universe $U(ag)$ where $ag_1 ag_2 ... ag_k \in Link(ag)$.
7. $Unc\_rel(ag)$ is the set of uncertainty relations unc_rel_i of type
$$(o_i, \rho_i, ag_1, st(ag_1), ag_2, st(ag_2), ...,$$
$$ag_k, st(ag_k), ag, st(ag), \mu_o(ag_1), ..., \mu_o(ag_k), \mu_o(ag))$$
where $ag_1 ag_2 ... ag_k ag \in Link(ag)$, $o_i(st(ag_1), ..., st(ag_k)) = st(ag)$ and ρ_i is such that

$$\rho_i((x_1, \epsilon_1), (x_2, \epsilon_2), .., (x_k, \epsilon_k), (x, \varepsilon))$$

254

holds for $x_1 \in U(ag_1), x_2 \in U(ag_2), .., x_k \in U(ag_k)$ and $\varepsilon_1, \varepsilon_2, .., \varepsilon_k \in [0,1]$
iff $\mu_o(x_j, st(ag_j)) = \epsilon_j$ for $j = 1, 2, .., k$ and $\mu_o(x, st(ag)) = \epsilon$
Uncertainty relations express the agents knowledge about relationships among uncertainty coefficients of any agent ag and uncertainty coefficients of its children. The relational character of these dependencies expresses their intensionality.

8. $Unc\_rule(ag)$ is the set of uncertainty rules unc_rule_j of type
$$(o_j, f_j, \mu_o(ag_1), st(ag_1),$$
$$\mu_o(ag_2), st(ag_2), ..., \mu_o(ag_k), st(ag_k), \mu_o(ag), st(ag))$$
of the agent ag where $ag_1 ag_2 ... ag_k ag \in Link(ag)$ and $f_j : [0,1]^k \longrightarrow [0,1]$ is a function (called *rough mereological connective*) which has the property that

if objects $x_1 \in U(ag_1), x_2 \in U(ag_2), .., x_k \in U(ag_k)$
satisfy the conditions $\mu_o(x_i, st(ag_i)) \geq \varepsilon(ag_i)$ for $i = 1, 2, .., k$

then $\mu_o(o_j(x_1, x_2, ..., x_k), st(ag)) \geq f_j(\varepsilon(ag_1), \varepsilon(ag_2), .., \varepsilon(ag_k))$.

Uncertainty rules provide functional operators for propagating uncertainty measure values from the children of an agent to the agent; their application is in negotiation processes where they inform agents about plausible uncertainty bounds.

9. $H(ag)$ is a strategy which produces uncertainty rules from uncertainty relations; to this end, various rigorous formulas as well as various heuristics can be applied.

10. $Dec\text{-}rule(ag)$ is a set of decomposition rules dec_rule_i of type

$$(o_i, \Phi(ag_1), st(ag_1), \Phi(ag_2), st(ag_2), ..., \Phi(ag_k), st(ag_k), \Phi(ag), st(ag))$$

where $\Phi(ag_1) \in L(ag_1), \Phi(ag_2) \in L(ag_2), .., \Phi(ag_k) \in L(ag_k), \Phi(ag) \in L(ag)$ and $ag_1 ag_2 ... ag_k ag \in Link(ag)$ such that $st(ag_i)$ satisfies $\Phi(ag_i)$ for $i = 1, 2, .., k$, $st(ag)$ satisfies $\Phi(ag)$ and $o_j(st(ag_1), st(ag_2), .., st(ag_k)) = st(ag)$.
Decomposition rules are decomposition schemes in the sense they describe the standard $st(ag)$ and the standards $st(ag_1), ..., st(ag_k)$ from which the standard $st(ag)$ is assembled under o_i.

We may sum up the content of $(1) - (10)$ above by saying that for any agent ag the possible sets of children of this agent are specified and, relative to each team of children, decompositions of standard objects at ag into sets of standard objects at the children, uncertainty relations as well as uncertainty rules, which relate similarity degrees of objects at the children to their respective standards and similarity degree of the object built by ag to the corresponding standard object at ag, are given.

5.2 The approximate logic of an agent

We present in this section a formal approach to reasoning by any agent ag in the form of an approximate logic $\mathcal{L}_{app}(ag)$. We recall that any agent ag is endowed with a label

$$lab(ag) = (A(ag), M(ag), L(ag), Link(ag), O(ag), St(ag),$$
$$Unc\_rel(ag), H(ag), Unc\_rule(ag), Dec\_rule(ag)).$$

Atomic formulae of the logic $\mathcal{L}_{app}(ag)$ are of the form $(ag; \Phi, \varepsilon)$ where $\Phi \in L(ag)$ and $\varepsilon \in [0, 1]$. The set of formulae of the logic $\mathcal{L}_{app}(ag)$ is defined as the smallest set containing all atomic formulae and closed under propositional connectives : $\vee$, $\wedge$, $\neg$. The approximate formula $(ag; \Phi, \varepsilon)$ has the intended meaning of a formula Φ satisfied in a degree ε; formally, we will say that a construct (object) $x \in U(ag)$ *satisfies* the approximate formula $(ag; \Phi, \varepsilon)$, symbolically: $x \models (ag; \Phi, \varepsilon)$, iff there exists a standard $st(ag)$ such that $st(ag)$ satisfies the formula Φ and $\mu_o(ag)(x, st(ag)) \geq \varepsilon$. We write $x \models_{st(ag)} (ag; \Phi, \varepsilon)$ in order to stress that the satisfiability is achieved with respect to the standard $st(ag)$. In particular, for a decomposition rule dec_rule_i as in (10) above x satisfies $(ag; \Phi(ag), \varepsilon)$ whenever $\mu_o(ag)(x, st(ag)) \geq \varepsilon$; clearly, $st(ag)$ satisfies the approximate formula $(ag; \Phi(ag), 1)$. For any pair of formulae α, β of the logic $\mathcal{L}_{app}(ag)$ and any $x \in U(ag)$, we let $x \models \alpha \vee \beta$ iff either $x \models \alpha$ or $x \models \beta$ and $x \models \neg\alpha$ iff it is not the case that $x \models \alpha$.

5.3 The approximate reasoning by a system of agents

We now consider a system S of agents over an inventory INV. We assume that the relation $\leq$, defined by $ag' \leq ag$ iff $ag_1 ag_2 ... ag_k ag \in Link(ag)$ and there exists $i \leq k$ such that $ag' = ag_i$, orders S into a tree; we assume that any agent ag in S has exactly n standards which satisfy the composition rule in the sense that if $ag_1 ag_2 ... ag_k ag \in Link(ag)$ and $ag_1^i ag_2^i ... ag_{k_i}^i ag_i \in Link(ag_i)$ for $i = 1, 2, .., k$ then for any $j = 1, 2, .., n$ the composition

$$o_j(ag) \circ (o_j(ag_1), ..., o_j(ag_k))$$

produces from standards $st(ag_1^1)_j, ..., st(ag_{k_k}^k)_j$ the standard $st(ag)_j$. We denote by the symbol $Root(S)$ the root agent of the scheme S and the symbol $Leaf(S)$ will denote the set of leaf (inventory) agents of S.

Let us recall that our approach is motivated by the following observations:

1. The knowledge of an agent in a scheme for reasoning under uncertainty is incomplete. In particular, an agent may not be able to distinguish among certain requirements(specifications, formulas etc.) and its understanding of requirements is approximate only.

2. The local decomposition knowledge of an agent may also be uncertain and this knowledge may not be understood fully by other agents as the agents possess incomplete fragments of the knowledge about the world.

3. The leaf agents having an access to the inventory of elementary objects may be able to select objects which satisfy the requirements not exactly but in an acceptable degree only.

4. Agents may be able to classify objects approximately only, in terms of their closeness to certain model objects (standards, logical values etc.).

5. The general form of an inference rule under uncertainty (inf_rule) of an agent ag whose children are $ag_1, ag_2, .., ag_k$ is of the form

$$\textbf{if } [x_1 \models (ag_1; \Phi_1, \epsilon_1) \wedge x_2 \models (ag_2; \Phi_2, \epsilon_2) \wedge ... \wedge x_k \models (ag_k; \Phi_k, \epsilon_k)]$$
$$\textbf{then } o(x_1, x_2, .., x_k) \models (ag; \Phi, \epsilon)$$

where $x_1, x_2, ..., x_k$ are objects submitted by, respectively, ag_1, $ag_2, ..., ag_k$ and $(ag_1; \Phi_1, \epsilon_1), ..., (ag_k; \Phi_k, \epsilon_k)$ are approximate specifications (formulas) at agents $ag_1, ..., ag_k$, $o(x_1, ..., x_k)$ is the object produced by ag from $x_1, ..., x_k$ by means of an operation o and $(ag; \Phi, \epsilon)$ is the approximate specification at ag.

The intended meaning of (inf_rule) is as follows: if the agent ag_1 can submit an object x_1 satisfying the approximate specification $(ag_1; \Phi_1, \epsilon_1)$ and ... and the agent ag_k can submit an object x_k satisfying the approximate specification $(ag_k; \Phi_k, \epsilon_k)$ then ag can apply the operation o to assembly the object $x = o(x_1, ..., x_k)$ which satisfies the approximate specification $(ag; \Phi, \epsilon)$.

6. Problem specifications are issued by the external agent cag (the *customer agent*) in a language understandable (up to some degree) to some agents in the scheme (in particular, to the root agent R). The specific form of the language depends on the particular synthesis process.

The object x synthesized by the scheme as an approximate solution to a requirement is evaluated by the agent cag with respect to its local knowledge. The process of learning the correct synthesis of solutions to a given specification is concluded when the two evaluations are consistent.

7. Universes of objects (universes of discourse) of agents are models of L_{rm} in which certain collections of objects, called *standard objects*, are distinguished. The rough inclusions of the universes induce rough mereological distance functions in their respective domains by means of which objects are perceived and characterized with respect to the standards in the respective universe.

8. The semantics of the approximate logic of formulas of the form $(ag; \Phi, \epsilon)$ of any agent ag is defined in terms of standards of ag and the rough mereological distance function in the universe of objects of the agent ag.

We observe that for any agent ag in S there exists a unique $v(ag)$ in $Link$

such that $v(ag)$ is a subtree of S; we denote this $v(ag)$ by the symbol $v_S(ag)$.

An *S-object assignment* is a mapping g which assigns to any agent ag in S an object $g(ag) \in U(ag)$. An S - object assignment g is *S-admissible* if for any agent ag in S there is an operation $o_g \in O(ag)$ satisfying

$$o_g(g(ag_1), g(ag_2), ..., g(ag_k)) = g(ag)$$

where $v_S(ag) = ag_1 ag_2 ... ag_k ag$.

An S - *selector* Θ is a mapping which assigns to any non - leaf agent ag in S a tuple

$$< o_\Theta(ag), f_\Theta(ag), \Phi_\Theta(ag), st_\Theta(ag), \epsilon_\Theta(ag) >$$

and to any leaf agent ag a tuple

$$< \Phi_\Theta(ag), st_\Theta(ag), \epsilon_\Theta(ag) >$$

such that if $v_S(ag) = ag_1 ag_2 ... ag_k ag$ then

$$(o_\Theta(ag), f_\Theta(ag), \mu_o(ag_1), st_\Theta(ag_1), ..., \mu_o(ag_k), st_\Theta(ag_k), \mu_o(ag), st_\Theta(ag))$$

is an uncertainty rule of ag and

$$(o_\Theta(ag), \Phi_\Theta(ag_1), st_\Theta(ag_1), ..., \Phi_\Theta(ag_k), st_\Theta(ag_k), \Phi_\Theta(ag), st_\Theta(ag))$$

is a decomposition rule of ag.

An S - selector Θ defines a $\Theta-$ *constructive subscheme* S_Θ if

(i) for any non–leaf agent ag in S with $v_S(ag) = ag_1 ag_2 ... ag_k ag$ we have

$$f_\Theta(ag)(\epsilon_\Theta(ag_1), ..., \epsilon_\Theta(ag_k)) \geq \epsilon_\Theta(ag);$$

(ii) $st_\Theta(ag)$ satisfies $\Phi_\Theta(ag)$ for any ag in S;

A Θ–constructive subscheme S_Θ is *compatible* with an admissible S–object assignment g if

(i) $o_\Theta(ag) = o_g(ag)$ for any non–leaf agent in S;
(ii) $\mu_o(ag)(g(ag), st_\Theta(ag)) \geq \epsilon_\Theta(ag)$ for any leaf agent in S.

For the root agent $R(S)$ of the scheme S, we say that a formula

$$(R(S); \Phi, \epsilon)$$

in the logic $\mathcal{L}_{app}(R(S))$ is *consistent* with a Θ–constructive subscheme S_Θ if

(i) $\Phi(R(s)) \Longrightarrow \Phi$;
(ii) $\epsilon(R(S)) \geq \epsilon$.

Let S_Θ be a Θ–constructible subscheme compatible with an S–admissible object assignment g. Then a formula $(R(S); \Phi, \epsilon)$ is satisfied by an S–object assignment g if

$$g(R(s)) \models_{st_\Theta(R(S))} (R(S); \Phi, \epsilon);$$

we write in this case $g \models_S (R(S); \Phi, \epsilon)$.

The following proposition which follows directly from the above definitions expresses a sufficiency criterium for synthesis of an object $x \in U(R(S))$ which satisfies an approximate requirement $(R(S); \Phi, \epsilon)$.

Proposition 5.2. If a formula $(R(S); \Phi, \epsilon)$ is consistent with a $\Theta-$ constructive subscheme S_Θ and the $\Theta-$ constructive subscheme S_Θ is compatible with an admissible S–object assignment g, then $g \models_S (R(S); \Phi, \epsilon)$.

It follows from this proposition that the object $x = g(R(S))$ which satisfies the approximate requirement $(R(S)); \Phi, \epsilon)$ can be constructed by the scheme S in the case when a $\Theta-$ constructive subscheme S_Θ and an S - object assignment g can be negotiated by the agents in S which are such that : the approximate requirement $(R(S); \Phi, \epsilon)$ is consistent with S_Θ and S_Θ is compatible with the S - object assignment g.

6 Approximate Synthesis of a Solution From Data

In this section, we present some examples concerning approximate reasoning by systems of intelligent agents along the scheme set above. The reader will find in [29] an example of a negotiation process based on boolean reasoning [4], [52] and in [30], [33], [36], [45] an idea of a rough mereological controller.

6.1 Rough inclusions from information systems

Rough inclusions can be generated from the information system $\mathbf{A}$; for instance, for a given partition $P = \{A_1, \dots, A_k\}$ of the set A of attributes into non-empty sets $A_1, \dots, A_k$, and a given set $W = \{w_1, \dots, w_k\}$ of weights, $w_i \in [0, 1]$ for $i = 1, 2, \dots, k$ and $\sum_{i=1}^{k} w_i = 1$ we let

$$\mu_{o,P,W}(x,y) = \sum_{i=1}^{k} w_i \cdot \frac{\|IND_i(x,y)\|}{\|A_i\|}$$

where $IND_i(x,y) = \{a \in A_i : a(x) = a(y)\}$. It is easy to check that $\mu_{o,P,W}$ is a pre-rough inclusion. We give an example illustrating this procedure.

Example 6.1. Consider an information system (H)

The table below shows values of the initial rough inclusion $\mu_{o,P,W}(x,y) = \frac{\|IND(x,y)\|}{3}$ i.e. we consider the simplest case when $k = 1$, $w_1 = 1$.

	hat	ker	pig
x_1	1	0	0
x_2	0	0	1
x_3	0	1	0
x_4	1	1	0

Table 1. The information system (H)

	x_1	x_2	x_3	x_4
x_1	1	0.33	0.33	0.66
x_2	0.33	1	0.33	0.00
x_3	0.33	0.33	1	0.66
x_4	0.66	0.00	0.66	1

Table 2. Initial rough inclusion for (H)

Example 6.2. In addition to information system (agent) (H) from Example 1, we consider agents (B) and (HB) . Together with H they form the string $\mathbf{ag} = (H)(B)(HB)$ in *Link* i.e. (HB) takes objects: x sent by (H) and y sent by (B) and assembles a complex object xy. The information systems of (B) and (HB) are shown below. The standards are taken as: x_1, x_2 at (H) and y_1, y_3 at (B) and in the table for (HB) we have only standards $x_1 y_1, x_1 y_3, x_2 y_1$ and $x_2 y_3$. The attributes at (HB) are related to those of (H) and (B) by formulas: $har = pis \land cut \land kni$, $lar = pis \land \neg cut \land \neg kni \lor \neg pis \land cut \land \neg kni \lor \neg pis \land \neg cut \land kni$, $off = hat \land pis$, $tar = kni \land pig \land \neg cr$ hence one can easily complete the table for (HB).

	pis	*cut*	*kni*	*cr*
y_1	1	1	1	1
y_2	1	0	0	0
y_3	0	0	1	0
y_4	1	1	1	0

Table 3. The information system (B)

The values of the initial rough inclusion $\mu = \mu_{o,P,W}$ are calculated for (B) and (BH) by the same procedure as in Example 1.

	har	*lar*	*off*	*tar*
x_1y_1	1	0	1	0
x_1y_3	0	1	0	0
x_2y_1	1	0	0	0
x_2y_3	0	1	0	1

Table 4. The information system (HB)

6.2 Uncertainty functions from data

We outline an algorithm which may be used to extract from information systems of agents in a scheme S approximations to uncertainty functions (rough mereological connectives).

Example 6.3. We will determine an approximation to the mereological connective at the standard x_1y_1 i.e. a function f such that:

for any pair ϵ_1, ϵ_2,

if $\mu(x, x_1) \geq \epsilon_1$ and $\mu(y, y_1) \geq \epsilon_2$ **then** $\mu(xy, x_1y_1) \geq f(\epsilon_1, \epsilon_2)$.

The following tables show conditions which f is to fulfill.

x	$\mu(x, x_1)$	y	$\mu(y, y_1)$	$\mu(xy, x_1y_1)$
x_1	1	y_1	1	1
x_1	1	y_2	0.25	0.5
x_1	1	y_3	0.25	0.25
x_1	1	y_4	0.75	1
x_2	0.33	y_1	1	0.5
x_2	0.33	y_2	0.25	0.25
x_2	0.33	y_3	0.25	0.00
x_2	0.33	y_4	0.75	0.5

Table 5. The conditions for f (first part)

This full set T_0 of conditions can be reduced: we can find a minimal set T of vectors of the form $(\varepsilon_1', \varepsilon_2', \varepsilon)$ such that if f satisfies the condition $f(\varepsilon_1', \varepsilon_2') = \varepsilon$ for each $(\varepsilon_1', \varepsilon_2', \varepsilon) \in T$ then f extends by the formula: for $(\varepsilon_1, \varepsilon_2, \varepsilon_3) \in T_0$ we let $f(\varepsilon_1, \varepsilon_2) = \varepsilon^*$ where $(\varepsilon_1^*, \varepsilon_2^*, \varepsilon^*) \in T$ and: **if** $\varepsilon_1 \geq \varepsilon_1', \varepsilon_2 \geq \varepsilon_2'$ for some $(\varepsilon_1', \varepsilon_2', \varepsilon) \in T$ **then** $\varepsilon_1^* \geq \varepsilon_1', \varepsilon_2^* \geq \varepsilon_2'$. This follows by definition of f.

The following algorithm produces a minimal set T of conditions.

Algorithm

Input : table T_0 of vectors $(\mu(x, x_1), \mu(y, y_1), \mu(xy, x_1y_1))$;

Output: table T of vectors of the form $row(\varepsilon)$.

x	$\mu(x,x_1)$	y	$\mu(y,y_1)$	$\mu(xy,x_1y_1)$
x_3	0.33	y_1	1	0.75
x_3	0.33	y_2	0.25	0.25
x_3	0.33	y_3	0.25	0.25
x_3	0.33	y_4	0.75	0.75
x_4	0.66	y_1	1	1
x_4	0.66	y_2	0.25	0.5
x_4	0.66	y_3	0.25	0.25
x_4	0.66	y_4	0.75	1

Table 6. The conditions for f (second part)

Step 1. For each pair $(\mu(x,x_1) = \varepsilon_1, \mu(y,y_1) = \varepsilon_2)$, find

$$\varepsilon(\varepsilon_1,\varepsilon_2) = \min\{\varepsilon : \varepsilon_1' \geq \varepsilon_1, \varepsilon_2' \geq \varepsilon_2, (\varepsilon_1',\varepsilon_2',\varepsilon) \in T_0\}.$$

Let T_1 be the table of vectors $(\varepsilon_1,\varepsilon_2,\varepsilon(\varepsilon_1,\varepsilon_2))$.

Step 2. For each ε^* such that $(\varepsilon_1,\varepsilon_2,\varepsilon(\varepsilon_1,\varepsilon_2) = \varepsilon^*) \in T_1$, find: $row(\varepsilon^*) = (\varepsilon_1^*,\varepsilon_2^*,\varepsilon^*)$ where $(\varepsilon_1^*,\varepsilon_2^*,\varepsilon^*) \in T_1$ and if $(\varepsilon_1',\varepsilon_2',\varepsilon^*) \in T_1$ then $\varepsilon_1' \geq \varepsilon_1^*, \varepsilon_2' \geq \varepsilon_2^*$.

One can check that the following table shows a minimal set T of vectors for the case of Tables 5,6.

ε_1	ε_2	ε
0.66	0.75	1
0.33	0.75	0.5
0.66	0.25	0.25
0.33	0.25	0.00

Table 7. A minimal set T of vectors

One can extract from the algorithm the synthesis formula of f from conditions T_0 :

$$f(\varepsilon_1,\varepsilon_2) = \min\{\varepsilon' : (\varepsilon_1',\varepsilon_2',\varepsilon') \in T_0, \ \varepsilon_1' \geq \varepsilon_1, \ \varepsilon_2' \geq \varepsilon_2\}.$$

We can now give an example of a synthesis.

6.3 Approximate synthesis from data: an example

We give an example of synthesis; in the synthesis process, we make use of pre - rough inclusions and approximations to rough mereological connectives which were found above.

Example 6.4. Assume that we want to apply the scheme S with $R(S) = (HB)$ and the unique $v_S((HB)) = (H)(B)(HB)$ in order to synthesize $x \in U(R(S))$ which satisfies the approximate requirement $((HB); \Phi(HB) = har \wedge off, \varepsilon(HB) = 0.5)$. It follows by Table 7 that we can take $((H); \Phi(H) = hat \wedge \neg pig, \varepsilon(H) = 0.33)$ as the approximate requirement at the agent (H) and $((B), \Phi(B) = pis \wedge cut \wedge kni, \varepsilon(B) = 0.75)$ as the approximate requirement at the agent (B), for the approximation f satisfying the set T of conditions. The $\Theta-$ constructive subscheme S_Θ is determined by selecting the standards: x_1 at the agent (H) and y_1 at the agent (B) and $\Phi(HB) = har \wedge off$, $\varepsilon(HB) = 0.5$. We can see from Tables 1, 3 that any S- object assignment g such that $g(< (H), (B) >$ equals one of the following: $(x_1, y_1), (x_1, y_4), (x_2, y_1), (x_2, y_4),$ $(x_4, y_1), (x_4, y_4)$ has the property that S_Θ is compatible with g and , according to Proposition 5.2. $g \models ((HB); \Phi(HB) = har \wedge off, \varepsilon(HB) = 0.5)$.

7 Exercises

1. Software quality factor *reusability* (R) (see e.g. [28]) is treated as dependent on the following criteria (features): *self–descriptiveness* (S), *generality* (G), *modularity* (M), *software systems independence* (SI) and *machine independence* (MI). Assuming that each of these attributes has *low, medium, high* as its possible values, construct a decision table **A** having $\{S,\ G,\ M,\ SI,\ MI\ \}$ as the set of condition attributes and R as its decision attribute.

2. For the table in Ex. 1, derive all decision rules. Are they consistent with your intuitions? If not, try to modify **A** and repeat the process of decision rules generation until their interpretation agrees with your intuitions.

3. For the table in Ex. 1, derive all dependencies among condition attributes. Check, whether they agree with your intuitions. If not, try to modify **A** and repeat the process of decision rules derivation until dependencies obtained agree with your intuitions.

4. For any condition attribute a in the set $\{S,\ G,\ M,\ SI,\ MI\ \}$ of Ex. 1, construct a decision table $\mathbf{A}_a$ with the decision attribute a and a set of "measurable" condition attributes (e.g. for the attribute SI you may use two binary condition attributes, say, UNIX, DOS, whose value is **YES** in case the analyzed software runs under UNIX, resp. DOS).

5. Define condition attributes S, G, M, SI, MI of Ex. 1 in terms of condition attributes form the union of condition attribute sets of tables in $\{\mathbf{A}_a : a \in \{S, G, M, SI, MI\}$.

6. Could you use the approach offered by rough mereology to find a more compressed description of attributes asked for in Ex. 5?

7. Outline a possible procedure in the case when attributes in Ex. 1 are real continuous random variables having e.g. normal distributions.

8 Some Remarks on Applications to Software Engineering

We would like to comment in a very concise manner on usage in software engineering of the methodology presented above. While discussing these topic in a satisfactory way would require an independent study, it might be useful for potential users to highlight some points.

1. Software quality assessment is a vital process bearing on the software development process. Software quality assessment is based on a judicious choice of quality attributes which characterize some aspects of software performance. Therefore quality assessment can be formalized as a decision attribute in a decision table whose condition attributes are some quality determining attributes.

2. Values of quality determining attributes are measured on some scale either introduced in an apriorical way or resulting from a process of quantization or discretization of continuous measurements, Therefore values of quality assessment can be determined from decision rules generated from decision tables of 1.

3. Quality determining attributes lend themselves to assessment process i.e. they usually depend on other, lower level, features and their values can be assessed from appropriate decision tables. This process may be continued until elementary quality factors are reached e.g. referring to Ex. 1–5 above, the quality factor *reusability* depends on the following factors: *self–descriptiveness, generality, modularity, software system independence, machine independence* and in turn, *software system independence* may be assessed in terms of attributes like X–*portability* where X stands for an operating system. Therefore one does arrive at a hierarchical multi - agent system in which agent names are attached to attributes of various levels.

4. A standard approach to quality measurement consists in evaluating values of some metrics providing a global information on collective behaviour of quality determining attributes. This approach is characterized by uncertainty due to subjective evaluation of values of these attributes and to often opposing influences of various of these attributes which have to be accounted for in a subjective way most often by a degree in which they conform to a certain "standard" points on a value scale.

5. Rough merological approach can offer an alternative to the approach outlined in 4. above viz. by characterizing the global quality assessment value of a given software by a vector of rough mereological distances derived from decision tables from a set of standards representing a chosen set of

industry standards each of them having a specified set of quality factor values. This approach makes it possible to discuss various factors influencing software quality at the same time globally as well as locally i.e. preserving the individuality of each factor. In examples 6.1–6.3 (Section 6) we show how to compute uncertainty measures of local agents in order to obtain global uncertainty measures and this approach may suit well the case of hierarchical systems for software quality assessment.

Acknowledgments

Authors would like to express their thanks to Professor Witold Pedrycz and Professor Jim F. Peters for the invitation to write a chapter on rough mereology to this book.

This work was partially supported by the grant No 08T11C01011 from National Committee for Scientific Research and by the ESPRIT project 20288 CRIT-2.

References

1. S.Amarel, PANEL on AI and Design, in: J.Mylopoulos and R.Reiter, eds., *Proceedings Twelfth International Conference on Artificial Intelligence* (Sydney, Australia, 1991) 563–565.
2. R. Axelrod, *The Evolution of Cooperation* (Basic Books, 1984).
3. T.P. Bowen, G.B. Wigle, J.T. Tsai: *Specification of Software Quality Attributes* (RADC–TR–85–37, 3 volumnes, U.S. Rome Air Development Center. 1985).
4. E.M. Brown, *Boolean Reasoning* (Kluwer, Dordrecht, 1990).
5. M. Burns, *Resources: Automated Fabrication. Improving Productivity in Manufacturing* (Prentice Hall, Englewood Cliffs, NJ, 1993).
6. J. Cavano, J.A. McCall, A framework for the measurement of software quality, in: *Proceedings of the Workshop on Software Quality Assurance* (1987).
7. B.L. Clarke, A calculus of individuals based on "Connection", *Notre Dame Journal of Formal Logic* **22** (1981) 204–218.
8. B.L. Clarke, Individuals and points, *Notre Dame Journal of Formal Logic* **26** (1985) 61–75.
9. S.H. Clearwater, B.A. Huberman and T. Hogg, Cooperative problem solving, in: B.A. Huberman, ed., *Computation: The Micro and Macro View* (World Scientific, Singapore, 1992) 33–70.
10. J.H. Connolly and E.A. Edmunds, *CSCW and Artificial Intelligence* (Springer-Verlag, Berlin, 1994).
11. R. Davis and R.G. Smith, Negotiations as a metaphor for distributed problem solving, *Artificial Intelligence* **20** (1989) 63–109.
12. K. Decker and V. Lesser, Quantitative modelling of complex computational task environments, in: *Proceedings AAAI-93* (Washington, DC, 1993) 217–224.

12. K. Decker and V. Lesser, Quantitative modelling of complex computational task environments, in: *Proceedings AAAI-93* (Washington, DC, 1993) 217–224.

13. D. Dubois, H. Prade and R.R. Yager, *Readings in Fuzzy Sets for Intelligent Systems* (Morgan Kaufmann, San Mateo, 1993).

14. E.H. Durfee, *Coordination of Distributed Problem Solvers* (Kluwer, Boston, 1988).

15. J.H. Holland, *Adaptation in Natural and Artificial Systems* (MIT Press, Cambridge, MA, 1992).

16. T. Ishida, *Parallel, Distributed and Multiagent Production Systems* (LNCS 878, Springer-Verlag, Berlin, 1994).

17. J. Komorowski, L. Polkowski and A. Skowron, Towards a rough mereology-based logic for approximate solution synthesis, Part 1, *Studia Logica* 58 (1997), 143-184.

18. S. Leśniewski, Foundations of the general theory of sets (in Polish) (Polish Scientific Circle, Moscow, 1916); also in: S. J. Surma, J. T. Srzednicki, D. I. Barnett and V.F. Rickey, eds., *Stanisław Leśniewski, Collected Works* (Kluwer, Dordrecht, 1992) 128–173.

19. B.T. Low, Neural-logic belief networks - a tool for knowledge representation and reasoning, *Procdings the 5-th IEEE International Conference on Tools with Artificial Intelligence* (Boston, MA, 1993) 34–37.

20. E.H. Mamdani and S. Assilian, An experiment in linguistic synthesis with a fuzzy logic controller, *International Journal of Man - Machine Studies* 7 (1975) 1–13.

21. J.A. McCall, Quality factors, in: L. J. Marciniak, ed., *Encyclopedia of Software Engineering* (John Wiley, New York, 1994).

22. E. Mendelson, *Introduction to Mathematical Logic* (Van Nostrand - Reinhold, New York, 1964).

23. Z. Pawlak, *Rough sets: Theoretical Aspects of Reasoning about Data* (Kluwer, Dordrecht, 1991).

24. Z. Pawlak and A. Skowron, Rough membership functions, in: R.R. Yager, M. Fedrizzi and J. Kacprzyk, eds., *Advances in The Dempster - Shafer Theory of Evidence* (Wiley, New York, 1994) 251–271.

25. J.W. Payne, J.R. Bettman and E.J. Johnson, *The Adaptive Decision Maker* (Cambridge University Press, Cambridge, 1993).

26. J. Pearl, *Probabilistic reasoning in intelligent systems: Networks of Plausible Beliefs* (Morgan Kaufmann, San Mateo, 1988).

27. W. Pedrycz, J.F. Peters III, Computational intelligence in software engineering, *Proceedings of the Canadian Conference on Electrical and Computer Engineering* (1997) 253–256.

28. J. F. Peters III, S. Ramanna: A rough set approach to assessing software quality: Concepts and rough Petri net models, in: S.K. Pal, A. Skowron eds., *Fuzzy Sets, Rough Sets and Decision Making Processes* (Springer-Verlag, Singapore) (in preparation)

29. L. Polkowski and A. Skowron, Rough mereology, in: *Proceedings ISMIS-94* (LNAI 869, Springer-Verlag, Berlin, 1994) 85–94.

31. L. Polkowski and A. Skowron, *Vagueness in the analysis and synthesis of complex objects: Rough set approach*, Manuscript of a textbook prepared in TEMPUS JEP-1943 (1994) 1–312.

32. L. Polkowski and A. Skowron, Logic of rough inclusion, Rough mereological functions, Rough functions (ICS Research Report 12/94, Institute of Computer Science, Warsaw University of Technology, 1994).

33. L. Polkowski and A. Skowron, Introducing rough mereological controllers: Rough quality control, in: T.Y.Lin and A.M.Wildberger, eds., *Soft Computing* (Simulation Councils, Inc., San Diego, 1995) 240–243.

34. L. Polkowski and A. Skowron, Rough mereology and analytical morphology: New developments in rough set theory, in: M. de Glass and Z. Pawlak, eds., *Proceedings of WOCFAI-95; Second World Conference on Fundamentals of Artificial Intelligence* (Angkor, Paris, 1995) 343–354.

35. L. Polkowski and A. Skowron, Adaptive decision-making by systems of cooperative intelligent agents organized on rough mereological principles, *Intelligent Automation and Soft Computing, An International Journal*, 2(2)(1996).

36. L. Polkowski and A. Skowron, Rough mereological approach to knowledge-based distributed AI, in: J. K. Lee, J. Liebowitz and J. M. Chae, eds., *Critical Technology* (Cognizant Communication Corporation, New York, 1996) 774–781.

37. L. Polkowski and A. Skowron, Implementing fuzzy containment via rough inclusions: rough mereological approach to distributed problem solving, in: *Proceedings of the Fifth IEEE International Conference on Fuzzy Systems* (New Orleans 1996) 1147–1153.

38. L. Polkowski and A. Skowron, Learning synthesis schemes in intelligent systems, in: *Proceedings of the Third International Workshop on Multistrategy Learning* (AAAI Press, Piscataway NJ 1996) 57–68.

39. R.B. Rao and S.C.-Y. Lu, Building models to support synthesis in early stage product design, in: *Proceedings of AAAI-93; Eleventh National Conference on Artificial Intelligence* (AAAI Press/MIT Press, Menlo Park, 1993) 277–282.

40. G. Shafer, *Mathematical Theory of Evidence* (Princeton University Press, Princeton, 1976).

41. G. Shafer and J. Pearl, *Readings in Uncertainty Reasoning* (Morgan Kaufmann, San Mateo, 1990).

42. A. Skowron and C. Rauszer, The discernibility matrices and functions in information systems, in: R. Słowiński, ed., *Intelligent Decision Support. Handbook of Applications and Advances of the Rough Sets Theory* (Kluwer, Dordrecht, 1992) 331–362.

43. A. Skowron, Boolean reasoning for decision rules generation, in: *Proceedings ISMIS-93; 7-th International Symposium on Methodologies for Intelligent Systems* (LNAI 689, Springer-Verlag, Berlin, 1993) 295–305.

44. A. Skowron, Synthesis of adaptive decision systems from experimental data, in: A.Aamodt and J.Komorowski, eds., *Proceedings SCAI-95; The Fifth Scandinavian Conference on Artificial Intelligence* (IOS Press, Amsterdam, 1995) 220–238.

45. A. Skowron and J. Grzymała-Busse , From rough set theory to evidence theory, in: R.R. Yager, M. Fedrizzi and J. Kacprzyk, eds., *Advances in The Dempster -*

Shafer Theory of Evidence (Wiley, New York, 1994) 193–236.
46. A. Skowron and L. Polkowski, Adaptive decision algorithms, in: *Proceedings Intelligent Information Systems III, The International Workshop* (Institute of Foundations of Computer Science PAS, Warsaw, 1995) 103–120; also in: Decision algorithms: A survey of rough set theoretic methods, *Fundamenta Informaticae* **30/3–4** (1997) 345–358
47. A. Skowron and L. Polkowski, Rough mereological controller, in: *Proceedings of the Fourth European Congress on Intelligent Techniques and Soft Computing* (Verlag Mainz, Aachen,1996) 223–227.
48. A. Skowron and L. Polkowski, Rough mereological foundations for design, analysis, synthesis and control in distributive systems, in:*Proceedings The Second Joint Annual Conference on Information Sciences* (Wrightsville Beach, NC, 1995) 346–349; also in: *Information sciences. An International Journal* (in print).
49. D. Sriram, R. Logcher and S. Fukuda, *Computer - Aided Cooperative Product Development* (LNCS 492, Springer-Verlag, Berlin, 1991).
50. A. Tarski, Zur Grundlegung der Booleschen Algebra.I, *Fundamenta Mathematicae* **24** (1935) 177–198.
51. A. Tarski, Appendix E, in: J.H. Woodger, *The Axiomatic Method in Biology* (Cambridge University Press, Cambridge, 1937).
52. I. Wegener, *The Complexity of Boolean Functions* (Wiley, New York, 1987).
53. A.N. Whitehead, *An Enquiry Concerning the Principles of Natural Knowledge* (Cambridge University Press, Cambridge, 1919).
54. L. A. Zadeh, Fuzzy sets, *Information and Control* **8** (1965) 338–353.
55. G. Zlotkin and J. Rosenshein, Negotiations and conflict resolutions in non-cooperative domains, in: *Proceedings of AAAI-90; Eight National Conference on Artificial Intelligence* (Boston, MA, 1993) 100–105.
56. G. Zlotkin and J. Rosenshein, Incomplete information and deception in multi-agent negotiations, in: *Proceedings IJCAI-91* (Sydney, Australia,1991) 225–231.

This article was processed using the LaTeX macro package with LMAMULT style

FOOD:

TOWARDS FUZZY OBJECT-ORIENTED SYSTEMS DESIGN

W. PEDRYCZ

Department of Electrical and Computer Engineering

University of Manitoba, Winnipeg R3T 2N2 Canada

E-mail: pedrycz@ee.umanitoba.ca

Z.A. SOSNOWSKI

Department of Computer Science

Technical University of Bialystok , ul. Wejska 45, Bialystok, Poland

E-mail: zenon@ai.pb.bialystok.pl

Imprecision or vagueness can be involved in data at two different levels: it can be related either to the type of data i.e., fuzziness in the data themselves, or to the knowledge of data, i.e. uncertainty in the information about the data. In this paper we define the Fuzzy Object Oriented Data (FOOD) model by generalizing, step by step, its two-valued counterpart that is an Object Oriented (OO) data model. The primary intent of this study is to thoroughly analyze some ways of augmenting the fundamentals of the generic object-oriented approach by the technology of fuzzy sets. In contrast to the previous studies, our thrust is to retain the very nature of object-oriented design (and its advantages) as much as possible while maximizing benefits stemming from the introduced generalization of the model. A usefulness of the proposed approach is illustrated in a problem of vehicle classification.

1   Introduction

There is no doubt that an object-oriented (OO) system design and analysis have deeply permeated the fundamental concepts of software design and radically changed a number of underlying design practices. By perceiving the external world through a hierarchy of objects and clearly realizing a panoply of the relationships occurring between such entities, we are at a position to describe the problem under consideration in a more coherent and transparent way. What the OO design brought into software engineering is a highly required rigor that, subsequently, promotes various systematic patterns of design. For instance, an identification of a hierarchy between objects helps a lot in carrying out the ensuing detailed design and coding. The property of inheritance sheds light on interrelationships between the objects and allows us to derive a number of interesting findings about the behavior of the individual instances. Dominantly, if not exclusively, OO design is based on notions of set theory and two-valued logic. The objects are linked by the inheritance relation that again can be regarded as a purely Boolean construct. Similarly, the values of attributes come as specific numbers or symbols. While such assumptions are valid in many cases, there are situations when it becomes worthwhile to revisit the paradigm of the OO design and place it in the setting of fuzzy sets, namely to admit notions that are lacking abrupt yes-no characteristics as well as those being described with the aid of linguistic terms.

The primary intent of this study is to analyze the fundamentals of the OO design and analysis involving the technology of fuzzy sets, or FOOD (Fuzzy OO Design), for short. We analyze the basic notions of the resulting OO concepts being augmented in such a way. Similarly, we contrast these extensions with the standard notions encountered in the OO setting.

While relatively new, there have already been a number of research endeavors dealing with various ways of extending the paradigm of object orientation to the domain of linguistic information. One may refer here to the results developed by Cross (1996), Dubois et al. (1991), George et al.(1991, 1993), Graham (1994), van Gyseghem et al. (1993). To produce a high level of coherency of the overall presentation, we confine ourselves to the well-known OMT (Object Modeling Technique) as introduced by Rumbaugh (1991). The experimental studies revolve around a data set of vehicles (more precisely, their silhouettes characterized by several features) available from the Turing Institute. There have been two reasons for the selection of this data set. Firstly, it provides with an interesting structure that helps establish hierarchies between classes and quantify relevant dependences. Secondly, the data set is available on the Web so that the interested reader who wishes to experiment with the data on his own, can easily accomplish that.

2   The fuzzy-orientation of classes and objects

In a nutshell, the object-oriented data model means that we organize data as a collection of interacting, discrete entities (objects) that incorporate both data structure and behavior. Objects are usually characterized by their identity and classification. Identity means, that any two objects are distinguishable. Classification means, that similar objects are grouped together into a single class, while the class is defined by its data structure (attributes) and behavior (methods) of the class instances (objects). A class is an abstraction that describes properties relevant to an application and ignores the rest. Any choice of classes is arbitrary and depends on application. To illustrate these ideas we confine ourselves to the description of objects in a small personal data base as they usually encountered in many enterprises. The class Person, see Figure 1 along with corresponding pseudocode (C++) is shown below.

Figure 1: Crisp class model: (a) pseudo C++ notation, (b) OMT notation

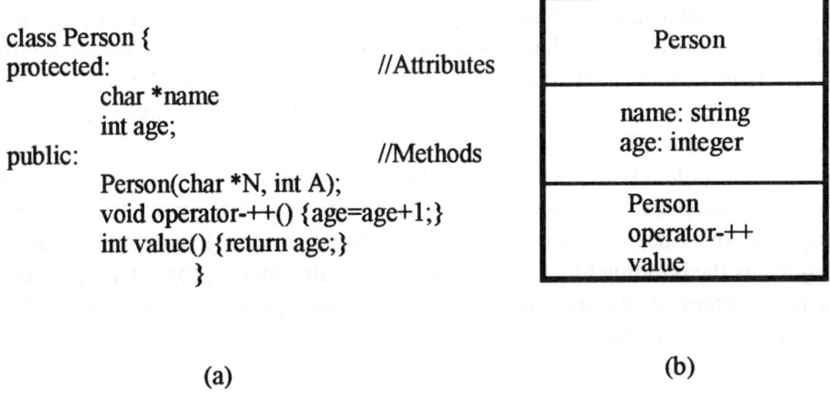

In the above example, a class Person is an abstract data type grouping all objects represented by name of the person and his/her age. All such objects are called instances of the class. Figure 2 shows two instances (two persons): Peter of age 18, and Barbara (age 20).

Figure 2: Crisp (two-valued) instances

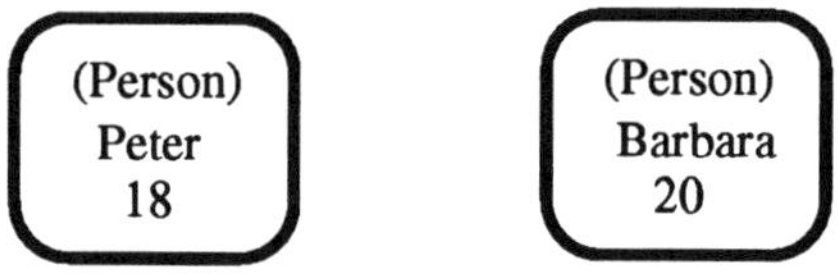

(Person)
Peter
18

(Person)
Barbara
20

The corresponding fragment of code reads as follows

```
Person  p1('Peter',    18);

Person  p2('Barbara'   , 20);
```

It is worth mentioning that in object oriented approach data and methods compose a fully protected data object. The data within the object are protected; nothing can change the data members. The data member can be changed only through the class method. It is said, that each object encapsulates a group of its data members (attributes) and member functions (methods) and acts as an autonomous entity whose internal characteristics are hidden from other objects. The term encapsulation is used in object-oriented approach to emphasize a different but related aspects of abstract data types represented by classes. A class combines methods (operations) and intended representation (data structure) putting these together into a single well-defined unit. Thus object-oriented data modeling presents a more flexible approach to knowledge representation. Encapsulation promotes modularity, meaning that objects must be regarded as the building blocks of a complex system. Once a proper modularization has been achieved, the designer of the object may postpone any final decision concerning the implementation of the object. The prime purpose of member functions (methods) is to control access to data. In principle, the data are invisible from the outside and may be modified only by invoking the corresponding method.

2.1.   Fuzzy domain of attributes

The domain of an attribute is the set of all values this attribute may assume, irrespective of the classes it falls into. A straightforward way of introducing fuzziness in an object oriented data scheme arises at the level of the domains of the individual attributes. This augmentation becomes necessary when the value of an attribute is not given precisely but vaguely as linguistic terms. For example, the attribute age of the class Person may not take on values which are numbers but it may assume linguistic values like young, old, very young, etc. Such an attribute can then be perceived as a linguistic variable. In brief, we can refer to them as linguistic attributes. For instance, the linguistic variable AGE is a fuzzy domain of an attribute age, and the linguistic variable AGE contains a set of linguistic terms as values. Figure 3 shows an example of a class whose attribute constitutes a linguistic variable.

Figure 3: A class with two instances

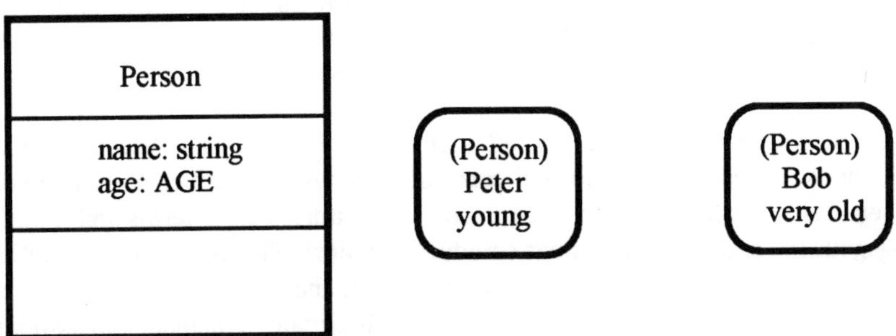

The respective portion of the pseudocode (C++) reads as

```
class Person {

        char * name;

        AGE age;

        ...

        }
```

Then we have

Person p1('Peter',   'young');

Person p2('Bob',   'very old');

In this class, the attribute AGE is specified as a linguistic variable. Before getting into the concept of object-orientation with fuzzy sets, it is instructive to summarize some underlying facts about linguistic variables.

274

2.2. *Linguistic variable*

Linguistic variables introduced by Zadeh (1975) form the basis of linguistic algorithms which use a qualitative kind of information. The values of the linguistic variables are not numbers, but words or sentences of a natural or formal language. The main advantage of the utilization of linguistic variables lies in their ability to cope with uncertainty of descriptors of real-world phenomena. This delivers a valuable possibility to create a new category of models. We will be referring to them as so called *verbal* models. The concept of the linguistic variable helps us approximate a description of the attributes' values, which otherwise cannot be captured in the language of plain numbers (numeric quantities) or sets.

Linguistic variables provide a fundamental mechanism to generate linguistic expressions. As usual to any formal construct, linguistic variables comprise syntax and semantics. As far as syntax is concerned, it embraces basic terms and modifiers along with the associated grammar (production rules). The aspects of semantics of the linguistic variable deal with the assignment the meaning to the individual expressions generated by the grammar and, as such, pertain to membership assignment and computations with the aid of the linguistic modifiers.

In what follows, we discuss some pertinent details. Denote by $T=\{t_1, t_2, \dots , t_n\}$ a collection of basic linguistic terms (such as Small, Medium, Big, etc.). Similarly, a collection of modifiers (hedges) comprises a finite set of terms $H=\{h_1, h_2, \dots , h_m\}$ (such as e.g. more or less, very, etc.). More formally, a linguistic variable is a system

$$L = \ <N, L(G), \mathbf{X}, G, M>$$

where N, L(G), $\mathbf{X}$, G and M denote respectively:

N - name of variable;

L(G) - set of labels of fuzzy sets defined in a given universe of discourse (the language generated by grammar G);

$\mathbf{X}$ - universe of discourse;

G - syntactic rules defined as generative grammar, that defines all well-formed sentences in L(G);

M - semantics, which consists of rules by which the meaning of the sentences in L(G) can be determined.

Semantics M is defined as a mapping

$$M : L(G) \rightarrow F(\mathbf{X})$$

that associates with each sentence of the language L(G) generated by the grammar G, its meaning as a fuzzy set in a universe of discourse $\mathbf{X}$. Here $F(\mathbf{X})$ stands for the family of fuzzy sets defined in $\mathbf{X}$.

The semantics M exhibits three key components:

(i) membership functions A_i of a generic primary terms $t_i \in T$. These arise as a result of an elicitation of domain knowledge.

(ii) linguistic modifiers (hedges) applied to the element of T. Their role in semantics M is to modify the membership functions. According to some previous studies, two main methods are exploited in this study:

- the modifiers affect the membership functions by taking their exponents meaning that

$$h(A(x)) = A^P(x)$$

where h(.) denotes some linguistic modifier, p > 0. Depending upon the value of the exponent, the modifier gives rise to a concentration or dilution effect: the first occurs when p >1 and the latter takes place for p <1. For example we get

$$\text{very } A(x) = A^2(x)$$

$$\text{more or less } A(x) = A^{0.5}(x)$$

- the modifiers shift the original membership functions yielding the effect

$$h(A) = A(x \pm \tau)$$

Depending upon the values of the shift parameter τ, the modifier can exhibit a substantial impact on the original membership function by shifting it to the left or right along the universe of discourse.

These two constructs can be easily combined by introducing a two-parametric class of the modifiers

$$h(A) = A^P(x \pm \tau)$$

(iii) to make the linguistic expressions meaningful, the grammar is aimed to generating the expressions of the form

$$e_1 \ \textbf{or} \ e_2 \ \textbf{or} \ ... \ \textbf{or} \ e_k$$

for k=1,2,...,s where s $\leq$ card(T) while e_i is an expression of the form

$$h_i \ t_j$$

i=1,2,...,m, j=1,2,...,s. In the above construct, the modifiers are optional.

The semantics of the expression of the form

$$e_1 \ \textbf{or} \ e_2 \ \textbf{or} \ ... \ \textbf{or} \ e_k$$

is defined through the expression

$$M(e_1) \cup M(e_2) \cup ... \cup M(e_k)$$

The syntax of the linguistic variable is given by a context-free grammar G defined as the four - element tuple:

$$G = \ < V, \Sigma, P, \delta>$$

where V and Σ are sets of terminal and nonterminal symbols, respectively. P stands for the set of productions (production rules), and δ denotes an initial symbol.

The set of terminal symbols V consists of primary terms t_i, modifiers h_j, and logical operator **or**. Hence we can write this down in the form

$$V = \{ \ t_1, t_2, ... , t_n, h_1, h_2, ... , h_m, \textbf{or}\}$$

The set of nonterminal symbols Σ contains all symbols used in the productions.

$$\Sigma = \{ \ \delta, \text{<simple expression>}, \text{<expression>} \ \}$$

The set of productions P as being represented in the standard BNF notations can be written down accordingly:

$$\delta ::= \text{<expression>}$$

<expression> ::= <simple expression> or <expression>|<simple expression>

<simple expression> ::= t_i | h_j t_i

for i=1,2,...,n, j=1,2,...,m.

Example 1. Let us consider the term set T = { small, medium, large} and H = {very, more or less}. Then the examples of valid sentences in the sense of the above grammar are:

very small

small or more or less medium or very large

etc.

2.3. *Linguistic approximation*

The fundamental problem exhibiting a primordial impact in any application is that of linguistic approximation. The essence of this concept is to approximate any notion Z (being either a fuzzy or numerical value) by the elements of L(G). As the name stipulates, Z is associated with Y* such that

$$\max_{Y \in L(G)} \| Y = Z \| = \| Y^* = Z \|$$

where $\|.\|$ denotes a similarity index. The similarity index can be defined in many different ways. The list of possible options, Table 1, includes four representatives. We assume that these are defined for fuzzy sets defined in a finite space, say $\mathbf{X} = \{x_1, x_2, \ldots, x_k\}$.

Table 1: Similarity index: some selected examples

$$\|A \equiv B\| = \frac{1}{\text{card}(X)}\sum_{i=1}^{k} \begin{cases} 1 \text{ if } a_i \leq b_i \\ \dfrac{b_i}{a_i} \text{ otherwise} \end{cases} \quad \textit{method 1}$$

$$\|A \equiv B\| = \frac{1}{\text{card}(X)}\sum_{i=1}^{k} \begin{cases} 1 \text{ if } a_i \leq b_i \\ 1-a_i+ b_i \text{ otherwise} \end{cases} \quad \textit{method 2}$$

$$\|A \equiv B\| = \frac{1}{\text{card}(X)}\sum_{i=1}^{k} \begin{cases} 1+a_i- b_i \text{ if } a_i \leq b_i \\ 1-a_i+ b_i \text{ otherwise} \end{cases} \quad \textit{method 3}$$

$$\| A \equiv B \| = \begin{cases} \text{Poss}(A,B) \text{ if } \text{Nec}(B, A) > 0.5 \\ \dfrac{\text{Nec}(B,A)}{2}\,\text{Poss}(A,B) \text{ otherwise} \end{cases} \quad \textit{method 4}$$

The rationale behind the two first methods is to emphasize a phenomenon of a (partial) inclusion of Z in Y. The difference between method 1 and 2 comes in the form of the implication operator (residuation) - in fact they happen to be of secondary nature. The third method uses the equality index implemented with the aid of the Lukasiewicz implication. The last method originates in the realm of fuzzy rule-based systems and uses possibility (Poss) and necessity (Nec) measures.

It is instructive to gain a better insight into the performance of linguistic approximation by completing more detailed simulation experiments.

Example 2. We consider a universe of discourse X=[26, 61], which is a domain of the 8-th attribute of the vehicle dataset at the Turing Institute. This attribute is called ELONGATEDNESS. The universe of discourse **X** is partitioned using a collection of generic linguistic terms obtained with the use of standard FCM algorithm (FUZZY ISODATA); see Bezdek (1980). We complete the linguistic approximation for an input datum Z characterized by a Gaussian membership function

$$Z(x) = \exp\left(-\left(\frac{x - x_0}{d}\right)^2\right)$$

centered at x_0, see Figure 4.

Figure 4: Generic linguistic terms A_i, and nonnumeric datum Z

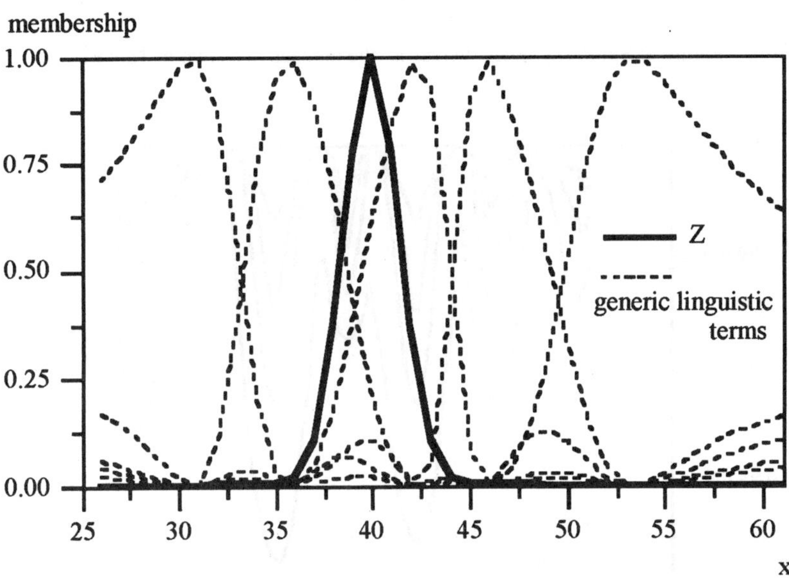

This nonnumeric datum is translated along the universe and for each of its position the result of approximation is returned in terms of the best expression derived and the value of matching. The experiment is completed for several levels of granularity of Z, (quantified by the spreads of the Gaussian function d=1, 5, 10, 20) and some selected number of linguistic terms. The syntax of the grammar is the same as defined before. More specifically, the grammar has k primary terms and two modifiers, hence the set of terminal symbols is given as

$$V = \{ A_1, A_2, A_3, \dots , A_k, \text{very}, \text{ more or less}, \text{or}\}$$

A_i, i=1,2,...k are fuzzy numbers generated by the FCM for the different number of fuzzy prototypes (k= 3,4,5,7) - number of linguistic terms. The modifiers are specified accordingly

$$\text{very } A(x) = A^2(x) \qquad \text{more or less } A(x) = A^{0.5}(x)$$

The series of plots of the similarity index for the sliding Z is contains in Figure 5. Similarly, Figure 6 includes a plot showing the result of approximation, Y* for the five linguistic terms and d=0.5, 1, 2, and 5 with the similarity index computed using the third method. There is clear and justifiable regularity: with an increasing granularity of Z, the results of this approximation loose their uniqueness. Simply, several terms can be regarded as the optimal approximators of Z.

Figure 5: Similarity index versus x, the indexes as shown in Table 1

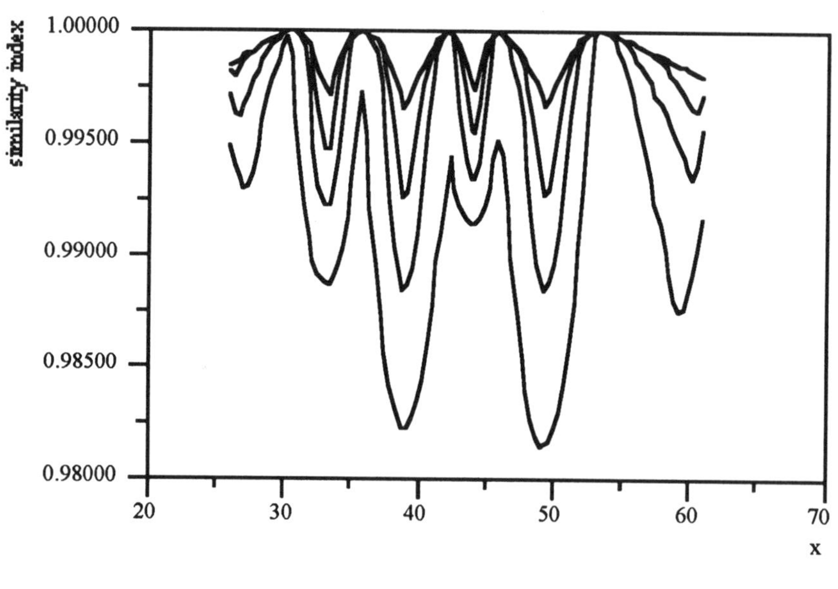

(a)

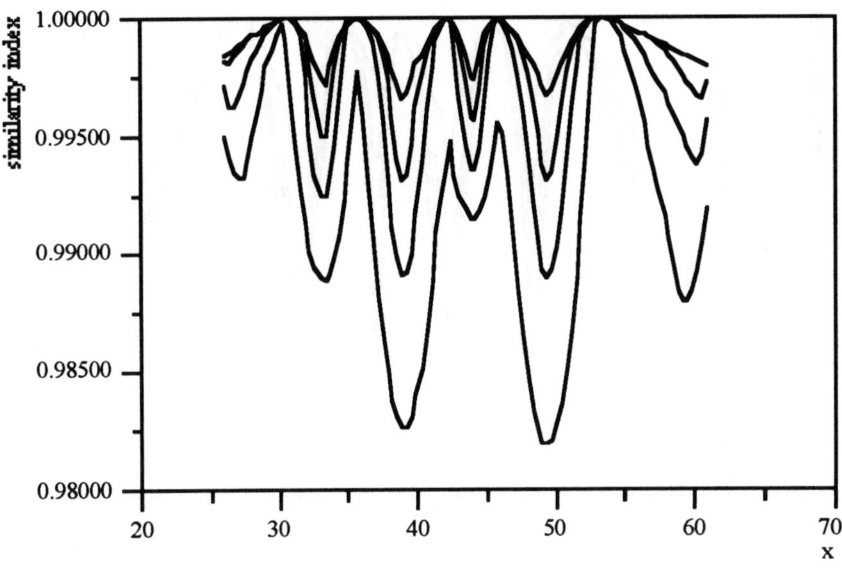

(b)

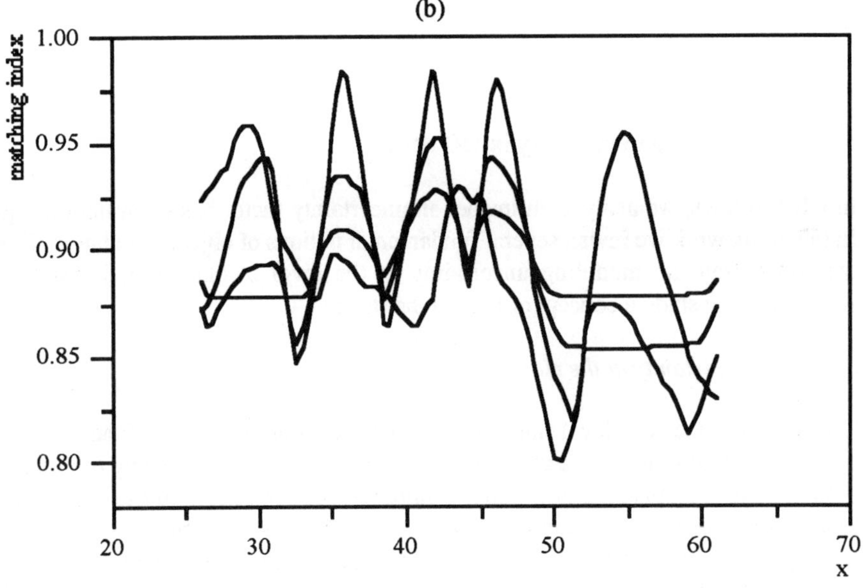

(c)

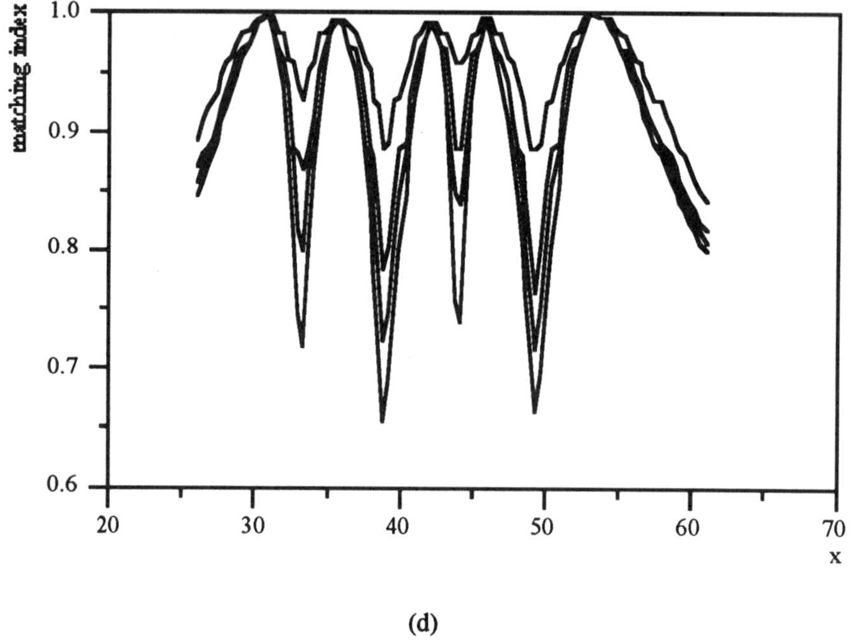

(d)

3 Modeling uncertainty in OO design

In what follows, we analyze an impact an uncertainty factor has on system design. In this framework we revisit several fundamental notions of object orientation. First, we concentrate on modeling uncertainty at the level of classes and instances. Afterwards we study a concept of fuzzy inheritance.

3.1 *Uncertainty at the class level*

Uncertainty at the class level can be introduced to give an indication of the relevance of a particular attribute to the concept being modeled by the class. In any information system there are situations in which it is important or even necessary to express this kind of relationship. For example, in an information system containing data about the experience, knowledge, and skill of people looking for a job it would be of great interest to be able to make a list of applicants with respect to their experience in the subject matters of interest to the potential employer. In the crisp, two-valued object oriented modeling this is not possible or becomes very much limited.

In order to express the degree to which a given attribute is relevant to the class we associate with each attribute inside the class a weight factor, calling it a relevance factor. Refer to Figure 7 containing an example of the relevant class.

Figure 7: Class with relevance factors

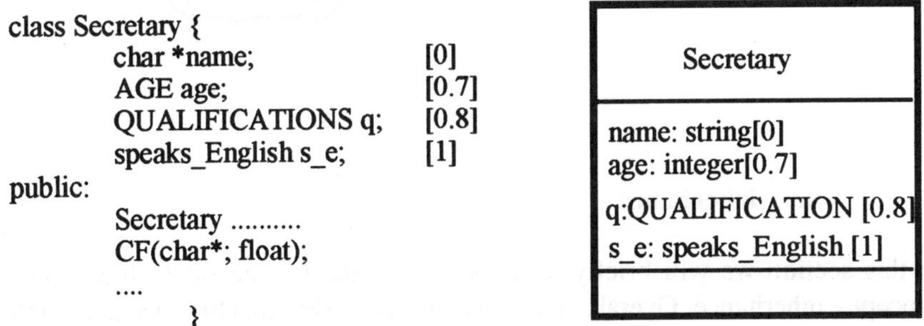


```
class Secretary {
        char *name;                    [0]
        AGE age;                       [0.7]
        QUALIFICATIONS q;              [0.8]
        speaks_English s_e;            [1]
public:
        Secretary ..........
        CF(char*; float);
        ....
                }
```

Each relevance factor models an influence of the attribute on the concept represented by the class.

3.2.   *Modeling uncertainty at the instance level*

Uncertainty occurs when one is not absolutely certain about a piece of information at hand. The degree of certainty at the level of instance will be represented by a certainty factor (CF) which may be attached to each attribute by invoking a special CF method with the name of the attribute and a number from the unit interval representing CF of a given attribute. Figure 8 shows an instance of the class Secretary with a confidence factor of 0.7 attached to the attribute speaks-English. This number represents our belief, that this person really speaks English.

284

Figure 8: Instance with certainty factors

Secretary s('Barbara','young');
s.CF('speaks_English', 0.7);

4   Fuzzy inheritance

In this section we will briefly describe one of the fundamental object oriented concept - inheritance. Overall, inheritance is about sharing attributes and methods among classes being in hierarchical relationship. Thus classes themselves can be placed in a subclass/superclass lattice. Each subclass incorporates, or *inherits*, all of the attributes and methods of the superclass and adds new structure and specializes in the inherited behavior. The properties of the superclass need not be repeated in each subclass. Inheritance forms a powerful abstraction for sharing similarity among classes while preserving their differences. Each object is an instance of one class, but is also a member of all superclasses of this class.

Figure 9 illustrates a hierarchy of classes of objects as they appear in the silhouette data set. The Big_vehicle class is a subclass of the class Vehicle and inherits methods from this class.

The concept of conventional inheritance hinges exclusively on binary logic. In other words, only complete inheritance or complete abortion for attributes and methods are allowed. More realistically, the subclass hierarchies can be intrinsically fuzzy, so is the notion of partial inheritance. Therefore it is essential to revisit the notion of fuzzy inheritance, considering the fact that this notion has been already introduced in the existing literature. Previously (Van Gyseghem et al, 1993) studied the representation of both uncertainty and fuzziness in an object oriented model. They have used conjunctive fuzzy sets for fuzzy information and captured uncertainty by generalized fuzzy sets. They assumed that uncertainty affects only the data and

Figure 9: Hierarchy of classes of vehicles

<table>
<tr><td colspan="2">Vehicle</td></tr>
<tr><td>elongatedness: ELONGATEDNESS [$E_1,E_2,E_3,E_4,E_5,E_6,E_7$]
rectangularity: RECTANGULARITY [R_1,R_2,R_3,R_4,R_5]
kurtosis: KURTOSIS [K_1,K_2,K_3,K_4,K_5]
hollows: HOLLOWS [H_1,H_2,H_3,H_4]</td></tr>
<tr><td>elongatedness
rectangularity
kurtosis
hollows</td></tr>
</table>

<table>
<tr><td>Big_vehicle</td></tr>
<tr><td>elongatedness: ELONGATEDNESS [E_1,E_5,E_6,E_7]
rectangularity: RECTANGULARITY [R_1,R_2,R_3,R_5]
kurtosis: KURTOSIS [K_1,K_2,K_4,K_5]
hollows: HOLLOWS [H_1,H_2,H_4]</td></tr>
</table>

not the structure of the data itself. As a consequence of this conjecture, they did not explicitly investigate class/subclass relationship. In the simple way (George et al., 1991) a membership degree is attached there to every subclass/superclass relationship: e.g., class Greco_Italo_Celtic is judged to be a subclass of class Indo_European but only to some degree. Dubois et al. (1991) have approached the representation of vagueness and uncertainty in class hierarchies using the possibility theory. They define an inclusion between classes to be the inclusion between their fuzzy ranges (which are possibility distributions). George et al. (1993) have considered uncertainty in hierarchies within databases management system for non-singular object attribute values that may be connected through logical operators such as logical AND (nested instances) and logical OR (merged instances). Having identified some close relationships between frame-based systems and object-oriented systems, one can also refer to alternative methods of representing fuzziness in this setting, cf. Di Nola et al. (1994).

286

4.1 Inheritance of fuzzy classes

The classical inheritance concept is based upon binary logic. In other words, only complete inheritance or complete abortion for attributes and methods are allowed. The superclass/subclass hierarchies can also be intrinsically fuzzy. This leads us to the notion of partial inheritance, that is a fuzzy inheritance between classes. The emphasis in our approach is to define a fuzzy class hierarchy which will allow us to refine knowledge on the basis of the results produced by the linguistic approximation.

Let us note that in the conventional inheritance mechanism, a subclass is derived from its superclass by "specialization". This effect is achieved by adding new attributes or by providing more specialized methods, which override the corresponding methods existing at the level of a superclass. Inheritance of parent class data structure means inheritance of attributes, or being more precise, inheritance of attributes types. In this point, we would like to emphasize that most of the existing attempts encountered in the fuzzy OO literature consider inheritance as inheritance of *instances*(objects), so they consider that the particular values of attributes are inherited. These approaches seem to be not quite compatible with the spirit of the object-oriented paradigm, where instances are considered to be autonomous entities with their own data structure and behavior.

Not trying to go beyond the object oriented paradigm, we are forced to keep the inheritance of attributes for fuzzy classes. In fuzzy class the type of an attribute is a linguistic variable so the set of possible values is defined by the language generated by the respective grammar attached to this linguistic variable. The fuzzy class can be specialized not only by adding new attributes or redefining more specialize methods. We can specialize fuzzy class by introducing some restrictions on the set of possible values an attribute in a class can take. In order to do this, we associate with each attribute a certain domain. This domain is defined as a subset of a family describing a type of an attribute. This subset is considered in the sense of inclusion of languages. Thus the language describing the domain of any given attribute of a superclass should contain the language describing the domain of this attribute in any resulting subclass, namely

$$L(G1) \supset L(G2)$$

where:

       $L(G1)$ - a language describing the domain of an attribute in a superclass

       $L(G2)$ - a language describing the domain of corresponding attribute in a subclass

For example, we can define a fuzzy class Van as a class derived from the fuzzy class (superclass) Big_Vehicle. Here, the number of primary terms of the linguistic variable ELONGATEDNESS in the subclass Van is less then the number of primary terms this variable has in a superclass Big_Vehicle, so the domain of an attribute ELONGATEDNESS in a subclass Van is included in a domain of an attribute ELONGATEDNESS in a superclass Big_Vehicle. This is visualized in Figure 10. In this example the lists of the corresponding primary terms are contained in the square parentheses.

4.2. Membership of instance to class

One of the profound applications of the hierarchies of classes of the objects is a classification of a new object. In contrast to commonly encountered schemes of pattern classification whose feature space is fixed for all the patterns under consideration, here we are faced with variable collections of features depending upon the level in the hierarchies. The lower the level in the hierarchy, the more features become associated with the objects, see Figure 11.

Figure 10: Fuzzy inheritance for classes of big_vehicles and vans

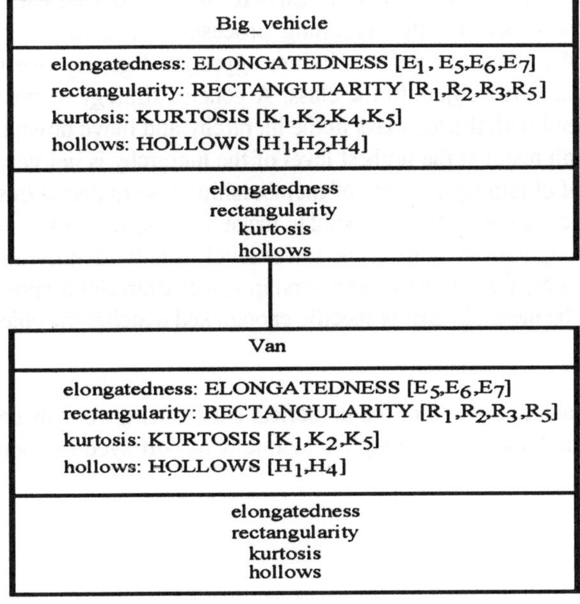

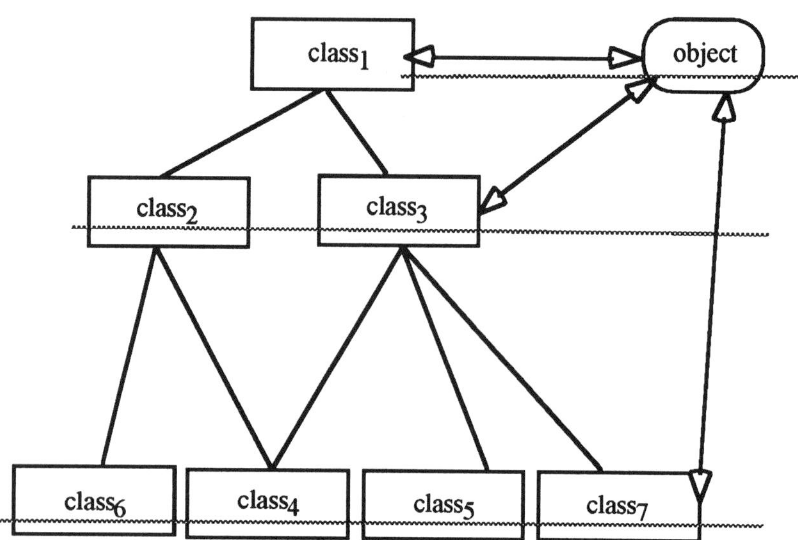

Figure 11. Classification mechanism in object-oriented systems

The classification of a given object is carried out considering each class in the hierarchy. More precisely, the matching process applies to the corresponding attributes. Finally, these partial results are aggregated giving rise to the overall degree of matching the object to the class. A general strategy of matching is top - down; we proceed with the top class in the hierarchy and move down this hierarchy. The classification result at the highest level of the hierarchy is not very informative; the likelihood of obtaining a degree of membership close to one at this level is very high however the class itself is too general to make the classification results meaningful enough. The computations done at the lower level usually identify a specific depth in the hierarchy beyond which the membership values drop significantly. This points out the class in the hierarchy that is specific enough and matches the object sufficiently well.

Example 3. As a continuation of the numerical experiment, we consider a collection of the vehicles and discuss the complete hierarchy as portrayed in Figure 12.

Figure 12: Hierarchy of vehicles and their description

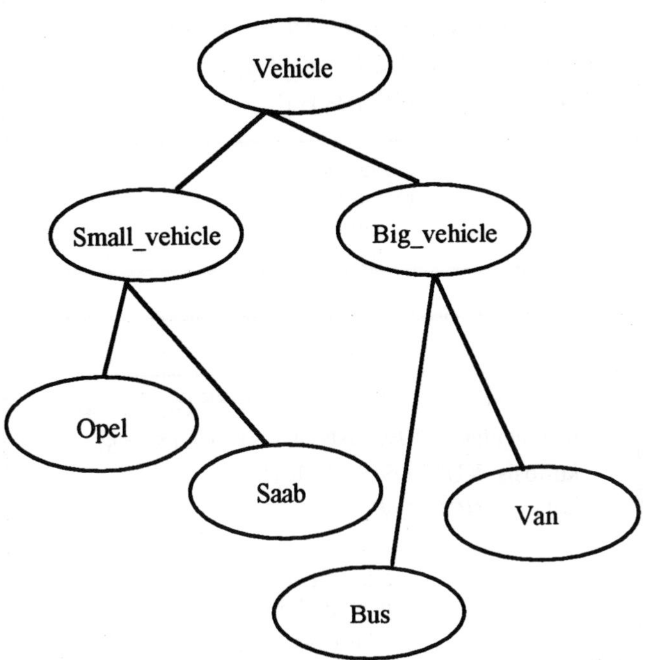

Vehicle
elongatedness: ELONGATEDNESS [E_1, E_2,E_3, E_4, E_5,E_6 E_7] rectangularity: RECTANGULARITY [R_1, R_2, R_3, R_4, R_5] kurtosis: KURTOSIS [K_1,K_2,K_3, K_4, K_5] hollows: HOLLOWS [H_1, H_2, H_3,H_4]
elongatedness rectangularity kurtosis hollows

Small_vehicle
elongatedness: ELONGATEDNESS [E_2, E_3, E_4] rectangularity: RECTANGULARITY [R_4, R_5] kurtosis: KURTOSIS [K_1, K_2, K_3] hollows: HOLLOWS [H_3, H_4]
elongatedness rectangularity kurtosis hollows

Opel
elongatedness: ELONGATEDNESS [E_2, E_3, E_4] rectangularity: RECTANGULARITY [R_4, R_5] kurtosis: KURTOSIS [K_1, K_2] hollows: HOLLOWS [H_3]
elongatedness rectangularity kurtosis hollows

Saab
elongatedness: ELONGATEDNESS [E_2, E_3, E_4] rectangularity: RECTANGULARITY [R_4] kurtosis: KURTOSIS [K_3] hollows: HOLLOWS [H_3, H_4]
elongatedness rectangularity kurtosis hollows

<table>
<tr><td align="center">Big_vehicle</td></tr>
<tr><td>

elongatedness: ELONGATEDNESS $[E_1, E_5, E_6, E_7]$
rectangularity: RECTANGULARITY $[R_1, R_2, R_3, R_5]$
kurtosis: KURTOSIS $[K_1, K_2, K_4, K_5]$
hollows: HOLLOWS $[H_1, H_2, H_4]$

</td></tr>
<tr><td align="center">

elongatedness
rectangularity
kurtosis
hollows

</td></tr>
</table>

<table>
<tr><td align="center">Van</td></tr>
<tr><td>

elongatedness: ELONGATEDNESS $[E_5, E_6, E_7]$
rectangularity: RECTANGULARITY $[R_1, R_2, R_3, R_5]$
kurtosis: KURTOSIS $[K_1, K_2, K_5]$
hollows: HOLLOWS $[H_1, H_4]$

</td></tr>
<tr><td align="center">

elongatedness
rectangularity
kurtosis
hollows

</td></tr>
</table>

<table>
<tr><td align="center">Bus</td></tr>
<tr><td>

elongatedness: ELONGATEDNESS $[E_1, E_5]$
rectangularity: RECTANGULARITY $[R_2, R_5]$
kurtosis: KURTOSIS $[K_1, K_4, K_5]$
hollows: HOLLOWS $[H_1, H_2]$

</td></tr>
<tr><td align="center">

elongatedness
rectangularity
kurtosis
hollows

</td></tr>
</table>

In the Turing database these objects were characterized by 18 attributes. For our experiment we choose 4 of them, namely:

- elongatedness

- principal axis rectangularity defined as area / (principal axis length*principal axis width)

- kurtosis about major axis computed as

$$(\text{4th order moment about minor axis})/\text{sigma\_maj}^2$$

where sigma_maj^2 is the variance along the major axis

- hollows ratio taken as the ratio of the form (area of hollows)/(area of bounding polygon)

The linguistic terms defined for the linguistic variables are calculated by FCM algorithm. The results of matching at the level of individual attributes derived with the use of Method 1 (see Table 1) for the first 25 objects from the data set are collected in Figure 13. What is profoundly visible, is a level of matching while traversing down the hierarchy of the classes.

Figure 13: Results of matching (averaged over 25 objects) for the class of vans

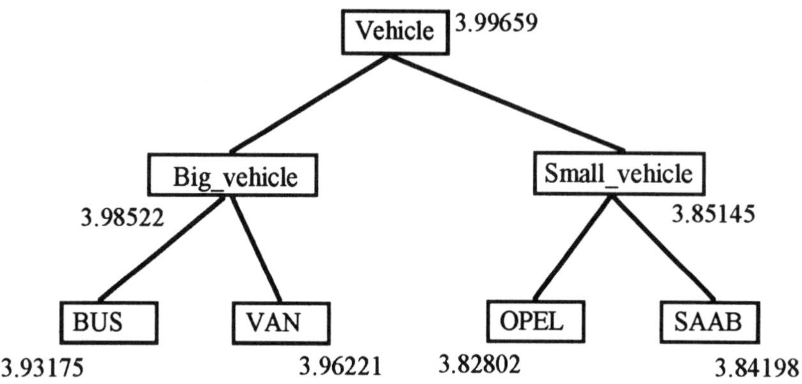

5   Conclusions

The fuzzy set - based extension of object-oriented paradigm retains the conceptual fundamentals of the OO approach. The realization of inheritance - the key idea of classes of objects, in the considered setting exploits the concept of linguistic approximation. The results of such approximation are used to identify objects. The introduced object-oriented approach is discussed in the applications to classification problems.

Acknowledgment

The support from the Natural Sciences and Engineering Research Council (NSERC) and the Technical University of Bialystok (grant No. W/II/3/96) provided to the first and second author, respectively, is gratefully acknowledged.

6   References

J.F. Baldwin, T.P. Martin, Fuzzy classes in object-oriented logic programming. Proc. 5th IEEE Int.Conf. on Fuzzy Systems, New Orleans, LA, September 8-11, 1996, pp. 1358-1365.

J.C. Bezdek, A convergence theorem for the fuzzy ISODATA clustering algorithm, IEEE Trans. Pattern Anal. Mach. Intell, vol. PAMI-2, pp.1-8, 1980.

V. Cross, A unifying framework for the fuzzy object model, Proc. 5th IEEE Int.Conf. on Fuzzy Systems, New Orleans, LA, September 8-11, 1996, pp. 1351-1357.

A. Di Nola, S. Sessa, W. Pedrycz, Fuzzy information in knowledge representation and processing for frame-based structures, IEEE Trans. on Systems, Man, and Cybernetics, 24, 1994, 918-925.

D. Dubois, H. Prade, J.-P. Rossazza, Vagueness, typicality, and uncertainty in class hierarchies, Int. J. Intelligent Systems, 6, 1991, 167-183.

R. George, B.P. Buckles, F.E. Petry, Integrating artificial intelligence and databases - where do we manage uncertainty, In: Proc. IJCAI-91 Workshop on Integrating Artificial Intelligence and Database Systems, August 1991, Melbourne.

R. George, B.P. Buckles, F.E. Petry, Modeling class hierarchies in the fuzzy object-oriented data model, Fuzzy Sets and Systems, 60, 1993, 259-272.

I. Graham, Object-Oriented Methods, Addison-Wesley, New York, 1994.

J. Rumbaugh et al., Object-Oriented Modeling and Design, Prentice Hall, Englewood Cliffs, NJ, 1991,

Turing Institute -The vehicle dataset, Turing Institute, Glasgow, Scotland.

N. Van Gyseghem, R. De Caluwe, R. Vandenbghe, UFO: uncertainty and fuzziness in an object-oriented model, In: Proc. 2nd IEEE Int. Conf. on Fuzzy Systems, March 1993, San Francisco, vol. II, pp.773-778.

L.A. Zadeh, The concept of a linguistic variable and its application to approximate reasoning, Information Sciences, part I:8,199-249, part II:8, 301-357, part III: 9, 43-80, 1975.

7   Problems

1 Characterize the most important features of object-oriented approach to system modeling. In which way fuzzy sets become instrumental in this setting?

2 Explain how object orientation reduces the complexity of the model to be developed

3 Characterize the advantages and disadvantages of object inheritance. Elaborate how inheritance may jeopardize encapsulation.

4 Discuss the problems of inheritance in knowledge representation arising due to some nonmonotonic aspects of reasoning.

5 Develop a class diagram describing a hierarchy of computers and their components. Consider several components such as mainframe, personal workstation, type of monitor, system box (CPU, RAM, etc.), pointing device, etc.

6 Propose a class diagram describing a hierarchy of planar geometric figures. Discuss the mechanisms of inheritance of methods (move, rotate, scale, display, etc.)

7 Extend the syntax of the linguistic variable discussed in this paper by adding a conjunction operator *and*. Introduce appropriate production rules.

8 Download the Turing database from the Web; experiment with other attributes and classify the objects using the methods discussed in this study.

KNOWLEDGE-BASED TECHNIQUES FOR SOFTWARE QUALITY MANAGEMENT

Christof Ebert

Alcatel Telecom, Switching Systems Division,
Fr.Wellesplein 1, B-2018 Antwerpen, Belgium
E-mail: christof.ebert@alcatel.be

Ekkehard Baisch

Alcatel Telecom, Switching Systems Division,
Lorenzstrasse 10, D-70445 Stuttgart, Germany
E-mail: ebaisch@stgl.alcatel.de

Cost-effective software project management has the serious need to focus resources on those areas with highest criticality. The article focuses on two areas important for practical application of criticality-based predictions in real projects, namely the selection of a classification technique and the use of the results in directing management decisions. The first part is comprehensively comparing and evaluating five common classification techniques (Pareto classification, classification trees, factor-based discriminant analysis, fuzzy classification, neural networks) for identifying critical components. Results from a current large-scale switching project are included to show practical benefits. Knowing which technique should be applied the second area gains even more attention: What are the impacts for practical project management within given resource and time constraints? Several selection criteria based on the results of a combined criticality and history analysis are provided together with potential decisions.

1. Introduction

> *As far as I can tell Engineering Judgement just means*
> *they are going to make up numbers.*
> *Richard Feynman*

In order to achieve an early indication of software quality, software is subjected to measurement. It would be of great benefit to predict early in the development process those components of a software system that are likely to have a high error rate or that need high development effort. Though the search for underlying structures and rules in a set of observations is performed in many scientific fields and effective solutions to refine forecasting methods based on past data have been suggested, their applicability to software development has been restricted [1,2]. Few references give insight that attention has been paid to a systematic analysis of empirical data (e.g. [3,4,5,6]).

This article compares different classification techniques as a basis for constructing quality models that can identify outlying software components that might cause potential quality problems. For example, when distinguishing modules that are more error-prone than others, a metric vector consisting of few metrics such as module size, cohesiveness and data fan-in can be determined during the design phase. Now, the goal is to determine those modules that belong to the rather small group of modules that potentially cause most of the errors, costs, and rework. Obviously, the best solution would be to filter out exactly the specific high-risk components in order to improve their design or start again from scratch.

Unfortunately, the metric vector usually provides rather continuous data, hence preventing clear frontiers between good and bad. Experts' knowledge in such cases covers this problem with linguistic uncertainty and fuzziness: "*if length is medium and cohesion is low the module is likely to cause trouble*". We will discuss techniques that allow to differentiate even between such linguistic attributes and come to an exact and reproducible decision.

Such classification models are based on the experience that typically a rather small number of components has a high failure rate and is most difficult to test and maintain. Our own project experiences for instance just recently showed that 20 % of all modules in large telecommunication projects were the origin of over 40 % of all field failures with high priority (fig. 1). Even worse is the fact that we could also show that it is not so difficult to identify these modules in advance - either by asking designers and testers and grouping their subjective ratings, or by applying classification rules based on simple structural software metrics [7].

The article investigates the hypothesis whether fuzzy classification applied to criticality prediction provides better results than other classification techniques that have been introduced in this area.

In this context the article addresses typical questions often asked in software engineering projects:

- How can I early identify the relatively small number of critical components that make significant contribution to faults identified later in the life cycle?
- Which modules should be redesigned because their maintainability is bad and their overall criticality to the project's success is high?
- Are there structural properties that can be measured early in the code to predict quality attributes?

- If so, what is the benefit of introducing a metrics program that investigates structural properties of software?
- Can I use the - often heuristic - design and test know-how on trouble identification and risk assessment to build up a knowledge-base to identify critical components early in the development process?

Fig. 1: Benefits of using early criticality prediction in a telecommunication project

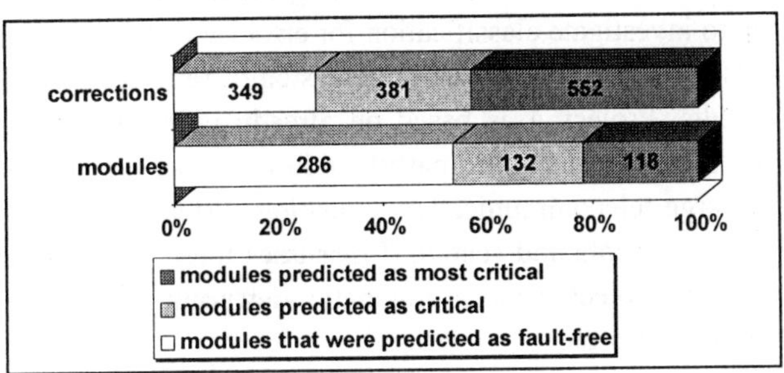

Beyond addressing such questions the article compares different approaches for identifying critical components and provides insight in the most common techniques for complexity-based classification of software modules. Quantitative data both from literature (in order to provide easy access to some quality data and thus to do own experiments and to validate results) and from telecommunication software development supports the underlying hypothesis that fault-prone modules can be identified best with fuzzy classification techniques based on their structure and contents.

The effects of applying complexity-based criticality prediction to a new project can be summarized based on results from telecommunication projects (fig. 1):
- 20 % of all modules in the project were predicted as most critical (after coding);
- these modules contained over 40 % of all faults (up to release time).

Knowing from these and many other projects that [11,23]
- 60 % of all faults can theoretically be detected until the end of module test and
- fault correction during module test and code reading costs less than 10 % compared to fault correction during system test,

it can be calculated that 24 % of all faults can be detected early by investigating 20 % of all modules more intensively with 10 % of effort compared to fault correction during system test, therefore yielding a 20 % total cost reduction for fault correction. Additional costs for providing the statistical analysis are in the range of two person days per project. Necessary tools are off the shelf and account for even less per project.

The article is organized as follows. The introductory section 2 presents a brief overview of background and problems associated with metric-based decision models. Section 3 introduces common classification methodologies and their applicability to software quality models, covering Pareto classification, crisp classification trees, factor-based discriminant analysis, neural network approaches, and fuzzy classification. Due to size limits we will concentrate on brief qualitative introductions with references on archive materials. Section 4 describes the construction of a classification system for software quality management. Section 5 provides the experimental setup to investigate classification for error- and change prediction.

Two projects from the area of real-time systems are introduced for comparing classification results. Project A is based on already published metric data which permits easy access for further (third party) studies. Project B is a collection of 451 modules from a large telecommunication switching system. Section 6 provides the results of these experiments and section 7 discusses these results in the context of applicability to other projects from a pragmatic viewpoint. Finally, section 8 gives an outlook on future research.

2. Metric-Based Quality Models

Although striving to reach high quality standards, only a few organizations apply true quality management. Quality management consists of proactively comparing observed quality with expected quality, hence minimizing the effort expended on correcting the sources of defect. In order to achieve software quality, it must be developed in an organized form by using defined methods and techniques and applying them consistently. In order to achieve an indication of software quality, software must be subjected to measurement. This is accomplished through the use of metrics and statistical evaluation techniques that relate specific quantified product requirements to some attributes of quality.

The approach of integrating software metrics and statistical techniques is shown in fig. 2. The CASE environment provides defined methods and process, and holds descriptions of different products developed during the software life-cycle. Multivariate statistical techniques provide feedback about relationships between components (e.g. factor analysis [8], principal component analysis [4]). Classification techniques help determining outliers (e.g. error-prone components) [2,9]. Finally, detailed diagrams and tables provide insight into the reasons why distinct components are potential outliers and how to improve them [10].

Quality or productivity factors to be predicted during the development of a software system are affected by many product and process attributes, e.g. software design characteristics or the underlying development process and its environment.

Fig. 2: Measures and statistical techniques in software engineering

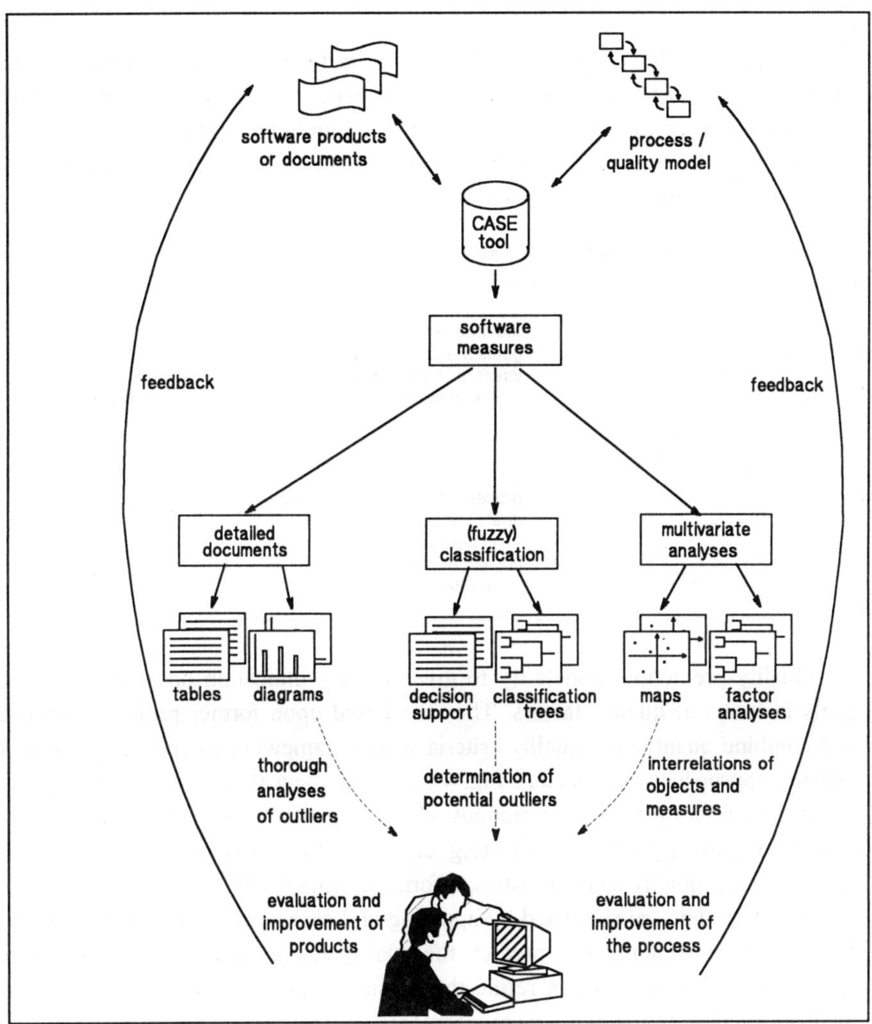

In order to achieve a distinct quality goal that is often only measurable at delivery time, quality criteria are derived that allow *In Process Quality Checks*. Such quality criteria if measured are indirect quality metrics because they do not directly measure the related quality factor (fig. 3). However, being available early in the development process they can be used to set up immediate targets for project tracking.

Quality criteria are measurable during the development process. An example is given in fig. 3. The quality factor reliability that is contracted based on the failure rate of 10 failures per month can only be measured after the product is deployed to the field.

The associated quality criteria, for instance test coverage, can be measured early and they can be kept within a distinct range if experience suggests so. These quality criteria are part of the development quality plan and can rather easy be checked at appropriate milestones. A comprehensive picture of how quality goals relate to each other and to quality criteria is given in ISO 9126.

Fig. 3: Quality factors, quality criteria and metrics

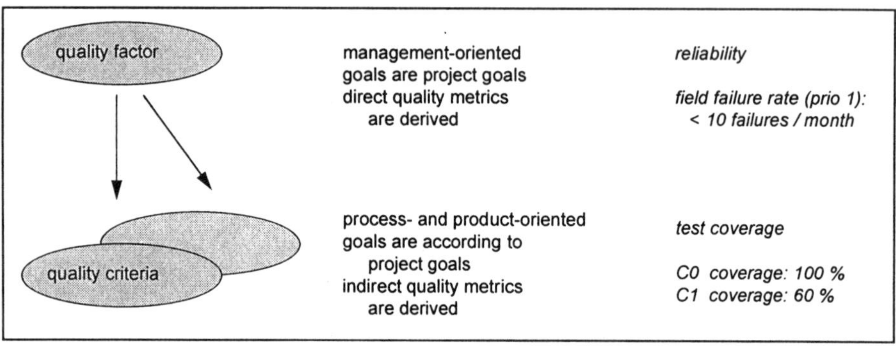

Quality prediction models try to give an early indication on achieving quality goals in terms of quality factors. They are based upon former project experiences and combine quantitative quality criteria with a framework of rules (e.g. limits for metrics, appropriate ranges etc.). Fig. 4 shows the typical approach of metric-based classification in a project environment. They are generated by combination and statistical analysis of product metrics (e.g. complexity metrics) and product or process attributes (e.g. quality characteristics, effort, etc.) [3,5,6,11].

These models are evaluated by applying and comparing exactly those invariant figures they are intended to predict, the quality factors (e.g. error rate). Iterative repetition of this process can refine the quality models hence allowing the use of them as predictors for similar environments and projects. Typical problems connected to data collection, analysis, and quality modeling are addressed and discussed comprehensively in [1,11, 23].

One of the few examples for a metric-based decision environment with expert rules has been suggested by Behrendt et al [13]. This tool is based on a factorial quality taxonomy that classifies the above mentioned quality factors (e.g. reusability) and related sub-factors (e.g. modularity) into linguistic categories (e.g. "not acceptable"). The proposed classification system takes measurable and nonmeasurable attributes as an input, such as design of control structures or number of system parameters. Another tool system for assessing risk factors of software components has been developed by Porter and Selby [2,9]. The proposed method generates metric-based models of high-risk components automatically, based on metrics from previous releases or projects.

Fig. 4: Criticality classification during software development

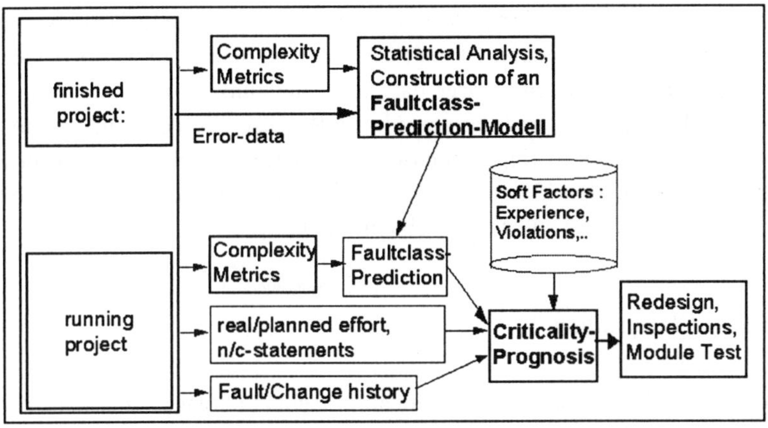

These models are built according to a classification tree with binary and multi-value decision nodes. While the first approach permits the use of linguistic descriptions and qualitative reasoning without describing how the classes had been created, the latter is based on history-based crisp decisions that do not indicate any intuition. Thus, both approaches try to solve the problem of metric-based decision support; however, it is often not clear how to justify the decisions. The most serious constraint imposed by classification trees and other crisp clustering techniques is their goal to identify *mutually exclusive subsets*, thus not allowing fuzzy memberships to several classes.

3. Classification Techniques

Classification or clustering algorithms are mathematical tools for detecting similarities between members of a collection of objects. Metric vectors assigned to the same cluster are in some sense similar to each other, more so than they are to other metric vectors not assigned to that cluster. Instead of predicting number of errors or changes (i.e. algorithmic relationships) we are considering assignments to groups (e.g. "change-prone"). While the first goal has been achieved more or less with regression models or neural networks predominantly for finished projects, the latter goal seems to be adequate for predicting potential outliers in running projects, where precision is too expensive and unnecessary for decision support.

Of course, the primary concern with the use of a classification algorithm is how well it has actually identified underlying structures that are present in the data (cluster validity). Classification algorithms may be constructed manually or automatically. Manual construction reflects intuitive knowledge about underlying structures and relations or influences of metrics on distinct factors to be predicted; automatic construction is applied to large data sets where unknown structures and a variety of interdependencies are to be considered. Because it is a difficult task to try all combinations of ranges of (input) metrics and determine their individual influence on the classification algorithm to predict quality factors, such automated techniques have been developed that solve this problem [9,19,20].

3.1 Pareto Classification

Pareto analysis is included as a classification technique that is common for quick quality analyses. The goal of a Pareto analysis is to identify those 20 % of all components that contribute heavily to all troubles. The principle is nicknamed '*80:20 rule*' because it assumes that the 20 % share is responsible for 80 % of the problems. It is amazing that this simple approach holds in most application domains. Software quality management methods, such as root cause analysis, typically also start by applying a Pareto analysis and identify the small amount of problems (20 %) that provide the biggest return on effort when resolved.

We consider Pareto analysis based on the software size (i.e. the top 20 % of all modules ranked according to module size are selected). In our comparison this type of analysis clearly performed well with volume as the only input metric for selecting the top 20 %. It is thus suggested to be applied as a quick rule of thumb to decide on further activities. The difference to crisp classification trees that could easily provide similar results is that the classification rule is not connected to static boundaries, but to a static rule of thumb with dynamic boundaries in terms of values.

3.2 Crisp Classification Trees

Classification trees have been widely used in many areas, for example in image recognition, taxonomy, or decision table programming. The trees are based on a set of metrics that are used to classify components according to how likely they are to have certain high-risk properties. They consist of several leaf nodes that contain binary or multivalue decisions to indicate whether a component is likely to be in a certain class based on historical data. Because each leaf describes values of a distinct metric such trees might be composed from a set of production rules.

Several methods for automatic tree generation have been described and used for real projects [9]. Each rule imposes crisp boundaries with the result being exclusively allocated to one set based on the values of the input metrics. They are all based on automatic learning from examples with distinct approaches for optimizing, controlling and supervising the learning process (e.g. pattern recognition). Features with more values can lead to decision trees that are unintelligible to human experts and require a larger increase in computation.

3.3 Factor-Based Discriminant Analysis

Factor-based discriminant analysis is an instrument to identify structures and suggest possible organizations of the data into meaningful groups [21,8]. Any given metric vector can be considered as a multidimensional space where each software component (e.g. a module) is represented as a point with distinct coordinates. We identify as a cluster any subset of the points which is internally well connected and externally poorly connected (i.e. components of a cluster are closely related to each other based on some similarities within the related input metrics). The underlying assumption is that objects under investigation may be grouped such that elements residing in a particular group or cluster are, in some sense, more similar to each other than to elements belonging to other groups.

Typically the classification consists of two steps. First factor analysis or a principal-components procedure is used for reducing the dimensionality of the metric vector to fewer metrics with orthogonal complexity domains. Discriminant analysis is then used to separate groups of software components according to one selected quality attribute (i.e. changes, error rate).

3.4 Neural Network Classification

To avoid unnecessary crispness while dealing with approximate knowledge, some recent research has focused towards employing *artificial neural networks* for metric-based decision support [17]. The multilayer perceptron is the most widely applied neural network architecture today. Neural network theory showed that only three layers of neurons are sufficient for learning any (non)linear function combining input data to output data. The input layer consists of one neuron for each complexity metric, while the output layer has one neuron for each quality metric to be predicted.

Because neural network based approaches are predominantly result-driven, not dealing with design heuristics and intuitive rules for modeling the development process and its products, and because their trained information is not accessible from outside, they are even less suitable for providing reasons for any result. To our point of view, any decision support system should contain the maximum amount of expert knowledge that is available. Neural networks can be applied when there are only input vectors (software metric data) and results (quality or productivity data), while no intuitive connections are known between the two sets (e.g. pattern recognition approaches in complicated decision situations). However, neural networks can currently not provide any insight *why* they arrived at a certain decision besides providing result-driven connection weights. It is interesting to note that feedforward neural nets can be approximated to any degree of accuracy by fuzzy expert systems [22], hence offering a new approach for classification based on neural fuzzy hybrids that can be trained and pre-populated with expert rules.

3.5 Fuzzy Classification

In the above mentioned classification techniques, expert rules are either completely ignored or not adequately covered because neither predicate logic nor probability-based methods provide a systematic basis for dealing with them [5,2,6]. Only recently, fuzzy classification techniques had been introduced to software quality management [12,18].

As a consequence, fuzzy facts and rules are generally manipulated as if they were non-fuzzy, leading to conclusions whose validity is open to question. As a simple illustration of this point, consider the fact [2]: "*If data bindings are between 6 and 10 and cyclomatic complexity is greater than 18 the software component is likely to have errors of a distinct type*". Obviously the meaning of this - automatically generated - fact is less precise than stated and might be provided by a maintenance expert as a fuzzy fact: "*If data bindings are medium and cyclomatic complexity is large then the software component is likely to have errors of a distinct type*." Of course, the latter fact requires the determination of the fuzzy attributes "medium" or "large" in the context of the linguistic variables they are associated with (i.e. data bindings and cyclomatic complexity).

Fig. 5: Fuzzy membership functions and inference rules for module design

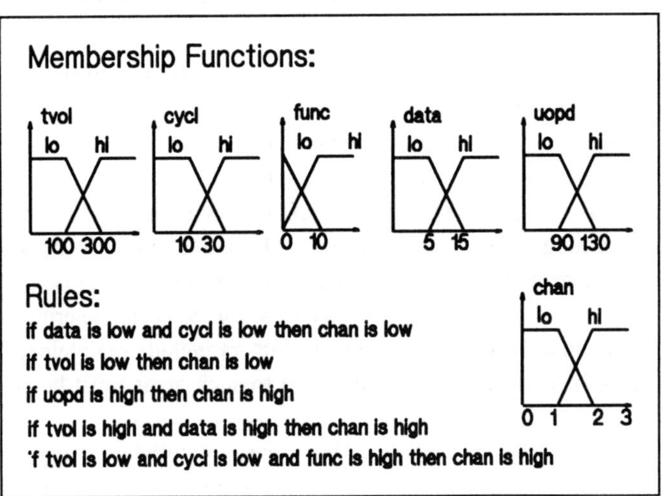

Fuzzy logic provides a method for representing the meaning of both fuzzy and non-fuzzy predicate modifiers or hedges (e.g. *not, very, much, slightly, extremely*) which permits a system for computing with linguistic variables, that is, variables whose values are words in a natural language [15]. For example, cyclomatic complexity is a linguistic variable when its values are assumed to be: *high, small, medium, very high, rather small*, etc., where each value can be interpreted as a possibility distribution over all integers. In order to permit rule-based approximate reasoning based on external input data from software products or documents and vague knowledge about the underlying process that produced the software components to be classified, it is necessary to permit the formulation of fuzzy (expert) rules. Fuzzy classification has been introduced to complexity-based criticality prediction in [18].

The combination of interacting fuzzy rules derived from expert knowledge is called a fuzzy expert system, because it is supposed to model an expert and make his or her knowledge available for non-experts for purposes of diagnosis or decision making [15]. Most fuzzy expert systems are using production rules that are used to capture both heuristic rules of thumb and formally known relations among the facts in the domain (fig. 5). These rules are represented as if-then-rules that associate conclusions to given antecedents. An example for a production rule that we use is "*if cyclomatic complexity is medium and statement count is medium then the component is error-prone*".

4. Developing a Metric-Based Classification System

The development of a classification system for software quality management consists of the following steps:

- Describe an exactly defined development process environment from which the software products under investigation are selected.
- Select a group of expert development staff who will be asked to develop a consensus concerning distinct quality factors. Of course, this jury should consist of people with respected knowledge in the areas that influence those projects being ranked (e.g. data-base or real-time experts for projects determined by such problem domains). If the selected quality factors include maintainability or testing effort, staff members that are assigned to such areas must be considered in the jury.
- Select a random, however representative sample of software components of past projects from the environment (e.g. modules, procedures, classes) which is used as training and validating data.
- Measure these components with respect to a metric vector $M = \{m1,...,mn\}$ based on n selected direct software product metrics that are available during the development process (e.g. cyclomatic complexity or number of input data to a module).
- Measure or have the jury cluster these software components with respect to quality or productivity factors in a quality vector F by comparing and evaluating them. Typically F considers aspects such as reliability, error-count, maintainability, or effort. It can have values such as number of errors or MTTF of a given group of software components. Usually F is unknown during the project development and therefore highest interest lies in its early and accurate prediction. To support accurate prediction is actually the task of the classification system. Because F is used for training and validation purposes, an associated metric vector M from the same past projects is required. The result of this step is a data set $\{M;F\}$ for each software module or component. If construction and validation of the prediction model is required, the associated data sets M and F need to be divided into two mutually exclusive sets $\{M';F'\}$ and $\{M'';F''\}$ before the classifi-

cation process takes place. One is the set used for training or construction of a distinct classification scheme, while the other one will be used to validate the scheme [5].

- Assign the elements of the set {M;F} to appropriate linguistic variables. Usually one linguistic variable is assigned to each metric and quality element of the vectors.
- Define values for each linguistic variable. Place membership functions for mapping the scale and (usually numeric) range of metrics or quality factors to membership degrees of these values.
- For construction of a rule-based system (e.g. pre-populated classification trees, neural-fuzzy hybrids, fuzzy classification) let the experts condense their design knowledge to a set of recursively refined predictive expert rules. The rules are usually dominated by fuzzy linguistic and qualitative descriptions in opposition to quantitative selection formulas that might be preferable on the first sight. Each rule must be explained exactly in order to permit a repeatable classification. When expert knowledge is not available or too expensive algorithmic fuzzy classification approaches may be used for the training data sets. Integrate this set of rules to a classification scheme that can be applied automatically to analyze other software components. Test the resulting set of production rules in terms of completeness (boundaries of ranges) and inconsistencies (several rules with similar antecedents, or similar consequences with contradictive antecedents, etc.).
- Validate the classification system by classifying the test data sets {M'';F''}.
- The final step is to improve the model by adjusting its properties to optimization goals (e.g. adjusting weights in neural networks, shifting membership functions in fuzzy classification systems, condensing classification trees). Such goals include reducing chi-square values which is equal to reducing misclassification errors (see section 5). Parameter tuning is measured by separating misclassification errors, either type I errors ("change-prone components" classified as "uncritical components") or type II errors ("uncritical components" classified as "change-prone components "; also called False Positives). The goal must be to reduce type I errors at the cost of type II errors because it is less expensive to investigate some components despite the fact that they are not critical compared to labeling critical components as harmless without probing further.

5. Experiment: Predicting Changes Based on Complexity Data

It is relatively easy to construct metric-based quality models that happen to classify data of past projects well, because all such models can be calibrated according to quality of fit. The difficulty lies in improving and stabilizing models based on historic data that are of value for use in anticipating future outcomes. While working on software for large real-time systems, we had the task of developing a quality model with predictive accuracy. The main interest of these quality models for metric-based software development was in detecting change-prone modules during the design. Changes include both corrective and additive maintenance, in any case they indicate components requiring more effort than others. The following two subsections introduce three experiments that had been conducted to investigate two hypotheses:

- Fuzzy classification applied to criticality prediction provides better results than other classification techniques that have been used in this area in the past.
- Fuzzy classification as introduced here does not necessarily need training (i.e. it could start completely untrained based on design heuristics), thus being more portable to other systems and easier to understand than other classification techniques.

While part A investigates already published data (thus providing access for further studies and validations) by applying the classification techniques introduced in section 3 and 4, part B shows how to use metric-based classification in an ongoing industrial project.

Both hypotheses have been tested with the Chi Square Test. Based on this test a hypothesis is rejected if the calculated χ^2 is bigger than the respective value of $\chi^2_{1;a}$ from χ^2-tables [25]. The population size was in both experiments sufficiently high to employ this test. An additional experiment for the investigation of the different classification techniques was performed based on a random selection of test sets that were then classified. Numbers of type I errors and type II errors are also used for evaluation. The success criteria are in all cases oriented towards low overall misclassification, sufficiently high χ^2-value and low number of type I errors. Due to outliers it is intrinsically impossible to optimize one classification method for both types of misclassification errors. Residual analysis was not performed because our goal was to predict change-prone modules and not number of changes. A sound statistical analysis of change or fault numbers would require a much larger data set with more modules and is usually not requested in practice.

5.1 Project A

To investigate the effectiveness of fuzzy classification we applied the classification techniques to data originally published by Kitchenham et al [1]. Given two sets of metrics from modules of the ICL general-purpose operating system VME, complexity-based classification was performed to estimate change-proneness of the modules. Both sets of data came from two different implementations of the same sub-system with identical functional requirements. As each program was coded, it was placed under formal configuration control and subsequent changes to modules were recorded. It was not distinguished between corrective and additive changes' intentions. Ten different software complexity metrics are provided together with change rates for 67 modules altogether. The complexity metrics' set includes machine code instructions, lines of code (executable), modules called (calls to external modules), data items (access to static data items by a program module), parameters, Halstead's unique operator count, Halstead's unique operand count, total operators in a module, total operands in a module, and McCabe's cyclomatic complexity.

Since these data sets had been investigated and used for other studies [4], we will only summarize some explorative outcomes. The given software complexity metrics are highly correlated, most Spearman rank correlation coefficients are above 0.5. For example the volume of the code in executable lines of code (without comments and without empty lines) is correlated with the cyclomatic complexity (0.90), and with unique operands (0.93) for all modules. Such relations between metrics are typical and were studied extensively [11]. Factor analysis was performed for reducing dimensions of the metric space resulting in three almost orthogonal factors: volume, control and parameterization. Based on these results we selected five complexity metrics as input values for the prediction models that are most common in complexity metrics application, namely lines of code (tvol), modules called (func), data items (data), unique operands (uopd), and cyclomatic complexity (cycl).

Two VME sub-systems had been described within the Kitchenham study with sub-system 1 containing 27 modules and sub-system 2 containing 40 modules. Since all changes to each module had been provided together with several complexity metrics, we first divided both sub-systems in two classes for each sub-system containing around 80 % of modules with few changes and the remaining 20 % with many changes. Then one sub-system was treated as the data set for training, while the other one was tested for validation purposes after having trained the classification system. For testing the robustness of different classification methods we treated the sets equally despite knowing about the presence of outliers. Compared to other studies [4] we did not eliminate outliers because no common agreement for such filtering exists [11].

Factor-based discriminant analysis could be performed rather easily because it only requires factor analysis for reducing metrics' dimensionality and afterwards discriminant analysis which needs just one learning cycle. This approach hence is the fastest way for classification. Both classification tree and neural network predictions need several thousand training cycles for optimization that are performed automatically on workstations or PCs. It was interesting to realize that classification tree results were similar to results from crisp cluster analysis with ten classes, although the latter approach takes almost no computational effort. For neural network classification a three layer perceptron (5, 12, 1 nodes) with backpropagation learning (100000 training cycles; learning rate: 0.5; momentum between 0 and 0.5) showed best results. Fuzzy classification was short-cut to only one given rule system without further optimization (as presented in fig. 5). Therefore the rules (weights = 1) and membership functions (trapezoid and symmetrical) provide good comprehension and portability. Optimizing the fuzzy classification resulted in reduction of misclassification errors by one or two (not presented here), however rules and membership functions looked very strange (i.e. asymmetric membership functions with overly precise boundaries, increasing the number of rules with individual weight factors). We hence discarded those results.

5.2 Project B

The second experiment was for portability of the classification methods to bigger projects. Training data was taken from several real-time telecommunication projects that had been developed according to a similar design approach. We will describe classification results for one telecommunication project in the area of switching systems called 'Project B' that was used for testing purposes. We investigated a selection of 451 modules that had been placed under configuration control since start of coding. The overall size of these modules is in the area of 1 Million lines of executable code. The specific project had been in field use for over a year thus showing stability in terms of features and failures. Software changes (comparative to those in project A) are given for each module together with several complexity metrics based on the *COSMOS* (*ESPRIT* funded) project [24].

Complexity metrics used in this project include number of (executable) statements, statement complexity, expression complexity, data complexity, depth of nesting (control flow), and data base access (number and complexity of data base accesses). Statement complexity, expression complexity and data complexity are simple metrics that count the use of distinct statements (e.g. different data types and their use is considered data complexity) according to given hierarchies of individual complexity assignments. Again Spearman rank correlations among different complexity metrics were considerably high. For all selected metrics they were above 0.8. Complexity metrics also correlated with number of changes (average over 0.4).

The second hypothesis being tested is that using fuzzy classification as introduced here does *not necessarily* need training (i.e. it could start completely untrained based on design heuristics), thus being more portable to other systems and easier to understand than the other methods. We tested this hypothesis in a third experiment for project B in order to achieve insight in portability of classification techniques without further training. Based on an earlier project that had been designed similarly we provided few expert rules for the fuzzy classification. The rules were as follows:
- if statement count is high then changes are high
- if data complexity is high then changes are high
- if expression complexity is high then changes are high
- if data base access is high then changes are high
- if depth of nesting is high then changes are high
- if data complexity is low then changes are low
- if statement count is low then changes are low

Membership functions remained unchanged from the former project which allows application of these expert rules as design heuristics or vice versa.

6. Results and Discussion

Table I shows a portfolio of predictions versus reality for both sub-systems of *project A*. Notions in quotation marks (in the first column) are the predictions. The upper half of the table investigates sub-system I, while the lower half analyses sub-system II. Instead of common portfolio tables the four values for predictions versus reality are put into single line entries. For example sub-system I consists of 27 modules. 21 of these modules (77 %) contain 5 changes or less, while 6 modules (23 %) contain more than 5 changes. This share reflects approximately the 80:20 ratio that is useful for predictions that require rework in terms of redesign or other approaches to improve maintainability. Applying the Pareto classification (second column) results in a selection of 6 modules that have the biggest volume (i.e. top 20 %). The remaining 21 modules are predicted as having 'few changes'. Now these two groups are compared with reality. 19 modules with few changes and 4 change-prone modules were classified correctly. 2 modules were misclassified as having few changes (type I error) and 2 modules were predicted as change-prone, while belonging to the class of modules with few changes (type II error). Taking these values gives the chi-square result of 8.82.

The last line of table I provides the average percentage of correct classifications for several runs when all data sets (both sub-systems) were mixed and then half of them were randomly selected for training or testing, respectively.

Table I: Classification Results for Project A with five Classification Methods

Project A: Two subsystems with 67 modules.	Pareto classification by volume (top 20 %)	crisp classification tree	factor-based discriminant analysis	neural network classification	non-optimized fuzzy classification
VME sub-system 1 (27 modules) used for testing (sub-system 2 for training)					
reality: ≤ 5 changes: 21 modules (77 %)					
prediction: "few changes"	19	19	20	19	20
prediction: "change-prone" (type II)	2	2	1	2	1
reality: > 5 changes: 6 modules (23 %)					
prediction: "few changes" (type I)	2	2	5	3	0
prediction: "change-prone"	4	4	1	3	6
χ^2	8.82	8.82	0.96	5.06	22.0
VME sub-system 2 (40 modules) used for testing (sub-system 1 for training)					
reality: ≤ 4 changes: 31 modules (78 %)					
prediction: "few changes"	28	30	28	30	30
prediction: "change-prone" (type II)	3	1	3	1	1
reality: > 4 changes: 9 mod. (22 %)					
prediction: "few changes" (type I)	3	4	1	4	3
prediction: "change-prone"	6	5	8	5	6
χ^2	13.0	15.0	15.5	15.0	19.4
random selection of test sets (percentage of overall correct classification)	83.0 %	78.3 %	73.2 %	80.7 %	92.5 %

Classification seems to be more difficult for sub-system 1 which contains more outlying data sets (i.e. complexity metrics and number of changes do not fit together). Fuzzy classification performed best in terms of χ^2 and overall misclassifications were altogether at a minimum. Fig. 6 shows a scatterplot of the complete Kitchenham data set (both subsystems) with changes (horizontal axis), lines of code (vertical axis), and cyclomatic complexity (shape). Outliers with small complexity and high change-rate can be clearly identified. It is obviously impossible to strive for zero misclassifications because several data sets are overlapping in a sense that they belong to the - intuitively - wrong group according to the delivered error count.

Fig. 6: Scatterplot of number of changes with volume and cyclomatic complexity for project A (both subsystems)

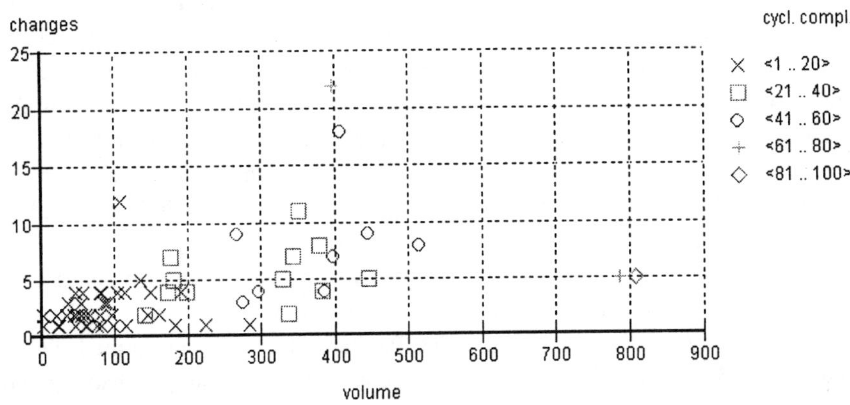

Fig. 7: Scatterplot of number of changes with volume and cyclomatic complexity for project B

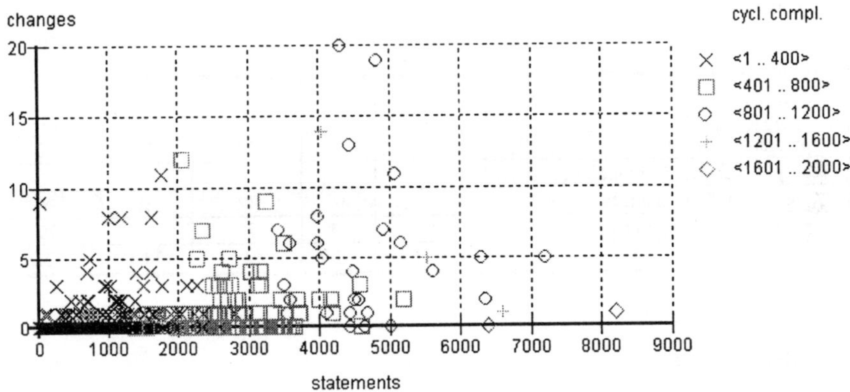

Applying the five different classification techniques to the switching system data of *project B* showed almost identical results in terms of overall correct classification of the modules (table II). Results showed highest overall correct classification for crisp classification trees (85 % of all modules). Pareto classification (83 % of all modules) and neural network classification (82.5 %) performed slightly worse. Factor-based discriminant analysis and non optimized fuzzy classification finally achieved 81 % correct classifications. Obviously there is no clear winner given this ranking which is due to a number of outliers that either increase type I or type II misclassifications when optimization of the other area is achieved (fig. 7).

A better indicator for comparing classification techniques is the number of type I misclassifications. The shaded area of table II provides these results. Fuzzy classification shows lowest misclassification results with only 8 modules indicated as having few changes while they actually were change-prone. Chi-square analysis also indicates that fuzzy classification is performing better than the other techniques ($\chi^2 = 52.2$). Automatic optimization of rules (e.g. more than two input values in one rule) and membership functions improved these results, however due to desired intuitiveness of rules we won't discuss such techniques.

Results of the third experiment on portability of classification techniques without further training are as follows: Fuzzy classification with data from a follow-on project provided $\chi^2 = 46.1$ for 200 modules. Pareto classification performed slightly worse ($\chi^2 = 35.7$), while the three remaining classification techniques had a χ^2 below 30.

Table II: Classification Results for Project B with five Classification Methods

Project B: 200 modules used for testing (163 modules with zero or one faults; 37 modules with more than one fault)	Pareto classification by volume (top 20 %)	crisp classification tree	factor-based discriminant analysis	neural network classification	non-optimized fuzzy classification
reality: $\leq$ 1 fault: 163 modules (81.5 %)					
prediction: "few changes"	146	149	137	149	133
prediction: "change-prone" (type II)	17	14	26	14	30
reality: > 1 faults: 37 modules (18.5 %)					
prediction: "few changes" (type I)	17	16	12	21	8
prediction: "change-prone"	20	21	25	16	29
χ^2	38.1	48.9	42.3	28.4	52.2

7. Conclusions

A comparison of different classification approaches suitable for metric-based decision support is presented in table III. Results as presented in this table are based on various applications of the four classification techniques to data sets from switching systems. Pareto classification is left out because this mere analytical technique needs neither training nor does it provide any constructive guidelines during design and coding. The upper part of this table presents a summary on learning and knowledge representation. The lower part gives the effects of using manipulated data values (i.e. two metrics are highly correlated, one metric is almost random; several data sets contain random values). The remaining two parts of table III provide portability results and - again - a short bibliography for improved orientation.

Based on the described experiments, fuzzy classification clearly performed best. Since there are some guiding principles for decision support available, we emphasize on utilizing expert-derived, however vague, knowledge that we included in a fuzzy expert system-type classification scheme. For the same reason (i.e. software engineering expert knowledge is available) we strongly oppose using learning strategies that are only result-driven (e.g. classification trees or mere neural network approaches). However, we see the necessity of such approaches when only few guiding principles are available and sufficient project data can be utilized for supervised learning.

Table III: Comparison of Different Classification Methods (without Pareto Classification)

	crisp classification tree	factor-based discriminant analysis	neural network classification	fuzzy classification
crisp data values as metric data values	x	x	x	x
fuzzy, vague, linguistic data values				x
algorithmic knowledge representation	(x)	x	(x)	(x)
rule-based knowledge representation	x			x
information represented by *intuitive* rules				x
learning is result-driven (as opposed to design heuristics)	x		x	(x)
learning can be performed automatically (0, +, ++)	++	0	++	+
reasons for decisions are given (0, +, ++)	++	0	0	++
effects of highly correlated metrics in input training data (0, +, ++)	++	++	+	++
effects of uncorrelated metrics in input training data (0, +, ++)	+	+	0	++
robustness to outlying data sets during training (0, +, ++)	++	+	0	++
portability to data sets from other projects with same design methodology (0, +, ++)	+	+	0	++
bibliography for applications and theory	[2,9,19,23]	[4,21]	[17]	[12,15,18,22]

*	dependent on learning approach or classification algorithm
0	bad results
+	medium results
++	good results

The choice of the proper approach to automatic decision support depends on the problem. To software classification problems, multibranching fuzzy classification provides a more comprehensive solution than crisp decision trees. Such multi-branching decision support is based on structures that are not necessarily trees but also networks that resemble expert systems' structures. When these classification schemes are applied to new data sets, the best solution is to provide not only a binary result, but fuzzy attributes that consider those results that lie in between a clear "yes" or "no". We emphasize the necessity of applying fuzzy concepts to the areas of metric-based software project and quality management because subjective and qualitative judgment plays an important role in this area.

The clear benefits of using the described fuzzy classification methodology are:
- Compared with other classification methods fuzzy classification shows best results in terms of both chi-square and reduction of type I misclassification errors.
- Expert rules that are already available (e.g. design heuristics, coding guidelines) can be directly included in the classification scheme.
- Rules can be used independent of the projects because membership functions may be tuned according to project environments without violating the rules.
- Derived classification schemes can be combined with CASE tools and automatic metrics generation for integrated design support.

The impacts of this study for other applications in software development projects are as follows:
- Complexity metrics together with history data sets of past projects must be utilized for criticality prediction of modules. They help identifying those few critical components that later are responsible for most of the faults that show up in integration and in the field.
- Criticality predictions are most effective before the start of system integration.
- For a quick overview, for instance in a project review, Pareto analysis should be applied to identify few highly critical modules.
- The best classification technique among five techniques that are currently applicable for complexity-based criticality prediction is fuzzy classification. This technique can easily be applied because tool environments are available off the shelf.
- The advantage of fuzzy classification in development projects is that available design heuristics can be reused. The technique thus is more intelligible for practitioners than other techniques.
- The outcome of each criticality prediction must be an intensive investigation of the identified modules in order to find out whether they indeed contain not yet detected errors.

8. Summary and Further Research

We have evaluated several classification techniques as an approach for predicting faults based on code complexity metrics. Given complexity metrics and quality data (fault rates) of several different real-time systems best results were achieved with fuzzy classification. Pareto analysis ('80:20 rule') generally showed good results which clearly underlie its importance as a rule of thumb for easy identification of the top 20 % of critical modules. Complexity-based classification has been applied to the design and testing of telecommunication systems. Its practical use was showed for detecting fault-prone components and assigning additional fault-detection effort.

As such the technique proves to be effective in early identification of critical components. It must be emphasized that criticality prediction techniques being used do not attempt to detect all faults. Instead they belong to the set of managerial instruments that try to optimize resource allocation by focusing them on areas with many faults that would affect the utility of the delivered product.

The trade-off of applying complexity-based predictive quality models is estimated based on:
- limited resources are assigned to high-risk jobs or components;
- impact analysis and risk assessment of changes is feasible based on affected or changed complexity;
- grey-box testing strategies are applied to identified high-risk components;
- less customer reported failures.

Especially the mentioned levels for reaction and the appropriate measures how to react most effective must be subject to continuous evaluation. They will improve over time with more projects being applied. Further research in the area of predictive quality models should focus on the areas:
- Investigation of more projects from different application areas in order to provide fundamental insight in the development of quality models and their influence on different project types. This should include analyses of different approaches for constructing classification schemes (e.g. decision trees) and optimizing their accuracy, intelligibility, and reproducibility.
- Model the processes contributing to fault injection, detection and correction (look for example on staffing, late feature changes, corrections affecting complex components, testing strategies and their coverage and distribution over the whole system).
- **Coping with noisy data sets for constructing predictive classification systems.** Solutions to this problem include robust feature selection and error-estimation

during the induction of classification schemes.
- Application to practical software project management based on predictive and
  dynamic classification models. Derived classification schemes must be combined with IPSE and CM thus providing automatic metric generation for integrated design and test management support.

Exercises

1. What does it mean if several software metrics are correlated? What is the impact
   of such correlation to statistical analysis? What is the impact on using such metrics as predictors?
2. Why are most non-normalized software metrics typically highly correlated?
3. Why do software defects cluster within components, modules or distinct procedures?
4. Describe some aspects of software complexity that are not measured by a pure
   size metric. What are the advantages and disadvantages of a size metric compared with for instance the McCabe code complexity metric?
5. Outline an experiment to validate a defect prediction technique that tries to predict criticality in terms of defects in a module from static code metrics. Explain
   the key assumptions or hypotheses. What can and can't be validated in such experiments?
6. Why do the different prediction techniques used in the described environment
   perform so differently? What does that mean for a simple rule of a thumb technique compared to a fuzzy prediction approach? What is the value of each in
   practical day-to-day management decisions?

References

[1]   Kitchenham, B. A. and L. Pickard: Towards a constructive quality model.
Software Engineering Journal, Vol. 2, No. 7, S. 114-126, Jul. 1987.

[2]   Porter, A. A. and R. W. Selby: Empirically Guided Software Development
Using Metric-Based Classification Trees. IEEE Software, Vol. 7, No. 3, S. 46-54,
Mrc. 1990.

[3]   Stark, G., R.C. Durst and C.W. Vowell: Using Metrics in Management Decision Making. IEEE Computer, Vol. 27, No. 9, pp. 42 - 48, 1994.

[4]   Munson, J.C. and T.M. Khoshgoftaar: Regression Modelling of Software
Quality: Empirical Investigation. Information and Software Technology, Vol. 32,

No. 2, pp. 106 - 114, 1990.

[5]   Schneidewind, N. F.: Validating Metrics for Ensuring Space Shuttle Flight Software Quality. IEEE Computer, Vol. 27, No. 8, pp. 50 - 57, 1994.

[6]   Selby, R. W. and V. R. Basili: Analyzing Error-Prone System Structure. IEEE Transactions on Software Engineering, Vol. 17, No. 2, pp. 141-152, 1991.

[7]   Ebert, C. and T. Liedtke: An Integrated Approach for Criticality Prediction. Proc. 6. Int. Symp. on Software Reliability Engineering ISSRE'95. IEEE Computer Soc. Press. Los Alamitos, CA, USA, 1995.

[8]   Ebert, C.: Visualization Techniques for Analyzing and Evaluating Software Measures. IEEE Trans. Software Engineering, Vol. 18, No. 11, pp. 1029-1034, Nov. 1992.

[9]   Selby, R. W. and A. A. Porter: Learning from Examples: Generation and Evaluation of Decision Trees for Software Resource Analysis. IEEE Trans. Software Eng., Vol. 14, No. 12, pp. 1743-1757, 1988.

[10]   Card, D. N. and R. L. Glass: Measuring Software Design Quality. Prentice Hall. Englewood Cliffs, N.J., USA, 1990.

[11]   Fenton, N. E. and S.L. Pfleeger: Software Metrics: A Practical and Rigorous Approach. Chapman & Hall, London, UK, 1997.

[12]   Pedrycz, W. and J. Waletzky: Fuzzy Clustering in Software Reusability. Software - Practice and Experience, Vol. 27, No. 3, pp. 245-270, Mrc 1997.

[13]   Behrendt, W., S.C. Lambert et al : A Metrication Framework for Knowledge-Based Systems. In: Proc. Eurometrics '92, pp. 197-210, Comm. of the E.C.: EUREKA, Brussels, April 1992.

[14]   Zimmer, A.C.: Verbal versus numerical processing. In: R. Scholz, Ed., Individual Decision Making Under Uncertainty. North-Holland, Amsterdam, NL, 1983.

[15]   Zimmermann, H.-J.: Fuzzy Set Theory and its Applications. Kluwer, Boston, 2nd edition, 1991.

[16]   Negoita, C.V.: Expert Systems and Fuzzy Systems. Benjamin/Cummings, Menlo Park, USA, 1985.

[17]   Khoshgoftaar, T. and D.L. Lanning: A Neural Network Approach for Early Detection of Program Modules Having High Risk in the Maintenance Phase. J. Systems and Software, Vol. 29, pp. 85-91, 1995.

[18]   Ebert, C.: Rule-Based Fuzzy Classification for Software Quality Control. Fuzzy Sets and Systems, Vol. 63, pp. 349-358, 1994.

[19]   Breiman, L., J.H.Friedman, R.A.Olshen, and C.J.Stone: Classification and Regression Trees. Wadsworth, Belmont, CA, 1984.

[20]   Shann, J.J. and H.C. Fu: A Fuzzy Neural Network for Rule Acquiring on Fuzzy Control Systems. Fuzzy Sets and Systems, Vol. 71, pp. 345-357, 1995.

[21]   Dillon, W. R. and M. Goldstein: Multivariate Analysis-Methods and Applications. John Wiley & Sons, NY, NY, USA, 1984.

[22]   Buckley, J.J. and Y. Hayashi: Neural Nets for Fuzzy Systems. Fuzzy Sets and Systems, Vol. 71, pp. 265-276, 1995.

[23]   Grady, R.B.: Practical Software Metrics for Project Management and Process Improvement. Prentice Hall, Englewood Cliffs, 1992.

[24]   Debou C., N. Fuchs und H. Saria: Selling believable technology. *IEEE Software*, Nov 1993.

[25]   Kendall, M.G. and A. Stuart: The Advanced Theory of Statistics. Vol. II. Griffin, London, 1961.

The article is based on an earlier article published by Chapmann & Hall. Permission is granted to use the material which originally appeared as: "Classification Techniques for Metric-Based Software Development", Software Quality Journal, Vol. 5, pp. 255-272, 1996.

FUZZY LOGIC TECHNIQUES FOR SOFTWARE METRIC MODELS OF DEVELOPMENT EFFORT

A. R. GRAY, S. G. MACDONELL
Software Metrics Research Laboratory
Department of Information Science
University of Otago, PO Box 56, Dunedin, New Zealand
Agray@commerce.otago.ac.nz

Software metrics are measurements that are made of software development processes and the resulting products. Once recorded they can be used as variables (both dependent and independent) in models for project management purposes, including prediction, monitoring, and assessing the development process. The most common types of these software metric models are those used for predicting the development effort required for a software system, usually in terms of developer hours/days, based on size, complexity, developer characteristics, and other relevant metrics. Despite the well-known, and considerable, financial and strategic benefits that can be acquired from developing accurate and usable models of effort estimation, there are a number of problems that have not yet been overcome by those using the traditional techniques of formal and linear regression models. These include taking full consideration of the non-linearities and interactions inherent in complex real-world processes such as software development and the lack of stationarity in such processes (as people, tools, and methodologies change). Other problems include over-commitment to precisely specified values, the small quantities of data often available, and the inability to use whatever knowledge is available where numerical values are unknown or are only known in some approximate manner. The usefulness of alternative techniques, especially that of fuzzy logic modeling, are investigated, some comparisons between the techniques are made, and some recommendations are suggested regarding the use of fuzzy logic for project management.

1 Introduction

In order to effectively and efficiently develop software in an increasingly competitive and complex environment, from both technological and commercial perspectives, many organizations are making increasing use of software metrics as part of their project management process. Software metrics are aspects of software development (either some part of the software product itself such as the code or documentation, or the development processes producing that product such as coding or testing phases) that can be measured [1]. These measurements can then be used as variables (both dependent and independent) in models for predicting or estimating some aspect(s) of the development process or product that are of interest (such as effort, errors remaining in the system after testing, user satisfaction, or system performance).

Models may also be developed in the same manner and used for monitoring (comparing predicted with actual values) or assessment (explaining the discrepancy between predicted and actual values) tasks. Often these activities are performed on each project at different stages of its life-cycle in order to facilitate learning more about the organization's software development process with the goal of iteratively improving project management. This is especially important given the often small quantities of data available and the changes that occur with an organization's development process over time. Many organizations do not have large quantities of data to calibrate their models initially and cannot delay their metrics program.

The most common application of software metrics is to develop models that predict the development effort (often measured in person-hours or person-days) that will be required to complete certain stages of a software system's development. Generally speaking, such models are most often developed once the users' requirements have been ascertained and the specifications outlining the system are completed, or are at least *reasonably* stable.

It is at this point that many of the traditionally used software metrics can be derived from the available information. Thus, the stages in the development life cycle that are modeled in terms of effort estimation are usually the programming, testing, and maintenance phases. There has also been some work towards even earlier modeling of effort based on requirements alone, such as [2], but the results are obviously less accurate since less information is available at these times. The number of attributes that can be *numerically* specified regarding a system increases with time as the product becomes more complete, with the level of accuracy also increasing.

Such effort-prediction models are of considerable importance to a number of quite diverse stakeholders. For the developer, manager, and user of any software product the prediction of project effort requirements is an extremely important activity [3,4]. The estimate arrived at frequently forms the basis for contract negotiations, resource and personnel allocation over the schedule, and charging for the project. Other higher-level issues involving strategic planning for the organization are also dependent on the timing of development. The use of such models enables the project manager to plan, monitor and control the subsequent development process. It may have run-on effects for the user, in that their operations may be planned around the delivery of a particular supporting software product at a certain time. Clearly then, an accurate and robust effort estimation model is desirable from all perspectives – for both financial and strategic reasons.

There are many other applications of software metric models, such as assessing reusability from previously developed systems and components, predicting maintenance frequency, estimating likely user satisfaction, and measuring system reliability. The remainder of this paper is concerned with predicting development effort, but the results presented here apply in general to other prediction tasks, and classification, and control models as well.

2 Software metric models for effort prediction

In order to illustrate the use of software metrics in an effort prediction system the following, somewhat abstract, example will be used. The size of a system could be measured in terms of the number of lines of source code, or the number of screens and reports contained in the specification. Similarly, the complexity may be measured in terms of the structure of the system, such as call paths or, for object-oriented systems, the depths and widths of inheritance hierarchies. Other metrics that may be of interest include the quality of developers working on the system, as may perhaps be assessed in terms of years of experience, and the types of development and support tools being used. These descriptive measures of the system and the development process are software metrics. In the same way, the potential variables of interest here such as the required developer effort for programming and testing are also software metrics. Such a model is shown in Figure 1.

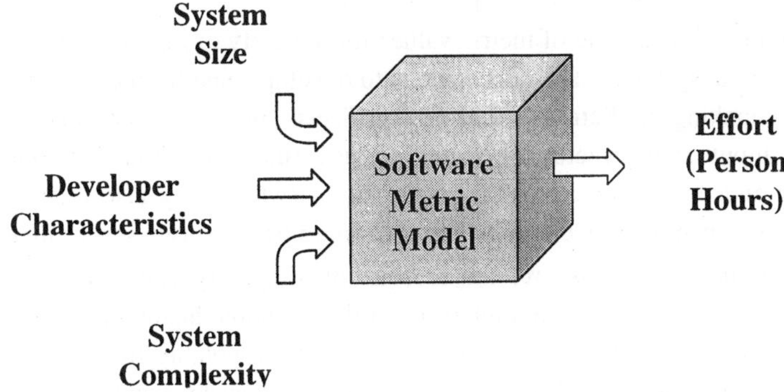

Figure 1. Software metric model for effort estimation

A software metric model may now be developed using data that contains some measures of system size and complexity, and developer ability in order to predict the effort required for various stages of the development life cycle. This is a fairly simple example of a model of an immensely complex and dynamic system (the process of developing software). Many other variables could be added, such as the reuse of previous systems, the demands and requirements for the system (such as maximum response time), the tools available, incentive schemes, the size of the team, and even the leadership style of the project manager. It should be noted that effort is the sum of developers' time spent on the project, and is distinct from the duration of the project. The duration does not allow for the fact that many designers, developers, and testers will work on a system simultaneously.

The data for these metrics are generally collected from project records, often based on educated guesses and possibly will be adjusted until they *feel* correct. Many problems with inadequate recording of project data, missing data, too coarsely recorded data, and simply incorrectly recorded data make this process very difficult in practice. It is common for employees to feel threatened and competitive when their *contributions* to the system are being determined, and this often leads to a biasing effect or a reluctance to participate in measurement programs. This is especially likely when precise values are ascribed to employees, making it easy to rank employees.

Most organizations will frequently change their development methodology, the tools used, and/or their development environment making it difficult to collect a large number of observations that are similar to the type of system that the predictive model is intended to work with. In some cases external data can be acquired to supplement the internal set, but small data sets are a problem familiar to most if not all software metrics researchers and practitioners alike.

The end result is a table of metric values for a variety of metrics, over a number of systems or subsystems. The next stage is to develop some form of model that can be used for making predictions about new projects. In generic terms such models accept as input some vector of metric values (including binary variables for categories) and produce a vector of metric values (which may also include binary variables). As such the model represents a mapping from the two sets of metrics.

Such predictive models are, for reasons of simplicity and tradition, usually developed using linear regression analysis on the available historical data, although there has been increasing use of other techniques, most notably fuzzy logic models [5], regression trees [6], neural networks [7], and case-based reasoning [8]. A useful summary of these techniques and their application to software metric modeling can be found in [9].

Linear regression models express the dependent variable (effort) as some linear combination of the independent variables (such as size, complexity, etc.) and can involve some transformations of these variables before being optimized by some cost function. Some software metrics models involve some scoring systems, such as for complexity, and then use an equation, often calibrated by regression, to predict effort. Some traditional models make some use of transformations to account for the increasing complexity of, say, larger systems. However the basic idea of numerical inputs to numerical outputs in a simple, some would say parsimonious, model has been the basis of software metric modeling for most applications. Predictions can then be made for new system development projects using the resulting model as the independent variables are estimated or become known for certain.

3 Difficulties with current models using software metrics

Some of the problems with collecting data and developing models have been briefly mentioned above. In this section a more complete list, although certainly not without its omissions, of the difficulties with the current use of formal and linear regression models are identified and discussed. Many other problems with software metric models exist, but here we will concentrate on those that result from the use of the traditional techniques described above.

3.1 Providing exact values for inputs

A major problem that exists with such models is the difficulty that project managers face in specifying the exact values for the metrics used as inputs. Often when using the developed models they must use values that they *anticipate* will eventuate, since for many metrics the actual value is never known with certainty until the project is completed. The accurate specification of such independent variables is next to impossible for lower-level metrics such as source code length and the number of transactions. Even higher level metrics such as the number of screens and reports can change greatly during development as the users' requirements are refined and better understood, or for some reason simply change. The values of these metrics, at best, tend to move towards their final value as the project progresses.

Using such models therefore often demands a level of accuracy in prediction from project managers that is rarely possible early in the project life cycle, the very time that planning is most crucial. While a manager may be quite capable of specifying the range within which the value will most likely fall, when faced with the need for a precise value they may struggle and end up guessing or choosing round numbers for convenience.

In addition, the use of numerical variables limits the opportunity for early estimation since the accuracy of the input metrics is greatly reduced in the early stages of the project's life cycle. Few project managers would be even willing to make numerical guesses at the very early stages of a project for any metrics at all, since those values will almost certainly be incorrect. It should be noted that we are not merely referring to the technical difficulties of specifying such values early in a project, but just as important are the psychological and organizational problems introduced by insisting that managers do make such estimates before they feel confident in their own values

3.2 Over commitment

The outputs from such models are almost always *crisp* (i.e. numerical) values and this often leads to overconfidence in both the accuracy and precision of the results. When, for example, the dependent variable is predicted as 7120 developer hours (or even worse as 7121.6 developer hours), there is a risk that this value becomes sacred. This can lead to development time being wasted in the event of an overestimate, and requirements remaining unfulfilled or the project going over schedule to an even greater extent where the effort is underestimated. In short, it is difficult to treat these outputs as what they really are, best guesses of the most likely required effort

While confidence intervals can be developed (for example, so that effort is predicted to range between 7000 and 7300 developer hours with some level of probability), this is rarely the case in either practice or research. In addition, given the small data sets that are often available, frequently with skewed distributions and outliers, the intervals can be questionable in any event. The practice of rounding such values can be used, but the more precise values are still generally available, and even rounded values can be taken as *accurate* even though *precision* is removed. This problem can not really be overcome by any modeling technique that returns numerical values.

3.3 The size of data sets

The next problem to be discussed here is that of the small data set size that is generally available for developing such models. While a larger organization may develop hundreds of systems in a year, they will often be so heterogeneous that only a relative few can be used for developing predictive models for certain types of systems. In addition, the non-stationarity of the contemporary software development process ensures that new programming languages, development environments, hardware platforms, and methodologies will emerge on a constant basis, making the available data less relevant as its generalisability declines. When high quality data is available in sufficient quantities, its proprietary nature generally leads to organizations being reluctant to allow its dissemination, although there have been moves towards databases of metrics data.

Many of the data sets used for software metrics research are collections of projects from different organizations, thereby introducing additional sources of variation. Even where a large number of data sets may have been collected on sufficiently similar systems to permit a proper model development process, the data is often contaminated by outliers (either through measurement error or unusual system or project characteristics) and inaccuracies.

Thus the developer of a software metric model is faced with the need to develop, calibrate, and validate a model of an exceptionally complex process without the benefit of large quantities of accurate or representative data. Unfortunately the techniques of choice, generally linear least-squares regression, are susceptible to small data sets with contaminated or unusual observations, further decreasing the generalisability of the resulting models.

3.4 Interpretability of models

The final problem discussed here is that of specifying models in such a way that they retain some intuitiveness while including a sufficient subset of influential independent variables, and their interactions, to provide the required level of accuracy. This is a direct tradeoff for any technique, the more complex the model the more difficult interpretation becomes – although different techniques allow movement along different tradeoff curves.

The intuitiveness of a software metric model is often vital for it to gain acceptance by project managers. In order to provide the necessary level of comprehensibility models in the past have often been linear equations with a small number of independent variables. These models usually ignore the potential non-linearity of the relationships, the interactions between the independent variables, and the less important, but nonetheless influential, variables that cumulatively may be capable of explaining considerable variation in the dependent variable. Such problems are exacerbated by small data sets where regression techniques cannot provide unique solutions for large numbers of variables where fewer observations are available.

4 A fuzzy-logic approach to software metrics and models

The potential solution that is suggested here to, at least partially, overcome the previously mentioned problems (and some others that were not mentioned) is to use fuzzy logic variables for the metrics and models. In general it is considered that project managers can fairly readily specify independent variables in software metrics models using linguistic labels, such as a *large* number of screens and a *low* level of system complexity, in the early stages of estimation – which as was mentioned earlier is the most crucial time for planning. It is also considered that such models provide considerable benefits in terms of reducing commitment, making full use of knowledge, and improving interpretability as will be discussed below. In [5] the bold statement is made, that not only is fuzzy logic useful for effort prediction, but that it is essential in order to improve the quality of current estimating models. While we endorse the use of this technique, we also feel that some pragmatism is required to determine exactly when and where this technique can be best used, not to mention the issues involved in educating practitioners in its use.

4.1 Fuzzy labels as independent variables

Since many of the independent variables in software metric models are either difficult to quantify (for example complexity), or are only known to a rough degree (such as system size), the use of fuzzy variables seems intuitively appealing. It is our conjecture here that project managers are in fact able to classify systems using fuzzy variables with reasonable levels of both accuracy and consistency. This also avoids the need for arbitrary measures of complexity, for example.

While complexity can be defined in an algebraic sense, and in fact it has been defined in a large number of ways in the past, such formal definitions are always to some extent arbitrary. The software metrics literature is filled with debates as to the relative merits, and demerits, of various definitions. It is instead suggested here that complexity is a multifaceted concept, but that experienced project managers would be able to make fairly consistent classifications of projects in terms of one or a small number of types of complexity. This has the added advantage of reducing the number of variables used as inputs into the model. This point is discussed further later in the paper in terms of work in progress.

4.2 Reducing commitment through fuzzy outputs

Particularly at the very early stages of a software development project, estimating to within one person-hour or person-day is simply not realistic. Instead, a fuzzy system may be used to transform linguistic labels, or numerical values, indicating system size and complexity, personnel experience, and other factors of influence into an equally imprecise (but adequate for its purpose) label indicating predicted effort, for example *very high*. While this approach may well be imprecise, this is justified and should ensure that personnel associated with the project do not attach unwarranted accuracy to the figures produced. As the project progresses and a greater degree of certainty is established in relation to the scope of the project (and also as data starts to become available), then more precise indicators of effort may be formulated, either through more and smaller membership functions or allowing for numerical defuzzification. There is an inherent trade-off in the development of effort estimation models; is it better to be approximately correct most of the time or precisely inaccurate all of the time? For the early stages of software development at least, we see the former as the preferred state.

4.3 Better use of knowledge and data

Since a fuzzy logic model can be initialized with expert rules, and given that the movement of membership functions and rules can be limited, it is possible that such a model will perform significantly better than alternatives such as regression and neural network models given small quantities of data. While it is possible to introduce some expert knowledge into regression models through variable selection, coefficient range limitation, including interaction, etc. these means require considerable skill with the technique, and it is felt that it would be an easier route to acquiring that knowledge via fuzzy logic rules.

4.4 Model interpretability

One final point that deserves mention is that the application of fuzzy logic to the estimation problem allows for *model transparency*. A fuzzy system provides the potential for those involved to view, evaluate, criticize, and even adapt the models. This is not always possible in statistical or other machine learning modeling approaches.

5 Empirical case study

The case study below is based on actual project data from [10]. Although the data is quite real, it is used here mainly to illustrate the capabilities and drawbacks associated with the various analysis methods available. Four approaches are compared: Function Point Analysis (which is a formal model), regression techniques, feedforward neural networks, and finally fuzzy logic. The results for the Function Point Analysis, regression models, and neural network models have been previously reported in more detail in [11]. The data set includes measures of a number of standard software metrics, namely:

330

- project effort
- project duration
- levels of experience with equipment
- levels of experience in project management
- numbers of basic transactions
- numbers of data entities
- raw and adjusted function point counts, which are a standard method for counting the functional size of a system, with adjustments for complexity also possible.

The issue of making the fullest use of information available, which is one area where fuzzy logic excels, is difficult to illustrate in a post-hoc case study. Since fuzzy variables are not available for earlier in the projects' life cycles, the accuracy of such models can not be shown here. It is regarded that such models would have performed comparatively well, since the other techniques depend more on the availability of data from later in the development life cycle. However, the actual use of fuzzy logic models throughout a series of projects is part of a current research project and so its effectiveness may soon be able to be judged.

Many different methods for estimating a model's goodness for prediction are available. These include the many forms of correlation (R^2, adjusted R^2, R^2 adequate), Akaike Information Criterion, Bayesian Information Criterion, and mean square error. A set of indicators that are commonly used in metrics analysis to indicate the adequacy of a predictive model are the mean magnitude of relative error and the threshold-oriented pred measure. Both of these are used in this case study on a validation data set (27 of the total 81 observations) for each technique.

The magnitude of relative error (MRE) is a measure of the difference between the actual values of the dependent variable (V_A) and the predictions of the model (V_F) as shown in Equation (1).

$$MRE = \frac{\left|V_A - V_F\right|}{V_A} \tag{1}$$

The mean MRE (MMRE) is therefore the mean value for this indicator over all observations in the sample. For software development project management relative errors are often claimed to be a better judge of the model's accuracy than absolute errors. The pred measure provides an indication of overall fit for a set of data points, based on the MRE values for each data point as shown in Equation (2).

$$pred(l) = \frac{i}{n} \qquad (2)$$

In Equation (2) l is the selected threshold value for MRE, i is the number of data point with MRE less than or equal to l, and n is the total number of data points. As an illustration, if pred (0.25) = 30%, then we can say that 30% of the fitted values fall within 25% of their corresponding actual values.

The various techniques for modeling that were examined with respect to the case-study data are now discussed in some detail with explanations provided as to how the final models were selected.

5.1 Function points

Function points are currently the most commonly used formal software metric modeling technique. Function Point Analysis (FPA) [12,13,14] provides a well-established method for the relatively early (post specification) assessment of system scope. Several versions of FPA have emerged, with specialized versions also created for particular types of systems. These are generally based on various transaction-oriented system requirements characteristics, although object-oriented and multimedia-based versions have also emerged.

In many respects FPA already contains some degree of *fuzziness*, with levels of complexity recognized for functions, albeit at a very crude level and with only binary memberships being used. Although FPA is not without its potential problems, especially with regards inter-rater consistency which tends to be very low, it remains one of the most widely used methods for modeling software development size and effort estimation.

Two versions of FPA are shown here. The standard use of FPA for effort prediction is to use the historical mean effort per function point. This is complemented here by the use of the median effort per function point, which is a more robust estimator.

5.2 Linear regression

Two forms of linear regression are illustrated here. Firstly, standard least squares (LS) is used as a demonstration of the most commonly used technique for developing software metric models. Secondly, least median squares (LMS, a robust regression technique that uses weighted regression to remove outliers) is illustrated.

The two cases differ only in terms of the goal function that they attempt to minimize, namely the mean square error and median square error respectively.

In both cases stepwise procedures were used to select linearly influential variables, with no interaction terms entered. This was felt to best approximate the usual course of model development taken. Both models resulted in a simple linear equation involving a constant term and the unadjusted function points, with other variables being found to offer non-significant improvements in model performance.

5.3 Feed-forward neural network

Neural networks have been applied to software metric modeling in a large number of papers and the results have, in general, been favorable to this particular technique where sufficiently large data sets have been available and the technique has been correctly used. Many forms of neural network models are suitable for the task of effort estimation, but we have here used only the simplest and most accessible, not to mention most commonly used.

The Multi-Layer Perceptron (MLP) networks were training using two-thirds of the 54 model-development observations for training, and one-third for a testing set. Training was stopped when the testing error was minimized, and the lowest testing error was also used to select the particular network architecture.

It should be noted that the third (validation) data set mentioned above, which was withheld for making an unbiased estimate of the generalisability of the model is not at all influential in model tuning or selection here. The same principle applies to all the techniques' results described in this chapter. The use of the model's performance on the training or testing data set gives a serious advantage to more complex techniques such as neural networks and can often be seen as contributing to their superior performance in the literature.

5.4 Fuzzy logic

A significant motivation for using fuzzy logic is not under the circumstances of the following post-hoc analysis, but rather in the ability to estimate development effort much earlier in the development process. Unfortunately, results are not yet available for how well this technique operates in what we regard as its most appropriate environment – early project estimation with iterative refinement.

For this analysis, the two most influential variables were selected as the raw function points count and the associated complexity adjustment factor. These were divided into three equi-spaced triangular membership functions for small, medium, and large size or low, medium, and high complexity. The same procedure was then carried out for the effort data, namely low, medium, and large effort. An experienced software developer was then asked to provide the initial set of nine rules (for the three by three input matrix). There rules were then hand-adjusted and weighted in consultation with an expert in fuzzy logic modeling, along with small changes to the membership functions, in order to achieve a better fit to the training data set. This process required only a small amount of time, with the developer quickly settling on the final set of rules.

While many other options for tuning the model, such as changing the shapes of the membership functions to be more complex (and therefore, presumably, better reflecting reality), and looking at the performance of various defuzzification schemes could have been used, one of the advantages of fuzzy logic lies in its simplicity and intuitiveness. As such the process was made as simple as possible. Much research is still required to determine how best to match the project manager's perceptions of the project and expert knowledge into a fuzzy logic model.

5.5 Comparison of techniques

Each technique's best model was then used to predict for the remaining 27 observations in the validation set. Again it is mentioned that the validation data set was withheld from having any influence on any of the model's development or selection, and thus provides an unbiased measure of each model's generalisability.

As can be seen in the results in Table 1 and Figure 2 the most accurate model in terms of MMRE is the neural network, followed by the fuzzy logic model. This is to a large extent due to the non-linearities and interactions present in the data, which is barely large enough for such features to be taken into account with regression analysis. However, in terms of *pred* accuracy, the neural network model is fairly comparable to the least squares regression model after outlier removal from the training and testing data based on residual analysis.

Table 1. Comparison of results

Method	MMRE	pred(10)	pred(25)
FPA estimation (mean-based)	0.70	4%	22%
FPA estimation (median-based)	0.89	19%	41%
LS regression	0.86	15%	41%
LS regression (no outliers)	0.88	30%	56%
LMS regression	0.85	7%	41%
Neural network	0.44	26%	63%
Fuzzy logic	0.54	7%	30%

Clearly these performance indicators are not in themselves very encouraging and one would have hoped for much more accurate predictions in order to effectively manage the software development process. The objective of this case study, however, was to compare a selection of analysis methods using the same data set, so as to emphasize the potential of the various analysis options and their capacity to provide effective general models for estimation. In relative terms the superiority of the neural network and fuzzy logic models is fairly apparent, at least in terms of MMRE. The question of which of these performance measures should be seen as most informative as far as real-world usefulness is concerned is still an open question.

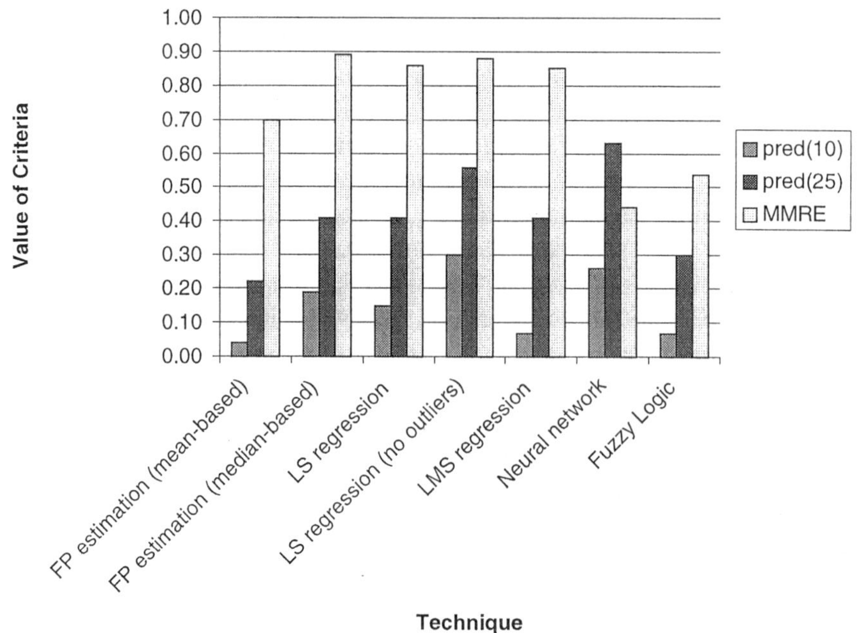

Figure 2. Comparison of results

Again it is stressed that the numerical accuracy of such models is not the only selection criteria that should be used. The ability of fuzzy logic to avoid over-commitment to particular predictions and its interpretability needs to be kept in mind, as does the simplicity of the regression models. We can not however easily ascribe ratings to the models for these characteristics.

6. Other aspects of using fuzzy variables for software metric models under investigation

The current study that has been presented here represents only the initial stage in a longer-term project to assess the suitability for, and develop models using, fuzzy logic in software metric models. A range of data sets have been collected and are currently being analyzed using a variety of modeling techniques including fuzzy logic. It is vital that the performance of each technique be compared over as wide a variety of software metrics data sets as possible in order to determine whether of not the rankings depend on certain types of system, the availability of certain metrics, data set size, and other possibly influential characteristics. It seems likely to be the case that each technique will find a *niche* in project management of software development, with different techniques being preferred depending on the circumstances.

In addition the use of fuzzy logic as a modeling technique from the start of real-world development projects is being used to assess the practical usefulness of the technique, as well as its academic appeal. As has been stated, the use of fuzzy logic as a very early estimation technique is perhaps one of its most appealing uses.

An important requirement for using models with linguistic inputs is that project managers are indeed able to specify such inputs in a reliable and consistent manner. In order to assess the truth of this assumption a number of experienced developers are being asked to describe aspects of systems based on specification documentation. The only known study of the consistency of such rankings is [15] where on a very small data set the authors found some consistency in metrics for source code analysis.

Work is also currently underway to ascertain how best to gather this information from software development and project management experts. Three main areas arise in this problem: the selection of appropriate experts, the techniques used to gather information from such experts, and the approach to performing the knowledge acquisition task [16]. The technique currently favored is providing the experts with some understanding of fuzzy logic, and then walking them through the creation of membership functions and matrices of rules.

Since any technique is unlikely to be used without tool support a fuzzy logic modeling system specifically developed for software metrics data analysis is currently being developed by the authors. This system will provide project recording facilities, data visualization and analysis, as well as fuzzy logic modeling with the emphasis being on the metrics application domain. The gathering of memberships and rules from a project manager without the necessity for a human expert to guide the collection will also be supported. While many good tools are available for fuzzy logic modeling, it is felt that these are not as user-friendly to the metrics community as will be necessary to encourage use of this technique.

Finally, work on automatically extracting the fuzzy rules from the available data and on fine-tuning expert-provided rules using such data is being investigated. Many options for automatically calibrating fuzzy logic systems are available, including fuzzy-neural networks, but these can detract from the intuitiveness and simplicity of the system.

Generally there is a tradeoff between the accuracy of the fuzzy system and the meaningfulness of the membership functions and rules – small changes in either of these may be able to improve accuracy, but if this requires changes to rule weights and membership functions that a human expert would not appreciate then the worth of the changes must be questioned.

7. Conclusions

The idea of using fuzzy logic for defining software metrics as linguistic variables and for the modeling process has been briefly outlined in this chapter along with a small empirical example comparing fuzzy logic to several other model-building techniques. The primary motivations for using this particular modeling technique, fuzzy logic, have been an attempt to overcome some of the difficulties faced by software metricians in terms of avoiding premature and costly commitment, using all available knowledge, having only small data sets to work with, and also the need for transparent models. The issue of early estimation of effort is also an important part of the motivation of this technique.

Compared to other techniques the fuzzy logic model developed for the case study shows good empirical performance, being out-performed in terms of accuracy only by the neural network model which used considerably more input variables. Given the other advantages of fuzzy logic models that have been outlined here this suggests that there is a place in the field of software metrics for the use of fuzzy logic. With further research into the practicalities of using fuzzy logic, the creation of practical guidelines for its use, and the development of support tools customized to the metrics application domain it is hoped that other researchers and practitioners will also start to contribute to this area of new growth in the metrics field.

Reference

[1]   N. Fenton. *Software Metrics, a Rigorous Approach.* Chapman & Hall, London, 1991.

[2]   T. Mukhopadhyay and S. Kekre. Software effort models for early estimation of process control applications. *IEEE Transactions on Software Engineering,* 18(10):915-924, 1992.

[3]   A.L. Lederer, R. Mirani, B.S. Neo, C. Pollard, J. Prasad, and K. Ramamurthy. Information system cost estimating: a management perspective. *MIS Quarterly,* 159-176, June, 1990.

[4]   B. Londeix. Deploying realistic estimation (field situation analysis). *Information and Software Technology,* 37:665-670, 1995.

[5]   S. Kumar, B.A. Krishna, and P.S. Satsangi. Fuzzy systems and neural networks in software engineering project management. *Journal of Applied Intelligence,* 4:31-52, 1994.

[6]   R.W. Selby and A.A. Porter. Learning from examples: generation and evaluation of decision trees for software resource analysis. *IEEE Transactions on Software Engineering,* 14:1743-1757, 1988.

[7]   K. Srinivasan and D. Fisher. Machine learning approaches to estimating software development effort, *IEEE Transactions on Software Engineering,* 21:126-137, 1995.

[8]   T. Mukhopadhyay, S.S. Vicinanza, and M.J. Prietula. Examining the feasibility of a case-based reasoning model for software effort estimation. *MIS Quarterly,* 16:155-171, 1992.

[9]   A.R. Gray, and S.G. MacDonell. A comparison of model building techniques to develop predictive equations for software metrics. *Information and Software Technology,* to appear, 1997.

[10] J.-M. Desharnais. *Analyse statistique de la productivitie des projects de development en informatique apartir de la technique des points des fontion.* Master's Thesis, Universite du Montreal, 1989.

[11] S.G. MacDonell and A.R. Gray. Alternatives to regression models for estimating software projects. *In Proceedings of the IFPUG Fall Conference,* Dallas TX, IFPUG 279.1-279.15, 1996.

[12] A.J. Albrecht. Measuring application development productivity. In *Proceedings of the IBM Applications Development Joint SHARE/GUIDE Symposium,* Monterey, CA, 83-92, 1979.

[13] J.E. Matson, B.E. Barrett, and J.M. Mellichamp. Software development cost estimation using function points. *IEEE Transactions on Software Engineering,* 20(4):275-287, 1994.

[14] J.J. Dolado. A study of the relationships among Albrecht and Mark II function points, lines of code 4GL and effort. *Journal of Systems and Software*, 37:161-173, 1997.

[15] R.I. Kilgour, A.R. Gray, P.J. Sallis, and S.G. MacDonell. A fuzzy logic approach to computer software source code authorship analysis. Submitted to The Fourth International Conference on Neural Information Processing -- The Annual Conference of the Asian Pacific Neural Network Assembly (ICONIP'97).

[16] Y.I. Liou. Knowledge acquisition: issues, techniques and methodology. *DATABASE*, 59-64, Winter 1992.

TIME-CONSTRAINED SOFTWARE COST CONTROL SYSTEM: CONCEPTS AND ROUGHLY FUZZY PETRI NET MODEL

James F. Peters III
Department of Electrical and Computer Engineering, University of Manitoba, Winnipeg, Manitoba R3T 2N2 Canada, jfpeters@ee.umanitoba.ca

Sheela Ramanna
Department of Business Computing, University of Winnipeg, Winnipeg, Manitoba R3T 2E9 Canada and Department of Electrical and Computer Engineering, University of Manitoba, Winnipeg, Manitoba R3T 2N2 Canada, ramanna@ee.umanitoba.ca

This paper introduces a rough set approach to constructing rules for a time-constrained feedback control system for software cost estimation. Decision rules capture dependencies between function points, project duration requirement, aggregation of granulations of multi-criteria evaluations of software development technologies with the Choquet integral, and magnitude of relative error in cost estimation. These rules spring from an approximate reasoning approach to making decisions about adjustments in the application of software development technologies for a particular software product. The method of rule derivation comes from rough sets. A fuzzy measure model of the importance of various coalitions of software technologies is introduced. The approximate character of the reasoning stems from the inherent imprecision of measurements of processing complexity. The approach is illustrated relative to software cost estimates for a collection of twenty-five software projects. The contribution of this paper is a formal description of a time-constrained software cost feedback control system based on an approximate reasoning approach to assessing software cost.

1 Introduction

At each stage in the life cycle of a software system, evaluation hinges on three basic measurements: cost, reliability and quality [1]. These measurements provide a basis for deciding whether to deploy or continue development of a software system. For a number of reasons, these measurements are approximate. The approximate character of software cost and quality measurements has been investigated in [2]-[5]. A prevalent problem in software system cost estimation models is the assessment of the impact of interacting system components on the total work (a Man Month (MM) measurement) required to complete a project. Usually, one MM equals 152 hours. In the case of Albrecht's Function Points (FPs), for example, total MM estimates are based on assessing the impact of Technical Complexity Factors (TCFs) on the functionality of software. TCFs are assumed to be independent of each other as well as independent of system size [6]. FP estimates of project MMs have been shown to have significant relative error, and to be sensitive to system size, particularly whenever the functionality of smaller projects is in the 50 to 100 MM range [2]. In addition, the TCFs used in FP analysis of a project fail to take into account the impact of coalitions of technologies such as integrated development environments, code generation, web browsers, applet viewers and concurrent engineering on MM project requirements. The key point to notice in FP analysis is that it depends on subjective multicriteria evaluation, and that it fails to take into the relation between factors underlying estimates of the functionality of a program as well as the importance of various coalitions of software development technologies on the software process. It has been shown that the fuzzy integral can serve as an aggregation operator in multicriteria decision making [7]-[9]. In particular, the Choquet integral has been used extensively in multicriteria evaluations [7]-[8], especially in software cost estimation in [2]-[4].

An approximate reasoning system for making software development decisions relative to the impact of applications of recent software development technologies and software cost estimates needs to be investigated. Such a system is introduced in this paper. For simplicity, this approximate reasoning system has been limited to measurements of processing complexity (the basis for cost estimates in Albrecht [6]). In this paper, Albrecht's approach to assessing processing complexity has been refined. Rather than attempt to estimate software development cost, the approach taken in this paper is based on the design of a software process which has been "sensitized" relative to a planned software cost. This is accomplished in a number of ways. To begin, a feedback system model of the of the software cost estimation process is given. A simplified view of this feedback system model is given in Fig. 1.

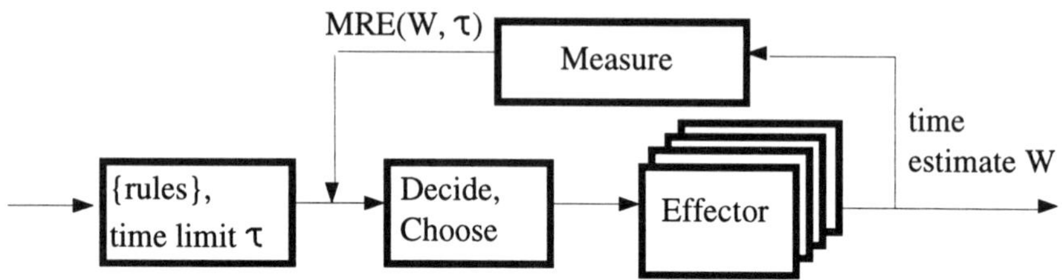

Fig. 1 *Feedback System Model of Software Estimation Process*

The approach to modeling the software cost estimation process introduced in this paper has been derived from Norbert Wiener's basic method of *control by information feedback* [10]. The estimation process is initialized with a reference duration, which is an upper bound on the time allowed to develop a product of a software process. The decider process in the feedback system model in Fig. 1 is governed by rules derived from decision tables which are part of a software process plan. The Choquet integral is used in a multicriteria evaluation of the impact of combinations of software development technologies on technical complexity as in [2]. Choquet integral values are granulated. The granulated Choquet integral values provide input to a roughly fuzzy Petri net relative to cut-off r and strength-of-connection w, which can be calibrated. A roughly fuzzy Petri net assimilates two technologies, fuzzy sets and rough sets, to facilitate description and analysis of decision systems and was introduced in [55]. This form of Petri net provides a high-level description of the construction of a decision table needed in the derivation of rules for the decider process. An approach to calibration of this form of Petri net is given in [11], which is based on a method described in [12]. An effector process in Fig. 1 represents a procedure designed to compute a result needed to continue the decision-making process. The output of the effector processes in Fig. 1 is W, which is an estimate of the man-months required to develop a planned software product. The measure process in Fig. 1 provides feedback to the decider. Feedback consists in measurement of the magnitude of relative error (MRE) relative to a required software development time limit τ and W. An unacceptable MRE value results in adjustments in the magnitude of usage of software development technologies used in arriving at an estimated man-month estimate for a project. The contribution of this paper is the introduction of a feedback system for estimating and controlling software cost.

The paper is organized as follows. In Section 2, a brief description of the methodology underlying the feedback system model for software cost estimation is given. A high-level Petri net model of the system is presented in Section 3. An application of the software cost estimation system is given in Section 4.

2 Basic Approach to Controlling Software Cost

The basic algorithm underlying the feedback system model for software cost estimation is given in Fig. 2. We begin by explaining the inputs to the feedback system. The functionality of a software system is assessed relative to what are known as Function Counts (FC) in [6]. Briefly, FC is a weighted sum of the form given in (1).

$$FC = \sum_{i=1}^{n} [(itemCount_i)(complexityLevel_i)] \qquad (1)$$

Each $itemCount_i$ equals the number of occurrences of an item in the behavioral (functional) description of software. Item counts can be obtained from software descriptions (e.g., statecharts or Petri nets) during the early phases of a software process, which makes it possible to use Albrecht's function points method to derive preliminary software cost estimates. A complexity level is assigned to each itemCount$_i$. The influence of FC is moderated by a Technical Complexity Factor (TCF) in arriving at W (a MM estimate) as shown in (2).

$$W = 54(FC)(TCF) - 13{,}390 \tag{2}$$

In Albrecht, TCF $\in$ [0.65, 1.35], which represents an estimate of the cumulative effect of sources of processing complexity on a software development effort. The formula in (2) comes from Albrecht [6]. This is one among many approaches to estimating W due to Halstead [58]. Notice that the TCF estimate in Albrecht does not take into account the aggregative effect of newer software development technologies, which tend to mitigate "processing complexity" and which significantly influence software design, accelerate the coding phase thanks to code generation, and contribute to speedup due to parallel processing. Notice in Fig. 2 that TCF is replaced by an adjusted TCF (adjTCF), which takes into account the influence of recent software development technologies.

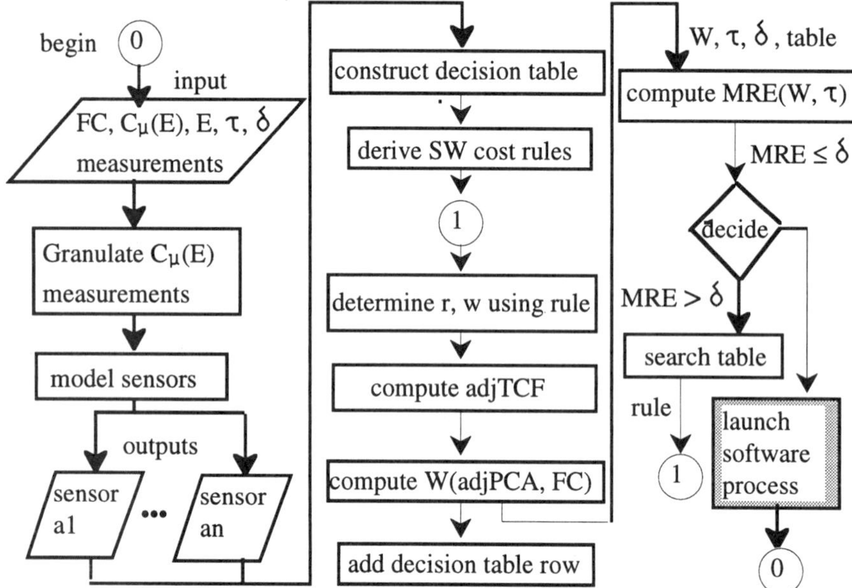

Fig. 2 *Algorithm for Software Cost Estimation Based on Feedback*

A multicriteria decision-making approach to assessing the impact of effort-reducing technologies is carried out using the Choquet integral, which we explain briefly in the next section.

2.1 Fuzzy Measures and the Choquet Integral

In an effort to provide an uncertainty measure of processing complexity in the context of more recent developments in software engineering, a subjective multicriteria evaluation methodology is introduced using the concept of fuzzy measure and the Choquet integral. This effort is in keeping with the original application of the fuzzy integral by Sugeno [13], and the use of the fuzzy integral as an aggregation tool in multicriteria decision-making [7]-[9]. This approach offers a means of assessing the combined influence of more recent software development methodologies on software cost. It is assumed that a universe of discourse X specifies a finite space $\{x_1, ..., x_n\}$ and $\aleph$ is the set of all subsets of X, which is called a class. A non-empty class F is called a σ-ring if, and only if (i) $\forall$ A, B $\in$ F, A - B $\in$ F, where $A - B = A \cap \overline{B}$ and (ii) $\forall A_i \in$ F, i = 1, 2, ..., $\cap_{i=1}^{\infty} A_i \in F$, i = 1, 2, ... A σ-algebra is a σ-ring that contains X. A *fuzzy measure* μ is a mapping $\mu: X \rightarrow [0,1]$, where X is a universe of discourse in a measure space (X, $\aleph$) with $\aleph$ forming a σ-algebra over X such that (i) $\mu(\emptyset) = 0$, $\mu(X) = 1$, and (ii) A $\subseteq$ B $\Rightarrow$ $\mu(A) \leq \mu(B)$ for each A, B $\subseteq \aleph$. The triple (X, $\aleph$, μ) constitutes a fuzzy measure space. Fuzzy integrals are aggregation operators on the hypercube $[0,1]^n$. In developing a multicriteria evaluation of processing complexity, fuzzy integration is defined in terms of [0,1]-valued functions.

Definition (Choquet integral [14])
Let (X, $\aleph$, μ) be a fuzzy measure space, f: X $\rightarrow$ [0,1], and let the indices of X be permuted so that $0 <= f(x_{(1)}) \leq ... \leq f(x_{(n)}) \leq 1$, and $A_{(i)} = \{x_{(i)}, ..., x_{(n)}\}$, $f(x_{(0)}) = 0$. The Choquet integral C_μ of f with respect to the fuzzy measure μ is defined by (3).

$$C_\mu(f(x_1),...,f(x_n)) = \sum_{i=1}^{n} (f(x_{(i)} - f(x_{(i-1)})\mu(A_{(i)}) \tag{3}$$

Let $C_\mu()$ be a Choquet integral where μ is a fuzzy measure defined on subsets of criteria $X = \{x_1, ..., x_n\}$. The fuzzy measure μ specifies weights on the criteria, which can be either a weight $\mu(\{x_i\})$ on an individual criterion x_i or a weight $\mu(\{x_i, x_{i+1}, ...\})$ on any group of criteria $\{x_i, x_{i+1}, ...\}$. This is a key feature of a Choquet integral (and of fuzzy integrals in general), namely, the fuzzy measure makes it possible to express effects of the interaction of criteria within a universe of discourse X. In the context of the software cost estimation method given in Fig. 2, let X be a collection of software development technologies. In this context, a criterion is viewed as some mode of software development in the sense of a method or manner in which software is developed. Let e map x $\in$ X to [0, 1] in estimating the per cent of reduction in effort resulting from the application of a new technology during software development. Let $C_\mu(e(x_1),...,e(x_n))$ be a Choquet integral value computed relative to the evaluation of various possible combinations of software development technologies. Values of $C_\mu()$ are granulated as a step toward arriving at an estimate of the adjusted TCF.

2.2 Granulating Choquet Integral Values

There is some justification for evaluating Choquet integral in the context of information granules, a clustering of measurements with vaguely defined boundaries. An information granule consists of a "clump" of similar values [15]-[16]. In the software cost estimation model investigated in this paper, Choquet integral values approximate the effect of software development technologies. By granulating Choquet integral values, we gain a means of interpreting integral values relative to the degree-of-membership of each value in selected granules. Consider, for example, the granules shown in Fig. 3.

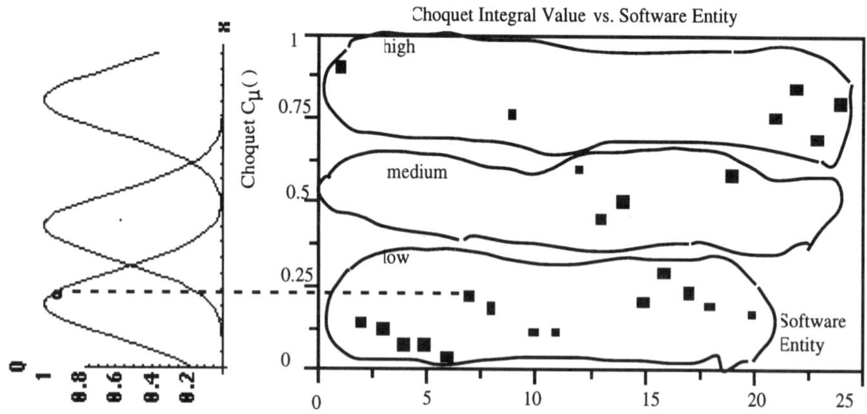

Fig. 3 *Sample Granulation of Choquet Integral Values*

In Fig. 3, it is assumed that Choquet integral values for evolving software modules are approximately normally distributed. For example, the degree-of-membership of a Choquet integral value in a granule labeled low is computed relative to a particular Gaussian distribution of the form given in (4)

$$low[x] = exp\left[\frac{-(C_\mu(e(x_1),...,e(x_n)) - m_{low})^2}{s_{low}^2}\right] \qquad (4)$$

The mean m_{low} and variance s_{low}^2 in (4) determine the modal point and spread in the graph of degrees of membership of Choquet integral values.   The modal point m_{low} and spread s_{low} of the Gaussian distribution in (4) will vary depending on the distribution of the data in a granule.   For example, let $m_{low} = 20$, $m_{med} = 45$, $m_{high} = 85$ be the modal points for three granules (each with s = 15) named low, med, and high, respectively.   The graphs of low, medium, and high are shown in Fig. 4.

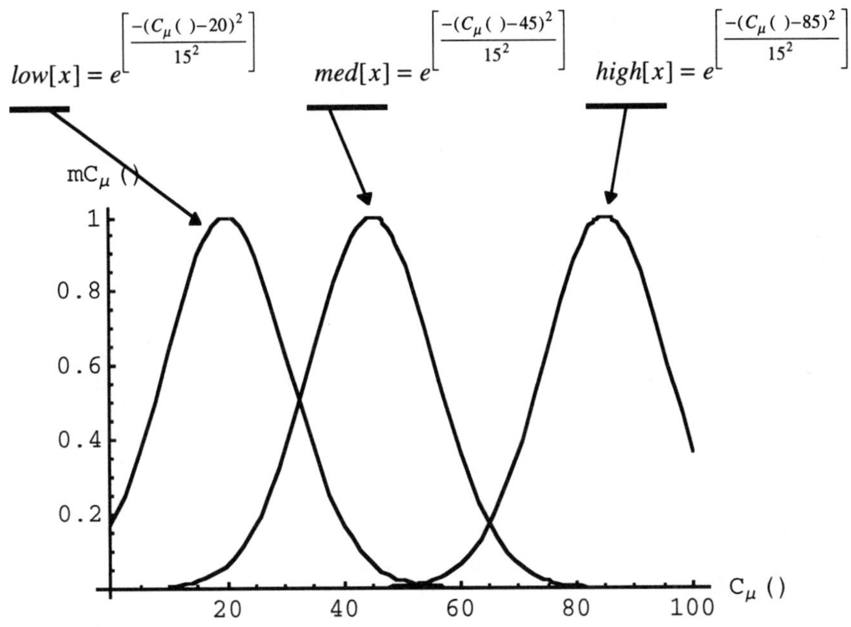

Fig. 4 *Sample Choquet Integral Measurement Distributions*

Let $mC_\mu()$ be the degree-of-membership of $C_\mu()$ in the granule named med.   We make the simplifying assumption

$$TCF = 1 - m\, C_\mu()$$

This approach to computing TCF stems from the view that a value of 1 for TCF represents maximum, "complete" technical complexity. Values less than 1 represent the beneficial influence of various combinations of software development technologies, which have the effect of decreasing technical complexity.   In computing an adjusted TCF, we introduce a fuzzy computational approach to deriving values of adjTCF using

$$adjTCF = ((TCF \rightarrow r) \; s \; w)$$

where TCF $\rightarrow$ r is a fuzzy implication, which computes a value in [0, 1] by various means relative to a cut-off or reference point r.   The value of TCF $\rightarrow$ r is aggregated relative to a strength-of-connection w using an s-norm operation.   The advantage to this approach is that adjTCF can be calibrated relative to r, w, and some software project duration target value.   The intuition behind this approach to computing adjTCF is that each calibration represents either increased or decreased application of software technologies as a means of adjusting estimated development time relative project deadlines.

2.3 Fuzzy Sets: Basic Concepts

Fuzzy sets are distinguished from the classical notion of a set (also called a crisp set) by the fact that the boundary of a fuzzy set is not precise [17].   The characteristic function for a set X returns a value indicating the degree of membership of an element x in X.   For a crisp set, the characteristic function returns a value in $\{0, 1\}$. A fuzzy set is non-crisp, and was introduced by Zadeh [18].   By contrast with a crisp set, the characteristic function for a fuzzy set returns a value in [0, 1].   Let U, X, $\tilde{A}$, x be a universe of objects, subset of U, fuzzy set in U, and an individual object x in X, respectively.   For a set X, $\mu_{\tilde{A}}: X \rightarrow [0, 1]$ is a function which determines the degree of membership of an object x in X.   A fuzzy set $\tilde{A}$ is then defined to be a set of ordered pairs as in (5).

$$\tilde{A} = \{ (x, \mu_{\tilde{A}}(x)) \mid x \in X \} \tag{5}$$

The set X is called the reference set.   The counterpart of intersection and union (crisp sets) are the t-norm and s-norm operators in fuzzy set theory.   For the intersection of fuzzy sets, the min operator was suggested by Zadeh [18], and belongs to a class of intersection operators (min, product, bold intersection) known as triangular or t-norms.   A t-norm is a mapping $t : [0,1]^2 \rightarrow [0, 1]$.   The algebraic sum (also called probabilistic sum) is commonly used for the union of fuzzy sets [18].   The probabilistic sum belongs to a class of union operators called triangular co-norms (or s-norms).   An s-norm is a mapping $s : [0,1]^2 \rightarrow [0, 1]$.   For example, let x, y belong to a fuzzy set $\tilde{A}$, and compute the s-norm relative to x and y as in (6)

$$\mu_{\tilde{A}}(x) \; s \; \mu_{\tilde{A}}(y) = \mu_{\tilde{A}}(x) + \mu_{\tilde{A}}(y) - \mu_{\tilde{A}}(x)\mu_{\tilde{A}}(y) \tag{6}$$

In fuzzy set theory, the symbol "$\rightarrow$" denotes a multivalued implication operation. Many forms of implication are possible [19]-[21]. For simplicity, the Lukasiewicz and Gaines forms of implication are compared in (7) and (8).

$$(r \rightarrow x)_{Lukasiewicz} = \begin{cases} 1 - r + x, & \text{if } r > x \\ 1, & \text{if } r \le x \end{cases} \tag{7}$$

$$(r \rightarrow x)_{Gaines} = \begin{cases} \dfrac{x}{r}, & \text{if } x < r \\ \min\left(1, \dfrac{x}{r}\right), & \text{otherwise} \end{cases} \tag{8}$$

In the case of Gaines, $r_i \rightarrow x_i = x/r$ for values of $x < r$ (see Fig. 5). Otherwise, $r_i \rightarrow x_i = \min(1, \frac{x_i}{r_i})$, $r \le x$, and the $\rightarrow$ is induced by the product operation. Hence, values of $r_i \rightarrow x_i$ rise smoothly along the r-axis to the $45°$ line. Notice, for example, that for $r = 0.5$ and $x = 0$, we have $r_i \rightarrow x_i = 0$. By contrast, the Lukasiewicz form of implication $r_i \rightarrow x_i = 1 - r_i + x_i$ for $r_i > x_i$ "ramps up" more rapidly than the Gaines form of implication (see Fig. 6). Otherwise for Lukasiewicz, $r_i \rightarrow x_i = 1$, $r \le x$, the $\rightarrow$ has a constant value of 1. As a result, for $r = 0.5$ and $x = 0$, we have $r_i \rightarrow x_i = 0.5$.

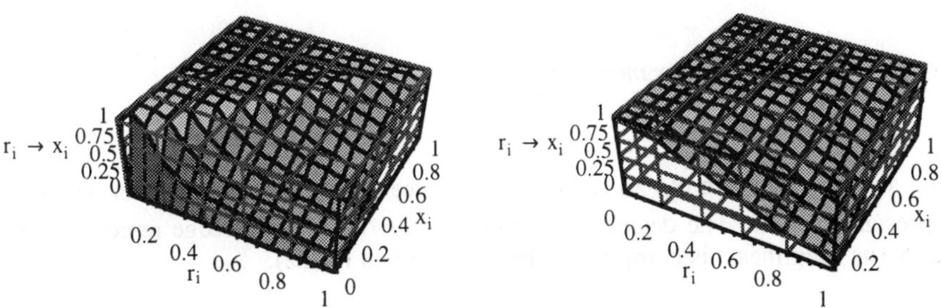

Fig. 5. $r_i \rightarrow x_i$ *[Gaines]*   **Fig. 6** $r_i \rightarrow x_i$ *[Lukasiewicz]*

Returning to the algorithm in Fig. 2, it should be mentioned that preliminary values of r and w reflect decisions made relative to FC, granulated Choquet integral values, adjTCF, project deadline τ, estimated project duration W, and magnitude of relative error (MRE).   These decisions are organized in decision tables constructed and analyzed with rough set theory.   From such decision tables, rules can be derived which guide the selection of appropriate values of r and w.

2.4 Rough Sets: Basic Concepts

Rough set theory offers a systematic approach to the conceptualization of decision systems and the derivation of rules useful in approximate reasoning [22]-[32].   To begin, let S = (U, A) be an information system with set U (universe of objects) and set A (attributes).   Then let R be a relation defined on U.   For x, y $\in$ U, let xRy indicate that x has relation R to y.   R is a tolerance relation, if xRx (reflexivity) for x $\in$ U and for all x, y $\in$ U, if xRy, then yRx (symmetry).   In the case where transitivity also holds, R is an equivalence relation over U.   The notation U/R (known as the quotient set) denotes the family of equivalence classes of R.   For x $\in$ U, the notation $[x]_R$ identifies an equivalence class in U/R.   The equivalence class $[x]_R$ is called an elementary category or concept of R [22].   A subset X in U is called a reference set, which can be approximated with two other sets in (9) and (10).

$$\underline{R}X = \{x \in U \mid [x]_R \subseteq X\}, \; lower \; approximation \tag{9}$$

$$\overline{R}X = \{x \in U \mid [x]_R \cap X \neq \varnothing\}, \; upper \; approximation \tag{10}$$

The pair $(\underline{R}X, \overline{R}X)$ is a rough set with reference set X.   The vagueness of a set stems from its borderline region.   A measure of the accuracy of a set X $\subseteq$ U is computed using $\alpha_R(X)$ (see (11)).

$$\alpha_R(X) = \frac{|\underline{R}X|}{|\overline{R}X|}, \; accuracy \; measure \tag{11}$$

The accuracy measure $\alpha_R(X)$ captures the degree of completeness of our knowledge represented by X.   The degree of incompleteness of our knowledge represented by a set X (its roughness) is computed using $\rho_R(x)$ given in (12).

$$\rho_R(X) = 1 - \alpha_R(X), \; R - roughness \; of \; X \tag{12}$$

Similarity among members of an equivalence class provides the basis for what is known as the indiscernability relation.   Let B be a subset of the set of attributes A, and let Ind(B) be the set of all elements of X that match each other relative to B (see (13)).

$$Ind(B) = \{(x,y) \mid \forall a \in B, a(x) = a(y)\} \tag{13}$$

The Ind(B) relation simplifies the investigation of a particular information system, where the representatives of U/Ind(B) are studied. Knowledge reduction is possible using the method shown in [22],[25],[27]-[32]. A minimal subset $B \subseteq A$ such that Ind(B) = Ind(A) is called a reduct of A. Any set of attributes has one or more reducts [33]. Let $a \in P$ in A. The attribute a is indispensable in P if Ind(P) $\neq$ Ind(P - {a}). The set of all indispensable attributes in P is called the core of P (denoted CORE(P)), which can be considered the most important part of knowledge [22]. For an information system S, the set of all reducts in S is denoted RED(S) [31].

In deriving decision system rules, the discernability matrix and discernabiliy function are essential [27]. Given an information system S = (U, A), the nxn matrix (c_{ij}) is called the discernability matrix of S (denoted M(S)) defined in (14).

$$c_{ij} = \{a \in A: a(x_i) \neq a(x_j)\}, \text{ for } i, j = 1, ..., n. \tag{14}$$

A discernability function fM(S) for information S is a boolean function of m boolean variables $a_1^*, ..., a_m^*$ corresponding to attributes $a_1, ..., a_m$ respectively, and defined in (15).

$$f_{M(S)}(a_1^*, ..., a_m^*) =_{df} \wedge\{\vee c_{ij}^* \mid 1 \le j < i \le n, c_{ij} \neq \varnothing\}, c_{ij}^* = \{a^* \mid a \in c_{ij}\} \tag{15}$$

Precise conditions for decision rules can be extracted from a discernability matrix as in [25]. For the information system S = (U, A), let $B \subseteq A$ and let $\mathcal{P}(V_a)$ denote the power set of V_a, where V_a is the value set of a. For every $d \in A - B$, a decision function $d_d^B : U \to \mathcal{P}(V_a)$ is defined in (16).

$$d_d^B(u) = \left\{ v \in V_d \mid \exists u' \in U, (u', u) \in Ind_B . d(u') = v \right\} \tag{16}$$

In other words, $d_d^B(u)$ is the set of all elements of the decision column of S such that the corresponding object is a member of the same equivalence class as argument u. The next step is to determine a decision rule with a minimal number of descriptors on the left-hand side. Pairs (a, v), where $a \in A$, $v \in V$ are called *descriptors*. A decision rule over the set of attributes A and values V is an expression of the form given in (17).

350

$$a_{i_1}(u_i) = v_{i_1} \wedge ... \wedge a_{i_j}(u_i) = v_{i_j} \wedge ... \wedge a_{i_r}(u_i) = v_{i_r} \underset{S}{\Rightarrow} d(u_i) = v \qquad (17)$$

where $u_i \in U$, $v_{i_j} \in V_{a_{i_j}}$, $v \in V_d$, $j = 1,...,r$ and $r \leq |A|$. Let $\| \tau \|_S$ denote the meaning of term τ. A rule is true in system S if (18) holds.

$$\| (a_{i_1} = v_{i_1}) \wedge ... \wedge (a_{i_r} = v_{i_r}) \| \subseteq \| (a_p = v_p) \| \qquad (18)$$

The fact that a rule is true is indicated by writing it in the form given in (19).

$$(a_{i_1} = v_{i_1}) \wedge ... \wedge (a_{i_r} = v_{i_r}) \underset{S}{\Rightarrow} (a_p = v_p) \qquad (19)$$

Let $R \in RED(S)$ be a reduct in the set of all reducts in an information system S. For an information system S, the set of decision rules constructed with respect to a reduct R is denoted OPT(S, R) [29]-[30]. Then the set of all decision rules derivable from reducts in RED(S) is the set in (20).

$$OPT(S) = \bigcup \{ OPT(S, R) \mid R \in RED(S) \} \qquad (20)$$

3 Petri Net Model of Cost Estimation Process

Considerable work has already been carried out in modeling decision system rules with Petri nets [25], [31]-[32], [34]. This aim of the earlier as well as the current research has been to simplify the analysis of large information systems, and the transformation of such systems as well as derived rules into corresponding concurrent models. The motivation for introducing rough Petri nets stems from an effort to capture the understandings and operations from rough set theory, which have been used to construct both general-purpose as well as highly-specialized decision systems. An overview of the types of Petri nets and related set theories leading to a Petri net of model of the software cost estimation process, is given in Fig. 7.

In what follows, it is assumed that the reader is familiar with classical Petri nets [35],[36] as well as the basic structure of coloured Petri nets found in [37]-[38]. Rough Petri nets are derived from coloured and hierarchical Petri nets as well as from rough set theory. The complete process of deriving rules for a decision system can be modeled with a rough Petri net at a sufficiently high level to facilitate an understanding of a particular rule-derivation process. In addition, the strengths of connections (weightings of attribute computations) in a rough Petri net can be calibrated. Fuzzy Petri nets are derived from classical Petri nets and fuzzy set theory

[40]. Fuzzy Petri nets can also be defined in the context of coloured Petri nets to facilitate implementation as in [12]. Roughly fuzzy Petri nets are derived from rough Petri nets and fuzzy Petri nets. This form of Petri net makes it possible to add learning capability to a decision-making rule-derivation process, which combines the use of fuzzy sets and rough sets in rule formulation.

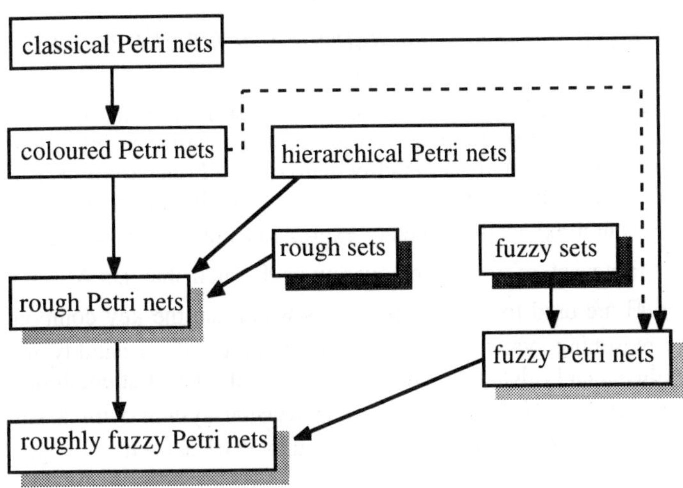

Fig. 7 *Lineage of Petri Nets*

3.1   Rough Petri Nets

A rough Petri net (rPn) is a structure $(\Sigma, P, T, A, N, C, E, I, W, \mathbb{R}, \rho)$ where Σ (data types), P (places), T (transitions), A (arcs), N (maps A to (PxT) $\cup$ (TxP)), C (maps P to Σ), E (maps A to expression E(a) of type C(p(a))), I (maps P to closed expressions p(a) of type C(p)) are as in a coloured Petri net (CPN). Strengths-of-connections (chosen from a finite set of weights W) are assigned to arcs with ρ: A $\rightarrow$ W. A *strength of connection* $w_i \in$ W specifies the relative importance of input to a sensor (a form of attribute in rough sets), and guarantees a certain magnitude of input to a transition. Weights are restricted to values in the interval [0, 1]. Let X, S, $\mathcal{E}$ be a set of inputs, information system S, and reduct $\mathcal{E}$ belonging to set of all reducts RED(S) of S, respectively. Let S = (U, A) be an information system and let R be an equivalence relation which forms the quotient set X/R, where R $\subseteq$ A and X $\subseteq$ U. Also, recall that the notation X/R (known as the quotient set) denotes the family of equivalence classes of R. The set $POS_R(X) = \underline{R}X$ is the set of all elements of U which can classified as elements of U - X.   Similarly, the set $NEG_R(X) = U - \overline{R}X$ is the set of those elements of U which can be classified as elements of X [22].   Further, let the set $\mathbb{R}$ consist of

$$\sigma_{X/R}, \; \rho_{POS_R(X)}, \; \rho_{NEG_R(X)}, \; \rho_{\inf_A(X)},$$
$$\rho_{dec_A(X)}, \; \rho_{M(S)}, \; \rho_{RED(S)}, \; \rho_{fM(RED(S))}, \; \rho_{OPT(S)}, \; \rho_{OPT(R,S)}$$

which identify distinguished procedures used to construct the quotient set X/R, set $POS_R(X)$ and set $NEG_R(X)$, as well as procedures to construct an information system table, decision system table, discernability matrix, set all rules for a decision system, and set of all rules relative to a reduct R, respectively.   The prescription of the elements of $\mathbb{R}$ is non-exhaustive. The arc expression function E has been specialized relative to a finite set of rough set operations $\mathbb{R}$ such that E: A $\rightarrow$ $\mathbb{R}$.   The operations in $\mathbb{R}$ are used to describe processes which are the key components of an approximate reasoning system, namely, decision tables, discernability matrices and functions, reducts, and rules.   Assume that each input x has a strength-of-connection w.   Further, let S = ({x}, a $\cup$ {d}) be a decision system with a single input, attribute a, and decision d. An example of a rough Petri net with a single transition is given in Fig. 8.

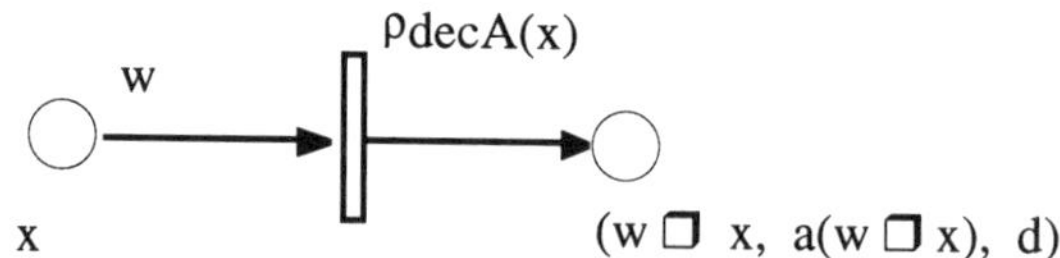

Fig. 8 *Single-Transition Rough Petri Net*

The output of the net in Fig. 18 is a tuple (w ⊡ x, a(w ⊡ x), d) representing a decision system table with a single row.   The computation w ⊡ a(x) aggregates w and x with the anonymous operation ⊡: $[0,1]^2 \rightarrow [0,1]$.   In the absence of a specific strength-of-connection, the default value of w is 0 and w ⊡ x equals x. This is the case in Fig. 9.   To construct a multi-transition rough Petri net, let a_1, $a_2,...,a_i,...a_n$, represent a collection of sensors A in a decision system S = (U, A $\cup$ {dec}).   Also, let dM, df, ε, {rule} represent discernability matrix, discernability function, reduct ε in RED(S) for a decision system S, and set of rules derived from ε.   The rough Petri net in Fig. 9 describes the process of constructing a set of rules derived from S.

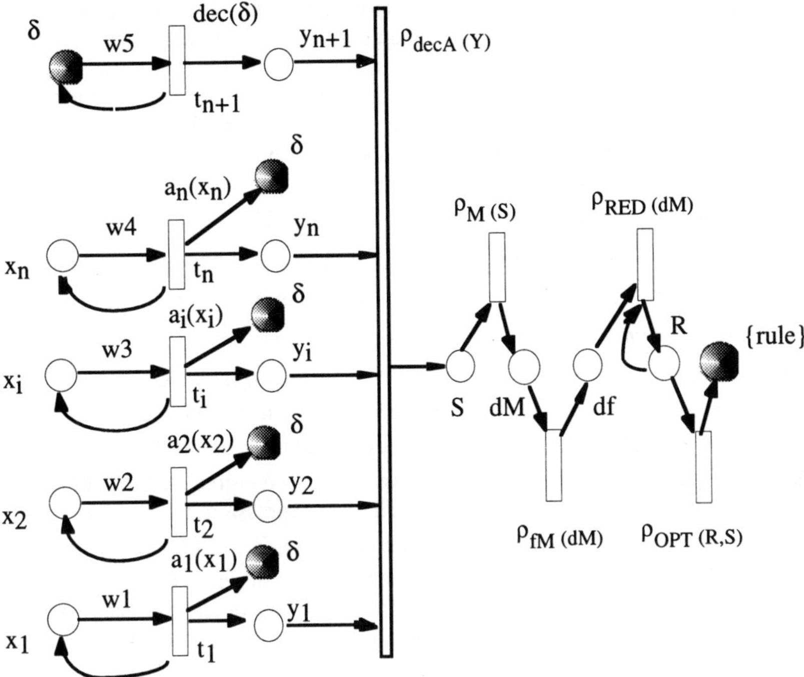

Fig. 9 *Sample Decision System Model*

To simplify the rough Petri net model in Fig. 9, aliasing of input place δ of transition t_{n+1} has been used.   Then the output place labeled δ of transitions t_1, t_2, ...,t_i, ..., t_n provides input to transition t_{n+1}. By allowing transitions in a rough Petri net to represent subnets, it is possible to model complex information systems concisely.   This is in fact what has been done in Fig. 9, where each of the transitions represents a subnet modeling a process needed to carry out necessary computations.   For example, the transition labeled $\rho_M(S)$ decomposes into a subnet designed to model the process which constructs a discernability matrix.

3.2 Fuzzy Petri Nets

Research concerning fuzzy Petri nets and their application is quite extensive [41]-[54]. Fuzzy Petri nets offer a concise means of modeling the interpretation of data points which have been granulated.   In the case where the objects of a universe are granulated, sensors in a decision system aggregate weighted degree-of-membership computations.   Further, a fuzzy Petri net makes it possible to model a form of neural processing where modulators and strengths-of-connections are calibrated [45]-[47].   Such calibrations make it possible to express the intentions of system designers in assessing software quality, and to construct a variety of highly-specialized software quality measurement frameworks.

A Fuzzy Petri Net (FPN) is a structure $(\Sigma,\ P,\ T,\ A,\ N,\ C,\ E,\ I,\ M,\ W,\ Z,\ \digamma,\ \rho)$ where $\Sigma,\ P,\ T,\ A,\ N,\ C,\ E,\ I$ are as in a CPN [38].   Annotations of arcs with strengths of connections chosen from a finite set of weights W are determined by ρ: $A \rightarrow W$, and *modulators* (also called reference points) chosen from the finite set M are determined by $\digamma\colon A \rightarrow M$.   A *strength of connection* $w_i \in W$ specifies the relative importance of input, and guarantees a certain magnitude of input to a transition.   A *modulator* $r_i \in M$ prescribes a certain magnitude of the level of marking of a place which must be maintained.   Weights and modulators are restricted to values in the interval [0, 1].   The arc expression function E has been specialized relative to a finite set Z such that $E\colon A \rightarrow Z$.   The expressions in Z make it possible to compute degrees of membership of values in a universe of discourse in fuzzy sets, to perform aggregations, and any other necessary operations for the functioning of a particular system.   Minimally, Z has four operations consisting of what are known as a dominance AND {OR} as well as conjunctive {disjunctive} ways of aggregating weighted inputs to a transition (see (21)).

$$Z = \{\ \mathop{T}_{i=1}^{n}((r_i \rightarrow x_i)\ s\ w_i) \qquad \text{--dominance AND operation,}$$

$$\mathop{S}_{i=1}^{n}((r_i \rightarrow x_i)\ t\ w_i), \qquad \text{--dominance OR operation,}$$

$$\mathop{S}_{i=1}^{n}(x_i\ t\ w_i) \qquad \text{--OR operation,}$$

$$\mathop{T}_{i=1}^{n}(x_i\ s\ w_i) \qquad \text{--AND operation}\} \qquad (21)$$

The operations in Z employ triangular norms s, t, as well as the implication operator $\rightarrow$ where r_i specifies a threshhold level which modulates the strength of firing coming from the ith input place.   Depending on the marking of the input places, a transition can fire. In contrast to two-valued Petri nets, the generalized version studied includes a gradual firing (strength of firing) of transitions together with level of marking of places.   First, let us discuss a generic model of a transition represented in Fig. 10. An elementary FPN has a single multivalued (fuzzy) transition z_i with inputs x_i (input signal), r_i (reference point), w_i (weight), and single output place out_k.

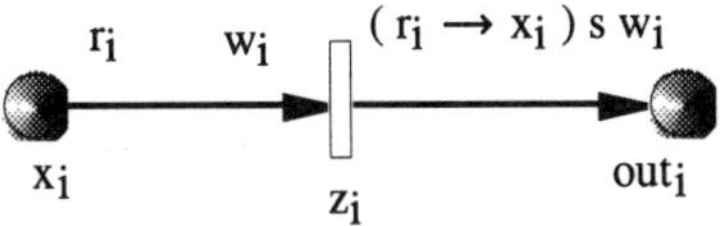

Fig. 10. *Elementary Fuzzy Petri Net*

Each input x_i is a fuzzy number (i.e., result of applying a membership function to an element of a universe of discourse which consists of real numbers). The results out_1, ..., out_n of elementary FPNs are aggregated. The level of firing of transition in a fuzzy Petri net is determined by (22).

$$Z = \mathop{T}_{i=1}^{n} [(r_i \rightarrow x_i) \text{ s } w_i]$$

$$(22)$$

For the computation (19) associated with transition Z, the limit "n" denotes the number of input places; x_i, a level of marking at the i-th place; r_i, a level of modulation of the input; and w_i, an associated degree of contribution of the x_i to the overall firing of the transition. Here "s" and "T" (or t) denote s- and t-norms. Similarly, "$\rightarrow$" denotes a multivalued implication operation. Many forms of implication are possible. For simplicity, the Gaines form of implication has been used in aggregating granulated software quality measurements.

3.3 Roughly Fuzzy Petri Nets

Roughly fuzzy Petri nets were introduced in [55]. In this section, roughly fuzzy Petri nets are presented as a straightforward extension of rough Petri nets. This form of Petri net provides a methodology for concise description of the construction, analysis and calibration of approximate reasoning systems relative to software cost estimation (see Fig. 11). The introduction of roughly fuzzy Petri Nets (rfPNs) is motivated by the need to develop mathematical models of decision-making systems relative to aggregations of granulated inputs such that the models are capable of learning, and are designed to react to dynamic changes in the reduct set for different samples of decision tables. A roughly fuzzy Petri net (rfPn) is a structure given in (23)

$$(\Sigma, P, T, A, N, C, E, I, M, W, \mathbb{R} \cup Z, \varsigma, \rho)$$

$$(23)$$

356

where Σ, P, T, A, N, C, E, I, W, $\mathbb{R}$, ρ are as in a rough Petri net. The set $\mathbb{R}$ is augmented with operations in Z from fuzzy Petri nets to handle aggregations of granulated inputs.

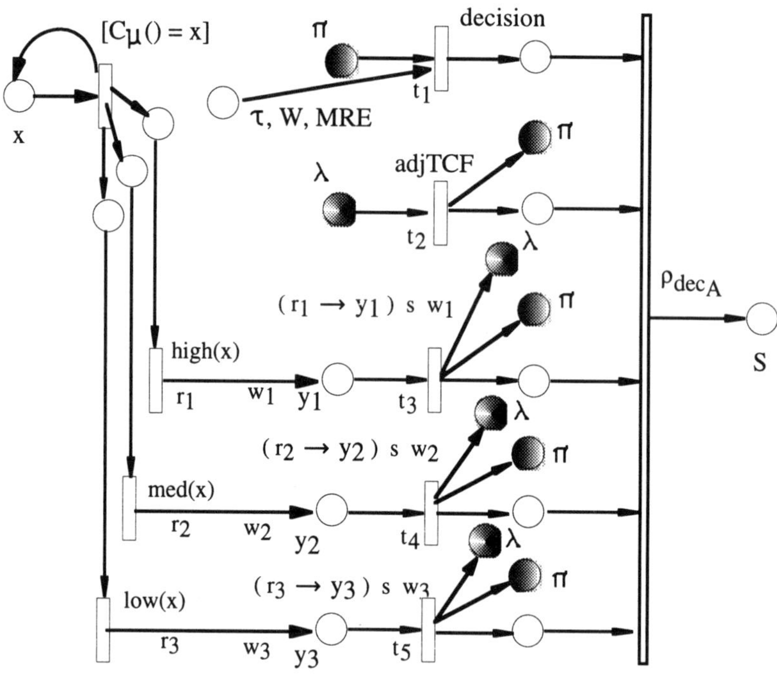

Fig. 11 *Petri Net Model of Software Cost Decision System*

The modulators (also called cut-offs or reference points) of operations in Z are in the set M. The operation ς maps arcs to modulators (or "cut-offs") chosen from the finite set M. In effect, a roughly fuzzy Petri net is an extension of the rough Petri net model, which provides a concise means of modeling the process of deriving rules for an approximate reasoning system for software cost estimation.

To simplify the roughly fuzzy Petri net model in Fig. 11, aliasing of input places λ and π of transitions t_1 and t_2, respectively, has been used. For example, the output place labeled λ of transitions t3, t4, t5 provides input to transition t2. The rfPn in Fig. 11 models the operations of the sensors for a decision system S. The place labeled S in Fig. 11 becomes input to the back end of the rough Petri net in Fig. 9. Observe that Choquet integral values are viewed relative to the extent that a multicriteria evaluation is a part of a granule, and this estimate of degree of membership initializes the roughly fuzzy Petri net in Fig. 10.   In the case where cut-offs and strengths of connections are incorporated into a roughly fuzzy Petri net for processing software cost measurements, then learning is possible.   Second, the outputs of sensors can be calibrated by a roughly fuzzy Petri net in providing inputs to a decision system table.   In this case, appropriate values of r and w are computed off-line as a result of supervised learning relative to target values as in [45]-[47].

4   Example Software Cost Estimation

The decider process in the feedback system in Fig. 1 implements a roughly fuzzy Petri net similar to the one in Fig. 11 with a number of enhancements. Rules are derived from a decision table based on rough set theory.   Whenever the decider is stimulated by new input, it selects a rule which comes closest to satisfying the conditions for the selection of necessary r, w values.   In each case where feedback of an MRE greater than some preset threshold δ, new r and w values are calibrated. This process continues until the MRE value is below δ.   In estimating W (man months needed to complete a project), negative values are excluded in

$$W = | \, 54 \, (FC) \, (adjTCF) - 13,390 \, |$$

The Magnitue of Relative Error (MRE) value is computed relative to W and required project duration τ in

$$MRE = \frac{| \, (\text{required time t}) \, - \, W \, |}{W}$$

Table 1 *Software Development Technologies*

Technology	Description
ide	integrated development environment (usually includes editor, error checker, debugger, graphical user interface, ability to link files, compiler)
team	cooperating software engineering teams, e.g., cleanroom engineering model.
av	applet viewer for web browser applications
web	use of web to maintain software requirement descriptions
awt	abstract windowing toolkit in Java programming

A collection of 25 Java programs have provided a testbed for the multicriteria decision-making approach to software cost estimation.   A collection of five software development technologies been found to influence the TCF in a significant way. These technologies are briefly described in Table 1. In effect, various combinations of these technologies are judged to have varying influence on a software development effort in saving time. Let X equal the set {ide, team, av, web, awt}.

The set X of five technologies in Table 1 results in a total of 2^5 coefficients of fuzzy measure relative to the power set of X. The values of the coefficients reflect preferences or judgments about the worth of each combination of technologies. Let $\mathcal{P}(X)$ denote the power set (set of all subsets) of X. To begin, it is necessary that these coefficients of fuzzy measure satisfy the rule

$$A \subset B \Rightarrow \mu(A) \le \mu(B), \text{ where A, B} \subseteq \mathcal{P}(X)$$

It is helpful to carry out multicriteria evaluation of elements of $\mathcal{P}(X)$ relative to a lattice of coefficients of fuzzy measure. In the case where X = {ide, team, av, web, awt}, we need to consider a lattice with 32 coefficients that will be used in Choquet integrations. Such a lattice is given in Fig. 12. Sample "scores" associated with coefficients are given in this lattice. Consider, for example,

$$\{web\} \subset \{team, web\} \Rightarrow \mu(\{web\}) \le \mu(\{team, web\})$$
$$0.28 \quad \le \quad 0.43$$

$$\{team, \subset \{team, \Rightarrow \mu(\{team, \le \mu(\{team,$$
$$web\} \quad\quad av, \quad\quad\quad web\}) \quad\quad av,$$
$$web\} \quad\quad\quad\quad\quad\quad\quad web\})$$
$$0.43 \quad \le \quad 0.59$$

In the context of software engineering, these scores reflect preferences concerning combinations of technologies. Notice that $\mu(\{ide, team, web\})$ equals 0.52 and $\mu(\{team, av, web\})$ equals 0.59, which suggests that combining an integrated development environment with an engineering team approach using the web is better than the combination of development methods {ide, team, web}. The heavier, shaded lines mark the paths in the lattice in Fig. 12 reflecting sample choices one can make in technology combinations relative to monotonically increasing coefficient values.

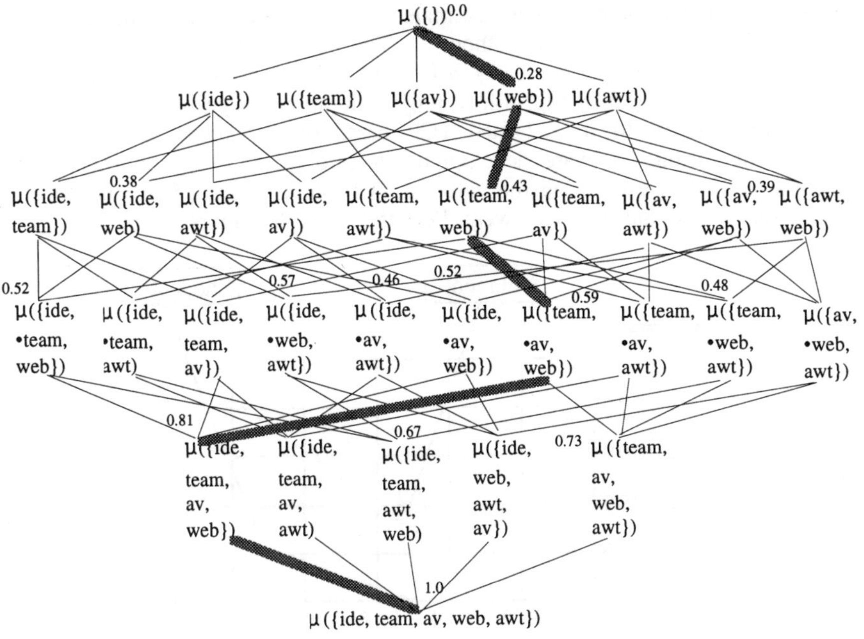

Fig. 12 *Lattice of Fuzzy Measure Coefficients*

To complete preparation for an application of the Choquet integral in software cost estimation, we introduce a function e used to estimate the per cent of usage of various combinations of technologies in a software project. That is,

$$e : X \rightarrow [0,1], \; X \subseteq \mathscr{P}(X)$$

The function e can be defined in a number of ways. For simplicity, assume that each value of e is computed relative to checklists serving as indicators of the per centage of project usage of each technology combination.

Next we consider sample data from a collection of 25 Java development projects with function counts varying between 200 and 1300, and target durations between 1800 and 9600 hours. Values of the degree-of-membership of Choquet integral considered in the granule named med (medium) ranged from 0.3 to 0.8. Each aggregation of a "normalized" Choquet integral value led to an adjusted TCF relative to cut-off r and strength-of-connection w. Estimates of the number of hours using the Choquet integral tend to be lower than estimates computed with Albrecht's method. A comparison of TCF and project duration estimates with these two methods is shown in Fig. 13. The dashed line in Fig. 13 indicates Albrecht's

360

estimates and, not surprisingly, these estimates are consistently higher than estimates (solid line) derived with the new method.   The contrast between estimates with these two methods is seen more clearly in Fig. 14.   For example, in the case where the function count is 750 in Fig. 14(a), project durations range between 2,800 and 27,000 hours relative to the adjusted TCF based on the fuzzy measure of the importance of various software development technologies.   By contrast, using Albrecht's method of estimating the value of TCF and assuming FC equal to 750, project duration estimates range between 12, 935 and 41,285 hours.

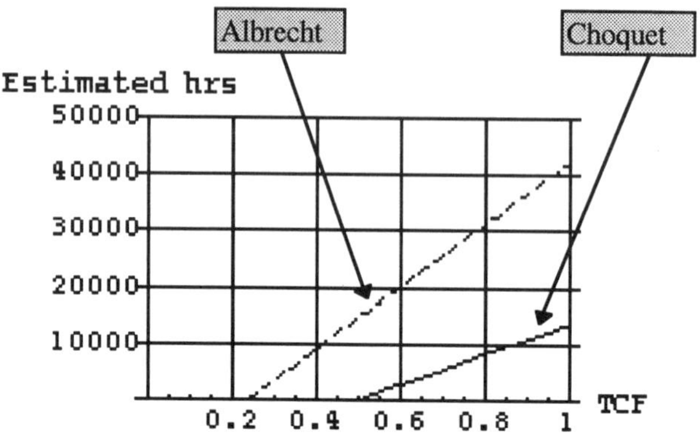

Fig. 13 *Comparison of Project Duration Estimates*

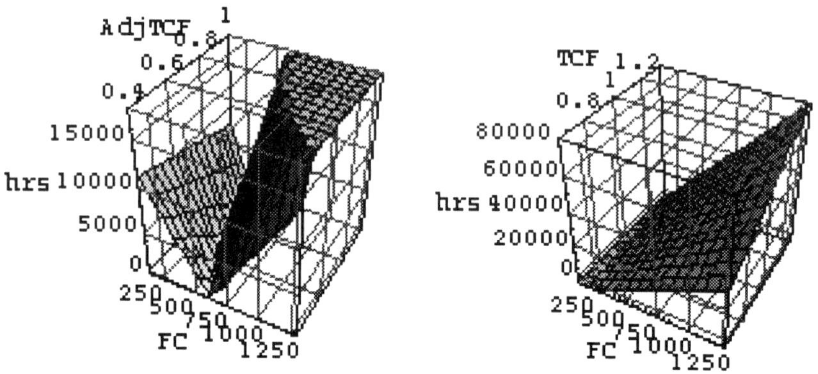

Fig. 14(a) *Choquet-based Method* **Fig. 14(b)** *Albrecht's Method*

Sample TCF and adjTCF estimates relative to a sampler of software development projects is given in Table 2.

Table 2 *Sample Software Cost Decision Table*

FC	TCF	τ (hrs)	nC_μ	adjTCF	$W(C_\mu)$	MRE	r	w
206	1.07	2960	0.4130	0.9354	2984.7	0.0083	0.64	0.22
215	1.26	2026	0.4130	0.9737	2042.8	0.0082	0.61	0.4
228	1.04	2339	0.4130	0.8960	2357.9	0.0080	0.68	0.24
281	1.35	2278	0.4130	0.7336	2257.9	0.0089	0.88	0.2
291	1.01	2110	0.4130	0.9853	2092.3	0.0085	0.6	0.32
351	1.15	2406	0.4130	0.8346	2428.7	0.0093	0.74	0.2
378	0.88	2182	0.4130	0.7620	2164.9	0.0079	0.84	0.21
400	0.98	1880	0.4130	0.5352	1882.9	0.0015	0.94	0.22
487	1.2	7350	0.7552	0.7802	7280.8	0.0095	0.32	0.09
479	1.25	7161	0.7552	0.7937	7140.9	0.0028	0.31	0.02
537	0.75	2780	0.3375	0.364	2834.7	0.0193	0.663	0.04
773	1.15	7650	0.7552	0.5045	7668.9	0.0025	0.49	0.01
1282	0.88	8500	0.7552	0.3167	8535.7	0.0042	0.79	0.01
1319	1.17	9650	0.7552	0.3247	9735.9	0.0088	0.77	0.01

A comparison of relative errors for a collection of 25 projects is given in Fig. 15.

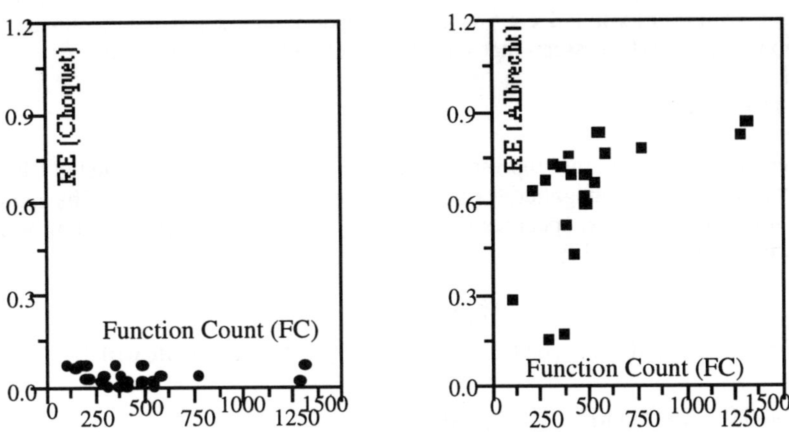

Fig. 15 *Relative Errors with Two Methods*

The relative error of cost estimates with Albrecht's method tends to increase as function count estimates increase, climbing to 0.9 for projects with function counts above 1200. By contrast, cost estimates with based on considerations of the coalition of software technologies have low, fairly uniform relative error measurements (in most cases, RE < 0.2).

Table 2 instantiates a decision system for software cost estimation. Values in the columns with FC, TCF headings represent function counts and technical complexity for actual software projects using Albrecht's method. The TCF column is given to facilitate comparisons with the adjusted TCF (adjTCF), which is a function of nC_μ, r and w. MRE values in Table 2 result from a comparison of upper bound τ and computed duration W. The feedback system in Fig. 1 is implemented with rules derived from a decision system table and provide a basis for selecting r and w. Rules derived from real-valued sensors like those in Table 2 are discretized relative to interval rather than individual sensor values. This is made possible by the quantization of the real values of software cost estimation sensors so that sensor values are partitioned into intervals. Let $\mathbb{R}$ be the set of real numbers, and let $\mathbb{R}^k$ be a k-dimensional affine space. An object in a decision table is treated as a point in $\mathbb{R}^k$ where k is the number of conditional sensors $a \in A$ such $a \neq d$ in $S = (U, A \cup \{d\})$. Then the objects in decision table are partitioned into r decision classes using the method described by H.S. Nguyen in [56]-[57]. The important consequence of this classification scheme is that all objects belonging to the same class have the same decision. This result has the effect of reducing the number of rules that must be considered in approximate reasoning. To illustrate this approach to rule formation in the context of software cost estimation, let x[*, b) for values of a sensor x so that $* \leq x < b$, where the lower bound * is indeterminate. Similarly, x[a, *) represents values of x in $a \leq x < *$ where the upper bound is left indeterminate. The notation $x(\{a < x \leq b\})$ asserts that sensor x is defined relative to the set

$$\{(a, b) \mid a < x \leq b\}$$

Further, let fc, tau, ncu, mre represent function count, time limit, granulated Choquet integral value, and magnitude of relative error, respectively. The notation fc([*, 400)), for example, specifies that $* \leq fc < 400$. Rules for selecting w have the form given in (x) and (y).

fc([*, 400.0)) AND tau([8500.0, *)) AND

ncu([*, 0.584)) AND mer($\{0.0025 < mer \leq 0.0085\}$) $\implies$ w(0.1) OR w(0.2)   (x)

fc([*, 400.0)) AND tau([*, 2100.0)) AND

ncu([*, 0.584)) AND mer($\{0.0025 < mer \leq 0.0085\}$) $\implies$ w(0.2) OR w(0.4)   (y)

In the case where selected columns of decision table 2 have been implemented in a feedback control system for software cost, rule (y) would result in the selection of trial values of w, either w = 0.2 or w = 0.4, in the case where project constraints have the form

FC	τ (hrs)	nC_μ	MRE	r	w
215	2026	0.4130	0.0082	?	?

Similarly, the decider in the feedback control system would make its selection of cut-off r values based on rules having a similar form. It is a straightforward task to derive these rules using Rosetta [59]. After encoding such rules, the decider process is governed by some form of rule-firing algorithm.

Decider Rule Firing Algorithm

step 1.   Let {fc, tau, nC_μ}, a_i, a_j, a_k, v_{ai}, v_{aj}, v_{ak} be experimental values for function counts, etc. observed during actual operation of a software cost feedback control system, sample decision system condition sensors for a sample control rule r $\in$ D(S), and sensor values from decision system table (U, A $\cup$ {d}, V), respectively. Let s be defined as a sum s = $(a_i(x) - v_{ai}) + (a_j(y) - v_{aj}) + (a_k(z) - v_{ak})$, where x is an input value (x is the observed function count fc; y, the time limit tau; z, the granulated Choquet integral value nC_μ) evaluated with sensors a_i, a_j, a_k in A (for example) to produce a particular value v_{ai}.

step 2.   Let n, m be the number of r, w rules, respectively. Let s_i, $1 \le i \le n$, s_j, $1 \le j \le m$ be sums of the form introduced in step 1 relative to n rules for r and m rules for w, respectively.   Then let m_{kp}, m_{kd} be functions defined as follows as follows:

m_{kp}: s_1, ..., s_i, ..., s_n $\longrightarrow$ i such that s[i] = $\min(s_1, ..., s_i, ..., s_n)$

m_{kd}: s_1, ..., s_j, ..., s_n $\longrightarrow$ j such that s[j] = $\min(s_1, ..., s_j, ..., s_n)$

In other words, m_{kp}, m_{kd} each finds the index of the smallest sum, which identifies the premise of a rule which is closest to the measured condition during the operation of a controller.

step 3. Let r := r[i], w := w[j] be the new values of cut-off and strength-of-connection used to estimate project duration W. Then compute W.

In the case where experimental values lead to an unacceptably high relative error, a new row is added to the initial decision table relative to adjusted values of r and w. Recalibration of r and w results in the introduction of new rules. For a collection of similar software projects, the feedback system eventually stabilizes.   Trial runs of the feedback system relative to the sample collection of software projects required between 400 and 1500 epochs to achieve a satisfactory relative error. For example, a trial run of the feedback system relative to one of the 25 Java projects required 400 epochs to achieve a relative error less than 0.01 based on FC = 537, τ (tau) = 2780, nC_μ = 0.449 (see Fig. 16).

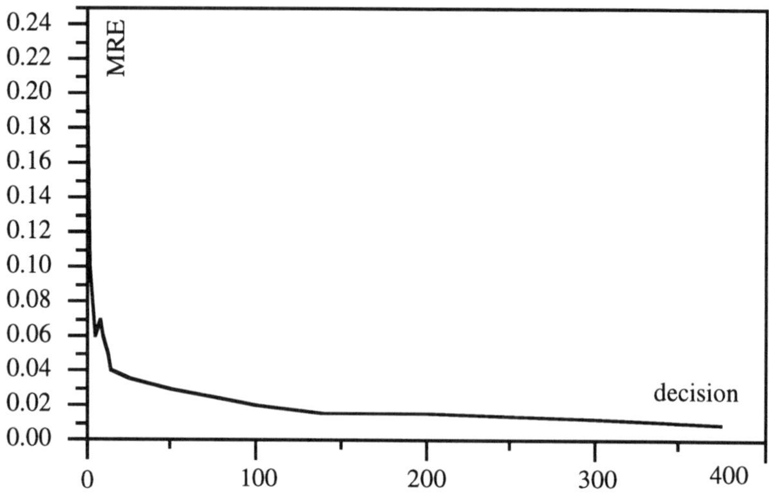

Fig. 16 *Sample Feedback System Performance*

5   Concluding Remarks

This paper presents a roughly fuzzy Petri net model of a real-time feedback control system useful in controlling the cost of products of a software process.   Since the basic approach to software cost estimation suggested by Albrecht requires a knowledge of software functionality, it is possible to estimate the cost of software entities early in a software process (see, for example, [60]).   Hence, it is possible to study the feasibility of a timing-constraint on a description of a software entity relative to possible coalitions of software development technologies.   The heart of the feedback system introduced in this paper is a fuzzy measure which models the importance or strength of each form of coalition of software development technologies in arriving at decisions about combinations of such technologies deliver the most benefit in controlling software cost.   In this context, the coalition means union, combination or fusion where the fuzzy measure of a combination can be greater than the fuzzy measure of coalition individuals.   The not-so-obvious advantage to this approach is that the importance $\mu(\{t\})$ of an individual development technology t in a software process may be less than the fuzzy measure $\mu(A \cup \{t\})$ for a coalition of development technologies A combined with t. Adequate representations of fuzzy measures suitable for multicriteria decision-making have presented in [7].

Also, notice that the feedback system algorithm in Fig. 2 is based on a hard real-time system design. This stems from the fact that the feedback system enforces a timing constraint imposed on each software product. The estimated completion time W is measured relative to duration τ. The subtlty of this approach is that by introducing various values of τ, a software development team can measure the required contribution of coalitions of software development technologies needed to satisfy a project timing constraint. In practice, the functionality of software as well as the availability and feasibility of coalitions of software technologies evolves and continuously changes. The feedback system described in this paper suggests how one might cope with these changes by adjusting the extent of change needed in the technical complexity factor to develop a software product within a required time. Finally, the design and analysis of the proposed feedback system will be aided by rough Petri net and roughly fuzzy Petri net models of decision table-building and rule derivation processes as well as models of the cost estimation rules themselves similar to rule-modeling in [34].

Acknowledgements   First, we thank Prof. Witold Pedrycz, Faculty of Engineering, University of Manitoba, Prof. Andrzej Skowron, Faculty of Mathematics, Computer Science and Mechanics, Warsaw University and Prof. Zbigniew Suraj, Institute of Mathematics, Rzeszow, members of the Institute of Mathematics at Warsaw University for discussions we have had related to this research. Second, we gratefully acknowledge the funding for this research provided by the Natural Sciences and Engineering Research Council of Canada (NSERC) operating funds for both authors, Canadian Space Agency, the University of Manitoba research grants committee, and the University of Winnipeg research grants committee.

References

1.   J.D. Musa, A. Iannino, K. Okumoto, K. Software Reliability: Measurement, Prediction, Application. New York, McGraw-Hill Publishing Co., 1990.
2.   J.F. Peters and S. Ramanna: Application of Choquet Integral in Software Cost Estimation. IEEE Int. Conf. on Fuzzy Systems, New Orleans, 1996, 862-866.
3.   J.F. Peters and S. Ramanna: A rough sets approach to assessing software quality: Concepts and rough Petri net models. In: Fuzzy Sets, Rough Sets, and Decision Systems edited by S.K. Pal and A. Skowron. Singapore, Springer-Verlag [accepted].
4.   J.F.Peters, S. Ramanna, Software Deployability Decision System Framework: A Rough Sets Approach, Proceedings IPMU'98, Paris, France, June, 1998.

5.   W. Pedrycz, J.F. Peters, S. Ramanna, Design of a software quality decision system: A computational intelligence approach, CCECE'98, Waterloo, Ontario, May 1998

6.   A. Albrecht and J.E. Gaffney: Software Function, Source Lines of Code, and Development Effort Prediction: A Software Science Validation. IEEE Trans. on Software Engineering, SE-9, 6 (1983) 639-647

7.   M. Grabisch: Alternative representations of discrete fuzzy measures for decision making. Int. J. of Uncertainty, Fuzziness and Knowledge-Based Systems 0, 0, 1997, 1-21.

8.   M. Grabisch, Fuzzy integral in multicriteria decision making. *Fuzzy Sets and Systems*, 69: 279-298, 1995.

9.   M. Grabisch, H.T. Nguyen, E.A. Walker: Fundamentals of Uncertainty Calculi with Applications to Fuzzy Inference. Boston, Kluwer Academic Publishers, 1995.

10. N. Wiener, Cybernetics: Or Control and Communication in the Animal and the Machine. Cambridge, MA, MIT Press, 1961.

11. J.F. Peters, Time and Clock Information Systems: Concepts and Roughly Fuzzy Petri Net Models. In: Knowledge Discovery and Rough Sets edited by J. Kacprzyk. Physica Verlag, a division of Springer Verlag (1998) [in press].

12. W. Pedrycz, J.F. Peters, Learning in fuzzy Petri nets. In: Fuzzy Petri Nets, Cardoso, J., Sandri, S. (Eds.). Berlin, Physica Verlag [in press]

13. M. Sugeno: Theory of fuzzy integrals and its applications. Ph.D. Thesis, Tokyo Institute of Technology, 1974.

14. G. Choquet, Theory of capacities. Annales de l'Institut Fourier, 5, 1953, 131-295.

15. L.A. Zadeh, Fuzzy logic = computing with words. IEEE Trans. on Fuzzy Systems 4/2 (1996) 103-111.

16. L.A. Zadeh, Toward a theory of fuzzy information granulation and its certainty in human reasoning and fuzzy logic. Fuzzy Sets and Systems 90/ 2 (1997) 111-128.

17. G.J. Klir, M.J. Wierman, Uncertainty-Based Information: Elements of Generalized Information Theory. Report, Center for Research in Fuzzy Mathematics and Computer Science, Creighton University, Omaha, Nebraska 63178, U.S.A., 1997.

18. L.A. Zadeh, Fuzzy sets, Information and Control 8 (1965) 338-353.

19. B.R. Gaines, Multivalued logics and fuzzy reasoning. BCS AISB Summer School, Cambridge, 1975.

20. J. Lukasiewicz, Logic and the problem of the foundations of mathematics. In: Jan Lukasiewicz, Borkowski, L. (Ed.), Amsterdam, North-Holland Pub. Co., 1970, 278-294.

21. D. Ruan, A critical study of widely used fuzzy implication operators and their influence on the inference rules in fuzzy expert systems. Ph.D. thesis, Gent, 1990.

22. Z. Pawlak, Rough Sets: Theoretical Aspects of Reasoning About Data. Boston, MA, Kluwer Academic Publishers, 1991.

23. Z. Pawlak, Rough sets: present state and future prospects. ICS Research Report 32/95, Institute of Computer Science, Warsaw Institute of Technology, 1995.

24. Z. Pawlak, Grzymala-Busse, J.W., Slowinski, R., Ziarko, W.: Rough Sets. Communications of the ACM 38 (1995) 88-95.

25. A. Skowron, Extracting laws from decision tables: a rough set approach. Computational Intelligence 11/2 (1995) 371-388.

26. A. Skowron, L. Polkowski, Rough mereology: A new paradigm for approximate reasoning. Journ. of Approximate Reasoning 15/4 (1996) 333-365.

27. A. Skowron, C. Rauszer, The discernability matrices and functions in information systems. In: Intelligent Decision Support, Handbook of Applications and Advances of the Rough Sets Theory, Slowinski, R. (Ed.), Dordrecht, Kluwer Academic Publishers, 1992, 331-362.

28. A. Skowron, Z. Suraj, A rough set approach to real-time state identification. Bulletin EATCS **50** (1993) 264-275.

29. A. Skowron, Z. Suraj, Synthesis of concurrent systems specified by information systems. ICS Research Report 39/94, Institute of Computer Science, Warsaw Institute of Technology, 1994.

30. A. Skowron, Z. Suraj, Discovery of concurrent data models from experimental data tables: a rough set approach. Institute of Computer Science Research Report 15/95, Warsaw Institute of Technology, 1995.

31. A. Skowron, Z. Suraj, A parallel algorithm for real-time decision making: a rough set approach. Journal of Intelligent Information Systems **7** (1996) 5-28

32. A. Skowron, Z. Suraj, A rough set approach to real-time state identification for decision making. Institute of Computer Science Research Report 18/93, Warsaw University of Technology, 1993.

33. J. Sienkiewicz, Rough sets for boolean functions minimization. Research Report, Warsaw Institute of Technology, 1995.

34. J.F. Peters, S. Skowron, Z. Suraj, S. Ramanna Approximate real-time decision-making: concepts and roughly fuzzy Petri net modeling. Int. Journal of Intelligent Systems [to appear].

35. T. Murata, Petri nets: properties, analysis and applications. Proceedings of the IEEE **77/4** (1989) 541-580.

36. C.A. Petri, Kommunikation mit Automaten. Schriften des IIM Nr. 3, Institut für Instrumentelle Mathematik, Bonn, West Germany. See, also, Communication with Automata (in English). Griffiss Air Force Base, New York Technical Report RADC-Tr-65-377, **1**, Suppl. 1, 1962.

37. K. Jensen, Coloured Petri nets. In: Advances in Petri Nets 254 (1986) 288-299.

38. K. Jensen, Coloured Petri Nets--Basic Concepts, Analysis Methods and Practical Use **1**. Berlin, Springer-Verlag, 1992.

39. P. Huber, K. Jensen, R.M. Shapiro, Hierarchies in coloured Petri nets. Proc. Int. Conf. Science on Application and Theory of Petri Nets. In: Rozenberg, G. (Ed.), Lecture Notes in Computer Science 483 (1986) 261-292.

40. W. Pedrycz, F. Gomide, A generalized fuzzy Petri net model. IEEE Trans. on Fuzzy Systems 2/4 (1994) 295-301.

41. P. Scrinivan, D. Gracarin, Approximate reasoning with fuzzy Petri nets. Proc. IEEE Int. Conf. on Fuzzy Systems, San Francisco, CA (1993) 396-401.

42. H. Scarpelli, F. Gomide, Relational calculus in designing fuzzy Petri nets. In: W. Pedrycz (Ed.), Fuzzy Modelling: Paradigms and Practice. Boston, MA, Kluwer Academic Publishers, 1996, 70-89.

43. H. Scarpelli, F. Gomide, Fuzzy reasoning and high level fuzzy Petri nets. In: Proc. First European Congress on Fuzzy and Intelligent Technologies, Aachen, Germany (1993) 600-605.

44. H. Scarpelli, F. Gomide, R. Yager, A reasoning algorithm for high-level fuzzy Petri nets. IEEE Trans. on Fuzzy Systems 4/3 (1996) 282-295.

45. W. Pedrycz, J.F. Peters, S. Ramanna, T. Furuhashi, From data to fuzzy Petri nets: generalized model and calibration abilities. Proc. of Seventh Int. Fuzzy Systems Association World Congress (IFSA'97) III (1997) 294-299.

46. W. Pedrycz, J.F. Peters, Learning in fuzzy Petri nets. In: Fuzzy Petri Nets, Cardoso, J., Sandri, S. (Eds.). Berlin, Physica Verlag [in press]

47. W. Pedrycz, J.F. Peters, Information Granularity Uncertainty Principle: Contingency Tables and Petri Net Representations. Proc. Proc. North American Fuzzy Information Processing Society NAFIPS'97, Syracuse, NY, (1997) 222-226.

48. M.L. Garg, S.I. Ahson, P.V. Gupta, A fuzzy Petri net for knowledge representation and reasoning. Information Processing Letters **39** (1991) 165-171.

49. H.S. Son, P.H. Seong, A safety analysis method using fuzzy Petri nets. Proc. North American Fuzzy Information Processing Society (NAFIPS'97), Syracuse, NY (1997) 412-417.

50. R. Gudwin, F. Gomide, Object networks--A modeling tool. Proc. IEEE World Congress on Computational Intelligence (WCCI'98), Anchorage, Alaska, 4-9 May 1998.

51. J. Cardoso, G. Bittencourt, L.L. Caimi, A frame-based representation for fuzzy Petri nets. Proc. IEEE World Congress on Computational Intelligence (WCCI'98), Anchorage, Alaska, 4-9 May 1998.

52. S. Sandri, J. Cardoso, Possibilistic timed safe Petri nets. Proc. IEEE World Congress on Computational Intelligence (WCCI'98), Anchorage, Alaska, 4-9 May 1998.

53. T. Furuhashi, J.F. Peters, W. Pedrycz, A stability analysis of fuzzy control systems using a generalized fuzzy Petri net model. Proc. IEEE World Congress on Computational Intelligence (WCCI'98), Anchorage, Alaska, 4-9 May 1998.

54. H. Ammar, L. Yu, A comparison of two analysis algorithms for fuzzy marking Petri nets. Proc. IEEE World Congress on Computational Intelligence (WCCI'98), Anchorage, Alaska, 4-9 May 1998.

55. J.F. Peters.: Time and clock information systems: Concepts and roughly fuzzy Petri net models. In: Rough Sets and Knowledge Discovery, Kacprzyk, J., Berlin, Physica Verlag, a division of Springer Verlag [in press].

56. H.S. Nguyen: Discretization of real-valued attributes: Boolean reasoning approach. Doctoral Thesis, Faculty of Mathematics, Computer Science and Mechanics, Warsaw University, 1997.

57. H.S. Nguyen, Rule induction from continuous data: New discretization concepts. Proc. of the Third Joint Conf. on Information Sciences, Raleigh, N.C., 1-5 March 1997.

58. M.H.Halstead, Elements of Software Science, North Holland, New York, 1977.

59. A. Skowron (Ed.), Handbook on Rough Sets and Rosetta. UK, Oxford University Press [to appear].

60. W. Pedrycz and J.F. Peters, Software Engineering: An Engineering Approach. NY, John Wiley & Sons, Inc. [to appear].

Exercises

1. Using Table 2, do the following.

(a) Granulate TCF values computed using Albrecht's method relative to several granules named low, med, high.

(b) Let mTCF be a degree-of-membership of a TCF value in a granule named med. Select appropriate r, w values for each value of mTCF. Then construct a table of adjusted TCF values using

$$\text{adjTCF'} = ((\text{mTCF} \rightarrow r) \, s \, w$$

(c) Compare and comment on the adjTCF' values in Part (b) relative to adjTCF values in Table 2.

2. Devise a new form of Albrecht's cost estimation formula by replacing the constants 54 and 13,390 with variables (say, a and b). Then do the following.

(a) Devise a means of selecting values of a and b.

(b) Experiment with the new cost estimation formula using adjTCF' from No. 1(b), and values of FC and τ in Table 2.

(c) Comment on the impact of this new cost estimation model.

3. Give an algorithm for calibrating r and w to be used by the decider process in the feedback system in Fig. 2 in cases where no rule is available which leads to an MRE value less than some preset minimum.

4.   Prove that the algorithm in No. 3 is correct.

5.   Use Table 2 in experiments with Rosetta to obtain a set of discretized rules for the feedback system.   Comment on how these rules can be implemented.

6.   Albrecht's method of computing the value of FC (function count) is based on table 3.

Table 3. *Template for Computing Function Count (FC)*

Id	Count Description	Simple complexity	Average complexity	High complexity	Total
IT	External Input	___ x 3	___ x 4	___ x 6	
OT	External Output	___ x 4	___ x 5	___ x 7	
FT	Logical Internal File	___ x 7	___ x 10	___ x 15	
EI	Ext. Interface File	___ x 5	___ x 7	___ x 10	
QT	External Inquiry	___ x 3	___ x 4	___ x 6	
FC	Total Unadjusted FPs				

Do the following.
(a)   Consider additions to columns 1 and 2 (count descriptions) relative to other indices of program functionality.
(b)   Let FC, countNew be traditional function count total from Table 2 and weighted sum of new additions to Table 3, respectively.   Then compute

newFC = FC + countNew

(b)   Replace the values of FC in Table 2 with values of newFC.

(c)   Assuming that nC_μ is unchanged in Table 2, recompute the values in Table 2, and compare the results with those obtained in the original Table 2.

7.   Give a rough Petri net model of a process which computes function count totals as aggregations of d-values based on the sensor evalutions of the results obtained in No. 5.

Computational Intelligence and Software Engineering

Expert System Design to Control the Information Provided to Pilots

MICHAEL S. MCCOY
The Boeing Corporation
Strategic Analysis and Planning
M.S. 064 2233
P.O. Box 516
St. Louis, Mo. 63166-0516

REUVEN R. LEVARY
Dept. Of Decision Sciences and MIS
School of Business and Administration
St. Louis University
3674 Lindell Blvd.
St. Louis, Mo. 63108

A rule based expert system program was used to model a fighter pilot's task and procedure execution. This model was developed to be incorporated into an intelligent cognitive decision support system to help maintain an estimate of pilot situation awareness, workload and general man-machine system performance. This model could be applied to augment operator procedures and information flow. Validation of the model was accomplished through direct comparison of critical predicted measures of merit against observed pilot performance in a high fidelity manned fighter simulation.

1. Introduction

One of the most important requirements for maintaining an operators situation awareness is to ensure that the proper information is presented for each given situation. Typically, displays are designed when the system is designed in anticipation of all potential situations. Often, not all situations can be anticipated early in system design. One way to help anticipate the environmental conditions of the human-machine situation is to perform a systems analysis of the missions to be performed by the system. This systems analysis includes functional analysis, task analysis and information requirements analysis. Given these peices of information, a human performance model can be developed which simulates the procedures and tasks performed by the operator given specific events. With the execution of procedures the operator must have appropriate information to make informed decisions. Therefore, the human performance model, which simulates the operators activity should contain detailed information requirements for the procedures also. In order to describe the mechanism, a discussion of human performance models is warrented.

Human performance models are computer based mathematical simulation models used to predict operator decision making, task and procedure execution, and mental workload. These models have been applied in the design of aircraft cockpits, nuclear power plant control stations, and air traffic control centers to anticipate problems with operability of the system. More recently proposed applications include supervisory control systems and decision aiding systems (Sheridan[1]). These new applications require a high level of precision in modeling the human decision making process and behavior.

Early human performance models were developed with the sensory, organism, and response construct (Siegel & Wolf[2] and Asiala, et.al.[3]). These models did not account for conflict between resource usage in the performance of tasks in parallel. Citing this deficiency, Wickens[3] developed a multiple resource theory that used expert subjective opinion to estimate the percentages of resources required to perform tasks. Then, when the sum of demanded resources exceeded the availability of resources, tasks were shed or delayed until resources became available. However, this method depended on a highly subjective estimate of the percentage of resources required by operator in performance of the tasks. In addition, Wickens did not account for the extra time required when operators performed tasks in parallel, rather than singularly, i.e., in sequential order. Therefore, using measured task performance times, a new method of modeling the relationship between task execution time and resource utilization was developed in this study to account for these deficiencies, and to more accurately simulate human behavior in a real-world, complex operating environment.

A human-machine system consists of a computer control system designed to provide an interface between a human operator and a task environment to achieve specific goals, such as, navigating through the sea in a ship, generating electricity in a nuclear power plant, managing air traffic in an airport, or flying an aircraft from an origin to a destination.

Human performance models have been classified into four major categories (a) information processing, (b) control theory, (c) task network, and, (d) knowledge based. Each type of model has advantages and disadvantages that must be weighed when selecting a technique for a specific application.

Little has been done to adapt knowledge- based technology to human performance models (Elkind, Card, Hochberg & Huey[4]). Hunt and Rouse[5] demonstrated the application of fuzzy sets and rule-based modeling in human problem solving. The concept required the definition of appropriate data structures, such as frames, schemas, and scripts (Minsky[6] and Schank & Abelson[7]). These data structures developed into the latest technology of object oriented programming that defined rules to relate patterns of objects or frames (data) and initiated changes in the database. Finally, a conflict resolution mechanism was required to determine which rules to use at any given instant. Expert system programs are now commercially available to provide the mechanization for this concept.

Rule-based models simulate cognitive processes, such as, decision making and problem solving. Rule-based models foster a better understanding of how people solve problems in a specific domain. This concept was deemed good for modeling cognitive activities in supervisory control (Baron, Kruser, & Huey[8]). In addition, these models allow representation of information requrements.

One disadvantage of rule-based models was that the process of extracting knowledge from experts (knowledge acquisition) did not readily apply across groups. Often there was conflict between experts on problem solving methodology. Because of the computational intensity of rule-based models, they typically were not applied to real-time processes (Pilot's Associate[9]). The extraction of knowledge has been a difficult process to construct (Nisbitt & Wilson[10]). Also, rule-based models were difficult to evaluate in terms of their fidelity to the acquired expertise they attempted to reproduce (Baron, Kruser, & Huey[8]).

Several network models were developed to account for parallel processing of tasks. Asiala, Miller, Wilper, and McCoy[3] developed a model that broke tasks into micro levels and associated a resource requirement with each subtask. No two subtasks could be executed simultaneously, if they shared the same resource. The resources available consisted of vision, audition, cognition, right hand and left hand. With this model, the operator (an aircraft pilot) could employ the right hand on the stick (controling attitude of aircraft), while looking at a display and thinking about a tactical situation simultaneously since they did not require the same resources.

The Human Operator Simulator (Harris, Iavecchia, Ross, & Shaffer[11])is currently being modified to account for parallel processing, in much the same way that the Pilot Simulation Model of Asiala and colleagues. However, as Wickens[12] noted, there is no method incorporated in either of these models to account for interaction between parallel tasks.

A human performance model that could adequately predict performance and workload, as well as fit into an "expert system" type of decision support system would be quite a beneficial design tool. If pilot workload and performance could be predicted accurately enough to provide reasonable indications of possible design deficiencies early in the aircraft design process, certainly the effort put forth developing such a model would be justified. A computer simulation model with the capabilities described would enable aeronautical design engineers to identify human-machine interaction problems and evaluate alternative designs with relative ease while the aircraft was still "on the drawing board". Thus the time and expense incurred in building a physical prototype of an inadequate aircraft could be avoided (Sage[13] and Sheridan[1]).

If the human performance model, developed early in the design process can be validated, this model can be used for two distinct purposes: evaluation of avionics systems and imbedded decision support. The model can be used during system design and deployment, a significant cost savings can be realized in system development. The model can also be incorporated into the decision support system to aid operator performance and manage workload during system deployment.

In order for complex human-machine systems to operate effectively and efficiently with humans, these systems must possess knowledge of both the humans' performance, workload and information requirements. Performance information allows the system to anticipate the human's actions, and workload knowledge helps the system judge when the human may need assistance (Sage[13]). Finally, information requirements help drive display change management. When good models have been incorporated in supervisory control systems, or other forms of decision support systems, they have enhanced the overall human-machine system performance (Morris, Rouse & Word[14]). Therefore, a good predictive model of human performance and workload can be critical for the efficient operation of a human-machine system (McCoy & Boys[15]).

2. The Pilot Performance Model

2.1 Model Development Process

The first step in the model development process consisted of defining the mission scenarios. These scenarios provided an objective of performing procedures in order to accomplish specific objectives. When the procedures were defined, they were analyzed to determine the functions and corresponding tasks that had to be performed to accomplish the mission. Two types of data requirements were defined, model input data and measures of merit for model validation. Each type of data required specific procedures to be executed in a realistic environment. Both part task and part mission simulation experiments were conducted to gather this data. A block diagram of the model development process is illustrated in Figure 1.

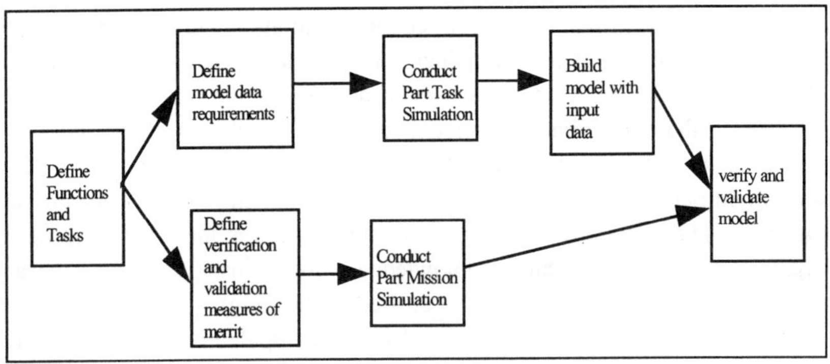

Figure 1. Model Development Process

Part mission simulation was the process of having piltos perform the entire mission scenario. This required the executions of multiple procedures simultaniously. In performing these procedures in parallel, conflict could arise between tasks competing for human resources (perceptual, cognitive or motor). If the model properly predicted pilot activity, it would also predict delays due to conflict between tasks. Therefore, measures of merit for validation were task exeuction times as well as delays due to conflict of tasks competing for human resources.

2.2 Task Decomposition and Analysis

In order to develop a simulation model of pilot activity, a task analysis had to be performed, generating data for input to the model and data to be used for validating the model. Initial task analyses for the F/A-18 aircraft were reported by Wise, et. al. (Wise & Asiala[16]; Wise, Asiala & Loy[17]). The data presented in these reports provided an initial base for developing the model. Additional data were collected in conjunction with experiments conducted at McDonnell Douglas Aerospace Company to satisfy the requirements of the Human Engineering Dynamic Simulation Plan (McCoy, Hunter, Seavers, & McClure[18]). The data collected during these exercises were reported in a series of White Papers that will be included in latter revisions of the Human Engineering Systems Analysis Report (McCoy & Seavers[19]).

Given the mission scenarios described, the pilot had to perform four major tasks, or functions (a) flight control, (b) communications, (c) identification, and (d) navigation. In order to determine which variables to measure and what tasks to model in the simulation, it was necessary to decompose the functional tasks. For flight control, the pilot primarily concentrated on manipulation of the stick. This required viewing the Head Up Display (HUD), comparing the heading to the desired flight path, and seizing the stick with the right hand to adjust the aircraft's flight path. The declarative knowledge for this task was the actual and desired heading.   The   procedural   knowledge   for   this   function   became:
If   (actual   heading   -   desired   heading)   is   too   large,
Then   adjust   heading   (by   manipulating   the   stick).
The type of data collected in the simulator were the mean time to manipulate the stick (adjust heading and altitude) and the mean time between adjustments.

The next function that was decomposed was communications. The pilot was instructed, via a radio transmission, to select a new radio frequency on the manual channel. In order to accomplish this procedure, several individual steps had to be performed. Using the Up-Front Control (UFC), the pilot selected the appropriate rotary "comm" knob, and then viewed the frequency set on the knob. If the frequency was not "manual" the pilot was required to rotate the knob and select "manual." The next step involved pulling the knob that changed the UFC to data entry mode to display the current frequency. Then, the pilot compared the current frequency to the desired one and chose to input the new frequency by using the mechanical keypad to input up to six digits. Finally the pilot pressed "enter" to signify that the old frequency had been overridden.

Another function the pilot performed was inputting the IFF code. Again, the pilot received a radio transmission instructing them to input this code. Upon receiving the command, the pilot pressed the appropriate button on the UFC to select the IFF input mode. The pilot compared the current with the desired four-digit code and chose to update it. Then, the pilot pressed "enter" to complete the operation.

The final, and by far the most complicated, procedure executed by the aircrew was changing the waypoint, or target location. After receiving a radio transmission with instructions to input the new target location the aircrew selected the data entry panel from the Horizontal Situation Indicator (HSI) display. Once the waypoint input mode was selected, the pilot entered the hemisphere "N" followed by a six-digit latitude. Next, the pilot entered "W" and a seven-digit longitude. Finally, the pilot selected and a three-digit elevation and pressed "enter." The data defined and collected for each task in the described procedures consisted of : task execution time (mean and standard deviation); information requirements; preconditions for execution; task goals or anticipated outcome; resource requirements; and, shed conditions.

Task times were measured by video taping the execution of procedures and recording the time needed to complete each component of the task. Since data input was being recorded by the computer, the time each button was pushed was also recorded. By using these data along with guidelines extracted from Card, Moran, and Newell[20], each task was measured for its perceptual, cognitive, and motor components. Then, this information was averaged across all pilots who participated in the data-gathering procedure. This produced an average execution time and a standard deviation for each task. Empirical distribution functions for each task were defined based on this data and used in the pilot performance simulation model (McCoy[21]).

The remaining data defined and collected for the model was gathered through pilot interviews. Pilots defined the information required to perform each task, the goals which prompted them to initiate the task and preconditions for task execution. In addition they defined reasons for abandoning a task (shed conditions).

2.3   Simulation Model Development

The human performance model developed for this study was comprised of a combination of conventional discrete event simulation modeling techniques and an activity scanning, or knowledge-based, representation of pilot decision making process. These two techniques were highly integrated to insure that they accurately represented the environment exerting demands on the aircrew, and the decision making and task execution processes that represented pilot activity. A description of the data generated from the model will be presented in section 3 to illustrate which variables compared favorably to observed pilot performance.

378

2.3.1 *Model Description*

The human performance model (HPM) used in this study was a special form of activity scanning model. The model was built using the 'C' Language Interactive Production System (CLIPS) program. CLIPS is an expert systems tool developed by the artificial intelligence section of the NASA/Johnson Space Center (Giarratano[22]). Although CLIPS is a language designed for writing expert systems, it could be used to develop and execute simulation models. The basic elements of CLIPS are (a) a fact base, (b) a knowledge base, and (c) an inference engine. A program written in CLIPS consists of facts and rules. The facts represent the major component of the declarative knowledge of the model, while the rules constitute the procedural knowledge of the model. The inference engine decides which rules should be executed.

2.3.2 *Declarative Knowledge*

CLIPs language has three basic components, declarative data, procedural data, and the inference engine that relates the two. Declarative data in CLIPs consist of facts. Facts can be simple structures, such as goals, or they can be complex structures called templates. A template defines a complex fact with associated fields or attributes. Two major templates were defined for this model, a resource template and a task template. Figure 2 illustrates the resource template.

The first line of Figure 2 defines the template for resources. A resource represents a class of objects that share the same fields. Therefore, this template was used to define those common fields for the class of objects assigned the name "resource."

The second line defines a name for each resource that was created. This name was distinct and was used for matching resource status in the rules. Lines 3 and 4 indicate that a limited number of resource names were allowed in the model: (a) vision, (b) audition, (c) cognition, (d) left-hand, (e) right-hand, and, (f) speech. This limitation enabled the model to check that only allowable names were used, otherwise no match could occur on the resource name.

Line Number	Code for CLIPs Resource Fact Template
1	(deftemplate resource "define the resource object"
2	(slot name (type SYMBOL)(default ?NONE)
3	(allowed-words vision audition cognition
4	right-hand left-hand speech none))
5	(slot status (type SYMBOL)(default idle)
6	(allowed-words idle busy))
7	(slot sum-used (type FLOAT)(default 0.0)
8	(slot sum used squared (type NUMBER)
9	(default 0.0))
10	(slot mean (type FLOAT)(default 0.0))
11	(slot stdev (type FLOAT)(default 0.0)))

Figure 2.   Resource Template

The status of the resource is addressed in lines 5 and 6. Either the resource status of "idle" or "busy" was allowed. Depending on the status, the system either implemented or delayed tasks requiring that resource. Execution time of the task as well as delay times were affected by the resource utilization state. The remaining five lines of code define statistical variables to be controlled. In order to collect statistics on the utilization of the resources, data had to be gathered on the amount of time the resource was busy. Therefore, two more fields were defined for this template, the sum-used and the sum-used-squared. These were used to compute the mean utilization rate and standard deviation by recording these times each time the resource changed status.

The second template in the model defined the tasks that the aircrew performed. Figure 3 presents the CLIPS coded task template. Again, templates are the mechanism for defining task attributes and are used by the rules to scan the tasks, or activities, for patterns of data that will allow task execution. The first attribute of the task is the name - again, an identifying keyword (see Figure 3, line 2).

Line Number	CLIPs Code for Task Template
1	(deftemplate task "define the network task template"
2	(slot name (type WORD)(default ?NONE))
3	(slot status (type WORD)(default null))
4	(allowed-words null planned enabled
5	activated executing completed))
6	(slot goal (type WORD)(default ?NONE)
7	(slot resource (type WORD)(default ?NONE)
8	(allowed-words vision audition cognition
9	right-hand left-hand speech))
10	(slot child-of (type WORD) (default none))
11	(slot parent-of (type WORD)(default none))
12	(slot predecessor (type WORD)(default none))
13	(slot successor (type WORD)(default none))
14	(slot start-time (type NUMBER)(default 0))
15	(slot end-time (type NUMBER)(default 0))
16	(slot priority (type WOrD)(default ?NONE)
17	(allowed-words survival effective
18	efficiency))
19	(slot mean (type NUMBER)(default 0))
20	(slot stdev (type NUMBER)(default 0))
21	(slot condition (type WOrD)(default no)
22	(allowed-words yes no))
23	(slot demand (type NUMBER)(default 0))
24	(slot repeat (type WORD)(default no)
25	(allowed-words yes no))
26	(slot information (type WORD)(default none)))

Figure 3. Task Template Code

The field illustrated on the third line of Figure 3 is the task status. When tasks were first defined, they had a status of "null'. However, rules in the model dictated when a task status would change. The task status and conditions for those allowable status values consisted of (Sacerdoti[23]):

    1. Planned = goal for task has been asserted.

    2. Enabled = predecessor task has been completed.

3. Activated = all preconditions have been met.

4. Executing = resource seized.

5. Completed = task conditions met.

In order for a task to be considered "planned", a goal must have been asserted. The goal field, described on line 6 of the task template, was used as part of the pattern-matching rules governing task planning. Defining the system in this way, made it a truly goal-oriented model of the pilot. Although, in this study project, one goal triggered a whole procedure, the model was defined with the ability to propagate goals throughout the procedure while integrating a variety of tasks. The major goals employed in this model consisted of: (a) fly-aircraft, (b) establish comm, (c) select IFF, and (d) select new waypoint. These goals were used to trigger (a) flying the aircraft, (b) inputting a manual frequency change, (c) inputting an IFF code, and (d) entering new waypoint coordinates, respectively.

The next set of fields (see Figure 3, lines 13 and 14) consists of predecessor and successor fields that allowed the model to traverse through a network of tasks that constituted a procedure. Rules were developed to examine the status of the predecessor and to insure that it was completed prior to activating the next task. Several tasks could be executed simultaneously, as long as they were members of different sub-networks. If a task was the first task of a procedure, it's predecessor was assigned the status of "nil". Also, if a task was the last task in a procedure, it's successor was set to "nil".

Task beginning and ending times were recorded when the task began execution and when it completed execution (see Figure 3, lines 15 and 16). Those data could be used to calculate average task execution times, if those data were deemed necessary. This proved particularly useful when tasks were repeated throughout a model execution. The repetitive tasks in this study were flight tasks.

Although resource availability and preconditions were used to dictate which tasks should be executed, there was also a priority scheme incorporated in the model. The priority could be (a) survival, (b) effectiveness, and (c) efficiency (see Figure 3, lines 17-19). In the rules, survival tasks have the highest priority, followed by effectiveness and, finally, efficiency. Therefore, as the activities were scanned, prioritization was employed. Another priority scheme, that may be implemented in the future involves defining a deadline for a task. Then, a criticality based on the time available to perform the task could be computed.

Once a task has met all conditions, including resource availability, the task completion must be scheduled. The next two fields, mean and standard deviation, were derived from the task analysis described in the earlier data gathering section. Those data were put into the task profile and employed using an appropriate distribution function to determine the random task execution times. Often, an empirical distribution was used.

2.3.3   Procedural Knowledge

The facts described in the previous section defined the state of the system at any time. The rules for the human performance model provided the mechanism for scanning all of these facts, recognizing a specific pattern of facts, and choosing which rule to execute. The types of rules available in this model consisted of (a) changing the status of a task or activity, (b) setting a new goal, and (c) advancing time in the simulated clock. When a rule was executed, new facts could be asserted and old ones could be either retracted or modified. New or modified facts could trigger execution of another rule by providing a pattern that matched the conditional part of the rule. This discussion of procedural knowledge describes the structure of rules employed in CLIPS as well as each of the rules developed for this pilot performance model.

If (conditions or rules are matched for pattern)

Then (execute statement)

Figure 4. Standard Rules for CLIPS

The standard rule employed for CLIPS is illustrated in Figure 4. The conditions on the conditional side of this rule structure typically represented a set of fact values that the model recognized. An inference engine, such as that imbedded in CLIPS, provided the most efficient algorithms for pattern recognition. Therefore, construction of the rules remained the most challenging activity for the modeler.

As mentioned before, the major rule types for the human performance model consisted of (a) changing task status, (b) setting new goals, and (c) advancing time. The potential task status consisted of (a) null, (b) planned, (c) enabled, (d) activated, (e) executing, and (f) completed. The first task status modification rule was:

If

status = null
goal of task is posted

> **Then**
>> modify task status to planned

The next rule developed for this model was the enabling rule that advanced the task to enabled status when a predecessor task was completed. If this was the beginning task, it became enabled automatically. The rule read as follows:

> **If**
>> the task status = planned
>> task predecessor = completed or nil
> **Then**
>> change status = enabled.

In order for a task to proceed to the next status and be activated, one of two conditions had to be true. Either a task had no preconditions to meet, so it was enabled, or the preconditions were met, and it was currently enabled. Although none of the current tasks had preconditions, this stage was incorporated into the model for future growth. When a task had assumed the activated status, it could become "executing." When a task became "activated," it was essentially waiting in a queue for the resources required to execute it.

When a task was in an activated state, and it required a resource to execute, the rule for changing the status of the task to "executing" checked the state of the demanded resource. If the demanded resource was idle, then the resource was "seized," (i.e., the state of the resource was modified to "busy" and the task status was modified to "executing"). Also, a random sample was used to schedule the task completion time. When the task began executing, the time of execution was recorded by the model for use in calculating total execution time and resource utilization time.

When the task completion time exceeded the clock time "tnow," then the resource was modified to the idle state and the task status was modified to the complete state. In addition, the running total of resource usage time was updated with the total time that the task was executed. This time factor was used at the end of the simulation execution to compute the statistics on resource utilization.

Another form of procedural knowledge investigated was the rule for advancing the clock. Every time a task was scheduled for execution, the event-time fact was asserted with the time of the completion of the task. A rule was developed to match on the latest event-time fact and update "tnow" when all activity had been completed for the current time. In this way the simulation was a

384

"next event" simulation, since it did not require the model to time step through the total modeling horizon. The rule was written as follows:

> **If**   event-time > tnow
>   event-time < other-event-time
> **Then**
>   assert new tnow = event-time

In addition, when "tnow" exceeded the target simulation cycle, the model terminated execution and report statistics of model execution and resource utilization.

A mechanism for predicting pilot workload was required. Wicken's[24] Multiple Resource Theory was deemed inappropriate due to the fact that it assumed several tasks using the same visual, cognitive or motor resource could be performed simultaneously (McCoy[21]). This same study found conventional single channel operator models to be inadequate because they did not address conflict between tasks being performed simultaneously using different resources. Therefoe, a technique was developed that combined these two methods to predict pilot workload, estimate the workload to performance relationship, and adjust task performance based on this relationship.

By using a single channel operator mechanism, the problem of multiple tasks using the same resource was eliminated. However, the conflict matrix was incorporated from the pilots associate program model (Pilots Associate[25]) and the workload calculation developed by North[26] was used to estimate workload each time a task began or completed execution. Next, a performance operating characteristic, as reported by Boff and Lincoln[27] was introduced into the model. This characteristic provided a threshold for comparison of pilot workload. When workload exceeded the threshold, all active task scheduled completion times were extended. When workload decreased below the threshold, all active task completion times were readjusted to reflect better performance (McCoy[21]).

Once the model was developed, verification and validation had to be performed. The process for verification and validation was fully described, along with the results in McCoy[21].

3. Display Change Management

Once the human performance model has been developed and verified, the knowledge about the human activity (tasks) and information requirements have been acquired and incorporated into a form useful for reasoning about the operators situation awareness. The next step is to develop an assessor and a planning system. The assessor is the mechanism of determining operator tasks requirements and goals. In addition, based on operator task goals, information requirements can be derived. These requirements must be asserted as a set of goals to present specific information to the operator in preparation for accomplishing the planning of information display.

Once the goal for information display change has been asserted in concert with anticipated operator activity, the display change management function must be developed. This system prioritizes the goals based on the appropriate criticality of the tasks being anticipated by the task planning system. Again, the priority of the information could be characterized as contributing to survival, effectiveness and efficiency. Another aspect of the planner must be to reason along three dimensions of presentation of information. The first dimension would be modal. The question becomes whether to show the information on a visual display or alert the operator through voice generated messages. If the operator is flying at low level, looking inside the cockpit may not be a reasonable thing to do. Verbal messages are then the better method of presentation of information.

The second dimension to reason about in the display change management planning system is spatial. If the information is to be presented visually, the question becomes whether to present it in a heads up display or heads down display. If in the heads down displays, which of the typical multiple display devices should be used to present the information, and which current information should be displaced.

Finally, the last dimension to reason about in display change management is temporal. The system needs to determine if the information is important enough, relative to all other current displays and plans to be presented immediately or can the presentation be delayed until other issues and tasks have been performed. In all of these situation, the display change management planning system can operator much like a typical planning system as described in Russell and Norbvig[28].

4. Conclusion

Expert systems can be used to regulate and aid the pilot in display change management. By using typical planning algorithms, display change management can reason across many dimensions in helping the pilot maintain situation awareness. These systems can then be used to aid in formulating the information and choosing the most efficient and effective method of presentation. When the pilot maintains a high degree of situation awareness, survivability is enhanced and effectiveness can be achieved.

5. Bibliography

1. Sheridan, T. B. (1992). <u>Telerobotics, automation, and human supervisory control</u>. Cambridge, MA: MIT Press.
2. Siegel, A. I., & Wolf, J. J. (1969). <u>Man-machine simulation models</u>. New York: John Wiley & Sons.
3. Asiala, C. F., Miller, J. T., Wilper, B. L., & McCoy, M. S. (1982). <u>Israeli ministry of defense pilot workload assessment users' reference guide</u> . St. Louis, MO: McDonnell Douglas Corp.
4. Elkind, J.I., Card, S.K., Hochberg, J., & Huey, B.M. (Eds.). (1989). <u>Human performance models for computer-aided engineering</u>. Washington, DC: National Academy Press.
5. Hunt, R.M. and W.B. Rouse (1984) A fuzzy rule-based model of human problem solving. <u>IEEE Transactions on Systems, Man and Cybernetics</u> SMC-14:112-120.
6. Minskey, M.L. (1968), Monitoring behavior and supervisory control. In K. Boff, L. Kaufmann, & J. Beatty, eds., <u>Handbook of Human Perception and Performance</u>. New York: John Wiley & Sons.
7. Schank, R. C., & Abelson, R. P. (1977). <u>Scripts, plans, goals, and understanding</u>. Hillsdale, NJ: Lawrence Erlbaum Associates.
8. Baron, S., Kruser, D. S., & Huey, B. M. (Eds.). (1990). <u>Quantitative modeling of human performance in complex dynamic systems</u>. Washington, DC: National Academy Press.
9. Pilots Aassociate Program, phase 1 -- Final report . (1991). (Report No. MDC 91B0012). St. Louis, MO: McDonnell Douglas Corp.

10. Nisbett, R. E., & Wilson, T. D. (1977) Telling more than we can know: Verbal reports on mental processes. Psychological Review, 84, 231-259.

11. Harris, R.M., Iavecchia, H. P., Ross, L. V., & Shaffer, S. C. (1987). Microcomputer human operator simulator (HOS-IV). Proceedings of the 32nd Annual Meeting of the Human Factors Society. Santa Monica, CA: Human Factors.

12. Wickens, C. D. (1989). Resource management and time-sharing. In J. I. Elkind, S. K. Card, J. Hochberg, & B. M. Huey (Eds.), Human performance models for computer-aided engineering. Washington, DC: National Academy Press.

13. Sage, A. P. (1991). Decision support systems engineering. New York: John Wiley & Sons.17. Wise J. & C. Asiala, (1977), F-18 Human Engineering Task Analysis Report (Fighter Task Analysis - Part 1), MDC A4276-1, St. Louis, Mo.: McDonnell Aircraft Co.

14. Morris, N. M., Rouse, W. B., & Ward, S. L. (1985). Experimental evaluation of adaptive task allocation in the aerial search environment. IFAC Man-Machine Systems, Varese, Italy.

15. McCoy, M. S., & Boys, R. (1987). Human performance models applied to intelligent decision support systems. National Aerospace and Electronics Conference (NAECON).

16. Wise, J., C. Asiale, (1977). F-18 Human Engineering Task Analysis Report (Fighter Task Analysis - Part 1), MDC A4276-1, St. Louis, Mo.: McDonnell Aircraft Co.

17. Wise, J., C. Asiala, & S. Loy, (1977). F-18 Human Engineering Task Analysis - Part II: Timeline and Workload Analysis (Fighter Task Analysis), MDC A4276-2, St. Louis, Mo.: McDonnell Aircraft Co.

18. McCoy, M. S., Hunter, M., Seavers, C., & McClure, A. (1993). Human engineering dynamic simulation plan (Report No. MDC 93B0082, Rev. A). St. Louis, MO: McDonnell Douglas Corp.

19. McCoy, M. S., & Seavers, C. R. (1993). Human engineering systems analysis report (HESAR) (Report No. MDC 93B0081, Rev. A). St. Louis, MO: McDonnell Douglas Corp.

20. Card, S. K., Moran, T. P., & Newel, A. (1983). The psychology of human-computer interaction. Hillsdale, NJ: Lawrence Erlbaum Associate..

21. McCoy, M. S. (1995). A Rule-Based Pilot Performance Model, Ph. D. Dissertation, St. Louis, Mo.: St. Louis University.

22. Giarratano, J.C. (1993). <u>CLIPS user's guide</u>. Houston, TX: NASA Lyndon B. Johnson Space Center, Information Systems Directorate, Software Technology Branch

23. Sacerdoti, E. D. (1977). <u>A structure for plans and behavior</u>. New York: Elsevier, North Holland, Inc.

24. Wickens, C. D. (1985). The multiple resource model of human performance: Implications for display design. <u>AGARD Conference Proceedings</u>, <u>371</u>, 17-1 to 17-6.

25. Pilots Associate Program, technical operating report (TOR) system design document . (1990). (Report No. MDC B2517). St. Louis, MO: McDonnell Douglas Corp.

26. North, R. A. (1985). WINDEX: A workload index for interactive crew station evaluation. <u>Proceedings NAECON</u>. New York: IEEE.

27. Boff, K., & Lincoln, J. (Eds.). (1988). <u>Engineering data compendium: human perception and performance</u>. Wright-Pattterson Air Force Base, OH: Harry G. Armstrong Aerospace Medical Research Laboratory.

28. Russell, S.J. and P. Norvig. (1995). <u>Artificial Intelligence: A Modern Approach</u>. Englewood Cliffs, New Jersey: Prentice Hall, Inc..

Problems

1. List potential procedures to be modeled in the following areas: Navigation, Flight Control, Communications, Sensor Management and Weapons Management.

2. Which of the following are examples of declarative knowledge?
Task execution time
Task predecessor
Task selection criteria
Information required for task
Time advance mechanism
Task priority
Resource Demand
Resource Selection

3. Which of the items in (2) are examples of procedural knowledge?

4. How would a human performance model be used in model based reasoning?

5. Give two examples of rules that could be incorporated into the model.

APPROXIMATING BLOCK ACCESSES IN DATABASE SYSTEMS

Lu Cui
Department of Computer Science
Florida State University
Tallahassee, FL 32306

A. Kandel
Department of Computer Science and Engineering
University of South Florida
Tampa, FL 33620
e-mail: kandel@csee.usf.edu

In this study, highly accurate, noniterative, closed form approximation formulas for calculating the expected number of block hits by a query in a database system are developed. The error bounds of the new formulas have been obtained in a thorough error analysis. The error bounds show that the approximations suggested in this study are almost identical to the exact value of the expected number and the accuracy of the approximations can be improved as the number of blocks in a database increases.

1 Introduction

Due to well known reasons such as limited core memory and the need for long time storage, data records of a database are often stored in the form of files and grouped into blocks in secondary storage devices, mainly disk drives. This is the case in both classical databases as well as in fuzzy databases [27].

Since this, the selection of the physical database organization used in a database system has a very important effect on the overall system performance. The right physical design can result in high efficiency and low cost of a database system in terms of execution and maintenance. This is especially meaningful for large databases. With respect to system performance, many design issues such as serial versus direct access search, indexing structures, and optimization of query processing are raised and subject to intensive studies (see [2], [3], [4], [6], [10], [12], [14], [16], [21] and [24]).

One way to determine which kind of physical organization should be used is as follows:

(i)   modeling the system analytically,

(ii)   estimating the costs of the system based on the model, and

(iii)   choosing the strategies which minimize the costs according to the design goal.

Usually the estimated costs can be expressed as cost functions or cost equations in the form

$$cost = h(\alpha, X) + g(\beta), \tag{1.1}$$

where α and β are vectors consisting of performance parameters, such as seek time, rotation latency, etc. which affect the system performance significantly, and where X is the number of blocks hit by a query. $h(\alpha, X)$ may be linear in X. Since in general X is a random quantity, instead of dealing directly with the cost functions, people usually use the average cost functions

$$cost = h(\alpha, E(X)) + g(\beta),$$

where $E(X)$ is the expectation of X under a certain assumption on the distribution of X. Many optimal design problems can be approached by minimizing the average cost functions (see [2], [4], [10], [12], [14], [21] and [24]). Also, instead of $E(X)$ a similar approach can be developed using the Fuzzy Expected Value (FEV) [8], [9], [15].

This approach provides a search for the typical membership grade in a fuzzy set from which one can identify typical elements. Typical membership grades are computed by the FEV expressed by

$$FEV = \sup_{0 \le \alpha \le 1} \left\{ \min\left(\alpha, \frac{|A_\alpha|}{n} \right) \right\}$$

where $|A_\alpha|$ is the cardinality of the α-cut of a fuzzy subset A and n is the number of items. Hence a typical element is viewed as one having a typical membership grade. This notion of a typical value in a set is directly related to both data summarization and approximate evaluations. The approach may be applied to sets of numerical data as well as to sets of symbolic data, and is of major interest in the area of knowledge discovery in databases (KDD) and data mining (DM).

Given the occurrence of the random variable X in (1.1), the following two factors play important roles in the applications of the cost functions:

(i)   the correct assumption on the distribution of X, and

(ii) the correct computation of $E(X)$.

Regarding (i), an assumption which is widely accepted and in many applications is being used by designers and researchers of database systems is that the records in a database system have equal probability to be hit by a query (i.e. a uniform distribution). The experiments have shown that this assumption is valid in many kinds of real world database systems (for example, the payroll database systems). It should be mentioned, however, that this is definitely not the case in inventory systems (e.g. supermarkets).

Issue (ii) attracts a lot of attention of database researchers (see [1], [4], [5], [11], [13], [18], [19], [20], [22], [25], [26]). Among them, J. Waters ([20]), S.B.

Yao ([25]), and P.C. Yue and C.K. Wong ([26]) independently derived the expressions of $E(X)$ under the assumption of uniform distribution. It was shown later that their formulas were equivalent ([13] and [22]). We give the well known formula for $E(X)$ obtained by Yao ([25]) as the following:

$$E(X) = m(1 - \frac{(n-k)!(n-p)!}{n!(n-p-k)!}),$$ (1.2)

where m = the number of the blocks, n = the total number of records in the database, p = the block factor, k = the number of records satisfying the query, and $k \leq n - p$ which guarantees the nontrivial case. Subsequent to Yao's ideal, slightly different formulas for expected hit numbers have been developed in slightly different design environments. For instance, the author of [1] considered deriving the expression of the expected number of distinct values in the projection of a relational database by taking the previous knowledge on the relations into account. The author of [5] considered computing $E(X)$ assuming that the duplication of tuples may exist in a database. Similar analysis can be performed with the Fuzzy Expected Value (FEV) and the theory of typicality [8], [9], [15].

All exact formulas for $E(X)$ have a common major disadvantage; the computation is difficult and expensive because of the factorials involved in the formulas. It is especially true when a database system has more than a hundred thousand records. This disadvantage makes the exact formulas almost useless in practice. Therefore, from a practical point of view, it is necessary to develop accurate, noniterative, closed form formulas to approximate the exact expectations. This has been the subject of considerable research ([4], [13], [18], [19], [20] and [22]). Among them, the authors of [22] suggested the following approximation to (1.2)

$$b^{(0)}_{m,p,k} = (1 - (1 - \frac{1}{m})^k) + (\frac{1}{m^2 p} \times k(k-1)(1 - \frac{1}{m})^{k-1}/2) +$$ (1.3)

$$+ (1.5/m^3 p^4 \times k(k-1)(2k-1)/6 \times (1 - 1/m)^{k-1}).$$

Although the existing approximation formulas can solve part of computation problems of $E(X)$ in (1.2), they all suffer the following deficiencies.

(i) In general, their accuracy depends on some nonessential restrictions on the relationship of p, k, and n or m. Only when those restrictions are satisfied, the formulas will have usable accuracy. This problem limits the scope of the use of such approximations.

(ii) No complete error analyses are given with the existing approximations except some simple numerical error checking at the special values of k, p, and n; especially for small n due to the difficulty of computing the exact value of $E(X)$.

For example, in [13] the error checking is done only for $p = 1, 5, 10$, and 15 with n as small as 300. Although the authors of [22] studied the accuracy of (1.3) through an intensive computation and observed that a 3.7% relative error may result, the maximum error of (1.3) still remains unknown. The computational error checking may answer how bad an approximation formula is by detecting the large errors.

394

However, the question of how good an approximation formula is, can not be answered by computational error checking without using certain optimization methods. The incomplete error analyses in the previous works cause confusion and hurt the credibility of the approximations. Unfortunately, those approximation formulas are still used in practice.

In this paper, we continue the study of the second issue and develop new and better noniterative approximations for Yao's exact value, $E(X)$ given in (1.2), which is extensively used in the literatures. Through a thorough error analysis we can see that our formulas achieve a high degree of accuracy. Without any special restrictions on p, k, and n, the values computed by our formulas are almost identical to the exact value of $E(X)$.

In section 2, we will derive our new noniterative, closed form formulas to compute the expected number of blocks hit by a query given in (1.2).

Let

$$f_{p,k,n} = \frac{(n-p)^{n-p+\frac{1}{2}}(n-k)^{n-k+\frac{1}{2}}}{n^{n+\frac{1}{2}}(n-p-k)^{n-p-k+\frac{1}{2}}} .$$

Let

$$u_1 = exp(\frac{12p+1}{12(n-p)(12n+1)} - \frac{12p-1}{12(n-k)(12(n-p-k)+1)})$$

and let

$$l_1 = exp(\frac{12p-1}{12n(12(n-p)+1)} - \frac{12p+1}{12(n-p-k)(12(n-k)+1)}).$$

The first approximation formula we suggest is

$$b_{p,k,n}^{(1)} = m(1 - f_{p,k,n}(\frac{u_1+l_1}{2})).$$

Now let

$$f'_{p,k,n} = \frac{\sqrt{2\pi}(n-p)^{n-p+\frac{1}{2}}(n-k)^{n-k+\frac{1}{2}}}{n^{n+\frac{1}{2}}(n-p-k)!e^{n-p-k}}$$

Let

$$u_2 = exp(\frac{1}{12(n-p)} + \frac{1}{12(n-k)} - \frac{1}{12n+1})$$

and

$$l_2 = exp(\frac{1}{12(n-p)+1} + \frac{1}{12(n-k)+1} - \frac{1}{12n}).$$

The second noniterative approximation formula to Yao's exact formula is

$$b_{p,k,n}^{(2)} = m(1 - f'_{p,k,n}(\frac{u_2+l_2}{2})).$$

We suggest the use of $b_{p,k,n}^{(1)}$ as an approximation of $E(X)$ in (1.2) if $n - p - k$ is large, (e.g. $n - p - k \geq 5$). If $n - p - k$ is small, especially $n - p - k = 0$, we may use $b_{p,k,n}^{(2)}$ as an alternative. In this case we note that the small factorial in the expression of $b_{p,k,n}^{(2)}$ is very easy to compute.

In section 3, we will do the error analysis on our formulas and discuss several other advantageous properties of those formulas.

Let E_1 and E_2 denote the absolute values of the relative errors of $b_{p,k,n}^{(1)}$ and $b_{p,k,n}^{(2)}$ respectively. The upper bounds of E_1 and E_2 can be given as

$$E_1 < 0.506(\frac{4}{72np} + \frac{1}{72k(n-p-k)} + \frac{13 \times min(\frac{n-p}{n-k}, \frac{p}{k})}{12 \times 144(n-p-k)^2}),$$

and

$$E_2 < 0.506(\frac{5}{144np} + \frac{1}{144(n-k)k}).$$

These error bounds are easy to use and they reveal some dependencies of the errors on p, k, and n. For our formulas, there are no special restrictions except the request that $m \geq 2$ and $k \leq n - p$, which guarantees the nontrivial case. The direct computations of the formulas for error bounds show that the absolute value of the overall relative error, using our first approximation, will not exceed 0.42% when the number of blocks exceeds nine. In this case, the absolute value of the overall relative error, when $b_{p,k,n}^{(2)}$ is used, will not exceed 0.22%. The achieved accuracy is such that our formulas can be regarded as the exact ones to use. In section 4, we will give a numerical comparison of the new and previous approximations.

2 Noniterative Formulas

In this section we will derive the alternative approximations for Yao's exact formula. In the next section we will see that those formulas achieve great accuracy and have some good convergent properties.

In this study, we will always assume that the number of blocks $m \geq 2$ and the number of records satisfying a query $k \leq n - p$. These assumptions prevent the trivial case that all blocks are always hit by a query. We also assume that the block factor $p = n/m$ is an integer, where n is the total number of records, since Yao's exact formula is true only for an integral block factor. We also assume the equal hit probability for the records of the database.

Let X denote the number of blocks hit by a query and let X' denote the number of blocks not hit by the query. We have

$$X + X' = m. \tag{2.1}$$

According to Yao (see [25]), the expected number of blocks not hit by a query is

$$E(X') = m\frac{C_k^{n-p}}{C_k^n}$$

$$= m\frac{(n-p)!(n-k)!}{n!(n-p-k)!}. \tag{2.2}$$

Hence the expectation of the number of blocks hit by a query is

$$E(X) = m - E(X') \tag{2.3}$$

$$= m(1 - \frac{C_k^{n-p}}{C_k^n}) \tag{2.4}$$

$$= m(1 - \frac{(n-p)!(n-k)!}{n!(n-p-k)!}). \tag{2.5}$$

In the following, we first get the approximations for $E(X')$ and then, according to (2.3), construct the noniterative formulas to approximate $E(X)$ using the obtained approximations. This strategy allows us to avoid the great difficulties both in the derivation and in the error analysis caused by the direct approximations to $E(X)$.

Define

$$\alpha_{p,k,n} = \frac{(n-p)!(n-k)!}{n!(n-p-k)!}.$$

According to (2.2),

$$E(X') = m\alpha_{p,k,n}.$$

Therefore, to approximate $E(X')$ we only need to approximate $\alpha_{p,k,n}$.

The following lemma is useful in our discussion.

Lemma 2.1. $\alpha_{p,k,n}$ monotonically decreases as p or k increases.

Proof. By the definition of $\alpha_{p,k,n}$

$$\frac{\alpha_{p,k,n}}{\alpha_{p,k-1,n}} = \frac{(n-p)!(n-k)!}{n!(n-p-k)!} \cdot \frac{n!(n-p-k+1)!}{(n-p)!(n-k+1)!}$$

$$= \frac{(n-k)!}{(n-k+1)!} \cdot \frac{(n-p-k+1)!}{(n-p-k)!}$$

$$= \frac{(n-p-k+1)}{(n-k+1)}$$

$$= 1 - \frac{p}{(n-k+1)}$$

$$< 1.$$

Hence $\alpha_{p,k,n} < \alpha_{p,k-1,n}$. It is that $\alpha_{p,k,n}$ monotonically decreases as k increases.

Similarly

$$\frac{\alpha_{p,k,n}}{\alpha_{p-1,k,n}} = \frac{(n-p)!(n-k)!}{n!(n-p-k)!} \cdot \frac{n!(n-p-k+1)!}{(n-p+1)!(n-k)!}$$

$$= \frac{(n-p)!}{(n-p+1)!} \cdot \frac{(n-p-k+1)!}{(n-p-k)!}$$

$$= \frac{(n-p-k+1)}{(n-k+1)}$$

$$= 1 - \frac{k}{(n-p+1)}$$

$$< 1.$$

Hence $\alpha_{p,k,n}$ monotonically decreases as p increases. ■

Remark. This result is true intuitively. Since $\alpha_{p,k,n}$ is just the probability that a block is not hit by a query (see [25]), and k and p are the number of records satisfying a query and the number of records in each block respectively, increasing either k or p will reduce the chance that a block will not be hit by the query i.e. reduce $\alpha_{p,k,n}$.

We also need the following lemmas.

Lemma 2.2.

$$\sqrt{2\pi} n^{n+\frac{1}{2}} e^{-n+\frac{1}{12n+1}} < n! < \sqrt{2\pi} n^{n+\frac{1}{2}} e^{-n+\frac{1}{12n}} . \tag{2.6}$$

See [7] for the proof and the discussion of (2.6).

Let

$$f_{p,k,n} = \frac{(n-p)^{n-p+\frac{1}{2}}(n-k)^{n-k+\frac{1}{2}}}{n^{n+\frac{1}{2}}(n-p-k)^{n-p-k+\frac{1}{2}}} . \tag{2.7}$$

Remark. To compute $f_{p,k,n}$ we can compute $log(f_{p,k,n})$, or we can rewrite $f_{p,k,n}$ as

$$f_{p,k,n} = (1 - \frac{p}{n})^{1/2} (1 - \frac{p}{n-k})^{-1/2} \frac{(1-\frac{k}{n})^{n-k}(1-\frac{p+k}{n})^{k}}{(1-\frac{k}{n-p})^{n-p}}$$

and then compute the logarithm of $f_{p,k,n}$.

Let

$$u_1 = exp(\frac{12p+1}{12(n-p)(12n+1)} - \frac{12p-1}{12(n-k)(12(n-p-k)+1)}) \tag{2.8}$$

and let

$$l_1 = exp(\frac{12p-1}{12n(12(n-p)+1)} - \frac{12p+1}{12(n-p-k)(12(n-k)+1)}). \tag{2.9}$$

Lemma 2.3. ∎

$$\alpha_{p,k,n} < u_1 f. \tag{2.10}$$

Proof. By *Lemma 2.2*, we have

$$(n-p)!(n-k)! < \left[\sqrt{2\pi}(n-p)^{n-p+\frac{1}{2}}e^{-(n-p)+\frac{1}{12(n-p)}}\right] \times$$

$$\left[\sqrt{2\pi}(n-k)^{n-k+\frac{1}{2}}e^{-(n-k)+\frac{1}{12(n-k)}}\right] \tag{2.11}$$

and

$$n!(n-p-k)! > \left[\sqrt{2\pi}n^{n+\frac{1}{2}}e^{-n+\frac{1}{12n+1}}\right] \times$$

$$\left[\sqrt{2\pi}(n-p-k)^{n-p-k+\frac{1}{2}}e^{-(n-p-k)+\frac{1}{12(n-p-k)+1}}\right]. \tag{2.12}$$

Combining (2.11) and (2.12) we get

$$\alpha_{p,k,n} < \frac{\sqrt{2\pi}(n-p)^{n-p+\frac{1}{2}}e^{-(n-p)+\frac{1}{12(n-p)}} \cdot \sqrt{2\pi}(n-k)^{n-k+\frac{1}{2}}e^{-(n-k)+\frac{1}{12(n-k)}}}{\sqrt{2\pi}n^{n+\frac{1}{2}}e^{-n+\frac{1}{12n+1}} \cdot \sqrt{2\pi}(n-p-k)^{n-p-k+\frac{1}{2}}e^{-(n-p-k)+\frac{1}{12(n-p-k)+1}}}. \tag{2.13}$$

The right hand side of (2.13) is

$$\frac{(n-p)^{n-p+\frac{1}{2}}(n-k)^{n-k+\frac{1}{2}}}{n^{n+\frac{1}{2}}(n-p-k)^{n-p-k+\frac{1}{2}}} exp(\frac{1}{12(n-p)} +$$

$$\frac{1}{12(n-k)} - \frac{1}{12n+1} - \frac{1}{12(n-p-k)+1})$$

$$= \frac{(n-p)^{n-p+\frac{1}{2}}(n-k)^{n-k+\frac{1}{2}}}{n^{n+\frac{1}{2}}(n-p-k)^{n-p-k+\frac{1}{2}}} exp(\frac{12n+1-12(n-p)}{12(n-p)(12n+1)} +$$

$$+\frac{12(n-p-k)+1-12(n-k)}{12(n-k)(12(n-p-k)+1)})$$

$$=\frac{(n-p)^{n-p+\frac{1}{2}}(n-k)^{n-k+\frac{1}{2}}}{n^{n+\frac{1}{2}}(n-p-k)^{n-p-k+\frac{1}{2}}}exp(\frac{12p+1}{12(n-p)(12n+1)}-$$

$$-\frac{12p-1}{12(n-k)(12(n-p-k)+1)}). \tag{2.14}$$

From the definitions of $f_{p,k,n}$ and u_1 together with (2.13) and (2.14), we get (2.10). The proof of *Lemma 2.3* is completed. ∎

Lemma 2.4.

$$\alpha_{p,k,n} > f_{p,k,n}l_1. \tag{2.15}$$

Proof. By *Lemma 2.2*

$$\alpha_{p,k,n} > \frac{\sqrt{2\pi}(n-p)^{n-p+\frac{1}{2}}e^{-(n-p)+\frac{1}{12(n-p)+1}}\cdot\sqrt{2\pi}(n-k)^{n-k+\frac{1}{2}}e^{-(n-k)+\frac{1}{12(n-k)+1}}}{\sqrt{2\pi}n^{n+\frac{1}{2}}e^{-n+\frac{1}{12n}}\cdot\sqrt{2\pi}(n-p-k)^{n-p-k+\frac{1}{2}}e^{-(n-p-k)+\frac{1}{12(n-p-k)}}}$$

$$=f_{p,k,n}exp(\frac{1}{12(n-p)+1}+\frac{1}{12(n-k)+1}-\frac{1}{12n}-\frac{1}{12(n-p-k)})$$

$$=f_{p,k,n}exp(\frac{12p-1}{12n(12(n-p)+1)}-\frac{12p+1}{12(n-p-k)(12(n-k)+1)}), \tag{2.16}$$

where $f_{p,k,n}$ is defined in (2.7).

Noting the definition of l_1, from (2.16) we get (2.15). The proof is completed. ∎

Now let

$$f'_{p,k,n} = \frac{\sqrt{2\pi}(n-p)^{n-p+\frac{1}{2}}(n-k)^{n-k+\frac{1}{2}}}{n^{n+\frac{1}{2}}(n-p-k)!e^{n-p-k}} \tag{2.17}$$

Remark. To compute $f'_{p,k,n}$ we can compute $log(f'_{p,k,n})$, or rewrite $f'_{p,k,n}$ as

$$f'_{p,k,n} = \frac{\sqrt{2\pi}}{(n-p-k)!}((n-p)(1-\frac{k}{n}))^{1/2}\frac{(1-\frac{k}{n})^{n-k}(\frac{e}{n})^k}{(\frac{e}{n-p})^{n-p}}$$

and then compute the logarithm of $f'_{p,k,n}$.

Let

$$u_2 = exp(\frac{1}{12(n-p)} + \frac{1}{12(n-k)} - \frac{1}{12n+1}) \tag{2.18}$$

and

$$l_2 = exp(\frac{1}{12(n-p)+1} + \frac{1}{12(n-k)+1} - \frac{1}{12n}). \tag{2.19}$$

Lemma 2.5.

$$\alpha_{p,k,n} < f'_{p,k,n}u_2. \tag{2.20}$$

Proof. Using *Lemma 2.2*, we have

$$\frac{(n-p)!(n-k)!}{n!} < \sqrt{2\pi}(n-p)^{n-p+\frac{1}{2}}e^{-(n-p)+\frac{1}{12(n-p)}} \times$$

$$\frac{\sqrt{2\pi}(n-k)^{n-k+\frac{1}{2}}e^{-(n-k)+\frac{1}{12(n-k)}}}{\sqrt{2\pi}(n)^{n+\frac{1}{2}}e^{-n+\frac{1}{12n+1}}}. \tag{2.21}$$

The right hand side of (2.21) is

$$\sqrt{2\pi}\frac{(n-p)^{n-p+\frac{1}{2}}(n-k)^{n-k+\frac{1}{2}}}{n^{n+\frac{1}{2}}e^{n-p-k}}exp(\frac{1}{12(n-p)} + \frac{1}{12(n-k)} - \frac{1}{12n+1}).$$

Hence

$$\frac{(n-p)!(n-k)!}{n!} < \frac{\sqrt{2\pi}(n-p)^{n-p+\frac{1}{2}}(n-k)^{n-k+\frac{1}{2}}}{n^{n+\frac{1}{2}}e^{n-p-k}} \times$$

$$exp(\frac{1}{12(n-p)} + \frac{1}{12(n-k)} - \frac{1}{12n+1}). \tag{2.22}$$

From (2.18), (2.17), (2.22) and the definition of $\alpha_{p,k,n}$, we have

$$\alpha_{p,k,n} < f'_{p,k,n}u_2. \tag{2.23}$$

The proof of the lemma is completed. ∎

Lemma 2.6.

$$\alpha_{p,k,n} > f'_{p,k,n}l_2. \tag{2.24}$$

Proof. Using *Lemma 2.2* again, we have

$$\frac{(n-p)!(n-k)!}{n!} < \sqrt{2\pi}(n-p)^{n-p+\frac{1}{2}}e^{-(n-p)+\frac{1}{12(n-p)+1}} \times$$

$$\frac{\sqrt{2\pi}(n-k)^{n-k+\frac{1}{2}}e^{-(n-k)+\frac{1}{12(n-k)+1}}}{\sqrt{2\pi}(n)^{n+\frac{1}{2}}e^{-n+\frac{1}{12n}}}. \tag{2.25}$$

The right hand side of (2.25) can be written as

$$\frac{\sqrt{2\pi}\,(n-p)^{n-p+\frac{1}{2}}(n-k)^{n-k+\frac{1}{2}}}{n^{n+\frac{1}{2}}e^{n-p-k}}\,exp(\frac{1}{12(n-p)+1}+\frac{1}{12(n-k)+1}-\frac{1}{12n}).$$

From this together with (2.17) and (2.19), we show that (2.24) holds. ∎

THEOREM 2.1. Given the above n, p, k, u_1, l_1, u_2 and l_2 we have

$$lim_{n-p-k\to\infty}\frac{u_1}{l_1}=1 \tag{2.26}$$

and

$$lim_{n\to\infty}\frac{u_2}{l_2}=1. \tag{2.27}$$

Proof. Since $p\le\frac{n}{2}$ and $\frac{p}{n-k}\le 1$, the quantities inside the exponential functions in the expressions of u_1 and l_1 approach zero when $n-p-k$ approaches infinity. Therefore (2.26) is true. A similar argument can be applied to show (2.27).

THEOREM 2.2. Let $\alpha_{p,k,n}^{(1)}$ be $(\frac{u_1+l_1}{2})f_{p,k,n}$ and let $\alpha_{p,k,n}^{(2)}$ be $(\frac{u_2+l_2}{2})f'_{p,k,n}$. Let $b_{p,k,n}^{(1)}=m(1-\alpha_{p,k,n}^{(1)})$ and $b_{p,k,n}^{(2)}=m(1-\alpha_{p,k,n}^{(2)})$. Then the absolute values of the differences from $b_{p,k,n}^{(1)}$ and from $b_{p,k,n}^{(2)}$ to the value computed from Yao's formula will not exceed $(\frac{u_1-l_1}{2})f_{p,k,n}m$ and $(\frac{u_2-l_2}{2})f'_{p,k,n}m$ respectively.

Proof. From *Lemma 2.3* and *Lemma 2.4*

$$m(1-u_1 f_{p,k,n})<m(1-\alpha_{p,k,n})<m(1-l_1 f_{p,k,n}).$$

Hence the value computed by Yao's formula falls into the interval I_1, $(m(1-u_1 f_{p,k,n}),m(1-l_1 f_{p,k,n}))$. Since

$$b_{p,k,n}^{(1)} = m(1-\alpha_{p,k,n}^{(1)})$$

$$= m(1-(\frac{u_1+l_1}{2})f_{p,k,n})$$

$$= \frac{m(1-l_1 f_{p,k,n})+m(1-u_1 f_{p,k,n})}{2},$$

i.e. the middle point of I_1, the absolute value of the difference between $b_{p,k,n}^{(1)}$ and the value computed by Yao's formula will not exceed half of the length of I_1, i.e. $(\frac{u_1-l_1}{2})f_{p,k,n}m.$

Using *Lemma 2.5* and *Lemma 2.6* and applying a similar argument on $b^{(2)}_{p,k,n}$, we can easily show the remaining portion of our theorem.

THEOREM 2.1 and *THEOREM 2.2* imply that we may take $b^{(1)}_{p,k,n}$, and $b^{(2)}_{p,k,n}$ as approximations of Yao's formula. According to *THEOREM 2.1*, we may expect that the absolute error of $b^{(1)}_{p,k,n}$ approaches as $(n-p-k)$ increases. When $n-p-k$ is small, especially when it is zero, we can use $b^{(2)}_{p,k,n}$ as an alternative approximation. In this case, the corresponding error could vanish as n increases. The issue of how good are our approximations will be studied in the next section.

3 Error Analysis

In this section, we will discuss issues related to the error analyses of our formulas, and for that we present the following lemmas.

Lemma 3.1 Let E_1 and E_2 be the absolute values of the relative errors of $b^{(1)}_{p,k,n}$ and $b^{(2)}_{p,k,n}$ respectively. Then

$$E_1 = \frac{\alpha_{p,k,n}}{1-\alpha_{p,k,n}} \cdot \frac{\left|\alpha_{p,k,n} - \alpha^{(1)}_{p,k,n}\right|}{\alpha_{p,k,n}} \tag{3.1}$$

and

$$E_2 = \frac{\alpha_{p,k,n}}{1-\alpha_{p,k,n}} \cdot \frac{\left|\alpha_{p,k,n} - \alpha^{(2)}_{p,k,n}\right|}{\alpha_{p,k,n}} \tag{3.2}$$

Proof.

$$\begin{aligned}
E_1 &= \frac{\left|m(1-\alpha_{p,k,n}) - b^{(1)}_{p,k,n}\right|}{m(1-\alpha_{p,k,n})} \\
&= \frac{\left|m(1-\alpha_{p,k,n}) - m(1-\alpha^{(1)}_{p,k,n})\right|}{m(1-\alpha_{p,k,n})} \\
&= \frac{\alpha_{p,k,n}}{1-\alpha_{p,k,n}} \cdot \frac{\left|\alpha_{p,k,n} - \alpha^{(1)}_{p,k,n}\right|}{\alpha_{p,k,n}} .
\end{aligned}$$

$$E_2 = \frac{\left|m(1-\alpha_{p,k,n}) - b^{(2)}_{p,k,n}\right|}{m(1-\alpha_{p,k,n})}$$

$$= \frac{\left| m(1-\alpha_{p,k,n}) - m(1-\alpha^{(2)}_{p,k,n}) \right|}{m(1-\alpha_{p,k,n})}$$

$$= \frac{\alpha_{p,k,n}}{1-\alpha_{p,k,n}} \cdot \frac{\left| \alpha_{p,k,n} - \alpha^{(2)}_{p,k,n} \right|}{\alpha_{p,k,n}} \, .$$

The proof is completed. $\blacksquare$

Remark. Note that the second factors in (3.1) and (3.2) are the relative errors of $\alpha^{(1)}_{p,k,n}$ and $\alpha^{(2)}_{p,k,n}$ to $\alpha_{p,k,n}$ accordingly. The next lemma gives the error bounds.

Lemma 3.2

$$E_1 < \frac{\omega}{2}(\frac{u_1}{l_1} - 1) \tag{3.3}$$

and

$$E_2 < \frac{\omega}{2}(\frac{u_2}{l_2} - 1), \tag{3.4}$$

where $\omega = min(\frac{n-p}{p}, \frac{n-k}{k})$.

Proof. First we show that

$$\frac{\alpha_{p,k,n}}{1-\alpha_{p,k,n}} < \omega. \tag{3.5}$$

By *Lemma 2.1* $\alpha_{p,k,n}$ decreases as p increases. thus

$$\alpha_{p,k,n} < \alpha_{1,k,n}.$$

Since

$$\alpha_{1,k,n} = \frac{(n-1)!(n-k)!}{n!(n-k-1)!}$$

$$= \frac{n-k}{n}$$

$$= 1 - \frac{k}{n},$$

$$\alpha_{p,k,n} < 1 - \frac{k}{n}.$$

Hence

$$1 - \alpha_{p,k,n} > \frac{k}{n}.$$

Therefore

$$\frac{1}{1-\alpha_{p,k,n}} < \frac{n}{k}.$$

Hence

$$\frac{\alpha_{p,k,n}}{1-\alpha_{p,k,n}} < \frac{1-k/n}{k/n} = \frac{n-k}{n}\frac{n}{k},$$

i.e.

$$\frac{\alpha_{p,k,n}}{1-\alpha_{p,k,n}} < \frac{n-k}{k}. \tag{3.6}$$

Because of the duality of p and k in our problem, we can replace k on the right hand side of (3.6) by p to get

$$\frac{\alpha_{p,k,n}}{1-\alpha_{p,k,n}} < \frac{n-p}{p}. \tag{3.7}$$

Inequalities (3.6) and (3.7) imply inequality (3.5). Now recall *Lemma 2.3* and *Lemma 2.4*. $\alpha_{p,k,n}$ falls into the interval $(f_{p,k,n}l_1, f_{p,k,n}u_1)$. Since $\alpha^{(1)}_{p,k,n}$ is the center of the interval (see its definition), the distance between $\alpha_{p,k,n}$ and $\alpha^{(1)}_{p,k,n}$ should not exceed the half of the length of the interval, i.e.

$$\left|\alpha_{p,k,n} - \alpha^{(1)}_{p,k,n}\right| \le \frac{f_{p,k,n}(u_1 - l_1)}{2}.$$

Hence

$$\frac{\left|\alpha_{p,k,n} - \alpha^{(1)}_{p,k,n}\right|}{\alpha_{p,k,n}} \le \frac{f_{p,k,n}(u_1 - l_1)}{2\alpha_{p,k,n}}$$

$$< \frac{f_{p,k,n}(u_1 - l_1)}{2f_{p,k,n}l_1}$$

$$= \frac{u_1 - l_1}{2l_1}, \tag{3.8}$$

where we have used *Lemma 2.4* to get the second inequality.

From this, using (3.5) and (3.1) we prove (3.3). Inequality (3.4) can be proved in a similar way.

With the help of *Lemma 3.2*, we come to the main results of this section.

THEOREM 3.1

$$E_1 < \frac{\omega}{2}(exp(\frac{1}{6n(12(n-p)+1)} + \frac{1}{6(n-k)(12(n-p-k)+1)} +$$

$$+ \frac{12p+1}{144(n-p)(12(n-p)+1)n} +$$

$$+ \frac{12p+1}{144(n-k)(n-p-k)(12(n-p-k)+1)}) - 1) \qquad (3.9)$$

and

$$E_2 < \frac{\omega}{2}(\exp(\frac{1}{12(n-p)(12(n-p)+1)} + \frac{1}{12(n-k)(12(n-k)+1)} +$$

$$+ \frac{1}{12n(12n+1)}) - 1). \qquad (3.10)$$

For short, we denote the quantities inside the exponentials of (3.9) and (3.10) by $\beta_{p,k,n}^{(1)}$ and $\beta_{p,k,n}^{(2)}$ respectively.

Proof. From the definition of u_1 and l_1,

$$\frac{u_1}{l_1} = \exp(\frac{12p+1}{12(n-p)(12n+1)} - \frac{12p-1}{12(n-k)(12(n-k-p)+1)}$$

$$- \frac{12p-1}{12n(12(n-p)+1)} + \frac{12p+1}{12(n-p-k)(12(n-k)+1)})$$

$$< \exp((\frac{12p+1}{12(n-p)12n} - \frac{12p-1}{12n(12(n-p)+1)}) +$$

$$(\frac{12p+1}{12(n-p-k)12(n-k)} - \frac{12p-1}{12(n-k)(12(n-k-p)+1)})). \qquad (3.11)$$

Since

$$\frac{12p+1}{12(n-p)12n} - \frac{12p-1}{12n(12(n-p)+1)}$$

$$= \frac{24(n-p)+12p+1}{12n \cdot 12(n-p)(12(n-p)+1)}$$

$$= \frac{1}{6n(12(n-p)+1)} + \frac{12p+1}{144n(n-p)(12(n-p)+1)}$$

and

$$\frac{12p+1}{12(n-p-k)12(n-k)} - \frac{12p-1}{12(n-k)(12(n-k-p)+1)}$$

$$= \frac{24(n-p-k)+12p+1}{12(n-k) \cdot 12(n-p-k)(12(n-p-k)+1)}$$

$$= \frac{1}{6(n-k)(12(n-p-k)+1)} + \frac{12p+1}{144(n-k)(n-p-k)(12(n-p-k)+1)},$$

from (3.11) and *Lemma 3.2* (3.9) holds.

To show that (3.10) is true, note

$$\frac{u_2}{l_2} = exp(\frac{1}{12(n-p)} + \frac{1}{12(n-k)} - \frac{1}{12n+1}$$

$$- \frac{1}{12(n-p)+1} - \frac{1}{12(n-k)+1} + \frac{1}{12n})$$

$$= exp(\frac{1}{12(n-p)(12(n-p)+1)} + \frac{1}{12(n-k)(12(n-k)+1)} +$$

$$+ \frac{1}{12n(12n+1)}). \tag{3.12}$$

Thus from *Lemma 3.2*, (3.10) is true.

By sacrificing a little accuracy, we can greatly simplify the error bounds so that the behavior of errors can be easily seen. To do this, we need the following lemmas.

Lemma 3.3

$$\beta_{p,k,n}^{(1)} < \frac{4}{72n^2} + \frac{1}{72(n-k)(n-p-k)} + \frac{13}{12 \times 144(n-p-k)^2}$$

and

$$\beta_{p,k,n}^{(2)} < \frac{5}{144n^2} + \frac{1}{144(n-k)^2}.$$

Proof. From the assumption that there are at least two blocks, the number of records in each block should not exceed $n/2$. Under such conditions, we can get the following inequalities:

$$\frac{1}{6n(12(n-p)+1)} < \frac{1}{6n(12 \cdot \frac{n}{2})},$$

hence

$$\frac{1}{6n(12(n-p)+1)} < \frac{1}{36n^2}, \tag{3.13}$$

$$\frac{12p+1}{144(n-p)(12(n-p)+1)n} < \frac{12(n/2)+1}{144\frac{n}{2} \cdot 12\frac{n}{2}n}$$

$$= \frac{1+\frac{1}{6n}}{72n^2}$$

$$< \frac{2}{72n^2}, \tag{3.14}$$

and

$$\frac{1}{6(n-k)(12(n-p-k)+1)} < \frac{1}{72(n-k)(n-p-k)}. \tag{3.15}$$

Therefore from (3.13), (3.14), (3.15) and the definition of $\beta_{p,k,n}^{(1)}$, we have

$$\beta_{p,kn}^{(1)} < \frac{4}{72n^2} + \frac{1}{72(n-k)(n-p-k)} + \frac{12p+1}{144 \times 12(n-k)(n-p-k)^2}. \tag{3.16}$$

Since $k \le n-p$, $\frac{p}{n-k} \le 1$. Hence

$$\frac{12p+1}{144(n-k)(12(n-p-k)^2)}$$

$$= \frac{12\frac{p}{n-k} + \frac{1}{n-k}}{144(12(n-p-k)^2)}$$

$$< \frac{13}{144(n-p-k)^2 \cdot 12}. \tag{3.17}$$

Now, from this (3.16), we get the first inequality in the lemma. To show the second inequality, we note that

$$\beta_{p,k,n}^{(2)} = \frac{1}{12(n-p)(12(n-p)+1)} + \frac{1}{12(n-k)(12(n-k)+1} + \frac{1}{12n(12n+1)}$$

$$< \frac{1}{(12 \cdot \frac{n}{2})^2} + \frac{1}{144(n-k)^2} + \frac{1}{144n^2}. \tag{3.18}$$

Therefore the second inequality holds.

Lemma 3.4 If $n-p-k \ge 1$, then

$$\frac{1 + \frac{\beta_{p,k,n}^{(1)} exp(\beta_{p,k,n}^{(1)})}{2}}{2} < 0.506.$$

If $n-k \ge 1$, then

$$\frac{1 + \frac{\beta_{p,k,n}^{(2)} exp(\beta_{p,k,n}^{(2)})}{2}}{2} < 0.506.$$

Proof. If $n-p-k \ge 1$, we have $n-p \ge 2$, $n-k \ge 2$ and $n \ge 3$. Then using the first inequality of *Lemma 3.3* we have

$$\beta_{p,k,n}^{(1)} < \frac{4}{72 \times 9} + \frac{1}{72 \times 2} + \frac{13}{12 \times 144}.$$

From this, the direct computation yields

$$\frac{1 + \frac{\beta_{p,k,n}^{(1)} exp(\beta_{p,k,n}^{(1)})}{2}}{2} < 0.506,$$

where we have used the fact that $x * exp(x)$ is increasing in x

It is easy to show the second inequality. From the expression of $\beta_{p,k,n}^{(2)}$, we have

$$\beta_{p,k,n}^{(2)} < \frac{3}{144}.$$

Then, as before, the straight forward computation yields

$$\frac{1 + \frac{\beta_{p,k,n}^{(2)} exp(\beta_{p,k,n}^{(2)})}{2}}{2} < 0.506.$$

Lemma 3.5

$$e^x - 1 < x(1 + \frac{xe^x}{2}),$$

where $x > 0$.

Proof. $e^x - 1$ can be expanded as

$$e^x - 1 = x + \frac{x^2}{2} e^{\theta x},$$

where $0 < \theta < 1$. Since $x > 0$

$$e^x - 1 < x(1 + \frac{xe^2}{2}).$$

THEOREM 3.2

$$E_1 < 0.506(\frac{4}{72np} + \frac{1}{72k(n-p-k)} + \frac{13 \times min(\frac{n-p}{n-k}, \frac{p}{k})}{12 \times 144(n-p-k)^2}) \quad (3.19)$$

and

$$E_2 < 0.506(\frac{5}{144np} + \frac{1}{144(n-k)k}). \quad (3.20)$$

Proof. First we use *THEOREM 3.1* and *Lemma 3.5* to get

$$E_i < \omega \frac{\beta_{p,k,n}^{(i)}(1+\frac{\beta_{p,k,n}^{(i)}e^{\beta_{p,k,n}^{(i)}}}{2})}{2},$$
(3.21)

where $i = 1,2$. Replacing

$$\frac{1}{2}(1+\frac{\beta_{p,k,n}^{(i)}e^{\beta_{p,k,n}^{(i)}}}{2})$$

in (3.21) by their upper bound 0.506 (see *Lemma 3.4*), we have

$$E_i < 0.506\omega\beta_{p,k,n}^{(i)},$$
(3.22)

where $i = 1, 2$.

Hence using (3.16) we get

$$E_1 < 0.506\omega(\frac{4}{72n^2} + \frac{1}{72(n-k)(n-p-k)} + \frac{12p+1}{144 \times 12(n-k)(n-p-k)^2})$$

$$\leq 0.506(\frac{n-p}{p}\frac{4}{72n^2} + \frac{n-k}{k}\frac{1}{72(n-k)(n-k-p)}$$

$$+\omega\frac{12p+1}{144 \times 12(n-k)(n-p-k)^2})$$

$$< 0.506(\frac{4}{72np} + \frac{1}{72k(n-p-k)} + \omega\frac{12p+1}{144 \times 12(n-k)(n-p-k)^2}),$$
(3.23)

where we have used the definition of ω. Now we only need to show that the last

term in (3.23) will not exceed $\dfrac{13 \times min(\frac{n-p}{n-k}, \frac{p}{k})}{12 \times 144(n-p-k)^2}$. In fact, we have

$$\omega\frac{12p+1}{144 \times 12(n-k)(n-p-k)^2}$$

$$\leq \frac{\frac{n-k}{k}(12p+1)}{144 \times 12(n-k)(n-k-p)^2}$$

$$= \frac{\frac{p}{k}(12p+\frac{1}{p})}{144 \times 12(n-p-k)^2}$$

$$< \frac{13\frac{p}{k}}{144 \times 12(n-p-k)^2}.$$

Also we have

410

$$\omega \frac{12p+1}{144 \times 12(n-k)(n-p-k)^2}$$

$$\leq \frac{\frac{n-p}{p}(12p+1)}{144 \times 12(n-k)(n-k-p)^2}$$

$$= \frac{\frac{n-p}{n-k}(12+\frac{1}{p})}{144 \times 12(n-p-k)^2}$$

$$< \frac{13\frac{n-p}{n-k}}{144 \times 12(n-p-k)^2}.$$

Hence (3.19) holds.

It is easy to show (3.20) as the following

$$E_2 < 0.506\omega\beta_{p,k,n}^{(2)}$$

$$\leq 0.506(\frac{n-p}{p}\frac{5}{144n^2} + \frac{n-k}{k}\frac{1}{144(n-k)^2})$$

$$< 0.506(\frac{5}{144np} + \frac{1}{144k(n-k)}).$$

The proof is completed.

    THEOREM 3.3

$$E_1 < 0.506(\frac{4}{72np} + \frac{1}{72(n-p-1)} + \frac{13}{12 \times 144(m-2)(n-p-k)}) \quad (3.24)$$

and

$$E_2 < 0.506(\frac{5}{144np} + \frac{1}{144(n-1)}). \quad (3.25)$$

Proof. Since $1 \leq k \leq n-p-1$, it can be shown that $\frac{1}{(n-p-k)k} \leq \frac{1}{n-p-1}$ and $\frac{1}{(n-k)k} \leq \frac{1}{n-1}$. From (3.19) and (3.20) we obtain

$$E_1 < 0.506(\frac{4}{72np} + \frac{1}{72(n-p-1)} + \frac{13p}{12 \times 144(n-p-1)(n-p-k)})$$

$$< 0.506(\frac{4}{72np} + \frac{1}{72(n-p-1)} + \frac{13}{12 \times 144(m-2)(n-p-k)})$$

and

$$E_2 < 0.506(\frac{5}{144np} + \frac{1}{144(n-1)}).$$

According to *THEOREM 3.3*, we note the relative errors of our approximations will approach zero as m approaches infinity. Based on (3.24) and (3.25), the direct computations yield the overall error bounds for our formulas. The absolute value of overall relative error using $b_{p,k,n}^{(1)}$, when $m \geq 10$ will not exceed 0.42%. When $n - p - k$ is small, for example $n - p - k \leq 5$, we can use $b_{p,k,n}^{(2)}$ as an alternative. The overall relative error of $b_{p,k,n}^{(2)}$ will not exceed 0.22% when $m \geq 10$.

As shown in [22], $b_{p,k,n}^{(0)}$ does not have such desired properties, because it may have a up to 3.7% error as long as p is small and k is close to $n - p$.

In *Theorem 3.2* of [22], The authors also showed that the relative error of $b_{p,k,n}^{(0)}$ denoted as *Erro*, satisfied

$$lim_{m\to\infty} Erro = 1 - \frac{(1 - e^{-p\lambda}(1 - \frac{\lambda^2 p}{2} - \frac{\lambda^3}{2p}))}{1 - (1 - \lambda)^p},$$

where $\lambda = \frac{k}{n}$ and p are fixed. In this case the error can not be reduced by increasing m. Without those restrictions we will see below the errors of our approximations indeed will approach zero as m approaches infinity.

THEOREM 3.4 For E_1 and E_2 above

$$\lim_{m\to\infty} E_1 \to 0 \text{ and } \lim_{m\to\infty} E_2 \to 0 .$$

Proof. From (3.24) and (3.25) we get the theorem immediately.

THEOREM 3.5 With fixed λ and m

$$\lim_{p\to\infty} E_1 \to 0 \text{ and } \lim_{p\to\infty} E_2 \to 0 .$$

Proof. The theorem follows (3.24) and (3.25).

A similar result holds for the formula of Whang et al in ([22]).

4 Numerical Study

In this section we will do a computational study to observe the performance of previous approximation formulas and our new approximation formulas.

There are three approximation formulas for Yao's exact value, Cardenas' formula

$$c_{p,k,m} = m(1 - (1 - \frac{1}{m})^k),$$

(see [4]),

Palvia, March and Waters' formula

$$\omega_{p,k,m} = m(1 - (1 - \frac{k}{mp})^p),$$

(see [13] and [20]) and Whang, Wiederhold and Sagalowicz's formula (see (1.3)). In this section we will compare our approximation $b^{(1)}_{p,k,n}$ with them numerically. We will first compare our formula with Yao's exact formula, and then we will compare our formula with the three previous formulas to see their departures from the exact one, both for small and large p, k, and m, since our formulas approximate Yao's exact value very well. The reason we will only focus on our first approximation $b^{(1)}_{p,k,n}$ is that our second approximation is designed primarily for the special case $k = n - p$ and is less relevant. As mentioned earlier, the numerical studies on the approximation formulas were formerly carried out basically for small m, p, and k due to the difficulty of computing the exact value.

In order to compare our formula with Yao's, exhaustive computer calculations were carried out. The absolute value of the relative error of $b^{(1)}_{p,k,n}$ was calculated for all $m = 2,3,\dots,100$; $p = 1,2,\dots,10$; and $k = 1,2,\dots,n-p-1$. The maximum error was observed as 0.0417% at $m = 3$, $p = 1$, and $k = 1$. We also noted that the error approached zero when the number of blocks increased, or the block factor increased, as observed through our error bound. Part of the results of the computation are given in *Table 1* in the appendix, where $E(X)$ and E_1 are the exact value and the absolute value of the relative error respectively, and Eb_1 is the error bound calculated from (3.19).

To study the three approximations, we only computed the absolute values of relative errors of $c_{p,k,m}$ and $b^{(0)}_{p,k,n}$ to $b^{(1)}_{p,k,n}$. Since $c_{p,k,m}$ can be written as

$$c_{p,k,n} = m(1 - 1(1 - \frac{p}{n})^k)$$

and $\omega_{p,k,m}$ can be written as

$$\omega_{p,k,n} = m(1 - (1 - \frac{k}{n})^p),$$

by the duality of $\omega_{p,k,n}$ and $c_{p,k,n}$, the error behavior of $\omega_{p,k,n}$ can be figured from $c_{p,k,n}$.

The computer calculation on $m = 10,100,\dots,1,000,000$; $p = 1,2,\dots,50$; and $k = 1,1+([0.01(n-p-1)]+1), 2+2([0.01 \quad (n-p-1)] +1,\dots,n-p-1$ showed that $c_{p,k,n}$ had the largest absolute value of relative error, 37% at $m = 1,000,000$, $p = 1$, and $k = 999,998$. The maximum absolute value of relative error of $b_{p,k,n}^{(0)}$, 3.4%, occurred at $m = 1,000,000$, $p = 2$, and $k = 1,999,997$, which was similar to the result reported in [22]. The computation also showed that the errors of $c_{p,k,n}$ and $b_{p,k,n}^{(0)}$ became smaller when p became larger. Repeating the same computation for $10 < p \leq 50$ gave maximum absolute value of error of $b_{p,k,n}^{(0)}$ 0.4% at $m = 1,000,000$, $p = 45$, and $k = 1$. In this case the maximum absolute value of error of $c_{p,k,n}$ was observed as 3% at $m = 1,000,000$, $p = 11$, and $k = 1,540,001$. *Table 2* and *Table 3* in the appendix show the error behavior of $c_{p,k,n}$ and $b_{p,k,n}^{(0)}$. In the tables *Err-Cad* and *Err-WWS* stand for the relative errors of $c_{p,k,n}$ and $b_{p,k,n}^{(0)}$ to our formula respectively.

5 Conclusion

In conclusion, we have found that the formulas suggested in this study achieve very good accuracy. The accuracy of the formulas can be improved as the number of the blocks of a database system increases. The formulas can serve several purposes:
(i) the direct application to the database design and optimization such as query processing optimization and optimal index selection,
(ii) the basis for deriving new approximation formulas under specific restrictions on p, k, and n, and
(iii) the basis for numerical error checking of other approximations.

As mentioned previously, due to the difficulty of computing $E(X)$ directly, many researchers performed computational error analyses only for small n. Since our approximations are very close to the value of $E(X)$, in order to check the error computationally for a new approximation formula, we only need to check the difference between the new approximation and our approximation.

One thing we have to emphasize is that the derivation and the error analysis of the formulas given in this paper imply a general method to derive approximation formulas for the expected numbers of blocks hit suggested in [1] and [5], since they involve a term consisting of the multiplication and division of factorials.

As for future investigations we are interested in the granulation of some of the measurements as well as considering other models that might deliver an alternative to the approach explored in this paper.

414

References

[1]   R. Ahad, K.V. Bapa Rao and D. Mcleod, On estimating the cardinality of the projection of a database relation, *ACM Trans. On Database Sys.*, 1 (1989) 28-40.

[2]   H.D. Anderson and P.B. Berra, Minimum cost selection of secondary indexes for formatted files, *ACM Trans. On Database Sys.*, 1 (1977) 68-90.

[3]   P.A. Bernstein, N. Goodman, E. Wong, C.R. Reeve and J.B. Rothnie, Query processing in a system for distributed databases, *ACM Trans. on Database Sys.*, 4 (1981) 602-625.

[4]   A.F. Cardenas, Analysis and performance of inverted database structures, *Communications of ACM*, 5 (1975) 253-263.

[5]   T.Y. Cheung, Estimating block accesses and number of records in file management, *Communications of ACM*, 7 (1982) 484-487.

[6]   J. Fedorowicz, Database performance evaluation in an index file environment, *ACM Trans. On Database Sys.*, 1 (1987) 85-110.

[7]   W. Feller, An introduction to probability theory and its applications, John Wiley and Sons, New York, 1968.

[8]   M. Friedman, M. Ma, A. Kandel, On the theory of typicality, Int. J. of Uncer. Fuzzy and Know.-Base Systems, Vol. 3, No. 2 (1995), 127-142.

[9]   A. Kandel, Fuzzy Mathematical Techniques and Their Applications, Addison-Wesley, Reading, MA. (1986).

[10]   W. Kiessling, Access path selection in databases with intelligent disc subsystems, *Computer J.*, 1 (1988) 41-50.

[11]   W.S. Luk, On estimating block accesses in database organizations, *Communications of ACM*, 11 (1983) 945-947.

[12]   P. Palvia, Batched searching in database organizations, *Information Sic.*, 45 (1988) 23-37.

[13]   P. Palvia and S.T. March, Approximation block access in database organizations, *Information Processing Letters*, 19 (1984) 75-79.

[14]   M. Schkolnick and P. Tiberio, Estimating the cost of updates in a relational database, *ACM Trans. On Database Sys.*, 2 (1985) 163-179.

[15]   M. Schneider and A. Kandel, Properties of the fuzzy expected value and the fuzzy expected interval in fuzzy environment, *Fuzzy Sets and Systems*, Vol. 28, (1988) 55-68.

[16]   K.F. Siler, A stochastic evaluation model for database organizations in data retrieval systems, *Communications of ACM*, 2 (1976) 84-95.

[17]   T.J. Teorey and J.P. Fry, Design of database structures, Prentice-Hall, Englewood Cliffs, 1982.

[18]   S.J. Waters, File design fallacies, *Computer J.*, 15 (1972) 1-4.

[19]   ____, Estimating magnetic disk seeks, *Computer J.*, 1 (1975) 12-17.

[20]   ____, Hit ratios, *Computer J.*, 1 (1976) 21-24.

[21]   K. Whang, Index selection in relational databases, *Foundations of Data Organization*, Edited by S.P. Ghosh et al, Plenum Press, New York, 1987.

[22] K. Whang, G. Wiederhold and D. Sagalowicz, Estimating block accesses in database organizations: A closed noniterative formula, *Communications of ACM*, 11 (1983) 940-944.

[23] G. Wiederhold, Database design, McGraw-Hill, New York, 1983.

[24] S.B. Yao, An attribute based model for database access cost analysis, *ACM Trans. On Database Syst.* 1 (1977) 45-67.

[25] ____, Approximating block accesses in database organizations, *Communications of ACM*, 4 (1977) 260-261.

[26] P.C. Yue and C.K. Wong, Storage cost considerations in secondary index selection, *International J. Comput. Information Sci.*, 4 (1975) 307-327.

[27] M. Zemankova-Leech and A. Kandel, Fuzzy Relational Data Bases — A Key to Expert Systems, Verlag TÜV Rheinland, Germany, (1984).

Appendix
Table 1

(Comparison of $E(X)$ and $b_{p,k,n}^{(1)}$)

m	p	k	$E(X)/m$	$b_{p,k,n}^{(1)}/m$	E_1	Eb_1
10	1	1	0.10000000	0.09999764	0.00002357925	0.003749
10	1	5	0.50000000	0.49997582	0.00004836798	0.003210
10	1	8	0.80000000	0.79991451	0.00010686181	0.004165
10	3	1	0.10000000	0.09999991	0.00000086778	0.000588
10	3	14	0.86206897	0.86206821	0.00000087601	0.000356
10	3	26	0.99901478	0.99901402	0.00000075803	0.001022
10	5	1	0.10000000	0.09999998	0.00000018688	0.000274
10	5	23	0.96189752	0.96189745	0.00000007773	0.000128
10	5	44	0.99999717	0.99999717	0.00000000243	0.000705
30	1	1	0.03333333	0.03333331	0.00000080772	0.001193
30	1	15	0.50000000	0.49999909	0.00000181725	0.000972
30	1	28	0.93333333	0.93330441	0.00003099439	0.001324
30	3	1	0.03333333	0.03333333	0.00000002970	0.000186
30	3	44	0.87078652	0.87078649	0.00000002972	0.000108
30	3	86	0.99996595	0.99996593	0.00000002620	0.000319
30	5	1	0.03333333	0.03333333	0.00000000641	0.000086
30	5	73	0.96660275	0.96660275	0.00000000249	0.000039
30	5	144	0.99999999	0.99999999	0.00000000001	0.000218
50	1	1	0.02000000	0.02000000	0.00000017163	0.000710

Table 1 — continued

m	p	k	$E(X)/m$	$b^{(1)}_{p,k,n}/m$	E_1	Eb_1
50	1	25	0.50000000	0.49999980	0.00000039143	0.000574
50	1	48	0.96000000	0.95998264	0.00001808765	0.000788
50	3	1	0.02000000	0.02000000	0.00000000631	0.000111
50	3	74	0.87248322	0.87248322	0.00000000632	0.000064
50	3	146	0.99999274	0.99999274	0.00000000558	0.000189
50	5	1	0.02000000	0.02000000	0.00000000137	0.000051
50	5	123	0.96747720	0.96747720	0.00000000052	0.000023
50	5	244	1.00000000	1.00000000	0.00000000000	0.000129
70	1	1	0.01428571	0.01428571	0.00000006211	0.000506
70	1	35	0.50000000	0.49999993	0.00000014242	0.000408
70	1	68	0.97142857	0.97141617	0.00001276863	0.000561
70	3	1	0.01428571	0.01428571	0.00000000229	0.000079
70	3	104	0.87320574	0.87320574	0.00000000229	0.000045
70	3	206	0.99999737	0.99999737	0.00000000202	0.000134
70	5	1	0.01428571	0.01428571	0.00000000049	0.000037
70	5	173	0.96784555	0.96784555	0.00000000019	0.000016
70	5	344	1.00000000	1.00000000	0.00000000000	0.000092
90	1	1	0.01111111	0.01111111	0.00000002911	0.000393
90	1	45	0.50000000	0.49999997	0.00000006694	0.000316
90	1	88	0.97777778	0.97776813	0.00000986686	0.000435
90	3	1	0.01111111	0.01111111	0.00000000107	0.000061

Table 1 — continued

m	p	k	$E(X)/m$	$b_{p,k,n}^{(1)}/m$	E_1	Eb_1
90	3	134	0.87360595	0.87360595	0.00000000107	0.000035
90	3	266	0.99999877	0.99999877	0.00000000095	0.000104
90	5	1	0.01111111	0.01111111	0.00000000025	0.000028
90	5	223	0.96804856	0.96804856	0.00000000009	0.000013
90	5	444	1.00000000	1.00000000	0.00000000000	0.000071

Table 2

(*Comparison of* $c_{p,k,n}$, $b_{p,k,n}^{(0)}$, *and* $b_{p,k,n}^{(1)}$ *for* $p \leq 4$)

m	p	k	$c_{p,k,n}/m$	$b_{p,k,n}^{(0)}/m$	$b_{p,k,n}^{(1)}/m$	Err-Cad	Err-WWS
10	1	1	0.100	0.100	0.100	-0.000	-0.000
10	1	6	0.469	0.606	0.600	0.219	-0.010
10	2	1	0.100	0.100	0.100	-0.000	-0.000
10	2	10	0.651	0.749	0.763	0.147	0.019
10	2	17	0.833	0.985	0.984	0.153	-0.001
10	3	1	0.100	0.100	0.100	-0.000	-0.000
10	3	15	0.794	0.878	0.888	0.106	0.011
10	3	26	0.935	1.021	0.999	0.064	-0.022
10	4	1	0.100	0.100	0.100	-0.000	-0.000
10	4	19	0.865	0.931	0.935	0.074	0.004
10	4	35	0.975	1.019	1.000	0.025	-0.019
100	1	1	0.010	0.010	0.010	-0.000	-0.000
100	1	51	0.401	0.517	0.510	0.214	-0.014
100	1	98	0.627	0.981	0.980	0.361	-0.001
100	2	1	0.010	0.010	0.010	-0.000	-0.000
100	2	100	0.634	0.737	0.751	0.156	0.019
100	2	197	0.862	1.030	1.000	0.138	-0.030
100	3	1	0.010	0.010	0.010	-0.000	-0.000
100	3	150	0.779	0.866	0.876	0.112	0.011

Table 2 — continued

m	p	k	$c_{p,k,n}/m$	$b_{p,k,n}^{(0)}/m$	$b_{p,k,n}^{(1)}/m$	Err-Cad	Err-WWS
100	3	296	0.949	1.032	1.000	0.051	-0.032
100	4	1	0.010	0.010	0.010	-0.000	-0.000
100	4	199	0.865	0.934	0.937	0.077	0.003
100	4	395	0.981	1.021	1.000	0.019	-0.021
1000	1	1	0.001	0.001	0.001	0.000	-0.000
1000	1	501	0.394	0.508	0.501	0.213	-0.014
1000	1	998	0.632	0.998	0.998	0.367	-0.000
1000	2	1	0.001	0.001	0.001	-0.000	-0.000
1000	2	1000	0.632	0.736	0.750	0.157	0.019
1000	2	1997	0.864	1.033	1.000	0.136	-0.033
1000	3	1	0.001	0.001	0.001	-0.000	-0.000
1000	3	1500	0.777	0.865	0.875	0.112	0.011
1000	3	2996	0.950	1.033	1.000	0.050	-0.033
1000	4	1	0.001	0.001	0.001	-0.000	-0.000
1000	4	1999	0.865	0.934	0.937	0.078	0.003
1000	4	3995	0.982	1.021	1.000	0.018	-0.021
10000	1	1	0.000	0.000	0.000	-0.000	-0.000
10000	1	5001	0.394	0.507	0.500	0.213	-0.014
10000	1	9998	0.632	1.000	1.000	0.368	-0.000
10000	2	1	0.000	0.000	0.000	0.000	0.000
10000	2	10000	0.632	0.736	0.750	0.157	0.019

Table 2 — continued

m	p	k	$c_{p,k,n}/m$	$b^{(0)}_{p,k,n}/m$	$b^{(1)}_{p,k,n}/m$	Err-Cad	Err-WWS
10000	2	19997	0.865	1.034	1.000	0.135	-0.034
10000	3	1	0.000	0.000	0.000	0.000	0.000
10000	3	15000	0.777	0.865	0.875	0.112	0.011
10000	3	29996	0.950	1.033	1.000	0.050	-0.033
10000	4	1	0.000	0.000	0.000	0.000	0.000
10000	4	19999	0.865	0.934	0.937	0.078	0.003
10000	4	39995	0.982	1.021	1.000	0.018	-0.021
100000	1	1	0.000	0.000	0.000	-0.000	-0.000
100000	1	50001	0.393	0.507	0.500	0.213	-0.014
100000	1	99998	0.632	1.000	1.000	0.368	-0.000
100000	2	1	0.000	0.000	0.000	0.000	0.000
100000	2	100000	0.632	0.736	0.750	0.157	0.019
100000	2	199997	0.865	1.034	1.000	0.135	-0.034
100000	3	1	0.000	0.000	0.000	-0.000	-0.000
100000	3	150000	0.777	0.865	0.875	0.112	0.011
100000	3	299996	0.950	1.033	1.000	0.050	-0.033
100000	4	1	0.000	0.000	0.000	0.000	0.000
100000	4	199999	0.865	0.934	0.937	0.078	0.003
100000	4	399995	0.982	1.021	1.000	0.018	-0.021
1000000	1	1	0.000	0.000	0.000	0.000	0.000
1000000	1	500001	0.393	0.507	0.500	0.213	-0.014

Table 2 — continued

m	p	k	$c_{p,k,n}/m$	$b^{(0)}_{p,k,n}/m$	$b^{(1)}_{p,k,n}/m$	Err-Cad	Err-WWS
1000000	1	999998	0.632	1.000	1.000	0.368	-0.000
1000000	2	1	0.000	0.000	0.000	-0.000	-0.000
1000000	2	1000000	0.632	0.736	0.750	0.157	0.019
1000000	2	1999997	0.865	1.034	1.000	0.135	-0.034
1000000	3	1	0.000	0.000	0.000	0.000	0.000
1000000	3	1500000	0.777	0.865	0.875	0.112	0.011
1000000	3	2999996	0.950	1.033	1.000	0.050	-0.033
1000000	4	1	0.000	0.000	0.000	0.000	0.000
1000000	4	1999999	0.865	0.934	0.937	0.078	0.003
1000000	4	3999995	0.982	1.021	1.000	0.018	-0.021

Table 3

(Comparison of $c_{p,k,n}$, $b_{p,k,n}^{(0)}$, and $b_{p,k,n}^{(1)}$ for $p = 6$, 8 and 10)

m	p	k	$b_{p,k,n}^{(0)} / m$	$c_{p,k,n} / m$	$b_{p,k,n}^{(1)} / m$	Err-Cad	Err-WWS
10	6	1	0.100000	0.100000	0.100000	-0.0000	-0.0000
10	6	28	0.984766	0.947665	0.981899	0.0349	-0.0029
10	6	53	1.006063	0.996243	1.000000	0.0038	-0.0061
10	8	1	0.100000	0.100000	0.100000	-0.0000	-0.0000
10	8	37	0.998613	0.979724	0.994998	0.0153	-0.0036
10	8	71	1.001409	0.999436	1.000000	0.0006	-0.0014
10	10	1	0.100000	0.100000	0.100000	-0.0000	-0.0000
10	10	46	1.001219	0.992145	0.998618	0.0065	-0.0026
10	10	89	1.000287	0.999915	1.000000	0.0001	-0.0003
100	6	1	0.010000	0.010000	0.010000	-0.0000	-0.0000
100	6	298	0.987754	0.949963	0.984139	0.0347	-0.0037
100	6	593	1.005254	0.997420	1.000000	0.0026	-0.0053
100	8	1	0.010000	0.010000	0.010000	-0.0000	-0.0000
100	8	397	1.000003	0.981500	0.995995	0.0146	-0.0040
100	8	791	1.001060	0.999647	1.000000	0.0004	-0.0011
100	10	1	0.010000	0.010000	0.010000	-0.0000	-0.0000
100	10	496	1.001684	0.993160	0.998989	0.0058	-0.0027
100	10	989	1.000192	0.999952	1.000000	0.0000	-0.0002
1000	6	1	0.001000	0.001000	0.001000	-0.0000	-0.0000

Table 3 — continued

m	p	k	$b_{p,k,n}^{(0)}/m$	$c_{p,k,n}/m$	$b_{p,k,n}^{(1)}/m$	Err-Cad	Err-WWS
1000	6	2998	0.988040	0.950188	0.984352	0.0347	-0.0037
1000	6	5993	1.005173	0.997511	1.000000	0.0025	-0.0052
1000	8	1	0.001000	0.001000	0.001000	0.0000	0.0000
1000	8	3997	1.000129	0.981666	0.996084	0.0145	-0.0041
1000	8	7991	1.001031	0.999663	1.000000	0.0003	-0.0010
1000	10	1	0.001000	0.001000	0.001000	0.0000	-0.0000
1000	10	4996	1.001722	0.993252	0.999020	0.0058	-0.0027
1000	10	9989	1.000185	0.999954	1.000000	0.0000	-0.0002
10000	6	1	0.000100	0.000100	0.000100	0.0000	0.0000
10000	6	29998	0.988069	0.950210	0.984373	0.0347	-0.0038
10000	6	59993	1.005165	0.997520	1.000000	0.0025	-0.0052
10000	8	1	0.000100	0.000100	0.000100	0.0000	0.0000
10000	8	39997	1.000142	0.981683	0.996093	0.0145	-0.0041
10000	8	79991	1.001028	0.999664	1.000000	0.0003	-0.0010
10000	10	1	0.000100	0.000100	0.000100	0.0000	0.0000
10000	10	49996	1.001726	0.993261	0.999023	0.0058	-0.0027
10000	10	99989	1.000184	0.999955	1.000000	0.0000	-0.0002
100000	6	1	0.000010	0.000010	0.000010	0.0000	0.0000
100000	6	299998	0.988072	0.950213	0.984375	0.0347	-0.0038
100000	6	599993	1.005164	0.997521	1.000000	0.0025	-0.0052
100000	8	1	0.000010	0.000010	0.000010	-0.0000	-0.0000

Table 3 — continued

m	p	k	$b^{(0)}_{p,k,n}/m$	$c_{p,k,n}/m$	$b^{(1)}_{p,k,n}/m$	Err-Cad	Err-WWS
100000	8	399997	1.000143	0.981684	0.996094	0.0145	-0.0041
100000	8	799991	1.001027	0.999665	1.000000	0.0003	-0.0010
100000	10	1	0.00001	0.00001	0.00001	-0.0000	-0.0000
100000	10	499996	1.00172	0.99326	0.99902	0.0058	-0.0027
100000	10	999989	1.00018	0.99995	1.00000	0.0000	-0.0002
1000000	6	1	0.00000	0.00000	0.00000	0.0001	0.0001
1000000	6	2999998	0.98807	0.95021	0.98437	0.0347	-0.0038
1000000	6	5999993	1.00516	0.99752	1.00000	0.0025	-0.0052
1000000	8	1	0.00000	0.00000	0.00000	-0.0001	-0.0001
1000000	8	3999997	1.00014	0.98168	0.99609	0.0145	-0.0041
1000000	8	7999991	1.00102	0.99966	1.00000	0.0003	-0.0010
1000000	10	1	0.00000	0.00000	0.00000	-0.0003	-0.0003
1000000	10	4999996	1.00172	0.99326	0.99902	0.0058	-0.0027
1000000	10	9999989	1.00018	0.99995	1.00000	0.0000	-0.0002

426

<u>Exercises</u>

1) By using the concept of the Fuzzy Expected Value (FEV) is there any deviation from the cost function discussed in the paper?
2) Provide detailed proof of Theorem 3.4.
3) Provide detailed proof of Theorem 3.5.
4) Discuss the problems related to the granulation of some of the measurements discussed in this paper.
5) Investigate the numerical correlation between the approximation formulas presented in this paper and results that can be obtained using the tools of the theory of typicality.
6) Discuss the applicability of the above to KDD and DM.

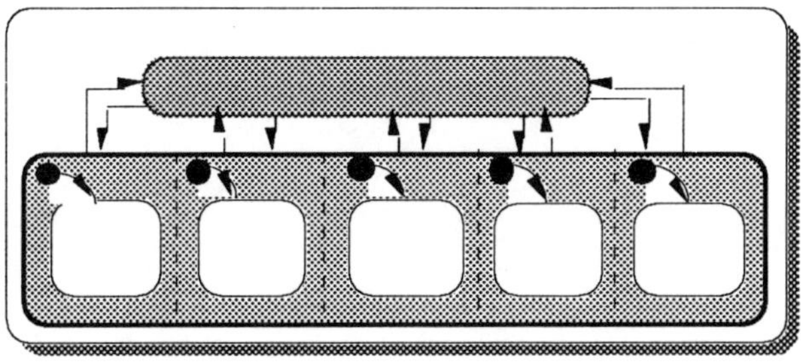

NON-CARTESIAN APPROACH
TO SOFTWARE ENGINEERING

This section introduces a non-Cartesian approach to software engineering, which is inspired by competences and the notion of a non-Cartesian robot. The article in this section suggests how the paradigms of non-Cartesian robotics can beneficially influence software engineering.

A competence consists of sensory input from one or more sensors coupled with one or more actuators providing a means of responding to specific situations. Each competence is carried out by a separate processor that runs asynchronously (there is no form of communication between processors, no shared global memory, no central control).   A non-Cartesian robot has a complex but hierarchical, non-deterministic structure which derives its intelligence through a process of self-organization among competences. Non-Cartesian robots are a direct result of research concerning situated robotics which stems from the work of Brooks.

IMPACT OF NON-CARTESIANISM ON SOFTWARE ENGINEERING

TAKASHI GOMI
Applied AI Systems, Inc.
Suite 600, Gateway Business Park
340 March Road, Kanata, Ontario Canada K2K 2E4
e-mail: gomi@Applied-AI.com

This paper proposes a novel way of looking at the concept of programs and programming by focusing on a recent development in the method of implementing the process structures necessary to operate intelligent robots and describing its characteristics in the context of Software Engineering. While still proven effective only in a new breed of robotics, there is a possibility the methodology is applicable to a wider range of embedded computing, realtime processes, and potentially to some parts of information processing, particularly if it is combined with evolutionary computational techniques such as GA. The approach could potentially become a crucial programming paradigm, forcing a new way of looking at the very concept of programming.

1 Introduction

The rise of Structured Programming[1,2] meant structuring the components of a program based on an organizational principle, a better encapsulation of program modules, and enforcement of coding disciplines on each of the modules. It also meant the introduction of new concepts in the manner the structure gets implemented. For example, Yourdon emphasized the importance of having all essential modules of a system to be developed identified and registered at the outset. This was encouraged even when it was not clear what their actual algorithm would be. In short, Software Engineering was a serious attempt to bring discipline into the theretofore black art of programming. Although programming still is largely a black art, the approach has been successful in the greater software engineering community and allowed practitioners of programming both in academia and industry easier comprehension of program structures and a more controlled manner of implementing and analyzing algorithms. Structured Programming also established a methodology to deal with the concepts of *module strength* and *module decoupling,* and hence significantly increased the reliability of software in general, and resulted in more efficient production of software. Object-Oriented programming, and some of the *agent* system concepts are the ultimate manner of expressing this approach to running computers. A computer is viewed as a form of automaton where every entity in the system is made accountable for its effects and every state transition traceable.

The move toward a more well-disciplined approach to running computers, however, did not solve the problem of rigidity of computation, and the problems associated with the need to have everything explicitly defined and instructed. Every bit in a program structure needed to be defined in its relationship to a global structure and its values accountable at all times. Computerized systems must be *perfect* at all times and failure to maintain these premises is invariably linked to a system failure. A screen of a personal computer that freezes, a banking network which can crash unexpectedly or an aircraft that can experience a sudden seizure on one of its control surfaces are just a few examples of such a failure. Since it is now common knowledge that total validation of even a moderately complex computerized system is impossible, this is particularly a serious drawback in realtime systems and embedded computing where a large risk, including potential loss of life, is involved. One can see this rigidity as a result of pursuing the Cartesian view on systems and machines. In Cartesian doctrine, which is in the backbone of traditional science, everything needs to be defined, every transition must be proven, and every event needs to be explained.

The notion of *soft computing* being pursued by a number of research groups today is obviously meant to ease the harshness we face by having to depend on the *perfectionism* insisted upon by computers. However, the movement still seems to center on the idea of easing up the restrictions of the hard and rigid framework of conventional computation using tools such as neural networks and fuzzy set theory. However, what is being sought now in terms of softening will not be satisfied by these "padding techniques". The softness must come from the architecture itself and the philosophy that underwrites the architecture. It is us humans who assumed machines and systems need to be *controlled* to the minutest detail and all their behaviors accountable to humans. A system is broken down, typically by its function, into major elements. Each of the elements is then broken down into smaller elements. The process is repeated recursively until all bits and their relationships to others in the system are explained and documented. This process of 'divide and conquer' is not only extremely costly, but also immutable in that once concepts, events, object, or ideas are defined any changes involve a considerable amount of time and effort on the part of the designer. Systems thus produced also lack in flexibility in operation and often cannot adapt to changes that normally happen in the environment where the system is put into use. They are hard to maintain and difficult to comprehend, often even by those who created the systems. Systems designed using the conventional concept of *control* are *closed.* The idea of *autonomy* is a key to get out of this bind and build systems that are *open.*

2 Non-Cartesian programming

2.1 Background

The 1980s saw the rise of an approach to tackle the issue of artificial intelligence (AI) from a new angle. Rodney Brooks of The Massachusetts Institute of Technology (MIT) proposed Subsumption Architecture in 1986[3] as a very unique, and controversial way of running intelligent robots. His approach is based on the principle of self-organization that results from dynamic activities of simple agents. This is not too different from what Stephanie Forrest proposed as a concept in the early 1990s as *emergent computation*[4]. Around that time the greater scientific community itself was also opening its eyes to the new manner of looking at the world and the reality as a *complex system* partly through a new discipline of research called Artificial Life [5].

As evident in most of the computerized systems in use and under development today, the whole purpose of creating a computer program is so that automation with some level of complexity and sophistication could be realized the way the instigator of the system and ultimately the programmer have wanted. In other words, no matter how complex and detailed the program appears, a computer is no more than an elaborate automaton that executes the intended algorithm. All steps executed are accountable and explainable. Necessary intelligence is said to be generated out of the explicit execution of known steps.

The non-Cartesian view on intelligence differs from that implied in conventional programming methodologies in a simple but fundamental manner. In his discussion on the nature of intelligence Brooks states, "Intelligence resides in the eyes of the beholder"[6]. Intelligence, as beauty, is viewed as a property detectable (visible, audible, touchable, etc.) only in a context, and in relation to an observer, and not as an independent entity by itself. Development of a system based on functional decomposition (the dominant design approach today) clearly ignores this view. Many researchers also misunderstood what intelligence really is, as eloquently pointed out by Rolf Pfeifer as "the frame of reference problem".[9] The failure to recognize this shift in epistemological stance on the nature of intelligence was one of the mistakes made by researchers in traditional AI for the past few decades. Table 2.1 summarizes a number of key AI researchers and roboticists who share the new view on intelligence or the approach in building systems.

Table 2.1 Key researchers active in "New AI"

Stephanie Forrest (Professor, U. New Mexico)	*Emergent Computation*
Pattie Maes (Associate Professor, MIT Media Laboratory)	*Action Selection Dynamics (ASD),* Agent-based Approach, Soft Robots, Interface Agents
Rodney Brooks (Professor/Director, MIT AI Lab)	*Subsumption Architecture (SA),* Behavior-Based AI
Chris Langton (Director Artificial Life Program, Sante Fe Institute)	*Collectionism*
Rolf Pfeifer (Professor, Head, Artificial Intelligence Lab, U. Zurich)	"Fungus Eater", *New AI*, non-Cartesian computation
Luc Steels (Director, Sony Computer Science Laboratory, Paris)	*Selectionism*
Thomas Christeller Director, German National Research Center for Information Technology	Social and Reflective Robots, Software agents
Ian Horswill (Assistant Professor, Northwestern University)	Habitat Constraint Computational Vision, non-Newtonian computation
Jean-Arcady Meyer Ecole Normale Supérieure	*Animat* Approach and *Biorobotics*
Inman Harvey (Research Fellow, Evolutionary Robotics Group, U. Sussex)	*SAGA* paradigm
Stewart Wilson (Roland Institute)	*Animat* Approach

2.2 What is non-Cartesian programming?

The basic unit of a non-Cartesian program is a simple expression of causality, such as a production rule consisting of an <if ... then ...> sentence. As explained further in Section 3 below, it can be implemented in a number of ways including hardware implementation. In non-Cartesian programming, an agent or the expression of causality, however implemented, is arranged in such a manner that it can be invoked, totally independent of other agents, by some external input(s) when a condition to invoke it is satisfied. In this regard, non-Cartesian programming is not just another agent system. There is no main routine to call an agent, no caller/callee relationships between an agent and another program body, no centralized scheduling of tasks that invoke agents, nor centralized control mechanism in the case of hardware implementation. And there is no hierarchical arrangement of the units, components, or agents in terms of the levels of abstraction which they represent or at which they operate. The agents are simply laid out side by side, each one of them independently *invokable* asynchronously and at its own initiative. In short, the system implemented in non-Cartesian programming is fully distributed in its structure, without a control mechanism, and its operation is autonomous. The lack of center of control is particulary important. A process can be invoked totally by an external condition perceived by an agent and does not require another entity to exert a control for it to be executed. The external condition for invocation could be any form of sensor inputs, signaling (reporting) by a human through an input device, or the arrival of a message via a communication channel of any sort.

The result of agents thus invoked is a process structure that emerges temporarily with its own dynamic and tentative control hierarchy and inter-process relationships as in the "bottom invoked top structure" in Langton's *Collectionism*. The structure is only dynamically supportable and, even in this form, in most cases cannot be sustained permanently due to changes that naturally occur in its own operational environment. The structure is not meant to execute an algorithm either. An algorithm to represent functioning of such a dynamic structure does not exist *a priori* and the simple causality that is described within each agent is too simple and minute to be termed an algorithm. The entire organization is a form of *complex system* in the sense that the total effect of the system is often greater than the sum of the effects of each process involved. In contrast, conventional computation based on algorithms is but a deterministic *simple system* no matter how complex the algorithms and/or their implementation could be. The designer of the program knows explicitly what is to be achieved and the programmer simply documents the process to cause the desired set of effects.

The conventional approach is also Cartesian as the algorithms involved are sought so as to establish computability of a proposed solution to a perceived problem. The entire scheme fits nicely in the Cartesian framework of deductively proving a hypothesis, as discussed in great detail by Descartes[8]. Indeed, conventional programming is Cartesian in its spirit and practice. It is a process of deductively proving an algorithms through top-down breakdown of functions, inputs, and outputs, and documenting the broken-down fragments until the last bit is documented. The proposed non-Cartesian scheme differs drastically from this approach, and works well at least when applied to intelligent robots which try to achieve practical tasks in a real environment. Such an implementation in the form of a robot is said to be *situated* and *embodied*. It is still not clear and at best debatable if and how a non-Cartesian program performs in conventional information processing which is *unsituated, unembodied*, or both.

2.3 An example non-Cartesian program

(1) A simple program to run a robot in a complex environment

Figure 2.1 shows the agent structure of an example non-Cartesian program implemented for a behavior-based robot called R2, and Figure 2.2 presents the actual code that was written to implement the agents and the structure. The robot's hardware was originally produced by Brooks' group at MIT. The experiment was designed by the author and the

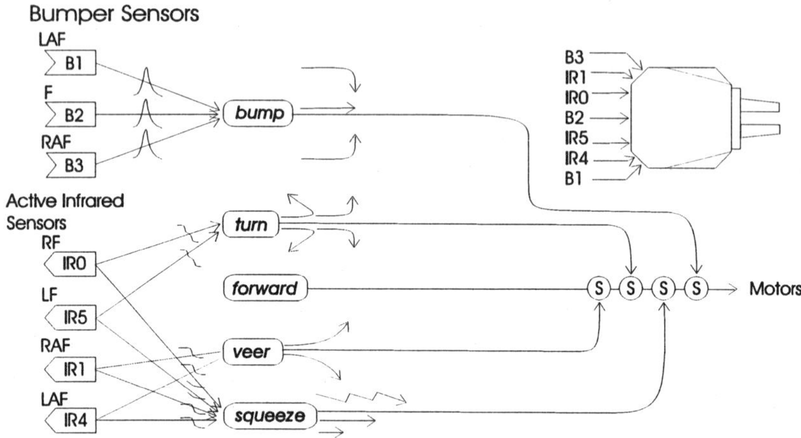

Figure 2.1 Agent structure of a program that allows passing of intelligent robots through a narrow passage

program was implemented by J-C Laurence[9] of Applied AI Systems, Inc (AAI) in the form of Subsumption Architecture. It describes agents collectively intended to give R2 the ability to run through a narrow passage, such as the one shown in Figure 2.3, avoiding contact with the walls, a bottleneck in the passageway, and later, another moving robot. Narrow corridors and passageways of this type are often found in factories and warehouses. In fact, the experiment was meant to test a prototype mobile platform for investigating effectiveness of behavior-based techniques in transportation applications such as AGV (Autonomous Ground Vehicle). An analysis of the tasks involved had been conducted and a set of component behaviors or agents to synthetically generate the behaviors of the robot in *all* circumstances anticipated in the set up was determined.

The behavior set is described as five independent agents that are not linked directly, but only through the environment via sensor inputs and output currents sent to two motors. The R2 robot, in this experiment, has 3 bump sensors, 4 active infrared sensors, and two motors. Left and right front wheels are differentially driven by these motors, while the rear of the robot is supported by two omni-directional casters. Other sensors which surround the circumference of the robot are ignored in defining the behaviors as they do not significantly contribute to the motions of the robot in this experiment. Each of the bump sensors generates an electronic pulse which manifests itself as a non-zero integer value in a register after an analog-to-digital (AD) conversion.

Each of the active infrared sensors emits an infrared signal at a specified duty cycle (at about 30 Hz) and returns an analog value on the receptor segment of the sensor. The value becomes the strength of the reflected signal as an integer in a register. These register values are then directly converted by a corresponding agent into a pair of values that designate the size and polarity of current fed to the motors using pulse width modulation (PWM). The actual energy sent to the motors is determined by associated servo controller circuitry.

The important aspect of this short example program is that it only defines a set of simple actions that the agents would take if invoked. Despite their simplicity, upon invocation, they collectively generate sufficient intelligence to drive the robot through the passageway and around any obstacles, including another mobile robot. The agents do not contain a description of how the robot avoids the walls, bottlenecks in the path, and other robots, or for that matter, how and in which direction it proceeds in the corridor in the first place. It only specifies at a very low level how and when the motors react in response to specific sensor inputs. The intelligence is generated through the phenomenon called *emergence*[10] as it is known in the study of *complex systems*. *Emergence* results from an asynchronous invocation of dynamic and non-linear processes. Although emergence is caused by a number of parallel agents in which the

```
(include "plsys;plutils.beh")
(include "r2sys;r2control.beh")

(defconstant $straight 0)
(defconstant $straight-hi 11)
(defconstant $1eft-turn 3)
(defconstant $right-turn 4)
(defconstant $1eft-veer 1)
(defconstant $right-veer 2)
(defconstant $halt 5)

(defbehavior init
  :outputs (start)
  :decls ((begin:init 0))
  :processes(
      (whenever (= begin 0)
          (setf begin 1)
          (delay .3)
          (set-force-mode)
          (finger-brake-off)
          (fingers-open)
          (delay 3.0)
          (finger-brake-on)
          (lift-brake-off)
          (lift-down)
          (delay 1.0)
          (lift-up)
          (delay 1.0)
          (lift-brake-on)
          (output start 1))))

(defbehavior feet
  :inputs (direction start)
  :decls ((begin:init 0))
  :processes(
    (whenever (received? start)
          (setf begin 1))
    (whenever (received? direction)
          (if (= begin 1)
             (sequence
             (cond
          ((= direction $straight) (move -22 -25))
          ((= direction $1eft-veer) (move -25 -12))
          ((=direction $right-veer) (move -12 -25))
          ((=direction $1eft-turn) (move -15 15))
          ((= direction $right-turn) (move 15 -15))
          ((= direction $halt) (move 20))
          ((=direction $straight-hi)(move -34)))))))))

(defbehavio bump
  :outputs (direction)
  :processes(
      (whenever (/= (bump 1) 0)
          (output direction $right-turn))
      (whenever (/= (bump 3) 0)            (output
direction $1eft-turn))
      (whenever (/= (bump 2) 0)
          (output direction $halt))))
```

```
(defbehavior turn
  :outputs (direction)
  :processes(
      (whenever (= (range 5) 4)
          (output direction $right-veer))
      (whenever (= (range 0) 4)
          (output direction $1eft-veer))
      (whenever (< (range 5) 4)
          (output direction $right-turn))
      (whenever (< (range 0) 3)
          (output direction $1eft-turn))))

(defbehavior forward
  :outputs (direction
  :processes(
      (whenever t
          (output direction $straight))))

(delbehavio veer
  :outputs (direction)
  :processes(
      (whenever (< (range 4) 5)
          (output direction $right-veer))
      (whenever (< (range 1) 5)
          (output direction $1eft-veer))))

(defbehavior squeeze
  :outputs (direction)
  :processes(
      (whenever (and (< (range 1) 5)
          (< (range 4) 5))
          (> (range 0) 4)            ;; speed.
          (> (range 5) 4))
        (output direction $straight-hi)))
      (whenever (or (and (= (range 4) 4)
                  (> (range 5) 4)
                  (> (range 0) 4)
                  (> (range 1) 4))
           (and (= (range 1) 4)
                  (> (range 5) 4)
                  (> (range 0) 4)
                  (> (range 4) 4)))
          (output direction $straight))
      (whenever (and (< (range 0) 3)
                  (< (range 1) 3))
          (output direction $left-turn))))

(connect (init start)(feet start))
(connect (default direction) (feet direction))
(connect (veer direction) (feet direction)
  ((inhibit (default direction))))
(connect (turn direction) (feet direction)
  ((inhibit (default direction)))
          ((inhibit (veer direction))))
(connect (squeeze direction) (feet direction)
  ((inhibit (turn direction)))
```

```
                    ((inhibit (veer direction)))
                    ((inhibit (default direction))))
(connect (bump direction) (feet direction)
((inhibit (default direction)))
                    ((inhibit (veer direction)))
                  ; ((inhibit (turn direction)))
                    ((inhibit (squeeze direction))))
```

Figure 2.2 Code that implements the agent structure of Figure 2.1

parameters have non-linear relationships among themselves, the emphasis is on *emergence,* **not** on *parallelism* per se.

In Figures 2.1 and 2.2, agent *bump* detects a contact with the environment through a set of contact sensors (B1, B2, B3) and generates a turn towards the opposite direction, or stops the robot if the collision is frontal. The *turn* agent prepares a pair of current values for the motors in response to the strength of reflection of two frontal infrared beams emitted by the active infrared sensors IR0 and IR5. The sharpness of the turn corresponds to the strength of the reflection and the direction of the turn corresponds to the direction of the reflection. The agent *forward* responds to a null sensor the value of which is always 'true' and issues a steady set of current values to drive the motors straight forward. The *veer* agent looks at the two front diagonal infrared sensors (IR1 and IR4) and generates a set of gradual opposite turn signals to the motors. This puts the robot into an oscillatory motion if two angular-front obstacles are located in a certain manner. The *squeeze* agent breaks the dead-lock by proceeding cautiously if there are obstacles front-diagonally (IR1 and IR4) but not frontally (IR0 and IR5). This allows the robot to 'sneak through' a narrow gap despite obstacle warnings from IR1 and IR4.

The outputs from these agents are put through a network to evaluate priorities. Each agent is given a priority at which its output is honored. The right-most output (output of the *bump* agent)in Figure 2.1 is given the highest priority while the left most output (of the *forward* agent) is treated at the lowest priority. The structure is implemented in the coding of Figure 2.2 using *connect* function.

(2) Adaptive trajectory of R2 robot

When the robot with the agents or component behaviors defined in Figures 2.1 and 2.2 is put into action in a narrow corridor illustrated in Figure 2.3, it proceeds forward (because *forward* process is always on) and maintains its course roughly straight in the approximate center of the corridor. This is because the process structure that emerges when *turn* and *veer* agents are executed tries to keep it so. If the R2 robot deviates from this established norm for whatever reasons, these processes work together to bring it to this dynamic equilibrium. The robot proceeds while constantly adjusting its position, orientation, and speed, or its relationship in this equilibrium. The equilibrium in turn changes in accordance with situations at hand. An equilibrium a moment (say, 100 milliseconds) ago is more often than not different from the one that exists now. Since infrared reflections from the walls of the corridor are not uniform along the length of the corridor and the floor does not have an even spread of friction against the rubber-capped drive wheels of the robot, the exact trajectory of the robot is not always straight, rigid, nor precise just as trajectories of an animal would not be. This is particularly true when the robot is traveling through the narrow passage (the bottleneck) formed by the protruding structure (an odd-shaped box placed in the mock-up corridor) and a wall on the opposite side. The exact trajectory of the robot also varies from run to run for a number of reasons such as variation in starting position and/or orientation of the robot, difference in friction between parts of the rubber tire and the specific spots on the floor the robot happens to be traveling, and changes in ambient infrared levels and their pattern of fluctuations, etc. The *uncertainty* associated with the runs is due to the robot's dependence on its relationship to the operational environment as it is detected through the robot's sensors and experienced through its wheels and casters. Therefore, the runs are totally dependent on how the robot detects various facets of the real world and how

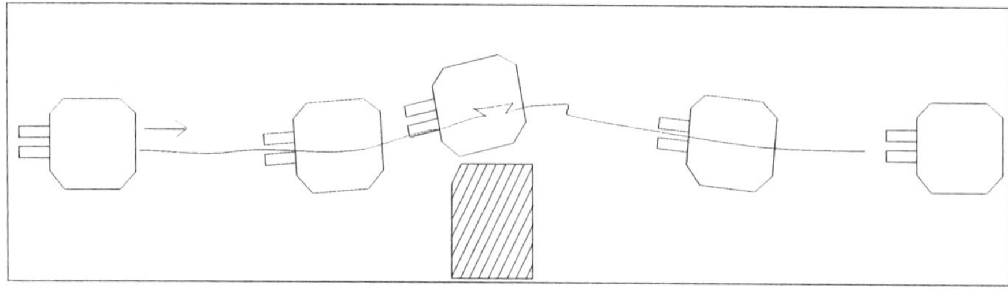

Figure 2.3 A narrow passage with an obstacle

it reacts to them. There is no 'theater of intelligence' which coordinates behaviors onboard the robot and manifests its authority by handing down the control to the drive wheels, as in most, if not all conventional mobile robots.

(3) The flexibility and the robustness of the robot's motion

To those accustomed to the concept of *control* as in control system theory where accuracy, rigidity, repeatability, exactness, assertiveness, and precision are a virtue, the volatile, non-deterministic, and fleeting nature of the robot's operation may seem undesirable. However, this is the same set of characteristics fully autonomous beings such as insects, animals, and humans who are expert in dealing with an uncertain *open world* possess and use. The R2 robot described above is not an automaton under a strict direction but an autonomous machine. R2 in this set up, despite a very simple agent structure, can cope with a much wider range of situations than an ordinary *controlled* robot with identical hardware and a similar amount of software could. Among others, it can quickly respond to changes in its operational environment. If a new obstacle of arbitrary type is thrown into its path, the robot can, without prior knowledge of the location, shape, and dimensions of the obstacle, quickly determine in its action if it can safely pass by it or not, and if it can, through which trajectory and at what speed! If it can't initially, it repeats the search for a passage automatically and perpetually like an animal trapped in a corner. If someone lifts the robot up during a run and relocates it somewhere else in the corridor, or any other floor space, it can instantly position itself away from obstacles, choose an orientation and initial speed, and resume operation immediately.

(4) The dynamic nature of the robot's run

These desirable characteristics for a mobile robot are all exhibited even in very dynamic real-life situations. When faced with a new set of conditions, the robot does not stop and 'think' but acts instantly to adjust to the changes. The dynamic nature of the robot's actions is especially clear when the robot encounters another mobile robot in action in a confined passage such as the one shown in Figure 2.3. Our repeated experiments show that R2 maintained a roughly straight course while avoiding walls and the bottleneck. It did so despite the complete lack of centralized structure that evaluates situations at hand, plans for the 'best' action sequence to take, and monitors the execution of the chosen set of actions. The nature of the exhibited intelligence here is in line with the notion of intelligence as an observed side-effect of a dynamic process[6,7]. If properly organized, an agent structure embedded on-board a fully autonomous robot can dynamically yield the necessary intelligence to cope with events, situations, and the intended or implied goal at hand.

(5) The open nature of design

The program that runs the R2 robot is not based on a fixed model but on a form of a volatile dynamic model that emerges from time to time as the robot tries to adjust its behavior to its changing relationship with the environment. In other words, the model is, as is the robot's behavior, emergent as a result of self organization. Since it is not fixed, the robot can perform a wider range of adaptive behaviors, most of which is not even designed nor intended by the designer of the robot or that of the agents. Even with a relatively small number of agents, the full combination of all internal states of each of the agents would rapidly grow with the number of agents. And because of the non-linear relationship between input and output parameters of such agents, the resulting dynamism will have a very wide range in a number of dimensions. That non-Cartesian robots have dynamism and adaptability beyond those perceived by the designer of the robot gives rise to the assumption that the robot is capable of adapting to more open situations than generally expected. In fact, as described below, the R2 robot has demonstrated its ability to cope in unexpected situations beyond what was originally intended for the experiment.

The R2 robot was eventually pitted against a T-2 robot in the same narrow passageway, as shown in Figure 2.4. The T-2 robot, which has similar dimensions and motion characteristics, was equipped with a similar set of sensors and agents as the R2. Now, not only do both R2 and T-2 have to negotiate a narrow passage, they have to deal with an additional moving obstacle which, if placed near the center of the path, is singularly capable of blocking the progress of the other robot. Without additional agents, the two robots were capable of avoiding and passing each other despite the fact that the relative speed between the robot and the obstacle is now about double. Speaking of the speed, the total time required to execute the code shown in Figure 2.2 is less than a millisecond, even if all the agents got activated in serial in this simulated parallelism set up. Since the active infrared (IR) sensors return the strength of reflection from obstacles at 30 Hz or every 33.3 millisecond, theoretically the robots could pass each other at more than 30 times the current speed of about 30 cm per second per robot, should one find strong enough motors to drive the robots and a way to construct the robots so that they can withstand very sharp turns.

The point to be made here is the achievement of the unprecedented code efficiency of the program and the program's even more remarkable performance when carrying out tasks which are known to be very difficult or impossible in conventional programming. When traveling the wider section of the corridor, typically a quick 'negotiation' takes place between the two robots and a set of two complementary spaces between the opposing robot and a wall is secured. Through repeated and quick adjustments of the heading and the relative position, each robot can find sufficient space and pass each other uneventfully. The result is impressive and amazing in a way, as the two robots repeatedly pass each other smoothly as if they are living animals with ample intelligence to negotiate the passage. When the agents were designed, there was not even a plan to try the robot against a moving obstacle. Yet, the same set of agents for solo runs collectively manage to yield enough intelligence to cope with this greatly more dynamic situation.

When the two robots meet at the bottleneck, as illustrated in Figure 2.5, each robot attempts to push its own way, and a deadlock between the two robots ensues. By adding a simple agent to R2 (called **back-off**) which forces the robot to back off for a few seconds when it frontally faces a moving obstacle, the R2 robot now momentarily retracts upon a face to face meeting with the T-2 robot. Because space is offered in front of the advance-only T-2 robot, it now proceeds. Depending on the situation, the R2 backs off further, often pushed backward past the bottleneck, and eventually leaves enough space on its side for T-2 to pass by. After the T-2 moves past R2, R2 can now proceed past the bottleneck.

(6) The graceful degradation

The R2 robot with the program shown in Figures 2.1 and 2.2 also demonstrated impressive graceful degradation characteristics. If the **veer** agent stops working for any reason (e.g., failure or deterioration of sensors, wrong threshold, electrical connections), the robot is still capable of making somewhat more jagged turns to avoid obstacles using the **turn** agent. If the **turn** agent and not the **veer** agent loses its ability, the **veer** agent would try to handle all avoidance turns except the ones due to collision with an obstacle, in which case the **bump** agent would generate recovery turns. The robot in this situation would travel among obstacles trying to avoid them by making only gradual turns that the **veer** agent generates. However, such large turns would sooner or later result in a collision with an obstacle since some of the obstacles are bound to be near the robot's course and the **veer** agent would not be able to issue sharp enough turns to avoid them. If the **bump** agent survives while both **veer** and **turn** are dead, the robot

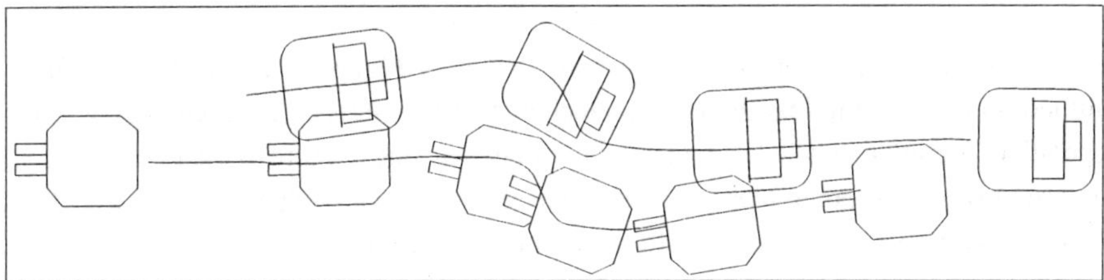

Figure 2.4 Two robots passing each other in a narrow corridor

would move *forward* until it hits an obstacle, and then try to continue moving forward after the **bump** agent forces it to turn away from the obstacle. This will result in a ricochet trajectory as often seen in behaviors of partially incapacitated insects or those of animals in stress. If only the ***bump*** agent survives, the robot would still try to avoid touching by a human by swinging the body away from the touch, like an animal seriously wounded which still tries to avoid human contact.

There are more possible combinations of able and disabled agents and in each case the robot will exhibit partially compromised behaviors that reflect the loss of specific agents. This is unlike most conventional computer-driven systems which, in most cases, stop working altogether upon an encounter with even the slightest of faults. In non-Cartesian programs, the system would continue to yield some actions towards the achievement of the effect of the original set of actions. Like animals, when deprived of some of their faculties, the system would still continue to maintain behaviors as close to the complete behavior set as possible. This form, level, and extent of graceful

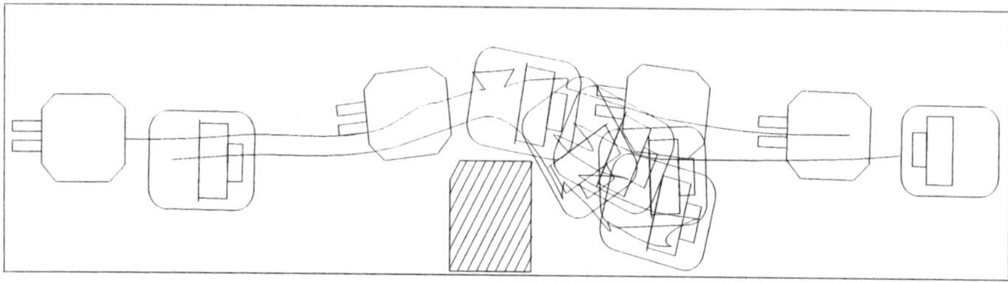

Figure 2.5 Two robots passing each other near a bottleneck

degradation has not been achieved in conventional computerized systems. But as shown here, it can be realized rather easily in non-Cartesian programming.

(7) The collection of agents as an autonomous system

The R2 or T-3 robot with agent structure shown in Figures 2.1 and 2.2 is a fully autonomous system in that there is no mechanism that exerts external control over its operation. Stimuli received through sensors can invoke one or more of the agents, which in turn moves the robot to a position itself where more stimuli might become detectible. If there is no change in stimuli pattern and/or level, it will stay put until a change in situation is detected. The system continues to operate autonomously just by reacting to situations at hand. The <if ... then ...> rules (coded in the example of Figure 2.2 as <Whenever (*condition*) (*action*)>) resemble in their appearance a production rule used in *expert systems* or *knowledge-based systems* of two decades ago. However, there is a crucial difference between the conventional AI systems mentioned and the system I have presented here. In fact, the driving principles of the two approaches to programming differ very significantly. In knowledge-based/expert systems, so-called 'reasoning' is said to take place as the result of the invocation of rules by a central execution control facility often called *inference engine*. It typically *forward chains* or *backward chains* production rules, and inference is assumed to occur when each of the chained production rules is explicitly executed.

In the execution of a non-Cartesian program, there is no involvement of a centralized facility such as an inference engine. There is no main routine or task scheduler to govern the execution of the agents. Each production rule can be invoked only by an event external to it as it is detected in the condition clause of the production rule. The condition clause often contains a description of the relationship between two or more sensor values, and/or sensor value(s) and fixed threshold(s). Values obtained through sensors assigned to the rule during the time of the rule's definition thus dictate the way the rule gets invoked.

The example non-Cartesian program discussed above demonstrates much of the preferable characteristics of the approach. It is clearly different from conventional programming in a number of ways. In seeking resemblance to conventional programs, one notices that each of the agents shown in Figure 2.2 runs like a device handler in a real-time operating system. Both an agent in non-Cartesian programming and a device handler in conventional programming are independent from each other and each has a priority assigned to it.

2.4 Nature of non-Cartesian programs

The manner in which the R2 and T-2 robots are run is quite unique in the field of intelligent mobile robotics. In conventional mobile robotics, robots are the target of *control* and their motions are under tight management of a control program built for that purpose. Robots run with non-Cartesian programs are an autonomous system. The fundamental difference manifests in almost all aspects of the running of the two types of robots. It is the algorithm that generates intelligence in conventional programs, whereas in non-Cartesian programs intelligence is only a side-effect of a process that self-organizes a series of dynamic equilibria in response to changing relationships between a system and its environment. Table 2.2 compares these and other aspects of the two approaches in robotics.

444

Table 2.2 Comparison of Cartesian and Non-Cartesian intelligent robots

Aspects	Cartesian intelligent robot	Non-Cartesian intelligent robot
Nature of operation	*Control*	*Autonomy*
Identification of entities involved	**Definitions** - Defining robot's position, work, operational environment movements, actions, and tasks	**No definitions** - Position, motion, plan, effective spheres of operation, and even goals are *emergent*
Method of representatioon of entities in robot	**Models** to visualize, structure, and document the **defined** entities	**No models** - instead, a robot maintains a collection of agents to cope with reality
Bases of generation of robot's actions	**Measurements** - position, velocity, momentum, mass, force, all need to be measured frequently and continuously	**No measurements.** Humans as an intelligent agent, for example, do not measure parameters in their execution of actions but seeks **affordance**
Nature of processing	**Computation** to verify compliance of robot's actions to the **definitions** and **models** through **measurements**	**No computation** but **reactive invocation** of agents to respond to changes in operational environment

Method of generation of action sequence	**Planning** - tasks and a detailed sequence of actions in each task need to be planned in advance mostly in explicit terms in accordance with preset **goals**. Any deviations from a **plan** must be checked and corrected through frequent **measurements**.	**Emergent goals** and **plans**. Serious real world tasks are too complex to be explicitly planned. Only rough task sequences (an **agenda**) could be maintained. The actual sequence of actions *emerges* through self-organization involving robot's condition and operational environment
Method of obtaining intelligence	By executing **algorithm** prepared to underwrite a **plan**	**No algorithm** -intelligence *emerges* as a result of self-organization involving *agent-invoked* processes
Format of execution	Explicit and/or implicit **centralized control** of execution of tasks and modules	**No centralization** nor **control** - spontaneous, asynchronous, and parallel invocation of independent *agents* in software or hardware
Distribution of action generation mechanism	Overt or covert **singularity** in system	**No singularity** - agents that implement processes can be distributed as needed through a system
Method of managing levels of abstraction	Explicit functional **hierarchy** designed and implemented in control structure	No predefined **hierarchy** - hierarchical structures may *emerge* dynamically in operation but none permanent
Nature of system	*Closed*	*Open*

3 Implementation options of non-Cartesian programming

I suspect that there are more than a few cases of earlier attempts of non-Cartesian programming prior to Brooks' Subsumption Architecture. However, it was

Subsumption Architecture that shed a clear light on the unique characteristics and capabilities of this type of programming, and made researchers and practitioners aware of the potential of the approach. That he implemented the concept as programs to run intelligent robots made it easy to manifest the true nature of the approach. Since his early attempts using Augmented Finite State Machines (AFSM), a large number of programming techniques in this approach have been tried successfully in running a wide range of intelligent robots, demonstrating the versatility of the approach and the coherence of the principles behind it. Below is a description of some of the options successfully attempted and still in use in implementing a 'program' that realizes a non-Cartesian process structure.

(1) Behavior Language option

In 1990, Brooks developed Behavior Language (BL) as a superstructure to LISP[11]. It has a syntax similar to LISP but with an added mechanism to define *behaviors,* or a causal relationship that links a condition described in terms of sensory input(s) to actuator output(s). Programs written in BL translate into LISP, then into assembler of a target computer. After assembly, the object module is linked to a customized real time operating system and supporting library modules prepared for the program, and then downloaded onto a microprocessor or micro-controller onboard a robot. The robot then executes the *behaviors* as defined under the supervision of the customized operating system within a simulated parallelism framework.

The BL system has been used in university courses, workshops, and engineering practices in industry for several years. It gave a convenient ready-made mechanism for implementing Subsumption Architecture, the dominant non-Cartesian programming method. Despite its shortcomings (basically integer arithmetic with limited ability to express equations, small number of available target processors despite the language system's multi-target architecture, quasi-multitasking architecture that depends on polling), it has been accepted as a convenient tool to create small-scale software structures that get embedded onto a behavior-based intelligent system with remarkable results. In our research alone, BL has been used in[9,12-16]. The language is still in use today in the development of software for some smaller mobile robots.

(2) LISP option

LISP is naturally non-Cartesian. Functions in LISP are all written as a causal relationship (as are functions in many other languages, but here in a very visible and consistent manner). LISP enforces a syntax that emphasizes the compactness of a causal relationship as the unit of programming, and this is also the unit construct in non-Cartesian programming that describes an agent. For this reason, a few attempts were made to build a software structure for behavior-based robots. In 1991, Koza implemented a notion of Subsumption Architecture in LISP on intelligent robots in simulation to demonstrate the power of Genetic Programming in evolving robots' behavior [17,18].

(3) L option

L is a dialect of full LISP language developed by Brooks in 1993 [19]. It is a language system which allows incremental compilation. It is considered as a successor to BL with additional features. Automatic generation of real time operating systems is also a main feature of the system. The processor-language structure was implemented typically using a Motorola 68332 processing board. The combined structure has been used in a number of behavior-based robots such as Hermes[20] and Pioneer[21] and in some non-robotic realtime intelligent system applications.

(4) C option

Most high-level symbolic languages, such as C, can be used to build an agent structure for a non-Cartesian program. In fact, almost all programs written for intelligent robots built by us have been written in C for the past few years. Functions (subroutines, procedures, or functions in other symbolic languages) are defined to express a causal relationship typically using an *if* statement. A *main* routine that governs the syntactic structure of the program is required in almost all high-level languages for a program definition to be complete. A program can only then proceed to *linking* the library and other logistic modules that compose an infrastructure for its run-time environment. Under this strictly von-Neumann top-down provision, some manipulation of the modules will be necessary to make a program non-Cartesian. For example, the *main* routine may have to act as a mechanism to support the *simulated parallelism* operation by monitoring invocation criteria of all agents in the system and invoking ones which meet the criterion. Or it could simply poll all defined agents serially and let each agent decide whether it is to be invoked during the current cycle or not. In a more grandiose manner, each of the agents in a structure can be defined as a task and let a real multi-tasking operating system look after management of the simulated parallelism. In any of these cases, as already shown, agents in non-Cartesian programs are all very short and sufficient effects of parallelism are obtainable out of the respective simulated parallelism attempt. Figure 3.1 is an example of a large-scale, polling-based, non-

448

Cartesian application written in C, with the exception of a few agents written in assembler. The program runs a motorized wheelchair autonomously through a complicated real world environment using landmark navigation. The total size of the software, including the vision processing, is only about 57 KBytes.

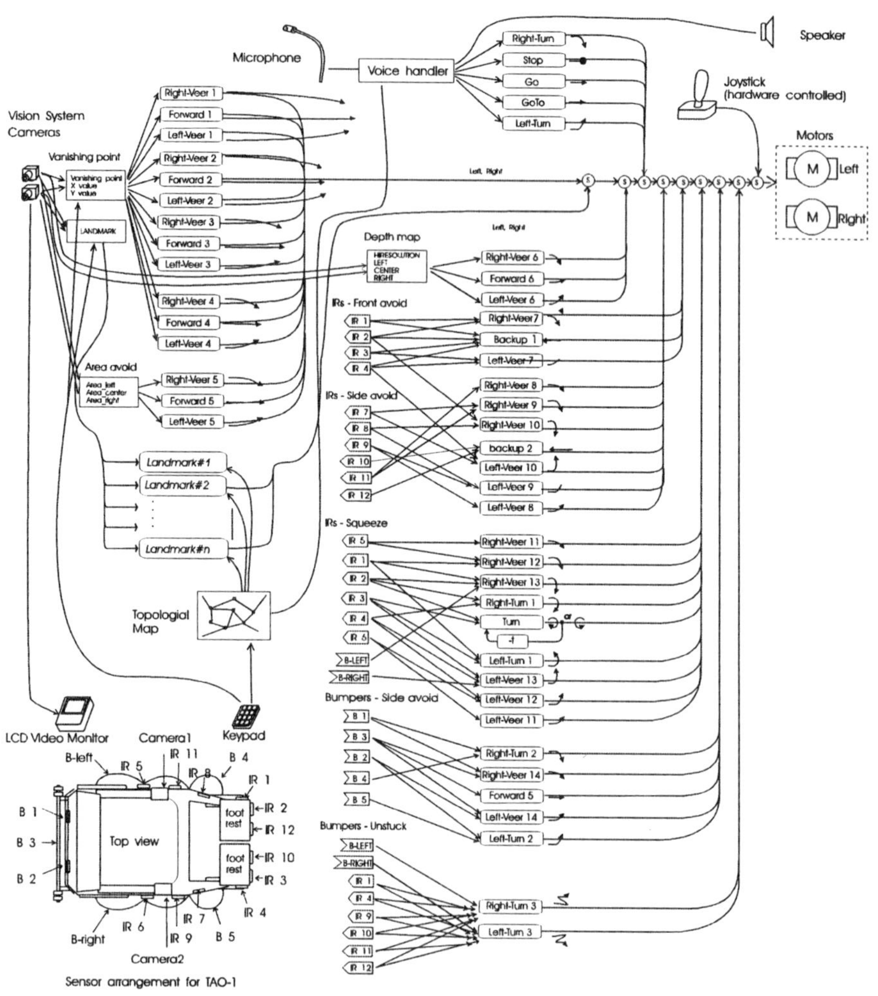

Figure 3.1 An example of a large non-Cartesian program implemented in C

(5) Assembler option

The non-Cartesian process architecture can easily be implemented in assembler languages. The same reasons for using languages which allow symbolic "high level" representation in conventional programming also exist in non-Cartesian programming. They are: lessening of cognitive load, efficiency in inter- and intra-programmer communication during development and maintenance, and the clarity of programs for explanation to the third parties that aid the management of the program development and maintenance processes. Nevertheless, as in conventional programming, certain programming tasks just have to be written in an assembler either due to unavailability of a suitable symbolic language for implementing minute tasks to be performed under tight temporal or spacial constraints. This was the case in some of our experience when we tried to implement a Subsumption Architecture structure on a vision processing board built around a DSP (Digital Signal Processor)[13,22] . In these cases, an efficient non-Cartesian program structure was obtained using assembler, with very satisfactory results.

(6) Neural network option

Several neural implementations of behaviors on robots have been attempted [23-26]. They are non-Cartesian in that they satisfy most of the characteristics shown in Table 2.2 above. Certainly, they are not Cartesian robots in that they do not render themselves to constant control from a system above such as a human operator or a fixed main routine. In fact, it seems easy and natural to materialize a non-Cartesian process structure using neural networks. However, there is a drawback in this approach in terms of lost agility and responsiveness when compared with a collection of reactive agents as discussed so far or as in Braitenberg vehicle[27]. Each time input patterns change, a considerable amount of time is needed until output of the network for the input pattern is obtained. It is suspected that the loss in responsiveness is due to processing time within the neural network.

The software implementation of a neural network is typically done by having a learning rule such as back propagation implemented in a language like C. This borders on the "execution of an algorithm" and results in slowed down processes. The hardware implementation of non-Cartesian programming combined with neural network technology could be achieved in the form of a collection of advanced neural network chips in which their ability to detect learned patterns can be executed in an insignificant period of time. The desirable speed of processing of such neuro-chips is of course relative to the speed of the rest of the non-Cartesian processing, such as the time

450

required to switch context at task level when a detection by a neural network occurs, or overhead caused by other so-called housekeeping functions conducted around the chip assembly. The effect of combining neural networks and non-Cartesian programming has not been fully explored except for a few attempts including our preliminary experiments[13,28]. This is expected to be a rich area of research to be fully investigated and analyzed in the future.

In some of the experiments we have conducted, one or more neural networks have been downloaded onto a robot so that it can run host-free[28-30]. The additional module strength and lowered dependence on external support the robot exhibits due to the embedding of software gives a heightened sense of autonomy.

(7) Graphic programming language option

Graphic programming languages are an effective tool to implement non-Cartesian programs. Developed mostly for conventional realtime applications such as process monitoring and control, they are also suited for describing process structures in non-Cartesian programs. An agent or a component behavior can be easily described often merely by clicking on icons displayed on the graphical list of available process types. LabView and PACLIB are good examples of this line of development tools readily available on the market. When using these tools, however, care must be given in composing processes in order to make the system truly non-Cartesian. The urge to introduce a procedural arrangement of icons to achieve the effects perceived in the mind of a programmer is very enticing. It is easy to visualize "what might be happening in the heart of an intelligent system" and think procedurally from there. This prevents one from freely composing a non-Cartesian program. Instead, the system must be broken down into a collection of small independent, self contained task-achieving processes. The icons that represent these processes needs to be structured in such a way that, when activated, they collectively form a cluster of parallel processes with minimal or no direct interactions among themselves but only interactions through their actions exerted onto the environment. When activated they should run in parallel and asynchronously, driven mostly by events which occur in the environment.

(8) The AFSM option

AFSM is a term used as a building block by Brooks when he first introduced Subsumption Architecture[3,31]. It is a finite state machine (FSM) with extensions such as a mechanism that allows the replacement of an input bit string with an alternative stream, suspension of output by an external signal, and auto-triggering of an event using a built in clock. Although a system of AFSMs can be designed manually, in the late 1980s Brooks used to maintain a behavior compiler which generated block diagrams of AFSMs which output diagrams detailed enough for immediate assembly in hardware. A number of intelligent robots were built this way [31-33]. This approach to programming has not been pursued in recent years possibly because the granularity of the building block is too fine to depict agents as the total agent structure has grown considerably since the earlier days of Subsumption Architecture robots. Figure 3.2 is an example AFSM structure for an intelligent robot[34].

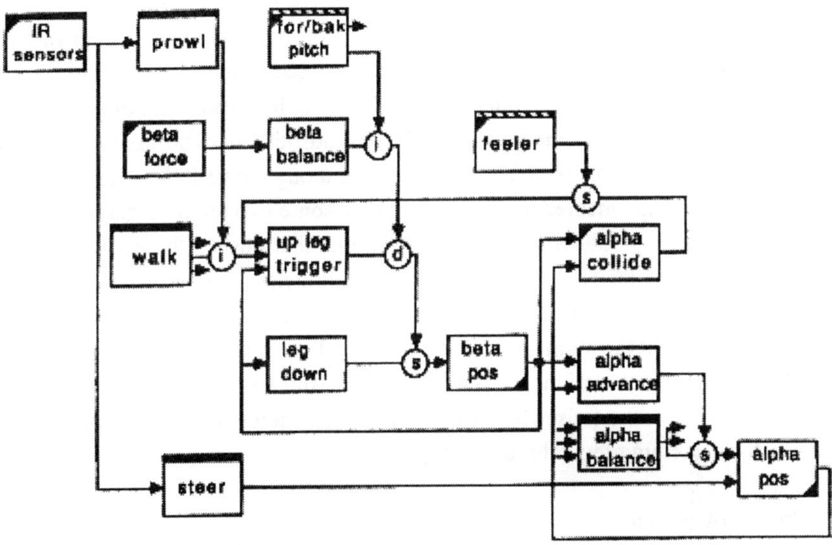

Figure 3.2 Example AFSM structure for an intelligent robot[34]

(9) The discrete component option

The non-Cartesian processing structure can also be implemented using discrete passive and active electronic components without going through the AFSM formality. Such electronic or electro-mechanical components as transistors, diodes, capacitors and registers, and even micro-switches and electro-mechanical relays are often used to build a non-Cartesian agent. A simple pressure-sensitive device can be embedded, for example, inside a bumper made of urethane and attached to the front of an autonomous vehicle. Upon contact, the sensor inside would generate a pulse, which is sent to an

452

analog-to-digital (AD) circuitry, and after amplification, converted into a set of drive currents sent to a steering motor. A set of discrete electronic components that supports this signal conversion process is an agent. A relay, having a primary and secondary circuit can readily represent a causal relationship, thus qualifying as a potential agent in non-Cartesian programming.

(10) The PAL option

As known, Programmable Array Logic (PAL) contains a set of components each of which performs a basic logic operation such as AND and OR. Each of these logical operators can run totally independent of the others. By programming these gates to depict a desired causal relationship, one can easily and very compactly implement a wide range of non-Cartesian programs including one that supports the behaviors of a small robot. In 1987, Jonathon Connell, then of MIT implemented a set of agents on a PAL[35]. The PAL is then mounted on a set of two modified toy radio-controlled cars. Four active infrared sensors were added to each car along with a PAL. The set of less than ten behaviors implemented on the device using some two hundred gates included ones that made the car follow a heat source and one that pushed the car back in the presence of an obstacle. The combined behavior mimicked the behavior of a kitten which plays with a human hand. The car would chase a human hand to the point of almost touching it, but the moment the hand got too close, it would quickly retract. As explained next, implementations similar to the successful attempt by Connell are now being reproduced by others elsewhere using similar in principle but more sophisticated hardware for describing logical relationships,.

(11) The FPGA option

In recent years, some researchers began to use Field Programmable Gate Arrays (FPGA) for generating robot motions [36,37]. FPGA is a collection of a large number of logic gates on a Very Large-Scale Integration (VLSI) chip. Input and output terminals of these gates are under the control of an on-chip processor. The user sends a set of instructions to this processor to have the desired connections established. Because the unit of non-Cartesian programming is a description of a simple causal relationship, it can be implemented by a combination of these logical gates. In applying FPGA to run behavior-based robots, input and output signals need to be formulated and pre-processed to meet the logical signal level and format defined for a specific FPGA device. In a typical robotic application, a set of sensor inputs are linked to the input side of the gate assembly after analog-to-digital conversions and level normalization. For example, a 3.2 volt blip at a bump sensor that means "left bumper touched" would be converted into a "logical on" on one of the input terminals of the FPGA. The condition that "infrared reflection is stronger than a threshold" would be connected as logical on or off on another input terminal. The logical output(s) from the gate assembly is converted into a necessary control signal and amplified before being sent to an actuator. Although the pre- and post-processing could be cumbersome, this way a large number of agents can be implemented on a single FPGA chip with regularity and at a very high density. A more important advantage here is that the logical structures involved will be placed under complete software control.

In conventional Cartesian processing, FPGA is just a very compact way of assembling a large number of logical gates mostly for sensing/control applications. It

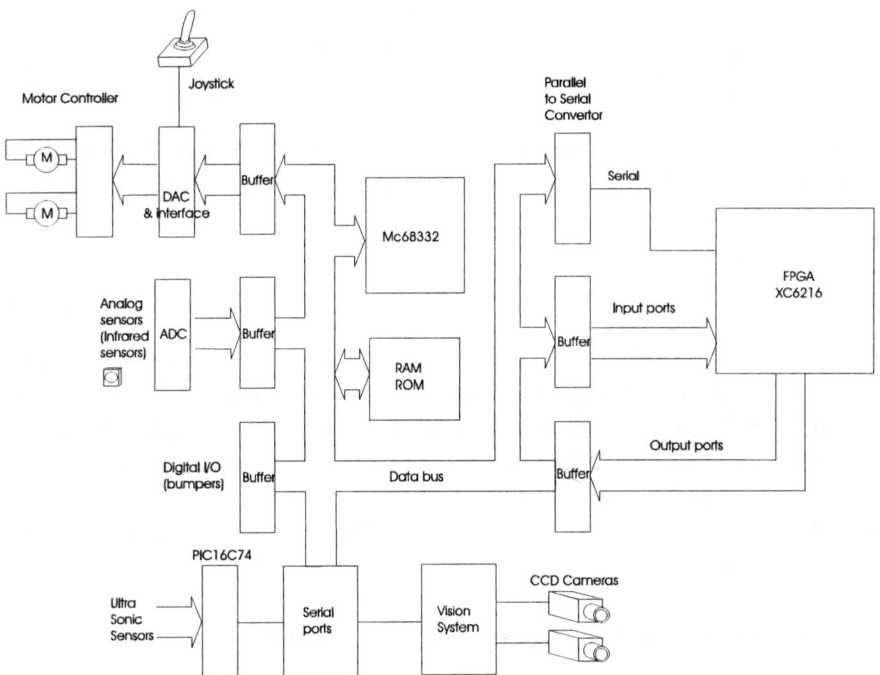

Figure 4.1 A framework for intelligent autonomy management for non-Cartesian programs with evolution

has been used as such in industry for the past few years and its use is expected to grow due to its convenience as an easily reconfigurable device. Designers of devices with a complex logical structure or simple but a large number of logical gates can now speed up the design-implementation-test cycle by putting a good part of the effort in software.

Using the latest FPGA, the reconfiguration can be executed even in run time. The term 'reconfigurable computation' is coined around this device for this reason. However, it is not computation itself that is reconfigured in the conventional sense because it is only a control structure around conventional processors (CPU's) that can be reconfigured using this device.

In non-Cartesian computation, the gates configured into agents themselves are the elements directly contributing to 'computation.' Thus the term reconfigurable computation carries a deeper meaning here. The researchers are now exploiting this potential further into a new dimension by applying evolutionary computational methods such as GA and GP to automatically reconfigure the FPGA. The new field of Evolutionary Robotics (ER) is viewing FPGA as a device for implementing a form of hardware evolution. The scheme is to automatically evolve the autonomy management structure of a robot at the hardware level and to successfully evolve connections between gates, inputs and outputs adjusted during operation. Figure 4.1 is a block diagram of the hardware structure to support this non-Cartesian 'software' structure we have developed and is being applied to a range of embedded systems from a miniature robot for experiments in Evolutionary Robotics to hardware evolution of behaviors onboard intelligent wheelchairs we have previously developed for the handicapped [30].

(12) Which option to choose?

The point to be made here is that in a non-Cartesian processing architecture, it is neither computer hardware nor software, let alone the medium, language or the detailed manner with which they are constructed, that signify the identity of the approach, but the architecture itself. As long as the architecture is maintained, it can be constructed using any of the methods discussed here and more. They can be combined at will to satisfy specific constraints a system must meet, as long as the local interface logistics are satisfied.

5 Benefits of non-Cartesian programs and programming

The example discussed in Section 2.3 and implementational issues covered in Section 4 above demonstrated some of the key aspects of non-Cartesian programs. In this section, I would like to summarize them and also like to describe other not so visible benefits of non-Cartesian programs and programming.

(1) Choices in implementation

It is advantageous to be able to implement the necessary process structure either in hardware or software, or in their mixture. The choice can be casual, such as the availability of suitable components; or practical, so that the implementation fits in available real estate; or theoretical, such as use of FPGA for serious hardware evolution. By having a wider range of selection, one can choose the format that best fits the application. In typical applications of non-Cartesian programming today, implementations that depend solely on software would satisfy most of the cases. However, in cases where space is limited, as in mobile robot applications, an optimal balance between hardware and software, selection of the best processing hardware, and availability of a language system play a significant role.

(2) Very small size of implementation

The programs or hardware structures implemented in non-Cartesian manner are a collection and encapsulation of small element causalities (*agents*) that often take the form of a production rule. As explained above, the <if ... then ...> rules are easily implemented in a large number of readily available computer programming languages and hardware arrangements. The size of each rule is normally very small, often occupying no more than a few to several hundred bytes of memory regardless of the language used. The total size of the program often amounts to no more than a few kilobytes. The size of a program that manages to run an intelligent motorized wheelchair that we developed, complete with vision processing for collision avoidance and landmark-based navigation[22] was about 51 kilobytes. The frugality is also the case when the implementation is in hardware. The size of the boards used and the number of components can get as small as one tenth or less of the hardware structure for similar functions implemented in conventional manner.

(3) Incremental nature of program development

The agents are implemented one at a time, either in software or hardware. Whereas a good deal of the entire system is necessary for the system to be tested in conventional system development, after implementing each agent, the entire system can be tested with the new addition. This means that the development of a system can be strictly incremental. An agent could be coded and integrated into the system one at a time without much regard for the history of the development. Contradictions between the existing body of agents and the one just added will manifest the moment the new system is tested, signaling a problem and clearly identifying the source of the problem. These are software engineering benefits one cannot expect in conventional programming where module structure has to be defined and built before coding starts.

(4) Modularity

The modules in non-Cartesian programming are modular in an ideal sense in that they do not have inter-module connections. They deal with each other only through the operational environment. There are no direct linkages between the agents other than those going through the environment. Thus, the program modules can enjoy very high *module decoupling*. It would also have very high *module strength* since a module contains only one fully independent causal relationship and nothing else. In short, this form of programming realizes ultimate modularity - maximum module strength and minimum module coupling. Unlike in object-oriented programming, which is a highly modularized version of Cartesian programming, there is no explicit communication or exchange of controls between modules.

(5) Evolvable structure

As mentioned in Section 3 (11) above, a new approach to develop agents that generate desired behaviors on robots using evolutionary computation is called Evolutionary Robotics. The field was established less than a decade ago[38]. Although earlier developments were dependent on software implementation of evolutionary computation methods such as GA, in recent years FPGA's are increasingly used to implement Evolutionary Robotics and other evolvable systems on hardware. Either way, because of the simplicity and the uniformity of the agent architecture that non-Cartesian programming is based on, it is greatly simpler to apply evolutionary computation methods to non-Cartesian programs than to conventional counterparts.

6 Issues with non-Cartesian programs and programming

(1) Non-Cartesian programming is non-algorithmic programming

As is obvious from the example examined above, the method of constructing a computer program discussed here is non-algorithmic. Whatever small steps that describe an agent or a component behavior is too short and simple to be called an algorithm (technically one can, but that is not the essence of the dynamic actions that take place when the module is activated). Programmers and system designers well abreast of conventional procedural programming would likely experience difficulties when grasping the concept, designing a system, and then implementing it. This is only because we have been systematically trained to think in terms of algorithms. The puzzlement a programmer would experience is not unlike the one felt by many programmers when faced with declarative programming such as the one with Prolog language over a decade ago. However, if one looks at the new programming as a process of simply identifying and documenting causal relationships that exist between inputs and outputs, as opposed to seeking procedures necessary for converting inputs to outputs, the confusion is well within the range of containment.

(2) Unruliness of the generated processes

The nature of the dynamic processes that happen when a non-Cartesian program is executed, is unruly. It is a very drastic departure from the way we are used to looking at programs. Programs governed all the actions, effects, and side effects that a computer generates to the last bit and to the finest system clock. In contrast, in non-Cartesian programming we depend solely on the side effects of activated simple agents operating over non-linear relationships. In a simple case such as the one described in Section 2.3, most, if not all, effects and side-effects of the processes that self-organize as a result of invoking the agent structure are containable. Impacts of a new agent incrementally added are immediately recognizable and its parameters can be easily adjusted according to observations. And one can even direct these effects and side-effects towards a useful goal, as shown in the example. However, in more involved cases, the process of creating a system based on non-Cartesian programming gets more tedious. There will be a large number of cut-and-try cycles of adding a new agent, testing it within the entire agent structure, modifying the agent, and then testing it again. The total amount of effort required to complete a system with similar functionality, however, is still far less than would be required using a conventional approach. Nevertheless, the uncertainty perceived in the method can work against the psyche of system designers who are trained in a certain way of viewing a system and system design. Evolutionary computation is an effective way to contain the processes and automate the process of perpetual and mundane process of revisions.

(3) Difficulty in explaining behaviors

The sequence of minute events that happen in the dynamic process that results from the execution of non-Cartesian programs is often not analyzable nor explainable. The theoretical analysis of the approach has barely begun as a part of the study of *complex systems* and of chaos. The process is viewed instead at a macroscopic level and only the global effects of the execution are analyzed. It is also very difficult to have a plan in the execution of non-Cartesian programs. Again, the inconvenience implied here is mostly because we view processes in a certain way, namely, procedurally. Therefore, to those researchers and practitioners trained in the conventional norm of analyzing all the unexplainable, the new method will appear less rational and even unacceptable. However, the lack of established methodology to explain the details of the operation is not always an issue at all in practicality. One can still construct systems using the approach and even put them into actual use in real world applications.

7 Conclusions

A new approach to programming computers has been described. With this method, computation becomes not only parallel but also non-von-Neumann and non-Cartesian. It has a number of desirable characteristics, especially when applied to robotics, and some drawbacks, when viewed from the conventional standpoint of computer programming. It will be a while before conventional programming practices are affected by this new approach but there is potential for a development that makes the hereto unmistakably clear concept of programming at least obscured.

Acknowledgments

I would like to thank more than a few dozen programmers, hackers, and hardware geniuses who have worked at AAI as an engineer, a coop student or a trainee, and those who are still there. Without their contribution in implementing ideas, it would never have been possible to visualize the emergence of the new way of running computers discussed here.

References

1. E. Yourdon *How to Manage Structured Programming* (YOURDON inc., 1976).
2. Zelkowitz *et al.*, *Principles of Software Engineering and Design* (Prentice-Hall Software Series, 1979).
3. R.A. Brooks, *A Robust Layered Control System for a Mobile Robot*, IEEE Journal of Robotics and Automation, **RA-2**, 14-23 (1986).
4. S. Forrest, *Emergent Computation*, (MIT Press, Cambridge, MA, 1991).
5. C.G. Langton, *Life at the Edge of Chaos* in Artificial Life II, ed. C.G. Langton,

C. Taylor, J.D. Farmer, S. Rasmussen, (Sanata Fe Institute Studies in the Sciences of Complexity, Volume X, Addison-Wesley, 1992).

6. R.A. Brooks, *Intelligence Without Reason*, Proceedings of International Joint Conference on Artificial Intelligence (IJCAI'91), 569-595, (1991).

7. R. Pfeifer and C. Scheier, *Introduction to "New Artificial Intelligence"* (Institut für Informatik der Universität Zürich, 1995).

8. R. Descartes, *Discourse on Method*, (Paris, 1637).

9. T. Gomi and J-C. Laurence, *Behavior-based AI Techniques for Vehicle Control* in Vehicle Navigation & Information Systems Conference (VNIS'93) (Ottawa, Canada, October 1993).

10. C.G. Langton, *Preface, The Artificial Life Workshop*, in Artificial Life ed. Christopher G. Langton, (Addison-Wesley Publishing Company, 1989).

11. R.A. Brooks, *The Behavior Language; User's Guide* MIT AI Memo **1227**, (April 1990).

12. T. Gomi *et al.*, *Elements of Artificial Emotion*, Presented at Robot Human Communication (RO-MAN'95), (Tokyo, Japan, July 1995).

13. T. Gomi *et al.*, *Vision-based Navigation for an Office Messenger Robot*, Chapter in Intelligent Robots and Systems, ed. V Graefe, (Elsevier Science, 1995).

14. T.Gomi *et al.*, *The Development of a Fully Autonomous Ground Vehicle (FAGV)"*, in proceedings, Intelligent Vehicles Symposium'94 (IV'94), (Paris, France, October 1994).

15. T. Gomi and K. Ide, *Emulation of Emotion Using Vision With Learning*, in proceedings, Robot and Human Communication (RO-MAN'94) (Nagoya, Japan, July 1994).

16. T. Gomi, and J. Ulvr, *Artificial Emotions as Emergent Phenomena*, Proceedings of Robot and Human Communication (RO-MAN'93), (Tokyo, Japan, November 1993).

17. J.R. Koza, *Evolution and Co-Evolution of Computer Programs to Control Independently Acting Agents*, European Conference on Artificial Life (ECAL'91), (Paris, France, December 1991).

18. J.R. Koza, *Genetic Programming: On the programming of computers by means of natural selection*, (A Bradford Book, The MIT Press, Cambridge, MA, 1992.)

19. R.A. Brooks, *L*, (IS Robotics, Sommerville, MA, 1993).

20. IS Robotics, Inc. *Hermes II Software Guide*, (IS Robotics, Somerville, MA, 1996).

21. RWI, *Pioneer User Guide,* (Real World Interface, Jaffrey, NH, 1996).

22. T. Gomi and K. Ide, *The Development of an Intelligent Wheelchair*, In proceedings, Intelligent Vehicles Symposium'96 (IVS'96), (Tokyo, Japan, September 1996).

23. B. Yamauchi and R. Beer, *Integrating Reactive Sequential, and Learning Behavior Using Dynamical Neural Networks*, From Animals to Animats III: Proceedings of the Third International Conference on Simulation of Adaptive Behavior, ed. D. Cliff, P. Husbands, J. Meyer, and S.W. Wilson, (MIT Press-Bradford Books, Cambridge, MA, 1994).

24. D. Floreano and F. Mondada, *Automatic Creation of an Autonomous Agent: Genetic Evolution of a Neural-Network Driven Robot,* From Animals to Animats III: Proceedings of the Third International Conference on Simulation of Adaptive Behavior, ed. D. Cliff, P. Husbands, J. Meyer, and S.W. Wilson, (MIT Press-Bradford Books, Cambridge, MA, 1994).

25. D.Floreano and F. Mondada, *Evolution of Plastic Neurocontrollers for Situated Agents*, From Animals to Animats IV: Proceedings of the Fourth International conference on Simulation of Adaptive Behavior, ed. P. Maes, M. Mataric, J-A. Meyer, J. Pollack, H. Roitblat, and S. Wilson, (MIT Press-Bradford Books, Cambridge, MA, 1996).

26. R. Naito *et al.*, *Genetic Evolution of a Logic Circuit Which Controls an Autonomous Mobile Robot*, in proceedings, International Conference on Evolvable Systems: From Biology to Hardware (ICES96), (Japan, October 1996).

27. V. Braitenberg, *Vehicles, Experiments in Synthetic Psychology* (Cambridge, MA: MIT Press, 1984).

28. K.M. Woon, *Landmark Detection Using Neural Networks*, Proceedings of IEEE Singapore International Symposium on Control Theory and Applications (Singapore, July 1997).

29. T. Gomi, *Fully Autonomous Ground Vehicle (FAGV) for Industrial Applications*, Proceedings of International Conference on Robotics, Vision, and Parallel Processing For Industrial Automation (ROVPIA'96) (Malaysia, November 1996).

30. T. Gomi and A. Griffith, *Developing Intelligent Wheelchairs for the Handicapped*, To appear in Lecture Notes in AI: Assistive Technology and Artificial Intelligence (Springer Verlag,1998).

31. R.A. Brooks, *A Robot that Walks; Emergent Behaviors from a Carefully Evolved Network*, Neural Computation, Vol **1**, No. 2, (Summer 1989).

32. J.H. Connell, *A Behavior-Based Arm Controller*, MIT AI Memo **1025**, (June, 1988).

33. R.A. Brooks and A. Flynn, *Robot Beings* IEEE/RSJ International Workshop on Intelligent Robots and Systems (IROS'89) (Tsukuba, Japan, 1989).

34. R.A. Brooks, *A Robot that Walks; Emergent Behaviors from a Carefully Evolved Network*, AI Memo 1091, February 1989)

35. J.H. Connell, *Creature Design with the Subsumption Architecture*, Proceeding of the International Joint Conference on Artificial Intelligence (IJCAI '87) (Milan, Italy, July 1987).

36. A. Thompson, *Evolving Electronic Robot Controllers that Exploit Hardware Resources*, Advances in Artificial Life: Proceedings of the 3rd European Conference on Artificial Life (ECAL'95), Springer-Verlag LNAI 929 (1995).

37. AAI, *Experimental Development in Evolutionary Robotics*, Internal document (1998).

38. Harvey *et al*, *Evolutionary Robotics and SAGA: the case for hill crawling and tournament selection*, in C. Langton, ed., Artificial Life III, Santa Fe Institute Studeis in the Sciences of Complexity, Proc. Vol. XVI, (Addison Wesley, 1993).

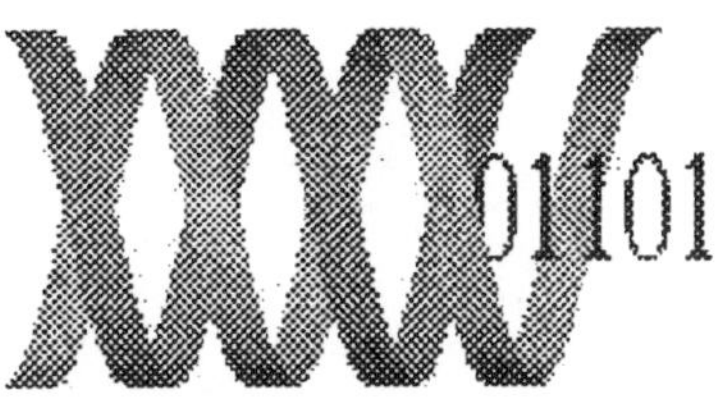
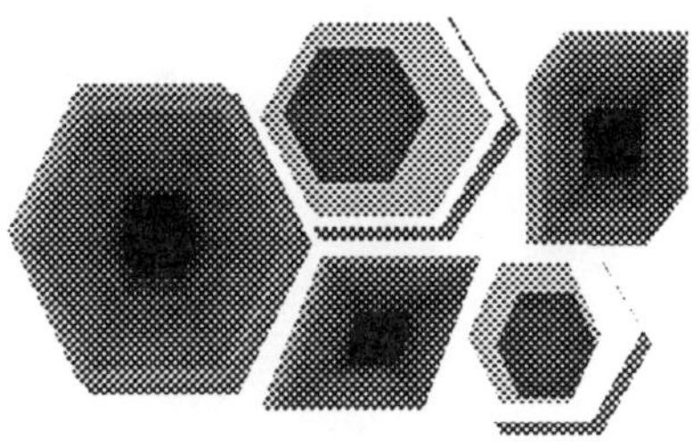
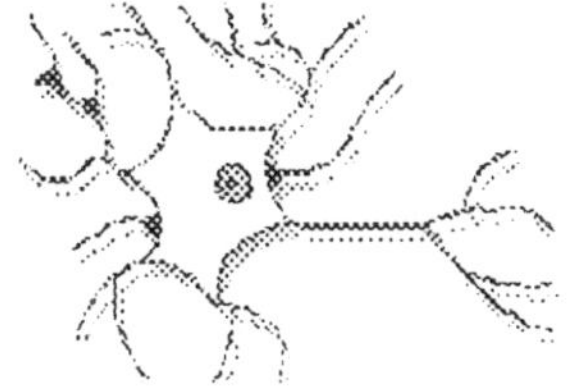

BIBLIOGRAPHY AND WWW RESOURCES

COMPUTATIONAL INTELLIGENCE AND SOFTWARE ENGINEERING:

A BIBLIOGRAPHY AND WWW RESOURCES

E. PEDRYCZ

Computational Intelligence Laboratory

University of Manitoba, Winnipeg R3T 2N2 Canada

E-mail: cilab@ee.umanitoba.ca

This paper includes an extensive bibliography concerning Computational Intelligence (CI) and Software Engineering (SE). It summarizes a list of pertinent World Wide Web resources that deal both with Software Engineering and the key components of CI such as neural networks, evolutionary computing, and fuzzy set technology. The paper highlights several main trends manifesting quite evidently in the development of the entire area.

1   Introduction

This chapter includes an extensive bibliography and WWW resources dealing with publications and other reference materials on Software Engineering and Computational Intelligence. It is obvious that the area of CI is at its early stage of development. Since the inception of the concept around 1992, there have been a number of important findings leading to the establishment of strong synergistic links between the contributing technologies as well as the emergence of several new domains whose existence hinges on a vital cooperation between neurocomputing, fuzzy sets, and evolutionary methods. The compiled bibliography concentrates on the entries that deal with all facets of Software Engineering *and* CI. There is a significant diversity of ways in which the contributing domains of CI become visible in SE. One among viable ways of looking at this is a distribution of the methodologies of CI across a lifecycle of SE products. This form of taxonomy helps identify the role of fuzzy sets, neural networks, and genetic methods in software development, assurance of software quality, and quantification and utilization of software measures. As far as fuzzy sets are concerned, this area has also embraced rule-based systems and rule-based methods. In this way, formed is a slight, yet inevitable overlap between fuzzy sets and Artificial Intelligence. Nevertheless, as of today, the rule-based computing constitutes an integral part of fuzzy set constructs. As a matter of fact, fuzzy sets enrich rule-based models to a high extent and enhance their usefulness in SE.

The summary of the publications sheds light on the entire area. The key components of CI are represented by 49 publications in fuzzy sets, 45 in neural networks, and 29 in evolutionary computing, Figure 1. The number of fuzzy set - related entries is slightly higher than the remaining two technologies due to the already mentioned inclusion of some publications on rule-based computing. There is a steady growth in the number of publications in the CI-SE area as visualized in Figure 2.

Figure 1: A distribution of publications in evolutionary computing, neural networks, and fuzzy sets in the CI-SE area

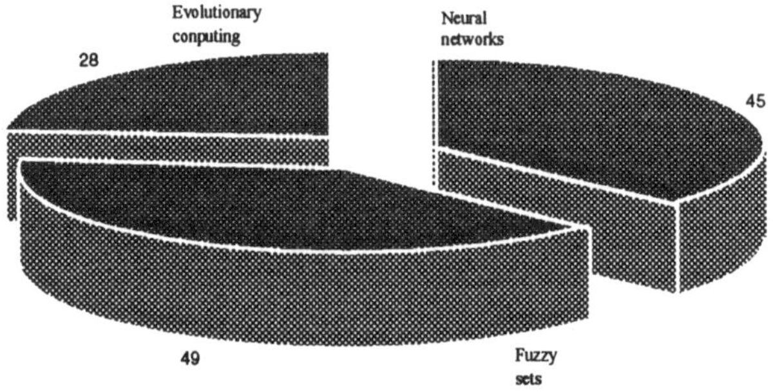

Figure 2: CI-SE publications year-by-year (1989-1997)

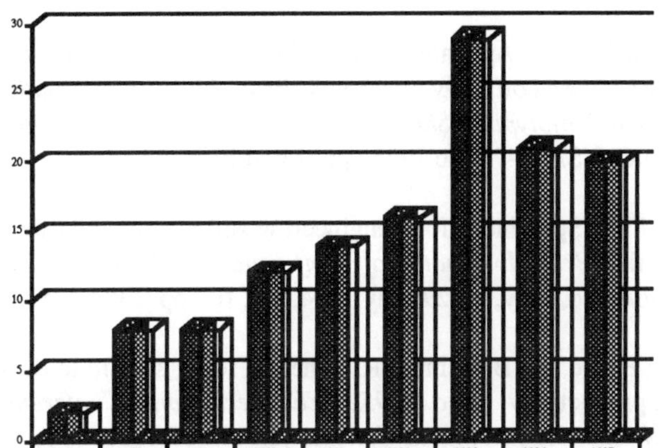

2 Bibliography

1. Agarwal, A.; Jairam, B. N.; Emrich, M. L.; Murthy, N. A knowledge-based manager for software projects. *Proc. 1st International Conference on Industrial and Engineering Applications of Artificial Intelligence and Expert Systems IEA/AIE - 88*;Tullahoma, TN, USA, 1-3 June 1988, vol. I, pp. 281-286.

2. Ahuja, S. P.; Kumar, A. A genetic algorithm approach for performance based reliability enhancement of distributed systems. *Proc. 7th International Conference on Parallel and Distributed Computing Systems*; Las Vegas, NV, USA, 6-8 Oct.1994, pp. 664-9.

3. Alvarez, J.; Castell, N.; Slavkova, O. Combining knowledge and metrics to control software quality factors. *Proc. Third International Conference on Achieving Quality in Software*, Florence, Italy, Jan 1996, p. 201-212.

4. Anderson, C.; von Mayrhauser, A.; Chen, T. Assessing neural networks as guides for testing activities. *Proc. 3rd International Software Metrics Symposium*; Berlin, Germany, 25-26 March 1996, pp. 155-165.

5. Antonakopoulos, T.; Agavanakis, K.; Makios, V., CASE tools evaluation: an automatic process based on fuzzy sets theory. *Proc. 6th IEEE International Workshop on Rapid System Prototyping. Shortening the Path from Specification to Prototype*; Chapel Hill, NC, USA, 7-9 June 1995, pp. 140-146.

6. Arseneau, J. B.; Spracklen, T. Reengineering software modularity using artificial neural networks. *Proc. International Conference on Artificial Neural Networks ICANN'94*; Sorrento, Italy, 26-29 May 1994, vol. II, pp. 1384-1387.

7. Baisch, E.; Bleile, T.; Belschner, R. A neural fuzzy system to evaluate software development productivity. *Proc. 1995 IEEE International Conference on Systems, Man and Cybernetics. Intelligent Systems for the 21st Century*; Vancouver, BC, Canada, 22-25 Oct. 1995, vol. V, pp. 4603-4608.

8. Balentine, B. J.; Zand, M. K.; Samadzadeh, M. H. Hybrid fuzzy metrics for software reusability. *Proc. 5th International Conference on Information Processing and Management of Uncertainty in Knowledge-Based Systems IPMU-94*, Paris, France, 4-8 July1994, pp. 522-533.

9. Bastani, F. B.; Ing-Ray Chen; Ta-Wei Tsao. A software reliability model for artificial intelligence programs. *International Journal of Software Engineering and Knowledge Engineering*; March 1993 Vol: 3 Iss: 1 p. 99-114.

10. Bleile, T.; Baisch, E.; Belschner, R. Neural fuzzy simulation to gain expert knowledge for the improvement of software development productivity. *Proc. Twenty-Seventh Annual Summer Computer Simulation Conference 1995*;Ottawa, Ont., Canada, pp. 317-322.

11. Boehm, B.; Bose, P. Critical success factors for knowledge-based software engineering applications. *Proc. Ninth Knowledge-Based Software Engineering Conference*; Monterey, CA, USA, 20-23 Sep.1994 pp. 166-171.

12. Budgen, D.; Marashi, M. Knowledge use in software design. *Proc. BCS CASE*; Cambridge, UK, 9-11 Sept. 1990, pp. 163-179.

13. Burnstein, I.; Jani, N.; Mannina, S.; Tamsevicius, J.; Goldshteyn, M.; Lendi, L. Intelligent fault localization in software. *Proc. Int. Test Conference*; Baltimore, MD, USA, 20-22 Sept. 1992, pp. 917-926.

14. Carlos Esteva, J. Learning to recognize reusable software by induction. *Proc. SPIE - The International Society for Optical Engineering*; Orlando, FL, USA, 17-19 April 1990 Vol: 1293 Iss: pt.2 p. 654-670.

15. Catania, V.; Fiorito, N.; Malgeri, M.; Russo, M. A soft computing approach to hardware software codesign. *Proc. Fifth Great Lakes Symposium on VLSI* ; Buffalo, NY, USA 16-18 March 1995, pp. 158-163.

16. Catania, V.; Malgeri, M.; Russo, M. Applying fuzzy logic to codesign partitioning. *IEEE Micro*; May-June 1997 Vol: 17 Iss: 3 p. 62-70.

17. Chang, K. H.; Cross, J. H. , II; Carlisle, W. H.; Shih-Sung Liao. A performance evaluation of heuristics-based test case generation methods for software branch coverage. *Int. Journal of Software Engineering and Knowledge Engineering*; Dec. 1996 Vol: 6 Iss: 4 p. 585-608.

18. Cheatham, T. J.; Yoo, J. P.; Wahl, N. J. Software testing: a machine learning experiment. *Proc. 23rd Annual 1995 ACM Computer Science Conference*; Nashville, TN, USA, 28 Feb.- 2 March, pp. 135-141.

19. Chen, Yiping; Singpurwalla, Nozer D. Unification of software reliability models by self-exciting point processes. *Advances in Applied Probability*; Jun 1997 Vol: 29 Iss: 2 p: 337-352.

20. Cheng, A. M. K. Measuring the structural complexity of OPS5 rule-based programs. *Proc.Twentieth Annual International Computer Software and Applications Conference (COMPSAC '96)*; Seoul, South Korea, 21-23 Aug.1996, pp. 522-527.

21. Clinkenbeard, R. A.; Feng, X. An unsupervised learning and fuzzy logic approach for software category identification and capacity planning. *Proc. IJCNN International Joint Conference on Neural Networks*; Baltimore, MD, USA, 7-11 June 1992, vol. III, pp. 358-63.

22. Croll, P. R.; Sharkey, A. J. C.; Bass, J. M.; Sharkey, N. E.; Fleming, P. J. Dependable, intelligent voting for real-time control software, *Engineering Applications of Artificial Intelligence*; Dec.1995 Vol: 8 Iss: 6 p. 615-23.

23. Cross, J. H. , II; Kai-Hsiung Chang; Homer Carlisle, W.; Brown, D. B. Expert system assisted test data generation for software branch coverage. *Data & Knowledge Engineering*; July 1991 Vol: 6 Iss: 4 p. 279-95.

470

24. Damiani, E.; Fugini, M. G. Fuzzy identification of distributed components. *Proc. Int. 5th Fuzzy Days.* Dortmund, Germany, 28-30 April 1997, pp. 550-552.

25. Debenham, J. A unified approach to requirements specification and system analysis in the design of knowledge-based systems. *Proc. 7th International Conference on Software Engineering and Knowledge Engineering*; 22-24 June 1995, Rockville, MD, USA, pp. 144-146.

26. Dellen, B.; Maurer, F.; Munch, J.; Verlage, M. Enriching software process support by knowledge-based techniques. *International Journal of Software Engineering and Knowledge Engineering*; 1997 Vol: 7 Iss: 2 p. 185-215.

27. Do-Hyoung Kim; Kiwon Chong. A method of checking errors and consistency in the process of object-oriented analysis, *Proc. Asia-Pacific Software Engineering Conference*, Seoul, South Korea, 1996 , pp. 208-216.

28. Ebert, Ch. An approach to fuzzy data analysis for software quality control. *Proc. 1st European Congress on Fuzzy and Intelligent Technologies, EUFIT'93*, Aachen, September 7-10, 1993, pp. 1156-1161.

29. Ebert, Ch. Rule-based fuzzy classification for software quality control, *Fuzzy Sets and Systems* ; May 1994 Vol: 63 Iss: 3 p. 349-358.

30. Ebert, Ch. Classification techniques for metric-based software development. *Software Quality Journal*; Dec.1988, Vol. 5, No. 4, p. 255-272.

31. Ellmer, E.; Merkl, D.; Quirchmayr, G.; Tjoa, A. M. Process model reuse to promote organizational learning in software development. *Proc. of the Twentieth Annual International Computer Software and Applications Conference (COMPSAC '96)*; Seoul, South Korea, 21-23 Aug.1996, pp. 21-216.

32. Etzkorn, L. H.; Davis, C. G. Automated object-oriented reusable component identification. *Knowledge-Based Systems*; 1996 Vol: 9 Iss: 8 p. 517-24.

33. Finnie, G. R.; Wittig, G. E. AI tools for software development effort estimation. *Proc. 1996 International Conference Software Engineering: Education and Practice*; Dunedin, New Zeland, 24-27 Jan.1996, pp. 346-53.

34. Forsyth, G. F.; Ali, M. (eds). *Proc. 8th International Conference on Industrial and Engineering Applications of Artificial Intelligence and Expert Systems,*

Melbourne, Vic., Australia, 1995, 857 pp.

35. Garcia, M.; Ellis, N.; Simmons, D. Intelligent Software Status Predictor. *Proc. Fuzzy Logic 95*. November 7-9 1995. San Francisco CA, USA, pp. 15-1 - 15-8.

36. Graham, P.; Nelson, B. Genetic algorithms in software and in hardware - a performance analysis of workstation and custom computing machine implementations *Proc. IEEE Symposium on FPGAs for Custom Computing Machines*; Napa Valley, CA, USA, 17-19 April 1996, pp. 216-225.

37. Guindon, R. The process of knowledge discovery in system design. Designing and Using Human-Computer Interfaces and Knowledge Based Systems. *Proc. Third International Conference on Human Computer Interaction*; Boston, MA, USA, 18-22 Sept. 1989 Vol.II p. 727-734.

38. Hakkarainen, J.; Laamanen, P.; Rask, R. Neural networks in specification level software size estimation. *Proc. Twenty-Sixth Hawaii International Conference on System Sciences*; Wailea, HI ,USA, 5-8 Jan. 1993, vol. IV, pp. 626-634.

39. Harmon, P. The evolution of software engineering for information management in the United States. *Genie Logiciel & Systemes Experts* Dec. 1992 Iss: no.29 p. 59-70.

40. Henninger,S. Case-based knowledge management tools for software development, *Automated Software Engineering*; 4, 1997, 319-340.

41. Henson, T.; Huxhold, W.; Bowman, D. Application of a simulated neural network to systems and software engineering. *Proc. Twenty-Fourth Annual Computer Simulationm Conference*; Reno, NV, USA, 27-30 July 1992, pp. 365-369.

42. Hidalgo, J. I.; Lanchares, J. Functional partitioning for hardware-software codesign using genetic algorithms. *Proc. 23rd Euromicro Conference: New Frontiers of Information*, Budapest, Hungary, 1-4 Sep. 1997, pp. 631-638

43. Hochman, R.; Khoshgoftaar, T. M.; Allen, E. B.; Hudepohl, J. P. Using the genetic algorithm to build optimal neural networks for fault-prone module detection. *Proc. of the Seventh Intenational Symposium on Software Reliability Engineering*, White Plains, NY, Oct.1996, pp. 152-162.

44. Hondo, N.; Iba, H.; Kakazu, Y. Sharing and refinement for reusable subroutines of genetic programming, *Proc. IEEE International Conference on Evolutionary Computation (ICEC'96)*; Nagoya, Japan, 20-22 May 1996 pp. 565-70.

45. Howe, A. E.; von Mayrhauser, A.; Mraz, R. T. Test case generation as an AI planning problem. *Automated Software Engineering*; Jan. 1997 Vol: 4 Iss: 1 p. 77-106.

46. Hsu, W.; Tenorio, M. F. Software engineering effort models using neural networks. Proc. *IEEE International Joint Conference on Neural Networks*; Singapore, 18-21 Nov. 1991, vol. II, pp. 1190-1195.

47. Hwee-Leng Ong; Long, S.; Hing-Yan Lee. Machine discovery of static software reuse potential metrics. *Proc. Second Singapore International Conference on Intelligent Systems. SPICIS `94*; Singapore, 14-17 Nov. 1994, pp. B286-291.

48. Jie Wei; Gao Zhongyi. Research of software structural test data generation based on genetic algorithms, *Journal of Beijing University of Aeronautics and Astronautics*; Feb. 1997 Vol: 23 Iss: 1 p. 36-40.

49. Jones, B. F.; Sthamer, H. -H; Eyres, D. E. Automatic structural testing using genetic algorithms. *Software Engineering Journal*; May 1995, Vol.12, No.5.

50. Karunanithi, N. A neural network approach for software reliability growth modeling in the presence of code churn. *Proc. 4th International Symposium on Software Reliability Engineering*; Denver, CO, USA, 3-6 Nov.1993, pp. 310-317.

51. Karunanithi, N.; Malayia, Y. K. Prediction of software reliability using feed forward and recurrent neural net, *Proc. IEEE International Conference on Neural Networks*, 1992, Vol 1, pp. 800-805.

52. Karunanithi, N.; Malayia, Y. K. The scaling problem in neural networks for software reliability prediction. *Proc. Symposium on Software Reliability Engineering*; 1992, pp.76-78.

53. Karunanithi, N.; Whitley, D.; Malayia, Y. K. Prediction of software reliability using neural networks. *Proc. IEEE International Symposium on Software Reliability Eng.*, May 1991, pp.124-130.

54. Karunanithi, N.; Whitley, D.; Malaiya, Y. Prediction of software reliability using connectionist models. *IEEE Trans. on Software Engineering*; 1992, Vol 18, p. 563-573.

55. Karunanithi, N.; Whitley, D.; Malaiya, Y. K. Using neural networks in reliability prediction. *IEEE Software*, July 1992 Vol: 9 Iss: 4 p. 53-59.

56. Khalid, H.; Obaidat, M. S. Simulation study of a novel cache replacement algorithm. *Simulation*; April 1997 Vol: 68 Iss: 4 p. 209-218.

57. Khoshgoftaar, T. M.; Allen, E. B.; Hudepohl, J. P.; Aud, S. J. Application of neural networks to software quality modeling of a very large telecommunications system. *IEEE Transactions on Neural Networks*; July 1997 Vol: 8 Iss: 4 p. 902-909.

58. Khoshgoftaar, T. M.; Lanning, D. L.; Pandya, A. S. A comparative study of pattern recognition techniques for quality evaluation of telecommunications software. *IEEE Journal on Selected Areas in Communications*; Feb.1994 Vol: 12 Iss: 2 p. 279-291

59. Khoshgoftaar, T. M.; Lanning, D. L.; Pandya, A. Neural network application in support of software reliability engineering *Proc.of the SPIE - The International Society for Optical Engineering*;Orlando, FL, USA, 17-21 April 1995 Vol: 2492 Iss: pt.1 p. 175-182.

60. Khoshgoftaar, T. M.; Lanning, D. L.; Pandya, A. S. A neural network modeling methodology for the detection of high-risk programs. *Proc. Fourth International Symposium on Software Reliability Engineering*; Denver, CO, USA, 3-6 Nov. 1993 pp. 302-329.

61. Khoshgoftaar, T. M.; Lanning, D. L. A neural network approach for early detection of program modules having high risk in the maintenance phase. *Journal of Systems and Software*; April 1995 Vol: 29 Iss: 1 p. 85-91

62. Khoshgoftaar, T. M.; Pandya, A. S.; Lanning, D. L. Application of neural networks for predicting program faults, *Annals of Software Engineering*; 1995 Vol: 1 p. 141-154.

63. Khoshgoftaar, T. M.; Szabo, R. M.; Guasti, P. J. Exploring the behaviour of neural network software quality models, *Software Engineering Journal* 1995 Vol: 10 Iss: 3 p. 89-96.

64. Khoshgoftaar, T. M.; Szabo, R. M.;Improving neural network predictions of software quality using principal components analysis. *Proc. 1994 IEEE International Conference on Neural Networks. IEEE World Congress on Computational Intelligence*, Orlando, FL, USA, 27-June-2 July 1994 , vol. V, pp 3295-3300.

65. Kingston, G.; Vernik, R.; Dart, P. Development of an expert assistant for software evaluation using a hybrid approach. *Proc. Eighth Knowledge-Based Software*

Engineering Conference;Chicago, IL, USA, 20-23 Sept.1993 pp. 186-195.

66. Knolmayer, G. F.; Gerber, J. -P. Experiences with applying a genetic algorithm to determine an information systems architecture, *OR Spectrum* ;1997 Vol: 19 Iss: 1 p. 47-53.

67. Kumar, S.; Krishna, B. A.; Satsangi, P. S. Fuzzy systems and neural networks in software engineering project management. *Applied Intelligence: The International Journal of Artificial Intelligence, Neural Networks, and Complex Problem-Solving Technologies* March 1994 Vol: 4 Iss: 1 p. 31-52.

68. Kurfess, F. J.; Welch, L. R. Categorization of programs using neural networks. *Proc. IEEE Symposium and Workshop on Engineering of Computer-Based Systems*; Friedrichshafen, Germany, 11-15 March 1996, pp. 420-426.

69. Lanning, D. L.; Khoshgoftaar, T. M.; Guasti, P. J. Improving neural network models of defect content in complex software systems, *Proc. of the SPIE - The International Society for Optical Engineering*;Orlando, FL, USA, 9-12 April 1996 Vol: 2760 pp. 713-724.

70. Lea, R. N. Applications of fuzzy sets to rule-based expert system development. *Proc. Telematics and Informatics*; Greenbelt, MD, USA, 16-17 May 1989 Vol: 6 Iss: 3-4 p. 403-436.

71. Lee, J. K.; Liebowitz, J.; Chae, Y. M. (eds.). *Third World Congress on Expert Systems*; Seoul, South Korea, 5-9 Feb. 1996.

72. Levary, R. R. , Lin, C. Y. Modeling the software development process using an expert simulation system having fuzzy logic. *Software - Practice and Experience*; 5-9 Feb. 1991, Vol. 21, pp.133-148.

73. Loomes, M.; Frank, R.; Davey, N. Theory building-a constructive approach to modelling neural network development processes, *Neural networks - producing dependable systems. Selected papers.* Issued by:ERA Technol.Ltd., Leatherhead, UK, Report No: ERA-97-0365, 1997 pp. 59-70.

74. Lowry, M. R.; Van Baalen, J. META-AMPHION: synthesis of efficient domain-specific program synthesis systems. *Automated Software Engineering*; April 1997 Vol: 4 Iss: 2 p. 199-241.

75. Man Leung Wong; Kwong Sak Leung. Applying logic grammars to induce sub-functions in genetic programming. *Proc. 1995 IEEE International Conference*

on Evolutionary Computation; Perth, WA, Australia, 29 Nov.- 1 Dec. 1995, vol. II, pp. 737-740.

76. Maskell, B.; Wilby, M. Evolving software agent behaviours, *Proc. IEEE GLOBECOM 1996. Communications: The Key to Global Prosperity*, 18-22 Nov. 1996, London, UK, vol. I, pp. 90-94.

77. Medsker, L.; Turban, E. Integrating expert systems and neural computing for decision support. *Proc. of the Twenty-Seventh Hawaii International Conference on System Sciences. Vol.III: Information Systems: Decision Support and Knowledge-Based Systems*; Wailea, HI, USA, 4-7 Jan., 1994, pp. 656-665.

78. Merkl, D. A connectionist view on document classification. *Proc. Australasian Database Conference (ADC'95)*, Adelaide, Australia, 1995.

79. Merkl, D.; Tjoa, A. The representation of semantic similarity between documents by using maps: Application of an ANN to Organize Software Libraries. *Proc. General Assembly Conference & Congress of the Int. Federation for Information and Documentation*; 1994 Oct. 2-9.

80. Meskens, N. A knowledge-based system for software quality analysis. *Proc. 6th International Conference on Software Engineering and Knowledge Engineering SEKE'94*; Jurmala, Latvia, 21-23 June 1994, pp. 180-187.

81. Mi, P.; Scacchi, W. A knowledge-based environment for modeling and simulating software engineering processes, *IEEE Transactions on Knowledge and Data Engineering*; 1990 Vol: 2 Iss: 3 p. 283-289.

82. Minohara, T.; Tohma, Y. Parameter estimation of hyper-geometric distribution software reliability growth model by genetic algorithms, *Proc. Sixth International Symposium on Software Reliability Engineering*; Toulouse, France, 24-27 Oct. 1995 pp. 324-329.

83. Navrat, P. A note on using artificial intelligence techniques is software engineering. *Journal of Electrical Engineering*; 1997 Vol: 48 Iss: 3-4 p. 105-112.

84. Partridge, D. Connectionism as a software-engineering paradigm. *AIS - Advanced Information Systems*; 1993 Vol: 1 Iss: 1 p. 7-14.

85. Partridge, D. Engineering multiversion reliability. *Neural networks - producing dependable systems. Selected papers*, Issued by ERA Technol. Ltd., Leatherhead, UK, Report No: ERA-97-0365, 1997, p. 27-36.

476

86. Partridge, D.; Sharkey, N. Neural computing: a new route to software reliability. *Proc. Third International Conference on Artificial Neural Networks*; Brighton, UK, 25-27 May 1993 pp. 66-70.

87. Paul, R. Metric-based neural network classification tool for analyzing large-scale software. *Proc. Fourth International Conference on Tools with Artificial Intelligence*; Arlington, VA, USA, 10-13 Nov. 1992 pp. 108-113.

88. Paul, R. A. Metrics based classification trees for software test monitoring and management. *Proc. Sixth International Conference on Tools with Artificial Intelligence*; New Orleans, LA, USA, 6-9 Nov. 1994, pp. 534-540.

89. Pedrycz, W.; Waletzky, J. Fuzzy clustering in software reusability. *Software-Practice and Experience*; March 1997, Vol.27, No.3, p. 245-270.

90. Petry, F. E.; Dunay, B. D. Automatic programming and program maintenance with genetic programming International *Journal of Software Engineering and Knowledge Engineering*; June 1995 Vol: 5 Iss: 2 p. 165-167.

91. Plant, R. T.; Gamble, R. Using meta-knowledge within a multilevel framework for KBS development. *International Journal of Human-Computer Studies* : April 1997 Vol: 46 Iss: 4 p. 523-547.

92. Porter A. A.; Selby, R. W. Empirically guided software development using metric-based classification trees. *IEEE Software*, March 1990, p. 46-54.

93. *Proc. International Computer Science Conference'88. Artificial Intelligence: Theory and Applications*; Hong Kong, 19-21 Dec. 1988.

94. *Proc. of 11th Knowledge Based Software Engineering Conference*, Syracuse, NY, USA, 25-28 Sept 1996.

95. *Proc. of Second International Conference on Knowledge Acquistion, Representation and Processing. KARP'95*, Auburm , AL, USA, 27-30 Sept. 1995.

96. Qureshi, A. Evolving agents; *Proc. First Annual Conference on Genetic Programming*, Stanford, CA, USA, 28-30 July 1996, pp. 369-374.

97. Ramachandran, M. Knowledge based support for reuse. *Proc 6th International Conference on Software Engineering and Knowledge Engineering SEKE'94*, Jurmala, Latvia, 21-23 June, 1994, pp. 382-386.

98. Reynolds, R. G.; Maletic, J. I.; Zannoni, E. Extracting procedural knowledge from software systems using inductive learning in the PM system, *Proc. Fourth International Conference on Software Engineering and Knowledge Engineering*, Capri, Italy, 15-20 June 1992 pp. 131-139.

99. Reynolds, R. G.; Maletic, J. I.; Zannoni, E. Operationalizing software reuse as a problem in inductive learning, *Proc. 5th Int. Conf on Industrial and Engineering Applications of Artificial Intelligence and Expert Systems, IEA/AIE-92*; Paderborn, Germany, 9-12 June 1992 pp. 143-153.

100. Reynolds, R. G.; Sverdlik, W. An evolution-based approach to program understanding using cultural algorithms. *International Journal of Software Engineering and Knowledge Engineering* Vol: 5 Iss: 2, June 1995, p. 211-226.

101. Reynolds, R. G.; Zannoni, E. Extracting procedural knowledge from software systems using inductive learning in the PM system, *International Journal on Artificial Intelligence Tools, Architectures, Languages, Algorithms* Sept. 1992 Vol: 1 Iss: 3 p. 351-367.

102. Reynolds, R. G.; Zannoni, E.; Posner, R. M. Learning to understand software using cultural algorithms. *Third Annual Conference on Evolutionary Programming*; San Diego, CA, USA, 24-26, Feb. 1994, pp. 150-157.

103. Robinson, G.; McIlroy, P. Exploring some commercial applications of genetic programming. Evolutionary Computing. *AISB Workshop*, Selected Papers, Sheffield, UK, 3-4 April 1995, pp. 234-264.

104. Rodriguez, A.; Martin, F. Knowledge-based systems development. *Cybernetics and Systems*; 1996 Vol: 27 Iss: 3 p. 213-222.

105. Roper, M. CAST with GAs-automatic test data generation via. evolutionary computation, *IEE Colloquium on Computer Aided Software Testing (Cast) Tools*; London, UK, 23 April 1996 pp. 7/1-5.

106. Roper, M. Computer aided software testing using genetic algorithms. Software Research Institute. Paper 9T1. *Proc.Tenth International Software Quality Week*; San Francisco, CA, USA, May 1997 (Software Research Institute. Paper 9T1).

107. Saha, D.; Mitra, R. S.; Basu, A. Hardware software partitioning using genetic algorithm. *Proc.Tenth International Conference on VLSI Design*, Hyderabad, India 4-7 Jan. 1997, pp. 155-160.

108. Schwanke, R. W.; Hanson, S. J. Using neural networks to modularize software. *Machine Learning*, 1994 Vol: 15 Iss: 2 p. 137-168.

109. Selby, R. W.; Porter, A. A. Learning from examples: generation and evaluation of decision trees for software resource analysis. *IEEE Trans.Software Eng.*;1988, Vol.14,No.12, p. 1743-1757.

110. Sharkey, N. E.; Partridge, D. The statistical independence of network generalisation: an application in software engineering. *Proc.Techniques and Applications of Neural Networks*; Liverpool, UK, 7-8 Sept. 1993 p. 21-33.

111. Sharp, H.; Robinson, G. The application of IKBS technology to software design measurement and improvement. *Proc. First International Conference on Software Quality Management*; Southampton, UK, 30 March- 1 April 1993, pp. 777-790.

112. Sheppard, J. W.; Simpson, W. R., Using a competitive learning neural network to evaluate software complexity. *Proc. 1990 ACM SIGSMALL/PC Symposium on Small Systems*; Arlington, VA, USA, 28-30 March pp. 262-267.

113. Smith, J.; Fogarty, T. C. Evolving software test data-GA's learn self expression. Evolutionary Computing. *AISB Workshop*. Selected Papers; Brighton, UK, 1-2 April 1996 pp. 137-146.

114. Smith, S.; Kandel, A. Verification and validation in fuzzy expert systems. *Proc. 1995 IEEE International Conference on Systems, Man and Cybernetics. Intelligent Systems for the 21st Century*; Vancouver, BC, Canada, 22-25 Oct., vol. IV, pp. 3647-3651.

115. Srinivasan, K.; Fisher, D. Machine learning approaches to estimating software development effort. *IEEE Transactions on Software Engineering*, 1995 Vol: 21 Iss: 2 p. 126-137.

116. Suzaki, K.; Kurita, T.; Tanuma, H.; Hirano, S. Adaptive algorithm selection method (AASM) for dynamic software tuning. *Proc. Seventeenth Annual International Computer Software and Applications Conference*; Phoenix, AZ, USA, 1-5 Nov. 1993, pp. 248-256.

117. Takada, Y.; Matsumoto, K.; Torii, K. A software reliability prediction model using a neural network. *Systems and Computers in Japan* Dec.1994 Vol: 25 Iss: 14 p. 22-31.

118. Tovar, E. Applicability of McCabe's complexity metric to knowledge engineering products. *Proc. 6th International Conference on Software Engineering and Knowledge Engineering SEKE '94*; Jurmala, Latvia, 21-23 June, 1994 pp. 508-515.

119. Tovar, E. An approach to measure the knowledge-based system development CC-AI, *The Journal for the Integrated Study of Artificial Intelligence, Cognitive Science and Applied Epistemology* 1996 Vol: 13 Iss: 4 p. 349-373.

120. Tsuhara, S. Automatic layout of dialogue components using fuzzy rules. *Transactions of the Institute of Electrical Engineers of Japan, Part C*; July 1993 Vol: 113-C Iss: 7 p. 479-487.

121. Valdes, R. What is biocomputing? *Dr. Dobb's Journal*; April 1991 Vol: 16 Iss: 4 p. 46, 108-109.

122. Van Bommel, P.; Van Der Weide, T.; Lucasius, C. B. Genetic algorithms for optimal logical database design. *Information and Software Technology*; Dec.1994 Vol: 36 Iss: 12 p. 725-732.

123.Von Mayrhauser, A.; Anderson, Ch; Mraz, R. Using a neural network to predict test case effectiveness. *Proc. IEEE Aerospace Applications Conference,* Snowmass, CO, Feb.1995.

124. Von Mayrhauser, A.; Jeon, T. CASE tools architecture for knowledge-based regression testing. *Proc. TRI-Ada '93*; Seattle, WA, USA, 18-23 Sept.1993 pp. 368-378.

125. Wakunda, J.; Zell, A. EvA: a tool for optimization with evolutionary algorithms. *Proc. 23rd Euromicro Conference: New Frontiers of Information Technology,* Budapest, Hungary,1-4 Sept.1997 pp. 644-651

126. Washburne, T.; Stachowitz, R.; Hawley, J.; Romsdahl, H. Automatic classification of software modules with probabilistic neural networks, *Proc. 1994 IEEE International Conference on Neural Networks. IEEE World Congress on Computational Intelligence*; Orlando, FL, USA, 27 June- 2 July 1994, vol. VI, p. 3894-3899.

127. Watkins, A. L. The automatic generation of test data using genetic algorithms. *Proc. of the 4th Software Quality Conference*, Dundee, UK, 4-5 July 1995, vol. II, pp. 300-309.

128. Welch, L. R.; Ravindran, B.; Henriques, J.; Hammer, D. K. Metrics and techniques

for automatic partitioning and assignment of object-based concurrent programs, *Proc. Seventh IEEE Symposium on Parallel and Distributed Processing*; San Antonio, TX, USA, pp. 440-447.

129. Wright, D. T.; Williams, D. J. Object-oriented software design techniques for process control. *Transactions of the Institute of Measurement and Control*; 1994 Vol: 16 Iss: 1 p. 48-56.

130. Zeephongsekul, P.; Xia, G. On fuzzy debugging of software programs. *Fuzzy Sets and Systems* Oct. 1996, 83, 2, 239-247.

3   Selected WWW sites

In this section we summarize selected WWW sites. They split into four categories. The first one lists these SE - oriented. The three remaining classes concern fuzzy sets, neural networks and neurocomputing, and evolutionary computing.

The compiled lists of the sites are not complete (and perhaps never will). The intent was to include the most relevant and easily accessible sites characterized by a wealth of pertinent materials (reports, updates on the existing methodologies) as well as well-linked to other sites of interest.

Software Engineering

WWW Virtual Library for Software Engineering, http://ricis.cl.uh.rdu/virt-lib/soft-eng.html
The Software Engineering Institute, CMU, http://www.sei.cmu.edu/
ASSET Source for Software Engineering Technology, A division of SAIC (Science Applications International Corporation), http://www.asset.com/WSRD/catalog.html
Australian Software Quality Research Institute, http://www-sqi.cit.gu.edu.au/
Cetus - Object Oriented Links Collection, http://www.rhein-neckar.de/~cetus/software.html
Case Tools, Computer Aided Software Engineering,
http://osiris.sunderland.ac.uk/sst/casehome.html
IBM Cleanroom Software Technology Center,
http://www.clearlake.ibm.com/MFG/solutions/cleanrm.html
NRC Software Engineering Group, Canada, http://wwwsel.iit.nrc.ca/
The Software Engineering Laboratory (SEL), NASA/Goddard Space Flight Center,

http://fdd.gsfc.nasa.gov/seltext.html
The WWW Formal Technical Review Archive
http://www.ics.hawaii.edu/~johnson/FTR/
Software Testing Online Resources (STORM), http://www.mtsu.edu/~storm/
Centre for Software Reliability, University of Newcastle upon Tyne,
http://www.csr.ncl.ac.uk/
Centre for Software Reliability, City University London,
http://albion.ncl.ac.uk/cabernet/members/uk-city.html

Fuzzy set technology

Internet's Resources for Neuro-Fuzzy and Soft Computing,
http://www.cs.nthu.edu.tw/~jang/nfsc.htm
Ostfold Regional College(Norway), ftp://ftp.hiof.no/pub/Fuzzy/
FAQ of fuzzy logic and fuzzy expert systems,
http://www.cs.tamu.edu/research/CFL
Fuzzy Logic and Neurofuzzy Research Group, http://www
isis.ecs.soton.ac.uk/research/nfinfo/fzrgroup.html
Ortech Engineering Inc..Fuzzy Logic Reservoir, http://www.ortech-
engr.com/fuzzy/reservoir.html
Lecture Notes:Fuzzy Decision Making, http://www.tucs.abo.fi/courses/95-
96/material/fuzzydec.html
Hybrid Intelligent Systems, http://www.cas.american.edu/research/his.html
Fuzzy Logic and Neurofuzzy Publication, http://www-
isis.ecs.soton.ac.uk/research/nfinfo/fzpub.html

Neural networks and neurocomputing

IEEE Neural Network Council, http://www.ieee.org/nnc/index.html
bibliographies on neural networks,
http://donkey.CS.Arizona.EDU:1994/bib/Neural/
The ISIS Group, http://www-isis.ecs.soton.ac.uk/
Neural Networks Archive, http://www.lpac.ac.uk/SEL-
HPC/Articles/NeuralArchive.html
Neuroscience, http://www.acsiom.org/nsr/neuro.html
Pacific Northwest National Laboratory,
http://www.emsl.pnl.gov:2080/docs/cie/neural/neural.homepage.html
NeuralNet Group, http://www.dice.ucl.ac.be/neural-nets/NNgroup.html
Neural Network Information, http://www.eeb.ele.tue.nl/neural/neural.html
UTCS Neural Networks Research Group, http://www.cs.utexas.edu/users/nn/
Neural Computing Research Programs Worldwide,

http://engine.ieee.org/nnc/research/nnworldprog.html
Machine Learning and Neural Networks, http://rtm.science.unitn.it/rms/nn-sites.html

Evolutionary computing

Evolutionary and Adaptive Systems CSRPs,
http://www.cogs.susx.ac.uk/adapt/easy/_csrps.html
Combination Fuzzy Logic-Genetic Algorithms Bibliography,
http://www.cs.orst.edu/~rpandey/info/libga.html
Bibliography on Evolutionary Computation,
http://cosmos.kaist.ac.kr/pub/bibliographies/Ai/EC-ref.html
Genetic Algorithms Group at George Mason University (Publication List),
http://www.cs.gmu.edu:80/research/gag/pubs.html
Evolutionary Computation,
http://www.etsimo.uniovi.es/ftp/pub/EC/FAQ/www/Q14.htm

INDEX

A

amplifier 145

analog circuit design 131

approximate block access 392, 400

approximate reasoning 238, 339

autonomy 430

C

classification 71, 119, 296, 301

cluster analysis 79, 306

cyclomatic complexity 189

D

database system 398

discriminant analysis 303

deductive logic 99-100

E

embryonic circuit 133

evolution 151

expert system 371

evolutionary system 228

F

function point system 331, 339

fuzzy expected value (FEV) 392

fuzzy measure 343

fuzzy set 270, 305, 321, 346

G

genetic programming 128, 132, 175, 178

granular computing 197

484

I

inductive computing 97

inductive logic 99, 103

information granularity 344

instruction set 153

L

learning, see neural network learning

linguistic approximation 277

linguistic variable 274

M

mereology 244

mutation 159

N

neural networks 35, 108, 304, 332, 449

neural network learning 7, 13, 38, 47, 76

non-Cartesian programming 431, 443

O

object

    system 212

    network 199, 214-215

    generic 200

    fuzzy 221, 270

object-oriented design 270

overfitting 8

P

Petri net 350

principal component analysis (PCA) 44

R

regression 331

retrieval 73

rough sets 243, 348

rule-based system 106

S

self-organizing map (SOM) 65, 74

software cost 339

software lifecycle 3

software measures 323

software quality 33, 184, 295

software testing 3-4, 10

software reuse 67

software libraries 66, 70, 77

standardization of data 43

structured programming 429

T

telecommunication system 40

test oracle 12

test generation 11

test reduction 15

U

unsupervised learning, see self-organizing maps

W

white box testing 17